This Book Belongs

NEUROPSYCHOLOGICAL ASSESSMENT

NEUROPSYCHOLOGICAL ASSESSMENT

Muriel Deutsch Lezak
Veterans Administration Hospital
and
University of Oregon Health Sciences Center
Portland, Oregon

New York / **Oxford University Press** / 1976

To Sidney

PREFACE

I have tried to make *Neuropsychological Assessment* the kind of comprehensive sourcebook in neuropsychology that psychologists and clinicians in the neurosciences need for training students, for communicating about the psychological aspects of brain dysfunction, and for their practice and research. Thus I wrote this book with several audiences and several purposes in mind.

My chief purpose has been to offer a practical approach to neuropsychological assessment that enables the clinician to be responsive to the individuality of his patients. An individualized approach, in which the examination's purpose and the patient's condition determine the content and conduct of the examination, recognizes the variety and range of problems and handicaps presented by brain damaged patients. Underlying such an approach is the assumption that when the neuropsychological examination is tailored to meet the requirements of the individual patient, it is most likely to provide useful answers to the questions that prompted it.

The extent to which the neuropsychological examination is patient-oriented depends in part on the examiner's understanding of both normal brain-behavior relationships and the psychological effects of brain dysfunction. The early chapters of this book review the psychological, neurological, and statistical bases of neuropsychology, providing a frame of reference for the selection and interpretation of assessment techniques.

Individualization of the neuropsychological examination also depends on the extent of the examiner's test repertory. In order to make the examination conform to the many different needs and limitations of his patients, the clinician must have available a large variety of tests and assessment techniques suitable for both wide-ranging and in-depth studies. Only with a full gamut of tests to choose from can the examiner, select, adapt, and innovate test procedures while conducting the examination, and thus explore problem areas as they appear without overtesting. The later chapters of this book present over 200 psychological test and assessment techniques, selected on the basis of their frequency of use, practicality, and appropriateness for examining neuropsychological problems. Included are descriptions, directions for administration, and norms of tests designed specifically for the evaluation of brain damage. Instructions are given for applying standard psychological assessment instruments—such as the Wechsler Adult Intelligence Scale, the Stanford-Binet Intelligence Scale, the Rorschach inkblot technique, and paper and pencil achievement, aptitude, and personality tests—to neuropsychological problems. Also reported are variations on the administration and scoring of such popular tests as the Bender-Gestalt and Draw-a-Person that make them applicable to neuropsychological studies.

While the need for a clinical sourcebook dictated the overall organization and content of this book, it is also intended for classroom use. For this purpose I have tried to avoid technical terminology peculiar to any one discipline, and to define it when it could not be avoided. The sections on brain structure and function and on psychological test and measurement theory were designed to introduce students and practitioners in psychology and the neurosciences to the methods and subject matter of the "other" discipline. The references cited in these introductory reviews should enable students to pursue their interests in these fields at more advanced levels.

I have also tried to make this book a resource to which medically trained persons can turn for clarification of psychological test material and for aid in working with psychologists. The explanations of test scores and psychological procedures, descriptions of the tests, and discussion of their applicability should help the medical clinician understand test reports, use psychological data appropriately, and better evaluate the quality of the psychological consultation he receives.

It would not have been possible to write a multipurpose book

without the stimulation, encouragement, and advice of many colleagues and students. Their clinical and training needs comple-
mented my own in setting a standard for developing its content and
organization. Their interests resulted in numerous additions to the
text and elaborations of specific topics. Their suggestions and criti-
cisms have contributed immeasurably to this book's readability,
practicality, and scientific soundness.

Joseph M. Wepman has played a special role in the realization of
this book. He introduced me to the mysteries of brain-behavior relations when, as a graduate student at the University of Chicago, I took
his course, then entitled, "Speech Therapy." Over the years I have
had a number of opportunities to continue to learn from him. Only
since I began to formulate my approach to clinical practice have I
come to appreciate how much his humanistic, pragmatic, and
openly inquiring orientation has influenced me. I am thus deeply
grateful to have also benefited from his apt and constructive critique
of the manuscript.

A number of persons gave a great deal of their time and expertise
to this book. I am especially indebted to John R. Painter, Jerry Deffen-
bacher, and John O. Lipkin for their conscientious and perceptive
help with this book's successive drafts. John Painter has also served
as psychological theoretician and statistical advisor; John Lipkin has
been the psychiatric consultant. I have received valuable assistance
in preparing the neurological portions of this text from James M.
Watson and from my colleagues in the Neurology Service of the Portland Veterans Administration Hospital, Luis Garcia-Bunuel and
Richard Olmscheid, and in the Department of Neurology of the University of Oregon Health Sciences Center, C. Conrad Carter and John
P. Hammerstad. Janice R. Stevens assisted in the presentation of
material related to epilepsy. Robert C. Marshall has been a most will-
ing and helpful advisor on aphasia and other disorders of communication.

An unexpected boon that came from writing this book has been the
contacts I have made—some in person, many by mail—with other
neuropsychologists. The authors and researchers whose data I have
reproduced have been, without exception, cooperative and encouraging. Without their help this book would be much less comprehensive.

I greatly appreciate the support given by members of the Portland

Veterans Administration Hospital staff, particularly that of my chief, Vincent Glaudin. The unstinting and, at times, heroic efforts of the hospital's chief librarian, Sandra C. Brayson and her staff to fill my hundreds of library requests were essential to the book's completeness. Nancy Temple and the Medical Illustration Service worked hard to help with the illustrative material.

I also want to express my gratitude to my editor, Jeffrey House. With good-humored patience, sensible advice, and painstaking care, he provided the guidance necessary to bring this work to fruition.

I have saved my final and most grateful "thank you" for my family. Their good-natured tolerance of a household turned topsy-turvy while a book was written in its midst flagged only occasionally during their two-year ordeal. Their good-will and encouragement never flagged. Additionally, each has contributed directly to the clarity and readability of this book, sometimes with a word or well-turned phrase, sometimes with an apt criticism or suggestion. Thank you Sidney, Annie, David, Miriam, Enrico Fletzer, and Jennifer Himmelsbach.

Portland, Oregon   M.D.L.
May 1976

CONTENTS

NEUROPSYCHOLOGICAL ASSESSMENT

1
THE PRACTICE
OF NEUROPSYCHOLOGY

Clinical neuropsychology is an applied science concerned with the behavioral expression of brain dysfunction. It evolved in response to practical problems of assessment and rehabilitation of brain damaged patients. These problems arose in a number of areas of clinical practice. Clinicians in the neurosciences wanted behavioral evaluations to aid in neurological diagnosis and in the documentation of the course of brain disorders or the effects of neurosurgery and other treatments. Psychotherapists needed to identify patients with underlying neurological disorders. Military medicine created its own neuropsychology programs to assist in rapid screening and diagnosis of brain injured soldiers during wartime and with rehabilitation afterwards. Child neuropsychology grew hand in hand with advances in the study of mental retardation, learning disabilities, and children's behavior problems[1] (Reitan and Davison, 1974, *passim*; E. M. Taylor, 1959).

The methods of clinical neuropsychology reflect the fact that its roots are in clinical psychology. However, unlike clinical psychology, which places its greatest emphasis on effecting behavior change, the emphasis in clinical neuropsychology has been on *assessing* behavioral change. In part this has occurred because so much of the demand on neuropsychology has been for assistance with diagnostic problems. Moreover, patients seen by neuropsychologists are often limited in their capacity to benefit from training programs

[1] The assessment of children and the consideration of brain disorders presenting prior to maturity have their own conceptual framework, methods, and data which are outside the scope of this book.

3

and counseling. Then too, as one of the clinical sciences, neuropsychology may be evolving naturally, for assessment tends to play
a predominant role while these sciences are relatively young; treatment techniques develop as diagnostic categories and etiological
relationships are defined and clarified.

Any of three different purposes may prompt a neuropsychological
examination: diagnosis, patient care—including questions about
treatment and planning, and research. Each purpose calls for some
differences in assessment strategies.

1. *Diagnosis.* Of the many practical applications of neuropsychological assessment, its diagnostic usefulness has probably received the most recognition. Diagnostic assessment is usually undertaken to discriminate between psychiatric and neurological
symptoms, to evaluate a possible neurological disorder in a
nonpsychiatric patient, or to aid in distinguishing between different
neurological conditions. When the focus of the neuropsychological
examination is on diagnosis, its scope may be limited to a search for
specific behavioral symptoms or patterns of performance aberrations. Although the extent to which behavioral findings can be related to neuroanatomical events is limited (see pp. 30–31 and
67–68), the neuropsychologist may be able to indicate possible
neuroanatomical correlates of the behavior he is evaluating.

2. *Patient care.* In some patients referred for neuropsychological
assessment, the presence of brain damage is obvious in histories of
prolonged periods of unconsciousness following head injury or
fever, scars or disfiguration of the face or skull, or a tell-tale weakness or loss of use of the limbs of one side of the body. Many other
patients have already been diagnosed by a neurologist, neurosurgeon, or other physician. For such a patient, referral questions usually concern the nature and extent of his behavioral impairment and
call for a descriptive use of the assessment techniques. The neuropsychological examination will aim to provide information about
the patient's psychological strengths and weaknesses and his needs
and attitudes that the patient and those responsible for his well-
being can use.

Descriptive evaluations may be employed in many ways for the
care and treatment of the brain injured patient. Precise descriptive

information about intellectual and emotional status is essential for careful management of many neurological disorders. Rational planning for the patient requires an understanding of the patient's capabilities, limitations, the kinds of psychological changes he is undergoing, and the impact of these changes on his experience of himself and on his behavior.

The relative sensitivity and precision of neuropsychological measurements make them well-suited for following the course of many neurological diseases. Data from successive neuropsychological examinations repeated at regular intervals can provide reliable indications of whether the underlying neurological condition is changing, and if so, how rapidly and in what ways. Repeated testing may also be used to measure the effects of treatment or retraining.

The brain damaged patient too must have factual information about his functioning if he is to understand himself and set realistic goals, yet his need for information about himself is often overlooked. Most people who sustain brain injury experience changes in their intellectual and emotional functioning; but because they are on the inside, so to speak, they may have difficulty appreciating how their behavior has changed and what about them is still the same. These misperceptions tend to heighten what mental confusion may already be present as a result of altered patterns of neural activity.

Distrust of their experiences, particularly their memory and perceptions, is another problem shared by many brain damaged persons, probably as a result of even very slight disruptions and alterations of the exceedingly complex neural pathways that mediate the intellectual functions. This distrust seems to arise from the feelings of strangeness and confusion accompanying previously familiar habits, thoughts, and sensations that are now experienced differently. The self-doubt of the brain injured person is usually distinguishable from neurotic self-doubts about life goals, values, principles, and so on, but can be just as painful and emotionally crippling. Careful reporting and explanation of psychological findings can do much to allay a patient's anxieties and dispel his confusion.

The following case exemplifies patients' needs for information about their psychological status.

An attractive, unmarried 24-year-old bank teller sustained a brain concussion in a car accident while skiing in Europe. She appeared to make an uneventful and practically complete recovery, with only a little residual facial numbness. When she came home, she returned to her old job but was unable to perform acceptably although she seemed capable of doing each part of it well. She lost interest in outdoor sports although her coordination and strength were essentially unimpaired. She became socially withdrawn, moody, morose, and dependent. A psychiatric consultant diagnosed depression, and when her unhappiness was not diminished by counseling or antidepressant drugs, he administered shock treatment which gave only temporary relief.

While waiting to begin a second course of shock treatment, she was given a neuropsychological examination at the request of the foreign magistrate who was responsible for awarding monetary compensation for her injuries. This examination demonstrated a small but definite impairment of immediate memory, concentration, and conceptual tracking. The patient reported a pervasive sense of unsureness which she expressed in hesitancy and doubt about almost everything she did. These feelings of doubt had undermined the young woman's trust in many of her previously automatic responses, destroying a lively spontaneity that was once a very appealing feature of her personality. Further, like many postconcussion patients, she had compounded the problem by interpreting her inner uneasiness as symptomatic of "mental illness," and psychiatric opinion confirmed her fears. Thus, while her intellectual impairment was not an obstacle to rehabilitation, her bewildered experience of it led to disastrous changes in her personal life. A clear explanation of her actual limitations and their implications brought immediate relief of anxiety and set the stage for sound counseling.

The concerned family also needs to know the patient's psychological condition in order to deal with him appropriately, understand his adjustment problems, and readjust to his changes. Family members frequently do not appreciate the nature and extent of the patient's disabilities. They then have difficulty adapting their demands and expectations to the patient's new performance levels. Overprotection, on the one hand, and denial or minimizing of the patient's psychological handicaps, on the other, are common family failings. The intangible, seemingly vague and puzzling mental changes of the neurological patient can spark family feuds, the opposing factions warring about whether the patient can be left alone or should be encouraged to return to work, is doing too much or too little, is being babied or neglected, and so on.

Often, other persons share responsibility for the brain damaged patient's care, such as physiatrists, speech pathologists, rehabilitation counselors, occupational and physical therapists, and visiting nurses. They need current appraisals of the patient's psychological functioning so that they can adapt their program and goals to the patient's changing needs and capacities.

3. *Research.* Neuropsychological assessment has been used to study the organization of brain activity and its translation into behavior and in investigations of specific brain disorders and behavioral disabilities. Research with neuropsychological assessment techniques also involves their development, standardization, and evaluation. The precision and sensitivity of neuropsychological measurement techniques make them valuable tools for investigating small, sometimes quite subtle behavioral alterations, such as those that may follow certain neurosurgical procedures or metabolic changes.

Neuropsychological research has had a very direct influence on the practice of clinical neuropsychology. Many of the tests used in neuropsychological evaluations—such as arithmetic tests or tests for visual memory and learning—were originally developed for the examination of normal intellectual functioning and were recalibrated for neuropsychological use in the course of research on brain dysfunction. Other assessment techniques—as for instance, certain tests of tactile identification or concept formation—were designed specifically for studies of brain dysfunction. Their often rapid incorporation into clinical use attests to the very lively exchange between research and practice. This exchange works especially well in neuropsychology because clinician and researcher are so often one and the same.

Usually neuropsychological studies serve more than one purpose. Even though the examination may be initially undertaken to answer a single question—most often, a diagnostic issue—the neuropsychologist may uncover vocational or family problems, or patient care needs that have been overlooked, or the patient may prove to be a suitable candidate for research. Integral to all psychological assessment procedures is an evaluation of the patient's needs and circumstances from a psychological viewpoint. When indicated, the neuropsychologist will redirect the scope of his inquiry to include problems he has defined as well as those stated in the referral.

When a single examination is undertaken to serve all three purposes—diagnosis, patient care, and research—a great deal of data may be collected about the patient and then applied selectively. For example, the examination of a patient complaining of immediate memory problems can be conducted to answer various questions. For a diagnostic determination of whether his immediate memory is impaired, it may only be necessary to find out if he remembers significantly fewer words of a list and numbers of a series than the slowest normal adult. To understand how he is affected by his memory dysfunction, it is important to know the number of words he can remember and under what conditions, the nature of his errors, his sensitivity and reactions to his performance, and the effect of his disability on his day to day activities. Research might involve studying his immediate memory in conjunction with blood sugar levels or brain wave tests, or comparing his performance to that of patients with other kinds of memory complaints.

The ways in which neuropsychological assessment has been employed in legal proceedings illustrate the usefulness of multipurpose studies. It has become quite commonplace in personal injury actions, in which monetary compensation is sought for claims of bodily injury and loss of function, for lawyers to request neuropsychological examinations of the claimant. In such cases, the neuropsychologist usually examines the claimant to evaluate the type and amount of behavioral impairment sustained and to estimate the claimant's rehabilitation potential and the extent of his need for future care. Occasionally, the request for compensation may hinge on the neuropsychologist's report.

In criminal cases, a neuropsychologist may assess a defendant when there is reason to suspect that brain dysfunction contributed to his misbehavior or when there is a question about his mental capacity to stand trial. The case of the murderer of President Kennedy's alleged assailant is perhaps the most famous instance in which a psychologist determined that the defendant's capacity for judgment and self-control was impaired by brain dysfunction (Kaplan and Waltz, 1965). Interestingly, the possibility that the defendant, Jack Ruby, had psychomotor epilepsy was first raised by Dr. Roy Schafer's interpretation of the psychological test results and was subsequently confirmed by *electroencephalographic* (brain wave) studies. At the sentencing stage of a criminal proceeding, the neuropsychologist may also be asked for his opinion about treatment of a convicted defendant or his potential for rehabilitation.

Knowledge of brain injury and brain functions underlies treatment programs for the rehabilitation of brain injured patients that have been developed by neuropsychologists. The works of K. Goldstein (1939, 1942) with brain injured World War I soldiers and Wepman (1951) with World War II aphasics relate some of the efforts of early rehabilitation programs based on neuropsychological research and clinical assessment. Following in this tradition, present-day neuropsychological rehabilitation projects continue to integrate clinical assessment and research with patient retraining (Diller et al., 1974; Lewinsohn, 1973).

The clinical neuropsychologist regularly deals with a variety of questions, a wide range of behaviors, and the very disparate capacities of his patients. This diversity of problems and persons presents an unending challenge to the examiner who wants to satisfy all the purposes for which the examination was undertaken and still test the patient at levels suited to his capacities and limitations. Moreover, in so new, complex, and broad-ranging a field he can take few facts or principles for granted, he has few techniques that cannot benefit from modifications, and few rules of procedure will not be bent or broken as knowledge and experience accumulate. The practice of neuropsychology calls for flexibility, curiosity, and inventiveness even in the most routine work. But even the routine work of the neuropsychologist holds the promise of new insights into the workings of the brain and the excitement of discovery.

2
BASIC CONCEPTS

NEUROLOGY AND PSYCHOLOGY

Neurology and psychology share much common ground for they are both concerned with behavior and both rely on behavioral observations and behavioral testing for much of their clinical data. Their differences lie in their focus and their methods. For neurology, the study of behavior is a means to an end: the understanding of the nervous system and the treatment of neurological disease. In psychology, the study of behavior is either an end in itself or a means of enhancing the prediction or control of behavior.

In clinical neurology, the full range of behavior, from discrete reflexes to complex acts, is studied extensively for the purpose of drawing or supporting inferences about the condition of the underlying neural structures. The neurologist looks for the typical behavior patterns generated by neuroanatomical subsystems, measuring the patient's responses in relatively coarse gradations or noting their absence.

In clinical psychology, on the other hand, behavior is studied intensively as the manifestation of such psychologically meaningful systems as intellect, personality, or emotionality. The psychological examination consists of assessment interviews, scaled tests, and questionnaires that can provide relatively precise and sensitive indices of behavior. The purpose of the psychological examination is the description, prediction, modification, or control of behavior, or some combination of these.

In clinical practice there is a great ideal of interaction between neurology and psychology. The clinical psychologists' needs for neurological consultation are obvious, since the initial symptoms of some brain diseases may appear in the form of personality or intellectual changes; and patients with early brain disease or bewildered family members often first seek psychological treatment for what they think are psychological problems. Neurologists may call on any one of a number of behavioral science practitioners— psychologists, psychiatrists, psychiatric social workers—for psychotherapy or counseling with their patients. Clinical neuropsychologists provide the behavioral measurement and appraisal needed for some of the problems of diagnosis, progress evaluation, or planning that neurological patients present.

The interaction between the two approaches is illustrated in this case history:

A 29-year-old air force technician with an excellent health history had a *grand mal* seizure hours after a tempestuous quarrel with his wife. When he had a second seizure several weeks later, he went to the base hospital where a thorough neurological examination revealed no abnormality. The seizures increased in frequency and were then controlled fairly well by anticonvulsive drugs, but he was given a medical discharge from service and was seen as an outpatient by neurologists at regular intervals thereafter.

He made a rapid adjustment to civilian life, becoming an electronic parts inspector and then foreman, jobs which required a great deal of precision in visual judgment and adeptness in handling complex machinery and delicate parts. Approximately three years after his first seizure, his supervisor noticed that he was slowing down and becoming clumsy and inaccurate in his work. His employer requested that he obtain a medical evaluation and the patient returned for another neurological examination. His wife then reported to the neurologist that he was sleeping much of the time, that he had lost interest in his usual activities, and that his sexual performance had become unsatisfactory. Once again, there were no "hard" neurological findings, but this time the patient was referred to a psychologist.

The patient was interviewed and given intellectual and personality tests. As expected from the history, the patient performed at *average* to *high average* levels (within the performance range of the upper 15 to 50% of the population) on almost all of the tests of intellectual ability, but scored lower on tasks involving organization, reproduction, and memory of complex visual perceptions. His personality test responses reflected a more than ordinary amount of preoccupation with physical concerns for a man his age but were otherwise unremarkable. Although the discrepancies between high and low test scores were not quite large enough to be statistically significant, they were sufficiently consistent to suggest an impairment pattern, particularly in the light of his having formerly excelled in work requiring fine visual discrimination and judgment.

Because of the psychological test pattern of impaired visual organization plus observations of slightly slurred speech and a barely perceptible flattening of the muscles on the left side of the nose and mouth, he was sent back to the neurologist with an urgent recommendation for further study of a possible right hemisphere lesion. Brain scan and radiographic studies of the cerebral blood vessels (angiography) revealed a mass in the front half of the right hemisphere. He was operated on within the week for removal of a malignant tumor.

The patient lived two more years, becoming increasingly childish. His judgment deteriorated, self-control gave way to impulsivity and rapidly shifting emotional ups and downs, and he became unsteady, weak, and ultimately bedridden. The psychologist counseled his wife and two school-age children as they coped with role changes, added responsibilities, frustrations, and fears. The patient was tested several times during this period to give the family an objective picture of his changing strengths and limitations. After his death the widow continued to see the psychologist for vocational and personal counseling.

DIMENSIONS OF BEHAVIOR

It is often useful to analyze behavior in terms of three functional systems: (1) *intellect,* which is the information handling aspect of behavior; (2) *emotionality,* which concerns feelings and motivation; and (3) *control,* which has to do with how behavior is expressed. Components of each of these three sets of functions are as integral to every bit of behavior as are length and breadth and height to the shape of any object. Moreover, like the dimensions of space, each one can be conceptualized and treated separately. The early Greek philosophers were the first to conceive of a tripartite division of behavior, postulating that different principles of the "soul" governed the rational, appetitive, and animating aspects of behavior. Present-day research in the behavioral sciences tends to support the philosophers' intuitive insights into how the totality of behavior is organized. These classical and scientifically meaningful functional systems lend themselves well to the practical observation, measurement, and description of behavior and constitute a framework for organizing behavioral data generally.

Organic behavioral disturbances rarely appear as defects of a single functional system. Typically they show up in the complex interactions between all three systems even when the immediate defect appears to be limited to just one of them.

These interactions occur in a variety of ways. Defects in one system can have repercussions on one or both of the others. For instance, blunted affect can compromise judgment, or loss of initiative may result in limited opportunities for intellectual stimulation and emotional satisfaction. More often, two or all three systems are directly affected by a brain injury and the impairments in each are mutually reinforcing. Behavior problems may also become more acute and the symptom picture more complex as secondary reactions to the specific problems created by the organic defect further involve each system. Additional repercussions and reactions may then occur as the patient attempts to cope with succeeding sets of reactions and the problems they bring.

The following case of a man who sustained relatively minor brain injuries demonstrates some typical interactions between impairments in different psychological systems.

A middle-aged clerk, the father of teen-aged children, incurred a left-sided head injury in a car accident and was unconscious for several days. When examined three months after the accident, his principal complaint was fatigue. His intelligence test scores were consistently high average (between the 75th and 90th percentiles). The only cognitive difficulty demonstrated in the psychological examination was a slight impairment of verbal fluency exhibited by a few word-use errors on a sentence building task. This verbal fluency problem did not seem grave, but it had serious implications for the patient's adjustment.

Because he could no longer produce fluent speech automatically, the patient had to exercise constant vigilance and conscious effort to talk as well as he did. This effort was a continuous drain on his energy so that he fatigued easily. Verbal fluency tended to deteriorate when he grew tired, giving rise to a vicious cycle in which he put out more effort when he was tired, further sapping his energy at the times he needed it the most. He felt worn out and became discouraged, irritable, and depressed. Emotional control too was no longer as automatic or effective as before the accident, and it was poorest when he was tired. He "blew up" frequently with little provocation. His children did not hide their annoyance with their grouchy, sullen father, and his wife became protective and overly solicitous. The patient perceived his family's behavior as further proof of his inadequacy and hopelessness. His depression deepened, he became more self-conscious about his speech, and fluency continued to be a problem.

INTELLECTUAL FUNCTIONS

Disturbances of the intellectual functions—those mental activities having to do with the processing of information—figure most prominently in the symptom constellations of brain damage. As a result, the intellectual functions have received the greatest part of neuropsychologists' attention.

It is often useful to divide intellectual functions into four major classes: (1) *receptive functions,* which involve the abilities to acquire, process, classify, and integrate information; (2) *memory and learning,* by means of which information is stored and recalled; (3) *cognition,* or thinking, which concerns the mental organization and reorganization of information; and (4) *expressive functions* through which information is communicated or acted upon. Each functional class comprises many discrete intellectual activities—such as immediate memory for spoken words, or color recognition. Although each function constitutes a distinct class of behavior, normally they all work in close, interdependent concert.

Generally speaking, within each class of intellectual function, a division may be made between those functions that mediate verbal/symbolic information and those that deal with data that cannot be communicated in words or symbols, such as complex visual or sound patterns. These subclasses of functions differ from one another in their neuroanatomical organization and in their behavioral expression while sharing other basic neuroanatomical and psychometric relationships within the functional system.

The identification of discrete functions within each class of intellectual functions varies somewhat with the perspective and techniques of the investigator (Poeck, 1969). Examiners using simple tests that elicit discrete responses can study highly specific functions. Multidimensional tests call forth complex responses and thus measure broader and more complex functions. Verbal functions enter into verbal test responses. Motor functions are demonstrated on tests involving motor behavior. When practical considerations of time and equipment limit the functions that can be studied or when relevant tests are not administered, then some functions remain unnoticed. However, even though different investigators may identify or define some of the narrower subclasses of functions differently, they agree on the major functional systems and the large subdivisions.

The Concept of Intelligence

Intellectual behavior was originally attributed to a single intellectual function, *intelligence*. Early investigators treated the concept of intelligence as if it were a unitary variable, which, like physical strength, increased at a regular rate in the course of normal childhood development (Binet, 1908; Terman, 1916) and decreased with the amount of brain tissue lost through accident or disease (Chapman and Wolff, 1959; Lashley, 1938). As refinements in testing and data handling techniques have afforded greater precision and control over observations of intellectual behavior, it has become evident that the behavior that tests measure is directly referrable to specific intellectual functions. The concept of intelligence becomes meaningful as an abstraction from common observation that reflects the tendency for each organism to process all kinds of information at a similar level of efficiency.

Neuropsychology and the concept of intelligence
Neuropsychological research has contributed significantly to this redefinition of the concept of intelligence. Although there is an overall tendency for the amount of general intellectual impairment to be associated with the sheer extent of the brain injury (Chapman et al., 1958; Lishman, 1968), in many patients, the presence of brain lesions, including some of considerable extent, is not reflected in lowered scores on tests of general intelligence (Hebb, 1942; Maher, 1963). When general intellectual impairment occurs in conjunction with large brain lesions, the broad deficits appear to be due to summation and interaction effects of tissue destruction at many local function sites.

Further, lesions involving at least some portion of the cerebral cortex usually result in impairment of one or more of the intellectual functions while sparing others (Blakemore et al., 1972; McFie, 1969; A. Smith, 1966b). A similar unevenness is generally seen in the effects of deteriorating brain diseases on psychological functions generally, for not only are some functions involved while others are spared, but the affected functions deteriorate at different rates (Klebanoff et al., 1954). Differential deterioration of diverse psychological functions also occurs in aging (Birren, 1963; Eysenck, 1945a, b; G. Goldstein and Shelly, 1975) (see Chapter 7). Moreover, there appears to be no evidence that a general intellectual function is served by any one part of the brain (Meyer, 1961; Piercy, 1964). In no area of the cortex of the brain does a discrete local lesion result in a generalized intellectual deficit.

The following case provides a telling example of how very specific organic impairment can be.

> A brilliant research scientist was struck on the right side of his head by falling rock while mountain climbing. He was unconscious for several hours and then confused for several days, but was able to return to a full research and writing schedule shortly thereafter. On psychological tests taken six weeks after the injury, he achieved scores within the top 1 to 5% range on all tests of both verbal and visuoconstructive skills, with the single exception of a picture-arranging test requiring serial organization of cartoons into stories. On this test his score, at approximately the bottom tenth percentile, was almost in the *borderline defective* ability range. He was then given a serial reasoning test involving letter and number patterns which he answered correctly, but only after taking about 25 minutes to do what most bright adults can finish in five. He reported that his previous high level of work performance was unchanged except for difficulty with sequential organization when writing research papers.

Mental ability factors and the concept of intelligence
For decades, many investigators have worked on the question of the nature and organization of the mental abilities covered by the global concept of intelligence. The statistical methods of factor analysis, pioneered by Spearman and Thurstone, have provided a fruitful approach to this complex problem.

Factor analytic studies of intellectual behavior have consistently demonstrated a hierarchical organization of *mental abilities* (intellectual functions defined by psychological measurements) (see Fig. 2-1). At the top of the hierarchy is the general mental ability factor g that represents the extent to which all intellectual activities are associated (Spearman, 1927).

> The earliest fundamental observation made was that the inter-test correlations, although widely varying in magnitude, were at least regularly positive in sign. On behalf of the old and charitable view, that a person's inferiority in one kind of performance is likely to be compensated by superiority in another, there was found no support whatever. On the contrary, it appeared that any failure in anything is rather a bad than a good augury for all other things (Spearman and Jones, 1950, p. 7).

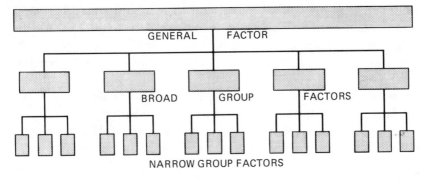

FIG. 2-1. A three-stage hierarchy. (Humphreys, 1962.) (Copyright 1962 by the American Psychological Association. Reprinted by permission.)

This commonly observed tendency for a person to perform at much the same level on a variety of different intellectual tasks gave an operational meaning to the concept of general intelligence (McNemar, 1965). Since this tendency was first documented at the turn of the century, it has been regularly demonstrated in clinical practice (H. L. Williams, 1962), in large sample standardization programs (Terman and Merrill, 1960; Wechsler, 1958), in longitudinal studies (Anastasi, 1965; Garrett, 1946; Jarvik et al., 1973), and in studies of individual abilities in which intraindividual correlations between scores on different skills and functions have been investigated (Bennett et al., 1972). Consistency of intellectual performance tends to appear even when uninvited. Test-makers have typically failed in their efforts to develop test batteries in which the commonality of performance on different kinds of mental tests would be minimal or eliminated altogether (R. W. Payne, 1961; L. L. Thurstone, 1948). However, g does not represent an intellectual function, for it is the one factor that is not defined by its own unique set of operations nor does it refer to any given activity.

At the next lower level of the mental ability hierarchy are group factors that are common to such broad classes of mental abilities as verbal, computational, or visual organization. The verbal group factor, for instance, appears in all factor analyses of tests of verbal skills, whether they be vocabulary tests, tests of grammar or fluency, tests of verbal abstraction, or writing tests. Under the broad group factors there may be subgroups of factors referrable to narrower ranges of abilities. Tests of grammatical skills, for example, would certainly be weighted with the general verbal group factor and would probably also contain a subgroup factor related to knowledge and use of grammar. What the factor analysis extracts, of course, depends on the tests studied. Obviously no computational factor will emerge when the test array contains no arithmetic tests, nor will clear differences between broad and narrow group factors appear unless there are many similar but not identical tests in the battery.

The performance of most adults on tests of intellectual ability reflects both the tendency for test scores generally to converge at the same level and for some test scores to differ in small, usually insignificant degrees from others (R. W. Payne, 1961; Vernon, 1950). In normal adults, specialization of interests and activities and singular experiences contribute to intraindividual differences. Social limitations, emotional disturbance, physical illness or handicaps, and brain dysfunction tend to magnify intraindividual test differences to significant proportions.

Intelligence remains a useful concept in intellectual assessment when it refers to the common tendency for an individual to perform many different intellectual tasks at about the same level of proficiency. Spiker and McCandless (1954) aptly define this tendency as "the transituational consistency of intellectual behavior." This tendency follows naturally from the conditions of normal development during which different parts of the brain are regulated by the same genetic material, receive the same nourishment, are subjected to the same diseases, and share similar levels of stimulation. Piercy summarizes this view well by defining intelligence as "a tendency for cerebral regions subserving different intellectual functions to be proportionately developed in any one individual. According to this notion, people with good verbal ability will tend also to have good non-verbal ability, in much the same way as people with big hands tend to have big feet" (1964, p. 341).

Classes of Intellectual Functions

Receptive Functions

The two main classes of receptive functions are *sensation* (visual, auditory, tactile, etc.) and *perception*, which concerns the integration of sensory impressions into psychologically meaningful data.

For example, light on the retina creates a visual *sensation;* the organization of the impulses transmitted by the aroused retina into a pattern of hues and shades and intensities recognized as a daffodil in bloom is *perception.*

Strictly speaking, sensory reception is not so much an intellectual function as it is an arousal process that triggers central registering and integrating activities. The organism receives sensation passively, shutting it out only, for instance, by holding the nose to avoid a stench. Even in the soundest slumber, a stomachache or a loud noise will rouse the sleeper. Perception, on the other hand, is an active intellectual process. It includes all the activities involved in filtering and modifying the continuous torrent of sensation from all the sense modalities and in integrating sensory stimuli with one another at each moment, successively, and with the organism's past experience.

Normal perception in the healthy organism is a complex process engaging many different aspects of brain functioning. Like other intellectual functions, the extensive cortical distribution and complexity of perceptual activities make them highly vulnerable to brain injury. Organic perceptual defects can occur indirectly through loss of a primary sensory input such as vision or smell and directly through impairment of specific integrative processes. Although it may be difficult to separate the sensory from the perceptual components of a behavioral defect in some severely brain damaged patients, sensation and perception each has its own functional integrity. This can be seen clearly when perceptual organization is maintained despite very severe sensory defects or when perceptual functions are markedly disrupted in patients with little or no sensory deficit. The nearly deaf person can readily understand speech patterns when the sound is sufficiently amplified, whereas some brain damaged persons with keen auditory acuity cannot make sense out of what they hear.

The perceptual functions include such activities as awareness, recognition, discrimination, patterning, and orientation. Since a disturbance in any one perceptual activity may affect any of the sensory modalities as well as different aspects of each one a catalogue of discrete perceptual disturbances can be quite lengthy. Reviewing auditory, visual, and *somatosensory* (body sensation) modalities, M. Williams (1970a) lists 17 different kinds of specific perceptual defects, the *agnosias* (literally, no knowledge). Her list of 17 agnosias could be expanded, for within most of these categories of perceptual defect there are functionally discrete subcategories (Nielson, 1962; Critchley, 1953). For instance, loss of the ability to recognize faces (*prosopagnosia*), one of the visual agnosias, may be manifested in at least two different forms: inability to recognize familiar faces and inability to recognize unfamiliar faces, each related to a different area of the brain (Warrington and James, 1967b).

Memory

Central to all intellectual functions and probably to all that is characteristically human in a person's behavior is the capacity for memory and learning. Memory frees the individual from dependency on physiological urges or situational happenstance for pleasure seeking; dread and despair do not occur in a memory vacuum. Severely impaired memory isolates the patient from emotionally or practically meaningful contact with the world about him and deprives him of a sense of personal continuity, rendering him passive, bland, and helplessly dependent. Mildly to moderately impaired memory has a disorienting effect.

Three kinds of memory are clinically distinguishable. Two are succeeding stages of *short-term storage* and the third is *long-term storage*. *Registration* is neither strictly a memory function nor a perceptual function but rather a selecting and recording process by which perceptions enter the memory system (Atkinson and Shiffrin, 1968; Lewinsohn et al., 1972). *Amnesia* (literally, no memory) refers to periods of total lapse of memory, in contrast to memory impairments that may involve specific deficits.

1. *Registration* has been called a "valve determining which memories are stored" (Nauta, 1966). It involves the programming of acquired sensory response patterns (perceptual tendencies) in the recording and memorizing centers of the brain (Nauta, 1964). The affective, *set* (perceptual and response predisposition), and attention-focusing components of perception play an integral role in the registration process (Brain, 1969; Pribram, 1969). Information in the registration process is either transferred to short-term memory or it quickly decays. Registration and the rate at which decay takes place are exceedingly rapid phenomena, measurable in milliseconds (Atkinson and Shiffrin, 1968).

2a. *Immediate memory*, the first stage of short-term memory storage, concerns the fixation of the information selected for retention by the registration process. It has been aptly called the "working memory": "On the one hand . . . (the short-term store) decouples the memory system from the external environment and relieves the system from the responsibility of moment-to-moment attention to environmental changes. On the other hand, STS (short-term store) provides a working memory on a temporary basis" (Shiffrin and Atkinson, 1969). Immediate memory is of sufficient duration to enable a person to respond to ongoing events when more enduring forms of memory have been lost (Talland, 1965; Victor et al., 1971). It lasts from about 30 seconds up to several minutes unless it is sustained by *rehearsal,* which is any repetitive process that serves to lengthen the duration of a memory trace. With rehearsal, a memory trace may be maintained for hours.

The preponderant evidence suggests that information in immediate memory is temporarily maintained in *reverberating neural circuits* (self-contained neural networks that sustain a nerve impulse by channeling it repeatedly through the same network) (Rosenzweig and Leiman, 1968; Thompson et al., 1972). It appears that, if not converted into a more stable biochemical organization for longer lasting storage, the electrochemical activities that constitute the immediate memory trace spontaneously dissipate and the memory is not retained. For example, only the rare reader with a "photographic" memory will be able to recall verbatim the first sentence on the preceding page although almost everyone who has read this far will have just seen it.

2b. Another kind of short-term memory may be distinguished from immediate memory in that it lasts from an hour or so to one or two days—longer than a reverberating circuit could be maintained by even the most conscientious rehearsal efforts, but not yet permanently fixed as learned material in long-term storage (Rosenzweig and Leiman, 1968). There may be some question as to whether this short-term memory is simply information transferred to long-term memory but so newly laid down as to be relatively vulnerable to interference effects, thus lacking the stability usually associated with long-term memory.

3. *Long-term memory*, or learning, refers to the organism's ability to store information. The process of storing information as long-term

memory begins as soon as one-half second after information enters short-term storage and it continues as long as that information remains there (Atkinson and Shiffrin, 1968). The consolidation of long-term memory traces generally is a slow procedure, which progressively strengthens the traces so that recently learned material or behavior is more vulnerable to disruption or dissipation than are older memories (McGaugh, 1966; Weiskrantz, 1966). Information in the long-term storage system appears to be organized on the basis of meaning, whereas the organization of information in the short-term storage system takes place in terms of sensory properties, such as similar sounds, shapes, or colors (Broadbent, 1970).

Long-term memory storage may be a biochemical process involving transformation of protein configurations in cortical nerve cells (Hydén, 1970; Magoun, 1966). These transformations, possibly in conjunction with the budding of new cell contact points (Hoffman, 1971; Rosenzweig et al., 1972), create the transmission patterns between cells that constitute the long-term memory trace. There does not appear to be a local storage site for stored memories; instead memories seem to involve neuronal contributions from many cortical and subcortical centers (Penfield, 1968; Thompson et al., 1972).

Recent and remote memory are clinical terms that refer respectively to memories stored within the last few hours, days, weeks, or even months and to older memories dating from early childhood (Brierley, 1966). In normal persons it is virtually impossible to determine when recent memory ends and remote memory begins, for there are no major discontinuities in memory from the present to early wisps of infantile recollection. Recent memory and remote memory become meaningful concepts when we consider those brain diseases in which the processes for registering or storing long-term memory are impaired (Milner and Teuber, 1968). In such diseases, the most recent of the remote memories may indicate the approximate time of onset of the memorization problem, since all later events will be very poorly remembered, if at all (Barbizet, 1970; Brain, 1969). When an amnestic period results from an accident or illness, memories stored after memorizing abilities return may be considered recent in contrast to the remote memories antedating the accident or illness. Following certain kinds of brain injury or disease, bits and chunks of remote memory may be lost (Adams et al., 1961; Goodglass, 1973). A global loss of remote memory rarely occurs without some alteration in level of consciousness as well (Ojemann, 1966; Whitty and Lishman, 1966).

The effectiveness of the memory system also depends on how readily and completely information can be retrieved. Information retrieval is *remembering*, which may occur through *recall* when an association triggers awareness of the stored information. The question, "What is the capital of Oregon?" tests the recall function. When a like stimulus triggers awareness, remembering takes place through *recognition*. The question, "Which of the following is the capital of Oregon: Albany, Portland, or Salem?" tests the recognition function. Retrieval by recognition is much easier than retrieval by recall for normal persons as well as brain damaged patients (Heilbrun, 1960; Lewis, 1961).

The dimensions of memory function become apparent in pathological conditions of the brain. Defective memory is usually thought of as a defect in the storage or recall of data that once was or could have been remembered. Difficulty or inability to recall specific information, such as a friend's name or the year Columbus discovered America, is an obvious memory defect. However, mental processes and behavioral activities are also learned, remembered, and subject to forgetting or to extinction by brain damage. Visceral responses, motor skills, rules and procedures, speech patterns and conceptual relationships can be lost through defects of memory too. Brain disease affects these different kinds of memories in long-term storage differentially so that a motor speech habit, such as organizing certain sounds into a word, may be wholly retained while rules for organizing words into meaningful speech are lost (Geschwind, 1970). Stored memories involving different sensory modalities and output mechanisms are also differentially affected by brain disease (Barbizet, 1970). For example, recognition of printed words or numbers may be severely impaired while speech comprehension and picture recognition remain relatively intact. The retention of learned material in long-term storage depends upon the integrity of the cortical areas that subserve the functions involved (Arnold, 1974; Barbizet, 1970). Only extensive cortical damage ordinarily disrupts long ingrained memories and habits (Brain, 1969).

Thinking

Thinking may be defined as any mental operation that relates two or more bits of information explicitly (as in making an arithmetic computation) or implicitly (as in judging that *this* is bad, i.e., relative to *that*). A host of complex cognitive functions is subsumed under the rubric of thinking, such as computation, reasoning and judgment, concept formation, abstracting and generalizing, ordering, organizing, and planning.

The nature of the information being mentally manipulated (e.g., numbers, design concepts, words) and the operation (e.g., comparing, compounding, abstracting, ordering) define the category of thinking. Thus, "verbal reasoning" comprises several operations done with words; it generally includes ordering and comparing, sometimes analyzing and synthesizing. "Computation" may involve operations of ordering and compounding done with numbers and distance judgment involves abstracting and comparing ideas of spatial extension.

The concept of "higher" and "lower" mental processes originated with the ancient Greek and Roman philosophers. This concept figures in the hierarchical theories of brain functions and mental ability factors in which "higher" refers to the more complex mental operations and "lower" to the simpler ones. Thinking is at the high end of this scale. The degree to which a concept is *abstract* or *concrete* also determines its place on the scale. For example, the abstract idea, "a living organism," is presumed to represent a higher level of thinking than the more concrete idea, "my cat Pansy"; the abstract rule, "file specific topics under general topics" is likewise considered to be at a higher level of thinking than the instructions, "file 'fir' under 'conifer,' file 'conifer' under 'tree'." It is interesting to note the the higher intellectual functions have traditionally been equated with "intelligence."

The higher intellectual functions of abstraction, reasoning, judgment, analysis, and synthesis tend to be relatively sensitive to diffuse brain injury even when most specific receptive, expressive, or memory functions remain essentially intact (Goodglass, 1973). They may also be disrupted by any one of a number of lesions in functionally discrete areas of the brain at lower levels of the hierarchy. Thus the higher intellectual functions tend to be more "fragile" than the lower, more discrete functions. Conversely, higher cognitive abilities may remain relatively unaffected in the presence of specific receptive, expressive, and even memory dysfunctions (Blakemore et al., 1972; Teuber et al., 1951).

Unlike the other classes of intellectual functions, cognitive functions have not been related to specific neuroanatomical systems. Rather, their impairment in the presence of brain damage proceeds from the disruption of the subsystems entering into the cognitive activity. "There is no . . . anatomy [of the higher cerebral functions] in the strict sense of the word. . . . Thinking is regarded as a function of the entire brain that defies localization" (Gloning and Hoff, 1969).

As with other kinds of intellectual functions, the quality of any higher cognitive operation will depend in part on the extent to which its sensory and motor components are intact at the central integrative (cortical) level. For example, patients with specific somatosensory perceptual defects tend to do poorly on reasoning tasks involving visuospatial concepts (Teuber, 1959); patients with perceptual disabilities that involve the visual system are more likely to have difficulty solving problems involving visual concepts (Milner, 1954). Verbal defects tend to have more obvious and widespread cognitive consequences than defects in other functional systems because task instructions are frequently verbal, self-regulating and self-critiquing mechanisms are typically verbal, and ideational systems—even for nonverbal material—are usually verbal.

Expressive functions
Expressive functions, such as speaking, drawing or writing, manipulating, physical gestures, facial expressions, or movements, make up the sum of observable behavior. All other mental activity is inferred from them.

Disturbances of expressive functions are known as *apraxias* (literally, no work). The apraxias typically involve impairment of voluntary action despite adequate motor innervation of capable muscles. Thus, when asked to pick up a pencil, an apraxic patient who has adequate strength and full use of his muscles may be unable to organize fingers and hand movements relative to the pencil sufficiently well to grasp it. He may even be unable to relate the instructions to hand movements although he understands the nature of the task (Vinken and Bruyn, 1969; M. Williams, 1970a).

Like perceptual dysfunctions, apraxias tend to occur in a cluster of disabilities that are usually associated with some specific sensory impairment and share a common pattern of localization (Critchley, 1953; Hécaen, 1962). For example, apraxias involving an inability to use objects appropriately and at will, *ideomotor apraxias*, are commonly associated with lesions near or overlapping speech centers and often appear concomitantly with communication disabilities (McFie, 1969). *Constructional apraxias*, "disturbance(s) in formulative activities such as assembling, building, drawing, in which the spatial form of the product proves to be unsuccessful without there being an apraxia of single movements" (Benton, 1969a), are more often associated with lesions of the nonspeech hemisphere of the brain than with lesions of the hemisphere that is dominant for speech and may accompany defects of spatial perception.

Also like agnosias, apraxias occasionally appear as disturbances of a single, discrete function. For example, Benton (1969a) distinguishes two different kinds of constructional apraxias that often but not always occur together, one having to do with difficulties in making two-dimensional constructions and the other with three-dimensional building tasks. However, expressive disabilities do not usually occur as disturbances of a single function; if such appears to be the case, the patient may not have been examined adequately.

Defects of symbol formulation, the *aphasias* and *dysphasias* (literally, no speech and impaired speech) have traditionally been considered to be apraxias, for the end product of every kind of aphasic or language disturbance is defective or absent speech or defective symbol production (Darley, 1967). The historical classification of aphasic disorders defines auditory and visual agnosias for symbolic material as *receptive* aphasias and defines verbal apraxias as *expressive* aphasias. The term "aphasia" is now reserved for those defects of symbol manipulation and concept formation at central integration levels that interfere with communication (Schuell, 1965; Wepman et al., 1960).

Like other kinds of intellectual defects, language disturbances usually appear in clusters of related dysfunctions. "Impairment of any of the cerebral systems essential to language processes is usually reflected in more than one language modality; conversely impairment of any modality often reflects involvement of more than one process" (Schuell, 1955, p. 308). Thus, *agraphia* (literally, no writing) and *alexia* (literally, no reading) only rarely occur alone.

They are most often found together and in association with other language disturbances, typically appearing as impairment (*dysgraphia, dyslexia*) rather than total loss of function (Piercy, 1964). Like other disturbances of intellectual functions, different forms of communication disabilities have also been associated with specific anatomical lesions (Geschwind, 1969; Hécaen, 1969).

Mental Activity Variables

Mental activity variables are behavior characteristics that concern the efficiency of mental processes. They are intimately involved in intellectual operations but do not constitute intellectual functions as they do not have a unique behavioral end product. They can be classified roughly into three categories, *attentional activities, level of consciousness,* and *activity rate.*

1. *Attentional activities* include *attention, concentration,* and *conceptual tracking.* Disorders of attention may arise from lesions involving any point in the perceptual system (Worden, 1966). Attention refers to the automatic, passive but focused, capacity for selective perception (J. Allison et al., 1968). Concentration is an effortful, usually deliberate, heightened and focused state of attention. Tracking involves unremitting attention to a stimulus or concentration on a directed train of thought (*conceptual tracking*) over a period of time. Complex conceptual tracking, which involves the ability to entertain two or more ideas or stimulus patterns simultaneously and sequentially without confusing or losing them, is necessary to solve problems requiring chained association, such as computing compound interest, interweaving the threads of a complicated story, or figuring distances from a road map (Gardner et al., 1960). Impairment of attention and concentration functions may result in a shortened attention span, distractibility, susceptibility to confusion, and unpredictable performance (Schulman et al., 1965).

Impaired attention and concentration are among the most common mental problems associated with brain damage (Reitan and Kløve, 1959). Not infrequently, such impairments are the only behavioral remnants of a brain disease or trauma. In such cases, although all the intellectual functions may be intact and the person may even be capable of better than average performance, overall intellectual productivity suffers from inattentiveness, faulty concentration, and consequent fatigue.

2. *Level of consciousness,* an organismic state, ranges in a

continuum from full alertness through drowsiness, sleep, and stupor, to coma. Even slight depressions of the alert state may significantly affect a person's mental efficiency, making him tired, inattentive, or slowed.

3. *Activity rate* refers to both the speed at which mental activities are performed and the motor response speed. Behavioral slowing is a common characteristic of brain damage. Motor response slowing is readily observable and may be associated with weakness or poor coordination. Slowing of mental activity shows up most clearly in delayed reaction times and in longer than average total performance times in the absence of a specific motor disability.

NONINTELLECTUAL FUNCTIONS

Personality characteristics, emotionality, and control are aspects of behavior that contribute significantly to a person's general effectiveness. Like intellectual functions, these capacities and characteristics may also be altered by brain dysfunction.

Personality/Emotionality Variables

Some personality or emotional change usually follows brain damage. Some changes tend to occur as fairly characteristic behavior patterns that relate to specific anatomical sites (Diller, 1968; Gainotti, 1972; Hécaen, 1964). The most common direct effects of brain injury on personality are emotional dulling, disinhibition, diminution of anxiety with associated emotional blandness or mild euphoria, and decreased social sensitivity. Heightened anxiety, depressed moods, and hypersensitivity in interpersonal interactions may also occur (K. Goldstein, 1939; Mulder and Daly, 1952).

Many persons suffer profound personality changes following brain injury or concomitant with brain disease, which seem to be not so much a direct product of their illness as a reaction to their experiences of loss, chronic frustration, and radical changes in life style. As a result, depression is probably the most common single emotional characteristic of brain damaged patients generally, with pervasive anxiety following closely behind. Some other common behavior problems of brain injured people are irritability, restlessness, low frustration tolerance, and apathy (Kostlan and Van Couvering, 1972; Ota, 1969).

Few brain damaged patients experience personality changes that are plainly either direct consequences of a brain injury or secondary reactions to impairment and loss. For the most part, the personality changes, emotional distress, and behavior problems of a brain damaged patient are the product of extremely complex interactions involving his neurological disabilities, present social demands, previously established behavior patterns, and his ongoing reactions to all of these.

Although most brain injured persons tend to undergo adverse emotional changes, brain damage seems to have beneficial effects for a few. These effects are most striking in those emotionally constricted, anxious, overly responsible people who become more easygoing and relaxed as a result of a pathological brain condition. While life seems to be more pleasant for some of the patients who experience release from anxiety and emotional disinhibition, their families may suffer instead. The following case illustrates this kind of personality change:

> A young Viet Nam veteran lost the entire right frontal portion of his brain in a land mine explosion. His mother and wife described him as having been a quietly pleasant, conscientious, and diligent sawmill worker before entering the service. When he returned home, all of his speech functions and most of his thinking abilities were intact. He was completely free of anxiety and thus without a worry in the world. He had also become very easygoing, self-indulgent, and lacking in general drive and sensitivity to others. His wife was unable to get him to share her concerns when the baby had a fever or the rent was due. Not only did she have to handle all the finances, carry all the family and home responsibilities, and do all the planning; but she also had to see that her husband went to work on time and that he didn't drink up his paycheck or spend it in a foolish shopping spree before getting home on Friday night. For several years it was touch and go as to whether the wife could stand the strain of a truly carefree husband much longer. She finally left him after he had stopped working altogether and begun a pattern of monthly drinking binges that left little of his rather considerable compensation checks.

One significant personality change that is rarely discussed but is a relatively common concomitant of brain injury is heightened sexual arousal (M. W. Buck, 1968). A married man or woman who has settled into a comfortable sexual activity pattern of intercourse two or three times a week may begin demanding sex two and three times a day from the bewildered spouse. Sometimes brain damaged men are unable to achieve or sustain an erection, or they may have ejaculatory problems secondary to nervous tissue damage, which, in turn, adds to their emotional disturbance and marital distress. Although sexual problems may diminish in time, for many patients they seriously complicate the problems of readjusting to new limitations and handicaps by adding another strange new set of impulses and reactions.

Control Functions

The critical dimension of *control* cuts across all behavior, intellectual and emotional alike. Control functions cannot be observed in themselves but must be inferred as qualitative aspects of all ongoing activity. Control is central to starting and stopping, speeding up and slowing down, inhibiting and exciting, modifying and regulating, and self-correcting activities. Grossly impaired control seriously compromises both intellectual and emotional behavior no matter how much intellectual ability or emotional capacity is retained.

Reliable and effective behavioral control requires an intact central nervous system. Some aspects of control are almost always affected by brain damage, no matter where the brain lesion is located, how small it is, or how negligible are the intellectual or emotional consequences. Among the more readily observable signs of impaired control are emotional lability, a heightened tendency to excitability, impulsivity, erratic carelessness, rigidity, and difficulty in making shifts in attention and ongoing behavior; deterioration in personal grooming and cleanliness; and decreased tolerance for alcohol. As with other kinds of functions, there is also some tendency for different kinds of control problems to relate to different brain areas (Diller, 1968; Luria, 1965a; Milner, 1964).

BRAIN PATHOLOGY AND PSYCHOLOGICAL FUNCTIONS

The relationship between brain and behavior is exceedingly intricate, frequently puzzling, yet usually taken for granted. Our understanding of this fundamental relationship is still very limited, but the broad outlines and many details of the correlations between brain and behavior have been sufficiently well explained to be clinically useful.

Brain activity underlying any behavior is not limited to one or a few neuroanatomical structures or neural circuits. Complex acts, such as swatting a fly or reading this page, are the product of countless neural interactions involving many, often far-flung sites in the neural network; their neuroanatomical correlates are not confined to any local area of the brain (Hebb, 1949; Luria, 1965a; Sherrington, 1955).

However, discrete psychological activities such as the perception of a pure tone or the movement of a finger can be disrupted by *lesions* (localized abnormal tissue changes) involving approximately the same anatomical area in most human brains. The disruption of complex behavior by brain lesions also occurs with enough anatomical regularity that inability to understand speech, to recall recent events, or to copy a design, for example, can often be predicted when the site of the lesion is known (Blakemore et al., 1972; Luria, 1965a; Penfield and Rasmussen, 1950; Piercy, 1964).

Knowledge of the *localization of dysfunction*, as this correlation between damaged neuroanatomical structures and behavioral functions may be called, also enables psychologists and neurologists to make educated guesses about the site of a lesion on the basis of abnormal patterns of behavior (McFie, 1961; Meyer, 1961; A. Smith, 1975).

Localization of dysfunction does not imply a "push-button" relationship between local brain sites and specific behaviors (Critchley, 1969; Poeck, 1964). Lesions at many different brain sites may alter or extinguish a single complex act, as can lesions interrupting the neural pathways connecting areas of the brain involved in the act (Poeck, 1969). Although it is tempting to adopt a simplistic, "push-button" kind of construction for the sense of knowledgeability and potential control it gives, the equation of empirically demonstrated regularities between functional disabilities and local brain sites with point-to-point neural circuitry can only obscure the very complex processes that underlie behavior.

3

THE BEHAVIORAL
GEOGRAPHY OF THE BRAIN

The first section of this chapter presents a brief (and necessarily superficial) sketch of some of the structural arrangements in the human central nervous system that are intimately connected with behavioral function and therefore of particular interest to neuro-psychologists. More detailed information can be gained by consulting such standard textbooks of neuroanatomy as Chusid (1973), Crosby, Humphrey, and Lauer (1962), and Gardner (1968).

THE CELLULAR SUBSTRATE

The nervous system carries out communication functions for the organism. It is involved in the reception, processing, storage, and transmission of information within the organism and in the organism's exchanges with the outside world. It is a dynamic system in that its activity modifies its performance, its internal relationships, and its capacity to mediate stimuli from the outside.

Estimates of the number of nerve cells (*neurons*) in the brain generally range from ten to 18 billion, and run as high as 25 billion. When well-nourished and adequately stimulated, tiny receptive organs at the neuronal tips proliferate abundantly, providing the human nervous system with an astronomical multiplicity of points of interaction between nerve cells. The vast number of these interaction sites is sufficient to provide a structural neural potential for the variability and flexibility of human behavior, and alterations in

32

spatial and temporal excitation patterns in the brain's circuitry can add considerably more to its dynamic potential.

Cells of the central nervous system differ from all other cells of the body in that they do not divide, multiply, or in any way replenish themselves. Once such a nerve cell is dead, connective tissue may fill its place or surrounding neurons may close in on the space left behind. New nerve cells cannot replace old ones.

When a nerve cell is injured or diseased, it may stop functioning and the circuits to which it contributed will then be disrupted. Some circuits may eventually reactivate as damaged cells resume functioning or alternative patterns involving different cell populations take over. When a circuit loses a sufficiently great number of neurons, the broken circuit can neither be reactivated nor replaced. Correlative behavioral alterations may indicate the locus and magnitude of the damage.

THE STRUCTURE OF THE BRAIN

The brain is an intricately patterned complex of small and delicate structures. Its bulk is composed of nerve cell bodies, fibers (*axons* and *dendrites*) that extend from the nerve cell bodies and are their transmission organs, and supporting cells (*glia*). In addition, an elaborate network of very fine blood vessels maintains a rich supply of nutrients to the extremely oxygen-dependent brain tissue.

The brain consists of the complex neural structures that grow out of the front end of the embryonic neural tube. The hind (lower, in humans) portion of the neural tube is the spinal cord. The brain stem and spinal cord serve as the throughway for communications between the brain and the rest of the body.

Three major anatomical divisions of the brain succeed one another along the brain stem: the *hindbrain*, the *midbrain*, and the *forebrain* (see Fig. 3-1). Structurally, the brain centers that are lowest (farthest back) on the neural tube are the most simply organized. In the brain's forward development there is a pronounced tendency for increased anatomical complexity and diversity culminating in the huge, elaborated outcroppings at the front end of the neural tube. The functional organization of the brain has a similar pattern of increasing complexity from the lower brain stem up through its succeeding

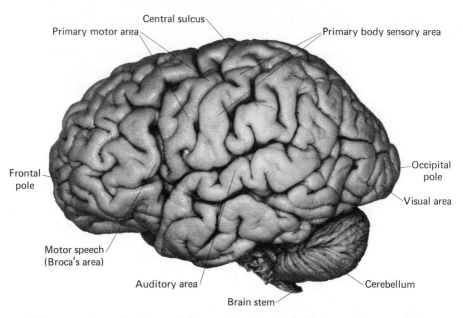

Central sulcus
Primary motor area
Primary body sensory area
Frontal pole
Occipital pole
Visual area
Motor speech (Broca's area)
Auditory area
Cerebellum
Brain stem

FIG. 3-1a. Lateral view of the cerebrum, cerebellum, and part of the brain stem.

parts. By and large, the lower brain centers mediate the simpler, more primitive functions while the forward part of the brain mediates the highest functions.

The Hindbrain

The medulla oblongata
The lowest part of the brain stem is the hindbrain, and its lowest section is the *medulla oblongata* or *bulb* (see Fig. 3-1). It is the site of such basic life-maintaining centers as those for nervous control of respiration, blood pressure, and heart beat. Significant injury to the bulb generally results in death.

The reticular formation
Running through the bulb from the upper cord to the *diencephalon* (see p. 36) is the *reticular formation,* a network of intertwined nerve cell bodies and fibers. The reticular formation is not a single functional unit but contains many nerve centers or *nuclei* (clusters of functionally related nerve cells). These nerve centers mediate impor-

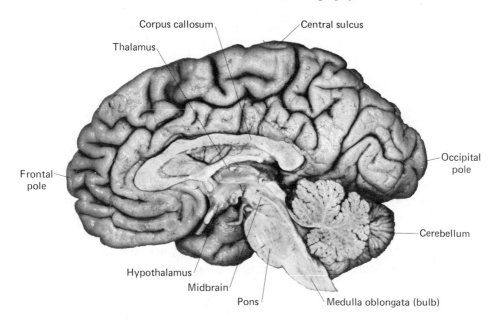

FIG. 3-1b. Medial view of the brain. (From DeArmond, Fusco, and Dewey, 1974.)

tant and complex postural reflexes, contribute to the smoothness of muscle activity, and maintain muscle tone.

The reticular formation is also the site of the *reticular activating system (RAS)*, which controls wakefulness and alerting mechanisms that ready the individual to react. The latter are a precondition for conscious behavior since they arouse the sleeping or inattentive organisms. Brain stem lesions involving the reticular activating system have been found to give rise to global disorders of consciousness, such as drowsiness, somnolence, stupor, or coma, which affect the organism's overall responsivity.

The pons and cerebellum
The *pons* and the *cerebellum* are structures high in the hindbrain (see Fig. 3-1). Together they correlate postural and *kinesthetic* (muscle movement sense) information, refining and regulating motor impulses relayed from the cerebrum at the top of the brain stem. The pons contains major pathways for fibers running between the cerebral cortex and the cerebellum. The cerebellum is attached to the brain

stem. Cerebellar damage is commonly reflected in problems of fine motor control and coordination.

The Midbrain

The *midbrain*, a small area just forward of the hindbrain that includes the major portion of the reticular activating system, contains both sensory and motor correlation centers (see Fig. 3-1). The sensory correlations that take place in midbrain nuclei contribute to the integration of reflex and automatic responses involving the visual and auditory systems. Motor nuclei play a role in the smooth integration of muscle movements and in the patterning of automatic posture. Midbrain lesions have been associated with specific movement disabilities such as certain types of tremor, rigidity, and extraneous movements of local muscle groups.

The Forebrain

The forwardmost part of the brain has two subdivisions. The *diencephalon* ("between-brain") comprises the structures that lie between the two halves of the *front* or *end* brain, the *telencephalon* (see Fig. 3-7).

The diencephalon
The most important of the diencephalic structures are the *thalamus* and the *hypothalamus*. The *thalamus* is a major sensory correlation and relay center (see Figs. 3-1 and 3-7). It is the way-station for all sensory data transmitted to the cerebral cortex, contributing significantly to the conscious experience of sensation (Brodal, 1969; Noback, 1967). It participates in most of the exchanges between cortical centers. That portion of it that enters into the *limbic system* (see pp. 60–62) also appears to be involved in emotional experience.

Thalamic lesions and thalamic degenerative disease may give rise to intellectual impairment associated with altered activation and arousal (Riklan and Levita, 1969). Moreover, the thalamus appears to play a central role in focusing and shifting attention (McGhie, 1969). Pronounced damage to certain thalamic nuclei can result in gross memory defects (see pp. 61–62). Another behavioral feature observed in some thalamic syndromes is a "withering" of the language mechanism with initial loss of spontaneous speech and, ultimately, mutism. Apathy, disorientation, and confusion characterize this behavior pattern (Brown, 1974; Riklan and Cooper, 1975).

The *hypothalamus* regulates such physiologically based drives as appetite, sexual arousal, and thirst. Behavior patterns having to do with physical protection, such as rage and fear reactions, are also regulated by hypothalamic centers. The hypothalamus is part of the *autonomic* subdivision of the nervous system that controls automatic visceral functions. Lesions to hypothalamic nuclei can result in a variety of symptoms including obesity, disorders of temperature control, and changes in drive state and behavior. Mood states may also be affected by hypothalamic lesions.

The cerebrum

The cerebrum, the most recently evolved and most elaborated brain structure, has two hemispheres that are almost but not quite identical mirror images of each other (see Figs. 3-1, 3-4, and 3-7). Within each cerebral hemisphere, at its base, are situated a number of nuclear masses known as the *basal ganglia* (ganglion is another term for nucleus). The largest is the *corpus striatum* (literally, striped body) consisting of several complex motor correlation centers that modulate both voluntary movements and autonomic reactions. The effects of injury to the corpus striatum vary with the specific site of injury, but lesions in this area may result in movement disorders.

Another prominent nuclear mass lying within each of the cerebral hemispheres is the *amygdala*, which has direct connections with the primitive centers involving the sense of smell. Semiautomatic visceral activities, particularly those concerned with feeding (e.g., chewing, salivating, licking, and gagging) and with the visceral components of the fear reactions, are affected by stimulation or ablation of the amygdala. Seizure activity and experimental stimulation of the amygdala provoke visceral responses associated with fright as well as mouth movements involved in feeding. Removal of the amygdala from both hemispheres may have a "taming" effect on animals and humans alike.

The internal white matter of the cerebral hemispheres consists of densely packed conduction fibers that transmit neural impulses between cortical points within a hemisphere (*association* fibers), between the hemispheres (*commissural* fibers), or between the cerebral cortex and lower centers (*projection* fibers). The *corpus callosum* is the great band of commissural fibers connecting the two hemispheres. Other interhemispheric connections are provided by some smaller bands of fibers. Section of the corpus callosum cuts off direct interhemispheric communication. When examined by special neuropsychological techniques, patients who have undergone section of commissural fibers (*commissurotomy*) exhibit profound behavioral discontinuities between perception, comprehension, and response, which reflect significant functional differences between the hemispheres (see pp. 43–46). Yet, direct communication between two cortical points occurs far less frequently than indirect communication relayed through lower brain centers, particularly the thalamus and the corpus striatum (Myers, 1967).

The *cortex* of the cerebral hemispheres, the convoluted outer layer of gray matter composed of nerve cell bodies and their synaptic connections, is the highest and most complexly organized correlation center of the brain (see Fig. 3-2). Since the late nineteenth century, it has been known that stimulation or destruction of certain sections of cortical tissue has regular, predictable effects on behavior (Hécaen, 1969). From this knowledge, some early investigators drew a picture of strict localization of function that assumed an almost one-to-one correspondence between highly specific behavioral functions and closely defined cortical areas.

More recent studies demonstrate that the specificity of cortical structures in mediating the different behavioral functions is neither as clear-cut nor as circumscribed as these early theorists held. Most cortical areas are involved to some degree in the mediation of any complex behavior (Gloning and Hoff, 1969). Studies of commissurotomized patients ("split-brain" studies) have shown that such functions as the comprehension of speech, once thought to be in the exclusive province of one or the other hemisphere, are also represented to some degree in both hemispheres (Nebes, 1974). Further, the boundaries of functionally definable cortical areas, or zones, are vague. Cells subserving a specific function are highly concentrated in the primary area of a zone, thin out, and overlap with other zones as the perimeter of the zone is approached (Polyakov, 1966). Moreover, even those functions that are subserved by cells located within relatively well-defined cortical areas have a significant number of components distributed outside the local cortical center. For instance, of the cortical cells subserving voluntary movement (the primary motor cells), only 40% are located in the primary motor area whereas 10 to 20% are situated in the primary sensory area (Brodal, 1969; Luria, 1965a). Further, lesions of a primary area do not always lead to permanent loss of the function subserved by that area as undamaged (perhaps secondary) areas may take over the function.

Cortical patterning of functionally defined behavioral systems emerges as a clear and consistent feature of cortical organization. However, the demonstration of functional zones within the cerebral cortex and their intricate interplay and connections with subcortical centers renders strict localization of function theories obsolete.

THE CEREBRAL CORTEX AND BEHAVIOR

"We do not know exactly what the cortex does." G. von Bonin (1962b)

The patterns of functional localization in the cerebral cortex are broadly organized along two spatial planes. The *lateral plane* cuts through *homologous* (in the corresponding position) areas of the right and left hemispheres. The *longitudinal plane* runs from the front to the back of the cortex, with a relatively sharp demarcation between functions that are primarily localized in the forward portion of the cortex and those whose primary localization is behind the *central sulcus* or *fissure of Rolando*.

Lateral Organization

Lateral symmetry
The primary sensory and motor centers are homologously positioned within the cerebral cortex of each hemisphere in a mirror-image relationship. With certain exceptions, such as the visual and auditory systems, the centers in each cerebral hemisphere mediate the activities of the *contralateral* (other side) half of the body (see Fig. 3-2). Thus, an injury to the primary *somesthetic* (body feeling) area of the right hemisphere results in decreased or absent sensation in the corresponding left-sided body part; an injury affecting the left motor strip results in a right-sided weakness or paralysis.

Point-to-point representation on the cortex.   The organization of both the primary sensory and primary motor areas of the cortex provides for a point-to-point representation of the body. The amount of cortex identified with each body portion or organ is proportional to the number of sensory or motor nerve endings in that part of the body rather than to its size. For example, the area concerned with sensation and movement of the tongue or fingers is much more extensive than the area representing the elbow or back.

The visual system is also organized on a contralateral plan, but it is one-half of each *visual field* (the entire view encompassed by the eye), which is projected onto the contralateral visual cortex (see Fig. 3-2). Fibers originating in the right half of each retina, which registers stimuli in the left visual field, project to the right visual cortex; fibers from the left half of the retina convey the right visual field image to the left visual cortex. Thus, destruction of either eye leaves both halves of the visual field intact. Destruction of the right or the left primary visual cortex or of all the fibers leading to either side results in blindness in each eye for that side of the visual field (*hemianopsia*). Lesions involving a portion of the visual projection fibers or visual cortex result in circumscribed *field defects,* such as areas of blindness (*scotoma;* pl. *scotomata*) within the visual field of one or both eyes, depending on whether the lesion involves the visual pathway before or after its fibers cross on their route from the retina of the eye to the visual cortex. The precise point-to-point arrangement of projection fibers from the retina to the visual cortex permits especially accurate localization of lesions within the primary visual system.

A majority of the nerve fibers transmitting auditory stimulation from each ear are projected to the primary auditory centers in the opposite hemisphere; the remaining fibers go to the *ipsilateral* (same side) auditory cortex. Thus, the contralateral pattern is preserved to some degree in the auditory system too. As a result of this mixed projection pattern, destruction of one of the primary auditory centers does not result in loss of hearing in the contralateral ear. A point-to-point relationship between sense receptors and cortical cells is also laid out on the primary auditory cortex, with cortical representation arranged according to pitch, from high tones to low ones.

Destruction of a primary cortical sensory or motor area results in specific sensory or motor deficits but generally has little effect on the

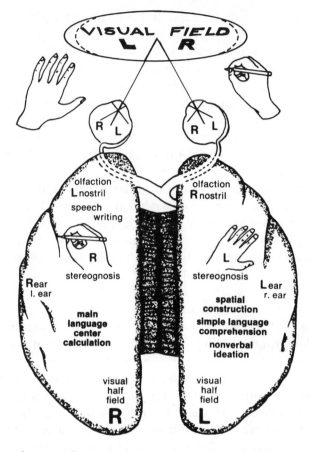

FIG. 3-2. Schematic diagram of visual fields, optic tracts, and associated brain areas, showing left and right lateralization in man (Sperry, 1970).

higher cortical functions. For instance, an adult onset lesion limited to the primary visual cortex causes cortical blindness while reasoning ability, emotional control, and even the ability for visual conceptualization may remain intact.

Association areas of the cortex.   Cortical representation of sensory or motor nerve endings in the body takes place on a direct point-to-point basis, but stimulation of the primary cortical association area gives rise only to meaningless sensations or nonfunctional movements (Gloning and Hoff, 1969; Luria, 1966). Modified and complex functions involve the cortex adjacent to primary sensory and motor centers. These secondary cortical areas and overlap zones are called association areas. Neurons in secondary areas integrate and refine raw percepts or simple motor responses. Overlap zones are areas peripheral to functional centers where the neuronal components of two or more different functions are interspersed, providing for integration of the functions mediated by them. Unlike damage to primary cortical areas, a lesion involving association areas and overlap zones typically does not result in specific sensory or motor defects; rather, the behavioral effects of such damage will more likely appear as a pattern of deficits running through related functions or as impairment of a general capacity. Thus, certain lesions that are implicated in drawing distortions also tend to affect the ability to do computations on paper; lesions of the auditory association cortex do not interfere with hearing acuity per se, but with the appreciation of patterned sounds.

Asymmetry between the hemispheres
A second kind of organization across the lateral plane differentiates the two hemispheres with respect to the localization of primary cognitive functions and to significant qualitative aspects of behavior processed by each of the hemispheres. These differences appear to have some structural foundation in that the left hemisphere of most right-handed persons is somewhat larger and heavier than the right (von Bonin, 1962a), the size differential being greatest in those areas that mediate language functions (Geschwind and Levitsky, 1968). However, right hemisphere cortical areas may also be larger than the corresponding areas on the left (Blinkov and Glezer, 1968).

The most obvious functional difference between the hemispheres is that left hemisphere lesions commonly give rise to speech and related language disorders—or, in the broadest sense, disorders of symbol formulation—whereas communication disturbances are rarely seen in patients with right hemisphere damage (W. R. Russell, 1961). Right hemisphere patients are more likely to experience difficulties in orienting themselves in space, in integrating the visual and spatial components of a percept or a task, and in handling complex or patterned material that cannot be readily conceptualized verbally. These observations have led to the conclusion that the left hemisphere in most people is *dominant* for speech (i.e., that language functions are primarily mediated in the left hemisphere) and that the right hemisphere predominates in the mediation of spatial transformations and complex nonverbal sensory integration. The right hemisphere has also been called the "minor" or "silent" hemisphere because the often subtle character of right hemisphere disorders had led observers to believe until quite recently that it played no specialized role in intellectual behavior.[1]

Until the development of the commissurotomy in the early 1960's for relief of certain kinds of epilepsy, the activities of the two hemispheres had to be studied indirectly through observations of behavioral impairments arising from lateralized lesions. Results from the study of the behavior of patients with intact but surgically separated hemispheres as well as data obtained with recently devised nonsurgical techniques (Dee and Fontenot, 1973) have confirmed earlier observations on the different functions subserved by each hemisphere. Thus, the left hemisphere mediates all verbal transformations including reading and writing, understanding and speaking, verbal ideation, and even comprehension of verbal symbols traced on the skin (Nebes, 1974). Moreover, left hemisphere lateralization of verbal functions extends to the musculature of speech, which appears to be under its sole control even though bilateral structures are involved. Yet it has relatively minor involvement in the perception of shapes, forms, and patterns whether by sight, sound, or touch, and in copying and drawing nonverbal figures (Bogen, 1969a; Gazzaniga, 1970).

The same studies show that the right hemisphere dominates nonverbal visual-spatial transformations, including the processing and storage of visual information, tactile and visual recognition of shapes and forms, perception of directional orientation and perspective, and copying and drawing geometric and representational designs and pictures. Native musical ability is also localized on the right. Under special test conditions, a few commissurotomized patients have demonstrated some limited verbal recognition and monosyllabic utterances associated with right hemisphere activity

[1] Because the left hemisphere is usually the dominant (speech processing) hemisphere for both right- and left-handed persons, it has become customary to conceptualize and refer to the dominant hemisphere as the left hemisphere and to use "right" hemisphere and "nondominant" hemisphere interchangeably. This custom is followed here. Thus, I call the dominant and nondominant hemispheres "left" and "right" respectively, despite the exceptions to the rule (see pp. 162–163).

(Moscovitch, 1973). Kinsbourne (1971) has reported that defective but recognizable speech may be produced, presumably under right hemisphere control, when the left hemisphere is badly damaged.

Not only are there differences between the hemispheres in *what* they process but also in *how* each processes the information at its disposal (Galin, 1971; Sperry, 1964). Nebes (1974) characterizes these differences by referring to the left hemisphere as the "analyzer," the right as the "synthesizer." The distinctive processing qualities of each hemisphere become evident in the mediation of spatial relationships. Left hemisphere processing tends to break the visual percept into details that can be identified and conceptualized verbally in terms of number or length of lines, size and direction of angles, etc. In the right hemisphere the tendency is to deal with the same visual stimuli as spatially related wholes. Thus, for most people, the ability to perform such complex visual tasks as the formation of complete impressions from fragmented percepts (the *closure* function), the appreciation of differences in patterns, and the recognition and remembering of faces, depends on the functioning of the right hemisphere.

> The painful efforts of a right hemisphere stroke patient to arrange plain and diagonally colored blocks according to a pictured pattern illustrate the kind of solutions available to a person in whom only the left hemisphere is fully intact. This glib 49-year-old retired salesman constructed several simple 2 × 2 block design patterns correctly by verbalizing the relationships: "The red one [block] on the right goes above the white one; there's another red one to the left of the white one." This method worked so long as the relationships of each block to the others in the pattern remained obvious. When the diagonality of a design obscured the relative placement of the blocks, he could neither perceive how each block fit into the design nor guide himself with verbal cues. He continued to use verbal cues, but at this level of complexity his verbalizations only served to confuse him further. He attempted to reproduce diagonally oriented designs by lining up the blocks diagonally (e.g., "to the side," "in back of") without regard for the squared (2 × 2 or 3 × 3) format. He could not orient any one block to more than another single block at a time, and he was unable to maintain a center of focus to the design he was constructing.
>
> On the same task, a 31-year-old mildly dysphasic former logger who had had left hemisphere surgery involving the visual association area had no difficulty on this task until he came to the first 3 = 3 design, the only one of the four nine-block designs that lends itself readily to verbal

analysis. On this design, he reproduced the overall pattern immediately but oriented the corner blocks erroneously. He attempted to reorient it but then turned a correctly oriented block into a 90° error. Though dissatisfied with this solution, he was unable to localize his error or define the simple angulation pattern.

Design 6

Design 7

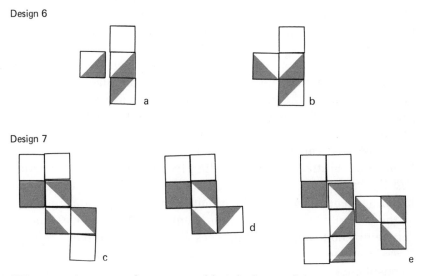

FIG. 3-3a. Attempts of a 51-year-old right hemisphere stroke patient to copy pictured designs with colored blocks. (a) First stage in the construction of a 2 × 2 chevron design. (b) Second stage: the patient does not see the 2 × 2 format and gives up after four minutes. (c) First stage in construction of 3 × 3 pinwheel pattern (see below). (d) Second stage. (e) Third and final stage.

Design 7

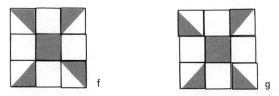

FIG. 3-3b. Attempts of a 31-year-old patient with a surgical lesion of the left visual association area to copy a 3 × 3 pictured pinwheel design with colored blocks. (f) Initial solution: 180° rotation of upper left corner block. (g) "Corrected" solution: upper left corner block rotated to correct position and lower right corner rotated 180° to incorrect position.

Hemispheric differences are not limited to visuospatial functions; they also may be found in other aspects of cerebral activity. Left hemisphere processing takes its special characteristics from the essentially verbal nature of the data it handles, in contrast to right hemisphere processing, which deals primarily with visuospatial aspects of information. From these fundamental differences in the kinds of information handled by each hemisphere, there appears to follow specialized processing and response patterns unique to each hemisphere.

Studies of both unilaterally lesioned and commissurotomized patients suggest that the left hemisphere codes data into verbal symbols, which it then manipulates and stores as verbal concepts. The formation of verbal concepts (i.e., the verbal coding process) involves the breakdown of percepts into meaningful elements (analysis), the search for similarities in meaning between elements (conceptual abstraction), the labeling (coding) of similar elements, and the categorization of coded elements for efficient storage and handling (generalization). The principle on which data are organized in the left hemisphere is *conceptual* similarity (Nebes, 1974). For the left hemisphere, apples and oranges are alike in that they are fruit. These fundamental operations characterize the activity of the left hemisphere at every level of complexity from simple coding of data to the generation of propositional speech and reasoning by logical steps.

In contrast, it appears that the right hemisphere deals with unverbalizable patterns and whole forms and thus manipulates and stores information as visual or spatial or, in the case of music or nonverbal sounds, auditory configurations (Kimura, 1966; Vignolo, 1969). Rather than analyzing data in a search for conceptual similarities, the right hemisphere reconstructs perceptual wholes from fragmented or incomplete sensory data and organizes its data on the basis of *structural* similarities. For the right hemisphere, apples and oranges are alike in that they are round. The fundamental synthesizing activity of the right hemisphere is apparent in depth perception, perspective, and perceptual constancy operations. Right hemisphere processing of percepts in terms of their structural similarity entails what Bogen (1969b) calls its "appositional" capacity because the right hemisphere handles its data in terms of comparing or *apposing* percepts or perceptual constructs that defy verbal description. The appositional capacity is fundamental to right hemisphere operations from the acquisition of simple configurational concepts to the identification and remembering of faces, musical passages, and cognitive maps.

The demonstration of two different kinds of cerebral processing of two distinct aspects of information fits in with long-standing conjectures about a duality in modes of thought. It supports a conceptual model of the duality of brain functions in which "reason" as formal logic, science-mindedness, or no-nonsense attention to details characterizes left hemisphere thinking; "intuition" as nonverbal perceptiveness, inspirational hunches, and uncritical imagination typifies right hemisphere thinking (Levy-Agresti and Sperry, 1968). Although oversimplified, this model has some clinical value. Loss of tissue in a hemisphere tends to impair its particular processing capacity. Damaged tissue in either hemisphere can exaggerate the thinking pattern characteristic for that hemisphere (Diller, 1968; Hall and Hall, 1968).

When the Wada technique of intracarotid barbiturate injections (Wada and Rasmussen, 1960) has been used for pharmacological inactivation of one side or another of the brain, the emotional reactions of the patients tend to differ depending on which side was inactivated (Gainotti, 1972; Galin, 1974; Rossi and Rosadini, 1969). Patients whose left hemisphere has been inactivated report feelings of depression more often than do their right hemisphere counterparts who are apt to feel euphoric.

There appear to be similar hemispheric differences in the emotional changes that may accompany brain injury. Anxiety is a common feature of left hemisphere involvement (Diller, 1968; Gainotti, 1972; Galin, 1974). It may show up in the patient's oversensitivity to his impairments and in a tendency to exaggerate his disabilities. It is frequently compounded by depression (M. W. Buck, 1968). Patients with left hemisphere lesions are more likely than those with right-sided brain damage to exhibit a *catastrophic reaction* (extreme and disruptive transient emotional disturbance). The catastrophic reaction may appear as acute, often disorganizing anxiety, agitation, or tearfulness disrupting the activity that provoked it. Typically, it occurs when the patient is confronted with his limitations, as when taking a test. The patient tends to regain his composure as soon as the source of frustration is removed. Yet, despite his tendencies to be overly sensitive to his disabilities, the patient with a left hemisphere lesion may ultimately compensate for them well enough to make a satisfactory adjustment to his disability and his living situation.

In contrast, patients with right-sided cortical involvement often tend to deny or make light of the extent of their disabilities and, in extreme cases, may be unaware of them (Denny-Brown, 1952; Gainotti, 1972). Patients whose injuries involve the right cortex are less likely to be dissatisfied with themselves or their performances than are those with left hemisphere lesions, and they are less likely to be aware of their mistakes (Hécaen et al., 1951). Although many patients with right hemisphere damage may at first appear to be free of emotional disturbance, particularly in comparison to those who have sustained left hemisphere damage, their complacency and diminished appreciation for their defective performances may result in irresponsible and childlike behavior. These patients are often unable to profit from experience and unlikely to improve very much (Knapp, 1959; Lezak, 1975; Warrington et al., 1966).

Fewer patients with right hemisphere lesions become depressed (Gainotti, 1972). In some depressed patients with right hemisphere involvement, the emotional disturbance does not seem to arise from awareness of defects so much as from the secondary effects of the patient's diminished self-awareness. Those patients with right hemisphere lesions who do not appreciate the nature or extent of their disability tend to set unrealistic goals for themselves, or to maintain their previous goals without taking their new limitations into account. As a result, they frequently fail to live up to their goals. Also, their diminished capacity for self-awareness tends to reduce their sensitivity to others so that they become more difficult to live with and thus are more likely to be rejected by family and friends than are patients with left hemisphere lesions. Depression in patients with right-sided cortical damage often takes longer to develop than it does in patients with left hemisphere involvement since it is less likely to be a reaction to immediately perceived disabilities than to their secondary consequences. When it does develop, however, it is apt to be more chronic, more debilitating, and more resistive to intervention.

These differences in the emotional behavior of right and left hemisphere damaged patients reflect observed tendencies and are not necessary consequences of unilateral brain disease. Neither are the emotional reactions reported here only associated with unilateral brain lesions. Mourning reactions naturally follow the experience of personal loss of a capacity whether it be due to brain injury, a lesion lower down in the nervous system, or amputation of a body part. Inappropriate euphoria and self-satisfaction may accompany lesions involving other than right hemisphere areas of the cortex. Further, premorbid personality colors the quality of the patient's response to his disabilities too (see pp. 163–164).

In fact, Milner (1967b) attributed all the emotional effects of pharmacological inactivation of one hemisphere to personality predispositions. Thus, the clinician should not be tempted to predict the side of damage from the patient's mood alone.

Longitudinal Organization

Although no two human brains are exactly alike in their structure, all normally developed brains share the same major distinguishing features (see Fig. 3-4). The external surface of each half of the cerebral cortex is wrinkled into a complex of ridges or convolutions called *gyri* (sing., *gyrus*), which are separated by two deep *fissures* and many

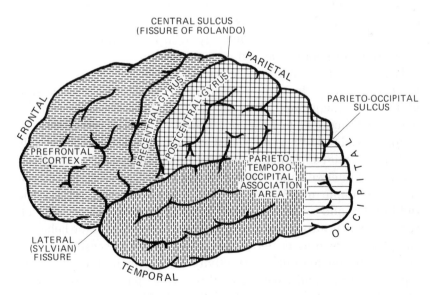

FIG. 3-4. The lobes and landmark structures of the cerebral cortex.

shallow clefts called *sulci* (sing., *sulcus*). The two prominent fissures and certain of the major sulci divide each hemisphere into four *lobes*, the *occipital, parietal, temporal,* and *frontal* lobes. These lobes received their anatomical delineations by virtue of the visual prominence of their identifying cerebral landmarks rather than any intrinsic functional or structural characteristics.

The *central sulcus* divides the cerebral hemispheres into anterior and posterior regions. Immediately in front of the central sulcus lies the precentral gyrus, which contains the *primary motor* or *motor projection* area. The entire frontal area forward of the central sulcus is also called the *precentral* or *prerolandic* area. The *primary somesthetic* or *sensory projection* area is located in the gyrus just behind the central sulcus. The area behind the central sulcus, excluding the lateral temporal lobe protuberances, is also known as the *retrorolandic* or *postcentral* area.

Certain functional systems have primary or significant representation on the cerebral cortex with sufficient regularity that the lobes do provide a useful anatomical frame of reference for functional localization, much as a continent provides a geographical frame of reference for a country. But, because the lobes were originally defined solely on the basis of their gross appearance, some functionally definable areas overlap two and even three lobes. For example, the boundary between the parietal and occipital lobes is arbitrarily defined by a minor sulcus, the *parieto-occipital sulcus,* lying in what is now known to be an overlap zone for visual and spatial functions.

The two-dimensional plan of the cortical organization of higher level behavior lends itself to a schema, which, although oversimplified and exaggerated, provides a crude framework for conceptualizing functional localization. The left and right sides may be characterized roughly as the verbal and nonverbal sides respectively and the posterior and anterior portions as the sensory and motor areas. The actual interweaving of different functional components complicates this simple model, for there is some minor verbal input into the right cortex and some nonverbal behavior is mediated by the left cortex. There is also a considerable motor component in the behavior complexes served by posterior cortical areas, just as sensory components contribute to frontal lobe activity. Yet even with the complicating interactions and exceptions, this overall pattern may make it easier to grasp the anatomical relationships between the different functional systems and their associated deficits.

Understanding of the functional patterning of the cerebral cortex has replaced "mass action" theories of cortical functioning, which related the degree of behavioral impairment simply to the size of the lesion (Luria, 1973; McFie, 1969; Talland, 1963). However, a strict pattern of functional organization of the cerebral cortex has not been clearly defined for portions of the frontal lobes where the extent of damage may have a more obvious effect on behavior than the side in which the damage is located (Hécaen, 1969; Piercy, 1964) (see pp. 66–67).

Functional organization of the posterior cortex
The primary visual cortex is located on the occipital lobe at the most posterior portion of the cerebral hemispheres (see Fig. 3-4). The postcentral gyrus, at the most forward part of the parietal lobe, contains the primary sensory (somatosensory) projection area. The primary auditory cortex is located on the uppermost fold of the temporal lobe close to where it joins the parietal lobe. Kinesthetic and vestibular functions are mediated by areas low on the parietal lobe near the occipital and temporal lobe boundary regions.

There are no clear-cut demarcations among any of the functions localized on the posterior cortex. Rather, although the primary centers of the major functions served by the posterior cerebral regions are relatively distant from one another, their secondary association areas gradually fade into tertiary overlap zones in which visual and body-sensing components intermingle.

As a rough general rule, the character of the defects arising from lesions of the association areas of the posterior cortex varies according to the extent to which the lesion involves each of the sense modalities. Any disorder with a visual component, for example, may implicate some occipital lobe involvement. If a patient with visual agnosia also has difficulty estimating close distances or feels confused in familiar surroundings, then parietal lobe areas serving spatially re-lated kinesthetic and vestibular functions may also be affected. Knowledge of the sites of the primary sensory centers and of the behavioral correlates of lesions to these sites and to the intermediate association areas enables the clinician to infer the approximate location of a lesion from the patient's behavioral symptoms.

Occipital lobe disorders.   Isolated lesions of the primary visual cortex result in discrete blind spots in the corresponding parts of the visual fields but do not alter the comprehension of visual stimuli or the ability to make a proper response to what is seen. Total destruction of the primary visual cortex causes complete blindness. For visual incomprehension or imperception (visual agnosias) or visual distortions to occur requires lesions in the visual association areas of the occipital lobe (Gloning et al., 1968). Only rarely do they result from lesions of other lobes or subcortical structures.

Visual agnosia refers to a variety of visual disturbances. In one common form associated with occipital lobe lesions, *apperceptive visual agnosia*, the patient sees but cannot synthesize what he sees. He may indicate awareness of discrete parts of symbols or symbol combinations, such as letters or words, or recognize elements of an object without organizing the discrete percepts into a perceptual whole. Drawings by such patients are fragmented: bits and pieces are recognizable but are not put together.

Luria (1965a) distinguishes an *associative visual agnosia* in which the patient can perceive the whole of a visual stimulus such as a familiar face or a personal possession but cannot recognize it. A third kind of visual agnosia associated with occipital lobe disease, *simultaneous agnosia* or *simultanagnosia*, appears as an inability to perceive more than one object or point in space at a time. Luria attributes the problem to difficulty in visual scanning, that is, shifting visual attention from one point in the visual field to another; but M. Williams (1970a) discusses it in terms of time needed to form a percept of a second object in the field. *Color agnosia*, the inability to relate colors to objects in the presence of intact color vision, may also accompany occipital lobe lesions. It rarely appears in a pure form but is usually found in association with other visual agnosias, most commonly with word blindness (Gloning et al., 1968).

Visual inattention associated with occipital lobe damage is similar to simultaneous agnosia in that the patient spontaneously perceives only one object in the field at a time. It differs from simultaneous agnosia in that the patient will see more than one object if others are pointed out to him; this is not the case in a true simultaneous agnosia. Visual inattention also refers to imperception of stimuli. Material in the left visual fields can be seen but remains unnoticed unless the patient's attention is drawn to it (see Fig. 3-5). This form of visual inattention, also known as unilateral spatial neglect, typically occurs only when there is right parietal lobe involvement as well as occipital lobe damage.

Copy these designs in the space to the right.

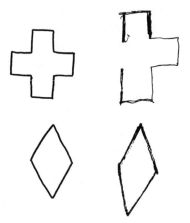

FIG. 3-5. Example of inattention to the left visual field by a 57-year-old college graduate with a right parieto-occipital lesion.

Left hemisphere visual agnosias interfere with reading and writing. With lesions confined to the occipital lobe, the reading problem stems from defects of visual recognition, organization, and scanning rather than from defective comprehension, which usually occurs only with parietal damage. Writing defects associated with occipital lobe lesions may result from inability to recall the visual image of the required symbol or the sequence of the discrete symbols that make up a number or word, or from faulty scanning. One form of *acalculia* (literally, no counting), a disorder that Grewel (1952) considered a primary type of impaired arithmetic ability in which the calculation process itself is affected, may result from visual disturbances of symbol perception associated with left occipital cortex lesions. Right occipital lesions are more likely to give rise to impaired object perception. For example, the ability to recognize familiar faces and objects is essentially a right hemisphere function.

The posterior association cortex. Association areas in the parieto-temporo-occipital region are situated just in front of the visual association areas and behind the primary sensory strip. They run from the *longitudinal fissure* (the deep cleft separating the two hemispheres) laterally to the areas adjacent to and just above the temporal lobe where temporal, occipital, and parietal elements commingle. These association areas include much of the parietal and the occipital lobes and some temporal association areas. Functionally they comprehend cortical mediation for all behavior involving vision, touch, body awareness, verbal comprehension, spatial localization, and for abstract and complex intellectual functions of mathematical reasoning and the formulation of logical propositions that have their conceptual roots in basic visuospatial experiences, such as "inside," "bigger," "and," or "instead of."

A variety of apraxias and agnosias have been ascribed to parieto-temporo-occipital lesions. Most of them relate to either a verbal or a nonverbal perceptual disability and thus are asymmetrically localized. A few are seen with lesions in either hemisphere.

The posterior association cortex: (a) Defects arising from lesions on either hemisphere. Constructional apraxia is one of the few predominantly parietal lobe disabilities that occurs with lesions on either side of the midline, but it appears in different forms depending on the hemispheric side of the lesion. Left-sided lesions are apt to disrupt the programming or ordering of movements necessary for constructional activity (Hécaen and Assal, 1970). Visuospatial defects tend to underlie right hemisphere constructional dyspraxias (Blakemore et al., 1972). Diagonality in a design or construction can be particularly disorienting to patients with right hemisphere lesions (Milner, 1971; Warrington et al., 1966). Defects in copying designs, for example, appear in the drawings of patients with left hemisphere lesions as simplification and difficulty in making angles, and in the drawings of patients with right-sided involvement as fragmented percepts, irrelevant overelaborativeness, and neglect of the left half of the page or the left half of elements on the page (Piercy et al, 1960; Warrington et al., 1966). (See Fig. 3-6a, b for free hand drawings of left and right hemisphere damaged patients showing typical hemispheric defects.) Puzzle construction in two- and three-dimensional space may be affected by both right and left hemisphere lesions. Constructional apraxia occurs almost twice as frequently (Hécaen, 1962) and with greater severity (Benton, 1967a) when the lesion is on the right side.

Hécaen (1969) associates difficulties in serial ordering with impairment of the parieto-temporo-occipital area of both the left and right hemispheres. Disruption of the sequential organization of

a

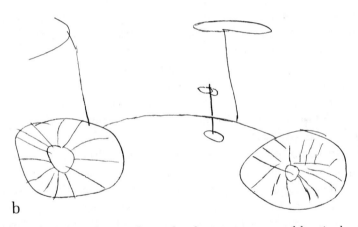

b

FIG. 3-6a. This bicycle was drawn by the same 51-year-old retired sales-man who constructed the block designs of Fig. 3 (a–e). This drawing demonstrates that neglect of the left visual field is not due to carelessness, for the patient painstakingly drew in the many details and was very pleased with his performance. b. This bicycle was drawn by a 24-year-old college graduate almost a year after receiving a severe injury to the left side of his head. He originally drew the bike without pedals, adding them when asked, "How do you make it go?"

speech associated with left hemisphere lesions may result in the language formulation defects of aphasia. Right-sided lesions of the parieto-temporo-occipital area appear to interfere with the comprehension of order and sequence so that the patient has difficulty seeing or dealing with temporal relationships and is unable to make plans (Lezak, 1975).

Lesions in either hemisphere involving the sensory association areas posterior to the postcentral gyrus can produce a *tactile agnosia* or *astereognosis* (inability to identify an object by touch). Astereognosis tends to be localized to the body side opposite the lesion. While some studies suggest that right hemisphere lesions may be associated with impairment of shape perception in both hands (Semmes, 1968), a high incidence of bilateral sensory defect has also been noted among patients with unilateral lesions of either hemisphere (Milner, 1975).

The posterior association cortex: (b) Defects arising from left hemisphere lesions. When they occur, aphasia and related symbol processing disabilities are generally the most prominent symptoms of left parieto-temporo-occipital lesions. Aphasia commonly follows cortical damage within this area where "the great afferent systems" of audition, vision, and body sensation overlap. W. R. Russell (1963) points out that even very small cortical lesions in this area can have widespread and devastating consequences for verbal behavior.

Communication disabilities arising from lesions in the left parieto-temporo-occipital region tend to involve impaired or absent recognition or comprehension of symbolic stimuli. Lesions overlapping both the parietal and occipital cortex may give rise to reading defects. Writing disabilities can occur with lesions limited to either the temporal or parietal lobe, but their severity increases significantly when there is damage to the parietal and any one of the other three lobes (Hécaen, 1969).

Two somewhat similar apraxias associated with the zone of overlap between kinesthetic and visual areas of the left hemisphere involve the carrying out of complex acts. *Ideomotor apraxia* refers to a disruption of the organization of complex acts in which the patient knows what he wants to do but cannot do it deliberately, although he can perform the desired act inadvertently. In *ideational apraxia* the patient is unable to recall or to demonstrate an activity when asked to perform it, but he can carry it out in the ordinary course of events. Acalculia and agraphia generally appear in association with other communication disabilities (Hécaen, 1962; Raghaven, 1961). When they occur with left-right spatial disorientation and an inability to identify one's own fingers, to orient oneself to one's own fingers, to recognize or to name them (*finger agnosia*), the symptom cluster is known as Gerstmann's syndrome (Fogel, 1962; Gerstmann, 1940, 1957), and the lesion is likely to involve the left parieto-occipital region. Acalculia associated with finger agnosia typically disrupts such relatively simple arithmetic operations as counting or ordering numbers.

Agnosias arising from left hemisphere lesions just anterior to the visual association area tend to appear as disorientation of either extrapersonal or of personal space. The spatial disorientation of left hemisphere lesions generally reflects impaired left-right directional sense and may involve a somatosensory defect as well (Denny-Brown et al., 1952).

Disabilities arising from left hemisphere lesions tend to be more severe when the patient is also aphasic. Although all of these disturbances can occur in the absence of aphasia, it is rare for any of them to appear as the sole defect.

The great importance of the left hemisphere for certain intellectual activities becomes apparent when reviewing the behavioral disturbances that can accompany a left parietal lobe lesion even when speech does not appear to be significantly affected or when the task seems to be essentially nonverbal. For example, patients with left parietal lesions did less well than those with right-sided involvement on a formboard memory task (De Renzi, 1968) and another group of left parietal patients displayed impairment on both visual and auditory learning tests (Butters et al., 1970), apparently because these patients had reduced recourse to verbal memory aids.

The posterior association cortex: (c) Defects arising from right hemisphere lesions.   The most commonly seen apraxia associated with the right parietal lobe is constructional apraxia. Patients with right hemisphere lesions frequently have vestibular and oculomotor disorders along with the constructional apraxia. A right hemisphere acalculia shows up on written calculations as an inability to manipulate numbers in spatial relationships, such as using decimal places or "carrying," although the patient still retains mathematical concepts and the ability to do problems "in his head" (Grewel, 1952). For instance, the 57-year-old college graduate with a right parieto-occipital mass lesion (see Fig. 3-5) gave correct answers to relatively complex oral multiplication problems, but when given a written column of five two-place numbers to add, he could not integrate the sum of the right-hand column with the sum of the left-hand one. *Apraxia for dressing,* in which the patient has difficulty relating to and organizing parts of his body to parts of his clothing, may accompany right-sided parietal lesions. There are other performance disabilities of patients with right parietal lobe involvement that are clearly the product of a perceptual disorder such as impaired ability to localize objects in space (Hécaen et al., 1951). For example, the chief complaint of a middle-aged rancher with a right parieto-occipital lesion was difficulty in eating because his hand frequently missed when he put it out to reach the cup, or his fork overshot his plate.

Many of the perceptual disorders arising from lesions of the right posterior association cortex are related to the phenomenon of inattention (Denny-Brown et al., 1952). Inattention may occur as a relatively discrete and subtle disorder apparent only to the examiner. When stimulated bilaterally with a light touch to both cheeks or fingers wiggled in the outside periphery of each visual field (*double simultaneous stimulation*), the inattentive patient consistently ignores the stimulus on the left if both stimuli are presented simultaneously, although he shows no difficulty noticing a stimulus on his left when it is presented alone. In its more severe forms, inattention arising from right parietal lobe lesions may amount to a complete agnosia for the left half of space or for the left half of the patient's body (*hemisomatagnosia*) Mild inattention to one's own body may appear as simple negligence: the patient rarely uses his left hand spontaneously, may bump into objects on his left, or may not use left side pockets. In more extreme cases in which the patient usually has a left hemiplegia as well, he may appear completely unaware of the left half of his body, even to the point of denying his left-sided disabilities (*anosognosia*) or being unable to recognize that his paralyzed limbs belong to him. One or more of these perceptual disorders generally accompany an apraxia for dressing in which the patient may put clothes on backwards or consistently misbutton his shirt. Other perceptual problems associated with lesions of the parieto-occipital cortex include visuospatial disturbances, such as the inability to recognize familiar faces (*prosopagnosia*) and impairment of topographical or spatial thought.

Temporal lobe defects.   Much of the temporal lobe cortex is concerned with hearing and related functions, such as auditory memory
storage and complex perceptual organization. Left-right asymmetry
follows the verbal-nonverbal pattern of the posterior cortex.

Cortical association areas of the left temporal lobe mediate the
perception of such verbal material as word and number and even
voice recognition (Milner, 1971). The farther back a lesion occurs on
the temporal lobe, the more likely it is to produce alexia and verbal
apraxias. *Auditory agnosia*, in which the ability to discriminate and
comprehend speech sounds is impaired, is associated with lesions in
the auditory association cortex (Wernicke's area), located in the
topmost (superior) temporal gyrus of the posterior third of the lobe
(see Fig. 3-4). This condition has been variously called *sensory
aphasia* (Luria, 1965a), *Wernicke's aphasia* (Geschwind, 1969), or
fluent aphasia (Benson, 1967). Severe auditory agnosia appears only
rarely in sufficient isolation to be distinguishable from more global
forms of communication disabilities. However, it is perhaps the most
crippling of the communication disorders since patients can understand little of what they hear, although motor production of speech
remains intact; many such patients prattle grammatically and syn-
tactically correct nonsense. The auditory incomprehension of patients with lesions in Wernicke's area does not extend to nonverbal
sounds for they can respond appropriately to sirens, squealing
brakes, and the like. Lesions lower down and farther forward on the
left temporal lobe may involve verbal memory, giving rise to difficulties in recalling words, which, when severe, can seriously disrupt
fluent speech (*dysnomia*). These patients find it hard to remember or
comprehend long lists, sentences, or complex verbal material; and
their ability for new verbal learning may be greatly diminished or
even abolished. Although they may no longer be able to perform any
but simple, one-step mental operations, they can still do arithmetic
on paper, handle abstract concepts, and, if the lesion is not too close
to the juncture with the occipital cortex, some patients may also be
able to read.

Patients with cortical lesions of the right temporal lobe are unlikely to have language disabilities; rather they tend to experience
comparable problems with nonverbal sound discrimination, recognition, and comprehension (Milner, 1962). If the lesion is forward on
the lobe, there may be an *amusia* (literally, no music), and the pa-

tient will be unable to distinguish tones, tonal patterns, beats, or timbre with resulting inability to appreciate or enjoy music or to sing or hum a tune or rhythmical pattern (Shankweiler, 1966). Spatial disorientation problems and difficulties in recognizing complex, fragmented, or incomplete visual stimuli have also been associated with right temporal lobe lesions (Lansdell, 1970).

The temporal lobes and the limbic system.   The cortex of the temporal lobe also appears to be the most common site of triggering mechanisms for recall of memories. Awake patients undergoing brain surgery report vivid auditory and visual recall of previously experienced scenes and episodes upon electrical stimulation of the exposed temporal lobe cortex (Penfield and Perot, 1963). Nauta (1964) speculates that these memories involve widespread neural mechanisms and that the temporal and, to a lesser extent, the occipital cortex play a role in organizing the discrete components of memory for orderly and complete recall.

A major component of the memory system, the *hippocampus*, runs within the inside fold of each temporal lobe for much of its length (see Fig. 3-7). The hippocampal structures have both recording and memory consolidation functions for putting new information into long-term storage (Barbizet, 1963; Nauta, 1964). Although destruction or surgical removal of one hippocampus generally has little permanent effect on information acquisition, bilateral destruction invariably results in the loss of the ability to learn anything other than new motor skills (Corkin, 1968). In unilateral destruction, hemispheric differences persist: loss of the left hippocampus impairs verbal memory in all of its modalities and destruction of the right hippocampus results in defective recognition and recall of "complex visual and auditory patterns to which a name cannot readily be assigned" (Milner, 1970, p. 30).

The hippocampus is one of several bodies of gray matter within the temporal lobes that are part of the *limbic system*. This system has its components in the temporal lobe, in the subcortical forebrain, and in midbrain areas. They form an anatomically linked circle of structures that appear to work together as a system (see Fig. 3-7). Limbic system structures mediate both memory and emotional behavior (Brain, 1969). They may be involved in those affect-laden and general behavioral attitudes that direct the focus of attention and

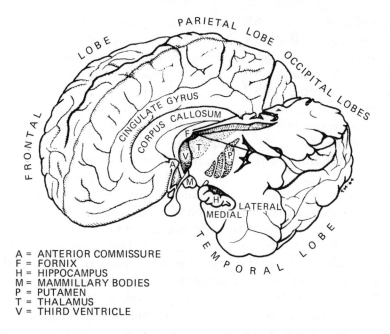

A = ANTERIOR COMMISSURE
F = FORNIX
H = HIPPOCAMPUS
M = MAMMILLARY BODIES
P = PUTAMEN
T = THALAMUS
V = THIRD VENTRICLE

FIG. 3-7. Cut-away perspective drawing of a human brain, showing the spatial relationships of most of the regions and structures thought to be related to general memory function. (The putamen is shown only as a landmark for readers familiar with the brain.) (Ojemann, 1966.)

thereby determine what is screened out of the perceptual field and what is selected for registration (Drachman and Arbit, 1966; Green, 1964). The hippocampus has been identified as one site of interaction between the perception and the memory systems. "The hippocampus appears to contain a mechanism capable of emitting a signal amounting to a 'Now print!' message without which no recording can take place. This 'Print!' message could be related to 'affective color or emotional tone'" (R. B. Livingston, quoted in Nauta, 1964, p. 19).

Other limbic system structures that have been specifically implicated in impairment of the recording and consolidation processes of memory are various portions of the thalamus, the mammillary bodies, and the fornix (Brodal, 1969). Massive *anterograde amnesia* (impaired ability for new learning including difficulty in remembering events after the onset of the amnesia) and some *retrograde amnesia* (difficulty in remembering events prior to the onset of the amnesia) result from diffuse lesions involving the mammillary bodies and the thalamus as well as from bilateral excision of the hippocampal structures. Recording of ongoing events may be mildly impaired by lesions of the *fornix* (Ojemann, 1966), a central forebrain structure that links the hippocampal and the mammillothalamic areas of the limbic system. When the fornix is cut or absent from birth, however, there appears to be no effect on memory function. This suggests that the hippocampus and the mammillothalamic structures may not be part of a unitary system despite their anatomical relationship and their similarity of function (Brierley, 1966).

Information storage is not confined to any single cortical area or brain structure. Rather, information involving each modality appears to be stored in the association cortex adjacent to its primary sensory cortex (Arnold, 1974; Samuels et al., 1972; Thompson et al., 1972). Thus, retrieval of visual information is impaired by lesions of the visual association cortex of the occipital lobe, impaired retrieval of auditory information follows lesions of the auditory association cortex of the temporal lobe, and so on. Frontal lobe motor association areas appear to provide the site for programming motor responses.

Disturbances in emotional behavior occur in association with seizure activity involving the hippocampus as well as the amygdala and *uncus* (the small hooked front end of the inner temporal lobe fold in which the hippocampus lies) (Pincus and Tucker, 1974). Abnormal electrical activity of the brain associated with *temporal lobe epilepsy* typically originates within the temporal lobe. This may give rise to a variety of transient behavior disturbances, such as changes in subjective feelings, behavioral automatisms, and bizarre posturing. Specific problems associated with temporal lobe epilepsy include alterations of mood; obsessional thinking; changes in consciousness; hallucinations and perceptual distortions in all sensory modalities including pain; and stereotyped, often repetitive and meaningless motor behavior that may comprise quite complex activities. Other names for these disturbances are *psychomotor seizures* or *psychomotor epilepsy*. Although psychiatric disorders are not necessarily associated with temporal lobe seizures, there is some tendency for patients subject to epilepsy, and particularly temporal lobe epilepsy, to display a schizophrenic-like psychosis (Pincus and Tucker, 1974). Mulder and Daly (1952) relate such psychic symptoms as anxiety, depression, and schizoid behavior either "specifically to a discharge focus in the temporal lobe . . . [or to] a reaction of the total personality to impairment of cerebral function" (p. 176). Hyposexuality (Pincus and Tucker, 1974) and hypersexuality (Harris et al., 1969) may occur with both temporal lobe seizures and surgical removal of temporal lobe limbic structures.

The precentral cortex: Frontal lobe disorders

In the course of the brain's evolution, the frontal lobes developed most recently to become the largest structures of the human brain. It was only natural for early students of brain function to conclude that the frontal lobes must therefore be the seat of the highest cognitive functions. For many years, and in fact until the latter half of this century, the highest and most uniquely human intellectual characteristics were assigned to the frontal lobes: "Even more important . . . [than manipulative ability] are the relations between the higher mental processes and the so-called frontal association areas of the frontal lobe. The capacity to form concepts, to organize the elements of a sequence of adjustments, to solve problems requiring central symbolic or 'recall' processes—all these mark the later stages of mammalian development, and in some cases it is rather clear that the frontal lobe is basic to the capacity" (Morgan, 1943, pp. 120–21). Although Morgan cited the 1939 article in which Hebb reported that surgical removal of the frontal lobes had virtually no effect on intelligence test performance, the association between highest functions and structures of most recent evolutionary origin apparently was too attractive to be easily set aside. The high incidence of World War II missile wounds and the popularity of psychosurgery on the frontal lobes for treatment of psychiatric disorders in the 1940's and 1950's ultimately provided enough cases of frontal brain damage without notable intellectual impairment to eliminate speculative misconceptions about frontal lobe functions.

Only the motor and motor association areas just forward of the central sulcus were correctly identified in the late nineteenth century when Fritsch and Hitzig studied the effects of direct electrical stimulation of the cerebral cortex in dogs (Tow, 1955). The motor strip or primary motor cortex lies on the first ridge in front of the central sulcus. The premotor cortex or secondary motor association area is on the adjacent forward ridge. Lesions in premotor association areas disrupt the integration of the motor components of complex acts, resulting in discontinuous or incoordinated movements and impaired motor skills. In the left hemisphere, for example, the lower portion of the motor association area (*Broca's area*) mediates the motor organization and patterning of speech, and lesions in this area may result in a motor pattern apraxia of speech some call *motor aphasia* (Luria, 1965a). Patients with this condition display disturbances in organizing the muscles of the speech apparatus to form sounds or in patterning groups of sounds into words. This may leave them incapable of fluent speech production, although their ability to comprehend language is not necessarily impaired. An ideational apraxia associated with diffuse frontal lobe lesions has also been described in which each motor element of a complex behavior pattern is adequately performed but the patient cannot integrate the elements into an overall plan of activity (Nielsen, 1948). *Expressive amusia* or *avocalia* (inability to sing) has been attributed to homologous lesions of the right hemisphere.

The anterior portions of the frontal lobes, the *prefrontal* areas, mediate a number of functions having to do more with the "how" than the "what" of both cognitive and emotional behavior. These are functions that organize and control actions and involve the activities of selective perception such as visual scanning. "Disturbances of behavior control in frontal lobe lesions is one of the basic factors in pathology of the frontal lobe system . . . behavior loses its selective character and early falls under the influence of outside associations. The effect of action is not evaluated, no signal of errors is actualized, mistakes are not corrected" (Luria and Homskaya, 1964).

Behavior problems associated with frontal lobe damage can be roughly categorized into four general groups with considerable overlap. These problems may also occur with lesions involving other areas of the brain, but in such cases they are apt to be associated with specific intellectual, sensory, or motor disabilities.

1. Problems of *slowing* appear as decreased spontaneity, decreased rate at which behavior is emitted, or decrease or loss of initiative. Severe slowing may appear as apathy, unresponsiveness, or mutism. In its milder forms, patients lack initiative and ambition, but may be able to carry through normal activities quite adequately.

2. Difficulties in making mental or behavioral shifts, whether they are shifts in attention, changes in movement, or flexibility in attitude, come under the heading of *perseveration* and are characteristic of

patients with frontal lobe lesions. Perseveration may sometimes be seen as difficulty in suppressing ongoing activities or attention to prior stimulation. In general, perseveration occurs as rigidity or stereotypy of behavior. Perseveration on intellectual tasks may be expressed in repetitive and uncritical perpetuation of a response that was once correct but becomes an uncorrected error under changed circumstances or in continuation of a response beyond its proper end point.

3. *Deficient self-awareness* results in an inability to perceive performance errors, to appreciate the impact one makes on others, or to size up a social situation appropriately. Defective self-criticism is associated with tendencies of some frontal lobe patients to be euphoric and self-satisfied, to experience little or no anxiety, and to be impulsive and unconcerned about social conventions.

4. A *concrete attitude* is also common among patients with frontal lobe damage. This appears in an inability to dissociate oneself from one's immediate surrounds and in a literal attitude in which objects, experiences, and behavior are all taken at their most obvious face value. The patient becomes incapable of planning and foresight or of sustaining goal-directed behavior.

Although difficulties in the control, integration, and regulation of behavior associated with frontal lobe lesions typically affect all aspects of the patient's behavior, cognitive defects tend to predominate when the lesion is on the top or outer sides of the frontal lobes. Lesions on the sides of the lobes between the hemispheres or subcortical lesions that involve pathways that connect the cortex between and just under the hemispheres with the drive and affective integration centers in the diencephalon are most apt to affect emotional and social adjustment (Valenstein, 1973).

Intellectual impairment associated with loss or disconnection of frontal lobe tissue usually does not appear as a loss of specific skills, information, or even reasoning or problem-solving ability (Landis, 1952; Teuber, 1964). In fact, patients with frontal lobe lesions typically do not do poorly on those formal intelligence tests in which another person directs the examination, sets the pace, starts and stops the activity, and makes all the discretionary decisions. The closed-ended questions of common fact and familiar situations and the well-structured puzzles with concrete solutions that make up standard tests of intellectual ability are not likely to present special problems for many patients with frontal lobe injuries. Perseveration or carelessness may lower a patient's scores somewhat but usually not enough to depress them significantly. Cognitive defects associated with frontal lobe damage tend to show up most clearly in the course of daily living and are more often observed by relatives and co-workers than by a medical or psychological examiner in a standard interview. Common complaints about such patients concern apathy, carelessness, poor or unreliable judgment, poor adaptability to new situations, and blunted social sensibility (Bonner et al., 1953).

Some specific cognitive defects may be ascribed to frontal lobe lesions. Difficulty in suppressing response tendencies may interfere with learning new associations to stimuli for which the patient has already learned associations or with performing tasks requiring delayed responses (Milner, 1971). Defective abstract thinking and trouble in making response shifts result in impaired mental efficiency (Tow, 1955). There appears to be a tendency for a dissociation to occur between language behaviors and ongoing activity so that the patient is less apt to use verbal cues (usually subvocalization) to direct, guide, or organize his ongoing behavior with resultant perservation, fragmentation, or premature termination of a response (Luria and Homskaya, 1964; Tow, 1955). Visual scanning defects appear as response slowing and inefficiency in the plan of search (Teuber, 1964). Patients with frontal lobe lesions show little of the imagination or innovative thinking that is essential to creativity (Zangwill, 1966). The ability to evaluate both incoming stimuli and one's own behavior may be affected by frontal lobe lesions. Sommerhoff (1974) relates this evaluative function to the inhibiting activity of the frontal lobe in its close relationship with major drive centers of the brain. Impaired registration of incoming stimuli resulting in a decreased short-term memory capacity has been associated with frontal lobe damage (Lewinsohn et al., 1972). The frontal lobes have also been implicated in defects of time sense, both with respect to recency and time-span judgments and, in patients with bilateral frontal lobe damage, to orientation in time (Benton, 1968).

Lateralization of cognitive functions appears to be less marked in the frontal lobes, although some of the verbal-nonverbal distinctions between left and right hemisphere functions obtain here too. Decreased verbal fluency and impoverishment of spontaneous speech tends to be associated with left frontal lobe lesions, although mildly depressed verbal fluency also occurs with right frontal lobe lesions. Constructional apraxia has been noted in patients with right frontal lobe lesions who have difficulty with the motor rather than the perceptual components of the task (Benton, 1968). Difficulties in making response shifts appear following loss of either right or left frontal lobe tissue, but this problem tends to be transient in right hemisphere patients who can learn to direct their behavior with verbal cues.

CLINICAL LIMITATIONS OF FUNCTIONAL LOCALIZATION

Early in this century pinpoint localizations of highly specific disturbances of intellectual functions was a popular undertaking (Luria, 1965b). However, variations in the size, position, and nature of the lesion and variations in cortical organization make it impossible to infer the location of a lesion from behavior alone with a high degree of certainty (Blinkov and Glezer, 1968; Bonin, 1962a) (see Chapter 7). Today, clinical investigators expend little effort in attempting precise localization of complex cognitive disturbances. Rather they use knowledge of the functions associated with the primary sensory projection areas, major sensory overlap zones, and prominent frontal areas to provide guideposts for making general estimates of the location and extent of the presumed cortical concomitants of organic behavior disorders.

A well-grounded understanding of functional localization strengthens the clinician's diagnostic capabilities so long as he takes into account the limitations of its applicability in the individual case. Common patterns of behavioral impairment associated with such well-understood neurological conditions as certain kinds of cerebrovascular accident tend to involve the same anatomical structures with predictable regularity. For example, stroke patients with right arm paralysis due to a lesion involving the left motor projection area of the frontal cortex will generally have an associated motor apraxia of speech. Yet, the clinician will sometimes find behavioral disparities between patients with cortical lesions of apparently similar location and size: some ambulatory stroke victims whose right arms are paralyzed are practically mute; others have successfully returned to highly verbal occupations (M. W. Buck, 1968).

Other apparent discontinuities between the patient's behavior and his neurological status may occur when a pattern of behavioral impairment develops spontaneously and without physical evidence of neurological disease. In such cases, "hard" neurological findings (e.g., such positive physical changes on neurological examination as primitive reflexes, unilateral weakness, or spasticity) or abnormal laboratory results (e.g., protein in the spinal fluid, brain wave abnormalities, or radiological anomalies) may appear in time, for instance, as a tumor grows or as arteriosclerotic changes block more blood vessels. Occasionally a suspected brain abnormality may be demonstrated only on postmortem examination; and even then correlative tissue changes may not always be found (Sklar, 1963; A. Smith, 1962a).

The uncertain relation between brain activity and human behavior obligates the clinician to exercise care in his observations and caution in his predictions, and to take nothing for granted when applying the principles of functional localization to diagnostic problems. However, this uncertain relation does not negate the dominant tendencies to regularity in the functional organization of brain tissue. Knowledge of the regularity with which brain-behavior correlations occur enables the clinician to determine whether a patient's behavioral symptoms make anatomical sense, to know what subtle or unobtrusive changes may accompany the more obvious ones, and to guide the neurosurgeon or neuroradiologist in further diagnostic procedures.

4
THE RATIONALE OF
DEFICIT MEASUREMENT

Neuropsychological assessment is similar to conventional psychological evaluation but with an important difference. In the usual psychological examination, the examiner studies a patient's intellectual performance, his personality characteristics, and his emotional state. He may also attempt to explain the patient's behavior in the light of common behavioral patterns and what he knows of the patient's history and his current life situation. Finally, the examining psychologist may draw a diagnostic conclusion for the purpose of facilitating treatment planning or other decision-making.

The neuropsychological examination proceeds in much the same manner. The neuropsychologist attends to the same aspects of behavior, relies on similar explanatory assumptions, and pursues the same kind of treatment or decision-making goals. The distinguishing characteristic of neuropsychological assessment is its emphasis on the identification and measurement of psychological deficits, for it is in deficiencies of intellect, emotionality, and control that brain damage is manifested behaviorally.

Brain damage always implies behavioral impairment. Even when psychological changes after head injury or concomitant with brain disease are viewed as improvement rather than impairment, as when there is a welcome increase in sociability or relief from neurotic anxiety, a careful assessment will probably reveal an underlying loss.

A 47-year-old postal clerk with a bachelor's degree in education boasted of having recently become an "extrovert" after having been painfully shy and socially uncomfortable most of his life. His wife brought him to the neurologist with complaints of deteriorating judgment, childishness, untidiness, and negligence of personal hygiene. The patient reported no notable behavioral changes other than his newfound ability to approach and talk with people.

On psychological testing, although his performance of many intellectual functions was at a *superior* level, in accord with his academic achievement and his wife's reports of his prior functioning, the patient also did poorly on tests involving immediate memory, new learning, and attention and concentration. The discrepancy between his best and poorest performances suggested that this patient had already sustained intellectual losses.

In some cases the loss, or deficit, may be subtle, becoming apparent only on complex judgmental tasks or under emotionally charged conditions. In other cases the direct behavioral effects of the impairment may be so slight or ill-defined as to be unobservable under ordinary conditions; the patient reports vague, unaccustomed, and unexpected frustrations or uneasiness while his family and friends are puzzled by his depression or heightened irritability or decreased frustration tolerance.

A physician's wife in her early 40's underwent a radical behavior change, from an active, socially well-adjusted, and apparently quite contented woman with many interests to a restless, dissatisfied, and irritable alcoholic, constantly embroiled in bitter fights with her husband and theatrical crises with her psychiatrist. Her problems were originally diagnosed as functional; but on psychological examination, a significant discrepancy between *superior* verbal functioning and *low average* visuopractic abilities was discovered, raising the suspicion of brain damage. On questioning, she reported that just before the behavior change she had received a head injury in a car accident, but routine x-ray and neurological examination were negative and neither she nor her husband had thought anything more about it.

Before the accident, she had done much creative needlework, deriving personal satisfaction from as well as obtaining attention and praise for her talent for sewing. After the injury, she lost interest in any kind of handcraft and stopped sewing altogether. She suddenly had a lot of time on her hands and lacked a significant source of self-esteem. She never associated her disinterest in sewing with the head injury and was not aware, until examined psychologically, that she suffered serious impairment of abilities involving visuospatial organization. Depression following the injury only compounded her self-doubt and bewilderment. She resisted treatment until her intellectual disability was discovered and a rational approach to her problems could be undertaken.

Although any psychological function may be affected by brain damage, the assessment of psychological deficit has focused on intellectual impairment for a number of reasons. First, some degree of intellectual impairment accompanies almost all brain dysfunction and is a diagnostically significant feature of many neurological disorders (Chapman and Wolff, 1959). Although emotional and social behavior may also be significantly altered by disease of or injury to the brain, defects affecting intellectual functioning—aphasias, failures of judgment, lapses of memory, etc.—tend to be most obvious to the casual observer and to interfere most radically with the patient's capacity to function independently.

Second, psychologists are better able to measure intellectual behavior than any other kind, except perhaps simple psychophysical reactions and sensorimotor responses. Certainly, intellectual behavior has been systematically scrutinized more times in more permutations and combinations and with more replications and controls than has any other behavior. Out of all these data have evolved numerous reliable and well-standardized techniques for identifying, defining, grading, measuring, and comparing the spectrum of intellectual behaviors. These technological achievements of intelligence and educational testing have provided the neuropsychologist with a ready-made set of operations and a technical frame of reference that have been fruitfully applied to deficit measurement. The deficit measurement paradigm can be applied to other kinds of behavioral impairments, such as personality change, decreased intellectual efficiency, or a defective capacity for self-control. However, personality is typically described rather than measured; and, in the clinical setting, impairments in efficiency and self-control are usually evaluated on the basis of their effect on specific intellectual functions or personality characteristics rather than studied in their own right.

COMPARISON STANDARDS FOR DEFICIT MEASUREMENT

The concept of behavioral deficit presupposes some ideal, normal, or prior level of functioning against which the patient's performance may be measured. This level, the *comparison standard*, may be *normative* (derived from an appropriate population) or *individual* (derived from the patient's history or present characteristics), depending on the patient, the kind of behavior being evaluated, and the purpose of the assessment.

Normative Comparison Standards

The population average

The normative comparison standard may be an *average*. For adults, the normative standard, or "norm," for many measurable psychological functions and characteristics is a score representing the average performance of some more or less well-defined population, such as white women or college graduates over 40. For many intellectual functions, variables of age and education or vocational achievement may significantly affect test performance and therefore are often taken into account in developing test norms. The measurement of children's behavior is concerned with abilities and traits that change with age, so the normative standard may be the average age or grade at which a given trait or function appears or reaches some criterion level of performance. Because of the differential rate of development for boys and girls, children's norms are likely to be given separately for each sex.

Normative standards based on either average performance level or average age of performance are available for a broad range of intellectual behaviors, from simple visual-motor reaction time or verbal mimicry to the most complex activities involving higher mathematics, visuospatial conceptualization, or sophisticated social judgments. Norms based on averages are also derived for social behaviors, such as frequency of church attendance or age for participation in team play; for vocational interests, such as medicine or truck driving; or for personality traits, such as assertiveness or hypochondria.

Species-wide performance expectations

The norms for some psychological functions and traits serve as species-wide performance expectations for adults, although they are age or grade averages for infants or children. This is the case for all intellectual functions that follow a common course of development, that are usually fully developed long before adulthood, and that are taken for granted as part and parcel of the normal adult behavioral repertory. Speech is a good example. The average two-year-old child can talk in two- and three-word phrases. The ability to communicate most needs and thoughts by means of speech is expected of four and five year olds. Seventh- and eighth-grade children can utter and comprehend word groupings in all the basic grammatical forms and their elaborations. Subsequent speech development mainly involves more variety, elegance, abstractness, or complexity of verbal expression. Thus, the adult norm for speech is the intact ability to speak, and all but a few adults function at the normative level. Some other mental abilities that are expected to be fully functional in adults are counting change, drawing a recognizable person, basic map reading, and using a hammer and saw or cooking utensils. Each of these skills is learned, improves with practice, has a common developmental history for most adults, and is sufficiently simple that its mastery or potential mastery is taken for granted. Anything less than an acceptable performance in an adult raises the suspicion of impairment.

Other species-wide normative standards are characteristic of people generally, regardless of their age, sex, or experience. Thus, binaural hearing, or the ability to localize a touch on the skin or to discriminate between noxious and pleasant stimuli, are capacities that are an expected part of the endowment of each human organism. These capacities are not learned in the usual sense, nor, except when impaired by accident or disease, do they change over time and with experience. They are not generally thought of as psychological functions or abilities; rather they are the simple or rudimentary behavioral components of more elaborate and complex psychological response patterns.

Customary standards
A number of assumed normative standards have been arbitrarily set, usually by custom. Probably the most familiar of these is the visual acuity standard: 20–20 vision does not represent an average but an arbitrary ideal, which is met or surpassed by different proportions of the population, depending on age. Verbal response latency—the amount of time a person takes to answer a question—has normative values of one or two seconds for informal conversation in our culture.

Applications and limitations of normative standards
Normative standards are used for most psychological purposes, including the description of intellectual status for both children and adults, educational and vocational planning, and personality assessment. In assessing brain damage in young children or persons whose impairment dates from infancy, the deficient behavior is generally measured against some normative standard of developmental expectations. The criterion may appear in the form of a "but for" hypothesis: "But for the [hereditary, metabolic, birth, etc.] defect, Johnny would be as [bright, attentive, sweet-tempered] as his [siblings, parents, the average child of his age]."

Normative standards, however, are of limited value in the assessment of behavioral deficit when the patient has suffered a significant decline from some prior level of intellectual competence. Here what is wanted is more than just a psychological description of the patient's present pattern of functioning, since a description gives no direct information about the pattern or extent of loss. Nor do comparisons with population averages add significantly to the information conveyed by the test scores alone, for most test scores are themselves numerical comparisons with population norms. In measuring deficit, the examiner must compare the patient's present with his prior functioning in order to assess the individual patient's real losses.

Thus, a first step in measuring intellectual deficit in an adult is to establish—or estimate, when direct information is not available—the patient's premorbid performance level for all of the functions and abilities being assessed. For those functions with species-wide norms, this task is easy. Any adult who can no longer name objects or copy a simple design or who appears unaware of one side of his body has an obvious deficit.

On the other hand, for all those functions and abilities for which the normative standard is an average, only an individual comparison provides a meaningful basis for assessing deficit. A population average is not an appropriate comparison standard since it will not ordinarily apply to the individual patient. By definition, one-half of the subjects achieve a score within the average range on any well-constructed psychological test; the remainder perform at many different levels both above and below the average. Although the average score may be, statistically, the most likely score a person will receive, statistical likelihood is a far cry from the individual case.

Individual Comparison Standards

As a general rule, *individual comparison standards* are called for whenever a psychological trait or function is evaluated for change. This rule applies both to deficit measurement and the measurement of behavioral change generally. Only on initial examination, and then only when dealing with functions for which there are species-wide or customary norms—such as finger tapping rate or accuracy of auditory discrimination—are normative standards appropriate for deficit measurement. And even for these functions, the results of repeated examinations will be compared to those of prior examinations of the same individual rather than to the normative standards.

The use of individual comparison standards is probably most clearly exemplified in rate of change studies which depend solely on intraindividual comparisons. Here the same battery of tests is administered three times or more at spaced intervals, and the differences between chronologically sequential pairs of test scores are compared.

The measurement of rate of change is important in child psychology as a method of demonstrating the rate of development. The rate of change approach also has very broad applications in neuropsychology. Knowledge of the rate at which the patient's performance is deteriorating can contribute to the accuracy of predictions of the course of a deteriorating disease. For purposes of rehabilitation, the rate of recovery of intellectual functions following cerebral insult may not only aid in predicting the ultimate extent of recovery, but provide information about the effectiveness of rehabilitative efforts. Rate of change studies are also important in research on the long range effects of injury to the brain on intellectual functioning since continuing changes have been reported months and even years after the injury occurred (Reitan, 1962; A. Smith, 1964).

THE MEASUREMENT OF DEFICIT

Direct Measurement of Deficit

Deficit can be assessed directly when there are normative comparison standards for the behavior in question. Inability to copy a simple
drawing or to follow a sequence of three verbal instructions are
obvious evidence of deficit in an adult. The extent of the discrepancy
between the level of performance expected for an adult and the level
of the patient's performance (usually given in terms of the age at
which the average child performs in a comparable manner) provides
one measure of the amount of deficit the patient has sustained.

Direct deficit measurement using individual comparison standards may appear to be a simple, straightforward operation: the
examiner compares premorbid and current samples of the behavior
he wishes to study and evaluates the discrepancies. Canter's study
(1951) of intellectual impairment in multiple sclerosis illustrates
this procedure well. He compared the scores that veterans with multiple sclerosis received on the Army General Classification Test
(AGCT) at the time of their induction into service with scores obtained on the same test battery after their illness was diagnosed. The
results of this direct comparison provided clear-cut, unequivocal
answers to questions of behavioral change over time. However, the
direct method using individual comparison standards presupposes
the availability of premorbid test scores or school grades or other
relevant observational data, and these may be either nonexistent or
difficult to obtain. Without full documentation of a patient's premorbid intellectual status, there is no direct comparison standard for
each and every intellectual function or skill being examined. Therefore, more often than not the examiner must use *indirect* methods of
deficit assessment in which the individual comparison standard has
been inferred.

Indirect Measurement of Deficit

In indirect measurement, the examiner compares the patient's present performance with an *estimate* of his original ability level. The
estimates may be made from a variety of sources. It is the examiner's

task to find defensible and meaningful estimates of the original (pre-traumatic or premorbid) ability level to serve as comparison standards for each patient.

Assumptions underlying the indirect measurement of deficit
The choice of a comparison standard is dictated by the rule holding that *the comparison standard is the one level of intellectual functioning that best represents the patient's premorbid level of general intellectual functioning*. This rule follows from a number of assumptions that also guide the examiner in its practical applications.

The assumptions rest on the premise that each person has an original intellectual potential inherent in and limited by his neural structures and metabolic efficiency (Maher, 1963). Hebb (1949) spells this out in his conceptualization of endowed capacity as "intelligence *A*, "the underlying potential out of which develops intelligence *B*," the manifested abilities. "Neither, of course, is observed directly; but *intelligence B*, a hypothetical level of development in brain function, is a much more direct inference from behavior than is *intelligence A*, the original potential" (p. 294). The level of general intellectual functioning inferred from observed behavior or evidence from premorbid performance represents Hebb's intelligence *B*.

One assumption underlies all methods for estimating the comparison standard for any particular patient: *Given reasonably normal conditions of physical and mental development, there is one intellectual performance level that best represents each person's intellectual abilities generally.* This assumption follows from the well-documented phenomenon of the transitional consistency of intellectual behavior, which is sometimes represented as the general ability factor g (see pp. 16–17). According to this assumption, the performance level of most normally developed, healthy persons on any single test of an intellectual function or skill probably provides a reasonable estimate of their performance level on all other kinds of intellectual tasks. A corollary assumption is that *marked discrepancies between the levels at which a person performs different intellectual functions or skills are evidence of disease, developmental anomalies, cultural deprivation, emotional disturbance, or some other condition that has interfered with the full expression of that person's intellectual potential.*

A second assumption is that *the general ability level provides the closest approximation to the upper limit of intellectual development set by each person's biological endowment.* According to this assumption, intellectual potential or capacity can either be realized or reduced by external influences; it is not possible to perform at a higher level than one's biological capacity will permit (J. M. Hunt and Cofer, 1944). Brain injury—or cultural deprivation, poor work habits, or anxiety—can only depress intellectual functioning (Rey, 1964). An important corollary to this second assumption is that, *for intellectually impaired persons, the least depressed abilities are the best remaining behavioral representatives of the original intellectual potential* (Jastak, 1949).

The phenomenon of overachievement (people performing better than their general intelligence would seem to warrant) appears to contradict this assumption, but in fact overachievers do not exceed their biological limitations. Rather, they expend an inordinate amount of energy and effort on developing one or two special skills, usually to the neglect of others. Overachievers generally know their material mostly by rote and cannot handle the complex intellectual operations or highly abstract concepts expected of people at their specialization level.

Another assumption is that *no person functions at his endowed maximum potential,* for everyone's intellectual effectiveness has been compromised a little here by a childhood illness, a little there by educational deficiencies, or understimulation in infancy, or impulsivity, or a bump on the head, or test anxiety, and so on (Cutter, 1957). With time and experience, each person's original intellectual potential becomes more or less obscured. Thus, a person's performance of any task, no matter how good it might be, only indicates the floor, not the ceiling, of his level of abilities involved in that task. There is no way to measure the ceiling, that is, to assess intellectual capacity directly.

A related assumption is that *within the limits of chance variations, a person's ability to perform a task is at least as high as his level of performance of that task.* It cannot be less. This assumption may not seem to be so obvious when a psychologist is attempting to estimate premorbid intelligence from remnants of abilities or knowledge. In the face of a generally shabby performance, the psychologist may be reluctant to extrapolate an estimate of *superior* intelligence from one or two indicators of superiority, such as a demonstration of how to use a complicated machine, or the apt use of several abstract or uncommon words, unless he accepts the assumption that prerequisite to the development of any skill or function is the ability to perform it. A patient who names "Washington, Jefferson, Adams, and Nixon" as four presidents since 1900 (approximately 95% of all adults can answer the question correctly) but then identifies correctly a relatively obscure religious book that fewer than 10% of American adults know is demonstrating a significantly higher level of prior intellectual achievement than he maintains. His poor response does not negate his good one; the difference between them represents the extent to which he has suffered intellectual deterioration.

It is also assumed that *a patient's premorbid ability level can be reconstructed or estimated from many different kinds of behavioral observations or historical facts*. Estimates of original intellectual potential may be based on interview impressions, reports from family and friends, test scores, prior academic or employment level, school grades, army rating, or an intellectual product such as a letter or an invention. Information that a patient is a physicist or that he designed and built his own cantilevered house is all that is needed to make an estimate of *very superior* premorbid intelligence, regardless of his present mental incapabilities. Except in the most obvious cases of unequivocal high achievement, the estimates should be based on a wide range of information from as many sources as possible to minimize the likelihood that significant data have been overlooked and the patient's premorbid ability level has been underestimated. For instance, verbal fluency can be masked by shyness or a highly developed graphic design talent lost to a motor paralysis. Such achievements might remain unknown without painstaking inquiry or testing.

Methods of indirect measurement
Different methods of inferring the comparison standard for each patient have been applied with varying degrees of success, depending on the examiner's sophistication and the individual patient's peculiar set of circumstances. Historical and observational data are obvious sources of information, and estimates of premorbid ability may be drawn from them directly. Estimates based on these sources will

be more or less satisfactory depending upon how much is known of the patient's past, and whether what is known or can be observed is sufficiently characteristic to distinguish this particular patient from other people. For example, if all that an examiner knows about a brain injured, intellectually impaired patient is that he was a logger with a ninth grade education and his observed vocabulary and interests seem appropriate to his occupation and education, then the examiner can only estimate a fairly low ability level as the comparison standard. If the patient had been brighter than average, if he could reason exceptionally well, tell stories cleverly, had been due for a promotion to supervisor, this information would probably not be available to the examiner who would then have no way of knowing from history and observations alone just how intelligent this particular logger had been.

Because premorbid ability estimates inferred from historical and observational data may be unpredictably low, indirect assessment of intellectual deficit is usually performed with current psychological test results. A number of different techniques have been developed for measuring intellectual deficit from test data. A common feature of all these techniques is that the premorbid ability level is estimated from the test data themselves.

For many years the most common method for estimating the premorbid ability level from test performance used a vocabulary score as the single best indicator of original intellectual endowment (Yates, 1954). This method was based on observations that many patients suffering various kinds of organic deterioration retained old, well-established verbal skills long after recent memory, reasoning, arithmetic ability, and other intellectual functions had deteriorated badly. A well-known example of this method is the Shipley Institute of Living Scale (Shipley and Burlingame, 1941), which contains both vocabulary and verbal abstraction items (see p. 445). It was expected that mentally deteriorated persons would show large discrepancies between their vocabulary and their reasoning scores. Wechsler and others used the same principle to devise "deterioration" ratios, which were mostly based on the comparison of vocabulary and other verbal skill scores with scores on timed tests involving visual-motor activities (see pp. 193–195).

Vocabulary and related verbal skill scores sometimes do provide the best estimates of the general premorbid intellectual ability level. However, the vocabulary scores of many patients tend to be more vulnerable to brain damage than the scores of other verbal tests (E. W. Russell, 1972b). Further, a significant proportion of patients with dominant hemisphere lesions suffer deterioration of verbal skills. Aphasic patients have the most obvious verbal disabilities; some are unable to use verbal symbols at all. Some patients with dominant hemisphere lesions are not technically aphasic, but their verbal fluency is sufficiently depressed that vocabulary scores do not provide good comparison standards (Lansdell, 1968a). Even among normal control subjects, vocabulary scores alone may not provide a good estimate of general ability level except in those persons who have superior verbal skills (Jarvie, 1960).

Other techniques have been devised for estimating the comparison standard (Thorp and Mahrer, 1959). For instance, one method compares the *variance* (a statistical measure of variability) of all the subtest scores (except the immediate memory subtest) obtained on the verbal section of the Wechsler test battery with the average of these scores, under the assumption that the wider the spread between the subtest scores (i.e., the higher the variance), the higher the estimate of original ability relative to the average of the obtained scores. Another method weights the three highest subtest scores obtained on the Wechsler subtests to provide an "intellectual altitude score." Thorp and Mahrer recommend "testing the limits" after the standard examination has been completed. For example, a patient who failed in his attempt to do arithmetic problems mentally may do them correctly if given paper and pencil. The estimate of original ability will then be based on the better arithmetic performance, although the lower score obtained for the mental calculations still reflects the patient's present functioning in that area. The discrepancy between the two scores indicates the amount of deficit.

The best performance method

A simpler method utilizes any test score as well as other observations and historical data. It follows from the assumptions that the patient's best performance provides the closest approximation to his original ability level and that no performance level can be higher than the performer's ability (except for minor chance score fluctuations and the performance of an occasional overachiever). This is the *best performance method* in which the level of the best performance—whether it be the highest score or set of scores, nonscorable behavior not necessarily observed in a formal testing situation, or evidence of premorbid achievement—serves as the best estimate of premorbid ability. Once the highest score or highest level of functioning has been identified, it becomes the standard against which all other aspects of the patient's current performance are compared.

This method has very practical advantages. The examiner is not bound to one battery of tests but can take his estimate from any test score or cluster of test scores, and from non-test behavior and behavioral reports as well. Thus, if a patient's general functioning is too low or too spotty for him to take a standard adult test, many children's tests or tests of specific skills or intellectual functions provide opportunities for him to demonstrate residual intellectual abilities.

There are two circumstances in which the examiner should not rely on a single high test score for his estimate of premorbid ability. One, which was referred to above, involves the overachiever whose highest scores are generally on vocabulary, general information, or arithmetic tests as these are the skills most commonly inflated by parental or school pressure on an ordinary student. The overachiever frequently has high memory scores too. He does not do as well on tests of reasoning, judgment, original thinking, and problem-solving, whether they are verbal or nonverbal. A single high score on a memory test should not be used for estimating premorbid ability level since, of all the intellectual functions, memory is the least reliable indicator of general intellectual ability. Dull people can have very good memories; some extremely bright people have been notoriously absent-minded.

It is rare to find only one outstandingly high score in a complete neuropsychological examination. Usually even severely impaired patients produce a cluster of relatively higher scores in their least damaged area of functioning so that the likelihood of overestimating the premorbid ability level from a single, spuriously high score is very slight. The examiner is much more likely to err by underestimating the original ability level of the severely brain injured patient who is unable to perform well on any task.

The Deficit Measurement Paradigm

Once the examiner has determined the comparison standard, whether directly from population norms, premorbid test data, or historical information, or indirectly from current test results and observation, he may assess deficit. To do so, he compares the level of the patient's present intellectual performance with the expected level, the comparison standard. Discrepancies between the expected level and the patient's present functioning are then evaluated for statistical significance (see Chapter 6, passim).

A statistically significant discrepancy between expected and observed performance levels for any intellectual function or activity represents an intellectual deficit. This procedure can be illustrated in a simple subtraction equation:

Premorbid intellectual functioning
− Present level of functioning
        = Intellectual impairment (provided that the difference between the estimated level of premorbid functioning and the present level of functioning is statistically significant)

This calculation is repeated for each function or ability being evaluated. For each patient for each comparison where premorbid test scores are not available, the comparison standard is the same estimate of original ability. By chance alone, a certain amount of variation (*scatter*) between test scores can be expected for even the most normal persons. However, chance variations tend to be small (Cronbach, 1970). If significant discrepancies occur for more than one intellectual function or activity, a *pattern* of deficit may emerge. By comparing any given pattern of deficit with patterns known to be associated with specific neurological or psychological conditions, the examiner may be able to identify etiological and remedial possibilities for the patient's problems. When differences between expected and observed performance levels are not statistically significant, deficit cannot be inferred.

For example, it is statistically unlikely that a person whose premorbid ability level was decidedly better than average cannot solve fourth or fifth grade arithmetic problems on paper or that he is unable to put together blocks to form any but the simplest patterns failed by only 2 to 9% of the adult population. If a patient whose original ability is estimated at the *high average* level produces this pattern of performance, then an assessment of impairment of certain arithmetic and practic functions can be made with confidence. If the same patient performs at an *average* level on tests of verbal reasoning and learning, then the discrepancy is not significant even though his performance is somewhat lower than expected. His slightly lowered scores on these latter two functions need to be considered in any overall evaluation in which significant impairment has been found in other areas. However, when taken by themselves, *average* scores obtained by patients of *high average* endowment do not indicate impairment, since they may be due to normal score fluctuations. On the other hand, just *average* verbal reasoning and learning scores achieved by persons of estimated original *very superior* endowment represent a statistically significant discrepancy so that in exceptionally bright persons, *average* scores indicate deficit.

Identifiable patterns of intellectual impairment can be demonstrated by the deficit assessment method. Although this discussion has focused on assessment of deficit where there is known or suspected neurological disease, this method can be used to evaluate the intellectual functioning of psychiatrically disabled or educationally or culturally deprived persons as well. The evaluation of children's intellectual disorders follows the same model (E. M. Taylor, 1959). It is of use not only as an aid to neurological or psychiatric diagnosis, but in educational and rehabilitation planning too.

5
THE NEUROPSYCHOLOGICAL
EXAMINATION: PROCEDURES

There are no hard and fast rules for conducting a neuropsychological examination. The enormous variety of neurological conditions, patient capacities, and examination questions necessitate a flexible, open, and imaginative approach. General guidelines for the examination can be summed up in the injunction: *tailor the examination to the patients's needs, abilities, and limitations.* By adapting the examination to the patient rather than the other way around, the examiner can answer the examination questions most fully at the least cost and with the greatest benefit to the patient.

THE INDIVIDUALIZED EXAMINATION

The neuropsychological examination can be individually tailored in two ways. The examiner can select tests and examination techniques for their appropriateness for the patient and for their relevancy to those diagnostic or planning questions that prompted the examination and that arise during its course. He can also apply these assessment tools in a sensitive and inventive way by adapting them to suit the patient's condition and enlarging upon them to gain a full measure of information.

Designing the Test Battery for the Patient

The examination questions
Like any other examination procedure, the purpose of a psychological examination is to provide answers to questions the patient or

others have raised concerning the patient. Examination questions give direction to the examination and determine its content. In order to design an appropriate neuropsychological test battery, the examiner must know what questions need to be answered.

Examination questions fall into one of two categories. *Diagnostic questions* concern the *nature* of the patient's symptoms and complaints in terms of their etiology and prognosis; i.e., they ask *what* is the patient's problem. *Descriptive questions* inquire into the *characteristics* of the patient's condition; i.e., they ask *how* the patient's problem is expressed. Within these two large categories are specific questions which may each be best answered through somewhat different approaches.

Diagnostic questions. Questions concerning the nature of the patient's condition are always questions of differential diagnosis. Whether implied or directly stated, these questions ask which of two or more diagnostic pigeonholes suits the patient's behavior best. In neuropsychology, diagnostic categorization can consist of coarse screening to differentiate the probably "organic" from "not organic" or "psychiatrically disturbed" patients, fine discrimination between a *presenile dementia* (early onset condition of intellectual deterioration) and mental deterioration associated with a tumor, or the even finer discrimination between the behavioral effects of a parietal lobe lesion from the effects of a lesion involving another part of the brain.

The simplest diagnostic question asks whether organic damage contributes to a patient's aberrant behavior. This is frequently the most difficult question to answer when patients have complaints and symptoms that are not distinctively neurological or psychiatric and are not obviously concocted for secondary gain. This question calls for gross screening of a wide range of functions in each of the major receptive and response modalities. Even when the patient complains of some specific disability such as poor immediate memory or a handwriting so shaky as to warrant a medical retirement, it is important to examine a variety of functions. A patient with a deteriorative condition may ask for an evaluation of his poor recent memory and be quite unaware of difficulties in information retrieval, problem-solving, and reasoning that more complete testing would demonstrate. The patient complaining of a tremulous hand may unwittingly draw designs from memory or write numbers with quick, firm lines.

When the data indicate that the patient may have a neurological condition, the examiner generally does not stop with the original referral question. Rather, he raises a new set of questions about the nature of the condition, its impact on the patient's situation, and so on. These questions in turn determine the further course of the examination.

Although the neuropsychological examination may be used to "rule in" the possibility of a neurological disorder, it cannot "rule out" such a possibility (Talland, 1963). That is to say, documentation of behavioral abnormalities in a neuropsychological examination may contribute significantly to a neurological diagnosis, but absence of evidence of behavioral impairment does not mean that the patient has no neurological disease. Nor does a neurological diagnosis preclude the possibility of functional contributions to the condition. Except when the neurological damage is so extensive that the patient's selfhood has been destroyed, there is likely to be some functional elaboration of the symptom picture in the form of exaggeration or denial, compensatory adjustments, behavioral alterations due to depression, anxiety, or other emotional reactions to the neurological disorder. The skillful examiner rephrases simple "either-or" diagnostic questions to take cognizance of the fact that organic defects alone rarely account for all the behavioral change associated with brain damage. When the results of a screening study are *negative*, i.e., when there are no abnormal findings, evidence of emotional or psychiatric disturbance may support a functional diagnosis, further reducing but not eliminating the likelihood that the patient's condition has an organic basis.

A second kind of diagnostic question is asked when the presence of brain damage has been established but a specific diagnosis has not been made. To answer questions concerning diagnostic classification, a comprehensive investigation of many functions in each of the major modalities is generally necessary as the examiner tests the likely diagnostic hypotheses to their limits. For instance, a patient complaining of a newly developed memory defect may have no other symptoms that would be readily demonstrated in a standard neurological examination. An in-depth study of the full range of memory functions evaluated in the context of the patient's overall intellectual status may enable the neuropsychologist to rule out some kinds of neurological conditions and identify others that are possible diagnoses. The neuropsychologist does not make the neurological diagnosis, but he may provide data and diagnostic formulations that contribute to the neurologist's diagnostic conclusions.

Both diagnostic questions may be considered together when the question of organicity cannot be settled without a specific diagnosis, whether it be neurological or psychiatric. However, each of these questions is frequently addressed separately. For many purposes, a specific diagnostic entity need not be named; e.g., a psychotherapist may decide aganist verbal insight therapy if he knows that the patient's poor memory or concrete thought processes are most likely of organic etiology, even though there is no definite diagnosis. On the other hand, patients who are thought to be brain damaged but have not received a positive diagnosis may be referred and re-referred for neuropsychological assessment until a diagnosable pattern manifests itself.

Descriptive questions.   Many kinds of questions cali for behavioral description. Questions about specific capacities frequently arise in the course of vocational and educational planning. They become particularly important to the recovering patient when he feels capable of reassuming normal adult rights and privileges as, for instance, when he applies for a renewal of his driving license or return of legal competency. In these cases, the neuropsychological examination may not be extensive, but rather will focus on the relevant skills and functions.

Longitudinal studies involving repeated measures over time are conducted when questions of deterioration or recovery are raised. In such studies, a broad range of functions usually comes under regular neuropsychological review. The initial examination, in which there is a full-scale assessment of each of the major functions in a variety of input and output modalities, is sometimes called a *baseline study* for it provides the standard set of data against which the findings of later examinations will be compared. Regularly repeated full-scale assessments give information about the rate and extent of recovery or deterioration, and about relative rates of change between functions.

Longitudinal studies can also be used to answer questions about the rate or extent of recovery of specific functional impairments associated with discrete or circumscribed brain lesions.

Test selection

Along with the examination questions, the patient's capacities and the examiner's test repertory determine what tests and assessment techniques will be used. In the well-tailored examination, the examiner rarely knows exactly which tests he is going to give before he begins working with the patient. He usually starts with a basic battery that touches upon the major dimensions of intellectual behavior and makes many of his choices as he proceeds. The patient's strengths and limitations and specific handicaps will determine how he uses the tests in the battery, which he must discard, and which require modifications to suit the patient's capabilities. As he raises and tests questions regarding possible diagnoses, areas of intellectual dysfunction, and psychosocial or emotional contributions to the total behavioral picture, he may need to go beyond the basic battery and use techniques appropriate to specific examination questions.

A basic test battery.   Within the limitations of available tests that are sufficiently well standardized or frequently used to provide reliable comparison standards, this battery offers a review of the major functions in the auditory and visual receptive modalities and the spoken, written, graphic, and constructional response modalities. It can be used to ascertain baselines and to make longitudinal comparisons in the major areas of intellectual activity.

The tests it contains screen for organicity at a relatively efficient rate. In many cases, information obtained from the battery alone will reflect the gross outlines of mental impairment patterns with enough clarity to permit the examiner to form a diagnostic impression. Moreover, the examiner can usually determine what areas need further exploration from the data provided by the basic examination.

This basic battery contains both individually administered tests and paper and pencil tests the patient can take by himself. The individually administered tests take two and one-half to three hours. Unless there is some compelling reason for doing them all at once, they should be given in two sittings, preferably on two different days to avoid fatiguing the patient unduly.

The following tests comprise the individually administered part of my battery:

1. The Wechsler Adult Intelligence Scale (WAIS): Information, Comprehension, Arithmetic, Similarities, Digit Span, Picture Completion, Block Design, Picture Arrangement, and Object Assembly subtests (see Chapter 8).
2. The Symbol Digit Modalities Test (SDMT) (instead of the WAIS Digit Symbol subtest, since the SDMT provides an opportunity to compare spoken and written responses to a symbol substitution test and allows patients with motor slowing or motor handicaps to be tested by this technique) (see pp. 427–428).
3. The Rey Auditory-Verbal Learning Test (see pp. 352–356).
4. Subtracting Serial Sevens (SSS) test (see pp. 425–426).
5. Draw a bicycle (pp. 330–331).
6. The Benton Visual Retention Test (BVRT), Administrations A and D (pp. 369–374).
7. The Purdue Pegboard Test (pp. 340–343).
8. The Trail Making Test (TMT) (pp. 429–432).
9. The Rorschach Inkblot Technique (pp. 287–290, 457–462).
10. The Bender-Gestalt Test (pp. 311–320).

The paper and pencil tests may be given by clerical or nursing staff. Patients generally take from three to six hours or more to complete them, depending on the extent to which the patient is motorically or mentally slowed and the amount of structuring, reassurance, or prodding he needs. Although some of the tests in this battery were developed as timed tests, none are timed in this administration. The person giving the test notes when the patient takes an unusual amount of time. Responsible patients who are fairly intact can often take the paper and pencil materials home and mail them back or return them at a later appointment. Irresponsible, immature, easily confused, or disoriented and poorly motivated patients should be given the paper and pencil tests under supervision.

The paper and pencil testing sessions should also be broken up. A patient may spend an hour or two doing paper and pencil tests and an hour or two with the examiner taking individually administered tests on the same day. If such a testing schedule is interrupted by coffee breaks and lunch, much of the testing can be accomplished in one day without tiring most patients to the point that their performance suffers.

My paper and pencil neuropsychological test packet includes:

1. The Self-Administered Battery (SAB). This is a collection of intellectual and personality tests and test samples suitable for adult patients generally. The SAB we currently use contains a set of 24 Wechsler-type information questions, ten Wechsler-type Arithmetic story problems, 25 multiple-choice vocabulary items, three Bender-Gestalt cards to be copied (pp. 311–320), the Draw-a-Person Test (DAP) (pp.328–330), a set of 20 sentence completion stems, one card from the Thematic Apperception Test (TAT) with instructions to write a story (see pp. 462–463), one Rorschach card with instructions to write three associations (pp. 457–462), three proverbs with instructions to "Write what each of these sayings mean" (pp. 394–395), two simple geometrical forms to copy and two to draw from memory, Sentence Building I or II of the Stanford-Binet (Form M), depending on the patient's apparent verbal skill level (p. 274).
2. The Arithmetic section of the Wide Range Achievement Test (WRAT) (pp. 232–234).
3. Raven's Progressive Matrices (RPM), Standard or Coloured Form, depending on the patient's apparent capabilities (pp. 248–251).
4. The Hooper Visual Organization Test (VOT) (p. 286).
5. Vocabulary and Comprehension subtests of the Gates-MacGinitie Reading Tests (usually Form F, but lower level forms can be substituted as needed) (p. 272).
6. The Personal History Inventory, a multiple-choice and fill-in biographical questionnaire (Lezak, 1968).

Selection of special tests.   The addition of special tests depends on continuing formulation and reformulation of the examination questions in the course of the examination as new data answer some questions and raise others. The tests in the basic battery will provide satisfactory answers for most examination questions. Those dealing with highly specific diagnostic issues or asking for full delineation of a dysfunctional behavior pattern require testing procedures that are not part of the basic battery. Sometimes the planning of a test battery for a particular patient evolves as examination questions call for special techniques that produce fresh data which in turn raise further questions requiring other special examination techniques, and so on until the examiner has answered the examination questions or must conclude that they are not presently answerable.

This procedure can probably be best explained by example. A good illustration is furnished by the examination of the research scientist mentioned in Chapter 2. Following ten days of hospitalization for his head injury during which he was confused, disoriented, and experienced symptoms of autonomic dysfunction (fever, excessive thirst, tachycardia), the acute symptoms subsided and he returned to work shortly thereafter.

The examination was undertaken in response to the patient's concern about his intellect. The principal examination question was whether he had sustained any significant brain damage that would affect his capacity to do research. A secondary question concerned the efficiency of his intellectual functioning generally. In order to answer these two questions, it was necessary to establish a comparison standard against which a broad range of functions could be evaluated. Therefore, the next question asked what comparison standard would apply.

In this case, the patient's educational background and professional achievements made it easy to establish the comparison standard. His original level of intellectual functioning was estimated to have been at the *very superior* level (the range of the top 2.2% of the population). On the paper and pencil tests of the basic test battery, the patient performed well and without any evident difficulty or aberrations. He was given all of the individually administered part of the battery excepting the Purdue Pegboard Test. His test performance supported the estimate of a *very superior* level of original, or premorbid, ability, since all but one of his test scores were in the *superior* or *very superior* ability ranges.

The second question was answered next. His overall pattern of high scores indicated that he had not experienced a general lowering of intellectual efficiency; or if he had, it was not of sufficiently large magnitude to be registered by the standard tests used in this examination. Very bright people such as this man sometimes report a loss of mental sharpness following brain injury that may be a very real concomitant of tissue damage. However, if their original abilities exceeded the upper limit of standard tests, and their present performance is close to or at the upper limit, the neuropsychologist as yet has no way of documenting the loss.

The presence of a single *borderline defective* score, significantly below his performance standard, on a test involving the ordering of cartoon pictures suggested that he had sustained some intellectual impairment although his generally intellectual functioning was not otherwise demonstrably affected by his injury. The nature of this impairment and its extent needed to be explored. Therefore, new questions were raised in order to make sense out of this one deviant observation.

The most obvious question concerned the reason for the one low test score. Usually, an impaired performance on this test results from a lack of social sophistication, defective visual perceptual functions including perceptual acuity and accuracy and the ability to comprehend complex visual stimuli, or simple motor slowing or incoordination. None of these possibilities was likely in this patient's case. His background and experience, observations of his behavior, and his excellent performance on a test of social judgment indicated that his poor performance was hardly due to social naïveté. Nor did his aberrant response pattern appear to be the result of either a visual perceptual defect or impaired motor coordination, for he consistently performed well on all other tasks involving visual stimuli and motor coordination.

Before considering the likelihood that the low score was a chance aberration, it was necessary to exhaust all reasonable explanatory possibilities. One of these was that his ability for serial organization was impaired. None of the other tests he had taken involve this special kind of organizing activity. However, the patient had mentioned in the preliminary interview that he was having difficulty putting together research papers although he was writing with ease, formulating problems, evaluating data, and drawing conclusions as well as ever. These two bits of data generated a new examination question regarding the patient's ability for serial organization. Once formulated, testing it was a relatively simple matter, for the question dictated the kind of tests required. He was given some tests involving sequential ordering activities: a test requiring the organization of words into sentences and two different forms of a serial reasoning test. He did manage to complete these tests correctly, but with much effort and in significantly greater than average amounts of time. Since these are tasks that persons at his intellectual ability level typically perform quickly and easily, it was concluded that the low score did reflect an impaired function. The original examination question asking whether his head injury affected his professional capacity in any way had to be answered affirmatively and the nature of his disability was clarified.

In the above case, there was no etiological question. When the examination questions involve differential diagnosis, the examiner asks questions in much the same manner as described above. The examination of the postal clerk discussed in Chapter 4 demonstrates this process as it is applied in testing diagnostic questions.

On the basis of his wife's complaints of subtle personality and intellectual changes primarily affecting judgment and social behavior, the patient was examined by a neurologist who diagnosed a form of presenile dementia characterized by fairly rapid intellectual deterioration (Alzheimer's disease). This diagnosis was supported by *pneumoencephalographic* (radiological air contrast) studies, which indicated enlarged cerebral *ventricles* (cavities of the brain containing cerebrospinal fluid). Much to the patient's chagrin, this diagnosis led to suspension of his driving license. He requested a reevaluation of the diagnosis in order to get his license back. When a second neurological examination, which did not include an air contrast study, was essentially normal except for documentation of some socially inappropriate behavior, he was referred for neuropsychological assessment.

Again, several examination questions were formulated. The first asked whether the patient had organic brain disease. A corollary question, which is standard procedure regardless of the reasons for the examination, concerned the patient's original general level of intellectual functioning. The fact that this college-educated man worked at a semi-skilled job raised another corollary question as to whether his present level of intellectual functioning was below a previous higher level. To answer this question, the examiner looks for any evidence of intellectual functioning that is significantly better than the rest of the performance. If such is found, the examiner can conclude that, for whatever reasons, the patient is functioning below his original or premorbid ability level. The examiner must then set up another series of examination questions about the nature of the discrepancy, i.e., whether it reflects socio-cultural or educational limitations, personality or emotional problems, or organic impairment.

A third question asked whether this patient displayed the characteristic symptoms of Alzheimer's disease. The answer to this latter question depended on two corollary questions regarding characteristics of this disease (Sim et al., 1966): (1) is the patient suffering impairment of immediate, recent, and remote memory, and (2) will his test performance deteriorate during the next six months or year?

On psychological tests the patient displayed judgmental impairment, social inappropriateness, and impaired learning ability. Conceptual and response rigidity appeared in the course of both the interview and his performance on the basic test battery, and raised the question of frontal lobe dysfunction. However, this tendency to behavioral rigidity was subtle and did not show up in markedly lower scores on the verbal tests of abstraction and concept formation of the WAIS or as frank perseverations. Evaluation of the possibility that this rigidity reflected a significant degree of impairment called for the testing of another corollary question. This question asked whether the patient suffered conceptual or response rigidity to a significant degree. He was given several tests requiring flexibility in shifting motor responses and set. Simple motor response shifting was within normal limits but he demonstrated an abnormal amount of difficulty in shifting his set in response to changing set requirements. Taken together, his significantly decreased learning ability, his inflexibility with respect to set, and his judgmental impairments led to a positive answer to the first question, i.e., that this patient probably was brain damaged.

With respect to the second question, since most of the patient's test scores ranged from *average* to *superior,* his original potential was estimated to be in the *high average* to *superior* range of intelligence and not significantly different from his present general level of intellectual functioning. However, the difference between his highest scores and lowest ones approached statistical significance suggesting that brain damage had affected at least several different aspects of intellectual functioning, although few were affected to any notable extent.

His test performance indicated that it was unlikely that he had Alzheimer's disease, for on tests of functions that commonly deteriorate first in this condition, he performed within his estimated original ability range. Further, on retesting six to 12 months later, there was no evidence of deterioration.

One further question had to be considered when it appeared likely that the patient was not suffering from Alzheimer's disease, at least in any usual form. (Alzheimer's disease can only be positively diagnosed postmortem since the diagnosis ultimately depends on the presence of well-defined pathological brain cell changes). This new question asked whether the patient's intellectual and personality changes were not symptomatic of a functional psychiatric disorder. This possibility could not be ruled out altogether, but it was rendered unlikely in that decreased learning ability had been consistently documented, the kind of inability to shift set that he displayed tends to be associated with frontal lobe disease, and the character of his personality changes and emotional aberrations was not typical for any commonly known psychiatric disturbance but was similar to the behavior of patients with frontal lobe disease.

The question of the patient's capacity to drive still remained. Such mental activity variables as alertness and response speed, as well as the relevant visuopractic functions were all within normal limits and thus there was no psychological contraindication to his driving. As a result, he was encouraged to take his driving test which he passed.

Questions as to diagnosis and prognosis for this man remain unanswered. Repeated semiannual neurological and neuropsychological study may eventually clarify this puzzling diagnostic problem.

This case gives a good example of how both diagnostic and descriptive questions come under consideration in the same case, each requiring some different tests. Even when the examination questions are strictly diagnostic or strictly descriptive, it is common for one question to lead to another as the examiner attempts to pin down a likely diagnosis or to define a possible problem area.

These two case studies do not provide an exhaustive review of possible examination questions, although they contain the most common types. Most examinations share one or more questions concerning the presence of organic damage, the estimation of an original potential or premorbid level of functioning, and the identification of a present level of general intellectual functioning. Many examinations also generate one or two questions peculiar to the specific case. There should be few examinations in which the questions and procedures are exactly identical. An examiner who does much the same thing with almost every patient he sees may not be attending to the implicit part of a referral question, to the patient's needs, or to the aberrations that point to specific defects and particular problems.

Selecting tests for patients with sensory or motor handicaps. Examination of a handicapped patient presents the problem of testing a variety of functions in as many modalities as possible with a more or less restricted test repertory. This is a relatively common problem for neuropsychological assessment, as there are many patients who suffer perceptual or motor disabilities and a few who are severely handicapped intellectually; all such patients require special tests for adequate evaluation.

Almost all psychological tests have been constructed with physically able persons in mind. When patients are handicapped, the examiner often has to find reasonable alternatives to the standard tests the patient cannot use, or he has to juggle test norms, improvise, or in the last resort, do without.

Although the examination of patients with sensory or motor disabilities is necessarily limited insofar as the affected input or output modality is concerned, the disability should not preclude at least some test evaluation of any intellectual function not immediately dependent on the affected modality. Of course a blind patient cannot be tested for his ability to organize visual percepts, nor can a patient with profound facial paralysis be tested for verbal fluency; but both can be tested for memory and learning, arithmetic, vocabulary, abstract reasoning, comprehension of spatial relationships, a multitude of verbal skills, and so on.

Ready-made tests that can be substituted for the standard ones are available for most general functions. Deaf patients can be given written forms of tests of verbal functions; blind patients can take orally administered forms. For verbal functions, there are a number of written and orally administered tests of arithmetic skills, vocabulary, and abstract reasoning in particular that have comparable norms. Other common tests of verbal functions, such as tests of background information, common sense reasoning and judgment, and verbal (reading) comprehension, do not have fully standardized counterparts in the other modality, whether it be visual or auditory. For some of these, similar kinds of alternative tests can be found although formats or standardization populations may differ. For others, the examiner may have to devise alternate forms on the spot. For instance, a test of background information that has been standardized for oral administration can be typed as a paper and pencil questionnaire; or a standardized reading comprehension test can be given orally, if the patient's level of verbal comprehension per se is under consideration.

There are fewer ready-made substitutes for nonverbal perceptual or practic tests, although some test parallels can be found, and the clinician may be able to invent others. The *haptic* (touch) modality lends itself most readily as a substitute for visually presented tests of nonverbal functions. For example, to assess concept formation, sizes, shapes, and textures of objects are testable dimensions for blind patients; to test pattern learning or searching behavior, tactile mazes may be used in place of visual mazes; three-dimensional block constructions will test constructional functions of patients who cannot see painted designs or printed patterns; and modeling in clay can be a substitute for human figure drawings. Even so, it is difficult to find a suitable nonvisual alternative for perceptual organization tests such as the Rorschach or Picture Arrangement series, or for a visuoconstructive task such as drawing a house or a bicycle, or for many others in the standard neuropsychological repertory.

The paralyzed patient presents similar challenges. Visual perceptual functions in these patients can be relatively easily tested since most tests of these functions lend themselves to spoken answers or pointing. However, drawing tasks requiring relatively fine motor coordination cannot be satisfactorily evaluated when the patient's dominant hand is paralyzed. Even when it is the nondominant hand that is paralyzed, some inefficiency and slowing on other practic tasks will result from the patient's inability to anchor a piece of paper with his nondominant hand or to turn blocks or manipulate parts of a puzzle with two-handed efficiency.

Some tests have been devised specifically for physically handicapped people (Delp, 1959). Most of them are listed in test catalogues or can be located through local rehabilitation services. One problem that these substitute tests present is normative comparability; but since this is a problem in any substitute or alternative version of a standard test, it should not dissuade the examiner if the procedure appears to test the relevant functions. Another problem is that alternative forms usually test many fewer and sometimes different functions than the original test. For example, multiple choice forms of design copying tests obviously do not measure the practic function. What may be less obvious is the loss of data about the patient's ability to organize, plan, and order his responses. Unless the examiner is fully aware of all that is missing in his alternative battery, he may overlook some important functions.

Selecting tests for the severely brain damaged patient. Another problem occasionally faced by the neuropsychological examiner is that, with a few notable exceptions, tests developed for adults have neither items nor norms for grading the performance of severely mentally impaired adults. On adult tests, the botton 1 or 2% of the normal noninstitutionalized adult population pass only the simplest items. These items leave a relatively wide range of behaviors unexamined and are too few to allow for meaningful performance gradations. Yet it is as important to know about the impairment pattern, the rate and extent of improvement or deterioration, and the relative strengths and weaknesses of the severely brain damaged patient as it is for the less afflicted patient.

For very defective patients, the simplest solution is to use children's tests. There are tests of all functions in every modality for children, as well as special children's norms for some tests originally developed for adults (see, for example, E. M. Taylor, 1959; Koppitz, 1964; Levitt and Truumaa, 1972). When given to retarded adults, children's tests require little or no change in wording or procedure. (See Chapter 6 for the application of children's test norms to adult patients.)

Occasionally a patient presents an assessment problem for which no well-standardized alternative test is suitable. Improvising appropriate testing techniques can then tax the imagination and ingenuity of any conscientious examiner. He may find a suitable test among the many new and often experimental techniques reported in the literature. A number of them are reviewed in this book. Many of these experimental techniques are inadequately standardized; some of them may not test the functions they purport to test; others may be so subject to chance error as to be undependable; and still others may have spurious norms. However, these experimental and relatively unproven tests may be useful in themselves or as a source of ideas for further innovations. Rarely can an examiner evaluate an unfamiliar test's standardization methodically, but with experience he can learn to judge reports and manuals of new tests well enough to know whether the tasks, the author's interpretation, the statistical norms, and the test's reliability are reasonably suitable for his purpose. It should go without saying that when making this kind of evaluation of a relatively untried test, clinical standards need not be as strict as research standards.

Order of presentation of the tests.   The order of presentation of tests in a battery has not been shown to have any appreciable effect on the patient's performance (Carter and Bowles, 1948; Cassel, 1962). The examiner, though, may have become accustomed to one or another presentation sequence and may be somewhat uncomfortable and feel less efficient if it is varied. In an examination tailored to the patient's needs, the examiner varies presentation of the tests to ensure his patient's maximum productivity. For example, he may give those tests he knows will be difficult at the beginning of a testing session when the patient is least fatigued; or he may follow a test that has taxed or discouraged the patient with one on which the patient can relax or recover his pride. Further, as testing proceeds, the patient's performance will also determine what other tests need be given. When using a test repertory flexibly, after completing the core—usually WAIS—testing, the only guides to the sequence of test presentation will be the questions to be tested, the patient's needs of the moment, and the examiner's convenience.

An aid to test selection: A compendium of tests and assessment techniques, Chapters 8 through 17.   In the last ten chapters of this book, most tests of intellectual function and personality in common use, and many relatively uncommon tests, are reviewed. These are tests and assessment techniques that are particularly well suited for *clinical* neuropsychological examination. Clinical examiners can employ the assessment techniques presented in these chapters for most neuropsychological assessment purposes in most kinds of work settings. The majority of these tests are well standardized;

those which have been insufficiently or questionably standardized were included because their clinical value outweighed their statistical weaknesses. W. L. Smith (1969) has compiled a long list of readings on neuropsychological tests including references to some of the tests not presented in this book. Space, time, and energy set a limit to the number of tests reviewed here. Selection favored tests that are in relatively common use, represent a subclass of similar tests, illustrate a particularly interesting assessment method, or uniquely demonstrate some significant aspect of behavior.

Psychophysiological tests of specific sensory or motor deficits, such as tests of visual and auditory acuity, of one- and two-point tactile discrimination, of perceptual inattention, or of motor response speed and strength are all also part of the standard neurological examination. Because they are well described elsewhere, this book will not deal with them. With few exceptions, the tests considered here are essentially psychological.

The selection criteria of availability and ease of administration eliminated those tests that require bulky, complicated, expensive equipment or material that cannot be easily obtained or reproduced by the individual clinician. These criteria cut out all tests that have to have a fixed laboratory installation, as well as all those demanding special technical knowledge of the examiner. The tests described in these chapters are portable for use at bedside, in jails, or anywhere the examiner might need to conduct a thorough examination. They are almost all relatively inexpensive to obtain and to administer. Most of the testing materials can be ordered from test publishers or they are easily assembled by the examiner; only a few must be ordered from the author or an unusual source.

A note on the use of ready-made batteries.   The popularity of ready-made batteries attests to the need for neuropsychological testing and to a general lack of knowledge about how to do it. The most popular batteries extend the scope of the examination beyond the barely minimal neuropsychological examination (which, in many places, consists of a WAIS and a drawing test of some kind). They offer reliable scoring methods for gross diagnostic screening (see Chapter 16). Ready-made batteries can be invaluable in research programs requiring well-standardized tests.

When batteries are used as directed, most patients undergo more testing than is necessary but not enough to satisfy the examination questions specific to their problems. Also, like most psychological tests, ready-made batteries are not geared to the patient's handicaps. The patient with a significant perceptual or motor disability may not be able to perform major portions of the prescribed tests, in which case the functions normally measured by the unusable test items remain unexamined. However, batteries do acquaint the inexperienced examiner with a variety of tests and with the importance of evaluating many different kinds of behaviors when doing neuropsychological testing, They can provide a good starting place for some newcomers to the field, who may then expand their test repertory and introduce variations into their administration procedures as they gain experience and develop their own point of view.

Conducting the Examination

The preparatory interview
The neuropsychological examiner usually uses the first 15 to 20 minutes of examination time to evaluate the patient's capacity to take tests and to ascertain his understanding of the purpose of the examination. He also needs time to prepare the patient for the tests. Occasionally, it is necessary to take longer, particularly with anxious or slow patients or with patients who have a confusing history or those whose misconceptions might compromise their intelligent cooperation. The examiner may spend the entire first session preparing a patient who fatigues rapidly and comprehends slowly, reserving testing for the subsequent days when he is no longer a stranger to the patient, and the patient is refreshed.

There are at least seven topics that must be covered with the competent patient before testing begins, if the examiner wants to be assured of the patient's best cooperation. (1) *The purpose of the examination:* Does the patient know why he was referred; and does he have questions of his own he would like answered? (2) *The nature of the examination:* Does the patient understand that the examination will be primarily concerned with his intellectual functioning and that being examined by a psychologist does not mean he is crazy? (3) *The use to which examination information will be put:* The patient must have a clear idea of who will receive the report and how it may be used. (4) *Confidentiality:* The competent patient must be reassured not only about the confidentiality of the examination, but of his control over his privacy. (5) *Feedback to the patient:* The patient should know before he begins who will report the test findings to him, and if possible, when he will get this information. (6) *A brief explanation of the test procedures:* Many patients are very reassured by a few words about the tests they'll be taking, such as,

> I'll be asking you to do a number of different kinds of tasks. Some will remind you of school, because I'll be asking questions about things you've already learned, or I'll give you arithmetic or memory problems to do, just like a teacher. Others will be different kinds of puzzles and games. You may find that some things I ask you to do are fun and some seem silly; some of the tests will be very easy and some may be so difficult you won't even know what I'm talking about or showing you; but all of them will help me to understand better how your brain is working, what you are doing well and what kinds of difficulties you are having, and how you might be helped.

(7) *How the patient feels about taking the tests:* This can be the most important topic of all, for unless the patient feels that taking the tests is not shameful, not degrading, not a sign of weakness or childishness, not threatening to his job or his legal status or to whatever else he may be worrying about, he cannot meaningfully or wholeheartedly cooperate on his own behalf. Sometimes the threat is real, when the patient's job or his competency, or custody of his children is at stake. It is then incumbent upon the examiner to give the patient a clear understanding of the possible consequences of his noncooperation as well as his full cooperation so that he can make a realistic choice.

The examiner can also conduct a brief mental status examination (see Chapter 17 for a detailed description) in this preliminary interview. The patient's contribution to the discussion will give the examiner a fairly good idea of the level at which he will have to conduct the examination. When beginning the examination with the WAIS or any number of other published tests, the examiner can ask the patient to answer the questions of date, place, birthdate, education, and occupation on the answer sheets, thereby getting information about the patient's orientation and personal awareness while doing the necessary record-keeping.

It is often useful to learn the patient's view of his condition, for although his inner experiences are not observable, this kind of self-report can offer important clues to disabilities the neuropsychologist will want to investigate. The patient should be asked for a brief history of his condition, for this too will aid the examiner in knowing what to look for and how to proceed. Other issues, such as fees, referrals, formal reports to other persons or agencies, should also be discussed at this time.

Patients who are not competent may be unable to appreciate all of the initial discussion. However, the examiner should make some effort to see that each topic is covered within the limits of the patient's comprehension and that the patient has had an opportunity to share his feelings about and understanding of the examination, and that he feels free to ask questions.

Examining the severely handicapped patient
When mental or physical handicaps greatly limit the patient's range of response, it may first be necessary to determine whether he has enough verbal comprehension for formal testing procedures. A set of questions and commands calling for one word answers and simple gestures will quickly give the needed information. Those that are simplest and most likely to be answered are given first to increase the likelihood of initial success. Questions calling for "yes" or "no" answers should be avoided since many patients with impaired speech cannot sound out the difference between "uh-huh" and "uh-uh" clearly; nor is it easy for a weak or tremulous patient to nod or waggle his head with distinct precision.

A patient with no speech impediment might be asked the following kinds of questions:

> What is your name?
> What is your age?
> Where are you now?
> What do you call this (hand, thumb, article of patient's clothing, coin, button, or safety pin)?
> What do you do with a (pen, comb, matches, key)?
> What color is (your tie, my dress, etc.)?
> How many fingers can you see? (Two or three trials.)
> How many coins in my hand? (Two or three trials.)
> Say the alphabet; count from one to 20.

Patients who do not speak well enough to be understood can be examined for verbal comprehension and ability to follow directions.

Show me your (hand, thumb, a button, your nose).
Give me your (left, right—the nonparalyzed) hand.
Put your (nonparalyzed) hand on your (other) elbow.

Place several small objects (button, coin, etc.) in front of the patient
and ask him to

Show me the button (or key, coin, etc.).
Show me what opens doors.
Show me what you use to write.

Place several coins in front of the patient.

Show me the quarter (nickel, dime, etc.).
Show me the smallest coin.
Give me (3, 2, 5) coins.

Patients who can handle a pencil may be asked to write their
name, age, where they live, and to answer simple questions calling
for "yes" or "no" or short word and simple number answers, and to
write the alphabet and the first 20 numbers. Patients who cannot
write may be asked to draw a circle, copy a circle drawn by the
examiner, copy a vertical line drawn by the examiner, draw a square,
and imitate the examiner's gestures and patterns of tapping with a
pencil.

Patients who respond to most of these questions correctly are able
to comprehend and cooperate well enough for formal testing. Patients unable to answer more than two or three questions probably
cannot be tested reliably. Their behavior is best evaluated by rating
scales (see Chapter 17).

Testing the limits
Knowledge of the patient's capacities can be extended by going
beyond the limits of the test set by the standard procedures. Arithmetic questions provide a good example. When a patient fails the
more difficult items on an orally administered arithmetic test because of an immediate memory, concentration, or conceptual tracking problem, the examiner still does not know whether the patient
understands the problem, can perform the calculations correctly, or
knows what operations are called for. If the examiner stops at the
point at which the patient fails the requisite number of items without
exploring these questions further, any conclusion he draws about
the patient's ability to do arithmetic is questionable. In a case like

this, the patient's arithmetic ability can easily be tested further by giving him pencil and paper and repeating the failed items. Some patients can do the problems once they have written the elements down; and still others do not perform any better with paper than without it.

Testing the limits does not affect the standard test procedures or scoring. It is done only after the test or test item in question has been completed according to standard test instructions. This method not only preserves the statistical and normative meaning of the test scores, but it can afford interesting and often important information about the patient's functioning. For example, a patient who achieves an arithmetic score in the *borderline defective* ability range on the standard presentation of the test and who solves all the problems quickly and correctly at a *superior* level of functioning when he can jot down the elements of a problem, demonstrates a severely crippling immediate memory problem but a continued capacity to handle quite complex computational problems as long as they are written down. From his test score alone, one might conclude that his competency to handle his own funds is questionable; on the basis of the more complete examination of his arithmetic ability, he might be encouraged to continue ordinary bookkeeping activities.

Testing the limits can be done with any test. The examiner should test the limits whenever he suspects that an impairment of some function other than the one under consideration is interfering with an adequate demonstration of that function. Imaginative and careful testing the limits can provide a better understanding of the extent to which a function or functional system is impaired and the impact this impairment may have on related functional systems. Much of the special testing done with handicapped patients is a form of testing the limits.

MAXIMIZING THE PATIENT'S LEVEL OF PERFORMANCE

It is not very difficult to get a patient to do poorly on a psychological examination. This is especially true of brain damaged patients, for the quality of their performance can be exceedingly vulnerable to external influences or changes in their internal states (Parsons and

Stewart, 1966). All an examiner need do is tire the patient, make him anxious, or subject him to any one of a number of distractions most people ordinarily do not even notice, and his test scores will plummet. In neuropsychological assessment, the difficult task is enabling the patient to perform as well as possible.

Eliciting the patient's maximum output is necessary for a valid behavioral assessment. Interpretation of test scores and of test behavior is predicated on the assumption that the demonstrated behavior is a representative sample of the patient's true capacity in that area. Of course, it is unlikely that all of a person's ability to do something can ever be demonstrated; for this reason many psychologists distinguish between a patient's level of test performance and an estimated ability level. The practical goal is to help the patient do his best so that the difference between what he can and what he does do is negligible.

Optimal versus Standard Conditions

In the ideal testing situation, both *optimal* and *standard* conditions prevail. Optimal conditions are those that enable the patient to do his best on the tests. They differ from patient to patient, but for most brain injured patients, they include freedom from distractions, a nonthreatening emotional climate, and prevention of fatigue.

Standard conditions are prescribed by the test-maker to ensure that each administration of the test is as much like every other administration as possible, so that scores obtained on different test administrations can be compared. To this end, many test-makers give detailed directions on the presentation of their test, including specific instructions on word usage, handling the material, etc. Highly standardized test administration is necessary when using norms of tests that have a fine-graded and statistically well-standardized scoring system, such as the WAIS. By exposing each patient to nearly identical situations, the standardization of testing procedures also enables the examiner to discover the individual characteristics of each patient's responses.

Normally, there need be no conflict between optimal and standard conditions. When brain damaged patients are tested, however, a number will be unable to perform well within the confines of the standard instructions.

For some patients, the difficulty may be in understanding the standard instructions. The Arithmetic subtest of the WAIS provides a good example. A problem similar to the third one of that subtest is, "How much is five dollars and three dollars?" Few talking patients cannot do this problem correctly. However, a number of mathematically adept and verbally competent but very concrete-minded brain injured patients will answer with a note of surprise in their voices that "five dollars and three dollars is five dollars and three dollars!" for the phrasing of the question does not specifically tell them to add. The examiner is then faced with a dilemma: whether to score the problem as failed, although the failure was on the basis of impaired abstract thinking and not a mathematical disability; or to repeat, and if need be, rephrase the question in order to test the patient's ability to add two one-place numbers. Should the patient pass the rephrased question, the examiner must next decide whether to give him credit. (In a case like this, the examiner can maintain a dual scoring system. Scoring strictly, he will obtain an estimate of the level of the patient's day-to-day performance on problems requiring mathematical skills as it is affected by his concrete thinking. Allowing the margin for nonconformity to the standardization requirements produces another—higher—score, which is his estimated arithmetic ability level.)

Memory tests are another kind of test on which instructional problems can occur with concrete-minded or poorly inhibited brain injured patients. When given a list of numbers or words, some patients are apt to begin reciting the items one right after the other as the examiner is still reading the list. Here too, additional instructions must be given if the patient is to do the test as originally conceived and standardized. In this case, a patient's immediate repetition may spoil the ready-made word or number series. When giving these kinds of memory tests, it is helpful to have a substitute list handy; particularly if the examiner does not plan to see the patient at a later date. Otherwise, the identical list can be repeated later in the examination, with the necessary embellishments to the standard instructions.

To provide additional information on immediate memory and allow the examiner to test the patient's comprehension of test questions, the examiner can ask the patient to repeat the question when he gives an erroneous response. It is particularly important to find out what the patient understood or retained when the patient's original response is so wide of the mark that it is doubtful he was answering the question the examiner asked. In such cases, subtle attention, memory, or hearing defects may emerge; or, if the wrong answer was due to a chance mishearing of the question, the patient has an opportunity to correct the error and gain the credit due him.

Many other comprehension problems of these kinds are peculiar to brain injured patients. They require a little more flexibility and looseness in interpreting the standard procedures on the examiner's part if he is to make the most of the test and elicit the patient's best performance. "The same words do not necessarily mean the same thing to different people and it is the meaning of the instructions which should be the same for all people rather than the wording" (M. Williams, 1965, p. xvii).

Other problems may arise from a patient's short attention span, fatigability, and distractibility. Occasionally patients cannot remember enough of a lengthy question to formulate a response. Some patients can only work for brief periods of time. Their examination may continue over days and even a week or two if their performance begins to suffer noticeably after ten or 15 minutes of concentrated effort, necessitating a recess. On occasion, a patient's fatigue may require the examiner to stop testing in the middle of a subtest in which items are graduated in difficulty or arranged to produce a learning effect. When the test is resumed in a day or two, the examiner must decide whether to start from the beginning and risk overlearning, or pick up where he left off, taking a chance that the patient will have lost the response set or forgotten what he had learned on the first few items.

Should the patient not answer a question for 30 seconds or more, the examiner can ask him to repeat the question, thus finding out if lack of response is due to inattention, forgetting, slow thinking, uncertainty, or unwillingness to admit failure. When the patient has demonstrated a serious defect of attention or immediate memory, it is necessary to repeat the format each time one of a series of similar questions is asked. For example, if the patient's vocabulary is being tested, the examiner must ask what the word means with every new word, for the subject may not remember how to respond without prompting at each question.

Scoring questions also arise when the patient gives two or more

responses to questions that have only one correct or one best response. When one of the patient's answers is correct, the examiner
should invite the patient to decide which of his answers he prefers
and then score accordingly.

Timing presents even greater and more common standardization
problems than incomprehension in that both brain damaged and
elderly patients are likely to do timed tests slowly and lose credit for
good performances. Many timing problems can be handled by testing the limits. With a brain damaged population, many timed tests
should yield two scores: the score for the patient's response within
the time limit and another for his performance regardless of time.

Street noises, a telephone's ring, or a door slamming down the hall
can easily break an ongoing train of thought in many brain damaged
patients. If this occurs in the middle of a timed test, the examiner
must decide whether to repeat the item, count the full time taken
including the interruption and recovery, count the time minus the
interruption and recovery time, do the item over using an alternate
form if possible, skip that item and prorate the score, or repeat the
test again another day. Should there not be another testing day, then
an alternate form is the next best choice; an estimate of time taken
without the interruption is a third choice; a prorated score is also
acceptable.

A record of the effects of interruptions due to distractibility on
timed tasks gives valuable information about the patient's efficiency.
Comparisons between his *efficiency* (performance under standard
conditions) and his *capacity* (performance under optimal conditions) are important for rehabilitation and vocational planning. In
some cases they may be used as indices of recovery or deterioration.
The actual effect of the distraction, whether it be in terms of increased response time, lowered productivity within the allotted
time, or more errors, should also be noted and reported.

Nowhere is the conflict between optimal and standard conditions
so pronounced or so unnecessary as in the issue of emotional support and reassurance of the test-taking patient. For many examiners,
standard conditions have come to mean that they have to maintain
an emotionless, standoffish attitude toward their patients when they
are testing them. The stern admonitions of test-makers to adhere to
the wording of the test manual and not tell the patient whether he
passed any single item have probably contributed to the practice of
coldly mechanical test administration.

From the viewpoint of any but the most severely regressed or socially insensitive patient, this kind of test experience is very anxiety-producing. Almost every patient approaches psychological testing with a great deal of apprehension. Brain injured patients and persons suspected of harboring a brain tumor or some insidious degenerative disease are often frankly frightened. When such a patient is then confronted with an examiner who maintains an impassive expression on his face and an emotionally toneless voice, who doesn't ever smile, and who responds only briefly and curtly to the patient's questions or efforts at conversation, the patient generally assumes that he is doing something wrong—failing, or displeasing the examiner—and his anxiety soars. The impact of such a threatening situation on intellectual performance can be seriously crippling. High anxiety levels may result in such mental efficiency problems as slowing, scrambled or blocked thoughts and words, and memory failure (Rabin, 1965; Wrightsman, 1962); they certainly will not be conducive to a representative performance.

Although standard conditions do require that the examiner adhere to the instructions in the test manual and give no hint regarding the correctness of a response, these requirements can easily be met without creating a climate of fear and discomfort. A sensitive examination calls for the same techniques which the psychologist uses to put a patient at ease in an interview and to establish a good working relationship. Conversational patter is appropriate and can be very anxiety-reducing. The examiner can maintain a relaxed conversational flow with the patient throughout the entire test session without permitting it to interrupt the administration of any single item or task. The examiner can give continual support and encouragement to his patient without indicating success or failure by smiling and rewarding the patient's *efforts* with words such as "Good," "Fine," and "You're doing well" or "You're really trying hard!" If the examiner takes care to distribute praise randomly, and not just following correct responses, he is no more giving away answers than if he remains stonily silent throughout. However, the patient feels comforted, reassured that he is doing something right and that he is pleasing—or at least not displeasing—the examiner.

When the examiner has established this kind of warmly supportive atmosphere, he can discuss with the patient his strengths and weaknesses and problems as they appear in the course of the examination. The interested, comfortable patient will be able to provide the examiner with information about his functioning that he might otherwise have forgotten or be unwilling to share. He will also be receptive to the examiner's explanations and recommendations regarding the specific difficulties he is encountering and which he and the examiner are exploring together. The examination will have been a mutual learning and sharing experience.

Special Problems of the Brain Damaged Patient

Sensory deficits

Many brain damaged patients with lateralized lesions will have reduced vision or hearing on the side opposite the lesion, with little awareness that they have such a problem. This is particularly true for patients who have *homonymous field cuts* (loss of vision in the same part of the field of each eye) or in whom nerve damage has reduced auditory acuity or auditory discrimination functions in one ear only. Their normal conversational behavior typically gives no hint of the deficit; yet presentation of test material to the affected side makes their task more difficult.

The neuropsychologist is often not able to find out quickly and reliably whether the patient's sight or hearing has suffered impairment. Therefore, when the patient is known to have a lateralized lesion, it is a good testing practice for the examiner to position himself either across from the patient or to the side least likely to be affected. The examiner must take care that the patient can see all of the visually presented material and the examiner should speak to the ear on the side of the lesion.

A visual problem that can occur after a head injury, stroke, or other abrupt insult to the brain, or that may be symptomatic of a degenerative disease of the central nervous system, is eye muscle imbalance resulting in double vision (*diplopia*). The patient may not see double at all angles or in all areas of the visual field. He may experience only slight discomfort or confusion when his head is tilted a certain way, or the diplopia may compromise his ability to read, write, draw, or solve intricate visual puzzles altogether. Young, well-motivated patients with diplopia frequently learn to suppress one set of images and, within one to three years, become relatively untroubled by the problem. Other patients report that they have been handicapped for years by what may appear on examination to be a minor disability. Should the patient complain of diplopia, the examiner may want a neurological or ophthalmological opinion on the actual extent of the problem before determining whether he can proceed with tests requiring visual acuity. He will also want to take into account the patient's attitude toward being examined, toward expending effort, and toward rehabilitation when making this determination.

Distractibility

A common concomitant of brain damage is distractibility: the patient has difficulty shutting out or ignoring extraneous stimulation, be it noise outside the testing room, test material scattered on the examination table, or a brightly colored tie or flashy earrings on the examiner. This difficulty may exacerbate problems in attention and concentration, interfere with learning, and increase the likelihood of fatigue and frustration. The examiner may not realize how his clothing or the location of the examining room or its furnishings are adding to the patient's difficulties, for the normal person screens out extraneous stimuli so automatically that most people are unaware that this problem exists for others.

To reduce the likelihood of interference from unnecessary distractions, the examination should be conducted in what is sometimes referred to as a *sterile environment*. The examining room should be relatively sound-proof and decorated in quiet colors, with no bright or distracting objects in sight. The examiner's clothing too can be an unwitting source of distraction. Drab colors and quiet patterns or a lab coat are recommended apparel for testing.

The examining table should be kept bare except for materials needed for the test at hand. When one test is completed, the materials should be cleared away and placed out of the patient's sight before the next materials are brought out. Clocks and ticking sounds can be bothersome; clocks should be quiet and out of sight, even when test instructions include references to timing. A wall or desk clock with an easily readable second indicator, placed out of the patient's line of sight, is an excellent substitute for a stopwatch and frees the examiner's hands for note taking and manipulation of test materials.

An efficient way to use a watch or regular clock for unobtrusive timing is to pay attention only to the second marker, noting in seconds the times at which a task was begun and completed. Minutes are marked with a slash. Total time is then 60 seconds for each slash, plus the number of seconds between the two times. For example, $53 \,/\,/\, 18 = ([60 - 53] + 18) + 120 = 145$ seconds. The examiner can count times under 30 seconds with a fair degree of accuracy by making a dot on the answer sheet every 5 seconds.

Fatigue
Brain damaged patients tend to fatigue easily, particularly when the condition is of relatively recent onset. Easy fatigability can also be a chronic problem, and many brain damaged persons are fatigued most of the time. Once fatigued, they take longer to recuperate than do normal persons.

Many patients will tell the examiner when they are tired, but others may not be aware themselves, or they may be unwilling to admit fatigue. Therefore, the examiner must be alert to such signs as slurring of speech, an increased droop on the paralyzed side of the patient's face, motor slowing, or restlessness.

Brain damaged patients, particularly those whose condition is of recent origin, are most apt to be rested and energized in the early morning and will perform at their best at this time. Even the seemingly restful interlude of lunch may require considerable effort of the patient and fatigue him. Physical or occupational therapy is exhausting for many patients. Therefore, in arranging test time, the patient's daily activity must be considered if the effects of fatigue are to be kept minimal. When necessary, the examiner may insist that the patient take a nap before being tested.

Depression and frustration
Depression and frustration are often intimately related to fatigue in brain damaged patients, and the pernicious interplay between them can seriously compromise the patient's performance. The patient who fatigues easily rarely performs well and may experience even relatively intact functions as more impaired than they actually are. He stumbles more when walking, speaking, and thinking and is more frustrated, which in turn drains his energies and increases his fatigue. This results in a greater likelihood of failure and leads to more frustration and eventual despair. Repeated failure to exercise previously accomplished skills, difficulty in solving once easy

problems, the need for effort to coordinate previously automatic responses further contribute to the depression that commonly accompanies brain damage, particularly in the first year. After a while, the patient may give up trying. Such discouragement will usually carry over into a patient's test performance and may obscure his intellectual strengths from himself as well as his examiner.

When examining a brain damaged patient, it is important to deal with the problems of motivation and depression. Encouragement is useful. The examiner can deliberately ensure that the patient will have some success, no matter how extensive his impairments. Frequently the neuropsychologist may be the first person to help the patient share his feelings and particularly to reassure him that his depression is natural and common to people with his condition and that it will probably dissipate in time. Many patients experience a great deal of relief and even some lifting of their depression by this kind of informational reassurance.

When a patient is depressed, it is important for the examiner to form a clear picture of his state at the time of testing. If the examiner cannot allay his patient's depression or engage his interested cooperation, then he not only must report this but he must take these problems into account in interpreting the test protocol.

PSYCHOTHERAPEUTIC ASSESSMENT

Every psychological examination can be a personally useful experience for the patient. Each patient should leave the examination feeling he gained something for his efforts, whether it was an increased sense of dignity or self-worth, insight into his behavior, or constructive appreciation of his problems or limitations.

When the patient feels better at the end of the examination than he did at the beginning, the examiner knows that he has probably helped him to perform at his best. When the patient understands himself better at the end of the examination than he did at the beginning, the examiner knows he conducted the examination in a spirit of mutual cooperation and treated the patient as a reasoning, responsible individual. It is a truism that good psychotherapy requires continuing assessment. By the same token, good assessment is also a psychotherapeutic endeavor.

6

THE NEUROPSYCHOLOGICAL
EXAMINATION:
TEST INTERPRETATION

THE NATURE OF PSYCHOLOGICAL TEST DATA

The basic data of psychological testing, like all other psychological data, are behavioral observations. Testing differs from other forms of psychological data gathering in that it elicits behavior samples in a standardized, replicable, and more or less artificial and restrictive situation. Its strengths lie in the approximate sameness of the test situation for each subject, for it is this sameness that enables the examiner to compare behavior samples between individuals, over time, or with expected performance levels. Its weaknesses too lie in this sameness, in that psychological test observations are limited to the behaviors occasioned by the test situation. They rarely include observations of patients in more familiar settings engaging in their usual activities.

To apply test findings to the problems that have brought the patient to him, the psychological examiner extrapolates from his test-limited observations to the patient's behavior in real life situations. Extrapolation from the data is a common feature of other kinds of psychological data handling as well, since it is rarely possible to observe a human subject in every problem area. Extrapolations are likely to be as accurate as the observations on which they are based are pertinent and precise, as the situations are similar, and as the generalizations are apt.

A 48-year-old advertising manager with originally *superior* intellectual abilities sustained a right hemisphere stroke with minimal sensory or

116

motor deficits. He was examined at the request of his company when he wanted to return to work. His verbal skills in general were *high average* to *superior*, but he was unable to construct two-dimensional geometric designs with colored blocks, put together cut-up picture puzzles, or draw a house or person with proper proportions. The psychologist did not observe the patient on the job but, generalizing from these samples, she concluded that the visual-perceptual distortions and misjudgments demonstrated on the test would be of a similar kind and occur to a similar extent with lay-out and design material. The patient was advised against retaining responsibility for the work of the display section of his department. Later conferences with the patient's employers confirmed that he was no longer able to evaluate or supervise the display operations.

Qualitative and Quantitative Data

Every psychological observation can be expressed either numerically as quantitative data or descriptively as qualitative data. Each of these classes of data can constitute a self-sufficient data base as demonstrated by psychiatry's almost exclusive reliance on qualitative data and experimental psychology's frequent equation of figures with facts. However, the neuropsychological examiner must consider them together in order to make maximum use of his observations.

Qualitative data are direct observations. These include observations of the patient's *test-taking* behavior as well as his test behavior per se. Observations of the patient's appearance, his verbalizations, gestures, tone of voice, mood and affect, personal concerns, habits, and idiosyncrasies can provide a great deal of information about his life situation and overall adjustment, as well as his attitude toward the examination and his condition (see pp. 448–450). More specific to the test situation are observations of the patient's reactions to the examination itself, his approach to different kinds of test problems, and his expressions of feelings and opinions about his performance. Observations of the manner in which the patient handles test material, the wording of his test responses, the nature and consistency of his errors and his successes, fluctuations in attention and perseverance, his emotional state and the quality of his performance from moment to moment as he interacts with the examiner and with the different kinds of test material are the qualitative data of the test performance itself.

Quantitative data consist of *scores* that are not direct observational data but are summary statements about the observed behavior. Scores may be obtained for any set of behavior samples that can be categorized according to some principle. The scorer evaluates each behavior sample to see how well it fits a predetermined category and then gives it a place on a numerical scale (Cronbach, 1970).

For example, a tester interested in grammar might ask his subjects to make up a paragraph of five sentences and then score each sentence on the basis of its grammatical correctness. Another tester could use the same five-sentence technique to evaluate vocabulary level. He would devise a scoring system that differed from the first so as to produce vocabulary rather than grammar scores from the original behavior samples.

The most commonly used scale for individual test items has two points, one for "good" or "pass" and the other for "poor" or "fail." Three-point scales, which add a middle grade of "fair" or "barely pass," are often used for grading intellectual test items. Few scales contain more than five to seven scoring levels because the gradations become so fine as to be confusing to the scorer and meaningless for interpretation.

Scored tests with more than one item produce a summary score that is usually the simple sum of the scores for all the individual items. Occasionally test-makers incorporate a correction for guessing into their scoring systems so that the final score is not just a simple summation. The five-sentence grammar test proposed in the example above would produce a summary score of zero to five if each sentence is scored on a two-point pass-fail basis. If the vocabulary test is scored on a three-point basis of "zero" for below average, "one" for average and "two" for above average, then its possible score range becomes zero to ten. And so on.

Thus, a final test score contains two sources of inaccuracy: it not only represents one narrowly defined aspect of a set of behavior samples, but it is two or more steps removed from the original behavior. Should that summation score be included in the calculations summing or averaging *all* the subtests of a test battery, the resultant "global," "aggregate," or "Full Scale" score is three to four steps further removed from the behavior it represents.

The inclusion of test scores in the psychological data base satisfies the need for objective, readily replicable data cast in a form that permits reliable interpretation and meaningful comparisons. By using standard scoring systems, the examiner can reduce a vast array of different behaviors to a single numerical system. This enables him to compare the score of any one test performance of a patient with all other scores of that patient or of any other person.

Completely different behaviors, such as writing skills and visual reaction time, can be compared on a single numerical scale: one person might receive a high score for elegant penmanship but a low one on speed of response to a visual signal; another might be high on both kinds of tasks or low on both. Considering one behavior at a time, a scoring system permits direct comparisons between the handwriting of a 60-year-old stroke patient and that of school children at various grade levels, or between the patient's visual reaction time and that of other stroke patients of the same age.

Problems in the evaluation of quantitative data

To be neuropsychologically meaningful, a test score should represent as few kinds of behavior or dimensions of intellectual functions as possible. The simpler the test task, the clearer the meaning of scored evaluations of the behavior elicited by that task. Correspondingly, it is difficult to know just what functions contribute to a score obtained on a complex, multidimensional test task. If the test score is overinclusive, as in the case of summed or averaged test battery scores, it becomes virtually impossible to know just what behavioral or intellectual characteristics it stands for. Its usefulness for highlighting differences in ability and skill levels is nullified, for the patient's behavior is hidden behind a hodge-podge of intellectual functions and statistical operations (Butler et al., 1963; A. Smith, 1966b).

When interpreting test scores, it is important to keep in mind their artificial and abstract nature. Some examiners come to equate a score with the behavior it is supposed to represent. Others prize standardized, replicable test scores as "harder," more "scientific" data at the expense of unquantified observations. Reification of test scores can lead the examiner to overlook or discount direct observations. A test-score approach to psychological assessment that minimizes the importance of observational data can result in serious distortions in the interpretations, conclusions, and recommendations drawn from such a one-sided data base.

The evaluation of test scores in the context of direct observations is particularly important in neuropsychological assessment. For many brain damaged patients, test scores alone give relatively little information about the patient's functioning. The meat of the matter is often *how* a patient solves a problem or approaches a task rather than what his score is (Critchley, 1969).

For instance, two patients who achieve the same score on the Arithmetic subtest of the WAIS may have very different problems and abilities with respect to arithmetic. One patient performs the easy, single operation problems quickly and correctly, but fails the more difficult items requiring two operations or more for solution because of an inability to retain and juggle so much at once in his immediate memory. The other patient has no difficulty remembering item content. He answers many of the simpler items correctly but very slowly, counting aloud on his fingers. He is unable to conceptualize or perform the operation on the more difficult items. The numerical score masks the disparate performances of these patients.

Or two patients receive very low scores copying geometric designs with colored blocks. One may never quite understand any but the simplest problem; he neither appreciates the 2 × 2 layout of the blocks nor figures out how to construct a diagonal pattern when the blocks are square. The second patient is able to do four or five of the designs correctly, but so slowly as to receive credit for only the first one or two problems. The first patient has a profound visuopractic disability or is retarded; the second patient's greatest problem is his slowness. Close observation should clarify whether his slow performance is due to a motor disability, sluggishness in processing information, or depression.

Limitations of qualitative data

Distortion or misinterpretation of information obtained by direct observation results from different kinds of methodological and examination problems. All of the standardization, reliability, and validity problems inherent in the collection and evaluation of data by a single observer are ever-present threats to objectivity (Bolgar 1965; Chassan, 1960). In neuropsychological assessment, the vagaries of neurological impairment compound these problems. When the patient's communication skills are questionable, the examiner can never be certain that he understood his transactions with the patient.

Worse yet, the communication disability may be so subtle and well-masked by the patient that the examiner is not aware of communication slips. There is a more than ordinary likelihood that the patient's actions will be idiosyncratic and therefore unfamiliar and subject to misunderstanding. Also, the patient may be entirely or variably uncooperative, sometimes quite unintentionally.

Further, the range of observations an examiner can make is restricted by the test. Many paper and pencil tests afford the patient limited opportunities for self-expression; and typically, no one observes the cooperative, comprehending, or docile patient when he takes a paper and pencil test. Multiple-choice tests presumably offer no behavior alternatives beyond making a mark in one of the few prescribed places. Qualitative differences in multiple-choice test performances occur only when there are frank aberrations in test-taking behavior, such as qualifying statements written on an MMPI answer sheet, or more than one alternative marked on a single answer multiple-choice test. For most paper and pencil tests, *how* the patient solves the problem or goes about answering the question remains unknown or, at best, a matter of conjecture based on such relatively insubstantial information as heaviness or neatness of pencil marks, test-taking errors, patterns of nonresponse, erasures, and the occasional pencil-sketched spelling try-outs, mathematical equations, or arithmetic computations in the margin.

The integrated use of qualitative and quantitative examination data treats these two different kinds of information as different parts of the whole data base. Test scores that have been interpreted without reference to the context of the examination in which they were obtained may be objective but meaningless in their individual applications; clinical observations unsupported by standardized and quantifiable testing, although full of import for the individual, lack the comparability necessary for diagnostic and planning decisions. Descriptive observations flesh out the skeletal structure of numerical test scores. Each is incomplete without the other.

TEST SCORES

Test scores can be expressed in a variety of forms. Rarely does a test-maker use a *raw* score—the simple sum of correct answers or correct answers minus a portion of the incorrect ones—for in itself a raw score communicates nothing about its relative value. Instead, test-makers generally report scores as values of a scale based on the raw scores made by a *standardization population* (the group of individuals tested for the purpose of obtaining normative data on the test). Each score then becomes a statement of its value relative to all other scores on that scale. Different kinds of scales provide more or less readily comprehended and statistically well-defined standards for comparing any one score with the scores of the standardization population. The most widely used scale is based on the *standard score*.

Standard Scores

The need for standard scores
The handling of test scores in neuropsychological assessment is often a more complex task than in other kinds of intellectual evaluations because there can be many different sources of test scores. In the usual intellectual examination, generally conducted for purposes of academic evaluation or career counseling, the bulk of the testing is done with one test battery, such as the WAIS or the California Test of Mental Maturity. Within such a battery, the scores for each of the subtests are on the same scale and standardized on the same population so that subtest scores can be compared directly.

On the other hand, there is no single test battery that provides all the information needed to adequately assess most patients presenting neuropsychological questions. Techniques employed in the assessment of different aspects of intellectual functioning have been developed at different times, in different places, on different populations, for different ability and maturity levels, with different scoring and classification systems, and for different purposes. Taken together, they are an unsystematized aggregate of more or less standardized tests, experimental techniques, and observational aids that have proven useful in demonstrating the loss or disturbance of some intellectual function or activity. Their scores are not directly comparable with one another.

To make the comparisons necessary for evaluating impairment, the many disparate test scores must be convertible into one scale with identical units. Such a scale can serve as a kind of test users' *lingua franca*, permitting direct comparisons between many different kinds of measurements. The scale that is most meaningful statistically and that probably serves the intermediary function between different tests best is one derived from the normal probability curve and based on the standard deviation unit (Anastasi, 1968; Lyman, 1963) (see Fig. 6-1).

The value of basing a common scale on the standard deviation unit lies primarily in the statistical nature of the standard deviation (s) as a measure of the spread or dispersion of a set of scores (X_1, X_2, X_3, etc.) around their mean ($\overline{X}$). Standard deviation units describe known proportions of the normal probability curve (see Fig. 6-1, "Per cent of cases under portions of the normal curve"). This has very practical applications for comparing and evaluating psychological data in that the position of any test score on a standard deviation unit scale, in itself, defines the proportion of people taking the test who will obtain scores above and below the given score. Virtually all scaled psychological test data can be converted to standard deviation units for interest comparisons. Furthermore, a score based on the standard deviation, a *standard score,* can generally be estimated from a percentile, which is the most commonly used nonstandard score in adult testing.

The likelihood that two numerically different scores are significantly different can also be estimated from their relative positions on a standard deviation unit scale. This use of the standard deviation unit scale is of particular importance in neuropsychological testing, for evaluation of test scores depends upon the significance of their distance from one another or from the comparison standard. Since direct statistical evaluations of the difference between scores obtained on different kinds of tests is rarely possible, the examiner must use estimates of the ranges of significance levels based on score comparisons. In general, differences of two standard deviations or more may be considered significant, whereas differences of one to two standard deviations suggest a trend (Field, 1960; R. W. Payne and Jones, 1957).

Kinds of standard scores
There are a variety of standard scores that are all translations of the same scale, based on the mean and the standard deviation. The *z-score* is the basic, unelaborated standard score from which all

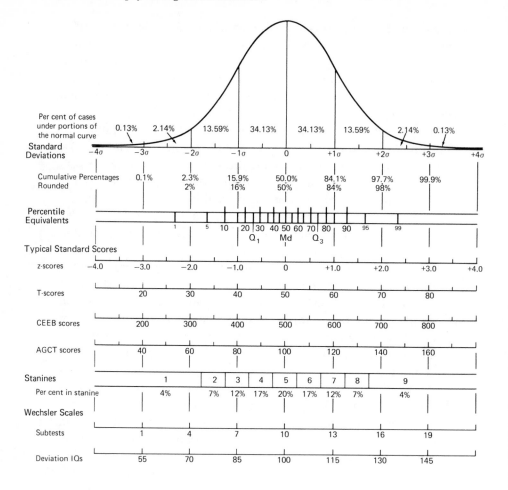

NOTE: This chart cannot be used to equate scores on one test to scores on another test. For example, both 600 on the CEEB and 120 on the AGCT are one standard deviation above their respective means, but they do not represent "equal" standings because the scores were obtained from different groups.

FIG. 6-1. The relationship of the most commonly used test scores to the normal curve and to one another. (Reprinted from the *Test Service Bulletin* of The Psychological Corporation, No. 48, 1955.)

others can be derived. The z-score represents, in standard deviation units, the amount a score deviates from the mean of the population from which the score is drawn $\left(z = \dfrac{X - \overline{X}}{s}\right)$. The mean of the normal curve is set at zero and the standard deviation unit has a value of one. Scores are stated in terms of their distance from the mean as measured in standard deviation units. Scores above the mean have a positive value; those below the mean are negative.

Elaborations of the z-score are called *derived scores*. Derived scores provide the same information as do z-scores, but the score value is expressed in scale units that are more familiar to some test users than z-scores. A test-maker can assign any value he wishes to the standard deviation and mean of his distribution of test scores. Usually he follows convention and chooses commonly used values.

Among the most widely used derived scores are T-scores, which are very popular in educational testing and paper and pencil personality tests. The T-score has a mean of 50 and a standard deviation of 10 (i.e., $T = 50 + 10z$). Some neuropsychologists working with scores from test batteries composed of many different tests report their findings in T-scores (Kiernan and Matthews, 1974; Lewinsohn, 1973; Reitan, 1964). Another popular standard score is based on a mean of 100 and a standard deviation unit of 15 (i.e., $SS = 100 + 15z$). Wechsler subtest scaled scores are computed with a mean of 10 and a standard deviation of 3 (i.e., $SS_w = 10 + 3z$). The College Entrance Examination Board uses a mean of 500 and 100 as the standard deviation size for their Scholastic Aptitude Tests (i.e., $CEEB = 500 + 100z$). Still other test means and standard deviations are set at other values. All of these different scores are directly comparable with one another, the standard deviation and its relationship to the normal curve serving as the key to translation (see Table 6-1).

Estimating standard scores from nonstandard scores
Since most published standardized tests today use a standard score format for handling the numerical test data, their scores present little or no problem to the examiner wishing to make intertest comparisons. However, there are still a few test-makers who report their standardization data in percentile or IQ score equivalents. In these cases, standard score approximations can be estimated.

Unless there is reason to believe that the standardization popula-

TABLE 6-1

Comparisons of Common Scoring Systems in Terms of Given z-score Values

When the z-score $\left(\dfrac{X - \bar{X}}{s}\right)$ =	−0.60	+0.80	+2.10
the T-score (50 + 10 z) =	44	58	71
SS (100 + 15 z) =	91.0	112.0	131.5
SS_w (10 + 3 z) =	8.0	12.4	16.3
CEEB (500 + 100 z) =	440	580	710
and the percentile =	27.4	78.8	98.2

tion is not normally distributed, a standard score equivalent for a percentile score can be estimated from a table of normal curve functions. Table 6-2 gives z-score approximations, taken from a normal curve table, for 21 percentiles ranging from 1 to 99 and the 19 five-point steps in between. The z-score that best approximates a given percentile is that one that corresponds to the percentile closest to the percentile in question. The mean percentile score of 50 is equivalent to a z-score of zero. All z-scores for percentiles above 50 are positive, those for percentiles below 50 are negative.

IQ scores can also be converted to standard score approximations without much difficulty. This is done by using the standard deviation of the distribution of test scores to measure the distance of any score from the test mean. The size of the discrepany between a score in IQ score units and the mean, when measured in standard deviation units, is the approximate z-score for that IQ score. Thus, if the IQ score is 123 and the standard deviation of the distribution is 16, the z-score estimate is 23/16 standard deviation units above the mean, or approximately +1.44. This kind of conversion is rarely necessary since most tests that give IQ score equivalents for their raw scores also provide percentile and standard score equivalents.

Exceptions to the use of standard scores

Standardization population differences. In evaluating a patient's performance on a variety of tests, the examiner can only compare scores from different tests when the standardization populations of each of the tests are identical or at least reasonably similar. Otherwise, even though their scales and units are statistically identical, the

TABLE 6-2
Standard Score Equivalents for 21 Percentile Scores Ranging from 1 to 99

Percentile Score	z-score	Percentile Score	z-score	Percentile Score	z-score
99	+2.33	65	+0.39	30	−0.52
95	+1.65	60	+0.25	25	−0.68
90	+1.28	55	+0.13	20	−0.84
85	+1.04	50	0	15	−1.04
80	+0.84	45	−0.13	10	−1.28
75	+0.68	40	−0.25	5	−1.65
70	+0.52	35	−0.39	1	−2.33

operational meanings of the different values are as different as the populations from which they are drawn. This restriction becomes obvious should an examiner attempt to compare a vocabulary score obtained on the WAIS, which was standardized on a cross section of the general adult population, with a score on the Graduate Record Examination (GRE), standardized on college graduates. A person who receives a mean score on the GRE would probably achieve a score of one to two standard deviations above the mean on the WAIS, since the average college graduate typically scores around two standard deviations above the general population mean on tests of this type (Anastasi, 1965). Although each of these mean scores has the same z-score value, the performance levels they represent are very different.

Test-makers usually describe their standardization populations in terms of sex, race, age, or education. The variables most likely to affect intraindividual comparability of test scores are education and age. For most intellectual functions, sex is not a significant variable in adult populations. Moreover, like race, sex rarely affects comparisons between test scores since *norms* (the score values of standardized tests) for any test in general use are not standardized on nonwhite or female populations alone. Thus, the test norms remain comparable for nonwhite and female subjects as long as all the tests involved in the score comparisons have been standardized on the same kind of population. Vocational and regional differences between standardization populations may also contribute to differences between test norms; however, vocational differences generally correlate highly with educational differences, and regional differences tend to be relatively insignificant compared to age and any variable highly correlated with income level, such as education or vocation (Anastasi, 1965).

Age can be a very significant variable when evaluating test scores of older patients. Functions such as immediate memory and learning which decline sharply with advanced age are also extremely susceptible to the effects of organic impairment (see Chapter 7, the section on aging). In patients over 50, the normal changes with age may obscure subtle intellectual changes that could herald early, correctable stages of a tumor or vascular disease. The use of age-graded scores puts the aging patient's scoring pattern into sharper focus. Age-graded scores are important aids to differential diagnosis in patients over 50 and are essential to the evaluation of test performances of patients over 65. Although not all tests an examiner may wish to use have age-graded norms or age corrections, enough are available to determine the extent to which a patient might be experiencing age-related deterioration.

Most tests of a single intellectual function, ability, or skill do not have separate norms for age, sex, education, etc. A few widely used tests of general intellectual abilities take into account the geographic distribution of their standardization population, the rest are usually standardized on local people. Tests developed in Minnesota will have Minnesota norms; New York test-makers use a big city population; and English tests are standardized on English populations. Although this situation results in less than perfect comparability between the different tests, in most cases the examiner has no choice but to use norms of tests standardized on an undefined mixed or nonrandom adult sample. Experience quickly demonstrates that this is usually not a serious hardship, for these "mixed-bag" norms generally serve their purpose adequately. Perhaps the chief normative fault of many single purpose tests is that they lack discriminating norms for the top 5 or 10% of the population.

Children's tests. Some children's tests are well-suited for the examination of patients with severe intellectual impairment or profound disability. There are also many good tests of academic abilities such as arithmetic, reading, and spelling that have been standardized for child or adolescent populations. The best of these invariably have standard score norms that, by and large, cannot be applied to an adult population because of the significant effect of age and education on performance differences between adults and children.

Senior high school norms are the one exception to this rule. On tests of intellectual ability that provide adult norms extending into the late teens, the population of 18 year-olds does not perform much differently than the adult population at large (Wechsler, 1955); and four years of high school is a reasonable approximation of the adult educational level. This exception makes a great number of very well-standardized and easily administered paper and pencil academic skill tests available for the examination of adults, and no scoring changes are necessary.

All other children's tests are best scored and reported in terms of mental age (MA) which is psychologically the most meaningful score derived from these tests. Most children's tests provide mental age norms or grade level norms (which readily convert into mental age). With mental age scores, the examiner can readily estimate the extent of impairment, or he can compare performances on different tests or between two or more tests administered over time, just as he does with test performances in terms of standard scores. Mental age scores are also useful for planning educational or living activity retraining programs.

A rough approximation to standard scores can be obtained for mental age scores of 5-3 (five years three months) and above by using the age 18 norms in the Conversion Tables (for converting mental age scores into standard scores) of the third revision of the Stanford-Binet Intelligence Scale (Terman and Merrill, 1960, pp. 257–335). In this test the standard score is entitled the "deviation IQ" (DIQ) and is based on a mean of 100 and a standard deviation of 16, i.e., $DIQ = 100 + 16 z$).

As with any other score, the examiner must make appropriate allowances for normal testing error so that he does not draw unwarranted conclusions about nonsignificant differences between mental age scores. When one or more of the scores to be compared are mental age scores, he can convert the MA to a standard score by using the DIQ conversion tables as long as the mental age is 5-3 or above. Care in evaluating the discrepancy between scores is particularly important when mental age scores are used, since differences that are quite significant for children may be well within the limits of chance variation for adults. At age four years three months, for example, an MA of 5-6 converts to a DIQ of 128, and an MA of 7-0 is equivalent to a DIQ of 164. Thus, at age four years three months, this one and one-half year mental age difference can be considered significant because the discrepancy is 2.25 standard deviations. At age 18, on the other hand, an MA of 5-6 converts to a DIQ of 23, and an MA of 7-0 converts to a DIQ of 42, a difference of only 10 DIQ points or 10/16ths of a standard deviation. Such small differences between scores are most likely due to chance.

Standard scores for mental age scores below 5-3 are not available for the 18-year-old norms. At this level, for age 18, the DIQ is 30, 4.38 standard deviations below the mean. Any adult mental age score below 5-3 can be considered significantly below any comparison standard for all but the frankly retarded.

Sometimes test norms for children's tests are given in standard scores or percentiles for each age or set of ages. The examiner can convert the score to a mental age score by finding the age at which the obtained score is closest to a score at the 50th percentile or the standard score mean (see Tables 6-3 and 6-4).

Small standardization populations. A number of interesting and potentially useful tests of specific skills and abilities have been devised for studies of particular neuropsychological problems in which the standardization groups are relatively small (often under 20) (Talland, 1965; Tow, 1955). Standard score conversions are in-

TABLE 6-3
Sample Table of Raw Scores for Converting Raw Scores into Percentiles for an Age-related Skill Test

Ages	Percentiles				
	10	25	50	75	90
3	3	5	7	9	12
4	5	7	10	12	14
5	8	11	13	15	18
6	10	14	16	19	22

If the patient receives a score of 10, his mental age is estimated to be 4, for 10 is the middle or most typical score for that age. A patient who gets a score of 14 on the same test is in the 5- to 6-year mental age range—approximately 5-4, by interpolation.

TABLE 6-4
Sample Table of Standard Scores for Converting Raw Scores into Standard Scores for an Age-related Skill Test[a]

Raw Scores	Mental Age Scores (years)			
	3	4	5	6
8	98	93	88	82
9	101	96	91	85
10	104	100	94	89
11	106	102	97	93
12	109	105	100	96

A raw score of 10 converts to a mental age score of 4 years, for 10 is the mean score for age 4. Similarly, a patient with a raw score of 11 would receive a mental age score between 4-0 and 5-0, or approximately 4-5 by interpolation.

[a] Mean = 100; Standard Deviation = 10.

appropriate if not impossible in such cases. If there is a clear relationship between the condition under study and a particular kind of performance on a given test, there is frequently a fairly clear-cut dichotomy between patient and control group scores. Any given patient's score can be evaluated in terms of how closely it compares with the score ranges of either the patient or the control group reported in the study.

On one verbal memory test (Running Digit Span, Talland, 1965; see p. 349, below), 24 patients with a severe memory disability (Korsakoff's psychosis) recalled an average of 8.4 (SD 3.3) out of a possible total of 20 numbers, compared with 28 control subjects' average recall of 13.9 (SD 3.0) numbers. The difference between the means of the groups was evaluated by a t-test and found to be significant at the .01 level. Thus, should a patient's score on this test be markedly below the control group's average, a memory disability may be suspected.

Reporting Scores

The practice of reporting test performances in terms of scores can be confusing and misleading, particularly since most recipients of test reports are teachers, guidance counselors, physicians, and lawyers who lack training in the niceties of psychometrics. One important source of faulty communication is the variability in the size of assigned standard deviations. This can be seen most clearly when one compares derived scores based on a mean of 100 but with standard deviations ranging from 10 to 20 (see Table 6-5). With four different common magnitudes of the standard deviation, a score of 110 can range as widely as from the 69th to the 84th percentile. Unless the person who receives the test report is statistically sophisticated and knowledgeable about the scaling idiosyncrasies of test-makers, it is unlikely that he will notice or appreciate these kinds of discrepancies.

Another difficulty in reporting scores lies in the statistically naive person's natural assumption that if one measurement is larger than another, there is a difference in the quantity of whatever is being measured. Unfortunately, few persons unschooled in statistics understand measurement error; they do not realize that two different numbers need not necessarily stand for different quantities but may be chance variations in the measurement of the same quantity. When a layman sees a report listing a WAIS Similarities score of 9 and an Arithmetic score of 11, he is likely to draw the possibly erroneous conclusion that the subject does better in mathematics than in verbal reasoning. Since most score differences of this magnitude are chance variations, it is more likely that the subject is equally capable in both areas (Doppelt, 1967).

Ignorance about the meaning of test scores has its gravest consequences in school testing programs in which children's test scores are reported as numerical "IQ's." Teachers and school administrators who really think that a child with an "IQ" score of 108 is not as bright as one with a score of 112 treat each child accordingly. Similar ignorance can compromise a nonpsychologist's understand-

TABLE 6-5
z-score and Percentile Values of a Score of 110 on Four Tests with Means of 100 and Different Standard Deviations

	$s = 10$[a]	$s = 15$[b]	$s = 16$[c]	$s = 20$[d]
z	+1.00	+0.67	+0.62	+0.50
Percentile	84	75	73	69

Among the tests with these four standard deviations are (a) the Wide Range Achievement Test; (b) the Wechsler Intelligence Scales; (c) the Stanford-Binet (Form L-M); and (d) the General Aptitude Test Battery.

ing of a psychological report, particularly a neuropsychological report in which conclusions often rest on proper interpretation of test score discrepancies.

Further, there has been a tendency, both within school systems and in the culture at large, to reify test scores. In many schools, this has too often resulted in the arbitrary and rigid sorting of children into different parts of a classroom, into different ability level classes, and onto different vocational tracks. In its extreme form, reification of test scores has provided a predominant frame of reference for evaluating people generally. It is usually heard in remarks that take some real or supposed "IQ" score to indicate an individual's personal or social worth. "Sam couldn't have more than an 'IQ' of 80," means that the speaker thinks Sam is socially incompetent. "My Harold's IQ is 160!" is a statement of pride.

Although these numerical metaphors presumably are very meaningful for the people who use them, the meanings are not standardized, objective, nor do they bear any necessary relationship to the meaning a test-maker defines for the scores in his scoring system. Thus, the communication of numerical test scores, particularly if the test-maker has labeled them "IQ" scores, becomes a very uncertain business since the examiner has no way of knowing what kind of meaning his reader has already attached to mental test scores.

One way to avoid the many difficulties inherent in test score reporting is to write about test performances in terms of the commonly accepted classification of ability levels (Terman and Merrill, 1960; Wechsler, 1955). In the standard classification system, each ability level represents a statistically defined range of scores. Both percentile scores and standard scores can be classified in terms of ability level (see Table 6-6).

Test performances communicated in terms of ability levels have generally accepted and relatively clear meanings. Should the examiner doubt whether such classifications as *average*, *high average*, and so on, make sense to his reader, he can qualify them with a statement about the percentile range they represent, for the public generally understands the meaning of percentiles. For example, in reporting WAIS scores of 12 and 13, the examiner can say, "the patient's performance on [the particular subtests] was within the *high average* ability level, which is between the upper 75th and 85th percentiles, approximately."

TABLE 6-6
Classification of Ability Levels

Classification	z-score	Percent Included	Lower Limit of Percentile Range
Very Superior	+2.0 and above	2.2	98
Superior	+1.3 to +2.0	6.7	91
High Average	+0.6 to +1.3	16.1	75
Average	±0.6	50.0	25
Low Average	−0.6 to −1.3	16.1	9
Borderline	−1.3 to −2.0	6.7	2
Retarded	−2.0 and below	2.2	—

This method also enables the examiner to report clusters of scores that may be one or two—or in the case of tests with fine-grained scales, several—score points apart but that probably represent a normal variation of scores around a single ability level. Thus, in dealing with the performance of a patient who receives scores of 8, 9, or 10 on each WAIS subtest involving verbal skills, the examiner reports that, "the patient's verbal skill level is *average*." Significant performance discrepancies can also be readily noted. Should a patient achieve *average* scores on verbal tests, but *low average* to *borderline defective* scores on constructional tasks, the examiner can note both the levels of the different clusters of test scores and the fact that discrepancies between these levels approach or reach significance.

INTERPRETING TEST DATA

Test data can be used for diagnostic decision-making, treatment, and planning purposes in several ways. *Screening techniques* are used to determine whether or not an organic defect is likely to be present. A *pattern approach* to test score analysis can provide diagnostically useful information as well as be a significant improvement over simple screening techniques in identifying organically impaired persons. *Integrated interpretation* takes into account test signs of brain damage and test score patterns in conjunction with the qualitative aspects of the examination. Each of these approaches will be discussed below.

Screening Techniques

The behavioral symptoms of brain damage differ not only in their nature and severity but in the extent to which a patient's behavior is affected generally. Some patients suffer only a single highly specific defect or a cluster of related disabilities with the greater part of their intellect remaining intact. Others sustain wide-spread impairment, usually of attention, memory, and cognitive functions. Still others display aberrations characteristic of brain damage (*signs*), most often along with some general intellectual or emotional deficits. Thus, brain damaged patients can be identified either in terms of a particular defect or set of associated defects, general impairment, or characteristic signs of organicity. Most brain damaged persons display two or three of the different kinds of symptoms and are likely to be identified by ordinary screening techniques. Those patients whose organic disabilities appear as discrete defects or in the form of relatively rare signs may not be recognized as brain damaged if only ordinary screening techniques are used.

As a rule, the more specific an intellectual defect, the more likely will it be associated with brain damage. Therefore, the most specific intellectual defects serve as quite reliable indicators of brain injury or disease. However, these specific symptoms of intellectual impairment occur relatively infrequently. For instance, *perseveration* (the continuation of a response after it is no longer appropriate, as in writing three or four "e's" in a word such as "deep" or "seen," or copying a 12-dot line without regard for the number, stopping only when the edge of the page is reached) is so strongly associated with brain damage that the examiner should suspect brain damage on the basis of this defect alone. However, since most brain damaged patients do not give perseverative responses, it is not a useful criterion for screening purposes. Use of a highly specific symptom, such as perseveration, as a screening criterion for brain damage results in few persons without brain damage misidentified as brain damaged (*false positive* errors), but such a narrow test of brain damage will let many persons who are brain damaged slip through the screen (*false negative* errors).

On the other hand, those defects that affect intellectual functioning generally, such as distractibility, impaired immediate memory, and concrete thinking, are not only very common symptoms of brain damage but tend to accompany a number of emotional disorders as well. As a result, a screening test that uses a defect impairing intellectual functioning generally will identify many brain damaged patients correctly with few false negative errors, but a large number of psychiatric patients will also be included as a result of false positive errors of identification.

Limitations in predictive accuracy do not invalidate either tests for specific signs or disabilities or tests that are sensitive to conditions of general dysfunction. Each kind of test can be used effectively as a screening device as long as its limitations are known and the information it elicits is interpreted accordingly. When testing is primarily for screening purposes, a combination of tests including some that are sensitive to specific impairment, some to general impairment, and others that tend to draw out diagnostic signs will make the best diagnostic discriminations.

Signs

The sign approach is based on the assumption that there are some distinctive behavioral manifestations of brain damage. In part this assumption reflects early concepts of brain damage as a unitary kind of dysfunction (Hebb, 1942; Shure and Halstead, 1958); and in part it results from observations of behavioral characteristics that do distinguish the test performances of many patients with organic damage.

Most "organic signs" refer to specific aberrant test responses or modes of response. Some signs are isolated response deviations which, in themselves, may indicate the presence of an organic defect. Rotation in copying a block design (Satz, 1966b) or a geometric figure (Fuller, 1969) has been considered a sign of brain damage. Specific test failures or test score discrepancies have also been treated as signs of organicity, as for instance, marked difficulty on a serial subtraction task (Ruesch and Moore, 1943) or a wide spread between the number of digits recalled in the order given and the number recalled in reversed order (Wechsler, 1958). The manner in which the patient responds to the task may also be considered an organic sign. M. Williams (1965) associated three response characteristics with brain damage: "stereotyping and perseveration"; "concreteness of behavior" defined by her as "response to all stimuli as if they existed only in the setting in which they are presented";

and "catastrophic reactions" of perplexity, acute anxiety, and despair when the patient is unable to perform the presented task.

Another common sign approach relies on not one but on the sum of different signs, i.e., the total number of different kinds of specific test response aberrations or differentiating test item selections made by the patient. This method has been widely used with the Rorschach test with some success (Harrower, 1965; Piotrowski, 1937) (see pp. 459–461) and has been attempted with the Minnesota Multiphasic Personality Inventory (Hovey, 1964; Zimmerman, 1965) (see pp. 467–469).

Cutting scores

The score that separates the "normal" or "not diagnostic" from the "abnormal" or "organic" ends of a continuum of test scores is called a *cutting score.* The use of cutting scores is akin to the sign approach, for their purpose is to separate patients in terms of the presence or absence of the condition under study. A statistically derived cutting score for organicity is that score that differentiates organic patients from others with the fewest instances of error on either side. A cutting score may also be derived by simple inspection, in which case it is usually the score just below the poorest score attained by any member of the "normal" comparison group.

Cutting scores are a prominent feature of most screening tests. However, many of the cutting scores used for neuropsychological diagnosis may be less efficient than the claims made for them (Meehl and Rosen, 1967). This is most likely to be the case when the establishment of a cutting score does not take into account the base rate at which the predicted condition occurs in the sample from which the cutting score was developed (Satz et al., 1970). The criterion groups are often not large enough for optimal cutting scores to be determined. Further, cutting scores developed on one kind of population may not apply to another one.

When the recommended cutting scores are used, these tests generally do identify the organically impaired patients better than by chance. They all also misdiagnose both organically intact persons (false positive cases) and persons with known organic defects (false negative cases) to varying degrees. The nature of the errors of diagnosis depends on where the cutting score is set: if it is set to minimize misidentification of organically sound persons, then a greater number of organically impaired patients will be called "normal" by the screening. Conversely, if the test-maker's goal is to identify as many patients with brain damage as possible, he will then include more organically sound persons in his brain damaged group (see Table 6-7). As a general rule, even when these tests screen brain damaged patients from a normal control group, they do not discriminate well between them and psychiatric patients (Lilliston, 1969). Only rarely does the cutting score provide a distinct separation between the two populations, and then only for tests that are so simple no nonretarded intact adult could fail. For example, there are no false positive cases screened in by the Token Test, which consists of verbal instructions involving basic concepts of size, color, and location (Boller and Vignolo, 1966).

Single tests for organicity
With the growing interest in brain damage as a diagnostic problem, there has been a proliferation of "tests of organicity" that comprise a single task or small set of tasks, usually of a similar character, and that purport to elicit evidence of organicity better than the psychodiagnostic techniques in general use. Some of them, like the Bender-Gestalt test, were originally developed for some other purpose (Bender, 1938) but soon entered the neuropsychological test repertory to become, for some examiners, a kind of psychological litmus paper for the detection of brain damage (Brilliant and Gynther, 1963; Hain, 1964) (see pp. 311–320). Other tests were developed especially for the detection of brain damage, without regard to anatomical or functional differences between organically impaired patients. Some of these tests, such as the Minnesota Percepto-Diagnostic Test, mainly involve visuopractic behavior (Fuller, 1969) (see pp. 321–322). Others emphasize visuoconceptual functions, as for instance, Elithorn's Mazes and Hooper's Visual Organization Test (see pp. 286 and 297–298). Still others include several different tasks, such as the Hunt-Minnesota Test for Organic Brain Damage (see pp. 444–445); or one relatively complex task, such as the Graham-Kendall Memory for Designs Test, which involves visuopractic *and* memory functions, and Satz's Block Rotation Test, which involves visuopractic *and* visuoconceptual functions (see pp. 333 and 375–376).

   The use of single tests for identifying brain damaged patients is

TABLE 6-7
Sample Table of Scores on a Timed Test for a Brain Damaged Group and a Normal Control Group

Performance Time (seconds)	Percent Achieving a Given Raw Score	
	Control Group	Brain Damaged Group
20	6	
25	12	1
30	23	0
35	29	2
40	20	6
45	8	15
50	2	24
55		28
60		16
65		5
70+		2

A cutting score set at 41 seconds misidentifies 10% of the control group and 9% of the brain-damaged group for the lowest number of total errors. If the cutting score is set at 51 to exclude all false positives, i.e., all normal controls, then 48% of the brain damaged patients will be excluded as well. A cutting score set to exclude all false negatives would exclude all but 6% of the normal control group.

also based on the assumption that brain damage, like measles perhaps, can be treated as a single entity. Considering the heterogeneity of organic brain disorders, it is not very surprising to find that single tests have high misclassification rates. Most single tests, including many that are not well standardized, can be rich sources of information about the functions, attitudes, and habits they elicit. But to look to any single one of them for decisive information about overall intellectual behavior is not merely foolish, but can be dangerous as well, for the absence of positive findings does not rule out the presence of a pathological condition. Neither does a lack of positive findings invalidate the test in any single case when there is known cerebral pathology. When an abnormal brain condition manifests itself in an abnormal test performance, the test contributes to the diagnosis or to an enhanced understanding of the condition. Should the patient's test behavior be within normal limits, the most that can be said about the test is that it contributed nothing to a clarification of this particular patient's problems.

The proportion of brain damaged patients identified correctly by single purpose tests increases with the number of functions they test (Teuber and Weinstein, 1956). Thus, tasks involving both perceptual *and* motor functions, such as the Bender-Gestalt and the Trail Making Test (see pp. 429–432), tend to identify organically impaired patients better than purely perceptual tasks (Zimet and Fishman, 1970). Tasks such as Raven's Progressive Matrices (see pp. 248–251) and Halstead's Category Test (see p. 440) that require both perceptual *and* conceptual activities also discriminate well between organic patients and normal control groups, although they are of questionable effectiveness in differentiating between brain damaged and psychiatric patients (Yates, 1954; Zimet and Fishman, 1970). Tests in which speed is a significant factor generally discriminate well too (Newcombe, 1969; Wechsler, 1958). Conceivably, the single test that would best identify the brain damaged members of any population would be one that incorporated all facets of intellectual behavior that are vulnerable to impairment by brain injury; then any impairment would affect performance adversely. Of course, the addition of each new function or variable renders the nature of the disability more obscure and increases the probability of misidentifying organically sound persons who tend to behave idiosyncratically on one aspect or another of the test.

Usefulness of screening techniques

Although dichotomizing screening techniques are useful in research for evaluating tests or treatments, or for comparing populations with respect to the presence or absence of organic defects, by themselves they have only limited clinical applicability. The extent to which screening techniques produce false positives and false negatives compromises their reliability for making decisions about individual patients (Spreen and Benton, 1965; Reitan, 1968). On the other hand, they can be of considerable clinical value in identifying psychiatric or medical patients who have a hitherto unsuspected brain condition. When screening tests are used along with tests that allow for many gradations of behavior, organic signs and positive cutting scores do lend support to findings suggestive of brain damage, although their absence does not weaken an interpretation of brain damage based on data from graded tests.

Once a patient has been identified by screening techniques as possibly having an organic disorder, the problem arises of what to do about him, for simple screening at best operates only as an early warning system. These patients still need careful neurological and neuropsychological study to evaluate the possibility of organicity and to diagnose organic conditions so that treatment and planning can be undertaken.

Pattern Analysis

Brain damage also shows up in sets of tests with graded responses as significantly large discrepancies between the patient's highest and lowest test scores. Any single discrepant score or response error can usually be disregarded as a chance deviation. A number of errors or test score deviations, however, may form a pattern that can then be analyzed in terms of whether or not it makes neurological sense; i.e., whether the score discrepancies fit neuroanatomically probable behavior patterns. The possibility that a given pattern of scores reflects an organic brain disorder is supported to the extent that the scores conform to a neuropsychologically reasonable discrepancy pattern.

The question of neuroanatomical or neurophysiological likelihood underlies all analyses of test patterns undertaken for differential diagnosis. As in every other diagnostic effort, the most likely explanation for a behavioral disorder is the one that requires the least number of unlikely events to account for it. Organicity is suspected when a neurological condition best accounts for the patient's behavioral abnormalities.

Intraindividual variability
Variability in the pattern of successes and failures in a test performance is called *scatter*. Variability within a test is *intratest scatter*; variability between the scores of a set of tests is *intertest scatter* (Wechsler, 1958).

Intratest scatter.   Scatter within a test is said to be present when there are marked deviations from the normal pass-fail pattern of a test. On tests in which the items are presented in order of difficulty, it is usual for the subject to pass almost all items up to the most difficult passed item, with perhaps one or two failures on items close to the last passed item. Rarely do nondefective persons fail very simple items, or fail many items of middling difficulty and pass several difficult ones. On tests in which all items are of a similar difficulty level, most subjects tend to do all of them correctly, with perhaps one or two errors of carelessness, or they tend to flounder hopelessly with maybe one or two lucky "hits." Variations from these two common patterns deserve the examiner's attention.

Efforts to relate intratest scatter to either organicity or emotional disturbance have not produced much evidence that intratest scatter patterns alone differentiate reliably between diagnostic groups (Guertin et al., 1966; Rabin, 1965). However, certain kinds of organic problems as well as some functional disturbances may manifest themselves in intratest scatter patterns. Hovey and Kooi (1955) demonstrated that when taking mental tests, those epileptic patients who suffered paroxysmal brain wave patterns (sudden bursts of activity) were significantly more likely to be randomly nonresponsive or forgetful than were psychiatric, brain damaged, or other epileptic patients. Some patients who have sustained severe head injuries respond to questions that draw on prior knowledge as if they had randomly lost chunks of stored information. For example, a high school graduate may recall the main theme of the Book of Genesis and the boiling point of water, but have no memory for the author of Hamlet or the capital of Italy, even though he is sure he once knew them. Psychiatric patients who tend to block or distort responses to verbalizations they perceive as emotionally threatening may also give highly scattered intratest performances (Rapaport et al., 1968). A review of the failed items will often give clues as to the nature of the failure: if the only items failed were those with potentially anxiety-arousing content, then the examiner can reasonably suspect a functional basis for the scatter. On the other hand, if premature failures occur in an apparently meaningless fashion, then organicity may account for them.

The presence of *intratest* scatter may aid psychodiagnosis, but its absence has no bearing on anything whatsoever. Since intratest scatter tends to be the exception rather than the rule, it is not relevant to the majority of test evaluations.

Intertest scatter. Probably the most common approach to the psychodiagnosis of organic brain disorders is through comparison of the test score levels obtained by the subject, in other words, analysis of the intertest score scatter (McFie, 1969; Reitan, 1964; Wechsler, 1958). By this means, the examiner attempts to relate variations between test scores to probable neuropsychological events. This technique can often provide clarification of a seeming confusion of signs and symptoms of behavioral disorder by giving the examiner a frame of reference for organizing and evaluating his data.

Consistency in the expression of intellectual functions is the key concept of pattern analysis. Damage to cortical tissue in an area serving a specific function changes or abolishes the expression of that function. Once a function is changed or lost, the character of all activities that originally involved that function will change to a greater or lesser degree, depending upon how much the function itself has changed and the extent to which it entered into the activity.

In analyzing test score patterns, the examiner looks for commonality of dysfunction. He first notes which functions contribute to the impaired test performances. Out of these he identifies which if any functions or functional systems are *consistently* associated with lowered test scores, for these are the possible behavioral correlates of an organic brain condition. When the pattern of lowered test scores does not appear to be consistently associated with a single pattern of intellectual dysfunction, then the discrepant scores can be attributed to psychogenic, developmental, or chance deviations.

Reliable diagnostic assessment based on impairment patterns requires a fairly broad review of functions (Harrower, 1965). This is particularly true when the impairment is relatively discrete, for a minor or well-circumscribed intellectual deficit may show up on only one or a very few depressed test scores if the test battery samples a narrow range of behaviors. Should this be the case, the examiner needs to give more tests to examine the implicated functions and others related to it. The examiner will then be better able to determine whether the function in question is consistently associated with defective performance, i.e., whether the disability has an organic basis. By means of the additional testing, the examiner may also be able to clarify the extent to which the defect is discrete or overlaps other functions (Milner and Teuber, 1968).

By and large, the use of pattern analysis has been confined to Wechsler subtests because of their obvious statistical comparability. However, by converting different kinds of test scores into comparable score units, the examiner can compare data from many different kinds of tests in a systematic manner, permitting the analysis of patterns formed by the scores of tests from many sources. Many neuropsychologists using the Halstead-Reitan test battery (see pp. 440–443) augment the Wechsler subtest score pattern with scores of the other tests in the Halstead-Reitan battery by converting the scores to the T-score scale (Kiernan and Matthews, 1975; Lewinsohn, 1973; Reed and Reitan, 1963). Lewinsohn also converts the scores of a number of memory, learning, and visual pattern recognition tests he devised into T-scores.

Charting the test performance graphically may enable the examiner to perceive performance patterns and trends more readily. A. E. Popov and I have developed a chart on which test performance levels can be laid out graphically. It is particularly useful when there are more than a handful of test scores and they do not all lie within a relatively narrow ability range. This technique for organizing the neuropsychological examination data also lends itself well to communicating the information to clinicians who are not familiar with psychological tests (see Fig. 6-2).

Most test performances can be charted easily. First the examiner converts the score to its appropriate ability level. This is a simple and direct procedure when the score comes from a standard test of intellectual ability (see pp. 133–134). Some tests present a conversion problem, particularly those that have been developed as neuropsychological screening tests in which the range of score classifications may be no more than "normal," "borderline" or "questionable," and "defective." The problem of fitting such a three-point classification system to a seven category scale can usually be solved by arbitrarily dividing the highest classification into "high average" and "average," and the middle classification into "low average" and "borderline," and assigning the obtained score to an ability level according to whether it was high or low within its classification. The lowest classification in each system, "defective," retains the same meaning in either system. Since bright patients generally tend to make better scores than duller ones when the involved function is intact, by using this technique, the examiner can usually avoid having to chart a very bright patient's unimpaired performance as *average* when, for that patient, *average* could represent a significant degree of impairment. Another scoring problem is presented by test performances that I do not score but evaluate qualitatively, such as the bicycle drawing test. Experience with these tests and familiarity with the literature usually enables the examiner to distinguish performances that are abnormally defective from the others and to develop standards for grading the others on a three- or four-point scale ranging from "poor" or "shoddy" through "fair" and "good" to "excellent," which grades roughly approximate ability levels from *low average* to *superior*. One other kind of scoring problem involves tests in which two classes of functions play significant roles, one of which may be intact and the other impaired. In this case, I chart the test twice, at the appropriate level for each of the functions [see "A(WAIS)" and "WCS," Fig. 6-2]. When all the functions involved in a test performance are intact, the patient's responses tend to be consistent and the test is usually charted only once under the most predominant of the functions in question.

The second step in charting test performances is to determine the predominant function(s) examined by the test. This too is a relatively simple task for most tests. Tests involving verbal skills, such as vocabulary, reading, or sentence construction tests or tests of information or reasoning in the verbal modality, can usually be subsumed under one of the two classes of "Verbal" functions; construction tasks belong under "Visuopractic" functions; and when memory and learning are emphasized, the predominant functional category is probably one of the classes of "Memory." Tests that do not lend themselves readily to a single classification can be charted twice. For example, a drawing task involving short-term memory may be represented under the "Visuopractic" category and under "Short-term Memory."

Arithmetic tests present a special problem because several functional classes may vie for the predominant role depending both on the format of the test and the nature of the patient's disability (see pp. 120 and 204–207). However, when a disability, such as defective concentration and mental tracking, interferes with the ability to perform oral arithmetic, or a visuospatial defect prevents a mathematically knowledgeable patient from doing paper and pencil calculations correctly, I chart the test performance under both "Arithmetic" and the other significant category [see "A(WAIS)" under "Arithmetic" and "Attention, Concentration, and Tracking," Fig. 6-2].

Intellectual Performance Chart   Name_____   Date_____   Examiner_____

Function / Level of Performance	VERBAL			NONVERBAL		MEMORY		Attention Concentration Tracking	Self-Regulation	Miscellaneous
	Old Learning and Verbal Skills	Reasoning and Judgment	Arithmetic	Perception and reasoning	Visuopractic	Short-Term	Learning			
Very Superior										
Superior										
High Average	Reading Vocab[1] Spelling Functional Vocab (writing and speech)	C[3] (except proverbs)								
Average	I (WAIS + SAB)[2]	S[4] Reading Compr.[5]	A (WAIS + SAB)[6]	PC[7] Mooney[8] Rorschach WCS[9] (sort)	Lady[13] BD[14] PA[15] Bender[16] (form)	DF[21] Rey I + B[22]			WCS (shift)	
Low Average				Raven[10]	Bicycle[17] DAP[17]		Rey V	DB[24]		
Borderline Defective					Mazes[18]		Rey VI Rey V-VI			
Defective		Proverbs (WAIS + SAB)		Hooper[11] Rorschach 3 rejects[12]	OA[19] Bender (space) PPT → (R)[20]	Benton nC + nE[23]		SDMT[25] WCS A(WAIS)		
Comment										Prepared by A.E. Popov and H.D. Lezak

FIG. 6-2. Charted performance of a 27-year-old high school graduate, recently demoted from a skilled to a semi-skilled position following onset of seizures and subsequent apathy, irritability, and complaints of memory problems. As can be seen from the chart, the most impaired functions were concentration and tracking, visual and spatial organization, and visual memory with some reduction of verbal learning capacity as well. On visual reasoning and visuopractic tests, his performance tended to vary directly with the degree to which the test is structured and therefore his performance level ranged from *average* on well-structured tasks to *defective* on those requiring very much organizing activity for success. On the Wisconsin Card Sorting Test (WCS), he demonstrated both good capacity for concept formation and the ability to shift concepts appropriately; but after the third shift, he lost track of the current concept, performing poorly because of defective concentration and tracking. This pattern suggests right hemisphere involvement, probably in the parieto-temporal region. Neuroradiological tests indicated a right anterior parietal lesion which, on surgery, proved to be a slow-growing tumor.

KEY: 1. Gates-MacGinitie Reading Test, Survey F. 2. Information subtest of the Wechsler Adult Intelligence Scale (WAIS) and of the Self-Administered Battery (SAB). 3. Comprehension (WAIS). 4. Similarities (WAIS). 5. Gates-MacGinitie Reading Test. 6. Arithmetic (WAIS and SAB). 7. Picture Completion (WAIS). 8. Mooney Closure Faces Test. 9. Wisconsin Card Sorting Test. 10. Raven's Progressive Matrices. 11. Hooper Visual Organization Test. 12. No response to three of ten Rorschach cards. 13. Lady Walking in the Rain. 14. Block Design (WAIS). 15. Picture Arrangement (WAIS). 16. Bender-Gestalt Test. 17. Draw-a-Person. 18. Maze Test from the Wechsler Intelligence Scale for Children. 19. Object Assembly (WAIS). 20. Purdue Pegboard Test performance discrepancy implicated right hemisphere dysfunction. 21. Digits Forward (WAIS). 22. Rey Auditory-Verbal Learning Test—Roman numerals and B on this and other Rey notations refer to different trials of the test. 22. Benton Visual Retention Test performance was defective according to both number correct and error score. 24. Digit Span Backward. 25. Symbol Digit Modalities Test.

When used to organize graphically a large set of data about a person, this charting technique can make very evident the presence—or the absence—of clear-cut performance patterns. However, the examiner must remember that ability level categories represent only rough approximations to performance levels, that his own arbitrary and subjective judgments enter into the construction of these graphic performance charts, and that, except as noted, qualitative aspects of the test performance are represented on the chart only indirectly if at all. The relative simplicity of the chart should keep the test-wise examiner from falling into the dangerous and all too common error of confusing graphic representations of psychological test scores with reality.

Common diagnostic patterns
Some patterns of test score scatter are fairly common but are not related in any regular manner to specific etiologies. When referring to them, the examiner must remain alert to the fact that although they probably can be used to *rule in* the presence of neurological abnormalities, their absence does not *rule out* the possibility of organic changes. Neither does the appearance of any one pattern rule out the possibility that a patient has a lesion involving any given area of the brain.

Right versus left lateralization.   The critical test score discrepancies implicating one hemisphere or the other are generally between tests of verbal skills and unverbalizable perceptual-practic activities. The presence of two or three significantly depressed scores related to functions associated with one side of the brain can be considered sufficient for suspecting lateralized dysfunction if the scores on tests of functions mediated primarily by the contralateral hemisphere are within or close to the patient's normal range.

If a consistent tendency for a verbal/perceptual-practic discrepancy appears throughout the examination, then the possibility of a lateralized lesion can be considered even when the discrepancies between the higher and the lower scores are not statistically significant. Further testing, increasing the sensitivity of simple verbal or perceptual-practic tasks by adding a memory dimension or scoring for response time differentials, can sometimes bring the discrepancy into sharper focus. Qualitative aspects of the performance, such as speech hesitancies or poor organization of penciled responses on a page, may also point up the presence of a lateralized abnormality. A statistically hefty discrepancy may be due to a chance deviation when it appears for only one or two lowered scores. When this occurs, the examiner can investigate the deviation to see if it represents a consistent impairment tendency by giving one or two more tests of the same function as were involved on the tests on which the patient received the low scores.

A concomitant disability can mask the differential effects of a lateralized lesion. This problem is common in older people. Among people under 60, it may occur when alcoholism or prior head injuries complicate the etiological picture.

When the lesion is in the minor hemisphere, and the dominant hemisphere is intact, scores of tests that include both verbal functions and immediate memory or concentration may also be low, whereas scores on tests of practic skills that do not require much immediate memory or concentration will not appear depressed relative to the verbal test scores. Patients whose specific defects are verbal may also have low scores on perceptual-practic tests when their activity rate has slowed so much that they lose test score points, even on tasks they can perform very well. Motor slowing or memory and concentration problems can also make specific deficits appear to be worse than they are. Careful inspection of the disability pattern and evaluation of the qualitative aspects of the performance will usually clarify the sources of the test score deviations.

Anterior versus posterior effects. As a general rule, postcentral lesions are associated with specific sensory or perceptual deficits or both. Lesions that do not involve the postcentral cortex are unlikely to produce specific sensory or perceptual disturbances. Motor dysfunctions and control problems are more apt to show up when lesions are precentral.

Focal versus diffuse effects. Focal (concentrated in one place) lesions of the brain typically produce relatively circumscribed and only partial intellectual losses. The simplest and most telling evidence of a focal lesion is lateralization; if the impairment pattern implicates functions associated with only one hemisphere, then in all probability, the condition is due to a discrete localized lesion. It may be more difficult to identify a focal lesion correctly if it involves both hemispheres, particularly if it is relatively large, extends into subcortical areas, or produces intracranial pressure. The intellectual effects of diffuse conditions tend to appear as nonspecific slowing; diminished ability for complex mental activities, such as reasoning, planning, and abstract conceptualization; general impairment of memory, concentration, and attention; and generalized mental deterioration (see pp. 153–154).

Integrated Interpretation

Pattern analysis is insufficient to deal with the numerous exceptions to characteristic patterns, with the many rare or idiosyncratically manifested neurological conditions, and with the effects on test performance of the complex interaction between the patient's intellectual status, his emotional and social adjustment, and his appreciation of his brain damage. For the examination to supply answers to many of the diagnostic questions and most of the treatment and planning questions requires integration of all the data—from tests, observations made in the course of the examination, and the history of the problem.

Many conditions do not lend themselves to pattern analysis beyond the use of large and consistent test score discrepancies to implicate brain damage. This is particularly the case with head injuries in which neither the location nor the extent of the damage can be definitively determined before autopsy and with malignant tumors, which are unlikely to follow a regular pattern of growth and spread. In order to determine which functions are involved and the extent of their involvement, it is usually necessary to evaluate the qualitative aspects of the patient's performance very carefully for evidence of complex or subtle aberrations that betray damage in some hitherto unsuspected area of the brain. Such painstaking scrutiny is often not as necessary when dealing with a fairly typical stroke patient, for instance, or a patient whose disease generally follows a well-known and regular course.

Test scores alone do not provide much information about the emotional impact of the patient's disease on his intellectual functioning. However, his behavior during the test is likely to reveal a great deal about how he is reacting to his disabilities and how these reactions in turn affect the efficiency of his performance. The common emotional reactions of brain damaged patients tend to affect their intellectual functioning adversely. The most prevalent and most profoundly handicapping of these are anxiety and depression. Euphoria and carelessness, while much less distressing to the patient, can also seriously interfere with full expression of a patient's abilities.

Brain damaged patients have other characteristic problems that generally do not depress test scores but must be taken into account in rehabilitation planning. These are motivational and control problems that show up in an inability to organize, to react spontaneously, to initiate goal-directed behavior, or to carry out a course of action independently. They are rarely reflected in test scores since almost all tests are well-structured and administered by an examiner who plans, initiates, and conducts the examination. Yet no matter how well the patient does on tests, if he cannot develop or carry out his own course of action, he is incompetent for all practical purposes. Such problems become apparent during careful examination, but they can only be reported descriptively; neither numbers nor ability levels tell anything about them.

7
DIAGNOSTIC ISSUES

A neuropsychological evaluation may be sought at any stage of the diagnostic process, from the time a brain disorder is first suspected to long after signs, symptoms, and laboratory studies have confirmed a diagnostic impression. Diagnostic questions are generally of two types—"*What* kind of condition does the patient have?" and "*How* is the condition manifested?"

Comparison of the patient's test performance with test and behavioral norms usually satisfies questions regarding the presence of organicity unless the diagnostic picture is complicated by a functional disorder or the changes of advancing age. Answers to questions about the degree of incapacitation, the nature of the disability, or the character of the patient's adaptation to his impairments require an understanding of the variables that affect the expression of brain damage.

VARIABLES AFFECTING THE EXPRESSION OF BRAIN DAMAGE

Like all other psychological phenomena, behavioral changes that follow brain injury are determined by multiple factors. The size, location, and kind of lesion certainly contribute significantly to the altered behavior pattern. Other important predisposing variables include the duration of the condition, the patient's age at the onset of the organic disorder, his pattern of cerebral dominance, his life situation, and his psychological makeup. Slight differences in the organization of brain function between the sexes have also been suggested (Lansdell, 1970, 1971; McGlone, 1976). As a rule, the more severe the cerebral insult, the less influence premorbid personality, ability, and skills exert on the behavioral manifestations of brain injury (Hillbom, 1960).

Diffuse and Focal Effects

The concepts of "diffuse" and "focal" brain injury are more clear-cut than their manifestations. Diffuse brain diseases do not affect all brain structures equally, and it is rare to find a focal injury in which some diffuse repercussions do not take place either temporarily or ultimately (Goodglass, 1973; A. Smith, 1975; Teuber, 1969).

Diffuse brain injury typically results from a widespread condition such as infection, *anoxia* (lack of oxygen), arteriosclerosis, intoxication (including alcohol intoxication, drug overdose, and drug reactions), and certain degenerative, metabolic, and nutritional diseases. Diffuse effects may also occur in closed-head injuries, particularly under conditions of fast acceleration or deceleration as in motor vehicle accidents or falls (Oppenheimer, 1968; W. R. Russell and A. Smith, 1961; Strich, 1969). Some aftereffects reflecting diffuse brain dysfunction are common to most of these injuries. These include memory, attention, and concentration disabilities; impaired higher level and complex reasoning resulting in conceptual concretism and inflexibility; and general response slowing. Affective dulling and disinhibition may also be present (McFarland, 1952; Wechsler, 1963). These symptoms tend to be most severe immediately after an injury or the sudden onset of a disease or they may first appear as subtle and transient problems that increase in duration and severity as a progressive condition worsens.

Trauma, space-displacing lesions (e.g., tumors, blood vessel malformations), localized infections, and cerebrovascular accidents (e.g., strokes, aneurysms) cause most focal brain injuries. Some systemic conditions too, such as a severe thiamine deficiency, may devastate discrete brain structures and result in a predominantly focal symptom picture (Bannister, 1973). Occasionally focal signs of brain damage accompany an acute exacerbation of a systemic disorder, such as diabetes mellitus, confusing the diagnostic picture until the underlying disorder is brought under control and the organic symptoms subside. Symptoms of diffuse damage almost always accompany focal lesions of sudden onset. Initially, cloudy consciousness, confusion, and generally slowed and inconsistent responsiveness may obscure focal residual effects so that clear-cut evidence of the focal lesion may not appear until later (W. R. Russell and A. Smith, 1961). On the other hand, the first sign of a progressive localized lesion such as a growing tumor may be some slight, specific behavioral impairment that becomes more pronounced and inclusive. Ultimately, diffuse behavioral effects resulting from increased intracranial pressure and circulatory changes may obliterate the specific defects due to local tissue damage.

Focal lesions can often be distinguished by lateralizing signs since most discrete lesions involve only one hemisphere. When the lesion extends to both hemispheres, the damage is apt to be asymmetrical, resulting in a predominance of one lateralized symptom pattern. In general, when one function or several related specific functions are significantly impaired while other functions remain intact and alertness, response rate, delayed memory, and orientation are relatively unaffected, the examiner can safely conclude that the cerebral insult is focal.

Nature of the Lesion

Differences in the nature of the lesion also affect the symptom picture. Where there has been a clean loss of cortical tissue, as a result of surgery or missile wounds, those functions specifically mediated by the lost tissue can no longer be performed. When white matter has also been removed, some disconnection effects may also occur. In short, when the lesion involves tissue removal with little or no diseased tissue remaining, repercussions on other, anatomically unrelated functions tend to be minimal and the potential for rehabilitation runs high (Newcombe, 1969; Teuber, 1969).

Dead or diseased brain tissue, which alters the neurochemical and electrical status of the brain, produces more extensive and severe behavioral changes than a clean surgical or missile wound that removes tissue (Deutsch, 1960; Diller, 1962; Weiskrantz, 1968). Thus the functional impairments associated with diseased or damaged tissue, as in strokes or closed-head injuries, tend to result in behavioral distortions involving other functions, to have high level cognitive repercussions and to affect personality. Hécaen (1964) found that fully two-thirds of his frontal lobe tumor patients presented with confused states and dementia, whereas patients who had had even extensive loss of prefrontal tissue were apt to be properly oriented and to suffer little or no impairment of reasoning, memory, or learned skills. *Distance effects,* technically known as *diaschisis,* may also occur as diseased or damaged tissue disrupts cerebral functions localized far from the site of the injury (A. Smith, 1975). The presence of diseased or dead brain tissue can also affect the circulation and metabolism of surrounding tissue both immediately and long after the cerebral insult has occurred, with continuing psychological dysfunction of the surrounding areas (Hillbom, 1960; A. Smith, 1960; Woltman, 1942).

Dynamic aspects of the lesion contribute to behavioral changes too (Fitzhugh et al., 1961; Reitan, 1966; A. Smith, 1966a). A fast-growing tumor is more likely to be accompanied by swelling of the surrounding tissues resulting in a greater amount of behavioral dysfunction with more diffuse effects than a slow-growing tumor. Other secondary effects of tissue damage, such as build-up of scar tissue, microscopic blood vessel changes or cell changes due to lack of oxygen following interference with the blood supply often complicate the symptom picture (Luria, 1966; A. R. Taylor, 1969; A. R. Taylor and Bell, 1966; Woltman, 1942).

Subcortical Involvement

Subcortical damage associated with a cortical lesion also contributes to the amount and kind of impairment the patient suffers. It compounds the symptom picture with the added effects of disrupted pathways or damaged lower integration centers. The depth and extent to which a cortical lesion involves subcortical tissue will alter the behavioral correlates of similar cortical lesions. Depth of lesion has been clearly related to the severity of impairment of verbal skills (Newcombe, 1969). The varieties of *anosognosia* (impaired awareness of one's own disability or disabled body parts, associated with right parietal lobe damage) illustrate the differences in the behavioral correlates of similarly situated cortical lesions with different amounts of subcortical involvement. Gerstmann (1942) reported three forms of this problem and their subcortical correlates: (1) Anosognosia with neglect of the paralyzed side, in which the patient essentially ignores the fact of his paralysis although he may have some vague awareness that he is disabled, is associated with lesions of the right optic region of the thalamus. (2) Anosognosia with amnesia for or lack of recognition of the affected limbs or side occurs with lesions penetrating only to the transmission fibers from the thalamus to the parietal cortex. (3) Anosognosia with such "positive" psychological symptoms as confabulation or delusions (in contrast to the unelaborated denial of illness or nonrecognition of body parts of the other two forms of this condition) is more likely to occur with lesions limited to the parietal cortex.

Subcortical lesions may cut cortical pathways, disconnecting one or another cortical area from the communication network of the brain. These disconnection problems can simulate the effects of a cortical lesion or produce an atypical symptom pattern. Even a small subcortical lesion can result in significant behavioral changes if it interrupts a critical pathway running to or from the cortex or between two cortical areas. Cortical involvement is not necessary for a cortical area to be rendered nonfunctional. Geschwind (1965, 1972) analyzed a case in which a patient with normal visual acuity suddenly could no longer read, although he was able to copy written words. Postmortem examination revealed that an occluded artery prevented blood flow to the left visual cortex and the interhemispheric visual pathways, injuring both structures and rendering the patient blind in his right visual field. His left visual field and right visual cortex continued to register words which he could copy. However, the right visual cortex was disconnected from the left hemisphere so that this verbal information was no longer transmitted to the left hemisphere for the symbol processing necessary for verbal comprehension and therefore he could not read.

Cognitive deficits tend to appear immediately following surgery performed on the thalamus or basal ganglia for relief of the tremor and muscle rigidity of parkinsonism (Reitan, 1976; Riklan and Levita, 1969). Several days after surgery, patients may display such specific defects as a marked reduction in verbal productivity and impaired verbal fluency, perceptual organization, and concept formation. These problems are more prominent and longer lasting in patients with bilateral lesions than those with only one lesion. Months later, both patients with unilateral lesions and those with bilateral lesions are likely to have regained their preoperative status on a wide variety of psychological tests. However, patients with bilateral lesions tend to continue to exhibit some behavioral slowing and inefficiency as well as dampened initiative after specific intellectual functions have returned to their preoperative levels (Blumer and Benson, 1975). These findings suggest that the subcortical structures associated with parkinsonism may be significantly involved in the activation and expression of the higher intellectual functions that are dependent on the "integration of two or more sensorimotor modalities, contribution by cortical association areas and energization by arousal systems" (Riklan and Levita, 1969, p. 268).

Time

There probably is no such thing as a static brain disorder. We take for granted that the impact of brain tumors and deteriorating diseases on the patient's behavior is continually changing, but the dynamic nature of head traumas, strokes, and other nonprogressive conditions has often been overlooked (Scherer et al., 1955; A. Smith, 1960; Newcombe et al., 1975).

Progressive brain diseases

In progressive brain disease, behavioral deterioration tends to follow an often bumpy but fairly predictable downhill course for particular sets of functions that may deteriorate at varying rates, depending on the disease (Ajuriaguerra et al., 1966; G. C. Fisher, 1958; Klebanoff et al., 1954). When the diagnosis is known, the question is not so much *what* will happen, but *when* it will happen. Past observations provide some rules of thumb to guide clinicians in their predictions. The clinical rule of thumb for predicting the rate of mental decline holds that conditions that are progressing rapidly are likely to continue to worsen at a rapid rate whereas slow progressions tend to remain slow.

For instance, most patients with multiple sclerosis can expect that, ultimately, higher level mental activities, vision, and motor functions will deteriorate. The rate at which the disease progresses in the early stages of the illness gives some indication as to whether these disabilities will occur in a few years or a few decades, for the rapid appearance of serious symptoms generally presages a rapid decline, and a slower course with long periods of remission is a favorable sign that deterioration will be slow and perhaps less profound (Grinker and Sahs, 1966; McAlpine et al., 1972). Similar progression patterns obtain in other degenerative disorders such as Huntington's chorea or Alzheimer's disease, although in these two conditions the time span from the appearance of the first symptom to severe disablement is more on the order of two to five or six years (English, 1942; Merritt, 1973).

Patients with newly diagnosed progressive brain disease may benefit from an early "baseline" assessment of their psychological status with one or two reexaminations at two- to four- or six-month intervals. Such a longitudinal study can provide a rough basis for forecasting the rate at which mental deterioration is likely to take place, to aid the patient and his family in their planning for his care.

Predicting the course of the behavioral effects of a brain tumor differs from making predictions about other progressively deteriorating diseases. Biopsy, performed in the course of surgery, takes some of the guesswork out of estimating the rate of progression, for different kinds of brain tumors grow at fairly predictable rates. The severity of the behavioral disorder, too, bears some relationship to the type of tumor; extensive edema, for instance, is more likely to accompany astrocytomas and glioblastomas than other tumorous growths and thus involve more of the surrounding and distant tissue (A. Smith, 1966b). On the other hand, the *direction* of growth is not predictable so that the neurologist cannot forewarn the patient or his family about *what* behavioral changes they can expect as the disease runs its course, short of terminal apathy, stupor, and coma.

Nonprogressive brain disorders
In this category can be found all brain disorders that have an end to their direct action on the brain. Head trauma, aneurysms, *anoxia* due to heart stoppage or the effect of anesthesia during surgery, infectious processes that are ultimately halted, temporary toxic conditions, and nutritional deficiencies are the usual sources of "nonprogressive" brain damage. Strokes may come under this heading, for the typical stroke results from a single cerebrovascular event that has a fairly predictable course that is similar in many respects to the course of other nonprogressive brain diseases. Strokes do not necessarily reoccur; or if there is another one, it may take place in a different part of the brain. However, once a patient has suffered a

stroke, the likelihood of reoccurrence is sufficiently great so that in some patients stroke can be considered a progressive brain condition in which the ongoing deterioration is irregularly slowed by periods of partial recovery.

Psychological characteristics of acute brain conditions.   With nonprogressive or single event brain disorders, the recency of the insult may be the most critical factor determining the patient's psychological status (Fitzhugh et al., 1961; Gronwall and Wrightson, 1974; W. R. Russell and Smith, 1961; Scherer et al., 1953). This is particularly evident in those stroke or trauma patients who are comatose or semiconscious for hours, days, and sometimes weeks as an immediate aftermath of cerebral damage. The duration of impaired consciousness following trauma generally bears a direct relationship to the rapidity and extent of ultimate recovery (Ruesch and Moore, 1943; A. Smith, 1961). The usual criterion of impaired consciousness in responsive patients is the presence of posttraumatic amnesia (PTA), which results from an inability to store memories of recent events.

Apart from specific functional defects that vary from patient to patient with the site and extent of the lesion, the most common behavioral characteristics of an acute brain condition in conscious patients are impaired retention, concentration and attention, emotional lability, and fatigability. The disruption of memory functions may be so severe that months later the patient can recall little or nothing of the acute stage of his condition although he appeared to be fully conscious at the time. So much of a patient's behavioral reintegration usually takes place the first month or two following a brain injury that psychological test data obtained during this time may be obsolete within weeks or even days. The rapidity with which change usually occurs plus the patient's great vulnerability to fatigue and emotional upset make premature testing inadvisable. As a general rule, formal psychological testing should not be initiated before six, or even better, eight weeks after the patient regains consciousness.

Psychological characteristics of chronic brain conditions.   Even after the acute stage has passed, the patient's condition rarely remains static. Intellectual functions, particularly those involving immediate memory, attention and concentration, and specific disabilities associated with the site of the lesion generally continue to improve markedly during the first six months or year, and improvement may go on for a decade and more following a stroke or other single event injury to the brain (Blakemore and Falconer, 1967; Diller, 1968; Newcombe et al., 1975; A. Smith, 1964). However, improvement rarely amounts to full recovery, even when the insult may appear to be slight (Milner, 1969; Weinstein and Teuber, 1957).

Conversely, some functions that appear to be intact in the acute stage may deteriorate gradually over the succeeding months and years (Hillbom, 1960; A. Smith, 1964). Behavioral deterioration generally involves the highest levels of intellectual activity having to do with mental flexibility and reasoning and judgment about abstract issues or complex social problems. It may be compounded by diminished self-control with consequent dilapidation of personal habits and performance standards (Lezak, 1975; McReynolds and Weide, 1960). These behavioral alterations have been associated with the build-up of scar tissue, secondary nerve fiber degeneration, and other local tissue changes involving blood supply and metabolic efficiency (A. Smith, 1960; Woltman, 1942). Brain injury also renders the patient more vulnerable to other brain diseases, such as stroke (Anttinen, 1960; Hillbom, 1960).

Few symptoms distinguish the behavior of persons suffering chronic brain damage of adult onset with sufficient regularity to be considered characteristic. The two most common complaints are fatigue and poor memory. Rest and a paced activity schedule are the patient's best antidotes to debilitating fatigue. Patients who read and write and are capable of self-discipline can aid their failing memory with notebooks; some patients have gained short-term improvement with mnemonic training, but the gains tend not to last for even a week (Lewinsohn et al., 1975).

However, the reality of memory complaints is not always apparent, even on careful examination. When this occurs, these complaints may reflect the patient's feelings of impairment more than an objective deficit. Care must be taken to distinguish true memory defects from attention or concentration problems, for patients may easily interpret the effects of distractibility as a memory problem. A common chronic problem is an abiding sense of unsureness about mental experiences. Patients express this problem indirectly with hesitancies and statements of self-doubt or bewilderment; they rarely understand that it is as much a natural consequence of brain injury as their fatigue. Reassurance that guesses and solutions that come to mind first are generally correct, and advice to treat the sense of unsureness as an annoying symptom rather than a signal that he must heed, often relieves the patient's distress.

Depression troubles most adults who were not rendered grossly defective by their injuries. It is usually first experienced within the year following the onset of brain damage. The severity and duration of the depressive reaction varies greatly among patients, depending on a host of factors both intrinsic and extrinsic to their brain condition (Merskey and Woodforde, 1972). Patients whose permanent disabilities are considerable and who have experienced no depression have either lost some capacity for self-appreciation and reality testing, or are denying their problems. In both cases, rehabilitation prospects are significantly reduced, for the patient must have a fairly realistic understanding of his strengths and limitations to cooperate with and benefit from any rehabilitation program. For most patients, the depression resolves or becomes muted with time. Some patients remain chronically depressed and, when their emotional distress is severe, may become suicidal (M. W. Buck, 1968).

Heightened irritability is another common complaint of both patients and their families. A greatly—and permanently—decreased tolerance for alcohol should also be anticipated following brain injury of any consequence.

Age at Onset

Although the relative recency of an acute brain condition has much to do with its impact on behavior, over all, the age of the patient when he incurs a nonprogressive brain injury is probably the greatest single factor determining how much recovery of psychological function can be anticipated (W. R. Russell, 1934; Sands et al., 1969; A. Smith, 1960, 1975). Severely injured adults in their late teens and early twenties often display remarkable recuperation both of specific functions and in their capacity for independent living. However, similarly injured patients over the age of 30 are rarely capable of returning to full independence, although the older patient too may enjoy a considerable return of specific functions.

Lateral Dominance

Speech functions, which are localized on the right rather than the left side of the brain in fewer than 1% of right-handed persons, occur on the right side in almost 10% of left-handed persons (Goodglass and Quadfasel, 1954; Penfield and Roberts, 1959). Thus, the possibility is always present that the patient's speech center is not localized in the left hemisphere, in which case there may be corresponding alterations in the location of cortical zones mediating auxiliary language and nonverbal functions (Miller, 1972). Estimates of the frequency of left hemisphere dominant persons range from approximately 92% (Rossi and Rosadini, 1967) to 96% (Geschwind and Levitsky, 1968; Zangwill, 1960). Rossi and Rosadini found that five of their 84 subjects were right dominant whereas two had equivocal dominance.

There are methods for determining dominance with considerable confidence. These include injection of a barbiturate directly into the common or internal carotid artery which creates a transient aphasia when the dominant hemisphere is inactivated, and direct electrical stimulation of the exposed cortex of patients prepared for brain surgery. In most cases, clinicians who want to determine the patient's dominant hemisphere do not have recourse to such exotic techniques. They may have to estimate dominance from handedness instead. Estimates of the frequency of right-handers run from 93 to 96% of the adult population, and of these, 98 to 99% have their dominant hemisphere on the left (Penfield & Roberts, 1959). Estimates of the proportion of left-handers whose right hemisphere is dominant for speech average about 10%, although Rossi and Rosadini report that five of their seven left-handed patients had dominant right hemispheres. Thus, for most clinical purposes, the assumption that a right-handed patient's speech is localized in the left hemisphere is acceptable and probably but not necessarily correct. With left-handed patients, this assumption is also probably correct, but at a lower level of confidence.

In left-handed persons, the questions of behavioral sidedness and of hemispheric dominance are often not clear-cut (Annett, 1967; Branch et al., 1964). Whereas right-handed people consistently tend to prefer the right eye for looking through a peephole, the right foot for kicking a ball, the right leg for leaning, and so on (Kreindler et al.,

1964), left-handed people show more diversity in right-left prefer-ences for different parts of the body and different activities (Hécaen and Ajuriaguerra, 1964). Some studies suggest that persons with mixed dominance patterns tend to perform less well than un-equivocal right-handers on tests involving visuospatial skills, al-though verbal performance levels do not differ between these two groups (Miller, 1971).

In left-handed and ambidextrous patients, aphasia occurs with greater frequency than in right-handers because both right and left hemisphere lesions may result in an aphasic condition (Humphrey and Zangwill, 1952), but it is also much more likely to be mild or transient (Gloning and Quatember, 1966), suggesting bilateral localization of speech functions. Lateralization of verbal functions may also play a role in determining the severity of deficits resulting from injury to one side of the head. Ten to 20 years post injury, right-handed persons who had sustained right-sided head injuries tend to perform more poorly on verbal fluency, memory and learning and several visuospatial tasks than do right-handed patients whose similar injuries were to the left side of the head. This difference may be due to a *contrecoup* (injury to an organ due to its rebound from a direct blow to the side of the organ opposite to the contrecoup lesion) effect (E. Smith, 1974).

Premorbid Psychological Status

Studies of head injury well support the observation that, "It is not only the kind of injury that matters, but the kind of head" (Symonds, 1937). Prior intellectual endowment tends to be directly related to intellectual achievement following brain damage (Chapman et al., 1958; Hillbom, 1960).

The premorbid personal and social adjustment of brain damaged patients also appears to have some effect, not only on the quality of their ultimate adjustment but on the amount of gain they make (Gloning et al., 1968; Symonds and Russell, 1943; A. E. Walker and Jablon, 1959). Premorbid personality contributes both directly and indirectly to the kind of adjustment a patient makes following brain injury (A. L. Anderson, 1950).

Direct effects are fairly obvious since premorbid personality characteristics are generally not so much changed as exaggerated by brain injury. Tendencies to dependent behavior, hypochondriasis, passivity, perfectionism, irresponsibility, etc., can be major obstacles to the patient whose rehabilitation depends on active relearning of old skills and reintegration of old habit patterns while he copes with a host of unrelenting and often humiliating frustrations.

The indirect effects of premorbid adjustment may not become apparent until the handicapped patient needs emotional support and acceptance in a protective but not institutional living situation. Patients who have conducted their lives in an emotionally stable and mature manner are also those most likely to be supported through their critical personal and social transitions by steadfast, emotionally stable and mature family and friends. On the other hand, patients with marked premorbid personality disorders or asocial tendencies are more apt to lack a social support system when they need it most. Many of this latter group have been social isolates, and others are quickly rejected by immature or recently acquired spouses, alienated children, and opportunistic or irresponsible friends who want nothing of the dependent patient who can no longer cater to their needs. The importance of a stable home environment to rehabilitation often becomes inescapable when determining whether a patient can return to the community or must be placed in a nursing home or institution in lieu of any alternative living situation.

PROBLEMS OF DIFFERENTIAL DIAGNOSIS

Many of the questions asked of the neuropsychologist concern problems of differential diagnosis. The most common ones, the ones in which differential diagnosis is the central issue, have to do with the possibility that brain disease may underlie an emotional or personality disturbance, or contribute to a premature senility.

Most often, these questions of differential diagnosis are asked as "either-or" problems even when lip service is given to the likelihood of interaction between the effects of a brain lesion and the patient's emotional predisposition or advanced years. In perplexing cases of differential diagnosis, a precise determination may not be possible unless an ongoing disease process eventually submerges the functional aspects of the patient's confusing behavior or "hard" neurological signs show up. The frequency with which neurological and neuropsychological diagnostic techniques mistakenly classify both organic and functional behavioral disturbances demonstrates how difficult differential diagnosis can be in some cases, particularly since the populations used in studies of diagnostic accuracy have already been identified by other means (Spreen and Benton, 1965; Filskov and Goldstein, 1974; Woody, 1968). Large test batteries that serve as multiple successive sieves tend to reduce but still do not eliminate neuropsychodiagnostic errors (K. Adams et al., 1975; Benton and Van Allen, 1972).

Organic and Functional Disorders

Problems of differential diagnosis involving the question of organic versus functional disorder tend to arise from two different referral sources. Neurologists and other medical specialists seek neuropsychological assistance when they suspect the patient's complaints have a significant functional—usually neurotic or personality— component. Professionals working with emotionally or behaviorally disturbed patients refer them when there appears to be a likelihood that the patient's psychiatric disturbance has an organic basis.

Neurotic and personality disorders
Patients who complain of headaches, dizziness, "blackout" spells, memory loss, mental slowing, peculiar sensations, or weakness and clumsiness usually find their way to a neurologist. These complaints can be very difficult to diagnose and treat: symptoms are often subjective and wax or wane with stress or attention; with regular events such as going to work, arriving home, or family visits; or unpredictably. The patient's complaints may follow a head injury or a bout with an illness as mild as a cold or as severe as a heart attack, or they may simply occur independently. When there are objective neurological findings, they may be unrelated to the patient's complaints or, if related, insufficient to account for his distress or incapacitation. Sometimes treatment—medication, psychotherapy, physical therapy, rest, activity, or a change in the patient's routine or living situation—will relieve the problem permanently. Sometimes relief lasts only temporarily, and the patient returns to his doctor again and again, each time getting a new drug or a different regimen

that may give him respite from his complaints for a while. The temptation is great to write off patients who present these kinds of diagnostic problems or who do not respond to treatment as neurotic, inadequate, or dependent personalities, or—if there is a pending law suit or disability claim—as compensation seekers.

However, many very serious and sometimes treatable neurological diseases first present with vague, often transient symptoms that can worsen with stress and temporarily diminish or even disappear altogether with symptomatic or psychological treatment. The first symptoms of multiple sclerosis and early cerebrovascular arteriosclerosis, for instance, are often transient, lasting hours or days, and may appear as reports of dizziness, weakness, ill-defined peculiar sensations, and fatigue. Diagnostically confusing complaints can herald a tumor and persist for months or even years before clear diagnostic signs emerge. Vague complaints are also common to post-concussion patients who may suffer headaches as well (Friedman, 1969; Merskey and Woodforde, 1972). Early diagnosis of neurological disease can be complicated by the fact that these are the same complaints expressed by many persons for whom functional disorders serve as a life style or a neurotic reaction to stress. Particularly when the patient's complaints and his reactions to them appear to be typically neurotic or suggestive of a character disorder may his neurological complaints have been discounted.

Neuropsychological opinions about the etiology of these symptom pictures rely on criteria for both functional and organic disorders. An inappropriate—usually bland or indifferent—reaction to the complaints, symbolic meaningfulness of the symptoms, secondary gains, perpetuation of a dependent or irresponsible life style, a close association between stress and the appearance of the patient's problem, and an unlikely or inconsistently manifested pattern of psychological impairment suggest psychogenic contributions to the patient's problems, regardless of his neurological status (Lynn et al., 1945). Occasionally, a happily unconcerned patient will maintain frankly bizarre and medically unlikely symptoms with such good will that their hysterical origin is indisputable. With more commonplace aches, weaknesses, and sensory disabilities, the patient's attitude of *la belle indifférence* may be the first clue to a conversion hysteria. Medical folklore has held that only women can suffer a conversion hysteria (*hysteria* means uterus in Greek, and was originally thought to result from a displacement of that organ). Occasionally this traditional thinking still leads to a misdiagnosis of an hysterical reaction in a male patient. Cheerfully unrealistic attitudes about visual or motor defects or debilitating mental changes may also mislead the examiner when they mask an appropriate underlying depressive reaction from the patient himself as well as others and result in an erroneous functional diagnosis.

Complaints of headache, dizziness, fatigue, and weakness can be accurate reports of physiological states or the patient's interpretation of an underlying depression. Still, the presence of depression in the absence of "hard" findings is not in itself evidence that the patient's condition is functional, for the depressive reaction may have resulted from the patient's awareness or experience of as yet subtle mental or physical symptoms of early neurological disease.

Identification of organicity in the differential diagnostic process is no different than when the diagnostic questions call for a simple yes or no. An organic behavior aberration may appear on neuropsychological examination as a single sign, such as rotation on a visuopractic task or perseverative writing, an otherwise inexplicable low test score or a few low scores on tests involving the same function, or a pattern of intellectual impairment that makes neuroanatomical or neuropsychological sense. Evidence of lateralized impairment lends strong support to the possibility of organic involvement. Should any of the behavioral aberrations associated with organicity be consistently evident, the examiner can suspect an organic brain disorder *regardless* of how much of the patient's problem is clearly functional in nature.

It is rare to find a case in which the behavioral manifestations of brain disease are uncomplicated by the patient's emotional reactions to the mental changes and the consequent personal and social disruptions he is experiencing (Small, 1973). As a rule, only the most simplistic or severely impaired persons will present clear-cut symptoms of brain damage without some functional contribution to the symptom picture.

Psychotic disturbances
An organic brain disorder can also complicate or imitate severe functional behavioral disturbances (Wahl et al., 1967). The primary symptoms may involve marked mood or character change, intellec-

tual confusion or disorientation, disordered thinking, delusions, hallucinations, bizarre ideation, ideas of reference or persecution, or any other of the thought and behavior disturbances typically associated with schizophrenia or the affective psychoses. The neuropsychological identification of an organic component in a severe behavior disturbance relies on the same criteria as are used to determine whether neurotic complaints have an organic etiology. Here too, a pattern of intellectual dysfunction selectively involving predominantly lateralized abilities and skills makes a strong case for organicity, as does an organic pattern of memory impairment in which recent memory is more severely affected than remote memory, or a pattern of lowered scores on tests involving attention functions and new learning relative to scores on tests of knowledge and skill. The inconsistent or erratic expression of cognitive defects suggests a functional disturbance. Organic behavioral disturbances are not likely to have symbolic meaning (Malamud, 1975).

Identifying those psychotic conditions that have an organic component is often more difficult than distinguishing neurotic conditions or character disorders from symptoms of brain damage because some functional psychoses are as likely to disrupt attention, concentration, and mental tracking as are some organic conditions. Functional psychoses may also disrupt perceptual, thinking, and response patterns as severely as organic conditions so that a single test sign or markedly lower score does not identify the organic patient in a psychotic population with the same degree of reliability as does a similar sign or lowered score among neurotic patients. Thus, in attempting to determine whether a psychotically disturbed patient is brain damaged, lacking a clear-cut pattern of lateralized dysfunction or organic memory impairment, the examiner will require a number of signs or a pattern of lowered test scores before concluding that brain damage is probably present.

Neuropsychological differentiation of organic and functional disorders tends to be easier when the condition is acute and to become increasingly difficult with chronicity for institutionalization tends to have a behaviorally leveling effect on organic and functional patients alike. The identification by neuropsychological techniques alone of long-term institutionalized patients with organic disorders in a chronic mental hospital population is often little more than a chance operation (DeWolfe et al., 1971; Watson et al., 1968). In some cases, the history is useful in differentiating the organic from the purely functionally disturbed patients. Organic conditions are more apt to appear during or following physical stress such as an illness, intoxication, head trauma, or some form of severe malnutrition. Emotional or situational stress more often precedes functionally disturbed behavior disorders. Unfortunately for diagnosticians, stress does not always come neatly packaged, for an illness that is sufficiently severe to precipitate an organic psychosis, or a head injury incurred in a family feud or a traffic accident, is also emotionally upsetting. Among diagnosed schizophrenic patients, those who tend to display symptoms of anxiety and emotionality are less likely to appear organic on neuropsychological testing than are the more apathetic patients and those with perceptual disorders (Lilliston, 1973).

The behavioral symptoms of some organic conditions are easily misinterpreted. Unlike many postcentral lesions that announce themselves with distinctive lateralized behavioral changes or highly specific and identifiable intellectual defects, the behavioral effects of frontal lobe tumors may be practically indistinguishable from progressive character or behavioral disturbances. Hécaen (1974) found that 67% of patients with frontal lobe tumors exhibit confused states and dementia, and almost 40% have mood and character disturbances. The confusion tends to be relatively mild and is often limited to time disorientation; the dementia, too, is not severe and may appear as general slowing and apathy which can be easily confused with chronic depression. Euphoria, irritability, and indifference resulting in unrealistically optimistic or socially crude behavior may give the appearance of a psychiatric disturbance, particularly when compounded by mild confusion or dullness. Tests of tracking behavior, motor and conceptual flexibility, response control, and verbal fluency and productivity may help identify those psychiatric patients who have frontal lobe involvement.

Another difficult to diagnose group is that of psychiatric patients with suspected temporal lobe lesions. These patients tend to be erratically and irrationally disruptive or to exhibit marked personality changes or wide mood swings (Pincus and Tucker, 1974). Severe temper or destructive outbursts, or hallucinations and bizarre ideation may punctuate periods of rational and adequately controlled behavior, sometimes unpredictably and sometimes in response to stress. Positive neuropsychological test results may provide clues to the nature of the disturbance when EEG or neurological studies do not. Memory for auditory and visual, symbolic and nonsymbolic, material should be reviewed as well as complex visual pattern perception and logical—propositional—reasoning.

Organicity and Old Age

Along with the "normal" mental decline of advancing years, there is an increased incidence of abnormal brain conditions (Kay, 1972; Malamud, 1972; Wang, 1973). The similarity between the patterns of intellectual change associated with senility and with diffuse brain disease has pointed toward some similarity in the anatomical and physiological changes that underlie both symptom pictures (G. Goldstein and Shelly, 1975; Reed and Reitan, 1963). Determining whether the mental slowing and dulling experienced by an elderly person represents the effects of the "normal" aging process or of an abnormal brain condition amounts to determining the extent to which the older person's mental disabilities either exceed those expected for his years or differ from the normal aging pattern (Bolton et al., 1966).

The pattern of normal decline is marked by both intellectual strengths and weaknesses (Baer, 1972). Most notable among retained abilities are verbal skills (Birren, 1963; Wechsler, 1958; M. Williams, 1970b). Not only do aging persons retain verbal skills and the ability to solve familiar, verbally presented problems—as shown by steady performance levels on Wechsler Comprehension, Arithmetic, and Similarities subtests—but some verbal skill scores, such as Vocabulary, continue to increase with age (G. Goldstein and Shelly, 1973; Traxler, 1972). Remote memory is also preserved in normal senescence, as are well-automatized elementary perceptual and motor skills (Ajuriaguerra et al., 1966; Ben-Yishay et al., 1971; Inglis, 1957; Reitan, 1967). Contrary to conventional belief, normal aging processes do not affect the immediate memory span (G. Goldstein and Shelly, 1973; M. Williams, 1970b); lowered Wechsler Digit Span subtest scores at older age levels result mainly in a greatly shortened span of recall for Digits Backwards, reflecting impaired concentration and mental tracking.

The normal intellectual decline associated with old age shows up most strikingly in four areas of intellectual activity:

(1) Memory of the recent past and learning ability tend to deteriorate with age and are among the most pronounced symptoms of senile dementia (Eysenck, 1945a; Hulicka, 1966; Inglis, 1957). Tests of delayed memory (M. Williams, 1970b) and rote learning tasks (Traxler, 1972) demonstrate this impairment clearly and help to illuminate the contrast between defective learning ability and a relatively intact immediate memory in a normally aging person. When senility is far advanced, severe impairment of recent memory and new learning may result in the psychotic reactions and confusional states of senile dementia (Hopkins and Roth, 1953; Roth and Hopkins, 1953). Noting that most senile dementia patients display more than one kind of memory problem, R. S. Allison (1961) categorized the predominant memory defects into (a) inability to recall names of absent objects and proper names, with recall stimulated by sight or touch; (b) time disorientation, including a confused sequencing of remembered events; (c) loss of memory of the spatial relationships of previously well-known places (topographic memory); and (d) "amnestic indifference" involving failure to use memory to aid thinking, orientation, etc.

(2) Impaired ability for abstract and complex conceptualization typifies the intellectual functioning of many elderly patients (Eysenck, 1945b; Hopkins and Post, 1955; Reitan, 1967). Impaired abstract reasoning tends to be a very sensitive and often the earliest indicator of senile deterioration (Bilash and Zubek, 1960; Clark, 1960; Eysenck, 1945a; Klebanoff et al., 1954).

(3) Mental inflexibility, appearing as difficulty in adapting to new situations, solving novel problems, or changing mental set, characterizes intellectual performance failures of old age (M. Williams, 1970b).

(4) General behavioral slowing is a predominant characteristic of aging affecting perceptual, cognitive, and all psychomotor activity (Birren, 1963; Eysenck, 1945a; Jarvik, 1975). The low scores of elderly subjects on Wechsler Performance Scale subtests and on the Trail Making Test have been attributed to mental inflexibility (G. Goldstein and Shelly, 1975; Reitan, 1967), but all of these tests are also timed tests. Accurate evaluation of an elderly patient's poor performance on any timed test must depend on careful observation and analysis of the effect of time limits on the scores, for the score alone will tell little about the effects of slowing per se (Lorge, 1936).

The most common problem complicating differential diagnosis of behavioral disturbances in the elderly is depression, which can mimic or exacerbate symptoms of senile dementia. Since the depressive features of the patient's disturbance may respond to psychiatric treatment, it is important to ascertain whether depression is contributing to the patient's symptoms. Most often, the disturbed behavior of an elderly psychiatric patient has a mixed etiology in which his emotional reaction to significant losses—of loved ones, of ego-satisfying activities, and of physical and intellectual competence—interacts with the behavioral effects of physiological and anatomical brain changes to produce a complex picture of behavioral dilapidation (Post, 1975).

The problem of differential diagnosis is most difficult in the presence of "garden variety" mental deterioration associated with the diffuse brain changes that tend to accompany advancing age. The identification of focal lesions in elderly patients proceeds along the same lines as in any other age group. Evidence of lateralization or a cluster of lowered scores on functionally related tests provides the best indication of a focal brain disorder, regardless of the extent to which the patient may also be suffering from general slowing, recent memory impairment, confused orientation, defective abstracting ability, or inflexibility in thinking and attitudes.

COMPLICATING CONDITIONS ASSOCIATED WITH ORGANIC BRAIN DAMAGE

Epilepsy

Seizure disorders can arise from any condition that heightens the excitability of brain tissue (Pincus and Tucker, 1974). The diagnosis of epilepsy relates to the observed seizure behavior and, in many but not all cases, to certain characteristic EEG patterns that reflect disturbances in the electrical rhythms of the brain. Epilepsy does not refer to a single disease entity or brain condition but to a large class of symptoms that have in common some form of episodic disturbance of behavior or perception arising from hyperexcitability and hypersynchronous discharge of nerve cells in the brain. The underlying cause relates to scarring or brain damage from birth trauma or head injury, the presence of a tumor, an infection, a metabolic disorder, a cerebrovascular accident, a deteriorating brain disease, or a host of other conditions (Glaser, 1973). In many cases, no physiological or anatomical abnormality appears to account for either the seizures or epileptiform brain wave patterns, but there may be a history of epilepsy in the family. Epilepsy of unknown etiology is commonly called *idiopathic* to distinguish it from *symptomatic* epilepsy for which the etiology is known.

The class of adult seizure patients includes persons whose seizures began in infancy and those whose seizures began yesterday, older persons who spent a considerable amount of time in an institution because modern medical techniques for controlling seizures were not available in their youth, and equally old persons who have enjoyed a lifetime of independent and productive activity in spite of a seizure disorder of long standing or before developing epileptic symptoms. Thus, it is not surprising to find that the seizure condition itself has no characteristic patterning effect on intellectual functioning (Klebanoff et al., 1954; Kløve and Matthews, 1974; Schmidt and Wilder, 1968).

Despite the plethora of conditions underlying the variety of epileptic phenomena that afflict the different kinds of persons who are seizure-prone, some kinds of seizure disorders tend to be associated with certain patterns of intellectual dysfunction. Not surprisingly, intelligence test scores tend to decline with increased brain wave abnormalities, reflecting the degree of underlying brain damage (Tarter, 1972). When the seizure activity arises from a localized cortical lesion, the seizure-prone patient is likely to display a pattern of test performance like that of patients with similar lesions who are not troubled by seizures (Milner, 1969). Thus, left hemisphere epileptic foci, whether due to chronic, acute, or progressive conditions, tend to be associated with impaired verbal function (Kløve, 1959; Kløve and Fitzhugh, 1962; V. Meyer and Jones, 1957). Patients with acute or progressive right hemisphere lesions and those whose right hemisphere lesion involves the parietal lobe are likely to display the visuopractic disabilities that tend to be associated with right hemisphere lesions (Kløve, 1959; V. Meyer and Jones, 1957). The test performance patterns of chronic seizure patients with right temporal lobe lesions show little if any difference from those of normal control subjects (Kløve and Fitzhugh, 1962; Dennerll, 1964), except that seizure patients with temporal lobe lesions may experience impaired recall of narrative material regardless of the side of the lesion (Glowinski, 1973).

Disrupted attention is a common but not universal problem of epileptic patients (J. Allison et al., 1968; Lansdell and Mirsky, 1964; Mirsky et al., 1960). It has been studied by EEG monitoring of patients taking standard psychological tests (Hovey and Kooi, 1955; Kooi and Hovey, 1957). Patients with petit mal epilepsy demonstrated a marked tendency to fail to respond at the moments when the EEG was recording the characteristic slow wave of the petit mal attack. They also tended to give "don't know" responses, to ask that questions be repeated, and to answer incorrectly at such moments; only rarely (14% of the time) did they give a correct answer during a brief seizure discharge. When the performance of a memory task was punctuated by paroxysmal activity, the item was usually failed regardless of its level of difficulty. These EEG abnormalities were also significantly related to response slowing in this group of patients. Attention problems underlie the distractibility factor extracted in a factor analytic study of the WAIS performance of brain damaged patients with an epileptogenic focus in the temporal lobe (Dennerll, 1964). This factor, which is not found in similar studies of Wechsler test results of normal populations, is weighted on Digit Span, Arithmetic, and Digit Symbol and appears to be related to the size of the associated brain lesion. Attention problems are probably related to a tendency for some epileptic patients to have lower scores on Digit Span, Arithmetic, and Digit Symbol, than on Comprehension, Block Design, and Object Assembly subtests of the Wechsler Scales (Tarter, 1972). Seizure patients also tend to do poorly on those General Aptitude Test Battery motor tasks that are scored for speed and require sustained activity, but their performance did not differ significantly from the norms on tests involving the more intellectual functions (Tellegen, 1965).

Alcoholism

Chronic alcohol abuse affects certain aspects of intellectual functioning while leaving the bulk of intellectual activities relatively unimpaired (G. Goldstein and Chotlos, 1965; Kish, 1970; Tarter, 1975). The severity of the specific intellectual deficits associated with chronic alcoholism tends to be directly related to the duration of the drinking problem (Tarter and Jones, 1971; Tarter, 1973). Complete recovery of impaired functions following prolonged sobriety appears to be limited to perceptual-motor skills (Tarter and Jones, 1971); memory tends to improve significantly but less than completely (Jonsson et al., 1962).

Intellectual deficits consistently appear on tasks involving functions associated with frontal lobe activity (Parsons et al., 1972; Talland, 1965; Tarter, 1975; Vivian et al., 1973). Thus, difficulties in maintaining a cognitive set, impersistence, defective visual searching behavior, deficient motor inhibition, perseveration, loss of spatial and temporal orientation, and impaired ability to organize perceptual-motor responses and synthesize spatial elements characterize the test behavior of chronic alcoholics. This pattern of intellectual deficits resembles many of the mental changes associated with aging (G. Goldstein and Shelly, 1975; J. D. Williams et al., 1973).

The perceptual-motor problems associated with chronic alcoholism may appear at first to implicate functions associated with the nondominant hemisphere. However, analysis of the perceptual-motor failures of chronic alcoholics suggests that they involve impaired motor control and integration. Furthermore, alcoholics show no consistent performance decrement on perceptual-motor tasks or motor coordination tasks that require little or no synthesizing, organizing, or orienting activity (Hirschenfang et al., 1968; Tarter, 1975; Vivian et al., 1973). The chronic alcoholic pattern of impaired frontal lobe functions without consistent involvement of other parts of the brain fits the neuropathological evidence (EEG and autopsy studies) of frontal lobe atrophy, particularly involving the anterior portion of the lobes and anterior-basal (diencephalic) areas.

The data on memory functions of chronic alcoholics are equivocal and probably vary with the length of period of abstinence at the time of testing (Jonsson et al., 1962). Serious memory defects are not a regular feature of chronic alcoholism. When they do occur, they are probably symptomatic of other specific neurological conditions that may be present in addition to the neuropathology of chronic alcoholism.

The most striking neuropsychological deficit associated with alcoholism is the gross memory impairment of Korsakoff's psychosis. The condition typically appears after a prolonged and unremitting bout with alcohol (usually two weeks or more) during which the patient eats little if any food. It is considered to be a nutritional disorder (Merritt, 1973; Victor et al., 1971). Clinically similar memory deficits can result from a variety of other cerebral diseases (Lewis, 1961; M. Williams and Pennybacker, 1954). Virtually no one but a chronic alcoholic can maintain the level and duration of alcohol consumption necessary to produce Korsakoff's psychosis, so that most patients who display the pathognomonic memory defect also suffer many of the intellectual deficits typical of chronic alcoholics (Victor et al., 1959; Talland, 1965).

The central problem of Korsakoff's psychosis appears as a defective ability to consolidate, retrieve, and utilize newly registered data (Buschke and Fuld, 1974; Butters, 1971; Butters and Cermak, 1974; Talland, 1968). This results in the patient's retaining access to much of the immediate experience of the past two or three minutes, with little or no ability to utilize whatever might have been stored in recent memory (i.e., since the onset of the condition), and a tendency toward inconsistent and poorly organized retrieval of remote memory. Many Korsakoff patients can perform Digit Span, Subtracting Serial Sevens, and other tasks involving immediate memory and attention quite well, although they are not likely to resume interrupted activities and show little if any learning curve on repetitive tasks (Talland, 1965). Even recall for immediate memory may be impaired in severely affected patients (Butters, 1971).

Behavioral defects specifically and consistently associated with the Korsakoff syndrome are disorientation for time and place; apathy characterized by a virtually total loss of initiative, disinterest, and a striking lack of curiosity about past, present, or future; and emotional blandness with a capacity for momentary irritability, anger, or pleasure that quickly dissipates when the stimulating condition is removed or the discussion topic is changed. In the early stages, many patients tend to produce unconsidered, frequently inconsistent, foolish, and sometimes quite exotic confabulations in response to questions for which they feel they ought to know the answer, such as "What were you doing last night?" or "How did you get to this place?" Although the patient may have retained many specific abilities and skills, unlike the chronic alcoholic whose memory functions remain relatively intact, the memory defects of the Korsakoff's syndrome render the severely impaired patient utterly dependent and call attention to the central organizing function of retention and recall for emotional and intellectual behavior alike.

SPECIAL PROBLEMS OF INTERPRETATION

Recovery and Deterioration

Brain damage is not a static phenomenon, even when the lesions are nonprogressive. There appear to be regular trends in patterns of recovery and deterioration, depending on the nature of the cerebral insult, the age of the patient, and the function under study. The length of time following the onset of the condition must be taken into account in any evaluation of neuropsychological examination data. Ideally, every patient would be examined more than once, for changes in intellectual status can be expected throughout the brain damaged person's lifetime.

Early stages
Most people experience confusion to some degree for days, weeks, and sometimes months following a head injury or stroke (Moore and Ruesch, 1944). This confusion is often accompanied by disorientation, marked difficulty in concentration, poor memory and recall for recent experiences, very easy fatigability, irritability, and labile affect. In very severe cases, there is marked behavioral regression as well. Testing during the early, acute stage is not only virtually certain to be invalid, but it is usually an unnecessary imposition on an emotionally vulnerable patient.

If there are significant cognitive disabilities, with few exceptions they will be most profound immediately after onset of the condition. They are also likely to improve most rapidly during the early post-traumatic period (Hillbom, 1960; Newcombe et al., 1975). Occasionally, the recovery rate is so rapid during this early stage that test scores obtained on a Monday bear little relationship to the ones achieved by the patient on Friday. The tendency for rapid improvement is most notable in young people; the older the patient, the less likely will he make great or rapid strides toward recovery (A. Smith, 1960). Also, the less severely impaired the patient, the better is his prognosis (Hillbom, 1960; Sands et al., 1969).

Testing done during the third to sixth months after severe brain injury may give a reasonably valid indication of what the patient's ultimate mental condition will be. Unless there has already been almost complete recovery, the patient will probably continue to improve significantly through much of the first year and into the second and third. Repeated testing during the first year following injury may give some indication of how much improvement can be expected. The rule of thumb for predicting extent of improvement is that the greater the rate of improvement, the more further improvement can be expected. According to this rule, patients who experience a rapid return of function are likely to make a fuller recovery than those whose progress is slow.

Both the rate of recovery and the nature of the improvement are almost always uneven. The recovery rate does not describe a smooth course but tends to proceed by inclines and plateaus, and different functions improve at different rates. Old memories and well-learned skills generally return most quickly; recent memory, ability for abstract thinking, mental flexibility, and adaptability are more likely to return at a slower rate. Of course, these general tendencies vary greatly depending upon the site and extent of the lesion and the patient's premorbid abilities.

Later stages

Findings from studies of traumatically injured patients (Anttinen, 1960; Hillbom, 1960) and of patients who underwent brain surgery for psychiatric disorders (North and Zubin, 1956; A. Smith and Kinder, 1959) suggest that for both these conditions, following an initial improvement and a plateau period of several years or more, a general mental deterioration tends to take place. Younger stroke patients with unilateral lesions who have had no recurrence of their condition are more likely to maintain their gains and even continue to improve over long periods of time (Sands et al., 1969; A. Smith, 1971). Patients with organic disorders who have been invalids or institutional patients over long periods of time tend to perform with a sameness characterized chiefly by poor memory and attention span, apathy, concrete thinking, and generally regressive behavior that often obscures the pronounced test performance discrepancies between differentially affected functions that are characteristic of acute and progressive brain conditions.

Social and cultural variables

The evaluation of neuropsychological data must take into account the contribution of educational, social, and cultural experiences to the patient's test performance and to his attitudes and understanding of his condition. When characteristics of cultural background or socioeconomic status are overlooked, interpretations of test scores are subject both to errors of overinclusion (false positives) and errors of overexclusion (false negatives). Poorly learned or insufficiently practiced skills can produce a test profile with a lot of scatter which may be misinterpreted as evidence of organic disease. Members of some subcultures that stress intellectual development at the expense of manual activities may be so clumsy and perplexed when doing tasks involving hand skills as to exhibit a large discrepancy between verbal and practic test scores. A bright but shy farm hand may fail dismally on any task that requires speaking or writing. On the other hand, the test performance of a patient whose intellectual development was lopsided and who sustained brain injury involving his strongest abilities may show so little intertest variability as to appear, on casual observation, to be intellectually intact.

Handedness

Although the incidence of right hemisphere dominance is low, and mixed dominance is infrequent in right-handed people (see pp. 162–163), test behavior must be evaluated with these possibilities in mind. The first hint that there has been an unexpected switch is often the examiner's bewilderment when a hemiplegic patient displays the "wrong" set of behavioral symptoms. Left-handed patients generally are less likely to conform to the common dominance pattern. Their behavior should be routinely scrutinized for evidence of an irregular dominance pattern. When deviations from the normal left-right organization of the brain appear, a very thorough study of all functional systems is necessary to delineate the nature of the patient's intellectual disabilities fully, for in these exceptional cases no systematic relationships between functions can be taken for granted.

Malingering

Malingering is a special problem in neuropsychological assessment because so many neurological conditions present few "hard" findings and so often defy documentation by clinical laboratory techniques, particularly in their early stages. The problem is complicated by the compensation and retirement policies of companies and agencies which can make poor health well worth some effort.

Inconsistency in performance levels or between a patient's reports of disability and his performance levels, unrelated to any fluctuating physiological condition, is the hallmark of malingering. Generally, but not always, a thorough neuropsychological examination performed in conjunction with careful neurological studies will bring out performance discrepancies that are inconsistent with normal neuropsychological expectations. If inpatient facilities are available, close observation by trained staff for several days will often answer questions about malingering. There are a number of special techniques for testing the performance inconsistencies characteristic of malingerers (see pp. 473–480). When malingering is suspected, the imaginative examiner may also be able to improvise tests and situations that will reveal deliberate efforts to withhold or mar a potentially good performance.

8

INTELLECTUAL ABILITY TESTS
1 / The Wechsler Adult Intelligence Scale (WAIS)

Although early psychological theorists treated intelligence as a unitary capacity, test makers have always acknowledged the multidimensionality of intellect by producing many-faceted measuring instruments. With few exceptions, the most widely used mental ability tests have been *composite tests* made up of a variety of tasks testing different skills and capacities.

Composite tests come in one of two formats. In *omnibus* composite tests, the order of task presentation varies so that each test item or subtest differs from its neighbors. For instance, an arithmetic problem may follow a verbal or pictorial reasoning item and be followed in turn by an immediate memory or a drawing task. Generally, different kinds of tasks reappear at different difficulty levels. Omnibus tests provide frequent activity changes to hold the interest of youngsters and mentally impaired persons of all ages. They also expose the subject to many different kinds of tasks in a practicable amount of administration time. However, their quick change format keeps the examiner so busy manipulating material and giving new instructions that he may find it difficult to observe the patient and keep track of the test performance. The patient who thinks, learns, and shifts slowly may be unable to acquire sufficient task familiarity to perform at his best. Furthermore, when a test contains a very wide variety of tasks, there is usually not enough time for each kind of task to be given at every ability level.

The other kind of composite test is actually a test *battery* comprising a number of distinct subtests. The battery format solves the administration problems of the omnibus approach. Fewer shifts from task to task reduce the amount of instructing and material handling to more manageable proportions and give the slow patient time to become oriented to the new task. Subtests with many similar items at different levels of difficulty permit relatively fine gradations in item scaling and development of highly standardized subtest norms for comparing performances on the various subtest tasks. These features have led to the now almost universal use of battery type ability tests (Lubin et al., 1971). Tests of the omnibus type still make up part of the usual test repertory, but they are apt to serve as a source of additional specific tasks that the standardized battery does not contain, or as a substitute for a battery type test when inattentiveness or restlessness become serious administration problems.

Both battery and omnibus type tests are available in individually administered and paper and pencil forms. For clinical decision-making, individually administered tests are essential. Paper and pencil tests can provide valuable supplementary information (see pp. 239–244).

The WAIS is an individually administered composite test in battery format (Matarazzo, 1972; Wechsler, 1955, 1958). For all but the most severely impaired adults, it ordinarily constitutes a substantial portion of the test framework of the neuropsychological examination. When paper and pencil tests of the basic communication, arithmetic, and drawing skills, and additional individually administered tests involving mental tracking, recent memory, and learning are administered along with the WAIS, the examiner will have obtained some information about the most important aspects of the patient's intellectual functioning. He will also have a great deal of information about how the patient behaves (J. Allison et al., 1968). Such a basic review of intellectual functions, in which the WAIS serves as the core instrument, is usually sufficient to demonstrate an absence of significant intellectual disability or to provide clues to altered functions.

Eleven different subtests make up the WAIS battery. Wechsler classified six of them as "Verbal" tests: Information (I), Comprehension (C), Arithmetic (A), Similarities (S), Digit Span (DSp), and Vocabulary (V). The other five he termed "Performance" tests. They include Digit Symbol (DSy), Picture Completion (PC), Block Design (BD), Picture Arrangement (PA), and Object Assembly (OA). (See pp. 201–224 for a detailed description of the WAIS subtests).

Wechsler's classification of the WAIS subtests roughly coincides with the results of factor analytic studies. Two functionally distinct subtest groups have consistently emerged on factor analysis of the WAIS. The first group shares a common *verbal* factor, weighting on the Information, Comprehension, Similarities, and Vocabulary subtests. The second group of subtests, always including Block Design and Object Assembly and sometimes including Picture Completion or Picture Arrangement, shares a common factor variously termed *perceptual organization* (J. Cohen, 1957b); *nonverbal organization* (Wechsler, 1958); *space performance* (Maxwell, 1960); *spatial* (McFie, 1961); and *performance* (E. W. Russell, 1972a). This will be called the *visuospatial* factor here. A general intellectual factor, akin to Spearman's g (see pp. 16–17), has been extracted as a discrete factor (J. Cohen, 1957a; E. W. Russell, 1972b) and also as part of the first, "verbal-intellectual" factor (Maxwell, 1960). A *memory* factor, weighting primarily on Digit Span and infrequently on Arithmetic has been identified with some regularity (J. Cohen, 1957b; McFie, 1961). J. Cohen reports two other, "minor specific" factors, one weighting primarily but inconsistently on Picture Arrangement and the other weighting primarily on Digit Symbol and occasionally on Digit Span and Picture Arrangement. Because of their tenuous intersubtest relationships, Cohen does not relate these two test-specific factors to intellectual functions. Wechsler suggests that the first of these minor specific factors may be a "measure of the individual's capacity to resist distraction," and the second may relate to relevance, or "the appropriateness of response" (1958, p. 126).

Although the WAIS's capacity to test different kinds of intellectual functions contributes much to its important role in neuropsychological assessment, the WAIS subtests assess neither pure nor readily defined functions, nor do they facilitate the systematic examination of the different functions. Still there are many reasons why the WAIS is the most commonly used psychological test (Zimmerman and Woo-Sam, 1973). Clinicians who become familiar with the virtues and limitations of each of the various subtests often are very sensitive to behavioral nuances and score relationships elicited by these subtests, both individually and in their many combinations. Furthermore, an enormous body of knowledge has grown up around the Wechsler tests. The WAIS and its predecessor, the Wechsler-Bellevue Scales, Forms I and II, have served as the primary test standards in all intellectual test development since shortly after the introduction of the Wechsler-Bellevue Scale in 1939. The Wechsler scales have also been the most commonly used tests of intellectual ability for research purposes. They have been the intellectual ability tests of choice for many neuropsychologists, who have incorporated them into both clinical and research batteries (e.g., Reitan and Davison, 1974; E. W. Russell et al., 1970; A. Smith, 1975). Finally, Wechsler tests and their translations have the advantage of being used throughout the world (Guertin et al., 1966).

It is certainly possible that another test maker will devise a set of tests for appraising adult intellectual functions that is more scientifically founded and systematic than the Wechsler scales. The question remains as to whether test efficiency would then supplant the hard-won achievements of familiarity and experience.

SCORING ISSUES

There are a number of issues involved in interpreting WAIS scores, such as item scaling, inter-examiner reliability, and the influence of testing conditions (Matarazzo, 1972; Zimmerman and Woo-Sam, 1973). Of them, those most relevant to neuropsychological assessment concern IQ scores, the effects of age, sex differences, and the evaluation of the significance of score discrepancies.

IQ Scores

Educators have found that the WAIS Full Scale IQ score, which is calculated from the sum of all the subtest scaled scores (or their prorated values if fewer than 11 subtests are given), is an excellent predictor of academic achievement. However, neither the IQ scores calculated for the Verbal or the Performance tests, nor the Full Scale IQ score, serve a purpose in neuropsychological testing. These IQ scores are averaged estimates of intellectual performance representing so many different kinds of functions that they become meaningless in the presence of a neuropsychological disorder.

> Omnibus IQ's are aggregate and often unreliable indices of organic intellectual deterioration. Specific defects restricted to certain test modalities, for example, may give a totally erroneous indication of severe intellectual impairment when actually intellectual functions may be relatively intact and lower total scores are a reflection of im-

pairment of test modalities. Conversely, IQ's may obscure selective defects in specific subtests (A. Smith, 1966b, p. 56).

Much neuropsychological research has focused on comparisons between Wechsler Verbal and Performance Scale IQ scores, under the assumption that differences between these scores would reflect impairment of one or the other major functional system and thus significantly aid in the diagnosis. Both Verbal and Performance Scale IQ scores, however, are based on averages of some quite dissimilar functions that bear no regular neuroanatomical nor neuropsychological relationship to one another (Parsons et al., 1969; J. Cohen, 1957a). This problem is compounded by the fact that "common sense" reasoning rather than factor analytic or neuropsychological studies dictated the assignment of the individual subtests to either the Verbal or the Performance Scale, resulting in considerable functional overlap between these two scales (Maxwell, 1960). Furthermore, although there is some general tendency for Verbal Scale IQ scores to be reduced relative to Performance Scale IQ scores when there is a lesion of the dominant hemisphere, the opposite case does not hold to the same degree; and even the Verbal Scale score dip associated with dominant hemisphere lesions does not occur regularly enough for clinical reliability (Satz et al., 1967; A. Smith, 1966a; Vega and Parsons, 1969). In addition, the Verbal Scale IQ score relative to the Performance Scale IQ score varies systematically as the Full Scale IQ score varies, with a strong tendency for Verbal Scale IQ scores to be relatively high at the higher Full Scale IQ score levels and for the tendency to be reversed in favor of higher Performance Scale IQ scores when the Full Scale IQ score is very much below 100 (A.Smith, 1966a).

In short, averaged scores on the WAIS provide just about as much information as do averaged scores on a school report card. There is no question about the performance of a student with a four-point average: he can only have had an A in each subject. Nor is there any question about individual grades obtained by the student with a zero grade point average. Excluding the extremes, however, it is impossible to predict a student's performance in any one subject from his grade point average alone. In the same way, it is impossible to predict specific disabilities and areas of intellectual competency or dysfunction from the averaged ability test scores. For these reasons, no IQ scores were computed for test data presented in this book.

Age-graded Scores

The WAIS takes account of age differentials in the computation of the IQ scores but not in the standard subtest scaled score equivalents (Wechsler, 1955, p. 77). These latter scores were ascertained for the whole standardization population of persons from ages 16 to 64, and therefore are not suitable for neuropsychological purposes. Instead, the examiner should use the Tables of Scaled Score Equivalents for Raw Scores by Age Group when converting subtest raw scores into standard scores. (See the Appendix of the WAIS Manual, Wechsler, 1955, pp. 99–110 for these tables and instructions on how to use them.) There are ten of these tables, for age groups from "16–17" to "75 and over." The number of years in each age group's range is not equal owing to the relatively rapid intellectual changes of the early and later adult years.

The standard subtest scaled score values are close to the age-graded score values for the middle score and young adult ranges of most of the subtests. A scaled score of 11 on a subtest, such as Information, which is relatively impervious to the effects of age refers to much the same number of correct items for the seven age groups from age 18 to age 69, whereas fewer correct responses are needed to achieve a scaled score of 11 at age ranges "16–17," "70–74," and "75 and over." The range of applicability of the standard scaled score values is much narrower for subtests such as Digit Symbol which are sensitive to age (Norman, 1966). The number of correct responses needed for a standard scaled score of 10 on Digit Symbol (52 to 57) is approximately the same for subjects from 16 to 35. At age 35 a raw score of 55 correct responses will earn a scaled score of 12. At age 65, however, 55 correct responses earn a scaled score of 18 (see Table 8-1).

Very occasionally, significant subtest performance differences in the younger age ranges may be sharpened by using the age-appropriate norms or, conversely, age-graded scores will nullify seeming differences. Below age 20 and above age 35, age-graded subtest scaled scores are necessary when making subtest comparisons. In these age ranges, for which the normal pattern of test behavior differs from the pattern of the large, mixed-age standardization group, it becomes difficult to interpret many of the subtest scores and virtually impossible to compare them or to attempt pattern

TABLE 8-1
WAIS Age-graded Scaled Score Equivalents of Raw Scores with a Standard Scaled Score Equivalent of 10

	Raw Score	Standard Score	Age		
			16–17	45–54	70–74
Information	16	10	11	11	12
Comprehension	18	10	11	11	13
Arithmetic	11	10	11	10	12
Similarities	14	10	11	11	13
Digit Span	11	10	11	11	13
Vocabulary	45	10	12	10	12
Digit Symbol	56	10	11	13	19
Picture Completion	14	10	11	12	14
Block Design	34	10	12	12	15
Picture Arrangement	25	10	10	13	16
Object Assembly	30	10	10	11	13

The effects of age are apparent in the changing pattern of test score deviations. Profound differences occur on the timed Performance Scale subtests, and of these, the scaled score equivalents of the single most time-dependent test—Digit Symbol—change most radically.

analysis unless the patient's performance has been graded according to the norms of his own age group (Simpson and Vega, 1971)(see Table 8-2).

In this book, Wechsler subtest scaled scores are reported in their age-graded equivalents; the standard scaled score equivalents are not used. Practical considerations may require the neuropsychological examiner to obtain both the age-graded and the standard scaled score equivalents. Although the standard scaled score equivalents distort the test data for neuropsychological purposes, they represent the patient's performance relative to the working population and thus can guide the psychologist in vocational and educational planning for his patient. For example, a 55-year-old former cabinetmaker who achieves a raw score of 24 on Block Design may be performing well in the *average* range for his age group; but compared to the working population as a whole, his score, in the *low average* range, is only at the 25th percentile. On the basis of his age-graded scaled score alone, he seems capable of working at his former occupation; but when compared to working people generally, his relative disa-

TABLE 8-2

Standard Scaled Score Equivalents for Age-graded Scaled Score Equivalents of 10 at Three Age Ranges

	16–17		45–54		70–74	
	Raw Score	Scaled Score	Raw Score	Scaled Score	Raw Score	Scaled Score
Information	18	9	15	10	12	8
Comprehension	16	10	17	10	14	8
Arithmetic	10	9	11	10	8	7
Similarities	13	10	13	10	9	8
Digit Span	10	9.5	10	9	9.5	8
Vocabulary	29	8	39	9	33	9
Digit Symbol	51	9	40	7	19	4
Picture Completion	13	9	11	8	7	6
Block Design	30	9	27	8	23	7
Picture Arrangement	22	9	17	7	12	6
Object Assembly	30	9	27	8	24	7

When the raw score is converted to standard scaled score equivalents, what appears to be a slight edge of Verbal Scale over Performance Scale scores at ages 45–54 becomes a large differential with the numerical discrepancy between one pair of scores (V-DSy) approximating statistical significance, in the overall trend toward higher verbal subtests. In a much younger person, this score pattern would be sufficiently suggestive of organicity to warrant further study. For people in their early 70's, the pattern of raw scores given above is most typical.

bility on the Block Design task (which tests visuospatial functions) puts him at a decided disadvantage.

Sex Differences

Although men and women perform differently on some WAIS subtests, the overlap between their scores is too great to allow these differences to enter into interpretations of the scores of the individual case. With few exceptions, studies of the original Wechsler tests found that men regularly obtained slightly higher full scale scores than women. This tendency has persisted in the WAIS (D. A. Payne and Lehmann, 1966; Wechsler, 1958). The men of the standardization sample for the 1955 WAIS revision of the Wechsler-Bellevue Scales achieved higher scores on Information, Comprehension, Arithmetic, Picture Completion, and Block Design, whereas the women had a small advantage on Similarities, Vocabulary, and Digit Symbol. However, only for Arithmetic and Digit Symbol were the combined age group differences greater than one scaled score point; one combined age group difference was approximately two-thirds of a scaled score point and all others were approximately one-third of a scaled score point or less.

The years since the WAIS was standardized have seen critical changes in the nature and extent of women's education and vocational pursuits. These changes have not been limited to younger women alone, for the proportion of working middle-aged women continues to grow, as does the number of older women returning to school. Thus, without more current data, it is not possible to estimate the presence or the pattern of sex differences more than two decades later. It is certainly likely that significant differences remain between the sexes in WAIS response patterns, but what these differences are and how they vary from age group to age group will have to be answered by another large scale standardization study.

Evaluating Significance

It is generally agreed that the psychodiagnostic meaningfulness of test score deviations depends on the extent to which they exceed expected chance variations in the subject's test performance. However, there is a lack of agreement about the standard against which deviations shall be measured.

Commonly employed comparison standards for the Wechsler tests are the subtest mean scaled score, which is 10 for all subtests; the patient's own mean subtest score, which can be broken down into Verbal Scale and Performance Scale subtest mean scores (Rabin, 1965; Wechsler, 1958); and the Vocabulary test scaled score (Gonen and Brown, 1968; McFie, 1969). Jastak developed an "intellectual altitude" measure by averaging the scores of the three highest subtests (Thorp and Mahrer, 1959). Wechsler uses deviations from the patient's subtest mean to obtain a pattern of scores that deviates in both positive and negative directions.

Neuropsychologically, the most meaningful comparison standard is the one that gives the highest estimate of the original ability level based on the patient's test scores (see Chapter 4). This is usually the highest WAIS subtest score, which then becomes the best estimate of the original general ability level. When the highest WAIS subtest score is used as the estimated comparison standard, lower scores are subtracted from it and all scaled score discrepancies will have a negative arithmetic value.

There are two exceptions to the use of the highest WAIS subtest score as the comparison standard. First, evidence that the patient once enjoyed a level of intellectual competency higher than that indicated by the Wechsler subtest scores, such as life history information, non-Wechsler test data, or isolated Wechsler item responses, takes precedence over Wechsler subtest scores in the determination of the comparison standard.

> A 52-year-old general contractor and real estate developer with severe progressive arteriosclerosis had successfully completed two years of the Business Administration program at an outstanding private midwestern university just after World War II when this school had a highly selective admissions policy. On the verbal subtests, his highest age-graded scaled score was 9, suggesting no better than an *average* original ability level. Knowledge of his previous academic experience led the examiner to estimate his original ability level as having been at least in the *superior* range, at the 90th percentile or above. The WAIS subtest scaled score at this level is 14, which became the comparison standard against which the obtained subtest scores were measured for significance. It is interesting to note that this same patient, who obtained an age-graded scaled score of 9 on the Arithmetic subtest, produced a highly variable arithmetic performance in which he also betrayed his original *superior* ability level by answering one difficult problem correctly while failing many easier items.

The second exception is that high scores on the test of immediate memory and concentration (Digit Span) and on a set of picture puzzle constructions (Object Assembly) are less likely to reflect the original general ability level than any other subtests. Correlational studies show that the highest correlation of Digit Span with any other subtest is .60 (with Vocabulary) and that six of the remaining ten subtest correlations range below .50. Although the highest intersubtest correlation of Object Assembly is .69 (with Block Design), six of its other ten subtest intercorrelations also are .50 or lower (Wechsler, 1955). In comparison, the highest correlation of Information is .81 (with Vocabulary) and none of the other subtest intercorrelations is lower than .54. Knowledge of the astonishing feats of memory of *idiots savants* should also make the examiner wary of using immediate memory scores as a basis for estimating original ability level (Anastasi, 1965). In clinical practice, the tendency for both Object Assembly and Digit Span to vary independently of other subtest scores becomes readily apparent as some rather dull people turn in excellent performances on these subtests and some bright subjects do no better than *average* on them. The symbol-number substitution task (Digit Symbol) also correlates as poorly with the other subtests as does Digit Span, but Digit Symbol is so rarely a subject's best subtest that the question of its score serving as a comparison standard is practically irrelevant.

Wechsler originally recommended that a subtest score deviation measured from the subject's mean should be of the magnitude of two subtest scaled score units to be considered a possibly meaningful deviation, and that a deviation of three be considered significant. The applicability of this rule of thumb depends to some extent upon the stability of the subtest scores. For most of the subtests, it is likely that the obtained score is within two to three scaled score points of the true score 95% of the time. Digit Span and Object Assembly are the only subtests that consistently vary so greatly that the 95% range of variability of individual scores exceeds three scaled score points. Picture Arrangement exceeds this range for some age groups but not for others. Vocabulary and Information scores display the least variability (Wechsler, 1955).

A discrepancy of three points between any two Wechsler subtest scores is generally significant at the 15% level (Wechsler, 1958) and therefore does not satisfy the usual minimum 5% significance level typically used in making psychological inferences. However, Wechsler measures deviations from the patient's mean, not from the highest score. When deviations of three points from the subject's mean occur, there would also usually be deviations of at least two points in the other direction. Thus Wechsler's two- and three-point deviations from the subject's mean generally would be of the magnitude of at least four to five points when measured from a high score comparison standard. Deviations of this magnitude accord with the discrepancy sizes that Field (1960) found to be reliable at the 1 and 5% significance levels (see Table 8-3).

TABLE 8-3
Reliability of Differences between Any Two Subtest Scores for Different Values of the Range (WAIS)[a]

Range	2		3		4		5		6		7		8		9		10	
Significance Level (percent)	5	1	5	1	5	1	5	1	5	1	5	1	5	1	5	1	5	1
Age (years)																		
18–19	3.5	4.7	3.7	4.9	3.9	5.0	4.0	5.1	4.0	5.2	4.1	5.2	4.1	5.3	4.2	5.3	4.2	5.4
25–34	3.6	4.8	3.8	5.0	4.0	5.1	4.0	5.2	4.1	5.3	4.2	5.4	4.2	5.4	4.3	5.5	4.3	5.5
45–54	3.5	4.6	3.7	4.8	3.8	4.9	3.9	5.0	4.0	5.1	4.0	5.2	4.1	5.2	4.1	5.2	4.1	5.3

[a] Adapted from Field (1960), p. 4. By permission.

To use Table 8-3,

a subject's scaled scores must first be arranged in order of magnitude. The two scores to be compared are located and their range is found by adding the number of intervening scores to the number of scores being compared, which is 2. The difference between the scores must be equal to or greater than one of the two values in the Table, under the appropriate Range and Age, to reach the level of significance shown in the second row of the Table (Field, 1960, p. 5).

For most practical purposes, the examiner can consider discrepancies of four scaled score points as approaching significance and discrepancies of five or more scaled score points to be significant, i.e., nonchance. This rough rule for estimating significance permits the examiner to evaluate the Wechsler test score discrepancies at a glance without having to resort to extra computations or formulae. Table 8-4 (p. 197) provides several examples of likely subtest score patterns.

IDENTIFYING THE PRESENCE OF BRAIN DAMAGE

Indices, Ratios, and Quotients

Most early studies of the neuropsychological diagnostic capabilities of the Wechsler tests were of mixed organic populations, with little or no regard for the nature, location, or extent of the brain lesion (Wechsler, 1944). A consistent pattern of subtest scores emerged from these studies in which subtests requiring immediate memory, concentration, response speed, and abstract concept formation were most likely to show the effects of brain damage. The performance of these same patients on tests of previously learned information and verbal associations tended to be least affected. While recognizing the inconstancy of relationships between Wechsler subtest patterns and various kinds of brain lesions, Wechsler and others noted the similarities between these apparently organicity-sensitive subtests and the subtests most prone to age-related changes. Efforts to apply this apparent relationship to questions of differential diagnosis resulted in a number of formulae for ratios on which to base cutting scores.

Wechsler devised a *deterioration quotient* (DQ), also called a *de-*

terioration index (DI), which enables the examiner to compare scores on those tests that tend to withstand the onslaughts of old age ("*Hold*" tests) with those that are most likely to decrease over the years ("*Don't Hold*" tests). His assumption was that deterioration indices that exceed normal limits reflect early senility, an abnormal organic process, or both. For the WAIS, calculation of the deterioration index uses age-graded scores in a comparison of "Hold" tests (Vocabulary, Information, Object Assembly, and Picture Completion) with "Don't Hold" tests (Digit Span, Similarities, Digit Symbol, and Block Design). The formula for the deterioration quotient is $\dfrac{Hold - Don't\ Hold}{Hold}$. The cutting score for "possible deterioration" is .10, and .20 is the suggested indicator of "definite deterioration" (Wechster, 1958, p. 211). Unfortunately, neither the earlier *mental deterioration index* (MDI) calculated on Wechsler-Bellevue subtest scores (using Information, Comprehension, Object Assembly, and Picture Completion as "Hold" tests and Digit Span, Arithmetic, Digit Symbol, and Block Design as "Don't Hold" tests) (Wechsler, 1944) nor the WAIS DQ proved effective in identifying patients with organic damage (V. Meyer, 1961; Rabin, 1965; Watson et al., 1968). Wechsler's 1944 formula classified anywhere from 43 to 75% of patients correctly (Yates, 1954), and the WAIS deterioration quotient has not produced better results (Bersoff, 1970; E. W. Russell, 1972b; Savage, 1970).

Dissatisfaction with the equivocal results of Wechsler's deterioration indices led to more elaborate efforts to develop a numerical touchstone for organicity. Other proposed formulae for ascertaining the presence of organic deterioration followed Wechsler's "Hold" versus "Don't Hold" subtest format. For the most part, these formulae involved rather slight variations on Wechsler's basic theme. W. L. Hunt (1949) and more recently Gonen (1970) recommended a deterioration quotient derived by using Information and Comprehension as the "Hold" and Digit Symbol and Block Design as the "Don't Hold" subtests, which Gonen describes as particularly sensitive to the effects of diffuse, nonlateralized cerebral atrophy. Allen (1947) developed a formula in which the sum of Digit Span and Digit Symbol scaled scores was subtracted from the sum of Information and Comprehension scaled scores; a difference between the two scores of five points or more raised the suspicion of organicity. When independently evaluated, Allen's formula misclassified too many normal individuals (34%) as brain damaged for it to be clinically useful (Blake and McCarty, 1948). R. D. Norman (1966) attributed some of the failures of Wechsler's deterioration index to differences between the sexes with respect to the "Hold" or "Don't Hold" qualities of subtests and offered a new formula for women based on Vocabulary, Information, Object Assembly, and Block Design as the "Hold" tests and Similarities, Digit Span, Digit Symbol, and Picture Arrangement as the "Don't Hold" tests, although he recommended retaining Wechsler's 1955 formula for men and the same cutting scores for both sexes.

Despite all these efforts, no one has yet devised a formula based on Wechsler's subtest scores that will separate organic patients from control or other patient groups to a clinically satisfactory degree. Recognizing the heterogeneity of the brain damaged population, Hewson developed not one but a set of ratios in hopes of using Wechsler subtest scores to identify organic patients (1949). This ratio method shuffles subtest scores into seven different formulae, each of which discriminates with more or less accuracy between normal control subjects, neurotic, and postconcussion patients. The ratios are applied sequentially to a set of Wechsler subtest scores until the appearance of a significant value for one of the seven ratio formulae raises the possibility of a diagnostic category; if none of the computed ratios results in a significant value, the subject is considered to be probably organically intact and without a marked neurosis.

A. Smith (1962b) has claimed relatively good success in identifying brain tumor patients by means of Hewson's ratios, classifying 81.3% of 128 of them correctly. However, he reports lower accuracy rates with other categories of patients. Whereas the ratios correctly identified as not organic 73.5% of 185 patients with functional disorders, 50% of the functional patients over the age of 50 and 64% of a group of hospitalized psychotic patients were misclassified as organic. Using eight ratios, Gutman (1950) reports that 71% of an organic population were correctly identified. In another study, age-graded subtest scaled scores were substituted for the standard scaled scores and this increased the accuracy of classification by means of the Hewson ratios from 67% to 71%; but the ratios still misclassified 23% of the patients with known cerebral pathology (Woolf, 1960).

Compared to other indices and ratios based on Wechsler subtest scores, the Hewson ratios screen for organicity relatively well; like the other indices and ratios, they misclassify too many cases for clinical application, and they also have the disadvantage of being rather complicated and time consuming to calculate.

Pattern Analysis

Wechsler and others have looked to the pattern of Wechsler subtest score deviations for clues to the presence of brain damage and, more recently, for evidence of specific kinds of brain damage (Matthews et al., 1962; McFie, 1969; Reitan, 1955b; E. W. Russell et al., 1970; Simpson and Vega, 1971). The most common Wechsler organicity patterns reflect the most commonly seen neuropathological conditions. A pattern of clear-cut differences between subtests involving primarily verbal functions on the one hand and those involving primarily visuospatial functions on the other is a likely product of lateralized brain injury (Lansdell and Smith, 1972; E. W. Russell, 1972a) (see Table 8-4). The rank order of the verbal subtests with one another and of the visuospatial subtests with one another need not follow a particular pattern, for discrepancies within subtest groups may reflect prior skills and interests. For example, an accountant with left hemisphere damage may do poorly on all verbal subtests but display least loss on Arithmetic because years of practice have made his arithmetic responses almost automatic, whereas a well-read and once competent housewife with a comparable brain lesion may do poorest on Arithmetic due to schoolgirl attitudes about arithmetic and her consequent inexperience with it. Not in-frequently, one or more subtests in the vulnerable group will not be significantly depressed. Occasionally a verbal subtest score will even be among the highest a patient with dominant hemisphere disease achieves. It is much less likely for a visuospatial subtest to be highest, regardless of the side of the lesion, because of the effect of motor slowing on these timed tests. Picture Completion, which has both verbal and visual components, may vary with either the verbal or the visuospatial tests, or take some middling position.

Other Wechsler subtest patterns may be superimposed on relatively clear-cut differences between verbal and visuospatial subtests. Immediate memory, attention, and concentration problems occur as

TABLE 8-4
Sample Subtest Score Patterns

	A	B	C
Information	8	10	8
Comprehension	7	10	6
Arithmetic	6	9	9
Similarities	7	8	6
Digit Span	8	9	7
Digit Symbol	6	8	6
Picture Completion	8	10	10
Block Design	6	8	13
Picture Arrangement	6	8	10
Object Assembly	8	13	12

A glance at pattern A shows that the greatest discrepancy between subtests is of a magnitude of two points and therefore probably due to chance. This could be a typical profile of an intact person who generally functions at a *low average* level (at approximately the 16th percentile). On pattern B, except for a *high average* score on Object Assembly, there are only chance variations between subtest scores. Since the single high score is Object Assembly, it too will be considered a chance deviation unless some other information suggestive of a better than *average* ability level becomes available. Sample pattern C, on the other hand, contains three six-point discrepancies, one five-point discrepancy, and one four-point discrepancy between score pairs, excluding the high score on Object Assembly. Taking the high Object Assembly score into account, since it is likely to be due to the same factors that contributed to the high Block Design score, strengthens this discrepancy pattern. Pattern C might be produced by a patient of originally *high average* to *superior* general ability who suffered impairment of verbal functions with some motor slowing.

depressed scores on Digit Span and Arithmetic, whereas problems involving attention and response speed primarily affect Digit Symbol scores (E. W. Russell, 1972b). These depressed scores are not necessarily associated with lateralized defect but also tend to characterize the Wechsler performance of many organically impaired persons with diffuse brain disease.

An additional feature that may appear with any kind of brain damage is concrete thinking. Concrete thinking—or the absence of the abstract attitude—is generally reflected in lowered scores on Similarities and Picture Completion, and in failures or one-point answers on the three proverb items of Comprehension when responses to the other Comprehension items are of good quality. Concrete behavior may also show up on Block Design as inability to conceptualize the squared format or appreciate the size relationships of the blocks relative to the pictured designs. Concrete thinking is also characteristic of persons whose general intellectual functioning tends to be low in the *average* range or below *average* and of certain kinds of psychiatric patients.

Concrete thinking associated with brain damage can be distinguished from the normal thinking of persons of lower intellectual ability when the examiner finds one or more scores or responses reflecting a higher level of intellectual capability than the patient's present inability to abstract would warrant. Further, in the brain damaged patient, concrete thinking is usually accompanied by lowered scores on subtests sensitive to memory defect, distractibility, and motor slowing, whereas these problems are not characteristic of people who are simply dull and not organically impaired. The concrete thinking of brain damage is distinguishable from that of psychiatric conditions in that the former tends to occur consistently, or at least regardless of the emotional meaningfulness of the stimulus, whereas the latter is more apt to vary with the emotional impact of the stimulus on the patient or with any number of factors external to the examination. Concrete thinking alone is not indicative of brain damage in patients of normally low intellectual endowment or in long-term chronic psychiatric patients. However, a concrete approach to problem-solving, which shows up in depressed Similarities and Picture Completion scores, with perhaps some lowering of Comprehension and Block Design scores, may be the most pronounced residual intellectual defect of a bright person who has had a mild brain injury.

Other than these fairly distinctive but not mutually exclusive patterns of lateralized and diffuse damage, the Wechsler-based evaluation of whether brain damage is present depends on whether the subtest score pattern makes neuropsychological sense. For instance, the widespread tissue swelling that often accompanies a fresh head injury or rapidly expanding tumor results in confusion, general dulling, and significant impairment of memory and concentration functions that appear on the WAIS as significantly lowered scores on almost all subtests, except perhaps time-independent verbal tests of old, well-established speech and thought patterns (Gonen and Brown, 1968). Bilateral lesions generally produce changes in both verbal and visuospatial functions; the amount of change will be related to the extent and location of the lesions as well as the patient's life experiences. In each case, evaluation of organicity by pattern analysis requires knowledge of what is neuropsychologically possible and an understanding of the patient's behavioral capabilities.

This kind of pattern analysis applies best to patients with recent or ongoing brain changes. The Wechsler subtest score patterns of patients with old, static brain injuries, particularly those who have been institutionalized for a long time, tend to be indistinguishable from those of chronic institutionalized psychiatric patients. In attempting to apply the rationale of pattern analysis for differential diagnostic purposes, the examiner must also take into account the patient's neuropsychiatric history (E. W. Russell, 1972b; A. Smith, 1966a; Watson et al., 1968).

THE WAIS SUBTESTS

Administration of the eleven subtests need not follow the standard order of presentation. Rather, the examiner may wish to vary the subtest order to meet the patient's needs and limitations. Patients who fatigue easily can be given more taxing subtests, such as Arithmetic or Digit Span, early in the testing session. If the patient is very anxious about the tests, the examiner will want him first to take tests on which he is most likely to succeed before he tackles more difficult material. If the patient is restless, the examiner may alternate one or more of the six question and answer type subtests with the puzzle-like ones to maintain interest.

The examiner also need not complete the WAIS battery in one sitting but can stop whenever he or his patient becomes restless or fatigued. In most instances, the examiner calls the recess at the end of a subtest and resumes testing at some later time. Occasionally a patient's energy or interest will give out in the middle of a subtest. For most subtests, this creates no problem; the test can be resumed where it had been stopped. However, the easy items on Similarities, Block Design, and Picture Arrangement provide some people the practice they need to succeed at more difficult items. If the examination must be stopped in the middle of any of these three tests, the first few items should be repeated at the next session so the patient can reestablish the set necessary to pass the harder items.

A verbatim record of the patient's answers and comments makes this important dimension of his test behavior available for leisurely review. The examiner who has learned short-hand has a great advantage in this respect. Slow writers particularly might benefit from an acquaintance with brief-hand or speedwriting.

The standard examination procedure calls for the administration of the eleven WAIS subtests in the order of their listing below. When all eleven tests are given, testing time generally runs from one and one-quarter to two hours, with the Verbal Scale subtests taking up about one-half to two-thirds of that time. The WAIS Manual gives the standard administration instructions in detail (Wechsler, 1955).

Many examiners routinely use only nine or ten of the eleven WAIS subtests (McFie, 1969; A. Smith, 1966b). In the examinations reported in this book, Vocabulary was not administered because the information it adds is redundant when the other verbal subtests have been given, it takes the longest of any of the verbal subtests to administer and score, and in these examinations a vocabulary test is usually included in the paper and pencil battery or a picture vocabulary test is substituted for patients unable to read or write. I usually exclude Digit Symbol and give the Symbol Digit Modalities Test instead. When Digit Symbol is given to patients with pronounced motor disability or motor slowing who will obviously perform poorly on this highly time-dependent test, their low scores add no new information, making this test redundant too.

When there are time pressures, the examiner may wish to use a "short form" of the WAIS; that is, a set of only three, four, or five subtests selected to give a reasonably representative picture of the patient's functioning (Duke, 1967). Short forms were originally developed to produce a quick estimate of the Full Scale IQ score. Selection of subtests for brief neuropsychological screening need not be made on the basis of how well the combined score from the small set of tests approximates the Full Scale score. So long as the subtests are handled as discrete tests in their own right, the examiner can include or exclude them to suit his patient's needs and abilities and the requirements of the examination. "Split-half" adminstrations, in which only every other item is given, also save time. However, with the exception of Vocabulary, the validity coefficient of split-half scores correlated with whole subtest scores range below .90; and of the Performance Scale subtests, only Block Design is above .80 (Zytowski and Hudson, 1965).

Many of the subtests present administration or scoring problems peculiar to that subtest (Zimmerman and Woo-Sam, 1973). These will be noted in the discussion of each subtest below.

Verbal Scale Subtests

Information
The 29 Information items test general knowledge normally available to persons growing up in the United States. The items are arranged in order of difficulty from the four simplest, which all but severely retarded or organically impaired persons answer correctly, to the most difficult, which only 1% of the adult population passes (Matarazzo, 1972).

Although the standard instructions call for discontinuation of the test after five failures, the examiner may use discretion in following this rule, particularly with brain injured patients. On the one hand, some neurologically impaired patients with prior average or above average intellectual achievements are unable to recall once learned information on demand and therefore fail several simple items in succession. When such patients give no indication of being able to do better on the increasingly difficult items and are also distressed by their failures, the examiner loses little by discontinuing this task early. If he has any doubts about the patient's inability to answer the remaining questions, he can give the next one or two questions later in the session after the patient has had some success on other subtests. On the other hand, bright but poorly educated subjects will often be ignorant of general knowledge but have acquired expertise in their own field which will not become evident if the test is discontinued according to rule. Some mechanics, for example, or nursing personnel, may be ignorant about literature, geography, and religion, but know the boiling point of water. When testing an alert person with specialized work experience and a limited educational background who fails five sequential items not bearing on his personal experience, I usually give all higher level items that might be work-related.

Information and Vocabulary are the best WAIS measures of general ability, that ubiquitous test factor that appears to be the statistical counterpart of learning capacity plus mental alertness, speed, and efficiency. Information also tests verbal skills, breadth of knowledge, and—particularly in older populations—remote memory. Information tends to reflect formal education and motivation for academic achievement (Saunders, 1960a). It is one of the few WAIS subtests that can give spuriously high ability estimates for overachievers, or fall below the subject's general ability level because of early lack of academic opportunity or interest. Information contains ten items that are not equally difficult for men and women, the difference favoring men to a significant degree.

In brain injured populations, even for patients whose condition is confined to the dominant hemisphere, Information tends to appear among the least affected WAIS subtests (Sklar, 1963). Although a slight depression of the Information score can be expected with brain injury of any kind, because performance on this subtest shows such resiliency it often can serve as the best estimate of original ability. However, the Information score does tend to drop when there is dominant hemisphere damage. In individual cases, a markedly low Information score suggests dominant hemisphere involvement, particularly if verbal tests generally tend to be relatively depressed and the patient's history provides no other kind of explanation for the low score. Thus, the Information performance tends to be a fairly good predictor of the hemispheric side of a suspected brain lesion (Reitan, 1955b; A. Smith, 1966b; Spreen and Benton, 1965).

Comprehension

This fourteen item subtest includes two kinds of open-ended questions: eleven test common-sense judgment and practical reasoning, and the other three ask for the meaning of proverbs. Comprehension items range in difficulty from a common-sense question passed by all nondefective adults to a proverb that is fully understood by fewer than 22% of adults (Matarazzo, 1972). The test normally begins with questions of practical and social judgment.

Except for the first two items, which are scored on a pass-fail basis, the subject can earn one or two points for each question, depending on the extent to which the answer is either particular and concrete or general and abstract. Scoring of Comprehension creates a judgment problem for the examiner since so many answers are not clearly of one- or two-point quality but somewhere in-between (R. E. Walker et al., 1965). There are even answers that leave the examiner in doubt as to whether to score two points or zero! I have found that scoring of the same set of answers by several psychologists or psychologists in training usually varies from two to four points in raw score totals. When converted to scaled scores, the difference is not often more than one point, which is of little consequence so long as the examiner treats individual subtest scores as likely representatives of a *range* of scores.

Comprehension is only a fair test of general ability, but the verbal factor is influential. Like Information, it appears to measure remote memory in older persons. Six of its fourteen items discriminate sexually with an overall tendency (at the 5% level of significance) for men to make slightly higher scores. Comprehension subtest scores also reflect the patient's social knowledgeability and judgment. Of all the WAIS subtests, Comprehension best lends itself to interpretation of content because the questions ask for the patient's judgment or opinion about a variety of socially relevant topics, such as marriage or taxes, which may have strong emotional meanings for the patient. Tendencies to impulsivity or dependency sometimes appear in responses to questions about dealing with a found letter or a movie theatre fire or finding one's way out of a forest.

Comprehension test scores hold up well as a record of the premorbid intellectual achievement of brain damaged patients generally, except that they are even more sensitive than other predominantly verbal subtests to dominant hemisphere damage. Thus, when damage is diffuse, bilateral, or localized within the minor hemisphere, the Comprehension subtest score is likely to be among the best test indicators of premorbid ability, whereas its vulnerability to verbal defects makes it a useful indicator of dominant hemisphere involvement. Impulsive answers to emotionally arousing questions may contrast vividly with well thought out judgments about land values or child labor laws, reflecting impaired self-control in once intellectually competent and socially sophisticated persons whose impulsivity is associated with brain injury. When premorbidly well-socialized adults recommend "Shout fire" or "Run for help" as proper responses to a movie house fire, they are demonstrating severely impaired social judgment that probably reflects a general personality regression. Childishness and impulsivity characterize the social behavior of such patients. The three proverbs give the examiner an opportunity to compare the patient's practical reasoning and common-sense judgments with his ability to think abstractly (see pp. 394–395).

Arithmetic

This subtest consists of fourteen items, but testing routinely begins with the third item since the first two are given only to persons who fail both items three and four. The simplest item, which calls for block counting, should also be given to patients with known or suspected right hemisphere lesions since they may be unable to count more than a few visually presented items correctly while still capable of performing fairly difficult arithmetic problems conceptually. All nonretarded, organically intact adults can answer the first of the routinely administered items correctly. A few brain damaged patients who can perform the simple addition respond incorrectly on this item because they interpret the question concretely (see p. 108). Approximately 20% of the adult population can do the last item (Matarazzo, 1972), which is like, "Four men can finish a job in eight hours. How many men will be needed to finish it in a half hour?"). Arithmetic items have time limits ranging from 15 seconds on the first four to 120 seconds on the fourteenth. A subject can earn raw score bonus points for particularly rapid responses on the last four items. As a result, all scores above a scaled score of 13 for ages 18 to 70 differ only in terms of time bonus increments.

When recording test data, the examiner will obtain more information by noting the patient's exact responses on the Record Form, rather than writing in "R" or "W" as the WAIS printed material suggests. I write in every answer, the correct ones as well as the incorrect, so that the subject gets no hint of failure from the pace or amount of the examiner's writing. Although all Arithmetic failures receive the same zero score, some approach correctness more closely than others, and a simple "W" tells nothing about this. On the last question, for example, an incorrect response of "32" indicates that the patient has sorted out the elements of the problem and used the appropriate operation, but has failed to carry it through to the proper conclusion; an answer of "48" suggests that he performed the correct operations but miscalculated one step; whereas an answer of "1½" or "16" reveals ignorance or confusion. Thus, although "32," "48," "1½," and "16" are equally incorrect as far as scoring is concerned, only a person with a reasonably good grasp of arithmetic fundamentals and ability to reason about a complex arithmetic idea could get "32" as an answer; a person who says "48" can handle mathematical concepts well but is either careless or has forgotten his multiplication tables.

The total Arithmetic score of a bright, intact person will usually be compounded both of number correct and time credit points. In the case of a slow responder who takes longer than the time limit to formulate the correct answer, the total Arithmetic score may not reflect his arithmetic ability so much as his response rate. Each of these persons may get the same number of responses correct, say 11; but the intact subject could earn a raw score of 12 and a scaled score of 11, whereas a neurologically impaired patient whose arithmetic skills are comparable might receive a raw score of only 8 or 9 and a scaled score of 7 or 8. To do justice to the slow responder and gain a full measure of data about him, the examiner should obtain two Arithmetic scores: one based on the sum of correct responses given within time limits plus time bonuses, and the other on the sum of correct responses regardless of time limits. The first score can be interpreted in terms of the test norms and the second gives a better indication of the patient's arithmetic skills in themselves. When testing for maximum productivity, the examiner will not interrupt the patient to give another item until he has indicated he cannot do it or he becomes too restless or upset to continue working on the unanswered item.

Difficulties in immediate memory, concentration, or conceptual manipulation and tracking can prevent even very mathematically skilled patients from doing well on the orally administered test. These patients typically can perform the first several questions quickly and correctly, since they involve only one operation, few elements, and simple, familiar number relationships; but when there is more than one operation, several elements, or less common number relationships requiring "carrying," these patients lose or confuse the elements or goal of the problems. They may succeed with repeated prompting but only after the time limit has expired, or they may be unable to do the problem "in their head" at all, regardless of how often the question is repeated. The standard WAIS Arithmetic procedure does not begin to test the Arithmetic skills of these patients. After discovering how poorly the patient performs when he has to rely on his immediate memory, the examiner can find out how well he can do on these problems by giving him paper and pencil and letting him work the problems out. I use one sheet of unlined paper for this purpose, handing it to the patient after each failure, *if the failure appears to be due to an immediate memory, concentration, or conceptual clarity defect.* Use of unlined paper has two advantages: spatial orientation problems are more apt to show up if there are no guide lines, and there is no visual interference to distract vulnerable patients. By providing only one sheet of paper, the examiner forces the patient to organize the two or three and sometimes more problems on the one page, a maneuver that may reveal defects in spatial organization, ordering, and planning. Here too, the examiner should obtain two scores: the one based on the patient's performance under standard conditions will give a good measure of the extent to which his memory and mental efficiency problems are interfering with his ability to handle problems mentally; the other compounded of all of his correct answers, regardless of timing or use of paper and pencil, will give a better estimate of the patient's arithmetic skills per se.

Arithmetic scores, like Comprehension scores, are of only mediocre value as measures of general ability in the population at large, but they do reflect concentration and "ideational discipline" (Saunders, 1960a). In early adulthood, the memory component plays a relatively small role in Arithmetic, but it becomes more important with age. Arithmetic performance, like Information, may suffer from poor early school attitudes or experiences. In the case of women generally, Arithmetic's vulnerability to culturally ingrained attitudes may well be reflected in their significantly lower scores.

When administered to brain damaged patients following standard procedure, the WAIS Arithmetic subtest results may be more confusing than revealing. The problem lies in the oral administration format which emphasizes the considerable memory and concentration components of oral arithmetic. This results in a tendency for Arithmetic scores to drop in the presence of brain damage generally (Morrow and Mark, 1955; Newcombe, 1969). In addition, using the oral format, the examiner may overlook the often profound effects of the spatial type of dyscalculia that becomes apparent only when the patient must organize arithmetic concepts on paper (i.e., spatially); or the examiner may remain ignorant of a figure or number alexia that would show up if the patient had to look at arithmetic symbols on paper (Hécaen, 1962). Further, a distinct verbal component emerges from the Arithmetic performance of organic populations which may account for the slight but regular tendency for dominant hemisphere patients to do a little worse on this subtest than those whose lesions are located within the minor hemisphere (Spreen and Benton, 1965; Warrington and Rabin, 1970). McFie found that patients with left parietal lesions tended to have significantly lowered Arithmetic scores (1960). A lowered Arithmetic subtest score should lead the examiner to suspect an immediate memory or concentration problem and to raise questions about verbal functions, but it does not necessarily reflect the patient's arithmetic skills, particularly if there are other indications of impaired memory, concentration, or verbal functions. To evaluate the patient's ability to do arithmetic, the examiner must turn to the untimed WAIS Arithmetic score, the paper and pencil score, qualitative aspects of the patient's performance, and other arithmetic tests.

Similarities
This is a test of verbal concept formation. The subject must explain what each of a pair of words has in common. The word pairs range in difficulty from the simplest ("apple-orange") which only retarded or impaired adults fail, to the most difficult ("fly-tree") on which less than 18% of the population perform well (Matarazzo, 1972). The test begins with the first item for all subjects and is discontinued after four failures. Here too, common sense should dictate whether to present the last one or two items to a patient who has ceased to comprehend the nature of the problem and is fatigued or upset. Items are passed at the two-point level if the patient gives an abstract generalization and at the one-point level if he responds with a specific concrete likeness.

There are fewer scoring problems on Similarities than on Comprehension, but some variation between scorers does occur. Deteriorated patients as well as persons whose general functioning is *borderline defective* or lower sometimes respond with likenesses to the first few items but name a difference, which is generally easier to formulate, when the questions become difficult for them. In such cases, I record the incorrect response, scoring the item zero, but repeat the request for a similarity the first time this happens. Sometimes this extra questioning will help the patient attend to the demand for a likeness on the next and subsequent questions.

Similarities is an excellent test of general intellectual ability, but through middle age it reflects the verbal factor only to a moderate degree. Since Similarities is virtually independent of any memory component, however, for older people whose memory assumes much more importance on other verbal tests, it becomes the best test of verbal ability per se. Of all the verbal subtests, Similarities is least affected by the subject's background and experiences. Unlike Information and Arithmetic, it does not depend on academic skills, so that a bright person with inadequate schooling may do significantly better on this than on the other, more school-dependent verbal subtests. Unlike Comprehension, Similarities is relatively independent of social or educational background and unaffected by the impulsivity and social misjudgments that accompany some kinds of brain injuries. Compared to schizophrenic patients and normal subjects, brain damaged patients tend to give many more "Don't know" responses to Similarities questions, and proportionately fewer brain damaged patients attempt conceptual responses (Spence, 1963).

Similarities tends to be more sensitive to the effects of brain injury regardless of localization than the other verbal subtests (Hirschenfang, 1960b). Its vulnerability to brain conditions that affect verbal functions compounds its vulnerability to impaired concept formation, so that a relatively depressed Similarities score tends to be associated with left temporal and with frontal lobe involvement (McFie, 1960; Newcombe, 1969; Sheer, 1956) and is one of the best WAIS predictors of dominant hemisphere disease.

Digit Span

This is more than a test of immediate memory, although that is one of its chief purposes. It has two sections, both consisting of seven pairs of random number sequences. In Digits Forward the examiner reads aloud number sequences that are from three to nine digits long and the subject's task is to repeat each sequence exactly as he hears them. The Digits Backward number sequences run from two to eight digits long and, on hearing them read, the subject's task is to say them in an exactly reversed order. Each section is discontinued when the subject fails to repeat both number sequences of a pair.

This test produces three scores: Digits Forward and Digits Backward scores are the number of digits in the longest correctly repeated sequence for each section, and the total Digit Span raw score is the sum of the scores of the two sections. In the general population, all but a few elderly persons can recall four digits forward and three reversed; but fewer than 1% get the maximum nine forward and eight backward. The average adult's raw score of eleven is most often based on six digits forward and five backward.

Although Wechsler's instructions suffice for most subjects, when dealing with patients who are known or suspected to have brain damage, some variants may help to elicit maximum performance on this test without violating the standardization. Many patients whose thinking is concrete or who become easily confused comprehend the standard instructions for Digits Backward with difficulty if at all. Typically, these patients do not appreciate the transposition pattern of "backwards" but only understand that the last number need be repeated first. To reduce the likelihood of this misconception, I introduce the Digits Backward task using the wording in the Wechsler Manual (1955, p. 41), but give as the first example the two-digit number sequence, which even very impaired patients can do with relative ease. Everyone who recalls two digits reversed on either the first or second trial then receives the following instructions: "Good! [or some other expression of approval]. Now I am going to say some more numbers, and once again, when I stop I want you to say them *backwards.* For example, if I say *1–2–3,* what would you say?" Most patients can reverse this three number sequence because of its inherent familiar pattern. If the subject fails this example, it is given again verbally with the admonition, "Remember, when I stop, I want you to say the numbers *backwards*—the last number first and the first one last, just as if you were reading them backwards." The examiner may point in the air from the patient's left to his right as he says each number, and then point in the reverse direction as the patient repeats the reversed numbers so as to add a visual and directional reinforcement to the concept "backwards." If the patient still is unable to grasp the idea, the examiner can write each number down as he repeats *1–2–3* the third time. The examiner needs to write the numbers in a large hand on a separate sheet of paper or at the top of the Record Form so that they face the subject and run from the subject's left to right, i.e., Ɛ–ᄅ–ƚ. Then when the examiner asks the patient to repeat the numbers backwards, he points to each number as the patient says or reads it. No further effort is made to explain the test. As soon as the subject reverses the *1–2–3* set correctly or has received all of the above explanations, the examiner continues the rest of Digits Backward according to Wechsler's procedure.

Another exception to Wechsler's instructions that encourages a maximum performance is to administer a third sequence of the same length after two failures. I do not do this routinely, but only in one of two circumstances: (1) When the patient's failure on at least one of the two trials of a sequence appears to be due to distraction, non-cooperation, inattentiveness, etc., I give the third digit series, usually taking the requisite number of digits out of one of the nine forward or eight backward sequences that are unlikely to be used. (2) When the patient recalls more digits reversed than forward, the examiner can assume that the patient is capable of doing at least as well on the much less difficult Digits Forward as on Digits Backward and that this rarely seen disparity probably reflects the patient's lack of effort on a simple task. Almost invariably, such a patient will pass a third trial and occasionally pass one or two of the longer sequences.

Digit Span certainly involves auditory attention and measures the immediate auditory memory span. Digits Backward measures immediate memory span plus the ability to store a few data bits briefly *and* at the same time juggle them around mentally. The reversing operation itself appears to depend upon a kind of internal visual scanning (Weinberg et al., 1972). Reversing a lengthy sequence requires that both the memory and the reversing operations proceed simultaneously, a feat of mental *double-tracking*. That Digits Forward and Digits Backward do not involve the identical operations is apparent in the raw score disparity of three or more between Digits Forward and Digits Backward that tends to occur in brain damaged patients with concentration problems. This is not a common response pattern of brain damaged patients who do not have concentration or mental tracking problems and is rarely seen in organically intact persons (Costa, 1975).

Factorial studies of Digit Span agree that memory is the chief functional component of this test, that verbal ability plays virtually no role, and that general intellectual ability correlates less well with this than with any other Wechsler subtest. There is only little evidence that anxiety or distractibility affect Digit Span performance of normal individuals, despite clinical speculation to the contrary (Guertin et al., 1966; Moldawsky and Moldawsky, 1952). When stress conditions do impair performance on this test, the impairment will show up on Digits Forward rather than Digits Backward, but a stress-induced lowering of the Digit Forward score will dissipate with practice (Pyke and Agnew, 1963). When the examiner suspects that a stress reaction is interfering with a subject's Digit Span performance, he can repeat the test later in the examination. If the scores remain low even when the task is familiar and the patient is presumably more at ease, then the patient's poor performance is probably due to something other than stress.

Digit Span tends to be more vulnerable to left hemisphere involvement than to either right hemisphere or diffuse damage (McFie, 1960; Newcombe, 1969). This vulnerability is reflected in factorial studies of brain damaged and aged subjects in which, contrary to the results of factor analytic studies of normal groups, the verbal factor contributes significantly to Digit Span while the prominence of the memory factor is reduced but not nullified. Because of its memory and attention components, Digit Span also remains one of the WAIS subtests most sensitive to the effects of any kind of brain injury. As a general rule, a disparity of three or more points between Digits Forward and Digits Backward reflects a concentration defect of organic etiology, and any Digits Forward score of five or less in a middle-aged or younger person suggests impaired immediate memory. Digit Span scores tend to be lowest immediately following brain injury and to increase in time, although even years later, Digit Span scores tend to remain low relative to other test scores (Hamlin, 1970; Scherer et al., 1957; Wheeler and Reitan, 1963).

Vocabulary.   This subtest consists of 40 words, arranged in order of difficulty, that the examiner reads to the subject in the question, "What does _____ mean?" The easiest word on the list is "bed," but the administration usually begins with the fourth word, "winter," which practically all adults can define. It continues until the subject fails five words consecutively or until the list is exhausted. The most difficult words are "impale" and "travesty" which fewer than 18% percent of the adult population can define (Matarazzo, 1972). Except for the first three words, which are scored two or zero, the subject can obtain one or two points for each acceptable definition, depending on its accuracy, precision, and aptness. Thus, the subject's score reflects both the extent of his recall vocabulary and the effectiveness of his speaking vocabulary.

Vocabulary normally takes 15 to 20 minutes to administer, and at least 5 minutes to score, which makes it the most time-consuming subtest by far. In clinical practice, particularly with easily fatigued brain damaged patients, the high time cost of administering Vocabulary rarely compensates for the information gain it affords. One kind of patient for whom the information gain may be uniquely relevant is the puzzling psychiatric patient who generally responds well to standard personality tests but exercises poor judgment and appears increasingly inefficient in his activities. The differential diagnosis is between a functional thought disorder and brain disease. With no other clear-cut findings, Vocabulary is the most likely of the WAIS tests to aid in discriminating between the two diagnostic categories, because patients with thought disorders occasionally let down their guard on this innocuous appearing verbal skill test to reveal a thinking problem in "clangy" expressions, idiosyncratic associations, or personalized or confabulatory responses. For any other purpose, another kind of vocabulary test will not only provide an estimate of the patient's vocabulary but will do so in terms of dimensions not tested by the WAIS, such as reading and writing, or visual recognition and discrimination (see pp. 244–248, 272).

Vocabulary has been identified as the single best measure of both verbal and general mental ability, although Information serves equally well as a measure of general ability and Comprehension does about as well as a measure of verbal functions. Early socialization experiences tend to influence vocabulary development even more than schooling, so that the Vocabulary score is more likely to reflect the patient's socioeconomic and cultural origins and less likely to have been affected by academic motivation or achievement than Information or Arithmetic.

When brain injury is diffuse or bilateral, Vocabulary tends to be among the least affected of the WAIS subtests (Gonen and Brown, 1968). Like all other highly verbal tests, it is relatively sensitive to brain lesions of the dominant hemisphere (Parsons et al., 1969). Among the WAIS verbal subtests, however, Vocabulary is generally not one of those most depressed by left hemisphere damage.

Performance Scale Subtests

Four of the next five tests require motor response, writing on Digit Symbol and manipulating material on the other three. The question arises as to the validity of scores obtained on these tests when the patient is hemiplegic and can use only one hand, which often will be the nonpreferred hand. Normal control subjects obtained no significant score difference on the three manipulation tasks when only one hand was used, whether or not it was the preferred hand, although both Picture Arrangement and Object Assembly showed a small scaled score point loss for either hand alone (Briggs, 1960). When the subject used only the nonpreferred hand, Digit Symbol suffered slightly but with enough consistency to produce a significant lowering of the score.

Digit Symbol
In the standard administration, this is the first of the Performance Scale subtests. This symbol substitution task is printed in the WAIS test booklet. It consists of four rows containing in all 100 small blank squares, each paired with a randomly assigned number from one to nine (see Fig. 8-1). Above these rows is a printed key that pairs each number with a different nonsense symbol. Following a practice trial on the first ten squares, the subject's task is to fill in the blank spaces with the symbol that is paired to the number above the blank space as quickly as he can. After 90 seconds he is stopped. His score is the number of squares filled in correctly. Of all the WAIS tests, this is the only one that I time openly, for in this case the importance of speed must be stressed.

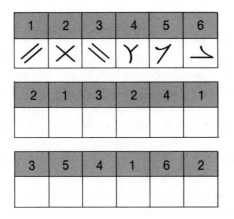

FIG. 8-1. The symbol-substitution format of the WAIS Digit Symbol subtest.

Persons unused to handling pencils and doing fine handwork under time pressure are at a disadvantage on this test. The great importance that motor speed plays in the scoring, particularly at ages below 35, renders Digit Symbol of doubtful validity for many low skilled manual workers and for anyone whose motor responses tend to be slow. This test should not be given to patients with pronounced motor slowing or to unskilled manual laborers who have not completed high school or who graduated more than 15 years before the examination, for these persons invariably do poorly regardless of their neuropsychological status. An exception to this rule is made for those few patients suspected of having visual perception or orientation problems whose defects might show up under the stress of this task.

Motor persistence, sustained attention, response speed, and visual-motor coordination play significant roles in the Digit Symbol performance. For most adults, Digit Symbol is relatively unaffected by intellectual prowess, memory, or learning (Murstein and Leipold, 1961). Some weak perceptual organization and memory components do show up in the performance of older persons.

This test is consistently more sensitive to brain damage than other WAIS subtests in that its score is most likely to be depressed even when damage is minimal, and to be the most depressed when other subtests are affected as well (Hirschenfang, 1960b). However, Digit Symbol tends to be affected regardless of the locus of the lesion and thus is of little use for predicting the laterality of a lesion.

Picture Completion
To give this test, the examiner shows the subject 21 incomplete pictures of human features, familiar objects, or scenes, arranged in order of difficulty, and instructs him to tell what *important part* is missing (see Fig. 8-2). The test always begins with the first picture (a knobless door) to which most mentally retarded persons respond correctly, and continues through the last picture (a profile lacking an eyebrow), which is correctly answered by about 22% of the population (Matarazzo, 1972). This test does not discriminate between *superior* and *very superior* ability levels.

Twenty seconds are allowed for each response. When testing a slow responder, the examiner should note the time of completion and whether the response was correct so that he can obtain a timed

FIG. 8-2. WAIS-type Picture Completion subtest item.

and an untimed score. The patient's verbatim responses on failed items may yield useful clues to the nature of the underlying difficulty. For example, the response "flagpole" to a picture of an American flag with 35 stars is a common error of persons with little initiative who respond to the obvious or who tend to think in simple, concrete terms; but the response "red in the stripes" to the eleventh of a black and white series is rare and more likely to be given by someone with a functional thought disorder than with an organic condition. Here too, I record the patient's words rather than merely noting whether or not his answer was correct.

Of all the Performance Scale subtests, Picture Completion has the highest weighting of the general ability factor with virtually no verbal components and minimal visuospatial ones. At the most basic level it tests visual recognition. The kind of visual organization ability needed to perform Picture Completion differs from that required by other Performance Scale subtests as the subject must supply the missing part from long term memory but does not have to manipulate the parts. Picture Completion correlates higher (.67) with the Information subtest than any other except Comprehension and is thus also a test of remote memory and general information. There are also reasoning components to this test involving judgments about both practical and conceptual relevancies (Saunders, 1960b). J. Cohen considers this test to be a nonverbal analogue of Comprehension (1957b). Picture Completion is biased to a slight but statistically significant degree in favor of men.

Picture Completion consistently demonstrates resilience to the effects of brain damage. Lateral damage does not have any consistent or significant differentiating effect. Picture Completion thus can serve as the best test indicator of previous ability, particularly when left hemisphere damage has significantly affected the ability to formulate the kinds of complex spoken responses needed for the Verbal subtests.

Block Design

This is a construction test. The subject is presented with red and white blocks, four or nine, depending on the difficulty of the item. His task is to use the blocks to construct replicas of ten red and white designs printed in smaller scale (see Fig. 8-3). The designs are given in order of difficulty with the exception of the second design, which has a difficulty level between designs five and six (Diller et al., 1974). The first six (four-block) designs have one-minute time limits and the last four (nine-block) designs two-minute limits. The subject can earn one or two bonus points for speed on the last four designs.

All subjects begin with the first item, which is presented and demonstrated as a block copying rather than a design copying test. The first and second items can be repeated should the subject fail to produce a correct design within the time limits, and the manual allows some leeway for demonstration and explanation of these items (Wechsler, 1955, p. 47). Only severely retarded or impaired adults are unable to succeed on either trial of the first two items. The third item, which is much easier than the second one, is also given to all subjects, regardless of their performance on items one or two, but no further demonstration is allowed. The test is normally discontinued after three failures. This test discriminates between subjects above the 75th percentile on the basis of their response speed alone.

The examiner may wish to vary the standard procedures to give the patient an opportunity to solve problems failed under standard conditions or to bring out different aspects of the patient's approach to the Block Design problems. As on the other timed tests, it is useful to obtain two scores if the patient fails an item because he exceeded

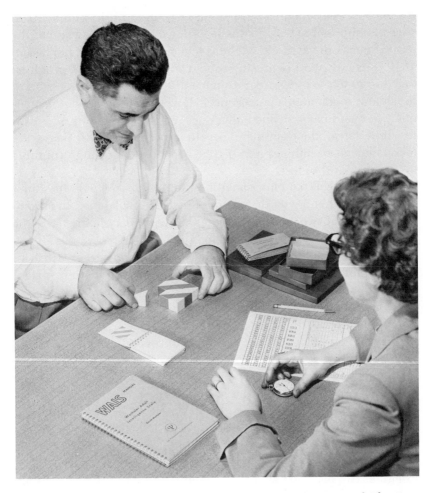

FIG. 8-3. Block Design subtest. (Reproduced by permission of The Psychological Corporation.)

the time limit. When the examiner times discretely, the patient remains unaware that he has overrun his time so that if he completes the design correctly, he will have the full satisfaction of his success. Usually, permitting the patient to complete the design correctly means waiting an extra minute or half minute beyond the allotted time. With a very slow patient, the examiner has to decide whether waiting the five or seven minutes the patient takes to work at a problem is time well spent observing him or providing an opportunity for success; whether the patient's struggle to do a difficult or perhaps impossible task distresses him excessively; or whether the patient needs the extra time if he is to succeed at this kind of task at all. It is usually worthwhile to wait out a very slow patient on at least one design to see him work through a difficult problem from start to finish and to gauge his persistence. However, if the patient is obviously in over his depth and either does not appreciate this or refuses to admit defeat, the examiner needs to intervene tactfully before the task so upsets or fatigues him that he becomes reluctant to continue taking any kind of test.

Brain damaged patients sometimes do not comprehend the Block Design task when given the standard instructions alone. An accompanying verbal explanation like the following may help clarify the demonstration: "This lower left-hand [patient's left] corner is all red, so I put an all red block here. The lower right-hand corner is also all red, so I put another all red block there. Above it in the upper right corner goes what I call a 'half-and-half' block [red and white halves divided along the diagonal]; the red runs along the top and inside so I'll put it above the right-hand red block this way (emphasizing the angulation of the diagonal), etc." Following completion of the test the examiner can bring out any design that puzzled the patient or elicited an atypical solution and ask him to try again. The examiner can then test for the nature of the patient's difficulty by having him verbalize as he works, by breaking up the design and constructing and reconstructing it in small sections to see if simplification and practice help, or by giving the patient blocks to copy instead of the smaller sized and unlined printed design. The examiner can test the patient's perceptual accuracy alone by asking him to identify correct and incorrect block reproductions of the designs (Bortner and Birch, 1962).

Block Design lends itself well to qualitative evaluation. The manner in which the patient works at Block Design can reveal a great deal about his thinking processes, work habits, temperament, and attitudes toward himself. The ease and rapidity with which the patient relates the individual block sides to the design pattern gives some indication of his level of visuospatial conceptualization. At the highest level is the patient who comprehends the design problem at a glance (forms a *gestalt* or unified concept), and scarcely looks at it again while putting the blocks together rapidly and correctly. Patients taking a little longer to study the design, who perhaps try out a block or two before proceeding without further hesitancy, or who refer back to the design continually as they work, function at a next lower level of conceptualization. Trial and error approaches contrast with the gestalt performance. In these the subject works from block to block, trying out and comparing his positioning of each block with the design before proceeding to the next one. This kind of performance is typical of persons in the *average* ability range. These people may never perceive the design as a total configuration, nor even appreciate the squared format, but by virtue of accurate perception and orderly work habits, many can solve even the most difficult of the design problems. Most people of *average* or better ability do form immediate gestalts of at least five of the easiest designs and then automatically shift to a trial and error approach at the point that the complexity of the design surpasses their conceptual level. Thus, another indicator of ability level on this perceptual organization task is the level of the most difficult design that the subject comprehends immediately.

The patient's problem-solving techniques reflect his work habits. Orderliness and planning are among the characteristics of working behavior that the block manipulating format makes manifest. Some patients always work in the same direction, from left to right and up to down for example, whereas others tackle whatever part of the design meets their eye and continue in helter-skelter fashion. Most subjects quickly appreciate that each block is identical, but some turn around each new block they pick up, looking for the desired side, and if it doesn't turn up at first they will set that block aside for another one. Some work so hastily that they misposition blocks and overlook errors through carelessness, whereas others may be slow but so methodical that they never waste a movement. Ability to perceive errors and willingness to correct them are also important aspects of the patient's work habits that can be readily seen on Block Design.

Temperamental characteristics, such as cautiousness, carefulness, impulsivity, impatience, apathy, etc., appear in the manner in which the patient responds to the problems. Self-deprecatory or self-congratulatory statements, requests for help, rejection of the task and the like betray the patient's feelings about himself.

The examiner should record significant remarks as well as the kinds of errors and manner of solution. For quick, successful solutions, he usually needs to note only whether the approach was conceptual or trial and error, and if trial and error, whether it was methodical or random. To some extent, time taken to solve a design will also indicate the patient's conceptual level and working efficiency since gestalt solutions generally take less time than those solved by methodical trial and error, which, in turn, generally are quicker than random trial and error solutions. The examiner can document the patient's difficulties, his false starts, and incorrect solutions by sketching them on the margin of the Record Form, on a piece of paper kept handy for this purpose, or on the WAIS Supplemental Record Form, which provides spaces for recording the designs. Of particular value in understanding and describing the patient's performance are sequential sketches of the evolution of a correct solution out of initial errors or of the compounding of errors and snowballing confusion of an ultimately failed design (e.g., Fig. 3-3a, p. 45).

Block Design is generally recognized as the best WAIS measure of visuospatial organization. It reflects general ability to a moderate extent so that intellectually capable but academically or culturally limited persons frequently obtain their highest WAIS score on this test.

Block Design scores tend to be lower in the presence of any kind of brain injury. They are likely to be least affected when the lesion is confined to the left hemisphere, except when the left parietal lobe is involved (McFie, 1960). They tend to be moderately depressed by diffuse or bilateral brain lesions and markedly depressed by right hemisphere lesions. For the latter, Block Design impairment is usually greatest with parietal lobe involvement, although it also occurs with right frontal and temporal lobe lesions (Milner, 1954; A. Smith, 1966b). Constructional apraxia with disorientation, design distortions, and misperceptions is more likely to occur with right parietal and parietal-occipital lesions, whereas patients with left parietal involvement tend more to confusion, simplification, and concrete handling of the designs. Patients with right hemisphere involvement also tend to be slower and to display much less activity than patients with left hemisphere damage in their efforts on this test (Ben-Yishay et al., 1971).

FIG. 8-4. WAIS-type Picture Arrangement subtest item.

Picture Arrangement

This test consists of eight sets of cartoon pictures that make up stories. Each set is presented to the subject in scrambled order with instructions to rearrange them to make the most sensible story (see Fig. 8-4). There are from three to six pictures in each set. Presentation is in order of increasing difficulty. Unless the subject fails both the first and second sets, all eight sets are administered. All but seriously retarded adults can do the first set (Matarazzo, 1972). The first six sets have a one-minute time limit and the last two a two-minute limit. On five of the sets there are two levels of accuracy and the subject can also earn time bonuses on the last two sets. Response speed accounts for all differences between subjects above the 90th percentile. As on other timed tests, the examiner should note correct solutions completed outside the time limits.

Like most of the other subtests, there are common failures made by patients whose functioning on this test is not organically impaired, and there are atypical failures that most likely result from conceptual confusion, perceptual distortion, or judgmental and reasoning problems. For example, many persons, particularly young men who have been arrested and detained for a minor offense, quite reasonably arrange item 3 incorrectly, for they were jailed briefly before appearing in court to be acquitted or placed on probation. Although this common incorrect arrangement receives zero credit, the examiner should take this "correct" solution into account when evaluating subtest scores. Another common failure involves displacement of the

last card to the beginning of the sequence on item 4. This arrangement reflects orderly sequential thinking in a person who misses the
point of the joke and needs to be interpreted differently than some
other erroneous sequence on this set. When the subject's failures are
unusual, suggesting that he has no appreciation of the task or no
awareness of his own misunderstandings, the examiner can gain
insight into the nature of his difficulty by asking him to "tell the
story" of his arrangement of the cartoons. The examiner may want to
hear each subject tell the story of one or two sets even when they are
correct, to sample his ability for verbal organization of a complex set
of visually presented data. Occasionally the subject will arrive at the
right solution for the wrong reasons, which will be revealed only by
a verbal explanation.

Other than a modest correlation with the general ability factor,
Picture Arrangement has little in common with other subtests or
with the prominent WAIS factors. It tends to reflect social sophistication so that, in unimpaired subjects, it serves as a nonverbal counterpart of that aspect of Comprehension. Its humorous content not
only enhances its sensitivity to socially appropriate thinking, but
provides an opportunity for a particular kind of social response and
interplay within the test setting. Sequential thinking—including the
ability to see relationships between events, establish priorities, and
order activities chronologically—also plays a significant role in this
subtest.

Picture Arrangement tends to be vulnerable to brain injury in general. Without regard to lobe of localization, right hemisphere lesions
tend to have a more depressing effect on these scores than do left
hemisphere lesions (McFie, 1960). A low Picture Arrangement score
in conjunction with a low Block Design score supports the implication of nondominant hemisphere involvement (Wheeler and Reitan,
1963). An extremely low Picture Arrangement score in itself is a
strong test indicator of right temporal lobe damage (Eigenbrod, undated; Milner, 1954; Piercy, 1964).

Object Assembly
This test contains four cut-up cardboard figures of familiar objects
given in order of increasing difficulty (see Fig. 8-5). In order of presentation, the objects are a manikin, a profile, a hand, and an
elephant. All responses are scored for both time and accuracy. Al-

FIG. 8-5. WAIS-type Object Assembly subtest item.

though each item has a time limit (two minutes for the two easiest puzzles, three minutes for the others), unlike Block Design and Picture Arrangement, partially complete responses receive credit too. All the items are administered to every subject.

Object Assembly has the lowest association with general intellectual ability of all the Performance Scale subtests and is second only to Digit Span in weakness on this factor. In normal individuals, the Object Assembly performance level tends to vary relatively independently of other subtest performances. Like Block Design, it is a relatively pure measure of the visuospatial organization ability. It requires little abstract thinking. Ability to form visual concepts is needed for an adequate performance on this test; ability to form visual concepts *quickly* and translate them into rapid hand responses is essential for an average or better score. Thus, Object Assembly is as much a test of speed of visual organization and motor response as it is of the capacity for visual organization itself.

The puzzles are relatively simple. Even moderately retarded adults can put the manikin together, and more than half of all adults can complete all four puzzles successfully (Matarazzo, 1972). Up to age 35, differentiation of performance levels above the 37th percentile depends solely on time bonuses; beyond that age, the importance of time diminishes, but even at age 70, all differentiations among the 25% of the population scoring above the 75th percentile occurs on the basis of time alone.

The speed component of Object Assembly renders it relatively vulnerable to brain damage generally. Like Block Design, it tends to be particularly sensitive to nondominant hemisphere lesions, so that a markedly low Object Assembly score, particularly if coupled with a similarly low Block Design score, suggests right hemisphere involvement. Unlike Block Design or Picture Completion, when the injury is localized within the dominant hemisphere, the Object Assembly score is usually not much higher than the relatively depressed verbal subtest scores because of the large role speed plays in Object Assembly scoring. The speed component probably underlies the association of lowered Object Assembly scores with frontal lobe lesions (A. Smith, 1966b; A. Smith and Kinder, 1959; Sheer, 1956).

9

INTELLECTUAL ABILITY TESTS
2 / Special Purpose Tests

COMPOSITE TESTS

Problems of learning and adjustment in school instigated the development of most tests of intellectual ability. These tests tend to reflect their educational origins in the age ranges to which they apply and in the type of questions they contain. Moreover, although the intellectual ability tests for adults usually have been developed to aid in job assignment or vocational counseling, the influence of school testing programs can be seen in formats that tend to emphasize academically acquired skills. Thus, intellectual ability tests are more likely to provide data about verbal than other kinds of functions; and those ability tests that purport to measure nonverbal functions have verbal instructions or have been validated on verbal criteria.

Wide Range Tests

"Wide range" refers to the age span covered by a test. In contrast to the WAIS, children's tests, and most paper and pencil ability tests, these tests provide items and norms for age levels ranging from early childhood into the adult years. Composite wide range tests meet the need for measures of different functions at many levels of difficulty.

The Stanford-Binet Intelligence Scale
The Stanford-Binet differs greatly from the WAIS. It is an omnibus test of intellectual abilities containing a very wide variety of short,

one- to six-item subtests (Sattler, 1974; Terman and Merrill, 1937, 1960, 1973). Its age span is from age two to the young adult.

Subtests are arranged in order of difficulty starting with year II at which the subject is asked to build a four-block tower, to identify pictures of three common objects by name (e.g., tree, plane, cup), to place three simple geometric wooden forms into a formboard, and to point out four body parts on a large cardboard doll (e.g., hair, mouth, feet). There are six subtests and an alternate at each level. The subtests are grouped into half-yearly age level intervals from years II to V. From V to XIV, subtest grouping continues by yearly intervals, The average child of a given age can pass most of the subtests at his own age level and few at higher levels so that the activities required at any given age level are typical for children of that age.

After year XIV, there are four more subtest groups, for Average Adult (AA) and Superior Adult (SA) I, II, and III levels. Sample SA III subtests are vocabulary test words "limpet," "flaunt," and "philanthropy"; interpretation of two proverbs such as "Let sleeping dogs lie"; and a mathematical reasoning test involving an arithmetic progression. Subtests at the AA level are equivalent in difficulty to WAIS items passed by adults of *average* intellectual ability. SA I level corresponds to the *high average* WAIS range, SA II to the *superior* WAIS range, and SA III to the *very superior* range.

Each subtest has its own administration and scoring instructions. At each level, the "pass" criterion for any given subtest is the subtest score achieved by a majority of persons at that age level. Some subtests are repeated at several age levels with a different "pass" criterion for each. For instance, Ingenuity I, which consists of three arithmetic reasoning problems, is one of the tests at levels XIV, AA, and SA II. At XIV, the "pass" criterion is one correct solution; at AA the criterion is two, and three correct solutions are required for credit at SA II.

The Binet also differs from the WAIS in that only 7 of its almost 120 subtests have time limits and that no bonuses are awarded for fast responses. Unlike the Wechsler tests, the Binet's emphasis on purely verbal functions varies at different ages. Below age VI, roughly two out of five subtests draw on visuospatial functions, but from age VI on, less than one subtest in seven has much of a visuospatial component. Thus adults with verbal impairments are at a decided disadvantage on the Binet, although the range and variety of verbal tasks permits testing of many more aspects of verbal functioning than does the WAIS. By the same token, although adult subjects whose disabilities are limited mainly to practic and visuospatial functions will fare relatively well on the Binet, it gives the psychologist little opportunity to examine their problem areas.

In selecting subtests for their 1960 revision of the Binet, Terman and Merrill favored those correlating highly with the general ability factor, which may account for the heavy bias toward verbal tests. A content analysis of this revision divided the subtests into seven categories: language, memory, conceptual thinking, reasoning, numerical reasoning, visual-motor, and social intelligence (Sattler, 1965). Table 9-1 lists the tests by category in the order of their appearance on the test.

The Binet contributes to the neuropsychologist's test repertory in two ways. First, it provides a wide enough range of difficulty for testing those patients who are so seriously impaired that they are unable to pass enough WAIS items to earn subtest scores that differ appreciably from the bottom of the scale. Second, many of the individual items are excellent tests of one or another of the functions and skills that come under investigation in neuropsychological studies. In reviewing Binet data from a series of patients who had had neurosurgery, Hebb (1942, p. 281) noted the sensitivity of such subtests as "Maze tracing, sentence completion, differentiation of abstract words, giving of opposites, analogies, speeded block-manipulation tasks, and picture absurdities" to the presence of brain injury. Some of these Binet subtests have similar counterparts in WAIS items, but many of them measure very different aspects of common mental activities. They may provide data to confirm or reject the presence of a specific kind of intellectual dysfunction or to clarify its nature or its functional relationships. Although few of the Binet items reoccur at enough levels of the test to allow discriminating scoring at every level, the item by item age or ability level grading enables the examiner to evaluate each Binet subtest performance separately and also to compare it with performance on other tests, whether they be from the Binet Scale, the WAIS, or another source.

To use the Binet Scale for a severely retarded adult, the examiner can simply follow the administration instructions in the manual. Neuropsychological evaluation does not require computation of the MA score or IQ score. The Binet examination can provide a richly

TABLE 9-1
Analysis of Functions Tested in the 1960 Stanford-Binet Intelligence Scale[a]

Language (L)

(1) II, 3:   Identifying parts of the body; (5) II-6, 2
(2) II, 5:   Picture vocabulary; (7) II-6, 4; (8) III, 2; (9) IV, 1
(3) II, 6:   Word combinations
  II, A: Identifying objects by name
(4) II-6, 1:   Identifying objects by use
(6) II-6, 3:   Naming objects
(10) IV, 4:   Pictorial identification; IV-6, A
(11) V, 3:   Definitions
(12) VI, 1:   Vocabulary; (13) VIII, 1; (15) X, 1; (19) XII, 1; (24) XIV, 1; (25) AA, 1; (28) SAI, 1; (31) SAII, 1; (32) SAIII, 1
(14) IX, 4:   Rhymes: New form
  IX, A: Rhymes: Old form
(16) X, 3:   Abstract words I; (20) XII, 5
(17) X, 5:   Word naming
(18) XI, 3:   Abstract words II; (22) XIII, 2
(21) XII, 6:   Minkus completion I
(23) XIII, 5:   Dissected sentences
(26) AA, 3:   Differences between abstract words
(27) AA, 8:   Abstract words III
(29) SAI, 3:   Minkus completion II
(30) SAI, 5:   Sentence building

Memory (M)

Meaningful Memory (mM)

(3) IV, 2:   Naming objects from memory
  IV, A: Memory for sentences I
(4) IV-6, 5:   Three commissions
(6) VIII, 2:   Memory for stories: The Wet Fall
(11) XI, 4:   Memory for sentences II
(13) XIII, 3:   Memory for sentences III
(16) SAII, 6:   Repeating thought of passage I: Value of Life
(17) SAIII, 6:   Repeating thought of passage II: Tests

Nonmeaningful Memory (nmM)

(1) II-6, 5:   Repeating 2 digits
  III, A: Repeating 3 digits
(5) VII, 6:   Repeating 5 digits
  VII, A: Repeating 3 digits reversed
(8) IX, 6:   Repeating 4 digits reversed
(9) X, 6:   Repeating 6 digits
(12) XII, 4:   Repeating 5 digits reversed
(15) SAI, 4:   Repeating 6 digis reversed

Visual Memory (vM)

(2) III, 4:   Picture memories
(7) IX, 3:   Memory for designs I; (10) XI, 1
  XII, A: Memory for designs II
(14) XIII, 6:   Copying a bead chain from memory

Conceptual Thinking (CT)

(1) IV, 3:   Opposite analogies I; (2) IV-6, 2
(3) VI, 2:   Differences
(4) VI, 5:   Opposite analogies II
(5) VII, 2:   Similarities: Two things
(6) VII, 5:   Opposite analogies III
(7) VIII, 4:   Similarities and differences
(8) XI, 6:   Similarities: Three things
(9) XIV, 6:   Reconciliation of opposites; SAI, A
(10) AA, 5:   Proverbs I
(11) AA, 7:   Essential differences; (124) SAII, 5
(12) SAI, 6:   Essential similarities
(13) SAII, 3:   Proverbs II
(15) SAIII, 2:   Proverbs III
(16) SAIII, 3:   Opposite analogies IV
  SAIII, A: Opposite analogies V

Reasoning (R)

Nonverbal Reasoning (nvR)

(1) II, 2:   Delayed response
(2) III-6, 1:   Comparison of balls
(3) III-6, 2:   Patience: Pictures
(4) III-6, 3:   Discrimination of animal pictures
(5) III-6, 5:   Sorting buttons
  III-6, A: Comparison of sticks

(6) IV, 5:   Discrimination of forms
(7) IV-6, 3: Pictorial similarities
               and differences I
(8) V, 5:   Pictorial similarities
               and differences II
(9) V, 6:   Patience: Rectangles
(10) VI, 3:   Mutilated pictures
(15) XIII, 1: Plan of search
(18) XIV, 5: Orientation: Direction I
(19) AA, 6:   Orientation: Direction II
(21) SAIII, 4: Orientation: Direction III

Verbal Reasoning (vR)

(11) VIII, 3: Verbal absurdities I
(12) IX, 2:   Verbal absurdities II;
               (14) XII, 2
     X, A: Verbal absurdities III
(13) XI, 2:   Verbal absurdities IV
(16) XIII, 4: Problems of fact
(17) XIV, 3: Reasoning I
(20) SAII, 2: Finding reasons III
     SAII, A: Codes
(22) SAIII, 5: Reasoning II

Numerical Reasoning (NR)

(1) VI, 4:   Number concepts
(2) IX, 5:   Making change
(3) X, 2:   Block counting
(4) XIV, 2:   Induction
(5) XIV, 4:   Ingenuity I; (6) AA, 2;
               (9) SAII, 4
     XIV, A: Ingenuity II
(7) AA, 4:   Arithmetical reasoning
(8) SAI, 2:   Enclosed box problem

Visual-Motor (VM)

(1) II, 1:   Three-hole form board
(2) II, 4:   Block building; Tower
     II-6, A: Three hole form board:
               Rotated
(3) III, 1:   Stringing beads
(4) III, 3:   Block building: Bridge
(5) III, 5:   Copying a circle
(6) III, 6:   Drawing a vertical line
(7) V, 1:   Picture completion: Man
(8) V, 2:   Paper folding: Triangle
(9) V, 4:   Copying a square
     V, A: Knot
(10) VI, 6:   Maze tracing
(11) VII, 3:   Copying a diamond
(12) IX, 1:   Paper cutting; XIII, A
     AA, A: Binet paper cutting

Social Intelligence (SI)

(1) II-6, 6:   Obeying simple commands
(2) III-6, 4: Response to pictures; VI, A
(3) III-6, 6: Comprehension I
(4) IV-6:   Comprehension II
(5) IV-6, 1: Aesthetic comparison
(6) IV-6, 4: Materials
(7) IV-6, 6: Comprehension III
(8) VII, 1:   Picture absurdities I
(9) VII, 4:   Comprehension IV;
               (10) VIII, 5
(11) VIII, 6: Naming the days of the week
     VIII, A: Problem situations I
(12) X, 4:   Finding reasons I
(13) XI, 5:   Problem situation II
     XI, A: Finding reasons II
(14) XII, 3: Picture absurdities II:
               The Shadow

Note:—Alternate items not designated by number.
[a] Form L-M (Sattler, 1965).

descriptive evaluation in which the age-grades of the subtests serve as points of reference. The summed MA or IQ scores can be computed as needed for legal purposes, to satisfy entry requirements into special programs, or for research; but like WAIS IQ scores, they obscure the strengths and weaknesses of the patient's performance. The examiner may prefer to use a battery type children's test for a wider range of difficulty and finer scaling of individual subtests and for their ease of administration and interpretation (see pp. 234–239 below for a discussion of children's tests).

Individual Binet subtests can be given as single tests, but there are few guidelines to direct the examiner looking for a test of some particular function or set of functions (see for example, Table 9-1). He must select most Binet subtests on the basis of their face validity and he can only draw a conclusion about the patient's performance relative to the average person at the age or ability level at which the subtest appears on the scale. Excepting those subtests that have counterparts at other levels of the scale, if the patient passes a subtest, the examiner does not know how much better he could do, and if he fails, the examiner does not know at what lower level he could pass it.

The neuropsychologist who wants an extensive repertory of easily administered and scored assessment techniques should familiarize himself with both the 1937 and 1960 revisions of the Binet Scale. A few subtests were omitted, mostly from Form M, when the two alternate forms of the 1937 revision were merged into the current Form L-M. Some of the omitted subtests are like Form L-M subtests, but their content puts them at different levels of difficulty. By making use of these Form M subtests, the examiner can evaluate similar test behavior at different levels of difficulty.

Individual Binet subtests fit well into larger test batteries constructed for specific research purposes or for the individual patient. Application of particular Binet subtests to specific problems in neuropsychological assessment will be discussed in Chapters 10 through 15 under the appropriate topic heading.

The Peabody Individual Achievement Test (PIAT)
This test battery measures academic achievement for school grades from kindergarten to grade 12 (Dunn and Markwardt, 1970). Its wide coverage of achievement levels makes it a valuable instrument for measuring residual intellectual competency of brain injured adults. By virtue of its focus on academic skills, the PIAT primarily tests verbal conceptual functions. However, the stimulus material is mostly visual—both verbal and pictorial in content—so that a variety of visual perceptual functions enter into the PIAT performance too. No complex motor responses are required of the subject, making this an excellent instrument for use with physically handicapped pa-

This test is carefully standardized with a full set of norms for each subtest. Level I has age norms for each half-yearly interval between ages 5 and 12. Level II age norms continue at half-yearly intervals from 12 to 16; from 16 to 20, they span two-year intervals, and from 20 to 45 they cover five-year intervals. All raw scores can be converted to school grades, standard scores, or percentiles. Thus this is a flexible test, adaptable for inclusion in any set of tests.

All three WRAT subtests are heavily weighted with the general ability factor, and the verbal factor contributes a large component to Reading and Spelling. Arithmetic has little of the verbal factor, but a "motivation" factor is involved.

The WRAT Arithmetic subtest provides an excellent means of testing the ability to perform written arithmetic. A feature of the WRAT Arithmetic test that is particularly valuable for neuropsychological assessment is the variety of mathematical problems it poses. These include application of the four basic arithmetic operations to two and three digit numbers, to decimals, percentages, fractions, and to algebraic problems, as well as the translation of Roman numerals, weights, and measures. Problems concerning squares, roots, and some geometric constructs are also presented. Thus, when a patient's mathematical performance is defective, the examiner can determine by inspection of his worksheet whether his difficulties are due to a dyscalculia of the spatial type, a figure or number alexia, or an anarithmetria in which number concepts or basic operations have been lost.

The Arithmetic subtest does have some drawbacks when used for neuropsychological purposes. Many brain damaged patients are unable to answer more than a few items within the allotted ten minutes. To evaluate a performance on the basis of the test norms, which take time into account, the examiner need only note how much of the test the patient completed at ten minutes, without disturbing the patient. Stopping the patient before he has finished may greatly restrict the amount of information that can be obtained about his ability to do arithmetic and the nature of any disability he may have in this area. The small print and scant space surrounding each problem can create some difficulty, particularly for older patients and patients with visual acuity problems. A larger scale version of this test, allowing for more computation space around each problem, would solve this difficulty and make it easier for the examiner to follow the patient's computational efforts. The standard score and percentile norms reflect intellectual decline from ages 25 to 50, but they do not take into account differences at older age levels.

Children's Tests

Patients with severe intellectual handicaps may give so few scorable responses to WAIS subtests that the examiner has little opportunity to assess their capabilities or the relative strengths and weaknesses of different functions. Such patients may be able to handle children's or infant's tests well enough to display a broader range of their behavior than they can on an adult test. The Binet satisfies the need for a measuring instrument at child and pre-school levels but lacks the advantages of battery tests. Three of the best known children's tests—the Wechsler Intelligence Scale for Children, The Wechsler Preschool and Primary Test of Intelligence, and the Pictorial Test of Intelligence—are in battery form. A fourth, the Leiter, is a nonverbal counterpart of the Binet intended for use with patients who have speech and hearing handicaps.

The Wechsler Intelligence Scale for Children (WISC AND WISC-R)
The WISC covers the age range from 5 to 15 years 11 months (Sattler, 1974; Wechsler, 1949), and the age range of its revision, the WISC-R, is 6 years to 16 years 11 months (Wechsler, 1974). They contain the same subtests as the WAIS in an almost identical format, but all of the subtests except Digit Span begin with considerably simpler items. Although most WISC and WISC-R items are the same, outmoded WISC items have been dropped from the WISC-R, and some of the new WISC-R picture items have black or female subjects. The WISC-R blocks conform to the two-color (red and white) WAIS blocks, replacing the four-color WISC blocks. The number sequences of the WISC and WISC-R Digit Span subtest are the same length and difficulty as those of the WAIS. There is an alternate form of Digit Symbol (called Coding on the WISC) for children under nine on the WISC, under eight on the WISC-R, and suspected mental defectives. Coding uses five geometric symbols (star, circle, etc.) instead of numbers, and the symbols to be written in are simpler than those of the more difficult WISC version or the WAIS. Administration instructions are similar, and for many subtests, identical, to those of the WAIS.

Standard score equivalents of WISC and WISC-R subtest raw scores are given for each four-month interval covered by the scale. However, in interpreting WISC and WISC-R scores for adult patients, the examiner should use the Table of Test Age Equivalents (p. 113 of the WISC *Manual,* p. 189 of the WISC-R *Manual*). This will give him the age equivalents of the patient's score on any of the WISC subtests.

The WISC contains a maze test that has no WAIS counterpart. It consists of printed mazes (eight on the WISC, nine on the WISC-R) of varying sizes and complexity which are given in order of difficulty. Scoring is based on the number of errors; there are no time bonuses. Mazes have been used to measure general ability as well as specific nonverbal reasoning and visuopractic functions. For further discussion of maze tests, see pp. 408–410 below.

Although there is no overlap between the WAIS and the WISC age norms, the WISC-R overlaps the WAIS at age 16; 16 year olds tend to obtain slightly higher scores on the WAIS than the WISC-R. There is also a considerable overlap in item difficulty. Thus some severely impaired patients cannot succeed on many more WISC or WISC-R than WAIS items, although several of the WISC-R subtests provide a fuller coverage than their WISC counterparts at the youngest age levels. Even the WISC's simpler items may be too difficult for the profoundly impaired patient.

Wechsler Preschool and Primary Scale of Intelligence (WPPSI)
This scale was developed to provide better Wechsler test norms at the lowest WISC levels where the original WISC standardization tends to be unsatisfactory for children of average or lower ability and to extend Wechsler test coverage downward another year below the WISC (Sattler, 1974; Wechsler, 1967). Its age range is four to six and one-half years.

Eight of the eleven subtests of the WPPSI have WISC counterparts, and of these eight, one-third to two-thirds of the test questions are similar or identical to WISC items. All the Verbal Scale subtests of the WISC and WAIS are represented on the WPPSI except Digit Span. Apart from the first four Arithmetic items, which use pictures to test quantity concepts, the formats of the verbal subtests are identical with those of their WISC and WAIS counterparts, differing only in range and difficulty level. The Sentences test substitutes for Digit Span as the test of immediate memory span.

Of the five Performance Scale subtests, Picture Completion, Mazes, and Block Design have WISC counterparts. Instead of cubes, Block Design uses two-sided flat blocks, some painted solid red or white, some half red and half white. Of the ten designs, only the last three are copied from pictures, the rest are copied from models the examiner builds. The flat blocks change the nature of the task radically so that, although the last three designs are from the WISC, this subtest is actually not an extension of the WAIS Block Design. The first six mazes are line mazes; the rest of the test consists of all but the most difficult of the WISC mazes. Animal House is new to the Wechsler tests. It presents a substitution format similar to Digit Symbol or Coding, but instead of being a paper and pencil test, it uses animal pictures and colored pegs. The child's task is to put the colored pegs into holes under the animal pictures following the pairing of animals and colored pegs displayed in a model at the top of the pegboard. Any slight motor clumsiness that slows performance penalizes the subject since the scoring is heavily dependent on time: a six year old who takes 4 minutes and 59 seconds to complete the test correctly receives a scaled score of 4; if he takes 1 minute and 59 seconds his scaled score is 9, and a 59-second performance earns him a scaled score of 14. Geometric Design is a copying task using ten simple geometric figures as models.

The WPPSI is not a test for the severely impaired patient, although a few items on each scale will be suitable for some patients who cannot handle the WISC. The added range afforded by this test is so small that few patients who are unable to perform WISC items could perform on the WPPSI instead.

The Pictorial Test of Intelligence (PTI)

This children's test in battery format was standardized on a well-randomized sample of American children from ages three to eight (French, 1964). It contains six subtests: (1) Picture Vocabulary tests comprehension of spoken words and picture recognition. (2) Form Discrimination is a design matching test. (3) Information and Comprehension measures the subject's understanding of the nature and use of common objects. (4) Similarities tests the ability to abstract and generalize. (5) Size and Number involves both quantity and number concepts. (6) Immediate Recall is a recognition test based on a 5-second exposure to a picture or design.

The PTI requires no verbal or fine motor response from the subject. He need only point to or otherwise indicate one of four designs, pictures, symbols, etc., printed on a large (27 cm × 27 cm) response card. All the printed materials are uncomplicated, clear black and white line drawings. This untimed test typically takes about one-half hour to complete. Each subtest has a short form covering a restricted range of the questions for three- and four-year-old children. These short forms are not appropriate for many profoundly impaired adults who may still possess some unexpected residual abilities enabling them to pass test items at higher levels than those represented on the short forms. Any given subtest can be discontinued after six consecutive failures.

The examiner may wish to change some of the wording to suit adult patients. For example, the recommended introduction to the test, "I believe that you will have a lot of fun looking at the pictures which I have in this box," might sound better to an adult as "I have a lot of pictures in this box for you to look at." Some of the Size and Number subtest questions in particular would benefit from rewording. For example, item 7 shows a picture of children in party dress and the examiner's introduction is, "Let's pretend that we are going to a party," which is more appropriately read to an adult as, "Let's pretend there is a children's party."

The Leiter International Performance Scale
This instrument was devised especially for testing verbally handicapped and foreign language-speaking children (Leiter, 1969a; 1969b). The instructions can be either spoken or pantomimed. This is not a test that is used frequently with adult populations, but it should be available as part of a standard neuropsychological battery. The Leiter was originally developed for ages 2 to 12, and it is well standardized for this group. The test also includes a set of upper level (ages 14 to Adult) subtests that are not as well standardized for validity or reliability. Test presentation follows the omnibus format.

The test material consists of a long wooden form with a slot on the top side for holding cardboard strips of varying length. Cut out squares form pockets along the length of the wooden form into which wooden block cubes can be fitted. Problems are printed on the cardboard strips. Each problem has its own set of blocks which carry the printed or painted "answers" on one side. The subject's task is to

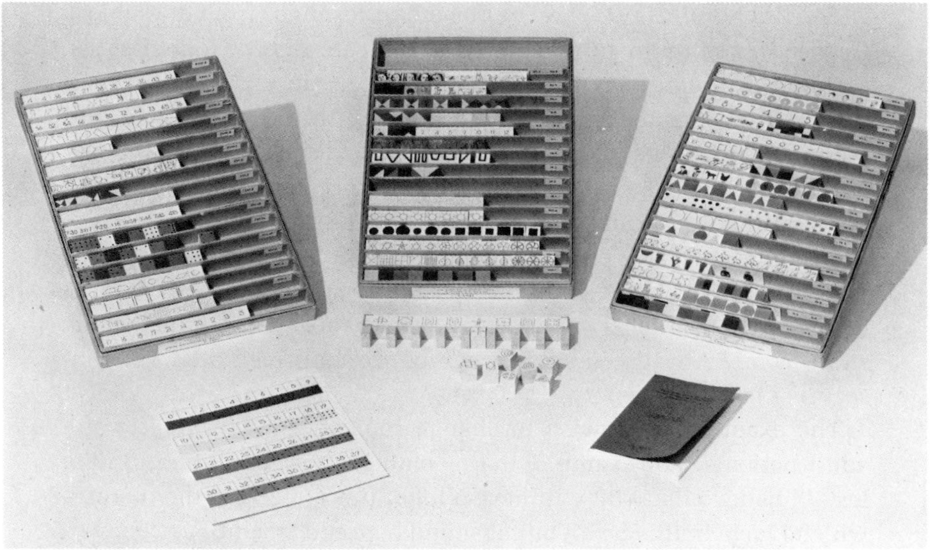

FIG. 9-2. The Leiter International Performance Scale test materials.

figure out the principle of the problem posed by the printed strip and insert the blocks correctly into the square pockets (see Fig. 9-2). Items include a wide variety of tasks involving pictures, colors, numbers, and geometric designs. Although this is a portable test, unfortunately its bulk and weight make transportation difficult.

Like the Binet, Leiter subtests are arranged and presented in age groups, ranging from year II to year XVIII, with four subtests in each group. After year X, only even-numbered years are represented, making 13 age levels and 52 subtests in all. As with the Binet, the examiner can estimate the patient's performance level from the age grade of passed subtests. Since a number of similar tests appear at different ages and levels of difficulty, this test does provide some differentiation of performance levels for some functions such as serial reasoning and two-dimensional visuopractic construction. The instructions recommend that the test begin at a level two years below the child's age to acquaint him with this unfamiliar activity on relatively easy tasks. When using the Leiter with adults, the examiner should follow the principle of beginning the test at an easily comprehended level. The examination stops when the subject has failed all the subtests of two consecutive age groups. The test is untimed except for four difficulty levels of Block Design, which allow from two and one-half to five minutes for the most difficult and easiest problems, respectively.

Many of the Leiter subtests are nonverbal analogues of tests that appear elsewhere, such as color, form, or picture matching; Block Design; Block Counting; and Similarities. Others are unique to the Leiter. These include tests of perceptual recognition, size and number estimation, and comprehension of sequences and progressions. For these latter subtests, the examiner must rely on his own content analysis when interpreting a patient's performance.

Paper and Pencil Tests

The large scale needs of academic and vocational selection, placement, and counseling programs occasioned the development of numerous paper and pencil tests designed to measure a variety of intellectual abilities. Although some of the earlier tests of intellectual ability followed the omnibus format, most group ability tests now are batteries with two, three, or more subtests of different skills and abilities.

Paper and pencil test batteries have rarely been used in neuropsychological assessment, except when premorbid test data were already available, as in the case of men who have been through the armed forces testing programs. However, composite paper and pencil tests can be a good source of information about the patient's reading, writing (sometimes), and ability to follow instructions and work independently. The content of many of them parallels or complements individually administered batteries for testing visuospatial functions as well as verbal ones, thus permitting the testing of similar functions with different input and output modalities. Further, their large scale, elaborate standardization procedures generally ensure statistically well-defined norms and high reliability.

Even though many of these batteries serve their purpose well, they do not substitute for individually administered tests. Many handicapped patients cannot take paper and pencil tests. Furthermore, the qualitative aspects of behavior rarely show up on multiple-choice answer sheets.

Armed services tests
Army General Classification Test (AGCT). This is like a battery test in that it contains three different kinds of test items, Vocabulary, Arithmetic Story Problems, and Block Counting, but it presents them in an omnibus format. The three kinds of multiple-choice items are sequentially rotated in sets of five or ten items, beginning with the ten easiest of each and continuing in order of difficulty, for a total of 150 items. The results are summed in one score.

The single score is based on a mean of 100 and a standard deviation of 20. Percentiles are also given for raw score conversions. Scores cover the entire range of nondefective adults from three standard deviations below the mean (AGCT Standard Score = 41) to three standard deviations above the mean (AGCT SS = 161). The examiner must inspect the answer sheet if he wants to find out whether there are marked performance differences between the subtests.

This test was designed to provide quick screening and classification of the intellectual ability of newly enlisted armed services personnel. Millions of young people took this test during the years 1940 to 1945. Scores from AGCT tests taken at induction were utilized in several brain function studies. The military stopped using this test in 1945, replacing it with an updated version, the *Armed Forces Qualification Test (AFQT)* (Montague et al., 1957). The AGCT then entered the civilian domain, like the Army Alpha a generation before (Army General Classification Test, 1948).

The single summed test score reduces reliable interpretation of AGCT data to the single dimension of general ability but does not restrict its sensitivity to brain damage. Brain injured patients generally tend to have lower postmorbid than premorbid AGCT scores (H. L. Williams et al., 1959). Significantly greater score depressions following frontal lobe and left hemisphere—particularly parietal and temporal lobe—injuries reflect the large role that language and speed play in this test (Teuber, 1964; Weinstein, 1964).

Army Classification Battery (ACB). The ACB (Montague et al., 1957) is not available for civilian examinations. However, all army recruits take it routinely and their scores are filed in their permanent service record. Although the test cannot be readministered in a civilian setting, data from this battery provide direct measures of premorbid intellectual functioning that can be invaluable in evaluating the extent of impairment in patients who have served in the army.

The ACB contains ten separately scored subtests. The first subtest, Reading and Vocabulary (RV), is a verbal skill test that correlates .76 with the Wechsler-Bellevue Information and Vocabulary subtests. Arithmetic Reasoning (AR) involves story problems and thus tests both verbal and arithmetic skills, as it correlates .71 with the Wechsler Information subtest and .70 with Arithmetic and Vocabulary. The Pattern Analysis test (PA) purports to measure spatial ability but it is actually a nonverbal test of general ability, correlating most highly with the Wechsler Full Scale score (.81) and more highly with Information (.63) than with Block Design (.58). The Army Clerical Speed test (ACS-1 and ACS-2), which includes a symbol substitution task like the WAIS Digit Symbol subtest, involves visual accuracy and graphomotor speed. The Army Radio Code Aptitude test (ARC-1) is an auditory learning test. The remaining five subtests measure different areas of technical information.

Vocational and educational guidance batteries
The batteries that are most highly recommended for vocational counseling contain many subtests covering a variety of skills and abilities. They are designed as multiple-choice tests with both machine and hand scoring keys to facilitate group administration. This limits their applicability to patients whose verbal skills and ability to follow directions and work independently are relatively intact. With such patients, they do enable the examiner to obtain a considerable amount of information with very little effort on his part. These advantages make them attractive research tools for the study of many kinds of brain damage. Examiners may also find them clinically useful, both for the broad range of data the complete battery can provide and for testing a specific function or ability by means of one or more of the individual subtests.

Differential Aptitude Tests (DAT). This test, now in its fifth edition, consists of eight separately scored subtests, each with its own norms (Bennett et al., 1972). Because it was designed for guidance in high schools, norms are given for each sex separately and for grades 8 through 12. Twelfth grade norms apply to young adults as well. There is a Spanish language form of the DAT.

Of the eight subtests, (1) is Verbal Reasoning (VR), a verbal analogies test. (2) Numerical Ability (NA) involves arithmetic calculation. (3) Abstract Reasoning (AR) concerns nonverbal conceptual sequences. (4) Clerical Speed and Accuracy (CSA) measures perceptual response speed. (5) Mechanical Reasoning (MR) tests the practical understanding of basic physical principles. (6) Space Relations (SR) requires translation of two-dimensional designs to three-dimensional figures. (7) Spelling (LU-1) requires identification of spelling errors. (8) Language Usage (LU-2) tests grammar. These are timed tests, the five longest taking 35 to 40 minutes each to explain and administer. Total testing time runs 300 to 330 minutes. Raw score conversion is to percentiles.

Recent studies of brain injured patients suggest that all DAT subtest scores are affected by the extent of the lesion (Lansdell, 1971). The scores of the verbal subtests (VR and LU-1 and 2) and the visuospatial tests show the greatest shift downward. The Abstract Reasoning Test may be particularly sensitive to temporal lobe damage.

General Aptitude Test Battery (GATB).   The main purpose of this battery, published by the U.S. Department of Labor (1965), is to provide information for job counseling and only secondarily for educational guidance. Like the armed services tests, the GATB is not available commercially. However, many patients have taken it when seeking vocational help from state employment and rehabilitation agencies either prior or subsequent to incurring their brain injury. Although most neuropsychologists do not have access to the test itself, they can use the scores obtained by a state agency in its testing program to augment their findings or to provide reliable premorbid test data.

There are twelve subtests in this battery, of which seven are multiple-choice paper and pencil tests. The five other subtests involve aspects of motor speed and coordination. The seven paper and pencil subtests are: (1) Name Comparisons, which involves comparing similar and different names on two lists, is associated with a factor called Clerical Perception (Q). (2) Computation consists of nonverbal arithmetic problems testing Numerical Aptitude (N). (3) Three-Dimensional Space requires the patient to relate two- and three-dimensional aspects of the same figure, like Space Relations on the DAT, and is associated with Spatial Aptitude (S). (4) Vocabulary tests identification of similar and different words and measures Verbal Aptitude (V). (5) Tool Matching involves perceptual accuracy and a Form Perception (P) factor. (6) Arithmetic Reasoning consists of story problems and is also a measure of Numerical Aptitude (N). (7) Form Matching is another test of perceptual accuracy associated with the Form Perception (P) factor. A general ability (G) factor score is compounded from the scores on the Three-Dimensional Space, Vocabulary, and Arithmetic Reasoning subtests. The eighth test, Mark Making, is a motor speed and accuracy test associated with a Motor Coordination (K) factor. Tests 9 through 12 require apparatus, a Pegboard for the (9) Place and (10) Turn subtests measuring Manual Dexterity (M); and a Finger Dexterity Board with rivets and washers for subtests (11) Assemble and (12) Disassemble, which are both tests of Finger Dexterity (F). Total testing time runs 120 to 150 minutes.

The five GATB motor tests involving motor speed tend to be particularly vulnerable to chronic seizure conditions (Tellegen, 1965) and chronic alcoholism (Kish, 1970). Alcoholics displayed little deficit on the Vocabulary subtest, and the seizure patients' performance on the nonmotor parts of the test was unremarkable. The thorough factorial analysis of these tests recommends their further application to both neuropsychological research and clinical problems.

Educational guidance tests
Several tests of academic ability are organized into a battery format with separate subtest scores. Because these are academically oriented tests, they provide data on a much narrower range of abilities than do the more vocationally oriented batteries.

Some of the academic ability tests, like the Cooperative School and College Ability Tests (SCAT) (1966) and the Scholastic Aptitude Test (SAT) of the College Entrance Examination Board, consist of just two subtests, one testing verbal and the other mathematical abilities. The College Qualification Test (CQT) (Bennett et al., 1961) has three subtests, V-verbal, N-numerical, and I-information. The California Short-Form Test of Mental Maturity, 1963 Revision (CTMM-SF) (Sullivan et al., 1963) gives norms for four factors: Logical Reasoning; Numerical Reasoning; Verbal Concepts; and Memory. All of the above-named tests except the SAT can be purchased by qualified individual examiners. The SAT battery is highly restricted and cannot be given in a clinical setting. However, for patients who took the test before the onset of an organic brain condition, they provide a very reliable measure of premorbid verbal and mathematical skills. The applicability of the College Qualification Tests is limited to persons who have completed high school and have not experienced a general retardation. The College Qualification Tests are best suited for estimating the premorbid general ability level of patients who have fairly specific nonverbal deficits. Since the SCAT norms begin at grade four and the CTMM test norms begin at the kindergarten level, these tests can assess residual verbal skills in moderately deteriorated patients.

There are also multiple-scale paper and pencil educational tests that purport to measure visual and spatial factors as well as verbal and quantitative ones. Unfortunately, claims for their performance have not been substantiated to an extent that warrants their regular use in neuropsychological studies (Buros, 1972).

SINGLE TESTS OF GENERAL ABILITY

Single tests for estimating the general intellectual ability level of intact persons typically measure some aspect of intellectual functioning associated with such evidence of mental prowess as school grades, academic attainment, or occupational status. Their usefulness in providing an estimate of the general ability of brain injured patients varies with the nature of the cerebral insult. When functions involved in one of these tests remain relatively unaffected, that test will serve its intended purpose well. When a function critical to the performance of one of these tests is impaired, the test can provide much information about the nature and extent of the intellectual disability when it is given as one of a set of different kinds of tests.

Vocabulary Tests

Vocabulary level has long been recognized as an excellent guide to the general intellectual performance of intact, well-socialized persons. Vocabulary tests have proven equally valuable in demonstrating the effects of dominant hemisphere disease. This dual function has placed vocabulary tests among the most widely used of all mental ability tests, whether alone or as part of test batteries.

Paper and pencil vocabulary tests

Single paper and pencil vocabulary tests are rarely used. Most of the time, the assessment of vocabulary takes place as part of an academic aptitude test battery, a reading test battery, or one of the multiple test guidance batteries. When neuropsychological studies have included a single vocabulary test in their paper and pencil battery, it has usually been the 100-word Atwell and Wells' Wide Range Vocabulary Test (Atwell and Wells, 1937) or the 80-word Mill Hill Vocabulary Scale (Raven, 1958). These multiple-choice tests take relatively little time to administer and are easily scored. The Atwell and Wells test gives grade level equivalents for raw scores with a range from grade three to college. Mill Hill raw scores convert to percentiles for age levels from 20 to 65. Both of these well-standardized tests have proven to be sensitive to dominant hemisphere disease (Costa and Vaughan, 1962; Lansdell, 1968a).

Nonverbal vocabulary tests

Vocabulary tests in which the patient signals that he recognizes a spoken or printed word by pointing to one of a set of pictures permit evaluation of the recognition vocabulary of many verbally handicapped patients. These tests are generally simple to administer. They are most often used for quick screening and for estimating the general ability level of intact persons when time or circumstances do not allow a more complete examination. Slight differences in the design and standardization populations of the picture vocabulary tests in most common use affect their appropriateness for different patients to some extent.

Peabody Picture Vocabulary Test (PPVT).   This easily administered vocabulary test was standardized for ages two and one-half to eighteen (Dunn, 1965). It consists of 150 picture plates, each with four pictures (see Fig. 9-3). There is one plate for each of the 150 words of the two equivalent word lists. The subject points to or gives the number of the picture most like the stimulus word, which is spoken by the examiner or shown on a printed card. The simplest words are given only to young children and obviously retarded or

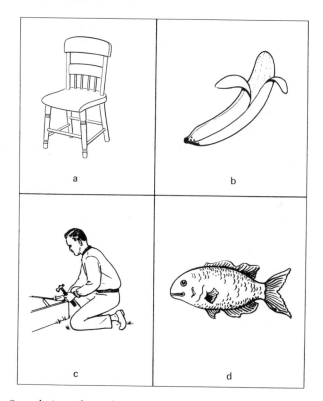

FIG. 9-3. Sample item from the Peabody Picture Vocabulary Test. The word to be matched is "Banana."

impaired adults. Care is taken to enter the word list at the level most suitable for the subject so that both basal (the highest six consecutive passes) and ceiling (six failures out of eight) scores can be obtained with minimum effort. Points for passed items are simply counted and entered into tables giving derived mental age scores, percentiles, and deviation IQ scores.

The PPVT spans both very low age ranges and levels of intellectual functioning and levels considerably above average adult ability. The simplicity of the pictures makes it eminently suitable for those brain damaged patients who have so much difficulty sorting out the elements in a complex stimulus that they are unable to respond to the intended problem. Of the three nonverbal vocabulary tests discussed here, the PPVT probably gives the purest measurement of recognition vocabulary per se. It is also the one on which the most seriously impaired patients have the greatest likelihood of success.

The Quick Test.   In contrast to the Peabody, Quick Test pictures each depict a complex scene or situation (Ammons and Ammons, 1962). This test consists of three 50-word lists, comparable in difficulty. Words are arranged in order of difficulty. For each series there is only one picture plate containing four pictures. The subject points or gives the number of that picture that can be best associated with each word as it is read aloud by the examiner or shown on a printed card. The entire list is given to all subjects. The raw score is the number correct for each list. Tables give the mental age equivalent, percentile, and deviation IQ score for each of the three raw scores separately as well as for each combination of two raw scores and for the summed raw scores for all three lists. The test takes into account the effects of age on intellectual functioning by adding from one to three points to the raw scores obtained by persons over age 45.

As its name implies, this test is quick. One word list takes ten minutes or less to administer; all three word lists rarely take more than 50 minutes. The intercorrelations between the lists are good so that a single list will give a reasonably reliable total score estimate. The Quick Test is geared for the borderline to the average range of the adult population. The pictures are sufficiently complex to be useful in making discriminations from age six through average adult. However, its ceiling is so low that it provides virtually no differentiation between bright and very bright adults.

The Quick Test's role in neuropsychology is primarily as an adjunctive technique, when language expression is impaired in an otherwise fairly intact person. Although not appropriate for severely impaired or retarded patients, it tests recognition vocabulary, ability to form relatively simple verbal associations, and ability to make sense out of a relatively complex visual stimulus.

The Full-Range Picture Vocabulary Test (FRPV).   This test combines the cartoon situation pictures and brief administration time features of the Quick Test with the wide range coverage of the Peabody (Ammons and Ammons, 1948). The stimulus word can be given orally or read by the patient. Besides the standard norms for ages two to adult, the FRPV offers separate norms for white farm children, Spanish-American children, black children, and black adults. Most reported correlations between the FRPV and the WAIS Vocabulary subtest and Verbal Scale IQ score run .85 or better, although a correlation with Vocabulary as low as .62 has been reported (Vellutino and Hogan, 1966).

Nonverbal Tests of General Intellectual Ability

There have been many attempts to devise a simple, easy to administer test that would predict academic success or vocational achievement as well as the Wechsler tests and the Binet. There are also many tests that claim to measure the general intellectual level of verbally handicapped persons. A few tests aim to accomplish both these goals. These various tests measure different sets of functions but have in common a nonverbal format.

Raven's Progressive Matrices (RPM)
This multiple-choice paper and pencil test was developed in England and has received widespread attention in this country and abroad (Raven, 1960). It was intended to be a "culture fair" test of general ability, but even though it requires neither language nor academic skills for success, educational level influences the RPM performance (Bolin, 1955; Colonna and Faglioni, 1966). The test consists of a series of visual pattern matching and analogy problems pictured in nonrepresentational designs. It requires the subject to conceptualize spatial, design, and numerical relationships ranging from the very obvious and concrete to the very complex and abstract (see Fig. 9-4).

Raven's Matrices is easy to administer. A secretary or clerk can give or demonstrate the instructions. It has no time limit; most people take from 40 minutes to an hour. It consists of sixty items grouped into five series, plus two sample items. Each item contains a pattern problem with one part removed and from four to eight pictured inserts of which one contains the correct pattern. The subject points to the pattern piece he selects as correct or writes its number on an answer sheet. The Coloured Progressive Matrices provides a simpler alternate three-series form of this test for use with children aged 5 to 11 and defective adults.

Norms are available for ages 8 to 65. Score conversion is to percen-

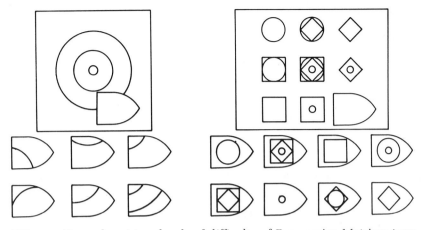

FIG. 9-4. Examples at two levels of difficulty of Progressive Matrices type items.

tiles. Seven percentile levels are given for age groups ranging from 20 to 65. For finer scaled scoring, the examiner can use Peck's table for converting raw scores into percentiles (see Table 9-2).

The Progressive Matrices correlates most highly with nonverbal tests and most poorly with tests that predict academic achievement (J. C. Hall, 1957a; Talland, 1965; Urmer et al., 1960). Although it fails to achieve its purpose as a test of general intellectual ability, it does assess reasoning in the visuospatial modality (Archibald et al., 1967; Colonna and Faglioni, 1966).

The effectiveness of the Progressive Matrices in identifying organically impaired patients appears to be related to the extent of the damage (Zimet and Fishman, 1970). It has old, rather loosely constructed norms, which may account for its limited usefulness in screening for brain damage (Newcombe, 1969). Cutting scores based on the observation that brain damaged patients tend to do much better on the first of the five series (which tests simple pattern discrimination) than on the other four series (which test the "capacity to educe new relations" at levels of increasing complexity) do not differentiate "organic" from schizophrenic patients to a clinically satisfactory degree (Knehr, 1965). Neither does this test discriminate well between undifferentiated groups of patients with right and left hemisphere damage (Arrigoni and De Renzi, 1964; Costa and Vaughan, 1962). However, poor performance on the Pro-

TABLE 9-2

Table for Converting Progressive Matrices Raw Scores into Percentiles

Raw Score	Age Group								
	25	30	35	40	45	50	55	60	65
13								2	5
14								5	7
15					2.5	3.0	5	8	10
16					3.0	3.5	7	10	13
17				2.0	4	5	8	13	17
18				3.0	5	6.5	10	15	20
19			2.0	4	7	7.5	12	18	25
20	2.0	2.0	2.5	5	8	10	15	22	30
21	2.5	3	3.5	7	10	12	20	25	34
22	3.0	4	5	8	12	15	24	28	38
23	3.5	5	7	10	15	19	28	32	42
24	4.0	7	9	12	17	21	32	36	46
25	5	8	11	15	20	25	36	40	50
26	8	10	14	17	23	28	40	45	55
27	9	12	16	20	25	32	44	50	60
28	10	14	19	23	28	36	48	54	64
29	11	16	21	26	31	40	50	59	68
30	12	18	25	28	35	46	54	63	72
31	14	20	28	31	39	50	58	66	75
32	15	22	30	34	43	54	62	70	78
33	17	25	34	37	47	58	64	73	81
34	19	28	38	40	50	61	68	58	83
35	21	30	40	43	54	64	71	78	85
36	24	32	42	46	57	67	73	80	87
37	26	34	45	50	60	70	76	82	88
38	28	38	48	53	63	72	78	84	89
39	32	40	50	57	66	74	80	85	90
40	35	42	53	60	69	76	83	87	91
41	38	45	56	64	72	78	86	89	93
42	42	48	60	68	75	80	88	90	94
43	45	50	62	71	78	83	90	92	95
44	48	54	66	75	81	85	92	93	96
45	52	58	70	79	85	87	93	95	97
46	56	62	74	82	87	90	94	96	98
47	61	66	77	85	90	92	95	97	>98
48	66	70	80	88	92	93	96	98	
49	70	74	84	90	94	95	97	>98	
50	74	78	86	92	95	96	98		
51	78	82	89	94	96	97	>98		
52	82	85	91	95	98	98			
53	85	90	93	96	>98	>98			
54	88	95	95	97					
55	94	98	>98	>98					
>56	>98	>98							

(From Peck, 1970.)

250

gressive Matrices appears to relate consistently to the presence of apraxia and visual field defects; RPM scores correlate significantly with performance on drawing and constructional tasks (De Renzi and Faglioni, 1965; Piercy and Smyth, 1962). One item analysis of RPM errors made by patients who have had cerebrovascular accidents showed that they tend to make many more random errors unrelated to difficulty level and more errors involving figure-ground reversal than do normal control subjects (Urmer et al., 1960).

Human figure drawing tests

The quality and complexity of children's drawings increases with age at a sufficiently regular pace to warrant the inclusion of drawing tests in the standard repertory of tests of intellectual development. In the United States, the Goodenough "Draw a Man" test and its recent revision utilizing drawings of a man and a woman have provided the most popular systems for estimating developmental level from human figure drawings (Harris, 1963). A similar test, developed in Europe, uses a system for scoring drawings of "A lady walking in the rain (une dame qui se promène et il pleut)" from which the child's developmental level can be estimated (E. M. Taylor, 1959). These tests have been particularly prized for measuring the intellectual potential of handicapped or neurologically impaired children. They have also been used as brief intellectual screening procedures with young children.

The upper age norms of both these tests end at 15, reflecting the normal leveling off of scores on drawing tests in the early teens. However, because drawing tests are relatively independent of language skills they can be used to obtain rough estimates of the general ability of adults with verbal impairments.

Each test is administered with verbal instructions to produce the desired drawing, a man and a woman, or a lady walking in the rain. Neither test is timed. The subject can achieve a maximum of 73 and 71 points for figures of a man and woman, respectively, whereas André Rey's standardization of "Lady" allows for a maximum 49 score points to provide a somewhat coarser grained scale than the Harris-Goodenough test (see Table 9-3).

The Harris scoring system converts the raw score points to standard scores based on a mean of 100 and a standard deviation of 15, for each year from 3 to 15. The Rey scoring system for "Lady" con-

TABLE 9-3
Rey's Scoring System for *Une dame qui se promène et il pleut*

Item	Points
1. Human form (head with legs)	1
2. Body distinct from arms and legs	1
3. Some clothing (buttons, scribbles on body)	1
4. A female figure	1
5. Profile: head and at least one other part of body in profile (body, feet, arms)	1
6. Motion indicated (gait, posture)	1
7. Rain roughly indicated	1
8. Rain properly indicated (touching ground, regularly distributed, raindrops on umbrella and lower parts of picture)	1
For drawing featuring umbrella	
9. Umbrella roughly indicated	1
10. Umbrella in two lines (round, oblong, top, handle)	1
11. Umbrella clearly shown (ribs, points, scallops)	1
12. Umbrella dimensions 1/3 to 2/3 of body length	1
13. Umbrella positioned to cover at least half of body	1
14. Umbrella attached to hand at end of arm	1
15. Position of arm adequate	1
For drawing featuring raincoat, raincape, hood, without umbrella	
16. Hood indicated (if there is a hood and an umbrella count only point 42—clothing)	1
17. Head well covered by hood	1
18. Raincoat or raincape	1
19. Shoulders, arms covered by coat or cape, hands showing only	1
20. Arms fully covered by cape, with shoulders clearly indicated	1
21. Shoulders not shown, but asked, "where are the arms?" child answers, "under coat."	1
22. Eyes shown (one line, dot)	1
23. Eyes in double lines, several parts	1
24. Nose shown	1
25. Mouth shown (one line)	1
26. Mouth shown in double lines, lips front or profile	1
27. Ears shown	1
28. Chin shown (front or profile)	1
29. Hair or headgear (except hood)	1
30. Neck or collar shown clearly	1
If the lady's face is covered by umbrella or if her back is turned, give credit for nose, mouth, eyes, etc. Credit 2 points if the quality of the picture suggests the more mature form of these details.	
31. Hands (credit one point if hands are in pocket)	1
32. Arms shown (one line)	1
33. Arms in double lines	1
34. Arms attached to body at shoulder level	1
35. Arms in proportion to body or slightly longer	1

TABLE 9-3 (Cont.)

Item	Points
36. Legs shown (one line)	1
37. Legs in double lines	1
38. Legs properly attached	1
39. Legs in proportion to body	1
40. Feet shown	1
41. Shoes shown clearly	1
42. Clothing: 2 articles (skirt and blouse, jacket and skirt; if the hood goes with an open umbrella, it is considered clothing)	1
43. No transparency, if such could be possible	1
For a picture that shows a definite artistic trend or technique (silhouette, etching, skilled schematization), credit total number of points possible up to here: 37 points.	
For landscape	
44. A baseline, a road, a path, in one line or dots	1
45. Figure clearly positioned on baseline or road	1
46. Road or path shown	1
47. Pavement or gravel shown	1
48. Flower border, tree, doorway, house shown	1
49. Special details showing imagination	1
	Maximum 43 points

(From E. M. Taylor, *Psychological appraisal of children with cerebral defects*, 1959, by courtesy of Harvard University Press and the Commonwealth Fund. Adapted from André Rey, *Monographies de psychologie appliquée*, No. 1, 1947)

verts the raw score to percentiles at five percentile levels for each age from 4 to 15+ (see Table 9-4). The age 15 norms of both tests should be used for adult patients.

Human figure drawings provide the neuropsychologist with a sample of behavior that is not only relatively culture free and language independent but also sufficiently complex and closely related to normal human development to afford some measure of the intellectual endowment of patients whose ability to draw has remained essentially intact. This method of assessing premorbid intellectual

TABLE 9-4
Rey's Norms for Ages 15 and Older for *Une dame qui se promène et il pleut*

Percentiles	0	25	50	75	100
Scores	17	30	33	37	43

(From E. M. Taylor, 1959.)

ability is not applicable to the many brain damaged patients with perceptual and practic disabilities or to those whose predominant mental symptoms include mental deterioration. The Harris and Rey scoring systems can greatly aid the assessment of impairment of those functions contributing to the free drawing performance. Use of these techniques in evaluating the nature and extent of an organic impairment is discussed on pp. 328–330.

10
VERBAL FUNCTIONS

TESTS FOR APHASIA

Any verbal test may be classified as an aphasia test since patients with aphasic disorders tend to perform verbal functions less well than do nonaphasic patients. However, aphasia tests differ from other verbal function tests in that they focus on disorders of symbol formulation and associated apraxias and agnosias (Benton, 1967b). They are designed to elicit samples of behavior in each communication modality—listening, speaking, reading, writing, and gesturing. The examination of the central "linguistic processing of verbal symbols" is their common denominator (Darley, 1972; Wepman and Jones, 1967). Other kinds of verbal tests measure aspects of verbal function that may be affected by perceptual or response disabilities, by learning and memory disorders, by defective reasoning or comprehension when symbol formulation remains essentially intact, or by impaired activity and control functions.

Aphasia Test Batteries

The most widely used aphasia tests are actually test *batteries* comprising numerous subtests of many discrete verbal functions. They are generally given only when aphasia is suspected or has already been diagnosed. Their product is not a score or index for diagnostic purposes but an orderly description of the patient's communication disabilities. Most aphasia tests involve lengthy, precise, and well-controlled procedures. They are best administered by persons, such as speech pathologists, who have more than a passing acquaintance with aphasiology and are trained in the specialized techniques of aphasia examinations.

Aphasia test batteries always include a wide range of tasks so that the nature and severity of the language problem and associated deficits may be determined (Brookshire, 1973). Because aphasia tests concern disordered language functions in themselves, and not their intellectual ramifications, test items typically present very simple and concrete tasks most children in the lower grades can pass. Common aphasia test questions ask the patient (1) to name simple objects ("What is this?" asks the examiner pointing to a cup or a pen or the picture of a boy or a clock); (2) to recognize simple spoken words ("Point to your ear," or "Put the spoon in the cup"); (3) to recognize simple printed letters, numbers, words, primary level arithmetic problems, and common symbols; (4) to give verbal and gestural answers to simple printed questions; and (5) to print or write letters, words, numbers, etc.

Aphasia test batteries differ primarily in their terminology, internal organization, the number of modality combinations they test, and the levels of difficulty and complexity to which the examination is carried. The five tests discussed here are both representative of the different kinds of aphasia tests and among the best known. Some clinicians devise their own batteries, taking parts from other tests and adding their own, so that apart from the published batteries, there are also a number of unpublished sets of tests (Eisenson, 1973; Osgood and Miron, 1963).

Examining for Aphasia
Although this test uses diagnostic categories that have generally been superseded by current formulations of the nature of aphasia, it offers a very thorough approach to the examination of communication dysfunction (Eisenson, 1954). Writing about it almost two decades after it first appeared, its author describes it as "a clinical instrument intended to provide a protocol of type and degree of severity of language and related deficits" (Eisenson, 1973, p. 100). It contains 37 discrete subtests, each differing from the others in modalities tested, content, or level of difficulty. Eisenson suggests the test can be used for aphasia screening by giving only the first item in each subtest, although administration of the full test permits

the examiner to determine gradations of dysfunction. The test may take anywhere from a half hour to two hours to complete. Eisenson offers no normative data since he considers a formal scoring system inapplicable to a condition for which inconsistency of response is a hallmark. Performances on each subtest can be summarized on a five-point scale rating the extent of impairment from "Complete" to "None."

The Porch Index of Communicative Ability (PICA)
The *PICA* was developed as a highly standardized, statistically reliable instrument for measuring a limited sample of language functions (Porch, 1967). This battery contains 18 ten-item subtests, four of them verbal, eight gestural, and six graphic. The same ten common items (cigarette, comb, fork, key, knife, matches, pencil, pen, quarter, toothbrush) are used for each subtest with the exception of the simplest graphic subtest in which the patient is asked to copy geometric forms. The examiner scores each of the patient's responses according to a 16-point multidimensional scoring system (Porch, 1971). Each point in the system describes performance. For example, a score of 1 indicates no response; a score of 15 indicates a response that was judged to be accurate, responsive, prompt, complete, and efficient. Qualified and trained PICA testers undergo a 40-hour training period after which they administer ten practice tests. This training leads to high interscorer reliability correlation coefficients. By virtue of its tight format and reliable scoring system, the PICA provides a sensitive measure of small changes in patient performance, which aids the speech pathologist in his treatment planning. Its statistically sophisticated construction and reliability make it a useful research instrument as well (Darley, 1972).

The Minnesota Test for Differential Diagnosis of Aphasia
This lengthy test involves 47 different subtests that thoroughly cover the breadth and depth of communication disturbances (Schuell, 1965). It focuses on many different aspects of each of five areas, defined by factor analysis, where aphasic patients commonly have problems: "auditory disturbances," "visual and reading disturbances," "speech and language disturbances," "visuomotor and writing disturbances," and "disturbances of numerical relationships and arithmetic processes." The battery usually takes from one to

three hours to administer, although profoundly impaired patients will finish much sooner because they are unable to respond to more than a few of the items. Each subtest is scored for errors. For each of the 47 subtests, Schuell reports percentages of unmatched patients in aphasic and control groups who make errors. In most instances, the percentages of the two groups are so disparate that the likelihood of overlap is slight. Data from this test provide a systematic description of the patient's language disability (Osgood and Miron, 1963; Schuell, 1955). This test is not standardized. The examination booklet also contains a six-point scale for rating extratest observations of comprehension of spoken speech, reading, writing, and *dysarthria* (impaired articulation).

Neurosensory Center Comprehensive Examination for Aphasia (NCCEA)

This battery consists of 24 short subtests, 20 involving different aspects of language performance, and four "control" tests of visual and tactile functions (Spreen and Benton, 1969). Most of the subtests normally take less than five minutes to administer. The control tests are given only when the patient performs poorly on a test involving visual or tactile stimuli. A variety of materials are used in the tests, including common objects, sound tapes, printed cards, a screened box for tactile recognition, and the Token Test "tokens" (see pp. 261–264). An interesting innovation enables patients whose writing hand is paralyzed to demonstrate "graphic" behavior by giving them "Scrabble" letters for forming words. All of the materials can be easily purchased, or they can be constructed by following instructions in the manual. Scores are entered on two profile sheets, one providing norms for the performance of normal adults on each subtest, the other norms based on the performance of aphasic patients. This double scoring enables the examiner to identify patients whose performance differs significantly from normal adults, while providing for score discriminations within the aphasic score range so that small amounts of change can be registered.

The Language Modalities Test for Aphasia

This test, which is presented in film strips, is also based on factor analytic studies of the language performance of adult aphasic patients (Wepman and Jones, 1961). It comes in two equivalent forms for retesting. Five statistically derived factors defined the test modalities: (1) oral response to visually presented stimuli; (2) oral response to orally presented stimuli; (3) written response to orally presented stimuli; (4) written response to visually presented stimuli; and (5) matching of auditory or visual stimuli to picture alternatives. Wepman and Jones introduced film strips into their test to ensure standardized presentation of the material. The testing procedures take about one hour. Responses are each scored according to a six-point scale of which the four middle positions refer to different kinds of errors reflecting the linguistic disturbances associated with the different types of aphasia (Wepman and Jones, 1967). This scoring system was devised to facilitate differentiation between a true aphasia involving defective symbol processing and *transmissive* (agnosic or apraxic) speech problems, as well as to indicate the kind of therapy the patient needs.

An "interview type" test: The Functional Communication Profile
This is a 45-item inventory that permits scaled ratings of a patient's practical language behavior (Sarno, 1969). Like the battery type aphasia tests, the *Functional Communication Profile* also requires an experienced clinician to apply it reliably and sensitively. Evaluation proceeds in five different performance areas: "Movement," "Speaking," "Understanding," "Reading," and "Other," not exclusively verbal, adaptive behaviors. Scoring is on a nine-point scale, and ratings are assigned on the basis of the patient's premorbid ability in that area. Scores are recorded on a histogram. Sarno recommends color coding to differentiate the initial evaluation from subsequent reevaluations for easy visual review (M. L. Taylor, 1965). She also offers a rather loose method of converting the item grades into percentages which may be too subjective for research purposes or for comparisons with clinical evaluations made by different examiners.

Aphasia Screening Tests

Aphasia screening tests do not replace the careful examination of language functions afforded by the test batteries. Rather, they are best used as supplements to a neuropsychological test battery. They signal the presence of an aphasic disorder and may even call attention to its specific characteristics, but they do not provide the fine discriminations of the complete aphasia test batteries (Eisenson, 1973). Since these tests do not require technical knowledge of speech pathology for satisfactory administration or interpretation, they can be given and interpreted reliably by clinicians familiar with aphasia syndromes.

The Aphasia Screening Test by Halstead and Wepman

This is the most widely used of all aphasia tests since it or its variants have been incorporated into many formally organized neuropsychological test batteries. As originally devised, the *Aphasia Screening Test* has 51 items which cover all the elements of aphasic disabilities as well as the most commonly associated communication problems (Halstead and Wepman, 1959). It is a fairly brief test, rarely taking longer than 30 minutes to complete. There are no rigid scoring standards, but rather the emphasis is on determining the nature of the linguistic problem, once its presence has been established. Erroneous responses are coded into a diagnostic profile intended to provide a description of the pattern of the patient's language disabilities. Obviously, the more areas of involvement and the more a single area is involved, the more severe the disability. However, no provisions are made to grade test performance on the basis of severity.

Reitan included the Aphasia Screening Test with a number of other, different, tests in the Halstead-Reitan neuropsychological test battery (see pp. 440–441). He pared down the original test to 32 items but still handled the data descriptively, in much the same manner as originally intended (Reitan, undated).

A second revision of the Aphasia Screening Test appeared in E. W. Russell, Neuringer, and G. Goldstein's amplification of the Reitan battery (1970). This latest version of the Halstead and Wepman test is called the "aphasia examination" and contains 37 items. It is essentially the same as Reitan's revision except that four easy arithmetic problems and the task of naming a key were added. E. W. Russell and his colleagues established a simple error counting scoring system for use with their computerized diagnostic classification system, which converts to a six-point rating scale. This scale indicates the severity of an aphasic disorder, but not its nature.

A very shortened version of the Halstead and Wepman Aphasia Screening Test consists of four tasks (Heimburger and Reitan, 1961):

1. Copy a square, Greek cross, and triangle *without lifting the pencil from the paper.*
2. Name each copied figure.
3. Spell each name.
4. Repeat: "He shouted the warning"; then explain and write it.

Although this little test does not "meet entirely ideal criteria for localizing lesions of the brain," it does aid in discriminating between patients with left and right hemisphere lesions, for many of the former can copy the designs but cannot write, while the latter have no trouble writing but many cannot reproduce the designs.

The Token Test
The Token Test is extremely simple to administer, to score and, for almost every nonaphasic person who has completed the fourth grade, to perform with few if any errors (Boller and Vignolo, 1966; De Renzi and Vignolo, 1962). Yet it is remarkably sensitive to the disrupted linguistic processes that are central to the aphasic disability, even when much of the patient's communication behavior has remained intact. It can also identify those brain damaged patients whose other disabilities may be masking a concomitant aphasic disorder, or whose symbolic processing problems are relatively subtle and not readily recognizable.

Twenty "tokens" cut from heavy construction paper or thin sheets of plastic or wood make up the test material. They come in two shapes—circles and rectangles*; two sizes—big and little; and five colors—red, yellow, blue, green, and white. The only requirement this test makes of the patient is that he comprehend the token names and the verbs and prepositions in the instructions. The diagnosis of those few patients whose language disabilities are so severe as to prevent them from cooperating on this task is not likely to depend on formal testing; almost all other brain injured patients can respond to the simplest level of instructions. The test consists of a series of oral commands, 62 altogether, given in five sections of increasing complexity (Table 10-1). Although this test seems easy to administer, the examiner must guard against unwittingly modifying his rate of delivery in response to the quality of the patient's performance (Salvatore et al., 1975).

---

* Square rather than rectangular tokens are recommended to reduce the number of syllables the patient must process (e.g., "Touch the green *square*.").

TABLE 10-1
The Token Test

PART 1

(Large rectangles and large circles only are on the table)

(1) Touch the red circle
(2) Touch the green rectangle
(3) Touch the red rectangle
(4) Touch the yellow circle
(5) Touch the blue circle
(6) Touch the green circle
(7) Touch the yellow rectangle
(8) Touch the white circle
(9) Touch the blue rectangle
(10) Touch the white rectangle.

PART 2

(Large and small rectangles and circles are on the table)

(1) Touch the small yellow circle
(2) Touch the large green circle
(3) Touch the large yellow circle
(4) Touch the large blue rectangle
(5) Touch the small green circle
(6) Touch the large red circle
(7) Touch the large white rectangle
(8) Touch the small blue circle
(9) Touch the small green rectangle
(10) Touch the large blue circle.

PART 3

(Large rectangles and large circles only)

(1) Touch the yellow circle and the red rectangle
(2) Touch the green rectangle and the blue circle
(3) Touch the blue rectangle and the yellow rectangle
(4) Touch the white rectangle and the red rectangle
(5) Touch the white circle and the blue circle
(6) Touch the blue rectangle and the white rectangle
(7) Touch the blue rectangle and the white circle
(8) Touch the green rectangle and the blue circle
(9) Touch the red circle and the yellow rectangle
(10) Touch the red rectangle and the white circle.

PART 4

(Large and small rectangles and circles)

(1) Touch the small yellow circle and the large green rectangle
(2) Touch the small blue rectangle and the small green circle
(3) Touch the large white rectangle and the large red circle
(4) Touch the large blue rectangle and the large red rectangle
(5) Touch the small blue rectangle and the small yellow circle
(6) Touch the small blue circle and the small red circle
(7) Touch the large blue rectangle and the large green rectangle

(8) Touch the large blue circle and the large green circle
(9) Touch the small red rectangle and the small yellow circle
(10) Touch the small white rectangle and the large red rectangle.

PART 5
(Large rectangles and large circles only)
(1) Put the red circle on the green rectangle
(2) Put the white rectangle behind the yellow circle
(3) Touch the blue circle with the red rectangle
(4) Touch—with the blue circle—the red rectangle
(5) Touch the blue circle and the red rectangle
(6) Pick up the blue circle or the red rectangle
(7) Put the green rectangle away from the yellow rectangle
(8) Put the white circle before the blue rectangle
(9) If there is a black circle, pick up the red rectangle
     N.B. *There is no black circle.*
(10) Pick up the rectangles, except the yellow one
(11) Touch the white circle without using your right hand
(12) When I touch the green circle, you take the white rectangle.
     N.B. *Wait a few seconds before touching the green circle.*
(13) Put the green rectangle beside the red circle
(14) Touch the rectangles, slowly, and the circles, quickly
(15) Put the red circle between the yellow rectangle and the green rectangle
(16) Except for the green one, touch the circles
(17) Pick up the red circle—no!—the white rectangle
(18) Instead of the white rectangle, take the yellow circle
(19) Together with the yellow circle, take the blue circle
(20) After picking up the green rectangle, touch the white circle
(21) Put the blue circle under the white rectangle
(22) Before touching the yellow circle, pick up the red rectangle.

(From Boller and Vignolo, 1966)

Items failed on a first command should be repeated and, if performed successfully the second time, scored separately from the first response. When the second but not the first administration of an item is passed, only the second performance is counted under the assumption that many initial errors will result from such nonspecific variables as inattention and lack of interest. Each correct response earns one point, so that the highest attainable total score is 62. When scoring, the examiner should note whether the patient makes the behavioral distinction between "touch" and "pick up" as directed in Part V.

Boller and Vignolo have developed a slightly modified version of De Renzi and Vignolo's original Token Test format. They give the full record of scores achieved by their standardization groups. Their cut-off scores correctly classified 100% of the control patients, 90% of nonaphasic patients with right hemisphere lesions, 65% of non-aphasic patients, for an overall 88% correctly classified. Table 10-2 summarizes these data.

It should be noted that Part V, which consists of items involving relational concepts, by itself identified only one less patient as a "latent aphasic" than did the whole 62-item test of Boller and Vignolo. This finding suggests that Part V could be used without the other 40 questions to identify those left hemisphere damaged patients misclassified as nonaphasic because their difficulties in symbol formulation are too subtle to impair their communication for most ordinary purposes.

Spreen and Benton (1969) developed a 39-item modification of De Renzi and Vignolo's long form, which is incorporated in the Neurosensory Center Comprehensive Examination for Aphasia. From this, Spellacy and Spreen (1969) constructed a 16-item short form that uses the same 20 tokens as both the original and the modified long forms and includes many of the relational items of Part V. The 16-item short form identified 84% of the aphasic and 76% of the nonaphasic brain damaged patients, screening as well as Part V of the 62-item long form, but not quite as well as the entire long form. These data suggest that for screening, either Part V or the 16-item short form of the Token Test will usually be adequate. Patients who achieve a borderline score on one of these shorter forms of the test should be given the entire test to clarify the equivocal findings.

Identifying objects by use

Asking patients the use of common objects is a feature of some aphasia tests (Eisenson, 1954; Porch, 1971). By this means, De Renzi and his colleagues (1968) studied the incidence of ideational apraxia in aphasic patients. They found that 34% of their patients with a diagnosis of aphasia were unable to give the use of objects, whereas only 6% of the nonaphasic patients with left hemisphere lesions and none of the patients with right hemisphere lesions were unable to do so. These results suggest that this technique can be used in rapid screening for aphasia so long as the examiner bears in mind that although failure on the task greatly strengthens the likelihood of an associated aphasic disability, success does not rule it out. De Renzi's group notes that in their patients, ideational apraxia was associated with lesions involving postcentral speech areas.

TABLE 10-2
*A Summary of Scores Obtained by the Four Experimental Groups
on the Token Test*

Partial scores	Control patients (n = 31)	Brain damaged patients:		
		Right	Left	
			nonaph.	aphasic
		(n = 30)	(n = 26)	(n = 34)
Part I				
10	31	30	26	30
9 & lower				4
Part II				
10	31	29	25	23
9 & lower		1	1	11
Part III				
10	29	28	25	13
9	2	2	1	10
8 & lower				11
Part IV				
10	29	25	21	5
9	2	3	3	4
8 & lower		2	2	25
Part V				
20 & above	28	22	14	3
18 & 19	3	7	5	2
17 & lower		1	7	29
Total score				
60 & above	26	21	14	2
58–59	5	6	4	1
57 & lower		3	8	31

(Adapted from Boller and Vignolo, 1966)

VERBAL FLUENCY

Following brain injury, many patients experience changes in the
speed and fluency of verbal production. Greatly reduced verbal productivity accompanies most aphasic disabilities, but it does not
necessarily signify the presence of aphasia. Impaired verbal fluency

is also associated with frontal lobe damage, particularly the left frontal lobe anterior to Broca's area (Benton, 1968; Milner, 1967a; Ramier and Hécaen, 1970; Tow, 1955). A fluency problem can show up in speech, reading, and writing; generally it will affect all three activities.

Fluency of Speech

Word Naming (Stanford-Binet)
One of the earliest fluency tests, *Word Naming,* simply requires the subject to say as many words as he can in one minute, but not in sentences or number series. In Terman and Merrill's 1960 standardization of the Stanford-Binet, 59% of the ten-year-olds tested gave a minimum of 28 words, which is the Binet Form L-M norm for that age.

Controlled Word Association Test
A. L. Benton and his group have studied production of spoken words beginning with a designated letter (Benton, 1973a). The associative value of each letter of the alphabet except X and Z was determined in a normative study using control subjects who were not brain damaged (Borkowski et al., 1967) (see Table 10-3). Control subjects of low ability tended to perform a little less well than brighter brain damaged patients (see Table 10-4). This result highlights the necessity of taking the patient's premorbid verbal skill level into account when evaluating his verbal fluency.

The *Controlled Word Association Test* (originally called the Verbal Associative Fluency Test) consists of three word naming trials, using the letters F, A, and S, respectively. The examiner asks the subject to say as many words as he can think of which begin with

TABLE 10-3
Verbal Associative Frequencies for the 14 Easiest Letters

	Words/minute		
	9–10	11–12	>12
Letters	A C D G	B F L M	P
	H W	R S T	

(From Borkowski et al., 1967)

TABLE 10-4
*Productivity Averages for Letter Pairs P T and F S for Brain Damaged
and Control Patients at Two Levels of Intelligence*

		Mean $\left(\dfrac{P\ T + F\ S}{2}\right)$	S.D.
High intelligence	Control	24.60	5.99
	Brain damaged	21.80	5.76
Low intelligence	Control	19.30	5.73
	Brain damaged	9.20	2.50

(From Borkowski et al., 1967)

the given letter of the alphabet, excluding proper nouns, numbers, and the same word with a different suffix. The score is the sum of all correct words produced in the three one-minute trials, adjusted for age, sex, and education (see Table 10-5). The adjusted scores can then be converted to percentiles (see Table 10-6).

Other verbal fluency tests
Studying the effect of set on the verbal productions of patients with

TABLE 10-5
Adjustment Formula for the Controlled Word Association Test

	Adjustment Formula: Female		
Education Years Completed	Age 25–54	Age 55–59	Age 60–64
Less than 9	+ 9	+ 10	+ 12
9–11	+ 6	+ 7	+ 9
12–15	+ 4	+ 5	+ 7
16 +	—	+ 1	+ 3

	Adjustment Formula: Male		
Education Years Completed	Age 25–54	Age 55–59	Age 60–64
Less than 9	+ 14	+ 15	+ 17
9–11	+ 6	+ 7	+ 9
12–15	+ 4	+ 5	+ 7
16 +	—	+ 1	+ 3

(From Benton, 1973a)

TABLE 10-6
Controlled Word Association Test: Table for Converting Adjusted Scores into Percentiles

Adjusted scores	Percentile range	Adjusted scores	Percentile range
54–62	95 & above	36	45–49
52–53	90–94	35	40–44
49–50	85–89	34	35–39
46–48	80–84	33	30–34
44–45	75–79	31–32	25–29
43	70–74	29	20–24
41–42	65–69	27–28	15–19
40	60–64	25–26	10–14
38–39	55–59	24	5–9
37	50–54	23 & lower	4 & lower

(Adapted from Benton, 1973a)

severe memory disorder (Korsakoff's psychosis, see pp. 175–177), Talland (1965) asked his subjects to "name as many different things as you can that one is likely to see in the street" in 60 seconds, and to "name as many different animals as you can" in 30 seconds. A control group of 17 normal persons with a mean Wechsler Vocabulary scaled score of 10 gave an average of 15.7 street sights and 12.5 animals, whereas patients named an average of 8.8 street sights and 9.1 animals.

The *Set Test* is another test of the effect of set on verbal fluency (Isaacs and Kennie, 1973). The subject is asked to name as many items as he can from four successive categories: colors, animals, fruits, and towns. He names items in the first category until he recalls ten items or can remember no more, at which point the next category is announced, and so on. His score is the total number of items recalled, forty being the highest possible score. This test has been given to a random sample of 189 persons aged 65 and older. Healthy old people averaged 31.2 names. Of the old people in this sample, 95% achieved scores of 15 or over; scores below 15 are considered abnormal for this age group. All of the 22 persons in the sample group who named fewer than 15 words had other symptoms of brain disease. Six persons diagnosed as demented achieved scores between 15 and 24, as did three depressed persons and 12 who were healthy and in good spirits. In contrast, only one of the

146 patients with scores of 25 or better was described as confused and 11 were considered "anxious or depressed."

Newcombe (1969) used another variant of these tests, asking her patients first to name objects, then animals, and then to alternate in naming birds and colors, each for 60 seconds. The first two tasks were scored for number of correct words emitted; the last for each correct alternation (e.g., B-C-B = 2, BB-C-B-CC = 3). She found that patients with left hemisphere lesions performed more poorly than those with right hemisphere lesions, but no regular performance differential related to the injured lobe (see Table 10-7). The fluency test discriminated between right and left hemisphere lesions better than most of the tests in Newcombe's considerable battery, but the data indicate that the overlap between groups is too large for this test to indicate much more than a tendency to impaired fluency in the individual case.

Writing Fluency

Word fluency
A written test for word fluency first appeared in the Thurstones' Primary Mental Abilities tests (1938; 1962). The subject must write as many words beginning with the letter S as he can in five minutes; and then he must write as many four-letter words beginning with C as he can in four minutes. The average 18-year-old can produce 65 words within the nine-minute total writing time. Milner (1964;

TABLE 10-7
Performance Averages of Patients with Left and Right Hemisphere Damage and of Controls on Three Verbal Fluency Tests

Group	Object naming	Animal naming	Alternations
Left hemisphere	24.25 (n = 50)	14.43 (n = 35)	12.00 (n = 50)
Right hemisphere	29.02 (n = 42)	18.00 (n = 31)	14.24 (n = 42)
Controls (n = 20)	30.20	16.95	16.95

(Adapted from Newcombe, 1969)

1967a) found that the performance of patients with left frontal lobectomies was significantly impaired on this test relative to that of other patients with left hemisphere lobectomies whose frontal lobes remained intact, and to that of patients whose surgery was confined to the right hemisphere.

Speed of writing

Talland (1965) measured writing speed in two ways: speed of copying a 12-word sentence printed in one-inch type and speed of writing dictated sentences. On the copying task, his 16 control subjects averaged 33.9 seconds for completion, taking significantly less time ($p < .05$) than patients with Korsakoff's psychosis. No significant score differences distinguished the control subjects from the patients in their speed of writing a single 12-word sentence. However, when writing down a 97-word story, read to them at the rate of one to two seconds per word, the control subjects averaged 71.1 words within the three-minute time limit, whereas the patient group's average was 53.1 ($t = 2.69$, $p < .02$). It would appear that when writing speed has been slowed by brain damage, the slowing will become more evident as the length of the task increases.

Reading Fluency

Talland (1965) used the *Stroop Test* to measure the effects of perceptual interference, but incidentally found that it provided data on reading fluency. The materials for this test include three white cards, each containing ten rows of five items. Randomized color names—blue, green, red, and yellow—are in black print on card A. Card B is identical, except each color name is printed in some color other than the color it names. Card C displays colored dots in the same array of four colors. There are four trials, each consisting of a different task. On trial I, the subject reads card A; on II he reads card B and ignores the color of the print; for III he names the colors on card C; and on IV he names the colors of the print on card B. The subject is instructed to read or call out the color "as fast as you can" (see Table 10-8).

Nehemkis and Lewinsohn (1972) administered the same tasks in the same order but, like Stroop's cards, the test cards they used contained 100 rather than 50 items. Their left hemisphere patients

TABLE 10-8
*Control Subject Performances (in Seconds) on Four Conditions of
the Stroop Test*

		Read black print	Read color print	Name color dots	Name color print
50-item[a]	Mean	24.7	32.9	40.9	71.8
cards	SD	8.7	12.6	8.1	19.4
100-item[b]	Mean	45.6	47.2	68.3	147.4
cards	SD	9.1	10.3	14.5	73.3

[a] Talland, 1965.
[b] Nehemkis and Lewinsohn, 1972.

took approximately twice as long as their control subjects to perform each trial, but the interference effect of the second and fourth trials was no greater for left than for right hemisphere patients.

In his original study (1935), Stroop used 100 words in a 10 × 10 format on two stimulus cards, one printed in black on white, and the other printed in red, blue, green, brown, and purple. (He excluded yellow because it was so much less intense than the other colors as to have a possible effect on its stimulus value.) "The colors were arranged so as to avoid any regularity of occurrence and so that each color would appear twice in each column and in each row." Mean reading time in seconds for his 70 undergraduate subjects was 41.0 on the black printed cards and 43.3 on the color interference card.

Oral reading was one of Newcombe's many subtests, but she scored only for errors and noted "unusual speech rhythm, pauses, and repetitions" (1969). She reported no significant differences between patients on the basis of localization of injury. However, 80% of the dysphasic patients and only 5% of those without dysphasia had difficulty performing this task. In almost every instance, the dysphasic patients did more poorly on oral reading than speaking.

Academic Skills

With the exception of aphasia tests, surprisingly few neuropsychological batteries contain tests of learned verbal skills such as reading, writing, spelling, and arithmetic. Yet impairment in these commonplace activities can have profound repercussions on a patient's vocational competence and ultimate adjustment; it can also provide clues to the nature of the underlying organic condition. Some standard tests measure a single skill and other tests measure more than one (see pp. 243–244, and Buros, 1972).

The *Gates-MacGinitie Reading Tests* (1965, 1969) are good examples of academic skill tests that lend themselves to neuropsychological assessment. These paper and pencil multiple-choice tests come in four primary levels and three grade and high school levels. The highest level, Survey F, contains norms for grades 10, 11, and 12. Grade level 11-8 (last quarter of the 12th year) norms are suitable for most adults, although the ceiling is apt to be too low for college graduates. Patients for whom Survey F is too difficult can take the test at a lower level. Survey D, for instance, extends down to grade 4. Patients who are unable to handle it should be given the individualized PIAT or an aphasia test for an evaluation of their reading skills.

The Gates-MacGinitie tests measure different aspects of reading separately. The first subtest, Speed and Accuracy, has a four-minute limit and determines how rapidly the subject reads with understanding. The second subtest, Vocabulary, involves simple word recognition. The last subtest, Comprehension, measures ability to understand written passages. Both Vocabulary and Comprehension scores tend to be lower when verbal functioning is impaired. When verbal functions remain essentially intact, but higher level conceptual and organizing activities are impaired, a marked differential favoring Vocabulary over Comprehension may appear between the scores of these two subtests. The norms of Speed and Accuracy are so time-dependent as to tell little about brain damaged patients except that they tend to be slow. The other two tests also have time limits, but they are more generous. They can be administered as untimed tests without much loss of information since most very slow patients fail a large number of the more difficult items they complete outside the standard time limits.

Writing and spelling can be readily assessed by obtaining written responses. I use a paper and pencil test battery which includes a number of tasks requiring written responses (see Fig. 10-1 and pp. 90–91). A self-report questionnaire, the *Personal History*

<u>SELF-ADMINISTERED BATTERY</u>

General Information Questionnaire

Name _____

Address _____

City _____   State _____

Phone _____   Age _____

Soc. Sec. # _____   Date _____

Circle by number the highest year you completed in school:

    <u>1 2 3 4 5 6 7 8</u>   <u>1 2 3 4</u>   <u>1 2 3 4 5 6</u>   _____
    Elementary School   High School   College   Graduate
                                                         Degree

<u>Please Circle:</u>

    Single   Married   Separated   Divorced

Number of children _____   Number of dependents _____

What date were you admitted
to the hospital? _____   What Ward _____

What is (or was) your occupation _____

When did you last work steadily
prior to coming to the hospital _____

What problems brought you to the hospital _____

_____

FIG. 10-1. Face sheet of the Self-Administered Battery.

Inventory (PHI) (Lezak, 1968), also provides incidental information about the patient's reading and writing skills.

The Stanford-Binet scales contain two tests applicable to writing skills which have proven useful in neuropsychological assessment. *Minkus Completion,* a sentence completion task involving prepositions, was one of several tests of verbal skills given as part of a study of language and intellectual function in patients with right hemisphere damage (Eisenson, 1962). The patients' performance was significantly poorer on this test than was that of matched control subjects. I have found *Sentence Building,* a task requiring the patient to compose a sentence around three given words, to be sensitive to slight impairments of verbal functions that may show up in occasional speech hesitancies or neologisms but are not reflected in significantly depressed WAIS verbal subtest scores. Sentence Building can be given as a written test, either as part of a paper and pencil test battery in which the instructions and words are printed on an answer sheet, or it can be orally administered with the request to "write" the sentence. Besides testing verbal and sequential organizing abilities and use of syntax, the written format elicits spelling, punctuation, and graphomotor behavior. The 1937 Revision, Form M version of the *Sentence Building* subtest at age level VII broadens the applicability of this test to adults with limited verbal skills.

11
PERCEPTUAL FUNCTIONS

The tests considered in this chapter are essentially perceptual, requiring no physical manipulation of the test material; verbal or gestural responses suffice. Some of these tests overlap with cognitive and memory tests, for the complexitities of brain function make such overlap both inevitable and desirable. Only by testing each function in different modalities, in combination with different functions, and under different conditions can the examiner gain an understanding of which functions are impaired and how that impairment is manifested.

VISUAL FUNCTIONS

Many aspects of visual perception may be impaired by brain disease. Typically an organic condition involving one visual function will affect a cluster of them. A major division in visual functions occurs between those having to do with verbal/symbolic material and those that deal with nonsymbolic stimuli. Some other stimulus dimensions that may highlight different aspects of visual perception are the degree to which the stimulus is structured, the amount of old or new memory involved in the task, the spatial element, and the presence of interference.

Color Perception

Tests of color perception serve a dual purpose in neuropsychological assessment. They can identify persons with congenitally defective color vision, or "color blindness," whose performance on tasks requiring accurate color recognition might otherwise be misinterpreted. Knowledge that the patient's color vision is defective will affect the examiner's evaluation of responses to colored material such as the color cards of the *Rorschach* technique (see pp. 290 and 459–461), and should militate against use of color-dependent tests such as the *Color Sorting Test* (see below and p. 399). They can also be used to test for color agnosia.

In neuropsychological assessment, the *Ishihara* (1954) and the *Dvorine* (1958) screening tests for the two most common types of color blindness are satisfactory. The *H-R-R Pseudoisochromatic Plates* (Hardy et al., 1955) screen for two rare forms of color blindness, which would not be correctly identified by the Ishihara or Dvorine tests, as well as for the two common types (Hsia and Graham, 1965). The stimulus materials of all three of these tests are cards printed with different colored dots, which form recognizable figures against a ground of contrasting colored dots. The Farnsworth-Munsell *100-hue and Dichotomous Test for Color Vision* (Farnsworth, 1943), which requires the subject to arrange colored paper chips according to hue, can be used to identify color agnosias and to screen for the purely sensory disorder too. The Color Sorting Test presents the patient with four different color identifying and sorting tasks with skeins of wool of different color and brightness (K. Goldstein and Scheerer, 1953a, b).

De Renzi and Spinnler (1967) put together a six-test battery for examining impaired response to color in patients with known lateralized lesions, including a color matching test, the Ishihara plates, color naming, point to color, verbal memory for color, and color drawing. They found that patients with visual field defects associated with right hemisphere lesions were most likely to have difficulty with the two purely perceptual tasks, color matching and the Ishihara plates, and to do poorly on the other tests as well. As might be expected, aphasic patients had more difficulty than any other group on tasks involving language. Battersby and colleagues (1956) used the H-R-R Plates for "Figure-ground" discrimination rather than color testing.

Visual Recognition

Interest in visual recognition has grown with the rapid expansion of knowledge of the different roles played by the hemispheres and with more precise understanding of the different functional systems. When the presence of brain damage is suspected or has been identified grossly, the examination of different aspects of visual recognition may lead to a clearer definition of the patient's condition.

Word recognition
Tests of written word recognition are usually not included in neuropsychological test batteries because impaired word recognition is predominantly an aphasic symptom; tests for it are included in aphasia test batteries. Two kinds of word recognition problems can trouble nonaphasic patients. Both aphasic and nonaphasic patients with visual field defects, regardless of which hemisphere is damaged, tend to ignore the part of a printed line or even a long printed word that falls outside the range of their vision when the eye is fixated for reading. This can occur in spite of the senselessness of the partial sentences they read. Patients with left hemisphere lesions may ignore the right side of the line or page, and those with right hemisphere lesions will not see what is on the left. This condition shows up readily on oral reading tasks in which sentences are several inches long. Newsprint is unsatisfactory for demonstrating this problem because the column is too narrow. To test for this phenomenon, Battersby and colleagues (1956) developed a set of ten cards on which were printed ten familiar four-word phrases (e.g., GOOD HUMOR ICE CREAM, NEWS PAPER HEAD LINE) in letters 1″ high and $\frac{1}{16}$″ in line thickness. Omission or distortion of words on only one side was considered evidence of a unilateral visual defect.

Visual inattention without a visual field defect usually occurs in patients with right hemisphere lesions and also results in imperception of stimuli to the patient's left. It differs from the visual deficit of hemianopsia in that the patient can see the ignored material when his attention is called to it without changing the direction of his gaze.

Picture recognition
Meaningful Pictures too was devised to bring out asymmetrical perceptual defects (Battersby et al., 1956). It requires a number of

colored magazine illustrations or photographs that are essentially symmetrical on either side of the median plane. Each picture is presented first as a verbal recall task in which, after a ten-second exposure, the subject is asked to name and indicate the relative position of the details he recalls. On completion of the recall task, the subject sees each picture again with instructions to describe all the details while looking at the card. Card sides are compared for the number of responses they elicit; a preponderance on one side or the other suggests a lateralized visual inattention to the opposite side.

Face recognition
Warrington and James' (1967b) demonstration that there is no regular relationship between inability to recognize familiar faces (*prosopagnosia*) and impaired recognition of unfamiliar faces has led to a separation of facial recognition tests into those involving a memory component and those that do not. Two kinds of facial recognition tests involve memory. All tests of familiar faces call on stored information. Typically, these tests require the subject to name or otherwise identify pictures of well-known persons (Milner, 1968; Warrington and James, 1967b). Two kinds of errors have been noted: left hemisphere damaged patients identified but had difficulty naming the persons whereas defective recognition characterized the right hemisphere damaged patients' errors.

Recognition tests of unfamiliar faces involving memory have appeared in several formats. Photos can be presented for matching either one at a time or in sets of two or more. When the initial presentation consists of more than one picture, this adds a memory *span* component, which further complicates the faces recognition problem. The second set of photos to be recognized can be presented one at a time or grouped; and presentation may be immediate or delayed.

To examine the ability to recognize faces without involving memory, Benton and Van Allen (1968, 1973) developed the *Test of Facial Recognition*. In this test, the patient matches identical front views, front with side views, and front views taken under different lighting conditions (see Fig. 11-1). The test calls for 54 separate matches. The scoring range is between 25 and 54 since 25 photos can be identified correctly by chance alone. The authors have tentatively defined scores of 35 and 36 as "raising the question of im-

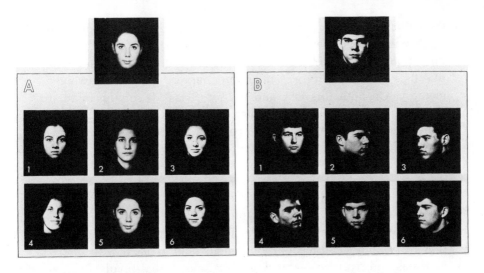

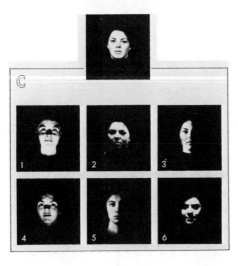

FIG. 11-1. Test of Facial Recognition (Benton and Van Allen.) These photographs illustrate the three parts of the test: a. Matching of identical front-views. b. Matching of front-view with three-quarters views. c. Matching of front-view under different lighting conditions.

pairment, a score of *33–34* as indicating impairment and a score *below 33* . . . as indicating severe impairment" (Benton and Van Allen, 1973, p. 11).

The material for *Unknown Faces* consists of two identical books of 16 4″ × 5″ photos of the head and shoulders of eight men and eight women (Warrington and James, 1967b). On this immediate memory task, the subject studies a photo in one book for ten seconds and then attempts to pick it out of the 16 photos in the second book. Patients with right parietal lesions performed most poorly on this test, more poorly than those with right temporal lesions, which suggests that the visuospatial processing component of this task outweighs memory. On both this task and the recall task involving familiar faces, patients with left hemisphere damage generally recognized more faces than right hemisphere patients. By having to match unfamiliar faces following a delay, patients with brain damage involving the right temporal lobe demonstrated significant performance decrements, again linking memory for unverbalizable material with the right temporal lobe.

Facial recognition problems typically implicate the right hemisphere. Neither visual field defects nor aphasia affect facial recognition scores, but facial recognition deficits tend to occur with spatial agnosias and dyslexias, and with dysgraphias that involve spatial disturbance (Tzavaras et al., 1970).

Figure and design recognition

Simple recognition.   Perceptual recognition of meaningless designs is usually tested by having the patient draw them from models or memory. When a subject's design reproductions contain the essential elements of the original from which they are copied and preserve their interrelationships with reasonable accuracy, his perceptual accuracy with this kind of material has been adequately demonstrated. A few correct responses to the WAIS Picture Completion subtest or a similar task show that the subject can recognize meaningful pictures. Only when the patient's graphic reproductions are inaccurate, markedly distorted or simplified, or have glaring omissions or additions, or when he is unable to respond correctly to drawings or pictures, is there further need to study his perceptual accuracy.

There are many techniques for examining simple perceptual recognition. A low level visual recognition task is *Discrimination of Forms* at age level IV of the Stanford-Binet. The patient is shown ten line drawings of common geometric figures such as a square, a circle, an oval, one at a time and asked to point out one like it on a card on which all ten geometric figures are displayed. Seventy-nine percent of the four-year-old normative group made correct responses on this test. The first 12 items of both forms of Raven's Progressive Matrices also test simple recognition of designs (Knehr, 1965). Newcombe (1969) devised a set of visual recognition tasks, *Visual Pattern-matching*, using ten black and white line drawings and ten black and white patterns (see Fig. 11-2). She timed responses and found a less than significant tendency for patients with right hemisphere lesions to take longer to respond than other brain injured patients. Newcombe suggests that tachistoscopic presentation might elicit more pronounced results. A 32-item multiple choice "experimental" version of Benton's *Visual Retention Test* discriminated significantly between apraxic and nonapraxic patients with respect to accuracy of perceptual recognition (Dee, 1970), with the wide spread between scores suggesting a pronounced difference in perceptual accuracy between these two groups. Hemisphere side of lesion also served to differentiate patients; those with lesions on the right performed more poorly than the left hemisphere group. Apraxic symptoms discriminated between right and left hemisphere patients better than perceptual accuracy, however, as right hemisphere patients were much more prone to apraxia.

Visual Organization

Tests requiring the subject to make sense out of ambiguous, incomplete, fragmented, or otherwise distorted visual stimuli call for perceptual organizing activity beyond that of simple perceptual recognition. Although the perceptual system tends to hold up well in the presence of organic brain changes for most ordinary purposes, any additional challenge may be beyond its organizing capacity. For this reason, tests of perceptual organization were among the earliest psychological instruments to be used for evaluating neuropsychological status. Roughly speaking, there are three broad categories of visual organization tests: tests requiring the subject to fill in missing elements; tests presenting problems in reorganizing jumbled elements of a percept; and those stimuli lacking inherent organization onto which the subject must impose structure of his own making.

Tests involving incomplete visual stimuli
Of all tests of visual organization, those in which the subject fills in a missing part, such as Picture Completion, are least vulnerable to the effects of brain damage, probably because their content is usually

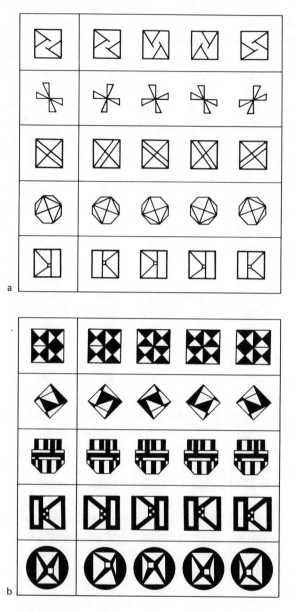

FIG. 11-2. Visual pattern-matching task: a. example of task I; b. example of task II.

so well-structured and readily identifiable. Thus, although technically they qualify as tests of perceptual organization, they are not especially sensitive to problems of perceptual organization except when the perceptual disorder is relatively severe.

Recognition of missing parts.   For most patients, the WAIS Picture Completion subtest is a good measure of the ability to fill in incomplete parts. An examiner who wants to assess the capacity for visual organization of a severely impaired patient can use *Mutilated Pictures* at age level VI of the Stanford-Binet. This test consists of one card with five simple line drawings of incomplete objects, such as a glove without a finger and a teapot without a handle. Three-quarters of all six-year-olds can identify the missing part correctly.

Recognition of shaded stimuli.   Another class of tests using incomplete visual stimuli consists of pictures shaded to varying degrees of ambiguity. One such set, originally developed to study maturation of the ability for perceptual organization, is the *Street Completion Test* (Street, 1931). Its two practice and 13 test pictures include several that are outdated today, such as an old-fashioned gas range and a steam locomotive. In a British study of normal perception based on test performances of 15-year-olds of average and high average intelligence, boys' performances on this test were weighted heavily with a closure factor having to do with the ability to form completed perceptions from incomplete stimuli (*closure*), whereas girls' performances were not (Beard, 1965). Talland's severely memory impaired patients tended to respond more rapidly on this test but with more errors than his control subjects, although the difference between the groups was not significant (1965).

Mooney's *Closure Faces Test* also made its first appearance in a study of perceptual development (Mooney, 1957) (see Fig. 11-3). Lansdell (1968a, 1970) rescored some of the pictures, rearranged the order of presentation, and by dropping four items and increasing the number of practice items from one to three, reduced the number of scorable items from 50 to 44. Newcombe (1969) used only the first 40 pictures in Lansdell's set. This test requires the subject to sort each shaded picture of a face into one of six piles: B (boy), G (girl), M (grown man), W (grown woman), O (old man), or X (old woman). The categories are not at all equally represented in the

FIG. 11-3. Mooney's Closure Faces Test. The upper-left-hand photograph shows one of the original pictures from which the black and white pictures were drawn. This picture and the two other sketches, along with their black and white counterparts, are shown to the subject to introduce test material.

cards, for 23 of them can be correctly sorted into the M pile and only 11 into W. B is also correct for three of the M sorts and O is correct for 14 of them; 28 of the items have two correct answers.

The three practice items are displayed with the original gray-toned sketch from which the black and white test cards were made. This enables the subject to perceive the black and white face readily and understand its construction. The subject can be left on his own to sort the pictures. Lansdell allows only a half hour and encourages his patients to sort the easiest pictures first (Lansdell, undated). Like many tests used in neuropsychological research, this one lacks standardization data. Until norms are available, there seems to be no necessary reason for setting a time limit to the test, other than the examiner's convenience and concern that his conscientious patients not become overly frustrated by the difficulty of some of the items.

Patients with right hemisphere lesions tend to identify fewer of the Mooney pictures correctly than do patients with left hemisphere lesions; and of the right hemisphere patients, those with parietal-temporal involvement do most poorly (Lansdell, 1968a; Newcombe, 1969). Lansdell's 19 patients with surgical ablations of the left temporal lobe averaged 36+ correct responses. In Newcombe's larger patient population, the right-left hemisphere differential between patient groups performing this task was significant ($p <$ .001), and there was no performance difference between left hemisphere patients and the normal control subjects. The right temporal-parietal patients, who had scored well as a group on intelligence and vocabulary tests, had the lowest mean score of all (21.36, using Lansdell's first 40 pictures) but the six right parietal patients had the highest mean score (27.83) of all right hemisphere groups. The lowest left hemisphere group mean score was made by the parietal lobe patients (28.67), and a "mixed" left hemisphere group achieved the highest mean score of all (33.40), higher than the mean of a matched control group (30.0).

Tests involving fragmented visual stimuli
Perceptual puzzles requiring conceptual reorganization of disarranged pieces test the same perceptual functions as does Object Assembly, but without the complicating motor response. This kind of test material can have either meaningful or meaningless visual content.

The Hooper Visual Organization Test (VOT). The *Hooper Visual Organization Test* was developed to identify those patients in mental hospitals with organic brain conditions (Hooper, 1958). Thirty pictures of more or less readily recognizable cut-up objects make up the test. The subject's task is to name each object verbally if the test is individually administered or by writing the object's name in spaces provided in the test booklet (see Fig. 11-4). This test does not correlate significantly with sex, education, age, or intelligence except at borderline defective and lower intellectual ability levels and at ages above 70. Intellectually intact persons generally fail no more than five VOT items. Persons who make six to ten failures comprise a "borderline" group that includes emotionally disturbed or psychotic patients as well as those with mild to moderate brain disorders. More than ten failures usually indicate organic brain pathology; when this many errors result from a psychotic rather than a neuropathological condition, qualitative aspects of the responses will generally betray their functional etiology.

Many brain injured persons perform well on the VOT. Rarely does it provide the first or only indication of an organic defect. However, when the patient's VOT score is low, it is likely that he has an organic brain disorder. The VOT is particularly useful in investigations of the nature of a patient's disability, since it provides a means for clearly separating the perceptual component from a patient's performance on Object Assembly and other visuopractic tests.

The Minnesota Paper Form Board Test. This test uses nonobjective material—fragmented circles, triangles, and other geometric figures—to elicit perceptual organizing behavior (Likert and Quasha, 1970) (see Fig. 11-5). It calls on perceptual scanning and recognition and on the ability to perceive fragmented percepts as wholes. In its standard form, it is a 64-item multiple-choice paper and pencil test with norms based on a 20-minute time limit. The manual gives norms for a variety of populations including high school students, men from various occupations and job applicant groups, and women factory worker applicants. By and large, eleventh and twelfth grade student groups averaged 39 to 40 correct responses, as did groups of adult males. Female groups had average scores of 34 or 35. Correlations with paper and pencil intellectual ability tests tend to be low, positive, and insignificant.

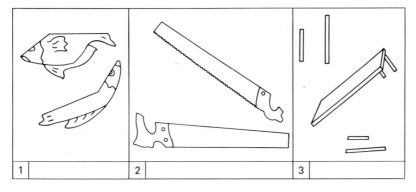

FIG. 11-4. Easy items of the Hooper Visual Organization Test. (By H. Elston Hooper, Ph.D. © 1958 by Western Psychological Services. Reprinted by permission.)

Dee (1970) views this test as measuring "a higher level of perceptual ability" than does a simple matching task. He simplified the original formboard test by enlarging the 2″ × 3″ items to 6″ × 9″ and presenting only the first 40 of them individually rather than side by side in a test booklet. Dee used a 25-minute time limit, thereby allow-

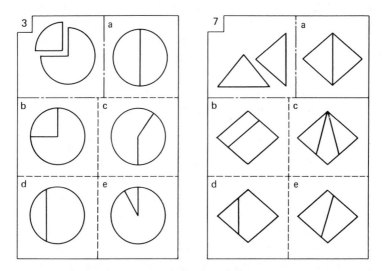

FIG. 11-5. Sample items from the Revised Minnesota Paper Form Board Test, Series BB. (Reproduced by permission. Copyright 1941, renewed 1969 by The Psychological Corporation, New York, N.Y. All rights reserved.)

ing approximately twice as much time for each item. With this format, nonapraxic patients averaged 32 correct responses and mean scores for apraxic patients were approximately 19, regardless of side of lesion. Statistical analysis of the data indicated a strong association between poor performance on this task and apraxia.

Tests involving ambiguous visual stimuli

Most tests that use ambiguous stimuli were developed as personality tests and not as tests of intellectual functioning. They were applied to neuropsychological problems as examiners became familiar with the kinds of responses made by different patient groups.

The *Rorschach* technique exemplifies how ambiguous stimuli, originally used for personality assessment, can provide information about a patient's perceptual abilities. When handling Rorschach responses as data about personality (e.g., behavioral predispositions), the examiner looks at many different aspects of the patient's test performance, such as his productivity, response style, and the affective quality of his associations. In neuropsychological assessment, Rorschach protocols can be evaluated for a variety of qualitative and quantitative response characteristics that tend to be associated with brain disease. Chapter 17 contains a discussion of the Rorschach as a projective technique and as a tool for making neuropsychodiagnostic discriminations. Although perceptual accuracy enters into both personality evaluations and diagnostic discriminations, it can also be treated in its own right, apart from these broader applications of the test.

Evaluation of the perceptual component of a Rorschach response can focus on four aspects of perceptual activity. The first of these is the accuracy of the percept. Since the Rorschach inkblots are ambiguous and composed by chance, no *a priori* "meaning" inheres in the stimulus material. Nevertheless, certain areas of the blots tend to form natural gestalts and to elicit similar associations from normal, intact adults. The test for perceptual accuracy, or "good form," is whether a given response conforms in content and in the patient's delineation of a blot area to common ways of looking at and interpreting the blot. Some Rorschach specialists leave the determination of good form to the examiner's judgment (Klopfer and Davidson, 1962; Rapaport et al., 1968). A more reliable method of determining whether a given response reflects a normal organization of the stimulus uses a frequency count, differentiating "good form" (F+) from "poor form" (F−) responses on a strictly statistical basis (Beck et al., 1961; Beizmann, 1970). Beck lists usual and rare responses to all the commonly used parts of the Rorschach ink blots so that the examiner need only compare the patient's responses with the listed responses to determine which are good and which are poor form. Of the hundreds of good form responses, 21 are given with such frequency that they are called "popular" (P) responses. They are thought to reflect the ability not merely to organize percepts appropriately but also to do so in a socially customary manner. The percentage of good form responses (F+%) and the incidence of popular responses thus can be used as measures of perceptual accuracy.

That these response variables do reflect the intactness of the perceptual system can be inferred from the consistent tendency for brain damaged patients to produce lower F+% and P scores than normal control or neurotic subjects (Aita et al., 1947; Brussel et al., 1942; Goldfried et al., 1971; Piotrowski, 1937). In normal Rorschach protocols, 75 to 85% of unelaborated form responses are of good quality. Brain damaged patients tend to produce fewer good form responses, generally from 40 to 70%. Their poor form responses reflect the kind of perceptual problems that are apt to accompany brain injury, such as difficulty in synthesizing discrete elements into a coherent whole, breaking down a perceptual whole into its component parts, clarifying figure-ground relationships, and identifying relevant and irrelevant details (Baker, 1956a). Patients' verbatim associations will often shed light on the nature of their perceptual disabilities. Their behavior too may betray the perceptual problems, for only brain damaged patients attempt to clarify visual confusion by covering parts of the blot with the hand.

A second aspect of perceptual organization that may be reflected in Rorschach responses is the ability to process and integrate multiple stimuli. Some organic brain conditions reduce the capacity for handling a large perceptual input at once, resulting in a narrowed perceptual field and simplified percepts. This shows up in relatively barren, unelaborated responses in which one characteristic of the blot alone dictates the content of the response, for the patient ignores or does not attempt to incorporate other elements of the blot into his percept. The reduced capacity for handling multiple stimuli also appears as difficulty in integrating discrete parts of the blot into a larger, organized percept, or in separating associations to discrete blot elements that happen to be contiguous. Thus, the patient may correctly interpret several isolated elements of card X as varieties of sea animals without ever forming the organizing concept, "underwater scene." Or, on card III, the side figures may be appropriately identified as "men in tuxedos" and the central red figure as a "bow tie," but the inability to separate these physically contiguous and conceptually akin percepts may produce a response combining the men and the bow tie into a single forced percept such as, "they're wearing tuxedos and that is the bow tie." Sometimes mere contiguity will result in the same kind of overinclusive response so that the blue "crab" on card X may be appropriately identified, but the contiguous "shellfish" becomes the crab's "shellfish claw." These latter two responses are examples of confabulation on the Rorschach.

In terms of specific Rorschach variables, the number of form responses that also take into account color (FC) is likely to be one per record for brain damaged patients, whereas normal subjects typically produce more than one FC response (Lynn et al., 1945). Some patients simply name colors (C_n), whereas normal subjects do not give this kind of response. There may be relatively few responses involving shading (FT, FY) and those introducing movement into the percept (M or FM) are apt to be minimal (Dörken and Kral, 1952; Hughes, 1948, Piotrowski, 1937).

A third aspect of perception is its reliability. Many brain damaged patients feel that they cannot trust their perceptions. Lack of certainty—the Rorschach term for expressions of doubt and confusion is *perplexity*—about one's interpretations of the ink blots is relatively common among brain damaged patients but rare for other patient groups or normal subjects (Baker, 1956a; Piotrowski, 1937).

Lastly, brain damaged patients tend to have slower reaction times on the Rorschach than do normal persons (Goldfried et al., 1971). Average reaction times of one minute or longer suggest impaired perceptual organization on an organic basis.

Visual Interference

Tasks involving visual interference are essentially visual recognition tasks complicated by distracting embellishments. The stimulus material contains the complete percept but extraneous lines or de-

FIGURES   DESIGNS

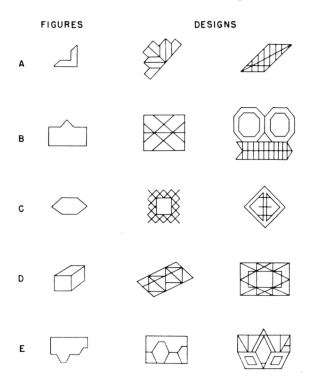

FIG. 11-6. Sample items from the Hidden Figures Test. (Talland, 1965, © Academic Press. Reprinted by permission.)

signs encompass or mask it so that the percept is less readily recognizable. Visual interference tasks differ from tests of visual organization in that the latter call on synthesizing activities whereas visual interference tests require the subject to analyze the figure-ground relationship in order to distinguish the figure from the interfering elements.

Figure-ground tests

Hidden figures. L. L. Thurstone's (1944) version of Gottschaldt's *Hidden Figures Test* has been used to study the perceptual disabilities of patients with traumatic brain injuries (Teuber et al., 1960; Weinstein, 1964), frontal lobectomies (Teuber et al., 1951), and severe memory disorders (Talland, 1965) (see Fig. 11-6). This 34-item test contains several different tasks each involving one or more simple figures and one or more relatively complex figures. The task requires the subject to identify the hidden figure by tracing the

Page A

P E M Y L W A O R A N G E T I S D V U B

Page B

R V L I N O K B C O A T M Q A L I W S N

Page C

L A S U M Y O P B O A T H R I W D G E Z

Page D

V O A L B I K C A R T N J F O W U H M E

Page E

X P O S H C E T Q I M V R Y B A L L O G

FIG. 11-7. Sample sentences for the Hidden Words Test.

outline of the simple figure embedded in the more complex one. At the most difficult levels, the subject has to determine which of two intricate designs contains the simpler figure. In Thurstone's study of normal perception, successful performance on this task was strongly associated with "the ability to form a perceptual closure against some distraction . . . [and] the ability to hold a closure against distraction" (L. L. Thurstone, 1944, p. 101).

Teuber and his colleagues found that all brain injured groups performed more poorly on the Hidden Figures Test than did normal controls and that those patients who had had surgery involving the frontal cortex and aphasic patients made significantly lower scores than other brain injured patients. Talland (1965) reports that patients with Korsakoff's psychosis performed very poorly on this test. He attributes their almost total failure to problems in perceptual shifting and focusing, for in order to perform successfully, the subject must shift his attention from the discrete figure to the inclusive design,

TABLE 11-1
Control Group Times (in Seconds) on the Hidden Word Test

	Page A	Page B	Page C	Page D	Page E
Mean	95.6	114.5	103.2	68.4	96.7
SD	50.6	43.6	35.7	37.1	33.2

(Adapted from Talland, 1965)

necessitating a change of perceptual set in the process. Perceptual flexibility also appeared to contribute significantly to the successful performance of normal teen-age youngsters on this test (Beard, 1965).

Hidden words.   Talland (1965) also studied embedded percepts using words. The *Hidden Words* test consists of five pages, each containing twelve lines of 20 typed capital letters (see Fig. 11-7). In the middle of each line of page A appears the name of a color. One clothing name is randomly positioned in each line of page B. Page C's words appear in the same position as those of page B, and are identical with those of page B except for a one- or two-letter change in each; thus *hat* becomes *ham*, *shoe* becomes *shop*, etc. Pages D and E both consist of different categories: D words appear in one of the four middle positions and E words are randomly placed along the lines. The instructions encourage the subject to underline the words as quickly as possible, but there is no time limit. Performance is scored for number of correctly underlined words and time taken per page. The 16 subject control group averaged 11+ words correct for each page. Talland's memory impaired patients achieved accuracy scores ranging from 8.5 to 9.8. Average response times of the memory impaired patients was more than double that of the control group (see Table 11-1). Although there is considerable overlap between the groups, very slow response times on this test may be interpreted as indicating impaired perceptual efficiency.

Optical illusions.   Optical illusions are variants of the embedded figure problem. L. Cohen (1959) used the number of figure-ground or alternate figure reversals, i.e., the "rate of apparent change (RAC)." to measure perceptual fluctuation in normal control subjects and a

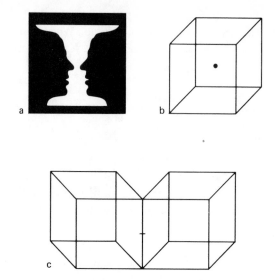

FIG. 11-8. Classical optical illusions: a. Rubin Vase, b. Necker Cube, and c. Double Necker Cube.

brain injured population. Brain injured subjects reported fewer reversals of the *Rubin Vase* and *Double Necker Cube* illusions (see Fig. 11-8) than did the control group. Of the brain injured population, those with lesions on the right reported fewer reversals than did those with left hemisphere damage. Frontal lobe patients differed from this pattern in that no right-left differential occurred, and except for those patients with bilateral frontal lesions, who saw the most reversals of all, the reversal rate of patients with frontal lobe lesions was the slowest (Teuber, 1964; Yacorzynski, 1965).

Visual masking problems
Cross-hatching or shading over simple drawings, letters, or words may destroy the underlying percept for some patients (see Fig. 11-9). Luria (1965a, 1966) found this disability among patients whose lesions involved the occipital lobe; left hemisphere patients experienced difficulty with letters and right hemisphere patients were unable to identify such simple drawings as a clock face or a table when they were shaded.

Another form of visual masking involves jumbled words or pictures which the subject must distinguish visually. André Rey's

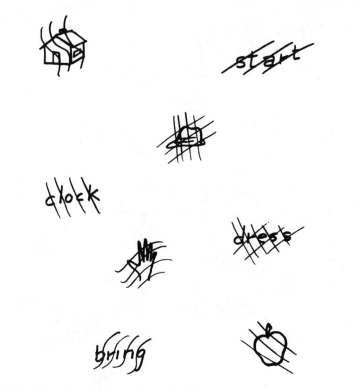

FIG. 11-9. Visual masked words and pictures.

Visual Word Discrimination Test (*Épreuve de ségrégation visuelle de mots*) (1964) consists of 25 common nouns printed over one another (see Fig. 11-10). The subject's task is to call out the words as rapidly as he can read them while the examiner writes down the words read, noting the number correctly identified after 30 seconds, one minute, and two minutes. Rey advises the examiner to show the patient the page on which the test is printed and then quickly remove it while giving the following instructions: "On this page you probably were able to make out a series of words that are printed in jumbled fashion one on top of another. When I place the page in front of you, you are to read aloud all the words as fast as you can." Rey's norms for this test are based on groups of approximately 35 subjects each. Besides the adult norms (see Table 11-2), he reports norms for the five years from ages eight to 12.

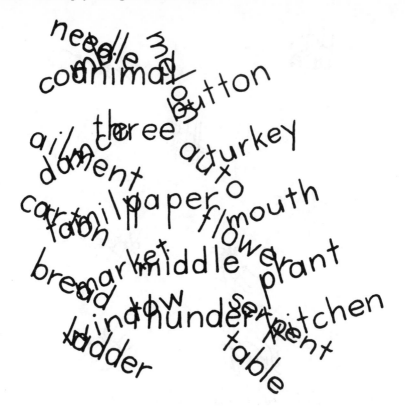

FIG. 11-10. Rey's Visual Word Discrimination Test.

Visual Scanning

The visual scanning defects that often accompany brain lesions can seriously compromise such important activities as reading, writing, performing paper and pencil calculations, and telling time (Diller et al., 1974) and are associated with accident prone behavior (Diller and Weinberg, 1970). They are most common and most severe in patients with right hemisphere lesions (Weinberg et al., 1976). Their relatively high incidence in brain damaged populations means that tests of visual scanning can be used to screen for brain damage. Picture description and reading tests and cancellation tasks (see pp. 432–433) will disclose many scanning problems. These deficits also show up on the purely perceptual tests involving scanning behavior.

TABLE 11-2
Norms for Visual Word Discrimination Test

| | Percentiles | | | | |
	10	25	50	75	90
Number of words read in first 30 seconds					
P[a]	9	12	14	16	17
S[b]	11	14	17	20	21
Number of words read in first minute					
P	16	18	21	23	24
S	18	21	22	24	25
Number of words read within two minutes					
P	19	22	23	24	25
S	21	23	24	25	25

(After Rey, 1964)
[a] P, adults with primary education only.
[b] S, adults who completed secondary school.

Visual search tests

Perceptual Maze Test.   Elithorn's Mazes are based on his view that "perceptual skills are phylogenetically fundamental components of intelligent behavior." Elithorn originally intended the *Perceptual Maze Test* to be a culture-free, nonverbal "intelligence test" (Elithorn, 1964) (see Fig. 11-11). One version of the test consists of 18 lattice-type mazes that require the subject to trace a line as quickly as he can from the top to the bottom of the lattice through as many of the randomly placed choice points as possible. Thus, besides perceptual activities, the patient must comprehend a somewhat complex task, count, keep track of several numbers and the paths they represent, and choose between alternate routes. The tests are scored on the basis of a one-minute time limit without informing the patient. Each maze has its own norms that give the percentage of control subjects who passed it.

In one large study, which included relatively few aphasic patients, this test discriminated well between brain damaged and control patients with more failures among right than left hemisphere pa-

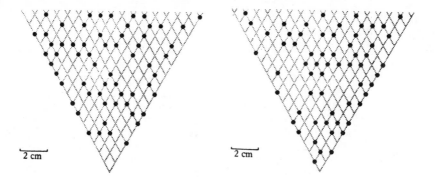

FIG. 11-11. Two patterns from Elithorn's Perceptual Maze Test. (Elithorn, 1964; reproduced by permission of the Cambridge University Press.)

tients (Benton et al., 1963). Aphasic patients consistently do poorly too (Archibald et al., 1967; Colonna and Faglioni, 1966). The Colonna and Faglioni study also demonstrated a low but significant relationship between the Perceptual Maze Test and education ($r = +.377$) and a higher significant correlation with Raven's Matrices ($r = +.668$). The intricacy of the Mazes' patterning and the complexity of the task limit the number of patients who can follow the instructions and handle the task. This problem probably accounts for the poor performance of aphasic patients. Thus, this test is not for general use with brain damaged patients. Whether the Elithorn Mazes add information that cannot be obtained through other perceptual and maze-type tests remains a question.

Field of Search. This visual search task uses a projector and screen to display the stimulus material, but its format lends itself to card presentation should mechanical equipment not be available or suitable to the examination situation. The *Field of Search* test (Teuber, 1964) consists of six slides each containing 48 different visual patterns scattered over all but the central area of a screen (see Fig. 11-12). A figure identical to one of the outlying figures is flashed on the screen and the time taken by the subject to locate its match is recorded. Teuber found that patients with frontal lobe lesions performed significantly more slowly than patients with posterior lesions. He also noted that patients with lateralized frontal lesions were slower in matching figures on the side of the screen opposite the side of the lesion.

FIG. 11-12. One of the six field tests in "field of search" procedures.

Counting dots.   This very simple device for testing visual scanning behavior can be constructed to meet the occasion (McFie et al., 1950). The subject is asked to count a number of dots, 20 or 30, widely scattered over a piece of paper. Errors may be due to visual inattention to one side, to difficulty in maintaining an orderly approach to the task, or to problems in tracking numbers and dots consecutively.

Visual tracking tests

Two tests for visual tracking do not differ greatly in their format. Rey's *Tangled Lines* (*Lignes enchevêtrée à suivre du regard*) test (1964) is printed on a single sheet placed before the subject with instructions to follow each of 16 numbered lines with his eyes from the left to the right of the page, where the ends of each line are also numbered (see Fig. 11-13). The subject reports the number at which each line ends. The examiner records errors and time taken. Each succeeding set of four lines represents successively greater degrees of visual complexity. Mean times decrease markedly with maturation; average time taken per line for five-year-olds is 16 seconds, for

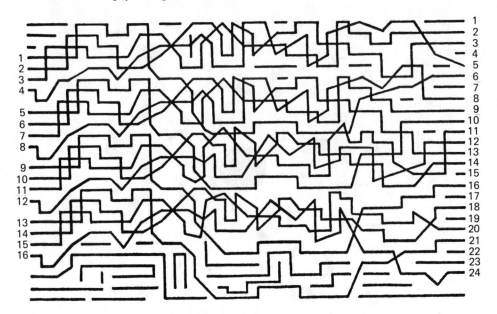

FIG. 11-13. Rey's Tangled Lines Test (*Lignes enchevêtrée à suivre du regard*). (Courtesy of Presses Universitaires de France.)

12-year-olds it is six seconds. Mean times increase with old age: 75% of an adult student group averaged four seconds per line, whereas the mean time per line for subjects 75 to 85 years of age was eight seconds. The error score decreases with maturation from an average of five for the 16 lines at age five to no errors at age 12 when only 10% of the subjects made any errors. Ninety percent of adult students made no errors, whereas the average number of errors made by aged patients was one. Rey identifies very long response times, more than a very few errors, or frequent false starts as signs of serious perceptual or oculomotor problems.

Talland's *Line Tracing* task (1965) consists of four separate tangled line patterns numbered only on the left (see Fig. 11-14). The subject's task is to write the number of each line beginning on the left in the empty space to the right of the line he thinks is the line's right end. The test patterns differ in the number of lines originating on the left, ending on the right, or both. These line problems are derived from those used by L. L. Thurstone in *A Factorial Study of Perception* (1944). Again, time is kept. Talland's 16 control subjects made no er-

FIG. 11-14. One of four patterns of the Line Tracing task. (Talland, 1965, © Academic Press. Reprinted by permission.)

rors on the two easiest patterns, less than one error on the next most difficult pattern, and less than two errors on the most difficult pattern. Average time taken per line on the simpler patterns was in the range of that taken by Rey's adult students but it more than tripled on the most difficult pattern.

AUDITORY FUNCTIONS

As is the case with vision, the verbal and nonverbal components of auditory perception appear to be functionally distinct (Kimura, 1967; Milner, 1962). Also as with vision, there are many psychological techniques for examining the verbal auditory functions. Unlike visual perception, however, psychologists have paid relatively little systematic attention to nonverbal auditory functions. Thus, although verbal tests involving audition are abundant, the psychological examination of nonverbal aspects of auditory perception is limited to a few techniques.

Auditory-Verbal Perception

Every thorough neuropsychological examination provides some opportunity to evaluate the auditory perception of verbal material. When the examiner orally presents problems of judgment and reasoning, learning and memory, he also has an opportunity to make an informal estimate of the patient's auditory acuity, comprehension, and processing capacity. Significant defects in the perception and comprehension of speech are readily apparent during the course of administering most psychological tests. For example, a patient must have a fairly intact capacity for auditory-verbal perception in order to give even a minimal performance on the WAIS.

If a few tasks with simple instructions requiring only motor responses or one- or two-word answers are given, however, subtle problems of auditory processing may be missed. These include difficulty in processing or retaining lengthy messages although responses to single words or short phrases may be accurate, inability to handle spoken numbers without a concomitant impairment in handling other forms of speech, or inability to process messages at high levels in the auditory system when the ability to repeat them accurately is intact. In the absence of a hearing defect, any impairment in the recognition or processing of speech usually indicates a lesion involving the dominant hemisphere (Milner, 1962).

When impairment in auditory processing is suspected, the examiner can couple an auditorally presented test with a similar task presented visually. This kind of paired testing enables the examiner to compare the functioning of the two perceptual systems under similar conditions. A consistent tendency for the patient to perform better under one of the two stimulus conditions should alert the examiner to the possibility of neurological impairment of the less efficient perceptual system. Test pairs can be readily found or developed for most verbal tests at most levels of difficulty. For example, I include both paper and pencil and orally administered personal history, information, arithmetic reasoning, and proverbs questions in my basic battery. Comprehension, sentence building, and vocabulary items and many memory and orientation tasks also lend themselves well to this kind of dual treatment.

Nonverbal Auditory Perception

So much of a person's behavior is organized around verbal signals that nonverbal auditory functions are often overlooked. However, the recognition, discrimination, and comprehension of nonsymbolic sound patterns—such as music, tapping patterns, and the meaningful noises of sirens, dog barks, and thunderclaps—are subject to impairment much as is the perception of language sounds. Defects of nonverbal auditory perception tend to be associated with lesions of the right temporal lobe (Bogen and Gordon, 1971; Milner, 1962, 1971).

Most tests for nonverbal auditory perception use sound recordings. The *Seashore Rhythm Test* is probably the one used most widely since Halstead (1947) incorporated it into his test battery and Reitan (undated) subsequently included it in his neuropsychological assessment program. This test, which is a subtest of the *Seashore Test of Musical Talent* (Seashore et al., 1960), requires the subject to discriminate between like and unlike pairs of musical beats. Milner (1971) has recorded a set of familiar sounds (train whistle, squealing brakes) for an auditory recognition test. Patients with right temporal brain damage tend to do poorly on both of these tests, whereas patients with brain lesions localized elsewhere rarely experience difficulty with them.

The examiner can improvise tests for nonverbal auditory perception. The Aphasia Screening Test (Halstead and Wepman, 1959) requires the patient to identify a tune ("America") the examiner whistles or hums. If the patient fails this simple task, the examiner should try several other simple popular melodies, such as "Yankee Doodle," "Oh Susanna," and "Silent Night." An adult raised in this country who recognizes none of these songs is demonstrating an *amusia* (literally, no music), which implicates damage to the right temporal lobe. The examiner can test pitch discrimination with a pitch pipe, asking the patient to report which of two sounds is higher or whether two sounds are the same or different. Recognition for rhythm patterns can be evaluated by requiring the patient either to discriminate similar and different sets of rhythmic taps or to mimic patterns tapped out by the examiner with a pencil on the table top. Adding a memory component to these tasks is likely to increase their sensitivity in demonstrating a perceptual defect. However, memory techniques can be included in perception tests only when the patient has demonstrated adequate memory in other perceptual modalities. The examiner should also note whether the patient seems to comprehend such extraneous noises as a door slamming, a plane flying overhead, or the ring of a phone.

When the perceptual task is as simple as asking for a discrimination between three evenly spaced taps and three taps spaced so that the first two are close together with a lag between the second and third taps, more than one failure suggests defective nonverbal perception. The patient who fails two or three of as many as five trials on this kind of discrimination task should be given another five to ten trials with similar material to clarify whether he misunderstood the instructions, was having difficulty concentrating on the task, or whether in fact he has a perceptual disability. Pairing similar tasks involving verbal and nonverbal material can help clarify the interpretation of a patient's failures. For example, the examiner can ask the patient to repeat four- and five-syllable sentences and to mimic four- and five-beat tapping patterns. Patients who display confusion on both tasks may have an attention defect or may not have understood the instructions. Those who fail to repeat only sentences or only tapping patterns correctly probably have a specific defect of auditory perception.

Sources of Defective Auditory Comprehension

The most common sources of defective auditory comprehension are deficiencies in auditory acuity resulting from conduction and/or sensorineural hearing losses, and deficits in auditory processing associated with aphasia.

Decreased auditory acuity

Most patients whose hearing is impaired are aware of their problem. Unfortunately, some individuals with mild to moderate deficits are embarrassed and do not report them to the examiner, or they may try to hide their disability even at the cost of a poor performance on the tests. Occasionally a patient incurs a reduction in hearing sensitivity as a result of his brain injury, in which case hearing on the ear opposite the side of the lesion is likely to be the more impaired. When such a hearing loss is slight, and particularly when it is recent or when aphasic defects also contribute to his speech comprehension problems, the patient may be unaware of it.

Usually, if the patient does not report that he is hard of hearing, his behavior will betray his problem. Persons whose hearing is better on one side tend to favor that side by turning the head toward the examiner and placing themselves so the better ear is closer to him.

The mild to moderately hard of hearing person may display erratic speech comprehension as the examiner's voice becomes louder or softer, or not hear well if the examiner turns away when speaking to the patient. The examiner who suspects that the patient has a hearing loss can test for it crudely by changing his voice level and noting whether the patient's level of comprehension varies. When the patient appears to have a hearing loss, the examiner should insist that the patient see an audiologist for a thorough audiological examination. An audiological assessment is of particular importance when a tumor is suspected, for an early sign of some forms of brain tumor is decreased auditory acuity. It is also important for the brain damaged patient with other sensory or cognitive defects to be aware of his hearing problems so that he can learn to compensate for them and, when indicated, get the benefits of a hearing aid.

Auditory discrimination problems

Some patients have difficulty discriminating sounds even when thresholds for sound perception remain within the normal hearing range and no aphasic disability is present. Auditory discrimination can be tested by having the patient repeat words and phrases spoken by the examiner, or by asking the patient to tell whether two spoken words are the same or different, using pairs of different words, such as "cap" and "cat," or "vie" and "thy," interspersed with identical word pairs (Wepman, 1958). Word lists for auditory discrimination are available in most textbooks on audiology and speech pathology. Auditory discrimination is evaluated routinely in audiometric examinations. When the problem is suspected, referral to an audiologist is indicated.

Aphasia

When the patient's comprehension problem clearly does not relate to deficits in auditory acuity, aphasia must be suspected. The neuropsychologist always looks for evidence of aphasia when the patient displays a right-sided weakness or complains of sensory changes on the right half of his body. Aphasia must also be considered whenever the patient's difficulty in comprehending speech appears to be clearly unrelated to hearing loss, attention or concentration defects, a foreign language background, or a functional thought disorder. The patient's performance on an aphasia screening test, such as that of Halstead and Wepman (p. 260), or the Token Test (p. 260) should help the examiner determine whether a more thorough study of the patient's language functions is indicated. The patient who has difficulty with more than one or two items on either of these tests should be referred to a speech pathologist for further assessment.

Dichotic Listening

Some patients with lateralized lesions involving the temporal lobe or central auditory pathways tend to ignore auditory signals entering the ear opposite the side of the lesions, much as other brain damaged patients exhibit unilateral visual neglect or *extinction* (unawareness of one of a pair of similar stimuli simultaneously presented to different parts of the body, different areas of the fields of vision, etc.) on the side contralateral to the lesion (Oxbury and Oxbury, 1969). Dichotic testing, in which the auditory recognition capacity of each ear is tested separately but simultaneously uses stimulus sets, such as digits, delivered through headphones by a dual track sound system (Kimura, 1961, 1967). By this means, the patient receives the stimulus pairs, one to each ear, at precisely the same time. Normally, when different digits or words are received by each ear, both of them are heard. When only one word set is heard clearly and the other is only poorly understood or not recognized at all, a lesion involving the auditory system on the contralateral side can be suspected.

TACTILE FUNCTIONS

Investigations into defects of touch perception have employed many different kinds of techniques to elicit or measure the different ways in which tactile perception can be disturbed. Most of the techniques present simple recognition or discrimination problems. A few involve more complex behavior.

Tactile Recognition and Discrimination Tests

The detailed examination for finger agnosia developed by Kinsbourne and Warrington (1962) includes three tactile tests that need no elaborate equipment. The patient closes his eyes and places his hand, palm down, on the working surface for all of these tests. These tests should first be given with the patient's eyes open so that he understands them. (1) In the *In-between Test*, the examiner touches two fingers simultaneously, having instructed the patient to tell the number of fingers in between the two that are touched. (2) The *Two-Point Finger Test* requires that the examiner touch two places on the same or different fingers and the patient reports whether one or two fingers were touched. (3) In the *Match Box Test*, the examiner slips a small match box between two of the patient's fingers or touches the sides of two different fingers with two match boxes. The patient must identify which fingers were touched. Of these three tests, the In-between Test was most useful for clinical purposes. Patients with finger agnosia consistently had difficulty differentiating their fingers or relating one to another. Twenty control patients, all of whom had some form of cerebral cortical disease without any evidence of finger agnosia, performed these tests without error.

Object recognition (testing for astereognosis) is commonly performed in neurological examinations. The patient closes his eyes and is asked to recognize by touch such common objects as a coin, a paper clip, a pencil, or key. Each hand is examined separately. Size discrimination is easily tested with coins. The examiner can use bits of cloth, wire screening, sandpaper, etc., for texture discrimination. Organically intact adults are able to perform tactile recognition and discrimination tests with complete accuracy: a single erroneous response or even evidence of hesitancy strongly suggests that this function is impaired. Somesthetic defects are generally associated with lesions of the contralateral hemisphere (Weinstein, 1955).

Skin writing, in which the examiner traces random letters or numbers on the palms of the subject's hands, is also used in neurological examinations. Rey (1965) formalized the skin writing procedure into a series of five subtests in which the examiner writes (1) the figures 5 1 8 2 4 3 on the dominant palm (see Fig. 11-15a); (2) V E S H R O on the dominant palm; (3) 3 4 2 8 1 5 on the non-dominant palm (Fig. 11-15b); (4) 1 3 5 8 4 2 in large figures extending to both sides of the two palms held one centimeter apart (Fig. 11-15c through h); and (5) 2 5 4 1 3 8 on the fleshy part of the inside dominant forearm. Each subtest score represents the number of errors. Rey provides data on four different adult groups: manual and

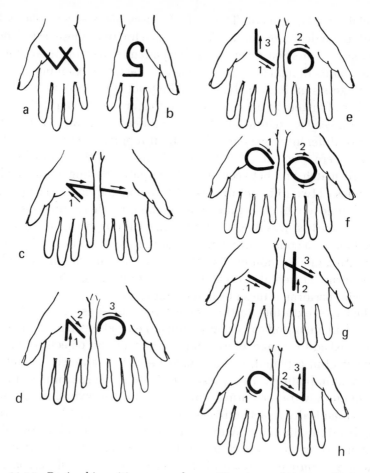

FIG. 11-15. Rey's skinwriting procedures. (Courtesy of Presses Universitaires de France.)

unskilled workers (M), skilled technicians and clerks (T), people with the baccalaureate degree (B), and persons between the ages of 68 and 83 (A) (see Table 11-3). In the absence of a sensory deficit or an aphasic condition, when the patient displays an error differential between the two hands, a contralateral cortical lesion is suspected; defective performance regardless of side implicates a tactile perceptual disability.

The *Tactual Completion Test* (Talland, 1965) was developed to test the closure phenomenon in a modality other than vision. Five

TABLE 11-3
Skin Writing Test Errors Made by Four Adult Groups

Group		Right Hand Numbers	Right Hand Letters	Left Hand Numbers	Both Hands Numbers	Forearm Numbers
M	Mdn	0	1	0	2	1
n = 51	CS[a]	2	3	2	5	3
T	Mdn	0	1	0	1	0
n = 25	CS	2	3	1	3	3
B	Mdn	0	1	0	0	0
n = 55	CS	1	2	1	2	2
A	Mdn	1	2	1	2	2
n = 14	CS	3	4	3	6	3

(Adapted from Rey, 1965)
[a] CS = Cutting Score.

stimulus figures—N, 5, R, 37, and TAX—are formed by pinheads or elevated ridges of baked clay on a small square board in three different stages of completeness. For each stimulus figure, the blindfolded subject begins with the least complete model, attempting to recognize it by touch within 90 seconds. If unsuccessful on either of the two incomplete models, he is given the next more complete one. Approximately three-quarters of Talland's control subjects recognized the single figure items on the first or second trial, almost two-thirds recognized "37" by the second trial, but only one-fifth of the group recognized "TAX" by the second trial, and more than one-quarter did not achieve the percept at all.

12

VISUOPRACTIC FUNCTIONS AND MANUAL DEXTERITY

VISUOPRACTIC FUNCTIONS

Tests of visuopractic functions combine perceptual activity with motor response and always have a spatial component. As a result, although persons with more than very mild perceptual disabilities will generally experience some difficulty on visuopractic tasks, the reverse does not obtain. Because of the complexity of functions entering into the visuopractic performance, numerical scores convey only a limited amount of information about the test performance. Careful observation is needed to distinguish between perceptual failures, apraxias, spatial confusion, or attentional or motivational problems.

The concept of visuopractic functions embraces two large classes of activities, graphic and constructional. The tendency for graphic and constructional disabilities to occur together, although significant, is so variable that these two classes of activity need to be evaluated separately.

Visuographic Tests

The major subdivisions within the class of graphic functions are copying and free drawing. The overlap between them is considerable and yet many persons whose drawing skills are impaired can copy with reasonable accuracy. Instances of the reverse case are relatively rare.

Visuographic tasks have achieved a central position in neuro-psychological testing by virtue of their sensitivity to many different

310

kinds of organic disabilities. This sensitivity may be the reason that the discriminating power of visuographic tasks at times has assumed mythic proportions. Unfortunately, it has not been uncommon for some psychologists to think that a complete neuropsychological examination consists of the WAIS and one or two drawing tests, usually the Bender-Gestalt and a Draw-a-Person test. (There are even a few intrepid purists who prefer to form their diagnostic opinions on the basis of a single drawing test.) However, although they are rich sources of data, drawing tests too have limits to the amount of information they can provide. The examiner who uses them needs to remember that every kind of drawing task has been performed successfully by brain injured patients including some with lesions that should have prevented them from doing the tasks. Furthermore, no matter how sensitive these tests might be to perceptual, practic, and certain cognitive and motor organization disabilities, they still leave many intellectual functions untouched.

Copying tests

   The Bender-Gestalt Test.   Of all visuographic tests, the *Bender-Gestalt* has been the subject of the most study, theory, and research. Conceptual approaches to the interpretation of nonobjective drawings that have evolved out of this work can be applied to the evaluation of visuographic performances generally. This test's quick and easy administration probably contributes to its first place position among the most frequently used psychological tests in the United States (Lubin et al., 1971). The fact that it serves as a projective technique for studying personality as well as a visuographic task for neuropsychological assessment also accounts for its popularity.

   The Bender material is a set of nine designs* originally used to demonstrate the tendency of the perceptual system to organize visual stimuli into *Gestalten* (configurational wholes) (see Fig. 12-1). The designs were assembled and numbered (A and 1 through 8) by Lauretta Bender for the study of mental development in children (Bender, 1938). She called this method a "Visual Motor Gestalt Test." Time and custom have grafted Dr. Bender's name onto the formal title of her test. Most clinicians simply refer to it as the "Bender."

---

* The set of Bender cards with the most evenly and clearly reproduced design elements is Hutt's adaptation of the Bender test figures (Hutt, 1969).

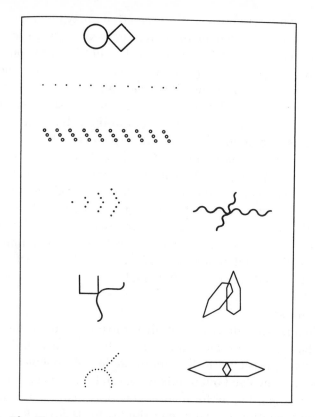

FIG. 12-1. The Hutt Adaptation of the Bender-Gestalt figures. (Hutt, 1969. Reproduced by permission.)

Almost every clinician who has written about the Bender at any length has prescribed at least one set of instructions. My administration of this test begins with laying three sharpened number one or two pencils and a small stack of unlined white typewriter size paper in front of the patient so that the short side is horizontal to him. Three pencils with good erasers ensure against having to interrupt the test when a heavy-handed, intense, or clumsy patient breaks one or more pencil points. Pencils any harder than a number two tend to resist pressure so that drawing becomes more effortful and the pencil marks are less apt to reflect individual pressure differences in their shading or thickness. The main purpose of putting out more than one piece of paper is to create a softer drawing surface that will increase ease of drawing and pick up pressure marks on the second sheet. Sometimes patients set aside the top sheet of paper on completion of the first drawing, or after three or four drawings. When they do so, I ask them to draw all the designs on the first sheet unless there is no usable space left, in which case I ask them to complete the test on the second sheet. Forcing the patient to confine his drawings to one or, at the most, two sheets provides one way to see how—or whether—the patient organizes the designs within limited space.

The instructions are: "I've got nine of these altogether (hold up the pack of cards with the back facing the patient). I'm going to show them to you one at a time and your job is (or "I want you") to copy them as exactly as you can. Here you go." The first card is then placed in front of the patient with its length running horizontally to him and its edges squared with the edges of the work surface. When the patient finishes the first drawing, the second card is placed on top of the first and so on to completion. When all the designs have been copied, I ask the subject to write his name and the date on the paper with no instructions about where these should be placed, and I offer no suggestions if asked.

These instructions afford the patient the barest minimum of structure and virtually no information on how to proceed. This method not only enhances the test's projective possibilities, but makes it a test of the patient's ability to organize his activities as well. By letting the subject know there are nine cards, the examiner gives him the opportunity to plan ahead for his space needs. By omitting any reference to the nature of the cards, i.e., by not calling them "designs," the examiner avoids influencing the subject's perceptual organization of the stimuli. By lining the cards up with the edges of the work surface, the examiner provides an external anchoring point for the angulation of the stimulus so that, should the subject rotate his copy of the design, the examiner knows exactly how much the drawing is angled relative to the original stimulus.

Many subjects need no more instruction than this to complete the tests comfortably. Others ask questions about how to draw the figures, whether they can be larger or smaller, have more or less dots, need to be numbered, lined up along the edge, or spread over the page, etc. To each of these questions, the answer is, "Just copy the card as exactly as you can." Should the subject persist in his questioning, the examiner may tell him that, "I can only give you these instructions; the rest is up to you." The subject who asks to erase is given permission without special encouragement. If the subject attempts to turn either the stimulus card or his sheet of paper, he should be stopped before he begins copying the card at an incorrect or uncommon angle, as the disorientation of the drawing might no longer be apparent when the paper is righted again. I do not let the patient turn the page more than is needed for a comfortable writing angle. The total time usually runs from five to ten minutes.

Besides different versions of the standard administration, there are a number of other ways to give the test, most of which were developed for personality assessment (Hutt, 1969). Those that enable the examiner to see how well the subject can function under pressure provide interesting neuropsychological data as well. For instance, in the "stress Bender," the patient is given the whole test a second time with instructions to "copy the designs as fast as you can. You drew them in ___ seconds (any reasonable time approximation will do) the first time; I want to see how much faster you can do them this time." The examiner then begins timing as noisily and ostentatiously as possible. Some patients who can compensate well for mild visuopractic disabilities when under no pressure will first betray evidence of their problem as they speed up their performance. Interestingly, many organically intact subjects actually improve their Bender performance under the stress condition. (Regardless of how much time the patient takes the second time, I always congratulate him on his speed and, if need be, shade a few seconds off his performance time in telling him about it.)

Wepman (personal communication, 1974) incorporates two recall procedures into his three-stage standard administration of the Bender. Each card is shown for five seconds, then removed, and the subject is instructed to draw it from memory. After this, the cards are shown again, one at a time, with instructions to copy them exactly. This second stage is the same as the standard copy administration. Finally, the cards are removed, the subject is handed one more blank sheet of paper, and asked to draw as many of the figures as he can remember. Wepman views difficulty with items 1, 2, 4, and 5 as particularly suggestive of a visuopractic disorder. He found that normal subjects typically recall five designs or more and he considers recall scores under five to be suggestive of brain injury. This impression is supported by Tolor's findings (1956, 1958) that functionally disturbed psychiatric patients recall six designs on the average, whereas organic patients average three and a half recalled designs.

Bender conceived of her test as a clinical exercise in which "(d)eviate behavior . . . should be observed and noted. It never represents a test failure" (1946). She did not use a scoring system. The Bender variables that can be scored are numerous and equivocal, and their dimensions are often difficult to define. The profusion of scoring possibilities has resulted in many attempts to develop a workable system to obtain scores for diagnostic purposes.

Probably the best known scoring system is the one devised by Pascal and Suttell (1941) who viewed deviations in the execution of Bender drawings as reflecting "disturbances in cortical function," whether on a functional or an organic basis. By assigning each deviant response a numerical value, they enabled the examiner to compute a score indicating the extent to which the drawings deviate from normal productions. As a general rule, the scores of neurotic patients are almost indistinguishable from those of normal subjects, the highest scores tend to be obtained by brain damaged patients, and the considerable overlap between groups of brain damaged and psychiatric patients makes differentiation between them on the basis of a Bender score alone a very questionable matter.

The Pascal-Suttell system identifies 106 different scorable characteristics of the drawings, from ten to 13 for each figure (excluding A) plus seven layout variables applied to the performance as a whole. Significant distortions of these characteristics earn score points. For example, there are twelve scorable characteristics for design 6 that yield scores for specific deviations: (1) Asymmetry (score 3); (2) Angles in the Curve (score 2); (3) Point of Crossing (score 2); (4) Curve Extra (score 8); (5) Double Line (score 1 for each); (6) Touch-up (score 8); (7) Tremor (score 4); (8) Distortion (score 8); (9) Guide Lines (score 2); (10) Workover (score 2); (11) Second Attempt (score 3 for each); and (12) Rotation (score 8). An examiner who knows this system can score most records in two to three minutes. The average mean raw score for seven age groups of men and women with high school education is 18.0 (SD 9.4); and for the same number of age groups of both sexes with college educations, the average mean score is 12.7 (SD 8.8).

Approaching the test performance as a whole rather than card by card, Hain (1964) developed a 15-category scoring system from inspection of the Bender protocols of brain damaged patients (see Table 12-1). Any single instance of a category characteristic earns the score points for that category. The total possible range of scores is from 0 for a perfect performance to 34 for a protocol in which every

TABLE 12-1
Hain's 15-Category Scoring System for the Bender Gestalt Test

The Scoring Categories Classified by Their Score Weights

4-points	3-points	2-points	1-point
Perseveration	Added Angles	Embellishments	Omission
Rotation or Reversal	Separation of Lines	Partial Rotation	Abbreviation of
Concretism	Overlap		Designs 1 or 2
	Distortion		Separation
			Absence of Erasure
			Closure
			Point of Contact on
			Figure A

(Adapted from Hain, 1963)

category of deviant response occurs at least once. Hain compared small groups of brain damaged, psychiatric, and "non-brain damaged" patients to obtain cut-off scores for discriminating between the brain damaged group and the others (see Table 12-2). He set the optimal cut-off point between scores 8 and 9, which identifies approximately 80% of all subjects correctly, but misidentifies 41% of the brain damaged patients and only 8% of the combined groups without brain damage.

Hutt designed a 17-factor Psychopathology Scale to measure the severity of psychopathology (1969). Although the scale was evaluated with groups of normal subjects and neurotic and schizophrenic patients, Hutt anticipated that scores of schizophrenic and brain damaged patients would overlap, with the highest scores going to the latter. Like Hain's scoring approach, this scoring system differs from the Pascal-Suttell system in treating the test performance as a whole. Thus, for a factor such as "curvature difficulty," Hutt has a four-point scale ranging from Severe (scale value = 10.0) scored when curves in all three figures containing curves are distorted, to Absent (scale value = 1.0) when all the curves are drawn well. In contrast, Pascal and Suttell's system scores for six different kinds of curve distortion on design 4, one kind of curve distortion on design 5, and two on design 6.

The first five of Hutt's factors relate to the organization of the drawings on the page and to one another: (1) Sequence, (2) Position (of first drawing), (3) Use of Space, (4) Collision, and (5) Shift of Paper.

TABLE 12-2
*Distribution of Hain Bender-Gestalt Scores for Brain Damaged
and Non-brain Damaged Groups*

Classification	Score	Brain damaged (%) (n = 21)	Non-brain damaged (%) (n = 84)[a]
Normal area	0–5	20	80
Borderline	6–12	41	18
Critical area	13–24	39	2

(Adapted from Hain, 1963)
[a] Includes 21 psychiatric patients.

The next factors concern changed gestalts: (6) Closure Difficulty, (7) Crossing Difficulty, (8) Curvature Difficulty, (9) Change in Angulation. Factors related to distorted gestalts are associated with severe psychopathology: (10) Perceptual Rotation, (11) Retrogression, (12) Simplification, (13) Fragmentation, (14) Overlap Difficulty, (15) Elaboration, (16) Perseveration, and (17) Redraw Total Figure. Scale values of each factor range from 10 to 1 with the exception of the second factor which has only two scale values, 3.25 for Abnormal and 1.0 for Normal. Score range is from 17 for a perfect performance (or at least a performance without serious imperfections) to 163.5 for a performance in which maximum difficulty is encountered in handling each factor characteristic.

Criteria for scoring each factor are presented in detail and are sufficiently clear to result in reliable judgments. Hutt reports that interjudge reliability correlations for the 17 factors for two judges scoring 100 schizophrenic records ranged from 1.00 to .76 with five factor correlations running above .90 and nine above .80. An interjudge reliability correlation of .96 was obtained for the total scale. Hutt reports that by means of this system the examiner can discriminate reliably between normal and neurotic, schizophrenic and organic groups, with all differences between groups significant beyond the .001 level except that between the last two, at the .05 level (see Table 12-3).

Hutt also describes a number of other characteristic distortions, such as size changes and line quality, which are not included in the scale but may be associated with organic conditions and have all been included in one or more other scales. He identifies eleven kinds

TABLE 12-3
Psychopathology Scale Values for Several Groups

Group	Mean	SD
Normal	33.8	3.2
Neurotic	57.8	5.6
Schizophrenic	100.3	10.1
Organic	103.8	11.4

(From Hutt, 1969)

of deviations which are particularly associated with brain damage: (1) Collision (and Collision Tendency), i.e., the running together or overlapping of two discrete designs, (2) Angulation Difficulty (marked), (3) Perceptual Rotation (severe, which increases in seriousness when the subject does not perceive or cannot correct it), (4) Simplistic, (5) Fragmentation (severe), (6) Overlapping Difficulty (moderate to severe), (7) Perseveration (of elements in a design and of elements of one design in another, especially if severe), (8) Elaboration (moderate), (9) Redrawing of a Total Figure, (10) Line Incoordination (both fine and coarse), and (11) Concreteness. He also regards sketching that is so loose or crude as to diminish the quality of the drawing or distort the gestalt, and expressions of feelings of impotence, as indicators of organicity. Hutt suggests that four or more of these deviant response characteristics in a record is strongly indicative of neuropathology. A careful reading of Hutt's description and interpretation of these deviant characteristics will enhance the examiner's perceptiveness in dealing with Bender data (see Hutt and Gibby, 1970, for examples).

Hutt's interest in the projective potentials of the Bender led him to develop a second scale, the Adience-Abience Scale, to measure "perceptual approach-avoidance behavior." The scale appears to add little to the study of visuographic functions although it may ultimately contribute information about the social and emotional adjustment of brain damaged patients.

Although some scoring system is necessary when doing research with the Bender, for clinical purposes formal scoring is usually unnecessary. Familiarity with one or more of the scoring systems will make the examiner aware of the common Bender distortions. Familiarity with the kinds of aberrations that tend to be associated with visuopractic disabilities and organic response styles will improve the examiner's accuracy in making discriminations on the basis of interpretations rather than scores of the Bender drawings. This was demonstrated in L. R. Goldberg's study (1959) comparing a group of psychology trainees, another group consisting of psychologists' secretaries, scores obtained by the Pascal-Suttell system, and Professor Max Hutt for accuracy in sorting the Bender protocols of subjects with and without brain damage. Trainees, secretaries, and the scoring system all did equally well; Professor Hutt made the most correct sorts.

Pascal and Suttell's mean score differences between high-school and college-educated populations suggested that the Bender-Gestalt performance correlates with general intellectual ability. In a psychiatric population, this was borne out by consistently significant correlations (around .50) between Pascal and Suttell and WAIS subtest scores, with only Digit Span and Object Assembly correlations running below .40 (Aylaian and Meltzer, 1962). On the other hand, a study of college students found "little if any" relation between an academic achievement test and Pascal and Suttell Bender scores, whereas Bender score differences in this relatively homogeneous, intellectually superior population were associated with GPA differences (Peoples and Moll, 1962). Since most nine-year-olds can copy the Bender designs with a fair degree of accuracy (Koppitz, 1964), Bender performance differences between competent intact adults apparently result from the same kind of temperamental or character traits that influence behavior in school or at work. Only when an organically intact group contains both dull and bright persons can intellectual differences be expected to show up in Bender score differences.

Neuropsychological research with the Bender has demonstrated its relative efficiency in making the frequently difficult discrimination between neurological and psychiatric patients (Yates, 1966). Brilliant and Gynther (1963) and Lacks and her colleagues (1970), each using Hutt's scoring system, found that the Bender identified members of each diagnostic group as well or better than any other instrument. In Brilliant and Gynther's study, the Bender-Gestalt showed a diagnostic accuracy of 82%, performing better than either of two visuographic memory tests. In the Lacks study, the Bender-Gestalt score identified organic patients as well or better (74%) than four of eight scores on the Halstead Battery and far and away better

(91%) than any of the Halstead Battery tests in identifying "non-organic" patients. In another study using the Pascal-Suttell scoring system (Korman and Blumberg, 1963), 74% accuracy in discriminating brain damaged from mixed psychiatric patients was reported.

It is impressive that the Bender is as effective as it is since many kinds of brain pathology simply do not affect the specific functions involved in this visuographic exercise. Perceptual functions are rarely so impaired as to affect Bender performance; and motor behavior alone does not account for the kinds of drawing distortions that brain damaged patients make. Rather, the complex visuographic copying task appears to require a high level of integrative behavior that is not necessarily specific to visuopractic functions but tends to break down with cortical damage.

Like other visuographic disabilities, difficulties with the Bender are more likely to appear with parietal lobe lesions (Garron and Cheifetz, 1965); and of these, lesions of the right parietal lobe are associated with the poorest performances (Diller et al., 1974; Hirschenfang, 1960a). The Bender response distortion that is most apt to be associated with organic defects, rotation, occurs with both right and left hemisphere lesions, but right hemisphere patients draw rotated Bender designs about twice as often as those with left hemisphere lesions (Billingslea, 1963; Diller et al., 1974).

Minnesota Percepto-Diagnostic Test (MPD). This copying task is designed to test for the presence of a tendency toward rotation in drawings (Fuller and Laird, 1963). It uses two of the designs included in the Bender-Gestalt test, A and 4, presenting each in three different combinations of design and card orientation. The instructions are simply, "Please copy the design." The examiner does not allow the subject to turn either card or paper. Scoring is based on the amount of rotation of the drawings, which is measured with a protractor. All rotations of 25° or more are scored as 25°; smaller rotations receive the exact number of degrees of the rotation as their score. The maximum possible score is 150° (6 × 25°); the theoretical minimum is zero. The manual gives norms for diagnostic groups of both children and adults. Much of the literature on this test pertains to studies of children with school or personal/social adjustment problems.

This test may be useful in discriminating between brain damaged and other patient and nonpatient groups (Uyeno, 1963; Yates, 1966).

Score differences on the MPD correctly identified 89% of the "Normal" subjects, 80% of a "Personality Disturbance" group (consisting of persons diagnosed as "neurotic," "sociopathic," and "psychotic" in unreported numbers), and 78% of the "Chronic Brain Syndrome" (CBS) group (described as "diagnosed CBS by the medical staff") of the standardization population, the latter group obtaining higher (error) scores (Fuller and Laird, 1963). However, the ages of these groups leave serious question as to their comparability for standardization purposes since the mean age of the Normal group was 29.11 (SD 10.94), of the Personality Disturbance group 43.21 (SD 14.20), and of the Chronic Brain Syndrome group 51.21 (SD 11.50), which brings the last-named group to the borderland of old age and all the normal functional changes of senility. Cultural background may also influence performance on this test (Harrison and Chagnon, 1966).

Rey-Osterrieth Complex Figure Test. A "complex figure" was devised by Rey (1941) to investigate both perceptual organization and visual memory in brain damaged subjects. Osterrieth (1944) standardized Rey's procedure, obtaining normative data from the performance of 230 normal children of ages ranging from four to 15 and 60 adults in the 16 to 60 age range. In addition to two groups of children with learning and adjustment problems, he studied a small number of behaviorally disturbed adults, 43 who had sustained traumatic brain injury, and a few patients with endogenous brain disease.

The test material consists of Rey's complex figure (see Fig. 12-2), two blank sheets of paper, and five or six colored pencils. The subject is first instructed to copy the figure which has been so set out that its length runs along the subject's horizontal plane. The examiner watches the subject's performance closely. Each time the subject completes a section of the drawing, the examiner hands him a different colored pencil and notes the order of the colors. Time to completion is recorded and both the test figure and the subject's drawings are removed. After three minutes, the examiner gives the subject the second sheet of paper and an ordinary pencil and asks him to draw the design from memory. The examiner records the time again and notes whether the subject follows the same procedural approach on this drawing as on his original one.

Osterrieth analyzed the drawings in terms of the patient's method

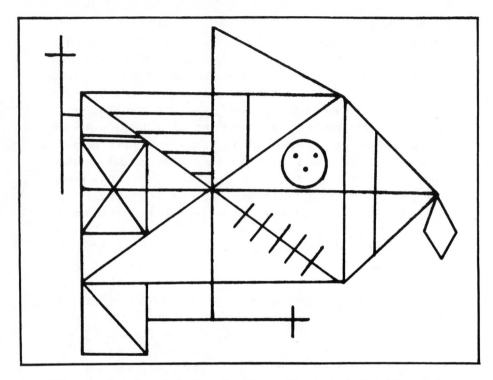

FIG. 12-2. Rey-Osterrieth Complex Figure Test (actual size) (Osterrieth, 1944).

of procedure as well as specific copying errors. He identified seven different procedural types: (I) Subject begins by drawing the large central rectangle and details are added in relation to it. (II) Subject begins with a detail attached to the central rectangle, or with a sub-section of the central rectangle, completes the rectangle and adds remaining details in relation to the rectangle. (III) Subject begins by drawing the overall contour of the figure without explicit differen-tiation of the central rectangle and then adds the internal details. (IV) Subject juxtaposes details one by one without an organizing structure. (V) Subject copies discrete parts of the drawing without any semblance of organization. (VI) Subject substitutes the drawing of a similar object, such as a boat or house. (VII) The drawing is an unrecognizable scrawl.

In Osterrieth's sample, 83% of the adult control subjects followed procedure Types I and II, 15% used Type IV, and there was one Type III subject. Past the age of seven, no child proceeded on a Type

TABLE 12-4
Scoring System for the Rey-Osterrieth Complex Figure Test

Units
1. Cross upper left corner, outside of rectangle
2. Large rectangle
3. Diagonal cross
4. Horizontal midline of 2
5. Vertical midline
6. Small rectangle, within 2 to the left
7. Small segment above 6
8. Four parallel lines within 2, upper left
9. Triangle above 2 upper right
10. Small vertical line within 2, below 9
11. Circle with three dots within 2
12. Five parallel lines with 2 crossing 3, lower right
13. Sides of triangle attached to 2 on right
14. Diamond attached to 13
15. Vertical line within triangle 13 parallel to right vertical of a
16. Horizontal line within 13, continuing 4 to right
17. Cross attached to low center
18. Square attached to 2, lower left

Scoring
Consider each of the eighteen units separately. Appraise accuracy of each unit and relative position within the whole of the design. For each unit count as follows:

Correct	placed properly	2 points
	placed poorly	1 point
Distorted or incomplete	placed properly	1 point
but recognizable	placed poorly	½ point
Absent or not recognizable		0 points
Maximum		36 points

(From E. M. Taylor, 1959, adapted from Osterrieth, 1944)

V, VI, or VII basis, and from age 13 onward, more than half the children followed Types I and II. No one, child or adult, produced a scrawl. More than half (63%) of the traumatically brain injured group also followed Type I and II procedures, although there were a few more Type III and IV subjects in this group and one of Type V. Three of four aphasic patients and one with senile dementia gave Type IV performances, one aphasic and one presenile dementia patient followed a Type V procedure.

An accuracy score based on a unit scoring system can be obtained for each test trial (see Table 12-4). The scoring units refer to specific areas or details of the figures that have been numbered for scoring

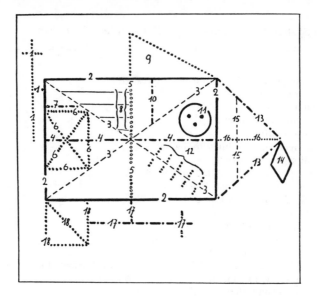

FIG. 12-3. Scoring units of the Rey-Osterrieth Complex Figure Test. (From Osterrieth, 1944.)

convenience (see Fig. 12-3). Since the reproduction of each unit can earn as many as two score points, the highest possible number of points is 36. From age eight onward, the average score is 30 or above; the average adult's score is 32. The memory trial of the test is scored in the same manner. A comparison of the scores on each trial will aid the examiner in determining the presence of visuographic or visual memory defects and their relative severity (see Table 12-5).

Although almost half of the traumatically brain injured patients in Osterrieth's sample achieved "copy" scores of 32 or better, one-third of this group's scores were significantly low. On the memory trial, fewer than one-third of the traumatically brain injured group were able to achieve the normal group's mean score of 22. In general, there was a wider disparity between the copy and memory scores of the brain injured group than the normal group. Four patients performed relatively better on the memory than the copy task, suggesting delayed perceptual organization or slowed ability to adapt to new tasks. Seven patients diagnosed as having a *syndrome d'automatisme mental* and *syndrome catatonique* produced a highly variable set of performances. They were the only adult patients to add bizarre embellishments to their drawings, in several cases re-

TABLE 12-5
Percentile Norms for Accuracy Scores Obtained by Adults
on Copy and Memory Trials of the Complex Figure Test

| | | Percentile | | |
Trial	25	50	75	100
Copy	31	32	34	36
Memory	18	22	27	35

(Adapted from Osterrieth, 1944)

interpreting details concretely, adding more but similar design elements, or filling in parts of the design with solid color. No behavior of this kind appeared among the brain damaged patients.

The Benton Visual Retention Test (BVRT): Copy Administration. The three alternate forms of this test permit the use of one of them for a copy trial (Benton, 1974). (See pp. 369–371 for a description and picture of the test.) The copy trial usually precedes the memory trials, which allows the subject to familiarize himself with the test and the test materials before undertaking the more difficult memory tests. Benton's normative population of 200 adults provides the criteria for evaluating the scores. Each patient's drawings must be evaluated in terms of his estimated original level of functioning. Persons of *average* or better intelligence are expected to make no more than two errors. Subjects making three or four errors who typically perform at *low average* to *borderline* levels on most other intellectual tasks have probably done as well as could be expected on this test; for them, the presence of a more than ordinary number of errors does not signify a visuographic disability. On the other hand, the visuographic functioning of subjects who achieve a cluster of test scores on other kinds of tasks in the ranges above *average* and who make four or five errors on this task is suspect.

   The performance of patients with frontal lobe lesions differs with the side of injury: those with bilateral damage average 4.6 errors; with right-sided damage, 3.5 errors; and with left-sided damage the average 1.0 error is comparable to that of the normative group (Benton, 1968). Other studies tend to support a right-left differential in defective copying of these designs, with right hemisphere patients two or three times more likely to have difficulties (Benton, 1969a).

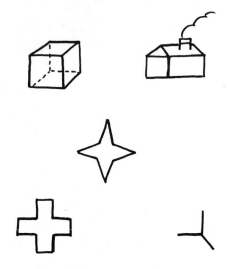

FIG. 12-4. Sample free-hand drawings for copying.

Miscellaneous copying tasks. Since any copying task can produce meaningful results, the examiner should feel free to improvise
tasks as he sees fit. He can learn to reproduce a number of useful
figures and then draw them at bedside examinations or in interviews
when his test material is not available. Hécaen and coworkers (1951)
and Bogen (1969a) give some excellent examples of how easily
drawn material for copying, such as a cube, a Greek cross, and a
house can contribute to the evaluation of visuographic disabilities
(see Fig. 12-4).

In a study of drawing disability and laterality of lesion, Warrington
et al. (1966) used line drawings of a four-pointed star, a square, and
a number of single lines, angles, and corners. A second subtest consists of a set of cards, each containing two dots variously positioned,
with instructions to copy the position of the dots. A third subtest
consists of 16 geometric figures, one-half containing internal "structure" lines, the other half identical in their outlines to the first eight
but without the inside lines (see Fig. 12-5). The material used in
these studies effectively elicited the different kinds of visuographic
disturbances commonly associated with the hemispheric side of a
lesion. Among their findings, Warrington and her colleagues particularly noted the following differences: (1) Left hemisphere pa-

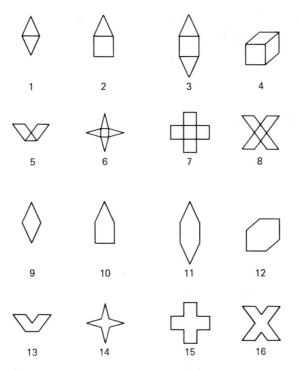

FIG. 12-5. "Structured" and "unstructured figures" (Warrington et al., 1966).

tients tend to improve with practice; right hemisphere patients do not. (2) Right hemisphere patients are significantly poorer than left hemisphere patients at estimating diagonal distances between dots, but both groups position horizontally placed dots equally well. (3) Left hemisphere patients tend to produce more—and right hemisphere patients tend to produce fewer—right angles than there are in the cube. (4) Right hemisphere patients consistently underestimate, and left hemisphere patients consistently overestimate, the angles of the star. (5) Right hemisphere patients produce more errors of symmetry than do left hemisphere patients. (6) Left hemisphere patients copied as much of the structure of the structured drawings as the right hemisphere patients but significantly failed to use it to build their drawings. (7) Visual inattention to the side opposite the lesion predominated among right hemisphere patients at a rate of six to one.

Another simple copying technique that is sensitive to visual inattention as well as preservation of relationships in space is *Copying Crosses*. Different investigators have used different numbers of crosses, two to six small ones arranged horizontally on a large (27 cm × 22 cm) sheet of paper (De Renzi and Faglioni, 1967) or ten small crosses, also arranged horizontally but in groups of five on either side of the paper's midpoint (Gainotti and Tiacci, 1970). The latter authors differentiate between "unilateral spatial inattention," which they define in terms of one or two absent crosses, and "unilateral spatial neglect," defined as the absence of five or more crosses. They also note whether the crosses are constructed in an organized or a piecemeal, fragmented fashion.

Free drawing tests

The absence of a model changes the perceptual component of free drawing from the immediate act of perception involved in copying tasks to arousal of a perceptual construct, a picture in the mind. This difference may account for the failure of Warrington et al. (1966), despite the many clear-cut differences between the drawings of right and left hemisphere damaged patients, to find a systematic way to sort free-hand drawings on the basis of the side of the lesion. Yet some differences do persist, such as a greater likelihood of left-sided visual inattention, an increased tendency to sketch over drawings, and more details—both relevant and inconsequential—among patients with right hemisphere lesions; whereas drawings of left hemisphere patients have fewer details, giving them an "empty" or poorly defined appearance. The closer the lesion is to the right occipital lobe, the greater is the likelihood that the patient will display some of the more pronounced drawing disabilities associated with right hemisphere lesions. The presence of these lateralizing characteristics will enable the examiner to identify some brain damaged patients on the basis of their free drawings.

Human figure drawings. Combining the number of times the test was mentioned for the *Draw-a-Person* test with those for the *House-Tree-Person* test in the most recent study of the frequency of test use (Lubin et al., 1971) brings the total mention of tests involving human figure drawing far ahead of the "technical" frontrunner, the WAIS. This is not surprising, since human figure drawing has long been a staple in personality and neuropsychological test batteries as well as a popular technique for the intellectual assessment of children. Among its virtues are the simplicity of administration, for it requires nothing more than pencils, paper, and the instructions to draw a person; the relative speed of administration, for few patients take more than five minutes to complete a drawing; and its applicability to all but those patients with such severe handicaps that they cannot draw.

Different kinds of scoring systems have been devised for evaluating human figure drawings. The Goodenough-Harris scoring system (D. B. Harris, 1963) and Rey's system for scoring *A lady walking in the rain* (*Une dame qui se promène et il pleut*) (E. M. Taylor, 1959) measure intellectual maturation in the child and the level of intellectual organization of the visuographic response when used in the neuropsychological assessment of adults (see pp. 251–254). Machover (1948) and J. N. Buck (1948) developed the best-known systems for appraising personality on the basis of human figure drawings. Both of these systems attend to dimensions and characteristics of the drawings that are, for the most part, irrelevant to neuropsychological questions. Reznikoff and Tomblen (1956) proposed a simple plus and minus scoring system they hoped would provide an indication of brain damage. Although their system did differentiate between brain damaged and other patient groups, the large overlaps preclude its use as a single screening technique for individual cases. Nevertheless, this study does identify six characteristics of human figure drawings that are strongly associated with organicity: (1) lack of details, (2) parts loosely joined, (3) parts noticeably shifted, (4) shortened and thin arms and legs, (5) inappropriate size and shape of other body parts (except the head), (6) petal-like or scribbled fingers.

Descriptions of human figure drawings by brain damaged patients with either specific visuographic disturbances or conditions of more generalized intellectual debilitation usually include such words as childlike, simplistic, not closed, incomplete, crude, unintegrated (Burgemeister, 1962; Hécaen et al., 1951). Asymmetry may appear either as a difference in the size of limbs and features of one side of the body relative to those on the other side, or in a tendency of the figure to lean to one side or the other. The absence of a portion of the figure is also more common in the drawings of brain damaged patients than in those of any other group but it does not necessarily imply visual inattention, for patients with somatosensory defects of a limb or side of the body may "forget" to draw the affected part although they perform well on visual field and visual attention tests (Cohn, 1953; Schulman et al., 1965). Perseverative loops also characterize the drawings of severely impaired patients (M. Williams, 1965). Patients with severe drawing disability may display acute emotional distress that subsides soon after the task is removed (*catastrophic reaction*). In evaluating human figures drawn by brain damaged patients, the impact of their emotional status should not be overlooked. This is particularly true for mildly impaired patients whose sensitivity to their loss has occasioned a highly anxious or depressed mental state that may lower the quality of their drawings or exaggerate the extent of their drawing disability.

Bicycle drawing test.   Most of the noncontent characteristics of the human figure drawings of brain damaged patients apply to other free drawings too. Bicycle drawings can serve as a test of mechanical reasoning as well as visuographic functioning (E. M. Taylor, 1959). The instructions are simply, "Draw a bicycle." The material consists of 8½ × 11-inch paper and pencils. When the drawing is completed, the examiner who is interested in whether the patient can think through the sequential operation of a bicycle can ask, "How does it work?" Mildly confused, distractible, and structure-dependent patients who consider their drawing complete when it still lacks a necessary element such as pedals or drive chain or a seat will usually note and repair the omission on questioning. Patients with problems of visual neglect, visual scanning, or more than mild confusion may refer to the missing component but remain satisfied with the incomplete drawing, or may overlook the missing part but add an inconsequential detail or superficial embellishments (see Figs. 3-7a and 3-7b).

The bicycle drawing task tends to bring out the drawing distortions characteristic of lateral damage. Right hemisphere patients tend to reproduce many of the component parts of the machine, sometimes with much elaboration and care, but misplace them in relation to one another; left hemisphere patients are more likely to preserve the overall proportions but simplify (McFie and Zangwill, 1960). Severely impaired patients, regardless of the site of the lesion, perform this task with great difficulty, producing incomplete and simplistic drawings.

Miscellaneous drawing tasks. Specific aspects of the visuo-graphic disability may be studied by means of other drawing tasks. *House* may elicit difficulties in handling perspective that are common among intellectually deteriorated patients; the alert, bright patient who struggles with a roof line or flattens the corner between the front and side of the house is more likely to have right than left hemisphere involvement. Patients who complain of difficulty in finding their way, getting lost even in familiar places, can be asked to reproduce a ground plan of their home or their ward. Drawings of such symmetrical objects as a *clock face* or a *daisy* may expose a unilateral visual inattention problem (Battersby et al., 1956). Even when they include all the numbers or petals on their drawings, right hemisphere patients may have a great deal of difficulty rounding out the left side of the clock, or spacing the numbers or petals properly, particularly on the left side of their drawing. Appreciation of the three dimensions and problems in drawing corners will show up on drawings of a *cube.*

Construction Tests

More than any other kind of test, construction tasks involve the spatial component in perception, at the conceptual level, and in motor execution. Inclusion of both construction and drawing tests in the test battery will help the examiner discriminate between the spatial and the visual aspects of a visuopractic disability and esti-mate the relative contributions of each.

With Block Design and Object Assembly, the Wechsler tests con-tribute two of the basic kinds of construction tasks to the neuro-psychological examination, both involving two-dimensional space. Three-dimensional construction tasks call upon a somewhat differ-ent set of functions, as demonstrated by patients who can put together either the two- or the three-dimensional constructions but not both (Benton and Fogel, 1962). Other construction tasks test the ability to execute reversals in space and to copy and reason about different kinds of visual-spatial maneuvers.

Two-dimensional block construction

Kohs Blocks.   This is the original block design test, differing from the WAIS Block Design subtest in that each block is four-colored—red, white, blue, and yellow (K. H. Goldstein and Scheerer, 1953). The 17 designs are different too, many of them more complex than the Wechsler designs, although the administration and interpretation of the test results are the same. This test has proven unsuccessful as a screening instrument, particularly in attempts to differentiate psychiatric from brain injured patients (Yates, 1954), but its sensitivity to postcentral lesions of the right hemisphere is well established (Benton, 1969a).

The almost universal use of the Wechsler scales has made the administration of the *Kohs Blocks* redundant in most cases. However, because it has some more difficult designs, this test may be useful in bringing out mild visuoconstructive deficits in very bright patients.

Grassi Block Substitution Test.   This test combines perceptual manipulation and the ability to switch response patterns with some of the visuoconstructive features of Block Design (Grassi, 1953). Using a set of Kohs-type blocks, the subject must first copy the design formed by another set of blocks exactly, and then copy it in different colors. Scoring is based on accuracy and time. Grassi also recommends that the examiner take account of qualitative aspects of the patient's performance in making his evaluation of the patient's clinical status. He offers the following ten-point evaluation schedule which can serve as a guide for behavioral analysis of the patient's performance: (1) time; (2) directions: ease of following; (3) reassurance: need for, request for; (4) perseveration; (5) recognition: insight; (6) trial and error; (7) corrections: perceive, make; (8) spatial disorientation; (9) diagonal relationship; (10) disturbed shifting.

Although Grassi claimed 100% success in identifying the brain damaged patients in his normal, schizophrenic, brain damaged, and postlobotomy standardization groups, serious questions about the handling of data and the intellectual level of the various groups have been raised (Yates, 1954) as well as questions about the test's usefulness in identifying individual patients (Thomas, 1963). When the composition of groups of left and right hemisphere damaged patients was controlled for the severity of their disorders, their performances on this test did not differ significantly (Archibald et al., 1967).

Block rotation. Because the rotational tendency appears almost exclusively among brain damaged patients, a number of constructional tests requiring rotation of the design have been developed. The *Block Design Rotation Test* consists of 40 four-block designs that tend to elicit rotational errors. It was standardized on a small group of matched pairs of brain damaged and psychiatric patients (Shapiro, 1953). It identified 14 of the 19 brain damaged patients while mistaking only one of the psychiatric patients. Replications resulted in similarly high proportions correctly identified (Spreen and Benton, 1965; Yates, 1954).

The *Block Rotation Test (BRT)* uses only blocks colored either red or white (Satz, 1966a). The subject's task is to make copies, rotated 90° to the right or left, of the 44 relatively simple designs the examiner constructs. The performance is scored for six rotation error variables. The rate of successful identification of brain damaged patients in a mixed population of patients with brain damage, functional complaints, or other medical problems was 60% in one study which produced 20% false positives and an overall correct identification rate of 70% (Satz et al., 1970). In another study, 82% of the 59 patients with organic brain disorders but only 35% of the 63 member mixed group comprising both psychiatric patients and normal control subjects were correctly identified by this test (Satz, 1966b). Satz suggests that on this test, "correct performance requires a displacement from the sensory stimulus cues and the activation of more complex brain-perceptual processes; that is, the ability to organize perceptually the figure-ground relationships of the various designs in the absence of a visual representation of the final arrangement."

Three-dimensional block construction

Cube construction. The simple block construction tasks described here will elicit three-dimensional visuoconstructive defects. The level at which age-graded tasks are failed provides a useful indicator of the severity of the disability.

The 1960 revision of the Stanford-Binet battery contains two simple block construction tasks: *Tower* at age level II is simply a four-block high structure; *Bridge* at age level II consists of three blocks, two forming a base with the third straddling them. At age three, most children can copy a four-block train (three blocks in a row with the fourth placed on one of the end blocks); most four-year-olds can build a six-block pyramid and a five-block gate (in which the middle block rests obliquely on the two bottom blocks); most five-year-old children can copy six-block steps; but ten-block steps are too difficult for most six-year-olds (E. M. Taylor, 1959). Hécaen and his colleagues (1951) used seven blocks in their cube construction task (four blocks, not touching, form the corners of a square; two blocks bridge a parallel pair of the bottom blocks, and the seventh block tops the middle two) which none of their six patients with severe visuoconstructive disabilities associated with right parietal lesions was able to perform correctly.

Test of Three-Dimensional Constructional Praxis. Benton includes six block constructions in his *Test of Three-Dimensional Constructional Praxis* (1973b), three on each of two equivalent forms (see Fig. 12-6). The number of (1) omissions, (2) additions, (3) substitutions, and (4) displacements (angular deviations greater than 45°, separations, misplacements) in the test constructions is subtracted from the total of 29 possible correct placements. There is no score for rotation of the entire model although Benton notes when this occurs. The scoring standard requires that the score represent the fewest corrections needed to reproduce an accurate copy of the original construction. When the construction is so defective that it is impossible to count errors, then the score is the number of correctly placed blocks. When the total time taken to complete all three constructions is greater than 380 seconds, two time-correction points are subtracted from the total score. Both control and brain damaged groups performed better with a block model presentation of the constructions than with photographic presentation (see Table 12-6).

Some of the construction problems exhibited by patients with three-dimensional apraxia parallel those made on two-dimensional construction and drawing tasks, such as simplification and neglect of half the model (see Fig. 12-6b). These kinds of errors are more characteristic of right hemisphere patients than left. Failure on this

TABLE 12-6
*Scores on Block Model and Photographic Presentations of the
Three-Dimensional Construction Tasks*

| | Block Model | | Photographic Presentation | |
| | Control Group (n = 120) | Organic Group (n = 40) | Control Group (n = 100) | Organic Group (n = 40) |
Score				
25 & above	120	30	92	10
17 to 24	0	3	8	17
16 & below	0	7	0	13

(Adapted from Benton, 1973)

task, defined as a performance level exceeded by 95% of the control group, occurs twice as frequently among patients with right hemisphere lesions (54%) than among those whose lesions are on the left (23%) (Benton, 1967a). A higher rate of defective performance on this task also distinguished right from left frontal lobe patients (Benton, 1968). An interesting finding was that, unlike other visuoconstructive tasks (e.g., block designs and stick construction), this test discriminates between groups of right and left hemisphere patients who are moderately impaired as well as between those who are severely impaired. One plausible interpretation of this finding is that visuoconstructive deficits may show up on this complex task when they are too mild to interfere with performance on a less challenging one.

Stick construction

Stick construction is a two-dimensional task requiring the subject to arrange sticks in patterns. It is usually presented as a copying task in which the subject is required to reproduce stick patterns arranged by the examiner (Fogel, 1962; K. H. Goldstein and Scheerer, 1953), but the subject can be asked to construct his own designs with them, to copy a drawing, or to compose simple geometric figures or letters (Hécaen et al., 1951: Hécaen and Assal, 1970). Twice as many right as left hemisphere patients show a severe deficit on stick construction tasks (14% to 7%). Approximately 20% of patients with lateralized lesions have some difficulty on this task regardless of the side of

FIG. 12-6a. Test of Three-Dimensional Constructional Praxis, Form A (A. L. Benton). The three block models successively presented to the subject.

lesion (Benton, 1967a). The six patients with severe visuoconstructive difficulties studied by Hécaen et al. made both copy and spontaneous stick arrangements that were close to being correct, but they

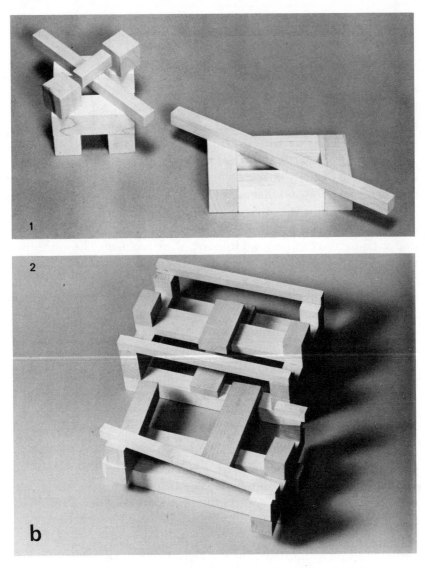

FIG. 12-6b. Illustrations of defective performances: (1) Simplified construction with inaccurate choice of blocks. (2) "Closing-in phenomenon" in which the patient utilizes part of the model in his own construction.

tended to take a long time. A later study brought out a difference between right and left hemisphere patients attempting to construct a cube pattern with the sticks; apraxic patients with left hemisphere lesions copied stick models best, whereas right hemisphere apraxic patients copied drawings best (Hécaen and Assal, 1970).

Stick test.   A relatively recent version of the stick construction task includes a rotation condition as well as a standard copy condition (Benson and Barton, 1970; Butters and Barton, 1970). This is a ten-item test, which is first administered as a copying task. The examiner remains seated *beside* the patient throughout the first "match condition" part of the test. He gives the patient four wooden sticks (approximately 5 inches long and ¼ inch wide with a ½ inch blackened tip) and then makes a practice pattern with two other sticks, instructing the patient to copy his pattern exactly. The examiner does not proceed until he is satisfied that the patient understands and can perform this two-stick problem. The examiner then gives the test by constructing each test design one by one in their numbered order (see Fig. 12-7) and requesting that the patient make his copy directly under that of the examiner. On completing the ten copy items, the examiner moves to the other side of the examining table so that he is seated opposite the patient. He constructs the same two-stick practice pattern he made originally, but this time asks the patient to "make your pattern look to you like mine looks to me." If the patient does not understand, the examiner demonstrates the right-left and up-down reversals with the practice pattern. Once again, when the examiner is confident that the patient knows what is expected of him, he gives the items of the test again in the same order as the first time. There is no time limit, but rather patients are encouraged to take as much time as they feel they need to be accurate. Each condition is scored for the number of failed items. On the reversal condition, the test is discontinued after five consecutive failures.

Again, the findings on the copy task implicate postcentral lesions, particularly those localized on the right hemisphere. However, on the rotation condition, there was a significant ($p < .05$) tendency for patients with left postcentral lesions to make more errors (mean = 2.74) than any other group. Those with right anterior lesions made the second greatest number of errors (mean = 2.13), and the left anterior group made almost as few (mean = 1.69) as did the 16 control subjects (mean = 1.59) (Benson and Barton, 1970). The need for verbal mediation to handle the rotation task successfully was sug-

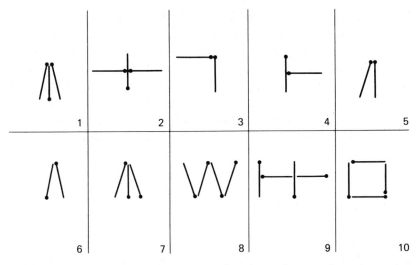

FIG. 12-7. The ten stick designs employed in the match and rotation conditions (Butters and Barton, 1970). (Copyright, Pergamon Press. Reprinted with permission.)

gested as one possible reason for the relatively poor performance of the left posterior patients. Regardless of hemispheric localization, when the apraxic condition is pronounced on other drawing and constructional tasks, it is likely to be present on the match condition and to be very pronounced on the rotation condition of this test (Butters et al., 1970).

Miscellaneous construction tasks

Paper Folding: Triangle. In *Paper Folding* at age level V of the 1960 revision of the Stanford-Binet, the subject is requested to copy a three-dimensional maneuver in which the examiner folds a square of paper along the diagonal into a triangle and folds that triangle in half. In Beard's previously mentioned factorial analysis of test performances of high school age children (1965), a set of three more complex paper folding tasks involved a number of different factors including a high weighting (.592) of a spatial factor involving "imagination of movement in space and awareness of orientation," and low weightings of a "speed of closure" factor (.290) and a verbal reasoning factor (.263).

A different kind of spatial maneuver is required by *Poppelreuter's*

Test, in which the subject must cut out a four-pointed star following a demonstration by the examiner (Paterson and Zangwill, 1944). Patients with right parieto-occipital lesions were unable to perform this task. Paterson and Zangwill also used simple "Mecano" models to test visual space perception. The possibility of using erector sets, "Leggo" type plastic blocks, which fit together, and "Tinker Toys" for testing visuospatial functions should not be overlooked even though they have not been reported as standard assessment procedures.

MANUAL DEXTERITY

Many neuropsychologists include tests of finger agility in their examination batteries. These are all timed speed tests that either have an apparatus with a counting device or elicit a countable performance. These tests may aid in the detection of a lateralized disability.

The Finger Tapping Test

Probably the most popular of these is the *Finger Tapping Test* (FTT) (S. G. Goldstein et al., 1973; Reitan and Davison, 1974; E. W. Russell et al., 1970), originally called the Finger Oscillation Test (Halstead, 1947), one of the tests in the Halstead-Reitan battery (see pp. 440–441). It consists of a tapping key with a device for recording the number of taps. Each hand makes five 10-second trials with brief rest periods between trials. The score for each hand is the average for each five trials. Normal right-handed control subjects average 50 taps per 10-second period for their right hand, 45 taps for their left. The presence of cortical lesions tends to have a slowing effect on finger tapping rate as, for example, one group of 50 brain damaged patients averaged 45.58 taps with their preferred hand (Halstead, 1947). Lateralized lesions may result in marked slowing of the tapping rate of the contralateral hand. However, these effects do not appear with sufficient distinctiveness or consistency (Lewinsohn, 1973) to warrant use of this test for screening purposes.

The Purdue Pegboard Test

This neuropsychologically sensitive test was developed to test manual dexterity for employment selection (Purdue Research Foun-

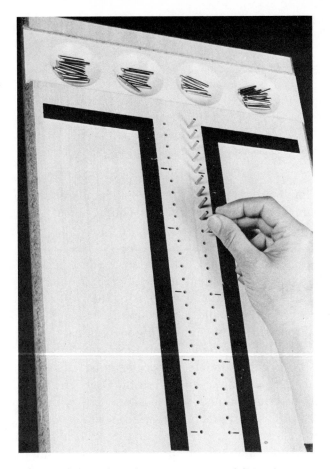

FIG. 12-8. The Purdue Pegboard Test. (Courtesy of the Lafayette Instrument Co.)

dation, 1948). The *Purdue Pegboard Test* has also been applied to questions of lateralization of lesions (Costa et al., 1963; Vaughan and Costa, 1962) and motor dexterity (Diller et al., 1974) among brain damaged patients. Following the standard instructions, the patients place the pegs with their left hand, right hand, and then both hands simultaneously (see Fig. 12-8). Each condition lasts for 30 seconds so that the total actual testing time is 90 seconds. The score is the number of pegs placed correctly. Average scores of normative groups, consisting of production workers and applicants for production work jobs, range from 15 to 19 for the right hand, from 14.5 to

TABLE 12-7
Purdue Pegboard Test Mean Scores

	Control Subjects	L Damaged Patients	R Damaged Patients
Right hand	14	9	10
Left hand	13	10	0

(Adapted from Vaughan and Costa, 1962)

18 for the left hand, from 12 to 15.5 for both hands, and from 43 to 50 for the sum of the first three scores (Tiffin, 1968). Averages for groups of women tend to run two or more points above the averages for men's groups.

Although brain damaged patients as a group tend to perform below the control group, patients with right hemisphere damage may be virtually nonfunctional when using their left hand (see Table 12-7). However, Diller found that group mean scores—averaged for the three 30-second trials—did not differ significantly for right and left hemiplegic stroke patients. Their mean scores ranged between 10.40 and 11.83 with standard deviations no smaller than 2.41.

In a study of the efficiency of the Purdue Pegboard Test in making diagnostic discriminations, cut-off scores were developed that proved 70% accurate in predicting a lateralized lesion in the validation sample, 60% accurate in predicting lateralization in the cross-validation sample, and 89% accurate in predicting brain damage in general for both samples (Costa et al., 1963). Since the base rate of brain damaged patients in this population was 73%, the Pegboard accuracy score represented a significant ($p < .05$) prediction gain over the base rate. Two separate sets of cutting scores were developed for older and younger age groups (see Table 12-8). Further, for patients of all ages, a brain lesion is likely to be present whenever the left hand score exceeds that of the right (preferred) hand, or the right (preferred) hand score exceeds that of the left by three points or more. One-sided slowing suggests a lesion on the contralateral hemisphere; bilateral slowing occurs with diffuse or bilateral brain damage.

With a total testing time—including instructions and a practice trial—that does not exceed five minutes, the Purdue Pegboard Test

TABLE 12-8
Purdue Pegboard Test Cutting Scores for Brain Damage for Two Age Groups

	Under Age 60	60 and Older
Right (preferred) hand	<13	<10
Left (nonpreferred) hand	<11	<10
Simultaneous (both hands)	<10	<8

(Adapted from Vaughan and Costa, 1962)

is a very efficient method of screening for brain damage and detecting lateralization of a lesion. Since it is both brief and unlikely to tax the patient, it can easily be included in any basic neuropsychological test battery, although its size and weight may limit its portability somewhat.

13
MEMORY

The assessment of memory requires a detailed examination of its many different aspects. The transient traces of immediate memory need to be distinguished from material more permanently stored by learning. Recent and remote memory must each be studied for both accuracy and continuity. Memory span and learning efficiency have to be dealt with separately. Modality specific impairments need to be identified. Furthermore, the examiner should attempt to separate retrieval from storage problems whenever a patient has difficulty with recall.

There are several standard examination procedures that together satisfy the requirements for a general review of memory functions. When the history, the patient's complaints, or his performance on any of the standard memory testing procedures suggests a memory problem, the examiner should explore the suspected disability further. He can do this by using more sensitive and specialized techniques. He may need to vary modes of presentation and response with the type of task to determine whether the defect is modality specific and whether there is an interaction between modality and the nature, difficulty, or complexity of the stimulus material. He may want to compare recognition with recall through the different input and output channels to give the patient a maximum opportunity to display his range of stored memories and to contrast the amount of stored memory with how much the patient can readily retrieve. The many memory tests presented here should enable the examiner to select tests that are appropriate for each patient's background, present comprehension and response capacities, and the specific questions that need to be addressed.

A GENERAL REVIEW OF MEMORY FUNCTIONS

At a minimum, the memory examination should cover span of immediate memory, addition of new information to recent memory, extent of recent memory, and capacity for learning (Barbizet and Cany, 1968; M. Williams, 1965). Ideally, these different memory functions would be systematically reviewed through the major input and output modalities with both recall and retrieval techniques. However, when memory problems do not appear to be central or unusual, thoroughness can be sacrificed for practical considerations of time and patient cooperation and fatigue.

For most adults, the WAIS is a good starting point for testing memory functions. It directly tests (1) *span* of immediate verbal memory and (2) *extent* of remote memory (Information) stored in verbal form. The longer Arithmetic and Comprehension questions also offer the observant examiner incidental information on (3) the duration and stability of the immediate verbal memory trace. The mental status examination (see pp. 448–450) augments the WAIS data with (4) a delayed verbal memory task requiring the subject to recall three or four spoken items—such as battleship, sidewalk, and schoolhouse; or New York, Denver, Boston, and Miami—after five minutes of interpolated interview, and with (5) personal orientation questions to assess the retention of ongoing experience at the minimal level necessary for independent living. The addition of (6) an immediate design memory and retention task, such as Wepman's administration of the Bender-Gestalt test (see p. 314) or the Benton Visual Retention Test (see pp. 369–374), and (7) a test of learning ability that gives a learning curve, such as Rey's Auditory-Verbal Learning Test (see pp. 352–356), completes a review of the major dimensions and modalities of memory.

When the patient's performance on these tasks is not significantly depressed relative to his best performance on other kinds of tests, and particularly when his performance on tests of remote memory is not significantly better than his handling of the learning tasks, the examiner can assume that memory and learning functions are fairly intact. Pronounced deficits on the general review of memory call for a detailed study involving systematic comparisons between functions, modalities, and the length, type, and complexity of the content.

A relatively poor performance only on tests of immediate memory and learning should alert the examiner to the possibility that the patient may be severely depressed (G. M. Henry et al., 1973; Sternberg and Jarvik, 1976). Impaired immediate memory and learning are also common early symptoms of many neurological conditions that ultimately result in general intellectual deterioration. As the still alert neurological patient experiences his failing competence, he may also be quite appropriately depressed, thus compounding the problem of differential diagnosis. However, depressed patients are unlikely to exhibit any other intellectual disabilities, except for slowed responses (A. S. Friedman, 1964), whereas a thorough neuropsychological examination will usually elicit other evidence of cortical involvement when the patient's memory problems stem from cerebral disease.

VERBAL MEMORY AND LEARNING TESTS

The almost unlimited possibilities for combining different kinds of verbal stimuli with input and output modalities and presentation formats have resulted in a proliferation of verbal memory tests. Many of them were developed in response to specific clinical problems or research questions. Only a few have received enough use or careful standardization to have reliable norms. Moreover, because of the lack of systematic comparisons between the different verbal memory tests, their relative usefulness and potential interchangeability remain unknown.

Therefore, the examiner's choice of memory tests must depend more on his clinical judgment than on scientific demonstration that this or that test is most suitable for answering the question under study. Even with many tests available, the examiner may occasionally find that none quite suits the needs of a particular patient or research question, and he will devise his own.

Verbal memory and learning tests are presented here by content. Under each content heading the reader will find a number of tests that differ in format, in emphasis on immediate memory or learning, and in the nature of the response. Not every kind of test is represented under every content heading; but taken altogether, the major techniques for examining memory and learning are reviewed. No effort has been made to separate learning and memory tests for there are few tests that treat immediate memory alone, and learning tests usually provide data on first stage immediate memory in the course of testing learning.

Verbal Automatisms

Patterned material learned by rote in early childhood and frequently used throughout life is normally recalled so unthinkingly, effortlessly, and accurately that the response is known as an *automatism*. Examples of automatisms are the alphabet, number series from one to 20 or 100 by 10's, days of the week and months of the year, and the Pledge of Allegience or a long-practiced prayer. Automatisms are among the least perishable of the learned verbal habits. Loss or deterioration of these well-ingrained responses in nonasphasic patients may reflect the attentional disturbances or fluctuations of consciousness of acute patients but occurs in nonacute conditions only when there is severe, usually diffuse, cerebral damage. To test for automatisms, the examiner simply asks the subject to repeat the alphabet, the days of the week, etc. More than one error usually indicates brain dysfunction; inability to begin, or if the subject does recall the first few items, inability to complete the response sequence, signifies that the dysfunction is severe.

Digits

Digit Span
The WAIS Digit Span subtest is the verbal immediate memory test format in most common use (see pp. 208–211). On the Binet, *Repeating of Digits* and *Repeating of Digits Reversed* appear at a number of difficulty levels from II-6 (2 digits forward) to SA I (6 digits reversed). The Binet format differs from Wechsler's Digit Span items only in allowing three rather than two trials for each span length (Terman and Merrill, 1960, 1973).

Point Digit Span
Along with the standard administration of Digit Span, A. Smith (1975) also has his subjects point out the digit series on a numbered card. The "point" administration parallels Digit Span in all respects

except that the response modality does not require speech, so that the verbal memory span of patients who cannot speak can be tested. When given with Digit Span to the speaking patient, marked performance differences favoring the "point" administration suggest a problem in speech production. A "point" performance much below the performance on the standard presentation suggests problems in integrating visual and verbal processes (A. Smith, personal communication, 1975).

Point Digit Span requires a large (approximately 30 cm × 30 cm) white cardboard card on which the numbers one through nine appear in a 3 × 3 arrangement in big (approximately 6 cm high) black print. The subject is instructed to *point out* the number sequence read by the examiner or the reverse sequence for Digits Backward. The procedure is identical with that of Digit Span; i.e., presentation begins with three digits (two for Digits Backward), and increases one digit following each success. The test is usually discontinued after two failures. The rate of presentation for all digit span tests is one per second unless otherwise stated.

Number Span

This technique tests the span of new verbal learning (Barbizet and Cany, 1968). The patient is given increasingly longer number sequences, each succeeding sequence differing from the one before it in its last number only; e.g., 8-3, 8-3-6, 8-3-6-1, 8-3-6-1-4, etc. Barbizet and Cany reported that 88 medical students retained an average of 9.06 numbers whereas the average retention of 51 persons over the age of 65 was 5.87.

Hebb's Recurring Digits

This is a disguised learning test. The subject is asked to recall orally presented digit lists, each of them one digit longer than his immediate memory span (Milner, 1970). He is not informed that every third list is identical whereas none of the intervening lists are alike. Normal subjects tend to learn the repeated lists but patients with verbal learning disabilities do not. This test was failed by patients who had had left temporal lobectomies but not by those with right temporal lobectomies, the extent of the defect varying with the amount of hippocampal involvement (Milner, 1971).

Running Digit Span
This immediate memory test also involves the "capacity to shift the focus of perception" (Talland, 1965). The examiner reads four lists of numbers (or letters), 10, 18, 8, and 12 items in length, at a one per two-second rate. Without foreknowledge of the length of each number list, the subject must recall the last *five* numbers of the list. Twenty-eight members of a control group recalled an average of 13.9 (SD 3.0) of the 20 possible numbers and 15.1 (SD 4.0) of the 20 possible letters in the identical *Running Letter Span* task. In contrast, the memory impaired patients' average recall was 8.4 (SD 3.3) numbers and 10.9 (SD 2.9) letters, recalling significantly fewer items than the control patients.

Letters

Letter Span
Every brain injured patient group in Newcombe's study (1969) had lower average scores on a simple letter span task, analogous to Digits Forward, than on the digit version of the task. However, the pattern of scores between groups was similar for both tasks. All left hemisphere damaged groups performed more poorly than any right hemisphere damaged group on Digits Forward; whereas on *Letter Span*, with the single exception of the left frontal group, the left hemisphere damaged groups also obtained lower average scores than the right hemisphere groups. The mean score range for the left hemisphere groups was from 5.00 (temporal or temporo-parietal, and mixed) to 5.75 (frontal); for the right hemisphere patients, group mean scores ranged from 5.50 (frontal and mixed) to 6.00 (temporal or temporo-parietal). Although patients with right hemisphere damage tend to recall more letters than their left hemisphere damaged counterparts, the overlap of scores of the different patient groups is too great to permit inferences about localization of the lesion in any individual case.

Consonant Trigrams
The verbal learning defect associated with left temporal lobectomy shows up on this learning task which requires recall of a spoken set of three consonants following the interpolated task of counting

backward from a given three-digit number by threes or fours (Milner, 1970). As in Hebb's Recurring Digits, the degree of the learning defect was related to the extent of removal of the left hippocampus, although patients with right temporal lobectomies suffered no pre- to postoperative performance loss on this test. The average recall accuracy of college students was 72% of 48 consonant sets when the recall came three seconds after the subject began counting backwards, and 38% when counting backwards continued for nine seconds (Peterson and Peterson, 1959).

Syllables

Nonsense syllables have been a popular medium for studying memory since Ebbinghaus first reported in 1885 on their use to explore retention and forgetting. They may be the stimulus of choice when the examiner wants to study verbal functions while minimizing or controlling the confounding effects of meaning. Noble's tables (1961) contain 2,100 nonsense syllables of the consonant-vowel-consonant (CVC) type along with their measured association and meaningfulness values for use in test syllable sets.

Nonsense Syllable Learning
This is a straightforward delayed recall test (Newcombe, 1969). Eight CVC syllables printed on a card in a vertical list are shown to the patient for three minutes, the card is removed, and the patient writes down as many syllables as he can remember. The next five minutes are occupied with other tests such as those for finger agnosia and right-left orientation. Then, without warning, the examiner asks the subject to name the syllables. On both trials of this test, left hemisphere damaged patients displayed deficits to a significant degree ($p < .001$ for immediate and $<.01$ for delayed trials) relative to the patients with right hemisphere lesions. The group with right posterior lesions obtained the highest scores of 6.43 and 4.86 on the immediate and the delayed presentations, respectively. Low group mean scores of 3.73 for immediate and 1.27 for delayed presentations were obtained by the left parietal and the left posterior groups respectively.

Successive Recall Test
Both CVC nonsense syllables and CVC words are used in this retention test (Talland, 1965). The patient has three minutes in which to
learn as many of a printed ten-item list of either nonsense syllables
with a low association value or a list of words (e.g., "dog," "bed").
He is then tested for recall without regard to order immediately
following the three-minute learning period, and again at 90 seconds,
180 seconds, 360 seconds, 540 seconds, and 720 seconds later with
no interpolated distraction. The control group of 16 subjects averaged around seven or eight nonsense syllables on each trial but
dropped from an average of over eight words on immediate recall to
a little more than six words at 720 seconds. The memory impaired
patients recalled an average of five meaningful words and three and
a half nonsense syllables immediately, but could remember fewer
than two words or syllables on the average after 720 seconds.

Words

Word Span
The number of words normal subjects recall remains relatively stable
through the early and middle adult years. Five age groups (20's, 30's,
40's, 50's, and 60's) comprising a total of 200 men, were tested with
familiar one-syllable words in lists ranging in length from four to
13 words (Talland, 1968). Beyond five-word lists, average recall
scores hovered around 5.0. The five age groups did not differ on
recall of lists of four to seven words. There was a very slight but
statistically significant tendency for the two oldest groups to do a
little less well than the youngest groups on the nine- and 11-word
lists, and the three oldest groups did less well on the 13-word list.
The greatest difference between the oldest and youngest groups was
on the nine-word list on which the 20–29 age group averaged 5.6
words and the 60–69 age group averaged 5.0 words. When tested in
the same manner as Digit Span—i.e., beginning with a two-word list
and adding a word with each successful repetition maintaining the
original word order—the word span of a group of control subjects
again averaged 5.0 (Miller, 1973). Control subjects learned word lists
of one, two, and three words longer than their word span in two,
four, and more than ten trials, respectively.

Rey Auditory-Verbal Learning Test (AVLT)

This easily administered test measures immediate memory span, provides a learning curve, elicits retroactive and proactive interference tendencies and tendencies to confusion or confabulation on memory tasks, and also measures retention following an interpolated activity (Rey, 1964; E. M. Taylor, 1959). It consists of six presentations of 15-word lists and a seventh recall trial which altogether take ten to 15 minutes.

It begins as a test of immediate word memory span. For trial I, the examiner reads a list (A) of 15 words (see Table 13-1) at the rate of one per second after giving the following instructions:

> I am going to read a list of words. Listen carefully, for when I stop you are to say back as many as you can remember. It doesn't matter in what order you repeat them. Just try to remember as many as you can.

The examiner writes down the words the patient recalls in the order recalled. In this way, he can keep track of the patient's pattern of recall, noting whether the patient has associated two or three words, whether he proceeds in an orderly manner, or whether recall is hit-or-miss. If the patient asks whether he has already said a word, the examiner should tell him, but the examiner should not volunteer that a word has been repeated because this tends to distract some patients and interfere with their performance.

When the patient indicates he can recall no more words, the examiner rereads the list following a second set of instructions:

> Now I'm going to read the same list again, and once again when I stop I want you to tell me as many words as you can remember, *including words you said the first time.* It doesn't matter in what order you say them. Just say as many words as you can remember whether or not you said them before.

This set of instructions must emphasize inclusion of previously said words for otherwise some patients will assume it is an elimination test.

The list is reread for trials III, IV, and V using trial II instructions each time. The examiner may praise the patient as he recalls more words; he may tell the patient the number of words he has recalled, particularly if the patient is able to use the information for reassurance or as a challenge. On completion of trial V, the examiner reads

TABLE 13-1
Rey Auditory-Verbal Learning Test Word Lists

	List A	List B	List C
	Drum	Desk	Book
	Curtain	Ranger	Flower
	Bell	Bird	Train
	Coffee	Shoe	Rug
	School	Stove	Meadow
	Parent	Mountain	Harp
	Moon	Glasses	Salt
	Garden	Towel	Finger
	Hat	Cloud	Apple
	Farmer	Boat	Chimney
	Nose	Lamb	Button
	Turkey	Gun	Key
	Color	Pencil	Dog
	House	Church	Glass
	River	Fish	Rattle

(Taken in part from E. M. Taylor, *Psychological appraisal of children with cerebral defects.* Copyright 1959 by Harvard University Press)

the second word list (B) with instructions to perform as on the first A list trial. Following the B list trial, the examiner asks the patient to recall as many words from the first list as he can (trial VI). The third word list (C) is available should either the A or B list presentations be spoiled by interruptions, improper administration, or confusion or premature response on the patient's part.

The score for each trial is the number of words correctly recalled. A total score, the sum of trials I through V, can also be calculated. Words that are repeated can be marked R; RC if the patient corrects himself, RQ if the patient questions whether he has repeated the word but remains unsure. Words that are not on the list are errors and are marked E. Frequently an error made early in the test will reappear on subsequent trials, often in the same position relative to one or several other words.

Rey gives norms for trials I through V and includes data on the performance of children and adolescents, ages five to 15 years. His adult norms differ according to social class and age groups (see Table 13-2).

TABLE 13-2
Average Recall on Each Learning Trial of the Rey
Auditory-Verbal Learning Test for Five Groups of Adults

Subject Groups		I	II	Trial III	IV	V	Recognition
Manual Laborers (n = 25)	Mean	7.0	10.5	12.9	13.4	13.9	14.5
	SD	2.1	1.9	1.6	2.0	1.2	0.8
Professionals (n = 30)	Mean	8.6	11.8	13.4	13.8	14.0	14.9
	SD	1.5	2.0	1.4	1.1	1.0	0.2
Students (n = 47)	Mean	8.9	12.7	12.8	13.5	14.5	14.8
	SD	1.9	1.8	1.5	1.3	0.7	0.3
Elderly Laborers (70–90 years) (n = 15)	Mean	3.7	6.6	8.4	8.7	9.5	11.9
	SD	1.4	1.4	2.4	2.3	2.2	1.8
Elderly Professionals (70–88 yrs) (n = 15)	Mean	4.0	7.2	8.5	10.0	10.9	13.6
	SD	2.9	2.9	2.5	3.3	2.9	1.3

(Adapted from Rey, 1964)

I gathered data on recall following the interpolated word list from 70 mixed brain damaged patients and 21 graduate and postgraduate students. On trial VI the patient group recalled 6.88 words, an average of 1.97 fewer words than on trial V; the average difference between the number of words recalled on trials V and VI for the graduate student was 1.52. The difference between these average differences was not significant ($t = 1.16$). However, for a significantly larger proportion of the patient group (one-third) than the student group (one-tenth), recall dropped by more than three words from trial V to trial VI ($\chi^2 = 5.66, p < .02$). These results suggest that a decrease of more than three words recalled from trials V to VI is an abnormal amount of shrinkage and probably reflects a retention or retrieval problem.

Ordinarily, the immediate memory span for digits and the number of words recalled on trial I will be within one or two points of each other, providing supporting evidence regarding the length of span. Larger differences usually favor the digit span and seem to occur in patients with intact immediate memory and concentration who become confused by too much stimulation. These patients tend to have difficulty with complex material or situations of any kind, but do well with simplified, highly structured tasks. When the difference favors the more difficult word list retention task, the lower digit span score is usually due to inattention, lack of motivation, or anxiety at the time the Digit Span was given.

Most brain damaged patients show a learning curve over the five trials. The appearance of a curve, even at a low level—i.e., from three or four words on trial I to eight or nine on V—demonstrates some ability to learn if some of the gain is maintained on the delayed recall trial, VI. Such a patient may be capable of benefiting from psychotherapy or personal counseling and may profit from rehabilitation training and even formal schooling since he can learn, although at a slower rate than normal. Occasionally a once bright but now severely memory impaired patient will have a large immediate memory span, recalling eight or nine words on trial I, but no more than nine or ten on V and very few on VI. Such a performance demonstrates the necessity of evaluating the scores for each trial in the context of the other trials.

Rey recommends a recognition trial immediately following the five learning trials. The recognition task requires the patient to indicate which of 30 words in a story read by the examiner were on the just learned list. The story uses all 15 words of the list, but not in their original order of presentation. For example, the following story could be told or shown to the patient.

> The *teacher* swallowed his *coffee* quickly and hurried down the *road* toward the *river*. He crossed the *bridge* and tipped his *hat* to the *farmer* cleaning his *turkey pen*. Every *minute* or so, he wiped his *forehead* and *nose* with his *kerchief*. He arrived at the *school house* just as the last *bell* rang. His *moon face* was the *color* of a *garden beet*. Through the *classroom curtain* he saw a *parent* pace the *floor* while the *children* played *soldier* with a *broomstick gun* and a *drum*.

Rey gives the average recognition scores for a similar 30-word story using the 15 words of the five-trial list (see Table 13-2).

I use the recognition trial when a patient's performance of the recall trial, VI, runs three or more words below the last learning trial, V. I give a typed copy of the story to patients who can read and ask them to circle with a pencil the words they recognize. Patients who are unable to read can raise a finger or say "yes" to indicate their recognition of a word as the examiner reads the story to them. This procedure will clarify the nature of the patient's recall problem, for if he has retained the data but cannot retrieve it easily, he will probably perform well on the recognition task. However, if his problem is simply that he has difficulty retaining new information, he will perform as poorly on the recognition task as on trial VI.

The five-trial learning format lends itself to use with pictures or printed words. I use 15 items of the Binet *Picture Vocabulary*, turning the picture cards at a rate of one per second, thereby exposing each picture for about a half second. Most patients recall two or three more pictures than words on the first trial and reach their ceiling—often 14 or 15—by the fourth trial.

Word learning tests

These two tests require the patient to learn definitions of unfamiliar words, thus sampling a common learning activity. The *New Word Learning and Retention Test* (NWLT) (Meyer and Yates, 1955; Meyer and Falconer, 1960) and the *Modified Word Learning Test* (MWLT) (Savage, 1970; Walton and Black, 1957; Walton and Mather, 1961; Walton et al., 1959) differ only in the length of the list of words to be learned.

Each of these tests uses a standard word list, either the Binet or Wechsler Vocabulary list (NWLT), or just the Binet Vocabulary (MWLT). Exceptionally bright subjects who have fewer than ten consecutive failures on these standard vocabulary subtests are given the most difficult words from the Mill Hill Vocabulary Scale, Form 1, Senior (Raven, 1958) (though American examiners might have more ready access to Atwell and Wells' Wide Range Vocabulary Test). The material of the NWLT consists of the first five consecutively failed words on the Vocabulary subtest list; the MWLT uses the first ten consecutively failed words. The examiner teaches the meaning of the failed words to the subject and asks him to define the words immediately afterwards. The criterion for success on the five-word test is three correct—not necessarily consecutive—definitions; on the ten-word list the criterion is doubled to six. If the subject is unable to meet the criterion, the meanings for all the words are given to him again and the testing repeated until he has given the required three or six definitions.

The MWLT has a scoring system that rewards speed of learning by giving the highest score (10) to subjects who learn six words on the first presentation of the ten-word list. One point is subtracted from the score for each additional presentation of the list until the subject succeeds at the task. Thus, if six words are learned on the second presentation, the subject earns a score of nine; if six words are not learned until the fifth presentation, the subject's score will be six.

Normal individuals generally learn three of the five words of the NWLT after hearing all of them defined just once. Without exception, 57 normal control subjects learned six of the ten-word series within three full repetitions, whereas only one of a 46-member organic group succeeded in fewer than five repetitions of the list (Walton and Black, 1957). A cutting score of five (success on the sixth repetition) identified 93.5% of the organic group and 97% of the normal control subjects and the 155 psychiatric patients with functional disorders (neuroses and psychoses). A cutting score of six (fifth repetition) produced no false positives among the normal control subjects and classified 71% of the organic patients correctly (Bolton et al., 1967). Because performance on this test does correlate significantly with level of intellectual ability, the scores of persons of *low average* or lower ability should be interpreted with caution. The MWLT also was found to misclassify a large number of schizophrenic patients when used on an elderly psychiatric population (Orme et al., 1964).

One variation of the MWLT uses neologisms to reduce the advantage of educated subjects who are more sophisticated about words and to provide items with concrete definitions that are easier for dull subjects to learn (Hetherington, 1967). This method uses the six out of ten criterion for success, discontinuing after ten repetitions. The use of neologisms produced a very large separation between control and organic group scores.

Word pairs
The paired-word learning test format permits a number of variations. Perhaps the most familiar of these is the *Associate Learning* task of the Wechsler Memory Scale (see pp. 384–385), which consists of ten

word pairs, six forming "easy" associations (e.g., baby–cries) and the other four "hard" word pairs that are not readily associated (e.g., cabbage–pen) (Wechsler, 1945). The list is read three times, with a memory trial following each reading. Total score is one-half the sum of all correct associations to the easy pairs plus the sum of all correct associations to the hard pairs, made within five seconds after the stimulus word is read. Thus the highest possible score is 21. The 20- to 29-year-old standardization group averaged 8.56 (SD .45) on the easy pairs and 7.15 (SD 2.63) on the hard pairs. The 40- to 49-year-old standardization group showed little difference on easy pairs with an average score of 8.26 (SD .24), but did less well on the hard pairs, averaging 5.70 (SD 2.73). From age 40, scores on this test tend to fall steadily (Hulicka, 1966). Differences between older (60 and above) and younger (30–39) age groups become significant ($p < .01$) as the summed scores drop from 15.48 (SD 3.48) at ages 30 to 39 to 11.49 (SD 4.53) at 60 to 69, 10.98 (SD 4.78) at 70 to 79, and 9.98 (SD 3.28) at 80 to 89.

Benton (1968) used eight easily associated word pairs in his *Verbal Paired Associate Learning* test. On the six trials following the original paired presentation, eight patients with right frontal lobe damage averaged 40.6 (SD 10.1) correct associations, the left frontal lobe damaged patients averaged 35.5 (SD 10.1) correct associations, whereas the bilaterally damaged patients' average score was only 18.7 (SD 14.1). However, Benton has not continued to use this test because it failed to discriminate between patients with right and left hemisphere disease (personal communication). A three-word pair list was used by Newcombe (1969) in her *Verbal Associative Learning* task. Wechsler's "hard" words make up the pairs. If, after initial presentation, the patient cannot give the correct association to the stimulus word within 10 seconds, he is told the correct response and the stimulus words are repeated until he can give three consecutive correct responses for each pair or has exhausted the maximum of 30 trials. The highest score is 30. One point is subtracted for each failed trial. Forty normal control subjects averaged 23.48 (SD 5.03). With the exception of the frontal lobe group, left hemisphere patients did more poorly than right hemisphere patients, the overall difference between hemispheres being significant ($p < .05$). Other variations on verbal paired associative learning use recognition instead of recall of the associated word, or visual presentation of the stimulus word (Meyer and Falconer, 1960).

Word Association Test.   A word association test devised to measure remote verbal memory presents common verbal associations (such as "dark–light") in a multiple-choice format (Lansdell, 1973). No significant difference appeared between a first and second administration of this test, nor between the sexes. However, two groups of male patients who had left hemisphere neurosurgery performed significantly worse on this test after surgery, although neither males with right hemisphere lesions nor females regardless of hemisphere showed a performance decrement. The results of this one reported study of word association memory suggests that it may be a sensitive technique for assessing old verbal habit patterns. It certainly deserves further study.

Sentences

The technique of evaluating memory by means of tests of sentence recall merits more attention than it has received. Unlike many memory tests, memory for sentences has a naturalistic quality that can be directly related to the patient's everyday functioning. Further, developmental norms provide ready-made criteria for evaluating a patient's performance when it is impaired. The average adult can correctly recall sentences of 24 or 25 syllables in length (M. Williams, 1965).

Comparing sentence span with word or digit span, the examiner can determine the extent to which meaning contributes to the patient's span of immediate memory. As on other verbal memory tasks, failure on memory for sentences is associated with lesions of the left hemisphere. McFie (1960) reported that left frontal, temporal, and parietal lobe lesions tend to result in impaired performance on this task with no similar deficits noted for patients with right hemisphere lesions.

Memory for Sentences

The Stanford-Binet scales include a sentence memory test at three age levels, beginning with 12-syllable sentences at age level IV. Each item in *Memory for Sentences* II at age level XI contains 20 syllables. At age level XII, the two Memory for Sentences III items contain 19 and 16 syllables, respectively, but the syntax and vocabulary are more complex than at age level XI.

TABLE 13-3
Memory for Unrelated Sentences

Sentences	Syllables
1. He had a book.	4
2. His father saw him leave.	6
3. They take their water from the well.	8
4. She went to the table to eat her food.	10
5. My brother does not like me to sleep in his room.	12
6. Each week they find a pretty flower and plant it in the garden.	16
7. During the winter when it is too cold, I go in the house and play with my friend.	20
8. The teacher sent the bad boy out because he did not want to sit down with the rest of the children.	24
9. Every day when school is out we run home as fast as we can so we can read a story to our little sister.	28
10. If I do not feel too well when I wake up in the morning, I ask my mother if I can rest in bed until I get better.	32

(From Ostreicher, 1973)

Memory for Unrelated Sentences
The effect of a simpler vocabulary on length of immediate retention span is demonstrated by Ostreicher's (1973) norms for his *Memory for Unrelated Sentences* test (see Table 13-3). Since the words of the sentences were taken from the Thorndike and Lorge (1944) list of the 500 most common English words, the average six-year-old girl can recall the 16-syllable sentence (see Table 13-4), although only 65% of 13-year-olds pass the Binet Memory for Sentences III, which contains one 16-word sentence. This test was developed for use with children and still lacks well-standardized adult norms. Data from a preliminary investigation suggest that the average adult performance on Ostereicher's sentences is in the 28- to 29-syllable range (A. Smith, personal communication).

Sentence Repetition
Newcombe (1969) varied the straightforward sentence repetition format by including among her five- to nine-word sentences "(a) fully grammatical and meaningful sentences, varied in syntactic complexity; (b) grammatically well-formed sentences that are semantically anomalous (e.g., 'colourless green ideas sleep

TABLE 13-4
Syllable Norms for Memory for Unrelated Sentences Test

Age	Male	Female
4	10	13
5	12	13
6	15	16
7	17	17
8	21	22

(From Ostreicher, 1973)

furiously'); (c) grammatically and semantically adequate sentences in which the possibility of semantic confusion exists, for example, subject and object nouns or adjectives could be interchanged ('The rich uncle was advised by the nice manager')." The 20th item was a string of random words ("Not in tree to the ran lake with") (p. 35). The percentage of sentences repeated accurately by control group members varied from 19.2 to 100. Both normal control subjects (n = 52) and patients with right hemisphere lesions performed similarly, although the patients had a little more difficulty with the meaningless sentences. Difficulty encountered by patients with left hemisphere lesions increased significantly with length, complexity, and especially with meaninglessness or semantic confusion.

Paragraphs

The quantity of words and ideas in paragraph tests takes them out of the class of tests that measure simple immediate memory span. Rather, they provide a measure of the amount of information that is retained when more is presented than the person can fully remember. In this sense, memory for paragraphs is analogous to the first trial of Rey's Auditory-Verbal Learning Test, for there too, more data are presented than can be totally grasped. The comparison of a patient's memory span on a paragraph test with that on sentences shows the extent to which an overload of data compromises his functioning. Thus, if a patient has an average recall for digits forward and can remember a 26- or 28-word sentence, but is unable to repeat as many as six words on the first presentation of the Rey word list and recalls only five or six ideas of a paragraph containing 22 or 24 memory units, then the examiner can better define the conditions under which the patient's immediate memory becomes ineffective. Like sentences, paragraphs afford a more naturalistic medium for testing memory than do smaller speech units.

Memory for stories
The Binet scales again provide several memory items in this category. These paragraphs, which appear at age levels VII (Form L-M, 1960, 1973), X (Form M, 1937 rev.), and XIII (Form M, 1937 rev.), vary in length, difficulty of vocabulary, and complexity of syntax and story. The easiest, *The Wet Fall,* contains fewer syllables than *The School Concert* at age level X, which in turn is shorter and simpler than *A Distinguished French Acrobat* at age level XIII. The subject looks at a card with the story printed on it while the examiner reads the story to him. Immediately after the reading, the examiner takes the card from the subject and asks a set of close-ended questions about the story, such as "What is the name of this story?"

Both the 1937 and 1960 Binet scales also contain two memory items, *Repeating Thought of Passage,* which are paragraphs dealing with abstract topics, *Value of Life* and *Tests* at SA II and SA III levels, respectively. These items differ from the easier paragraph memory tasks in that the subject cannot read the passage and is asked for a free recall, i.e., "You don't need to remember the exact words, but listen carefully so that you can tell me everything it says."

Logical Memory
Free recall immediately following auditory presentation characterizes most story memory tests. The *Logical Memory* test of the *Wechsler Memory Scale* (Wechsler, 1945), probably the most widely used story memory test, employs this format. The examiner reads two paragraphs, stopping after each reading for the patient to give his immediate free recall. Paragraph A contains 24 memory units or "ideas" and paragraph B contains 22. The subject gains one point of credit for each "idea" he recalls; the total score is the average number of ideas recalled for each paragraph. Young adults (20–29) averaged 9.28 (SD 3.10) out of the maximum possible score of $23 \left(\dfrac{A + B}{2} \right)$; older adults (40–49) retained a little less, achieving an

average score of 8.09 (SD 2.52). Hulicka (1966) extended Wechsler's norms to include both younger and older age groups. Performances of the youngest group and each of the three oldest groups differed significantly. The youngest subjects (15–17) averaged 10.37 (SD 3.50) "ideas" recalled whereas the 60- to 69-year-old group recalled 7.34 (SD 2.90) "ideas," the 70- to 79-year-olds an average of 7.35 (SD 3.83) "ideas," and the 80- to 89-year-old group an average of 6.80 (SD 3.19) "ideas."

Other paragraph memory tests

The two paragraphs included in the *Memory Battery* of the *Centre de reéducation de la memoire et du langage de l'Hôpital Albert Chenevier* contain 22 memory units each (Barbizet and Cany, 1968). One of the paragraphs is a French version of Wechsler's paragraph A with two fewer memory units; the second is called "The Story of the Lion":

> A lion,/ called Sultan,/ escapes from his cage,/ through the door/ left unlocked by the careless attendant./ The large crowd of visitors/ on that Sunday/ runs to the nearest buildings./ A woman, dressed in blue/ drops her/ one-year-old baby/ which she carried/ in her arms./ The lion takes him./ The woman goes back/ and crying,/ implores the lion/ to give her baby back./ The animal stares/ at her a long time./ Finally, he lets the baby go/ without hurting it. [Barbizet and Cany, 1968, p. 49]

The patient's recall for these paragraphs is tested four times, immediately and after one hour, one day, and one week. Medical students recalled an average of 14.2 memory units (marked by stroke lines) on the immediate trial. Data on delayed recall of normal subjects is available only for two older age groups (see Table 13-5).

TABLE 13-5
Average Number of Memory Units Recalled by Older Normal Subjects Immediately and on Three Later Trials following Reading of a 22-Unit Story

	Trial			
Age Group	Immediate	1 hour later	1 day later	1 week later
50–64	11.8	11.0	10.9	10.8
65 & older	9.5	9.1	9.1	8.4

(From Barbizet and Cany, 1968)

Talland (1965) makes a welcome distinction between verbatim and content recall of paragraphs. For this purpose, he used the "Cowboy," a story which dates from 1919. He divided it into 27 memory units for quantitative verbatim recall, and identified 24 content *ideas* (italicized words or phrases), which are credited as correctly recalled if the subject substitutes synonyms or suitable phrases for the exact wording.

> A *cowboy*/ from *Arizona*/ went to *San Francisco*/ with his *dog*,/ which he *left*/ at a *friend's*/ while he *purchased*/ a *new* suit of *clothes*./ Dressed finely,/ he *went back*/ to the *dog*,/ *whistled* to him,/ *called him* by name/ and *patted* him./ But the dog would *have nothing to do* with him,/ in his new *hat*/ and *coat*,/ but gave a *mournful*/ *howl*./ *Coaxing* was of no effect/; so the cowboy *went away*/ and donned his *old garments*,/ whereupon the *dog*/ *immediately*/ showed his wild *joy*/ on *seeing his master*/ as he thought he *ought* to be./ [pp. 235–236]

On immediate recall testing, a 22-subject control group gave an average of 8.32 of the 27 verbatim memory units; their average content recall score was 9.56.

NONVERBAL MEMORY TESTS

Most nonverbal memory tests involve visual memory. In order to test recall without resorting to verbalization, these tests must include a practic response, usually drawing. This, of course, complicates the interpretation of defective performances, for the patient's failure may arise from a practic disability or impaired visual or spatial memory, or it may represent an interaction between these disabilities and include others as well. Even on recognition tasks, which do not call for a practice response, such perceptual defects as visuospatial inattention may compound memory problems. Therefore, the examiner must pay close attention to the quality of nonverbal memory test performance in order to estimate the relative contributions of memory, perceptual, and practic components to the final product.

To reduce the possibility of verbal mediation, most visual recall test stimuli consist of designs or nonsense figures. However, unless they are quite complex or unfamiliar, geometric designs do not fully escape verbal labeling. Moreover, it is virtually impossible to design a large series of nonsense figures that do not elicit verbal associations. One series of 180 random shapes includes values for frequency and heterogeneity of verbal associations which allow the examiner to take into account the stimulus potential for verbal mediation (Vanderplas and Garvin, 1959).

Visual Memory: Recognition Tests

Recurring Figures Test

In this test, the stimulus material consists of 20 cards on which are drawn geometric or irregular nonsense figures (Kimura, 1963). After looking at each of these cards in succession, the patient is shown a pack of 140 cards one by one for three seconds each. This pack contains seven sets of eight of the original 20 designs interspersed throughout 84 one-of-a-kind-design cards. The patient must indicate which of the cards he has seen previously. A perfect performance would yield a score of 56. False positive responses are subtracted from right responses to correct for guessing. The 11 control subjects in Kimura's study, with an average age in the 20's, obtained a mean net (correct minus false positive responses) score of 38.9. There was essentially no difference in the gross average scores of right and left temporal lobectomized patients (43.4 and 44.4, respectively), although the right temporal lobe patients had more than twice as many false positive responses as the left temporal lobe group, resulting in a net score difference that significantly favored the left hemisphere patients. The members of both groups remembered geometric figures much better than nonsense figures, and the left hemisphere patients remembered a much larger proportion of the nonsense figures than did the right hemisphere patients, although the two groups did not differ greatly in their recognition of geometric figures.

An older group of 28 control subjects, most of them in their forties, averaged 28.5 (SD 6.92) on this task (Newcombe, 1969). The tendency for patients with left hemisphere lesions to fare better on this test than patients with comparable right hemisphere lesions also appeared in Newcombe's study, with an almost ten point difference in the average scores of nine left parietal injured patients (31.22) and six right parietal injured patients (21.83).

In a variant of Kimura's original task, the stimulus set consists of eight meaningless figures interspersed with 12 other nonsense figures in three 20-card sets and the identical instructions and right minus wrong scoring system are used (De Renzi, 1968). The maximum possible score is 24. Right hemisphere damaged patients with visual field defects displayed a striking tendency toward poor performance (mean score = 0.13) relative to 16 left hemisphere patients with visual field defects (mean score = 6.70), 52 left hemisphere patients with intact visual fields (mean score = 6.37), and 31 right hemisphere lesioned patients with intact visual fields (mean score = 5.69).

Visual Retention Test (Metric Figures)

With the goal of minimizing verbal mediation, Warrington and James (1967a) developed a different kind of multiple choice recognition task. Twenty 5 × 5 inch white squares, each containing four blackened squares variously positioned so that no two stimulus figures are alike, comprise the test material (see Fig. 13-1). Following a two-second exposure of each stimulus figure, the patient must choose the identical figure from a set of four similar figures. A second administration follows the first, differing in duration of exposure (10 seconds) and in a 180° rotation of the stimulus figures. Three error scores result, one for each administration and one for their sum. Ten control subjects made an average of 3.3 errors on the first and 2.2 errors on the second administration for an average total of 5.5 errors out of a maximum possible error score of 40.

Although the 37 left hemisphere patients' average total error score (8.6) differed by very little from that of the 40 right hemisphere patients (10.2), ten right parietal damaged patients made significantly more errors on the two-second administration than eight left parietal lobe patients. A significant association between performance on Block Design and this test attests to its usefulness for evaluating visuospatial perceptual processing. The nature of the right hemisphere damaged patients' errors on this test suggests that unilateral spatial neglect may contribute significantly to the higher error score of the right parietal lobe patients, since patients who demonstrated unilateral neglect on a drawing task tended to select their answers from the two choices on the right side of the multiple choice set (Oxbury et al., 1974).

Paired associate learning

The *Berkeley Paired-Associate Learning Test*, a recall task involving simply drawn pictures of common objects, was developed to

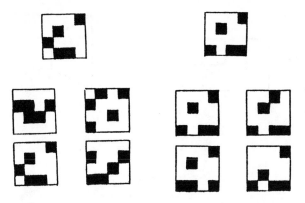

FIG. 13-1. Visual Retention Test (Metric Figures) (Warrington and James, 1967). (Copyright, 1967, Pergamon Press. Reprinted with permission.)

assess the learning ability of young children (Davidson and Adams, 1970; Lambert et al., 1974). The test material consists of cards with picture pairs, such as a door and a wagon, a tire and a hat. The examiner exposes each card for four seconds, naming each pictured object as it is displayed. To test learning, the subject is shown a single picture and asked to recall the object with which it had been paired. After a demonstration trial, the subject is given two learning trials of 20 picture pairs each. Each learning trial is followed by a test trial. The second trial series contains the same picture pairs as the first trial, but arranged in different order. The highest possible score for each trial is 20. The final score is the average for each trial.

This test reflects the development of learning ability in young children for the averaged final score of seven-year-olds is more than two points higher than that of four-year-olds (11.00 and 8.75, respectively) (Kee et al., 1971). Studies comparing the performances of younger with older and normal with mentally retarded children suggest that older and brighter children tend to facilitate their performance with mnemonic devices and that the performance of younger and retarded children improves when they are given mnemonic devices (Rohwer, 1970). Although no data on this test are available for adult subjects, it appears to hold considerable potential for studying both normal and disrupted memory functions. The use of a similar paired associate technique to train patients with impaired memory in the use of mnemonic devices has resulted in marked

 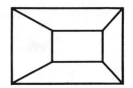

IX- and XI-year level

XII-year level

FIG. 13-2. Memory for Designs models (Terman and Merrill, 1960). (Courtesy of Houghton Mifflin Co.)

improvement on the day of the training, but no lasting gains (Lewinsohn et al., 1975).

Visual Memory: Recall Tests

Design reproduction
There are any number of abbreviated tests of memory for designs that call for a five- or ten-second exposure followed immediately, or after a brief delay, by a drawing trial in which the subject attempts to depict what he remembers. Probably the most popular designs are the two of the Binet *Memory for Designs* I task at age levels IX and XI (see Fig. 13-2). They are among the four designs of the Wechsler Memory Scale and appear in other batteries as well (e.g., Gainotti and Tiacci, 1970; Wood and Shulman, 1940). Both the Binet and the Wechsler Memory Scale administrations call for a ten-second exposure followed by an immediate response. A third Binet design, composed of embedded diamonds, appears at age level XII (see Fig.

13-2). The Binet item scaling permits some discrimination between performance levels but far less than the detailed scoring breakdown for the four Wechsler Memory Scale designs. However, the larger and more carefully selected Binet standardization population probably makes the Binet norms more reliable. Memory for design tests requiring reproduction of the design are particularly sensitive to right hemisphere damage. McFie (1960) found a significant number of impaired Binet design reproductions associated with right hemisphere lesions regardless of their specific site, although this disability was not associated with left hemisphere patients.

The Benton Visual Retention Test (BVRT). This widely used visual memory test is most often called by its originator's name alone (Benton, 1963; 1974). The *Benton* owes its popularity to a number of virtues. It has three roughly equivalent forms, which permit variations in administration. Its norms include both age and estimated original intellectual capacity. The three-figure design format is particularly sensitive to unilateral spatial neglect (see Fig. 13-3). The complex but easily learned scoring system helps the examiner identify error patterns. Benton furnishes adult norms for three administration procedures: Administration A allows a ten-second exposure to each card with immediate recall by drawing (and has norms for children ages 8 through 14); Administration B, like A, is also a simple recall test but follows a five-second exposure; and Administration C is a copying test in which the subject is encouraged to draw the designs as accurately as possible (and C also includes children's norms). No norms are given for Administration D, which requires the subject to delay his response for 15 seconds after a ten-second exposure.

All but two of each ten-card series have more than one figure in the horizontal plane; most have three figures, two large and one small, with the small figure always at one side or the other. Besides its sensitivity to visual inattention problems, the three-figure format provides a limited measure of visual memory span, since some patients cannot retain the third or both of the other figures while drawing the first or second one, even though they may be able to do a simple one-figure memory task easily. Further, spatial organization problems may show up in the handling of size and placement relationships of the three figures.

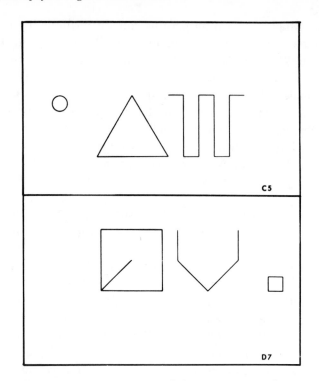

FIG. 13-3. Two representative items of the Benton Visual Retention Test. (Reproduced by permission. Copyright, 1955, by The Psychological Corporation, New York, N.Y. All rights reserved.)

The examiner should give the patient a fresh sheet of paper, approximately the size of the card, for each design. To avoid the problem of a patient "jumping the gun" on the memory administrations—and particularly on Administration D—I remove the pad of paper after completion of each drawing and do not give it back until it is time for the patient to draw the next design. The drawings should be numbered in some standard manner to indicate the orientation of the drawing on the paper. Although usually there is no question as to the orientation of the paper relative to the subject, when there are numerous errors of omission, perseveration, and particularly rotation, it can be difficult to tell from the drawing alone not only which side was up, but even which design was copied.

When the copy administration is given first, the examiner is able to determine the quality of the visuographic performance per se and also familiarize the subject with the three-figure format. Well-oriented, alert patients generally do not require the practice provided by Administration C, so that it need not be given if there is also a straight visuographic test in the battery. Patients who have difficulty following instructions and lack "test-wiseness" should be given at least the first three or four designs of a series for copy practice.

Each administration is scored for both the number of correct designs and the number of errors. Six types of error are recognized: omissions, distortions, perseverations, rotations, misplacements (in the position of one figure relative to the others), and errors in size. Thus there can be, and not infrequently are, more than one error to a card. Both the Number Correct Score and the Error Score norms for Administration A take into account intelligence level and age (see Table 13-6).

Interpretation of performance is straightforward. Taking the subject's age and intellectual endowment into account, the examiner can enter the normative tables for Administration A and quickly determine whether the Number Correct or the Error Score falls into the impairment categories. Benton considers a score of two points below the subject's expected Number Correct Score to "*raise the question*" of impaired memory or visuomotor function; three points below the expected Number Correct Score presumably "*suggests*" the presence of such impairment; and a Number Correct Score that is four or more points below the expected score may be interpreted as giving a "*strong indication*" of impairment. Error Scores can be evaluated on a similar scale. Those that exceed the expected score by three or more points also "*raise the question*" of impairment; four more than the expected number of errors "*suggests*" impairment, and when an Error Score is five points or more above the expected score, it becomes a "*strong indication*" of impairment. On Administration B, the normal tendency for persons in the age range 16 to 60 is to reproduce correctly one design less than under the ten-second exposure condition of Administration A. The examiner who wishes to evaluate Administration B performances need only add one point and use the A norms. Only Error Score norms with no age or intelligence corrections are available for Administration C (see p. 325). The Number Correct Scores of Administration D for normal control subjects are, on the average, 0.4 point below their Administration A score.

TABLE 13-6
BVRT Norms for Administration A: Adults
Expected Number Correct Scores, by Estimated Premorbid IQ and Age

Estimated Premorbid IQ	Expected Number Correct Score, by Age		
	15–44	45–54	55–64
110 and above (Superior)	9	8	7
95–109 (Average)	8	7	6
80–94 (Low Average)	7	6	5
70–79 (Borderline)	6	5	4
60–69 (Defective)	5	4	3
59 and below (Very Defective)	4	3	2

BVRT Norms for Administration A: Adults
Expected Error Scores, by Estimated Premorbid IQ and Age

Estimated Premorbid IQ	Expected Error Score, by Age			
	15–39	40–54	55–59	60–64
110 and above (Superior)	1	2	3	4
105–109 (High Average)	2	3	4	5
95–104 (Average)	3	4	5	6
90–94 (Low Average)	4	5	6	7
80–89 (Dull Average)	5	6	7	8
70–79 (Borderline)	6	7	8	9
60–69 (Defective)	7	8	9	10
59 and below (Very Defective)	8	9	10	11

Tabulation of errors by type allows the examiner to determine the nature of the patient's problems on this test. Impaired immediate memory or an attention defect appear mostly as simplification, simple substitution, or omission of the last one or two design elements the patient draws. Normal subjects exhibit these tendencies too; the difference is in the frequency with which they occur. The question whether the poor performance is due to an immediate memory or a concentration and attention problem can be resolved directly by giving the patient a simplified visual memory task, such as the Graham-Kendall Memory-for-Designs test (see pp. 375–376). An adequate Graham-Kendall performance indicates that simple visual memory is intact but that the patient cannot retain complex memory traces through an ongoing activity, such as drawing; forgetting the Graham-Kendall figure indicates an immediate memory problem. The Benton test, too, provides some data about simple immediate memory in that the first two designs of each series consist of only one figure so simple and easily named that it is rare for even patients with significantly impaired visual memory to forget them.

Other error characteristics also lend themselves to direct interpretation. Thus, unilateral spatial neglect shows up as consistent omission of the figure on the same side of the design. Practic disabilities appear as defects in the execution or organization of the drawings. Rotations and consistent design distortions generally indicate a perceptual problem. Perseverations on this test should alert the examiner to look for perseveration on other kinds of tasks. Widespread perseveration suggests a monitoring or activity control problem; perseveration limited to this test is more likely evidence of a specific visual or immediate memory impairment in a patient who is trying hard to compensate for or cover up his defect. Simplification of designs, including disregard of size and placement, may be associated with over-all behavioral regression.

When given with Administration A, Administration D (10-second exposure, 15-second delay) sometimes provides interesting information about the patient's memory processes that is not obtainable elsewhere. The average loss from D to A by brain damaged patients seen in a general clinical practice has been reported as 0.7 (Benton, 1974). Occasionally, the 15-second delay elicited a gross memory impairment when memory defects were not pronounced on Administration A. A few severely brain injured patients do better on Administration D than on A, apparently profiting from the 15-second delay to consolidate memory traces that would dissipate if they began drawing immediately (Peterson, 1966). Fewer errors on the delay administration (D) compared with the immediate recall administration (A) were made by every patient in a study of five stroke patients and five other elderly men hospitalized for non-neurological conditions (Crow and Lewinsohn, 1969). Fewer errors were also made by the two of a group of 11 right hemisphere damaged patients who scored low on Administration A with Number Correct Scores of 2 and 3 (Lezak, 1975). Each of these patients improved his Administration D performance by three correct reproductions, although the remaining nine patients had an average loss of 0.45 on Administration D relative to Administration A. Patients who improve their performance when they have the quiet delay period may be suffering attention and concentration problems rather than memory problems per se.

The preponderance of research on the BVRT shows that it performs better than other tests for brain damage in distinguishing patients with cerebral brain damage from those with psychiatric disorders (Benton, 1974; Brilliant and Gynther, 1963), but not well enough for individual diagnostic decisions (Watson, 1968). Benton reports that it also shows some promise in distinguishing between patients with lesions involving the cerebral hemispheres and those whose lesions are localized below the hemispheres. As on other visuographic tests, patients with right hemisphere lesions tend to perform more poorly than patients with left hemisphere lesions, and patients with parieto-occipital lesions are more likely to make errors than patients whose lesions are more anterior. However, these are only statistical tendencies and not hard and fast rules permitting conclusions about localization of a lesion to be drawn from interpretation of a Benton performance.

Although multiple-choice forms (Forms F and G) of the Benton were designed to test the visual memory of patients with motor handicaps (Benton, 1950, 1965), the *Multiple-Choice BVRT* can also be used to sort out the perceptual, practic, and memory components of a defective performance of the standard BVRT. Each form of the Multiple-Choice BVRT consists of 15 stimulus cards with their corresponding multiple-choice card. Benton has published norms that are identical for both the five- and the ten-second exposure administrations with immediate response; again both intelligence level and age are taken into account. Correlations between Administration A of the standard Benton and the multiple-choice administration are significant but run approximately 30 points below correlations between any two forms using the same administration. The multiple-choice version also correlates significantly with both memory and visuopractic tests, but not with verbal tests. Multiple-choice administrations of the BVRT also identify brain injured patients, but at a much lower rate, as must be expected when a major set of functions has been eliminated from the test task.

The Graham-Kendall Memory-for-Designs Test (MFD). This test consists of 15 geometric designs varying in complexity from an equilateral triangle to a complex line with two squared humps and

FIG. 13-4. Memory-for-Designs performance by a 39-year-old minister one year after a car accident in which he sustained a cerebral concussion and was unconscious for 16 days. The MFD scoring system gives this performance a "perfect" score of zero, although reproduction errors of three of the designs (3, 14, and 15), the line quality, handling of erasures, and the size and placement of the designs on the paper are distortions common to design reproductions of brain damaged persons.

squares with tails at either end (F. K. Graham and Kendall, 1960) (see Fig. 13-4). They are shown to the subject one at a time for five seconds. Immediately after each exposure, the subject draws what he remembers of the design.

The reproductions are scored for errors, based on a point system that awards one point for two or more errors when the essential design is preserved, two points when the configuration of the design has been lost or a major element is missing or greatly distorted, and three points for rotations and reversals. Surprisingly, no points are given for designs that have been completely forgotten. Thus, the error score of patients with extremely defective immediate memory who forget some or all of the designs may not be significantly elevated. On the other hand, the three-point penalties placed on rotations and reversals expand some patients' scores disproportionately (Grundvig et al., 1970). A correction for age and general ability level (based on the Wechsler-Bellevue or Binet Vocabulary subtest score) is recommended when evaluating the performance of children or mentally dull or aged adults. For all other adults, raw scores may be interpreted directly.Test norms were developed from 535 normal control subjects and a very mixed sample of 243 "brain-disordered" patients.

Studies of the efficiency of the MFD test as a predictor of brain damage have most often compared it with the Bender-Gestalt and found that the two tests have similar accuracy rates that usually vary only by a few percentage points (Brilliant and Gynther, 1963; Quattlebaum, 1968). A correlation of .851 between the MFD and the Bender (scored by the Hain method) suggests that although the MFD involves immediate memory, by and large these two tests measure the same functions (Quattlebaum, 1968). This might be expected from the MFD scoring system since it penalizes the same kinds of drawing distortions as do Bender scoring systems and it does not take blatant memory lapses into account. While cautioning against overgeneralizations, Korman and Blumberg (1963) reported that this test was 90% accurate in discriminating between 40 mixed brain damaged patients and 40 control subjects using a cutting score between 5 and 6. McFie associated poor performance on the MFD with right hemisphere lesions regardless of lobe (1960).

For clinical purposes, the MFD scoring system tends to be too stringent. Not infrequently, patients will produce a set of MFD reproductions that appear frankly defective on inspection but that earn scores within the "Normal" (0–4) or "Borderline" range (5–11) (see Fig. 13-4). Because the scoring system is so strict, this test yields very few false positives: short of deliberate faking, it would be difficult for an organically intact subject to earn a score in the "Brain Damage" range (12 error points or more).

Topographical memory

Defective memory for familiar routes or for the location of objects and places in space is a specific defect of visual memory (Benton, 1969b). Testing for this defect can be difficult, for it typically involves disorientation around home or neighborhood, sometimes in spite of the patient's ability to verbalize the street directions or descriptions of the floor plan of his home. When an alert patient or his family complain that he gets lost easily, or seems bewildered in familiar surroundings, his topographical memory can be tested by asking him first to describe the floor plan of his house or his ward and the route to the nearest grocery store or gas station from his home, and then having him draw the floor plan or a map, showing how to get from home to store or station, or a map of the downtown or other familiar section of his city (Paterson and Zangwill, 1944). Topographical memory can be further tested by requesting the patient to locate prominent cities on a map of the country. An outline map of the United States of convenient size can be easily made by tracing the Area Code map in the telephone directory.

Failure on any of these tasks does not necessarily indicate impaired topographical memory. Visuographic disabilities, unilateral spatial inattention, or impaired orientation may also interfere with the drawing performance (Battersby et al., 1956). Evaluation of the source of failure will depend largely on the nature of the patient's errors on this task and the presence of visuographic, perceptual, or orientation problems on any other tasks.

Miscellaneous recall tests of visual memory

Block-tapping. Milner (1971) described a *Block-tapping* task devised by P. Corsi for testing memory impairment of patients who had undergone temporal lobe resection. It consists of nine black 1½-inch cubes fastened in a random order to a black strip of wood. Each time the examiner taps the blocks in a prearranged sequence, the patient must attempt to copy his tapping pattern. By adding one tap to each succeeding successful sequence, the examiner ascertains the patient's memory span. Then the 24 test trials of tapping sequences one tap greater than the patient's immediate memory span are conducted. As in Hebb's Recurring Digits task, the same sequence is repeated every third trial. Normal subjects gradually learn the recurring pattern during the 24 test trials, as do patients with both large and small left temporal resections, but patients whose right temporal resections included significant amounts of the hippo-campus show no learning on this task.

Knox Cube Imitation Test. Corsi's Block-tapping test is a variant of the *Knox Cube Imitation Test,* one of the nonverbal tests in the *Arthur Point Scale of Performance* battery (Arthur, 1947). The four blocks of the Knox Cube Test are affixed in a row on a strip of wood. Again, the examiner taps the cubes in prearranged sequences of in-creasing length and complexity, and the subject must try to imitate the tapping pattern exactly. Administration time runs from two to five minutes. Mean scores of a large general hospital population of middle-aged and elderly men tested twice on four different ad-ministrations of this test correlated significantly ($p < .01$) with the WAIS Digit Span, Arithmetic, Block Design, and Picture Arrange-ment tests, but less highly with Vocabulary (Sterne, 1966). The ease of administration and simplicity of the required response recom-mend this task for memory testing of patients with speech and motor disabilities and low stamina, and elderly or psychiatric patients (Inglis, 1957).

Memory subtests of the Stanford-Binet Scales. The Binet scales contain two very simple visual recall tasks suitable for very regressed patients, the nonverbal *Delayed Response* at age level II and *Naming Objects from Memory* at age level IV. The former involves a small cat figurine and three small boxes. On each of the three trials, the examiner hides the cat under a different one of the three boxes, screens the boxes for a count of ten, and then invites the patient to point to the box hiding the cat. The latter test uses a box and nine different small objects, such as the cat, a thimble, and a spoon. On each of three trials, three of the objects are set out and named by (or named for) the patient, who then keeps his eyes closed while the examiner covers one of the three objects with the box. The patient's task is to recall which object is hidden. Two correct responses satisfy the passing standard for each of these tests.

At the XII year level of the Stanford-Binet, the patient must copy a nine-bead pattern made by stringing differently shaped wooden beads onto a shoestring. After the subject observes the examiner make the chain, it is exposed for five seconds more and then re-moved. The subject must replicate it in two minutes. This task

TABLE 13-7
Average Recall of Objects on the KIM test for Older Normal Control Subjects

Age Group	Immediate	1 hour	1 day	1 week
50–64	13.2	14.6	14.0	13.0
65 & older	11.4	12.8	12.2	12.5

(Adapted from Barbizet and Cany, 1968)

proved relatively easy for the 13-year-old standardization group, since 70% of them passed it.

Cross on a line.   Another nonverbal task failed by patients with significant loss of right or bilateral hippocampal tissue but performed successfully by patients with similar left-sided lesions involves drawing a cross on a line (Milner, 1970). In this test, the patient observes the examiner mark a cross on a line, the examiner's drawing is removed, and the patient counts backwards from ten. At zero, the patient attempts to draw a cross in the same relative position on the line as the examiner's cross.

7/24.   Barbizet and Cany (1968) include a completely nonverbal memory task—the 7/24 test—in their memory test battery. Seven poker chips are randomly placed on a 6 × 4 checkerboard. Presentation is in 10-second units. After each 10-second exposure, the subject attempts to reproduce the original seven chip pattern with nine chips and an empty board. Learning trials are repeated until the subject masters the task or has exhausted 15 trials. After each trial, the examiner notes the number of correctly placed chips; on the first trial this number represents the immediate visual memory span. The total number of trials and the time taken to learn the task is also recorded. Retesting is conducted after five minutes, 30 minutes, and 24 hours. Patients who cannot learn 7/24 in 15 trials are tested a week later with five chips. If they fail this simpler task after 15 trials, the following week the test is repeated with three chips. Normal control subjects between the ages of 41 and 79, averaging 58 years of age, recalled four chips correctly on the first trial. At five and 30 minutes, and at 24 hours, these subjects averaged a little over six correctly placed ships on the first trial.

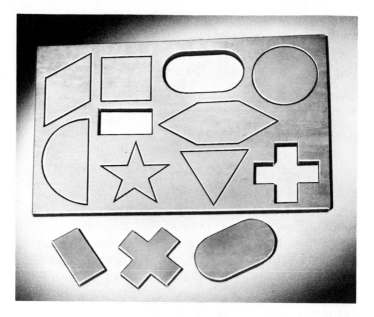

FIG. 13-5. One of the several available versions of the Seguin-Goddard Form-board used in the Tactual Performance Test. (Courtesy of The Stoelting Co.)

KIM. This is another visual learning test in Barbizet and Cany's battery, but unlike 7/24, *KIM* requires a verbal response. Twenty familiar objects are laid on a tray for the patient to view for 90 seconds. During this time he must name all the objects, and then name as many as he can as soon as the tray has been removed. The 90-second exposure, naming, and immediate recall are repeated once. Retention is tested by recall after one hour, one day, and one week with no further exposure of the test material. Norms are given for older control subjects only (see Table 13-7). It is interesting to note that for each age group, the average recall after one hour was better by more than one than the immediate recall, and that the older group maintained the improvement over a week's time.

Tactile Memory

Tactual Performance Test
Like the Knox Cubes, the material for this test, the *Seguin Form-board* came from the Arthur (1947) battery of nonverbal tests (see

TABLE 13-8
Tactual Performance Test Norms

	Total Time (minutes)	Memory	Localization
Average performance of normal subjects	10.56	8.17	5.92
Cutting Score	15.6	6	5

(From Halstead, 1947)

Fig. 13-5). Although originally administered as a visuopractic task, Halstead (1947) converted it into a tactile memory test by administering it to blindfolded subjects and adding a drawing recall trial. Reitan incorporated Halstead's version of this test into the battery he recommends for neuropsychological testing. Three trials are given in Halstead's administration, the first two with the preferred and nonpreferred hands, respectively; the third with both hands. The score for each trial is the time to completion, which Halstead records to the nearest tenth of a minute. Halstead computes a "Total Time" score.

On completion of the Formboard trials and only after the formboard has been concealed does the subject remove the blindfold. He is handed paper and pencil with instructions to draw the board from memory, and to indicate the different shapes and their placement relative to one another. Two scores are obtained from the drawing: the *memory* score is a simple count of the number of shapes reproduced with reasonable accuracy, i.e., a four-pointed star earns credit so long as the drawing preserves the essential star shape; the *localization* score is the total number of blocks placed in proper relationship to the other blocks and the board.

The cutting scores developed by Halstead have been retained by Reitan for predicting the likelihood of organic impairment (see Table 13-8). These cutting scores become questionable when applied to persons over the age of 40 (see p. 442). Lewinsohn (1973) found that his normal control group over age 40 averaged a Total Time score of approximately 18 minutes, which is well above Halstead's cutting score.

Teuber and Weinstein (1954) handle this test somewhat differently than Halstead and Reitan. They give only two trials to blindfolded subjects, one with the board in the usual position and one with the board rotated 180°. Like Halstead and Reitan, they follow the Formboard task with a drawing recall, but score only for memory, not for location. Performances of their frontal lobe injured patients were consistently superior to those of patients whose injuries involved other cortical areas (Teuber, 1964). The frontal lobe patients recalled more forms on the drawing trial than any other group and the occipital lobe patients recalled the fewest. Left frontal lobe patients also showed a "positive transfer for time," performing the second trial faster than the first, in contrast to the right temporal lobe patients whose average time on the second trial was longer than on the first.

Although there appears to be little doubt that markedly slowed or defective performances on the Formboard test or the memory trials are generally associated with brain damage, the nature of the organic defect remains in dispute. Some investigators have found a right-left hemisphere differential favoring performance by patients with left hemisphere lesions (Reitan, 1964; Teuber and Weinstein, 1954). However, opposite results on the recall task, in which the left hemisphere damaged group tended to do a little worse than the right hemisphere group, have also been reported (De Renzi, 1968). The better recall scores of right hemisphere patients were attributed to their access to verbal mediators. Halstead (1947), Reitan (1964), and Scherer and his colleagues (1957) consider this test to be particularly sensitive to frontal lobe lesions; yet Teuber and Weinstein's posterior brain injured patients performed least well and their anterior brain injured patients made the best scores of their three brain injured subgroups (1954; Teuber, 1964). Teuber notes that their findings are "not unreasonable, in view of the known symptomatology of parietal and temporal lesions. What is difficult to understand is that this formboard task should have been considered a test of frontal pathology at all" (1964, p. 421). That Reitan's significant anterior-posterior differences occurred between *right* frontal and *left* nonfrontal, and between *left* frontal and *right* nonfrontal groups— and not between groups of patients whose anterior and posterior lesions were on the same side—may account for the magnitude of his findings but still does not explain the contradiction between the relatively poor performance of his right frontal group and the relatively good performance of Teuber and Weinstein's patients whose lesions were similarly located.

Time differences between trials also yield important information.

The difference between the time taken on the preferred hand and that on the nonpreferred hand trials may provide a clue to the side of the lesion. Normally, if learning takes place, trial II takes a little less time than trial I even though it is performed with the nonpreferred hand, and trial III takes the least amount of time. When trial I runs much more than seven or eight minutes while trial II is in the three- to five-minute range, taking three or more minutes less, the possibility of a dominant hemisphere lesion can be considered. On the other hand, if trial II takes approximately as long or longer than trial I and a much shorter trial III plus good recall indicates that learning has taken place, the possibility of a lesion on the hemisphere contralateral to the nonpreferred hand must be considered. By adding one more trial, the Formboard task can be used to establish a learning curve. In my administration of this test, the fourth trial is a preferred hand trial identical with the first so that the overall amount of learning that has taken place can be measured directly as decrement of time from trial I to trial IV.

Other tactile memory tests
Four pieces of wire, each twisted into a distinctly different nonsense shape (see Fig. 13-6), comprise the material for a tactile test of immediate memory (Milner, 1971). The patients never see the wire figures. After several training trials on matching the figures with no time delay, matching follows an increasing delay length up to two minutes. Six out of seven commissurotomized patients performed better with their left than with their right hand, indicating that complex perceptual learning can take place without words and that it is mediated by the right hemisphere. Shaped wire has also been used in a paired recognition task in which pairs of wire patterns, placed in the palm of the blindfolded subject, are first learned, following which recognition for the learned pair is tested as a paired-asso-

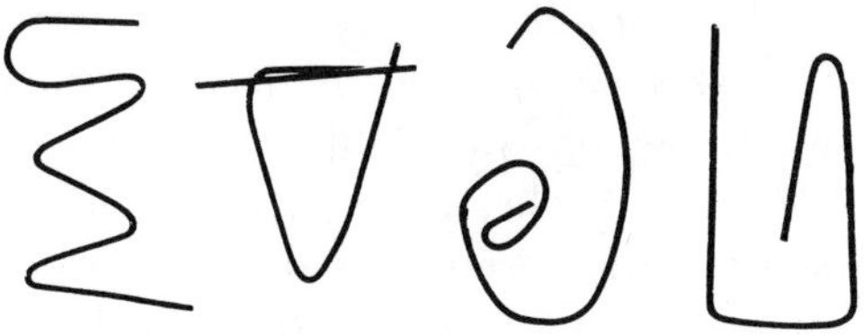

FIG. 13-6. Tactile nonsense figures (Milner, 1972). (Copyright, 1972, Pergamon Press. Reprinted with permission.)

ciates task (Meyer and Falconer, 1960). Using simple geometric designs projecting above a block to test tactile discrimination learning of 36 patients with unilateral brain injuries, Ghent and her coworkers (1955) found that learning took place when the patient used the hand on the same side as the injury, but no learning occurred with the contralateral hand.

MEMORY BATTERIES

To provide a thorough coverage of the varieties of memory disabilities, several batteries of memory tests have been developed. Of these, only the Wechsler Memory Scale has more than the most haphazard norms, and even the Wechsler norms are not satisfactory (see below). Thus, although these batteries contain some useful tests and provide practical guidelines for the conduct of a memory examination, their norms can only be advisory, and may not be used as unequivocal statements of performance criteria for the subtests.

Wechsler Memory Scale (WMS)
This scale contains seven subtests (Wechsler, 1945). The first two consist of questions common to most mental status examinations: *I Personal and Current Information* asks for age, date of birth, and identification of current and recent public officials (Who is president of the United States? Who was president before him?); and *II Orientation* has questions about time and place. *III Mental Control* tests automatisms (alphabet) and simple conceptual tracking (count by 4's from 1 to 53). *IV Logical Memory* tests immediate recall of verbal ideas with two paragraphs (see pp. 362–363). *V Digit Span* differs from the WAIS Digit Span subtest by omitting the three-digit trial of Digits Forward and the two-digit trial of Digits Backward, and not giving score credits for performances of nine forward or eight backward. *VI Visual Reproduction* is an immediate visual memory drawing task (see pp. 368–369). *VII Associate Learning* tests verbal retention (see pp. 357–358).

The Wechsler Memory Scale's normative population is relatively small (approximately 200) and composed of an unreported number of age groups between the ages 25 and 50. Wechsler gives no information about the intellectual ability of the normative subjects. Its very restricted age range stops at the point where the greatest normal changes in memory function begin to take place and where the incidence of central nervous system abnormalities increases. This serious deficiency in normative data has been remedied by Hulicka (1966) who has reported the average scores made by five groups of normal subjects at five different age levels (15–17, 30–39, 60–69, 70–79, and 80–89) for all of the subtests except II.

The reliability of the Wechsler Memory Scale has been questioned on a number of counts, including the low internal consistency of subtests and the disparate difficulty levels between the subtests. Subtest intercorrelations are so low as to nullify the assumption that intact subjects will perform the various subtests at a sufficiently similar level that subtest deviations may predict brain pathology (J. C. Hall, 1957b). These defects in test construction may underlie the demonstrated inability of Wechsler Memory Scale scores to discriminate between organic patients and other groups, including normal control subjects (Parker, 1957) and psychoneurotic and schizophrenic patients (J. Cohen, 1950). Hulicka (1966) found that many more subtests at the various age levels correlated significantly with the WAIS Vocabulary score than with scores on independent tests of learning and delayed recall.

An alternate scale, the Wechsler Memory Scale, Form II, is also available (Stone et al. 1946). It contains the same number and kinds of questions as Form I. No data on its standardization are offered beyond the total score means and the mean differences between total scores on two administrations of the test given two weeks apart, made by three young adult student groups. Total score means for only two of the three groups did not differ significantly, raising doubts about the reliability of Form II.

Memory Battery of the Centre de réeducation de la memoire et du langage de l'Hôpital Albert Chenevier
The rationale behind the selection of tests for this battery represents a neuropsychologically sound approach to the study of memory dysfunction (Barbizet and Cany, 1968). The subtests are grouped according to input and output modalities, directing the examiner's attention to this important dimension of memory dysfunction. Unfortunately, the authors do not follow through with their good intentions of providing a fully systematic review of different aspects of memory as mediated by the different input and output modalities.

This battery consists of three subtest groupings. The four tests with "auditive entry and verbal response" include *Span I* which is Digits Forward; *Span Ia* (see *Number Span*, p. 348); *Story*, a two-paragraph story recall test (see p. 363); and Rey's *Auditory-Verbal Learning Test* followed by his *Story Recognition Test* (see pp. 352–356). The battery also includes one test with "visual and auditive entry" and verbal response (*KIM*, see p. 379) and one strictly non-verbal visual-motor response test (*7/24*, see pp. 378–379). Normative data have been collected on a catch-as-catch-can basis, so that they have only a very limited applicability and lack the necessary standardization for comparing patients' performances on different subtests. However, the individual subtests are interesting and appear worthy of further study.

Learning Test Battery

Unlike the Wechsler Memory Scale and Barbizet and Cany's test battery, the one used by Meyer and Falconer (1960) tests neither remote nor immediate memory but focuses on retention of newly learned material. The subtests systematically differ in their input and output modalities to provide thorough coverage of modality-specific learning defects. There are seven tests in this battery: (1) the New Word Learning Test (see pp. 356–357) and six other learning tests in the paired associates format: (2) Auditory-Verbal Recall, (3) Auditory-Verbal Recognition; (4) Visual-Verbal Recognition; (5) Visual-Design Recognition; (6) Visual-Design Recall (a drawing test in which pictures of objects and designs are paired); and (7) Tactile Design Recognition (see p. 383).

Memory Test Battery

A set of tests and testing patterns that provide a comparison between immediate recall and retention (with and without rehearsal) was developed to study the memory impairment and effects of psychiatric treatment of depressed patients (Cronholm and Molander, 1957; Cronholm and Ottoson, 1963; Sternberg and Jarvik, 1976). The battery consists of three sets of material—each with two equivalent forms, A and B—that the subject learns: (1) 15 word pairs with a low (under 1%) association value (the *15 word-pair test*); (2) 15 drawings of familiar objects (the *15 figure test*); and (3) three fictitious facts associated with each of three photographs of persons (the *9 personal data test*). Both the 15 word-pair test and the 9 personal data test require a recall response; on the 15 figure test, the patient must recognize the learned material when it appears in a larger picture with drawings of 15 other objects.

Testing with each set of material involves six steps: (1) The patient learns Form A. (2) The patient is immediately tested on Form A. (3) The patient then learns Form B. (4) He waits three hours. (5) The patient is tested on Form B. (6) The patient is tested on Form A. Obviously, this testing pattern can be applied to other learning tasks. The addition of a second learning trial, using the *savings* method (see below) adds a more sensitive test of retention for evaluating the patient's retrieval ability.

SPECIAL MEMORY PROBLEMS

In his efforts to define the nature of a memory defect, the examiner may wish to explore several aspects of learning and memory that are not covered in the usual neuropsychological examination. These include the rate of forgetting, differentiation of storage and retrieval problems, and input and output modality differences studied by parallel techniques. Most tests that explore these problems have been developed through use with hospitalized patients. Many of them are not adaptable to general clinical use because they either take an impracticable amount of time to administer or require many hourly or daily repetitions on a schedule that is virtually impossible for the clinical practitioner to maintain, particularly when working with outpatients. However, innovative practitioners will be able to modify these tests to conform with the demands of an active practice and needs of his outpatients.

Forgetting

Forgetting curves require repetition over time. Several subtests (paragraph recall, KIM, and 7/24) of Barbizet and Cany's Memory Battery include recall trials as long as a week after presentation. Talland (1965) used the delayed recall format too, with recall trials of hours, days, and up to a week to establish forgetting curves for many different kinds of material.

The *savings* method provides an indirect means of measuring the amount of material retained after it has been learned. This method involves teaching the patient the same material on two or more occasions, which are usually separated by days or weeks but the second learning trial may come as soon as 30 minutes after the first. The number of trials the patient takes to reach criterion is counted each time. Reductions in the number of trials needed for criterion learning (the "savings") at a later session is interpreted as indicating retention from the previous set of learning trials. Ingham (1952) devised a formula for expressing savings based on the proportion of relearning to learning trials: $10 \left(\dfrac{N_1 - N_2}{N_1} \right) + 5$, where N_1 = the number of repetitions needed to learn the material completely, and N_2 = the number of repetitions required to relearn it completely at a later time. Ingham added the constant to make all scores positive in case N_2 is greater than N_1. Warrington and Weiskrantz (1968) demonstrated some retention in severely amnesic patients over one- and four-week intervals by using the savings method with both verbal and nonverbal material. No other method they used gave evidence that these patients had retained any material from the initial exposure to the tests.

Differentiation of Storage and Retrieval

The amount of material a patient recalls depends upon both the amount of information he has stored and the efficiency of his retrieval processes. Direct evaluation of the relative contributions of storage and retrieval to what is recalled is not possible. However, there are ways to differentiate between these two functions.

One method of evaluating the relative efficiency of a patient's storage and retrieval capacities compares performance on a test requiring the patient to *recall* the answers with a multiple-choice test, comparable to the first in difficulty level and content, in which the patient need only *recognize* the correct answer. Vocabulary tests are useful for making this comparison; for example, the patient's performance on the WAIS or Stanford-Binet Vocabulary subtest (both recall tests) can be compared with his performance on the Vocabulary subtest of the Gates-MacGinitie Reading Test or the SCAT (both multiple-choice recognition tests). A score on the paper and pencil test that is very much higher than the score on the orally administered test suggests a retrieval problem. (When the score of the orally administered test is notably higher than that on the paper and pencil test, the patient's capacity for self-direction or independence may be compromised.)

Another method for differentiating storage and retrieval is to compare recall with savings, inasmuch as the method of savings measures storage indirectly. If the memory impairment is due to retention problems, then recall will be down and there will be little savings on later learning trials. If the problem is one of retrieval, recall will be down, but relearning at a later time will occur rapidly, indicating that the material had been stored.

A test of recognition and recall

A learning test for the assessment of retention that also enables the examiner to compare recall and recognition involves printed words and drawings with written or drawn responses (Nyssen, 1957). Three cards, each with a printed word such as Boston, Rabbit, and Tuesday, or Merchant, Wagon, and Bubbles, comprise the verbal stimuli. The nonverbal stimuli are three simple one- or two-line figures, each drawn on a card, taken from Raven's 1938 Matrices designs. The test proceeds in a series of trials:

1. The three verbal or nonverbal stimulus cards are shown together for the subject to COPY.

2. Ten seconds after copying, the subject is asked to RECOGNIZE the three words or three figures from a list of 12 inscribed on one card, four to a row. For each recognition trial, there is a different test card on which the order of the words and figures differs from that of the other test cards.

3. A second COPY trial is given in which the placement of the three stimulus cards is changed.

4. After five minutes of intervening conversation or work on a simple task, the subject is asked to RECALL by writing or drawing the three stimuli.

5. Ten seconds after completing the recall trial, another RECOGNITION trial is given . . .

6. Followed by one more COPY trial.

Twenty-four hours later, the subject is given another series of trials in the following order:

1. RECALL by drawing or writing.

2. RECOGNITION from the card of 12 words or 12 simple figures.

3. COPY trial.

4. RECALL following five minutes of intervening conversation or activity.

5. RECOGNITION trial.
6. Another COPY trial if testing will be repeated the next day.

The methods of selective reminding and restricted reminding
The differentiation of retention, storage, and retrieval can be facilitated by the methods of *selective reminding* and *restricted reminding* (Buschke and Fuld, 1974; Fuld, 1975). In selective reminding, the subject recalls as many words as he can in any order from a list just read to him. After each trial, the examiner repeats all the words the patient omitted in that trial. The reminding and the recall trials continue until the patient recites the whole list. This technique tends to facilitate learning by focusing attention on unlearned items only. Normal subjects typically recall ten of ten-word lists of animals or articles of clothing by the third trial, all ten without any immediately prior prompting on the fourth trial (Buschke and Fuld, 1974).

In restricted reminding, following the first reading of the word list, the examiner again repeats those words the subject did not recall and tells him to recall as many words as he can. All subsequent reminding is limited to words not recalled on any trial. Recall trials and reminding continue until he has named each word at least once. Thus, the first recall tests immediate retention span. Spontaneous recall is demonstrated each time he recalls a word he had previously named. Retrieval problems become evident when a once-named word is recalled only sporadically thereafter. Once all words have been named, the stability of storage can be tested by the method of *extended recall* in which the patient is given 12 more recall trials without any further reminding. The patient's response can be evaluated for the number of items recalled and the consistency with which items are recalled. With a 20-word list of animal names, normal control subjects named an average of 16 items on extended recall and tended to recall items consistently once they were named during the extended recall trials (Fuld, 1975).

Modality Differences

Rey (1959) developed a simple technique for comparing the relative dominance of the visual and auditory modalities as measured by retention. On the first trial, the subject is shown ten common objects, such as a cup, a brush, a button, glasses, etc., one by one at a two-

TABLE 13-9
Quartile Values for Recall of Words and Objects

Trial	Stimulus Material	Q 25	Q 50	Q 75
I	Objects only	8	8	9
II	Words only	7	8	9
III	Objects and	5	7	7
	Words	4	5	6

(Adapted from Rey, 1959)

second rate and then he is asked to name as many as he can recall. Then a list of ten common words, such as dog, drum, hat, sugar, is read to the subject who again must recall as many words as possible. On the third trial, a list of ten words is read at the same time as each of ten unrelated objects is shown to the subject who then must name both objects and words from memory. Rey found a consistent tendency for normal young adults to recall one or two more objects than words (see Table 13-9). Sixty-seven percent recalled from one to as many as six more objects than words, 21% recalled the same number of words and objects, whereas only 12% recalled more (one to three) words than objects. The tendency for more objects than words to be recalled was even greater among 41 neurological patients with known or suspected memory disorders.

14
COGNITIVE FUNCTIONS

Unlike receptive or expressive defects, cognitive dysfunction is not necessarily associated with injury to a particular cortical area but tends to be sensitive to the effect of brain injury regardless of its site (Yacorzynski, 1965). This is not surprising since cognitive activities always involve at least (1) an intact system for organizing perceptions even though specific perceptual modalities may be impaired; (2) a well-stocked and readily available store of remembered learned material; (3) the integrity of the cortical and subcortical interconnections and interaction patterns that underlie "thought"; and (4) the capacity to process two or more mental events at a time. In addition, the translation of cognitive activity into overt behavior requires (5) a response modality sufficiently integrated with central cortical activity to transform conceptual experience into manifest behavior; and (6) a well-functioning response feed-back system for continuous monitoring and modulation of output.

Concrete thinking is the most common sign of cognitive impairment. It usually appears as an inability to think abstractly. The patient may have difficulty forming concepts, using categories, generalizing from a single instance, or applying procedural rules and general principles, be they rules of grammar or conduct, mathematical operations, or good housekeeping practices. Loss of the abstract attitude often results in a preference for obvious, superficial solutions. The patient may be unaware of subtle underlying or intrinsic aspects of a problem and thereby be unable to distinguish what is relevant from what is irrelevant, essential from unessential, and appropriate from outlandish. To the extent that the patient cannot conceptualize abstractly, he must deal with each event as if it were novel, an isolated experience with a unique set of rules.

Conceptual inflexibility frequently occurs in association with concrete thinking. It may show up in *stimulus-bound* behavior in which the patient cannot dissociate his responses or pull his attention away from whatever is in his perceptual field. It may appear as inability to shift perceptual organization, train of thought, or ongoing behavior to meet the varying needs of the moment. The stimulus-bound, conceptually rigid patient is usually unable to plan ahead, initiate activity, think creatively, or adapt to the demands of changing circumstances.

Conceptual concreteness and mental inflexibility are sometimes treated as different aspects of the same disability. When they occur together, they tend to be mutually reinforcing in their effects. However, they can be separated. Although both are associated with extensive or diffuse damage, significant conceptual inflexibility can be present without much impairment of the ability to form and apply abstract concepts, particularly when there is frontal lobe involvement (Zangwill, 1966). Furthermore, conceptual concreteness does not imply impairment of specific reasoning abilities. Thinking may be concrete even when the patient can perform many specific reasoning tasks well, such as solving arithmetic problems or making practical judgments. On the other hand, thinking is likely to be concrete when the patient has specific reasoning disabilities.

Most tests of cognitive functions are designed to probe for concrete thinking in one form or another, usually testing concept formation by itself or in conjunction with mental flexibility. Tests of other cognitive functions, such as planning and organizing, or problem solving and reasoning, do not treat concrete thinking as the primary examination object, but they often supply information about it. Tests that deal with mental flexibility per se are discussed later (see pp. 399–405 and 434–437).

TESTS OF CONCEPT FORMATION

Tests of concept formation differ from most other mental tests in that they focus on the *quality* or *process* of thinking more than the content of the response. Many of these tests have no "right" or "wrong" answers. Their scores stand for qualitative judgments of the extent to which the response was abstract or concrete, complex or simple, apt or irrelevant. Tests with right and wrong answers belong in the category of tests of abstract conceptualization to the extent that they provide information about *how* the patient thinks.

Patients with moderate to severe brain damage or with a diffuse injury tend to do poorly on all tests of abstract thinking, regardless of their mode of presentation or channel of response. However, patients with mild, modality specific, or subtle organic defects may not engage in concrete thinking generally, but only on those tasks that directly involve an impaired modality, are highly complex, or touch upon emotionally arousing matters. Furthermore, concretism takes different forms with different patients, and varies in its effect on mental efficiency with the type of task. The examiner who is interested in finding out how his patient thinks will use more than one kind of concept formation test involving more than one sensory or response modality.

Verbal Abstraction Tests

Proverbs
Tests of interpretation of proverbs are among the most widely used techniques for evaluating the quality of thinking. The Wechsler tests, the Stanford-Binet scales, and the mental status examination include proverb interpretation items. Their popularity rests on their usefulness in indicating where the patient's thinking lies on an abstract-concrete dimension. Further, all but mentally defective patients and those with serious communication disabilities can make some response without a great deal of effort or loss of dignity.

Although it is assumed that the abstract-concrete dimension is a continuum, interpretations of proverbs are usually evaluated dichotomously, as either abstract or concrete. The three-point scoring system of the Wechsler tests preserves this dichotomy. It is also implicit in informal evaluations of patients' responses in mental status examinations. In this system, appropriate abstract interpretations earn two points (e.g., *A rolling stone gathers no moss:* "You will have nothing if you keep on moving"); concrete interpretations earn one point (e.g., "Most turning objects never gather anything" or "Because of moss will fall off"), or no points if the response misses the gist of the proverb or misinterprets it (e.g., "If you keep busy you will feel better"). Usually this scoring system creates no problems, but occasionally patients' interpretations will be borderline or difficult to classify.

The *Proverbs Test* formalizes the task of proverb interpretation, presenting it as an important source of information about the quality of thinking in its own right rather than as a part of another examination (Gorham, 1956). Its standardization reduces variations in administration and scoring biases and provides norms that take into account the difficulty level of individual proverbs. This test has three forms, each containing 12 proverbs of equivalent difficulty. It is administered as a written test in which the subject is instructed to "tell what the proverb *means* rather than just tell more about it." The three-point scoring system is used. Mean scores for each form of the test do not differ significantly. A second, multiple-choice version of the Proverbs Test contains 40 items, each with four choices of possible answers. Only one of the choices is appropriate and abstract; the other three are either concrete interpretations or common misinterpretations.

Proverbs Test scores vary with education level (and probably social class) (Gorham, 1956). Using the multiple-choice version in a study of frontal lobe functions, Benton (1968) reported very poor performance by seven patients with bilateral frontal lobe disease (mean = 11.4, SD 6.1), a somewhat better performance by eight patients with right frontal lobe disease (mean = 20.1, SD 6.8), and unexpectedly adequate scores achieved by ten patients with left frontal lobe disease (mean = 26.4, SD 9.4). On the multiple-choice form of the Proverbs Test, the scores of groups of schizophrenic and organic patients are significantly lower than those of normal control subjects but they do not differ significantly among one another (Fogel, 1965).

Word usage tests
Tests calling for abstract comparisons between two or more words provide a sensitive measure of concrete thinking. However, word usage is also very dependent upon both the integrity of the patient's communication system and the level of his verbal skills. Thus patients who have even a mild aphasic disorder and those who have always been intellectually dull or educationally underprivileged will

do poorly on this test, regardless of the extent to which their cognitive functions have been preserved.

When ability to form verbal concepts is evaluated, the patient's verbal skill level must always be taken into account. Easy items (such as those through age level XII on the Binet) can be used with most adults who have completed the sixth grade. Difficult items may elicit evidence of cognitive dysfunction in bright, well-educated adults when their performance on easier words would seem to indicate that their ability to make verbal abstractions is intact.

The Abstract Words Test.   As in the Similarities subtest of the WAIS, the *Abstract Words Test* (Tow, 1955) calls for comparisons between two words, but instead of giving likenesses, the subject must tell how two words differ from one another, which is usually a simpler task (see Table 14-1). This test is part of a battery given pre- and postoperatively to evaluate the effects of psychosurgery (frontal leucotomy) on intellectual functioning. The patients scored significantly lower on this test after surgery.

Stanford-Binet subtests.   The Stanford-Binet scales test verbal abstraction in a number of ways. All of the Binet items are scored on a pass-fail basis; unlike Wechsler's and Gorham's three-point scoring system, both concrete interpretations *and* misinterpretations of words and proverbs receive no credit.

There are three *Similarities* subtests: *Two Things* at age level VII contains such questions as, "In what way are *wood* and *coal* alike?" *Three Things* at age level XI is identical with the lower level similarities test except that likenesses have to be found for three words, i.e., "In what way are *book, teacher,* and *newspaper* alike?" *Essential Similarities* at the SA I level is a two-word similarities test requiring a high level of abstraction for credit.

There are also three *Differences* subtests in the Binet. At age VI, *Differences* consists of three items asking for the differences between two words with fairly concrete referents, i.e., "What is the difference between a *bird* and a *dog?" Differences between Abstract Words* at the AA level and *Essential Differences* at levels AA and SA II both ask for the differences between two abstract words. The only difference between these two subtests, besides the content of the word pairs, is the insertion of the word "principal" in the ques-

TABLE 14-1
Abstract Word Test: Word List

Instructions: What is the difference between _____ and _____?

1.	MISTAKE	and	LIE
2.	THRIFT	and	AVARICE
3.	MURDER	and	MANSLAUGHTER
4.	LAZINESS	and	IDLENESS
5.	COURAGE	and	BOLDNESS
6.	POVERTY	and	MISERY
7.	ABUNDANCE	and	EXCESS
8.	TREACHERY	and	DECEIT
9.	CHARACTER	and	REPUTATION
10.	EVOLUTION	and	REVOLUTION

(From Tow, 1955)

tion, "What is the (principal) difference between . . . ?" on the Essential Differences subtest.

There are three *Similarities and Differences* subtests on the Binet. The simplest, *Pictorial Similarities and Differences I* at age level IV-6 presents six pictures, each with four figures, of which three are alike (e.g., crosses) and one different (e.g., a dash); the subject's task is to point to the one unlike figure. At year V, *Pictorial Similarities and Differences II* consists of 12 cards, each containing two figures that are either the same (e.g., two trees) or different (e.g., a circle and a square); the subject must tell whether the figures are the same or different. At year VIII, *Similarities and Differences* is completely verbal; the subject has to tell how two familiar objects, such as a *baseball* and an *orange*, are alike and how they differ.

In addition to the word comparison subtests, the Binet scales contain three subtests asking for definitions of *Abstract Words,* with scoring standards for years X and XII (*Abstract Words I*), XI and XIII (*Abstract Words II*), and the AA level (*Abstract Words III*). Word difficulty ranges from words of emotion such as "pity" at the X and XII year levels to words like "generosity" and "authority." The definitions too are scored on a two-point pass-fail basis.

Opposite Analogies is another form of word abstraction test. The Binet scales carry it in five versions spread over six age and ability levels from age level IV ("Brother is a boy; sister is a _____") to SA III ("Ability is native; education is _____").

Symbol pattern tests
Deductive reasoning combines with ability for conceptual sequencing in symbol pattern tests, exemplified by the Thurstones'
Reasoning Tests in the *Primary Mental Abilities* (PMA) battery
(1962) or their *American Council on Education Psychological Examination* (ACE), (1953, 1954). These tests are composed of such
number or letter patterns as 1-2-4-2-4-8-3-_ or A-B-D-C-E-F-H-__.
The subject must indicate, usually by selecting one of several
choices, what symbol should follow in the sequence. Both the ACE
and the PMA have norms for different age and education levels.
This kind of reasoning problem seems to require an appreciation of
temporal or consequential relationships for success.

Nonverbal Concept Formation

Sorting tests
Sorting tests are the most common form of nonverbal tests of abstraction and concept formation. In sorting tasks, the subject must sort
collections of objects, blocks, tokens, or other kinds of items into
subgroups following instructions such as "sort out the ones that go
together" or "put together the ones that have the same thing in common." Most sorting tests assess the patient's ability to *shift* concepts
as well as his ability to use them. The manner in which the subject
proceeds will give some indication of his ability to form and handle
abstract concepts.

Few sorting tests produce numerical scores, for it is more the patient's procedures than his solutions that interest the examiner. Attention is paid to whether the patient sorts according to a principle,
whether he can formulate the principle verbally, whether it is a
reasonable principle, and whether the patient follows it consistently.

Although sorting tests demonstrate how the patient thinks and
handles certain kinds of abstraction problems, they have not proven
successful in differentiating brain damaged from functionally psychotic patients (K. Goldstein and Scheerer, 1941, 1953; Yates, 1954).
On scored sorting tests, few significant differences show up between
the mean scores obtained by groups of brain injured patients and
normal control subjects (De Renzi et al., 1966; McFie and Piercy,
1952; Newcombe, 1969). This does not invalidate sorting tests except for screening purposes. It does suggest, however, that deficits

registered by these tests occur only mildly or infrequently in many brain injured populations. When marked impairment of performance does appear, an organic brain disorder is likely to be present.

Simple Sorting Tests.   There are two well-known nonverbal tests of concept formation that are simply sorting tests. Both highlight the processes used by the patient to solve concept formation problems. Neither is scored. The *Color Sorting Test* (K. Goldstein and Scheerer, 1941, 1953; Weigl, 1941) consists of 61 little skeins of wool, each of a different combination of hue, shade, and brightness. There are about ten skeins in each of the major colors—green, red, blue, and yellow, plus shades of brown, gray, purple, and other combined hues. The test requires the patient (1) to sort to sample; (2) to match two of three different skeins, two of which are similar in hue and two in brightness; (3) to explain the sameness principle underlying groupings of six skeins of the same hue but different shades and six skeins of different hue but the same brightness; and (4) to select all skeins of the same hue such as "red" or "green," giving his reasoning for the selection. The examiner judges the patient's level and his ease of abstract thinking from his own observations and from the patient's accompanying explanations.

The *Kasanin-Hanfmann Concept Formation Test,* also called the *Vigotsky Test,* was designed to "evaluate an individual's ability to solve problems by the use of abstract concepts and provide information both on the subject's level of abstract thinking and on his preferred type of approach to problems" (Hanfmann, 1953, p. 731). The Concept Formation Test consists of 22 different blocks varying in color, size, shape, and height. On the underside of each is printed one of four nonsense words (or a number, in a variant of the test) designating the group to which the block belongs when the blocks are sorted by both shape and height (see Fig. 14-1). The subject continues to group and regroup the blocks, with a correcting clue given following each incorrect attempt, until he combines both the principles of shape and height to achieve the correct sorting solution, which may take anywhere from five minutes to one hour. He is encouraged to "think aloud" as he works, and the examiner is encouraged to keep a detailed record of both performance and verbalizations

Sort and shift tests.   Sorting tests, which include a requirement to shift concepts, spread a wider screening net than the simple sorting

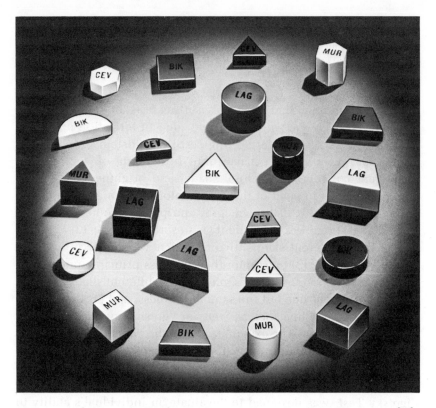

FIG. 14-1. The Kasanin-Hanfmann Concept Formation Test. (Courtesy of The Stoelting Co.)

tests. Observation will clarify whether the patient's primary diffi-culty is in sorting or in shifting. For those sort and shift tests which produce a numerical score, the need to augment numerical data with behavioral description is obvious.

The *Color Form Sorting Test,* sometimes called *Weigl's Test,* is made up of twelve cardboard tokens or blocks, colored red, blue, yellow, or green on top and all white underneath, which come in one of three shapes—square, circle, or triangle (K. Goldstein and Scheerer, 1941, 1953; Weigl, 1941). The patient is first asked to sort the test material. On completion of his first sort, he is told to "group them again, but in a different way." On completion of each sort, the examiner asks, "Why have you grouped them this way?" or "Why do these figures go together?" If the patient has difficulty in his second attempt at sorting, the examiner can give clues such as turning up the white sides for the patient who spontaneously sorted by color, or showing the patient who sorted by form a single grouping by color and asking if he can see why the three blocks belong together. The inability to sort conceptually or to shift from one sorting principle to another is presumed to indicate impaired mental functioning. McFie and Piercy (1952) found that many more patients with left hemisphere lesions (8 out of 17) fail on this test than those with right hemisphere lesions (2 of 32); the presence or absence of aphasia did not appear to affect the ratio of poor performances among patients with left hemisphere brain disease.

Modifications of this test have increased the number of possible sorts. The *Object Classification Test* (Payne and Hewlett, 1960) also uses 12 tokens, but besides differing in shape and color, they are of different weights, thicknesses, sizes, materials, hue, and brightness, which permit up to ten different sorts (including a sort by surface area and one by presence or absence of curved corners). The instructions are identical to those of the Color Form Sorting Test; following each correct sort the patient is asked to sort the tokens another way. The patient's score is the number of abstract (A) sorts he makes. A standardization group of 20 normal control subjects made an average of 4.20 (SD 1.61) different sorts on this test, the average score of a group of schizophrenics was 2.80 (SD 2.62), and the average scores of three groups of patients with neurotic or affective disorders fell in-between. The number of acceptable sorts made by Newcombe's brain injured population (1969) did not differ greatly from the mean of the normal control subjects. In fact, four patients with mixed right hemisphere lesions made an average of 4.25 sorts, and five patients with posterior right hemisphere lesions averaged 4.00 sorts. The lowest average scores attained by her patient groups were 2.70 and 2.80 for the left parietal and right frontal groups respectively.

Another modification (*Weigl's Test, modified version*) increases the number of possible sorts to five, using thickness, size, and "suit" (a club, heart, or diamond printed at the block's center) in addition to the four standard colors and three common shapes (De Renzi et al., 1966). The first part of the test proceeds much as the original and the Payne modifications, except for a three-minute time limit. When the patient is unable to make an acceptable sort within three minutes, the examiner makes each of the sorts not used by the patient and

FIG. 14-2. The Object Sorting Test. (K. Goldstein and Scheerer, in *Contributions toward Medical Psychology*, edited by A. Weider. © Ronald Press, New York.)

allows the patient one minute to identify the principle. Spontaneous patient sorts earn three score points each; correct classification of the examiner's sort earns one point. Scores can range from 0 to 15. Forty control subjects achieved a mean score of 9.49. The presence of aphasia tended to result in markedly depressed scores, but other kinds of brain dysfunction had little effect on performance of this test. This finding receives support from the other sorting test studies that associate left hemisphere lesions with relatively lower scores.

The *Object Sorting Test* (K. Goldstein and Scheerer, 1941, 1953; Weigl, 1941) is based on the same principles and generally follows the same administration procedures of the block and token sorting tests, except that the materials consist of 30 familiar objects (see Fig. 14-2). The objects can be grouped according to such principles as *use, situation* in which they are normally found, *color, pairedness, material,* etc. Variations on the basic sorting task require that the patient find objects compatible with the one preselected by the examiner, to sort objects according to a category named by the examiner, to figure out a principle underlying a set of objects grouped by the examiner, or to pick out one object of an examiner-selected set of objects that does not belong to the set. Most variations also ask for a verbal explanation. By providing a wider range of responses than most sorting tests, the Object Sorting Test allows the examiner more flexibility in the conduct of the examination and more opportunities to observe the patient's conceptual approach. The use of common objects also eliminates any need to familiarize the patient with the test material, or devise names for unfamiliar objects.

Weigl and K. Goldstein and Scheerer emphasize the qualitative aspects of the patient's performance, but Tow (1955) emphasized the number of different solutions. Preoperatively, his frontal leucotomy patients averaged 2.5 spontaneous solutions for a total of 3.2 solutions including both spontaneous ones and those achieved with clues. Postoperatively, these same patients' average number of spontaneous solutions was 1.8, and the average number of combined solutions was 2.1. Tow concluded that frontal leucotomy interfered with concept formation.

The *Wisconsin Card Sorting Test* was devised to study "abstract behavior" and "shift of set" (Berg, 1948; Grant and Berg, 1948). The subject is given a pack of 64 cards on which are printed one to four symbols, triangle, star, cross, or circle, in red, green, yellow, or blue. No two cards are identical (see Fig. 14-3). The patient's task is to place them one by one under four stimulus cards—one red triangle, two green stars, three yellow crosses, and four blue circles—according to a principle that the patient must deduce from the pattern of the examiner's responses to the patient's placement of the cards. For instance, if the principle is color, the correct placement of a red card is under *one red triangle*, regardless of the symbol or number, and the examiner will respond accordingly. The subject simply begins placing cards and the examiner tells him whether each placement is correct. After a run of ten correct placements in a row, the examiner shifts the principle, indicating the shift only in the changed pattern of his "right" and "wrong" statements. The test begins with color as the basis for sorting, shifts to form, then to number, returns again to color, and so on. The test continues until the patient has made six runs of ten correct placements or has placed more than 64 cards in one category. If the pack is exhausted before six successful runs, the card order is rearranged and the pack is used again. I usually discontinue the test after 30 or 40 cards have been misplaced and the patient seems unlikely to comprehend the task. If

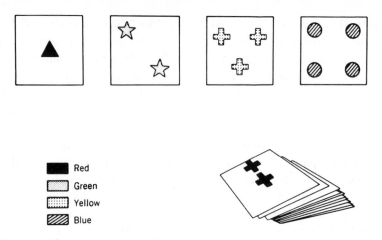

FIG. 14-3. The Wisconsin Card Sorting Test (Milner, 1964).

the patient makes four correct runs of ten consecutively (not count-ing the one or two trials between runs for determining the new prin-ciple), I ask the patient to state the general principle and discontinue if he is correct. Milner (1963) used a 128-card pack and discontinued after six runs or when all 128 cards were placed. She counted both the number of categories achieved and the number of erroneous responses for scores.

A poor performance on this test can result from different kinds of intellectual deficits. The patient may have difficulty sorting according to category, which suggests an impaired ability to form concepts. This problem occurs most often in patients with frontal lobe—particularly left frontal lobe—damage involving the medial area (Drewe, 1974). Difficulty in shifting when the category changes, i.e., perseveration, is another common error made by Drewe's brain injured patients regard-less of the side or site of lesion. It also characterizes the performance of long-term alcoholics (Parsons, 1975). Parsons calls attention to a third common error that he refers to as "difficulty in maintaining . . . [the] set," in which the patient may be able to form categories easily and shift readily, but after several shifts he loses track of the present category and may end up in hopeless confusion. (See Fig. 6-2, p. 146, for an example of the overall performance pattern of a patient with a right anterior parietal tumor who could not maintain a set after the third shift.)

Milner (1963, 1964) reported that both before and after surgical removal of brain tumors, the performance of patients with frontal lobe lesions was significantly poorer than that of patients with lesions localized elsewhere. The frontal lobe patients achieved fewer sorting categories and made more errors than the other brain tumor patients (see Table 14-2). Teuber and his colleagues (1951) also found a marked deficit in 20 frontal lobe patients (mean error score = 21.2), but 20 patients with parieto-temporal lobe lesions had a slightly more pronounced deficit (mean error score = 25.8); a group of 40 control subjects averaged the least number of errors (14.8) in 60 trials.

Other nonverbal concept formation tests

The Organic Integrity Test (OIT). This easily administered test consists of ten pairs of cards, one with two pictures and the other a single picture similar in color to one of the two pictures of its pair, and also similar in some formal characteristic (e.g., category, texture) to the other of the matching two pictures (Tien, 1960). The patient's task is to indicate which of the two pictures is more like the single picture. A numerical value for each form-dominant choice is recorded, the value differing for each card. The total possible score is 100; the lowest possible score (all color-dominant choices) is 0. The OIT is based on the assumption that categorization by color reflects a more primitive level of mental organization than categorization by form; the predominance of color responses over form responses in an adult presumably indicates intellectual regression due to a cortical disturbance or disease.

The OIT's diagnostic usefulness is questionable, although Tien's

TABLE 14-2
Effects of Surgery for Brain Tumor on Card Sorting Performance

Locus of Lesion	Categories Achieved		Total Errors	
	Preop. Mean	Postop. Mean	Preop. Mean	Postop. Mean
Dorsolateral frontal (n = 18)	3.3	1.4	54.9	73.2
Posterior cortex (n = 46)	4.5	4.6	39.8	31.0

(Adapted from Milner, 1964)

claims for his test are enthusiastic. He has reported that 94.5% of organically intact adults score above the cutting score of 50, whereas only 7% of a very mixed organic group achieved scores over 50. In a study of almost 1,000 army recruits, however, 25.9% obtained scores of 50 or less (Watts and Haerer, 1970). In another study, the scores of four groups of psychotic, organic, and other hospitalized patients without brain damage or psychiatric disturbance, and normal control subjects differed in the expected directions but not to a significant degree (Snelbecker et al., 1968). Wepman generally begins his testing sessions with the OIT because he considers it a good "icebreaker" (Wepman, personal communication, 1974). He also reports that a *shift* from form dominated to color dominated responses in the course of testing usually signals the presence of some kind of thinking problem.

Sequential concept formation tests. Talland (1965) used two decks of playing cards without aces in his most complex test of *Sequential concept formation.* He considered this task to be conceptually similar to maze learning. The black and red cards are arranged in 16 runs of B-B-R-B-R-R. The subject must discover the pattern in order to predict the color of the next card as he turns the cards up one by one. The subject proceeds at his own pace until he correctly predicts three sequences (18 cards) in a row. To add a dimension of immediate memory to this task, the examiner interjects a moment or two of verbal praise after the subject has completed a three-run sequence correctly and then permits him to resume the task. A final task requires the subject to reconstruct the pattern from a pack of disarranged cards. If a patient fails to see the pattern before going through both decks (16 six-card sequences), the examiner shows it to him, gives several demonstrations, and then if the patient still is unable to perform the task independently, the examiner has him copy the sequence from a model placed in front of him. All of Talland's 20 control subjects succeeded by the third trial and ten were not set back by the interruption. However, only two of the 20 patients with severe memory disorder solved the problem, one after two trials and one after five.

An easier sequential concept formation test uses five geometric figures drawn in black ink on white cards, a 1-inch circle, two small circles, a triangle, a square, and a 2-inch circle. The goal is to predict when the large circle will appear. Talland devised three different patterns: (A) With a varying number of intervening cards, the combination 1-inch circle, double circle, 1-inch circle heralded the 2-inch circle. (B) With a varying number of intervening blank cards, the combination 1-inch circle and two blank cards preceded the large circle. (C) Again a varying number of blank cards appeared, among which one square and one triangle were placed in different position; the 2-inch circle immediately followed the appearance of the second of these two figures. All of the 21 control subjects solved patterns A and B but four of them had to be told the rule for pattern C before they could apply it. Eighteen of the memory impaired patients solved pattern A, ten solved pattern B, but only seven solved C. Several of the patients verbalized C correctly but failed to apply the rule.

The easiest of these tests also uses playing cards, sorted into suit sequences, i.e., D-S-C-H. The subject has to anticipate the next suit that will be turned up. The 20 control subjects deduced the principle within the first three four-card sequences. The 17 (of 20) memory impaired patients who solved this problem took an average of 8.41 four-card sequences to do so.

TESTS OF ORDERING, ORGANIZING, AND PLANNING

The ability for both practical and conceptual organization, ordering, and planning involves an appreciation of the categories and relationships of whatever it is that needs organizing, be it objects, situations, concepts, activities, or combinations of these. It also requires the creative flexibility to perceive alternatives and the ability to conceptualize change from present circumstances.

Use of Standard Testing Procedures

There are few formal tests of these abilities. However, the patient's handling of many of the standard psychological tests will provide insight into how he performs these important conceptual activities. For example, his layout of Bender designs on the page indicates his awareness of space use and spatial relations. Responses to story telling tasks, such as the Thematic Apperception Test (see pp. 462–463), reflect the patient's handling of sequential verbal ideas. For example, stories may be complex and highly organized, have simple and straight story lines, be organized by accretion, or be loose or disjointed associations or descriptions (Henry, 1947). Even the patient's approach to such highly structured tests as Block Design will provide information about whether he orders and plans ahead naturally and effectively, laboriously, inconsistently, or not at all (see p. 219). Sentence Building at SA I of the 1960 Revision of the Stanford-Binet, and age level VII on the 1937 Form M of the Binet scales affords the patient a good opportunity to demonstrate how he organizes his thoughts into a sensible and linguistically acceptable construct.

I usually ask questions about everyday problems and future planning in my introductory interview. How a patient who is living alone or a housewife describes food purchasing and preparation may reveal how well he or she can organize and plan. Other issues that may bring out the organizing and planning aspects of thinking concern personal care, how the patient's illness affects his activities and his family, what accommodations he has to make to his disabilities, to his altered financial and vocational status, etc. Some patients, particularly those whose brain lesions affect the nondominant hemisphere, may give lucid and appropriate answers to questions involving organization and planning of impersonal situations or events but show poor judgment in unrealistic, confused, often illogical or nonexistent plans for themselves, or lack the judgment to recognize that they need to make plans if they are to remain independent (Lezak, 1975).

Nonverbal Tests involving Ordering and Planning

Porteus Maze Test

The maze tracing task was designed to yield data about the highest levels of mental functioning involving planning and foresight, i.e., "the process of choosing, trying, and rejecting or adopting alternative courses of conduct or thought. At a simple level, this is similar to solving a very complex maze" (Porteus, 1959, p. 7).

There are three sets of the *Porteus Maze Test* currently in use: the Vineland Revision, which contains 12 mazes for years III through XII, year XIV, and Adult; the eight-maze Porteus Maze Extension

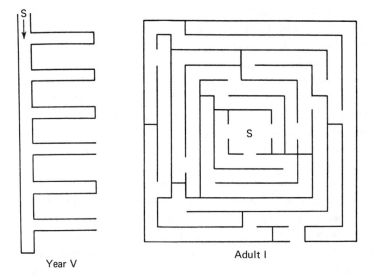

FIG. 14-4. Two of the Porteus mazes. (Reproduced by permission.) (Copyright 1933, 1946, 1950 by S. D. Porteus. Published by The Psychological Corporation, New York. All rights reserved.)

covering years VII through XII, year XIV, and Adult; and the Porteus Maze Supplement, which also has eight mazes for years VII through XII, XIV, and Adult (Porteus, 1965) (see Fig. 14-4). The latter two series were developed to compensate for practice effects in retesting, so that the maze at each year of the Porteus Maze Extension is a little more difficult than its counterpart in the Vineland Revision, and each year of the Porteus Maze Supplement is more difficult than its corresponding test in the Extension series. Tests for years III and IV of the Vineland Revision consist essentially of double lines testing the subject's ability to comprehend the rudiments of the task. Adult testing should not begin below year V except when the patient is significantly impaired; normally, adults begin at age VII.

To achieve a successful trial, the subject must trace the maze without entering any blind alleys. The test is not timed and may take some patients an hour or more to complete. A score is given in terms of test age (TA), which is the age level of the most difficult maze the patient completes successfully. The upper score is 17 for success on the Adult level maze. The test can be done with either hand without lowering the score although the nondominant hand makes about twice as many qualitative errors—such as crossing a line or lifting the pencil—as the dominant hand (Briggs, 1963).

The Porteus Maze Test is quite sensitive to the effects of brain damage (Klebanoff et al., 1954). Perhaps the most notable research was undertaken by A. Smith and Kinder (1959) and A. Smith (1960) who did an eight-year follow-up study of psychosurgical patients, comparing younger and older groups who had undergone superior or orbital topectomy with younger and older patient controls. Following a score rise in a second preoperative testing, scores on tests taken within three months after surgery were lower than the second preoperative scores in all cases. The superior topectomy group's scores dropped still lower during the eight-year interval to a score significantly $(p < .05)$ lower than the original. The control group mean scores climbed slightly following the first and second retest (10.87, 11.89, and 12.59), but the eight-year and the original maze test scores were essentially the same. Maze test scores have also successfully predicted the severity of brain damage (Meier, 1974). Those patients who achieved test age (TA) scores of VIII or above during the first week after a stroke made significant spontaneous gains in return of lost motor functions, whereas those whose scores fell below this standard showed relatively little spontaneous recovery. Tow (1955) found that frontal leucotomy patients tested pre- and postoperatively were significantly slowed $(p < .02)$ in their maze test performance by the psychosurgery and averaged more errors; their preoperative mean time for mazes VI to XII plus XIV of the Vineland Revision was 313 seconds whereas postoperatively their mean time lengthened to 546 seconds.

The Wechsler Intelligence Scale for Children contains a shorter maze test with time limits and an error scoring system (see p. 235).

REASONING TESTS

Reasoning tests call for different kinds of logical thinking, comprehension of relationships, and practical judgments. The WAIS furnishes examples of different kinds of reasoning tests in Comprehension, Arithmetic, Picture Completion, and Picture Arrangement. Tests of other functions may also provide information about the patient's reasoning ability, such as the Progressive Matrices, the

Reading Comprehension subtest of the Gates-MacGinitie Reading Test, and the Bicycle drawing test. The Stanford-Binet scales contain a variety of reasoning tests, some of which have counterparts in other tests. All the Stanford-Binet subtest references in this section are to the 1960 revision except as otherwise noted.

Verbal reasoning test problems

Although these reasoning tests have not had enough neuropsychological use to result in published studies, they are effective in drawing out defects in reasoning. The verbal reasoning tests of the Binet cover a sufficiently broad range of difficulty to provide suitable problems for patients at all but the highest and lowest levels of intellectual ability.

The *Verbal Absurdities* subtest items are little stories containing logical impossibilities the subject is asked to point out. At the IX year old level, for example, one item is, "Bill Jones's feet are so big that he has to pull his trousers on over his head." There are four forms of Verbal Absurdities with scoring standards for five age levels, VIII (VA I), IX (VA II), X (VA III), XI (VA IV), and XII (VA II). *Problem Situations* I and II at ages VIII and XI, and *Problems of Fact* at age XIII involve little stories for which the patient has to supply an explanation, such as "My neighbor has been having queer visitors. First a doctor came to his house, then a lawyer, then a minister (preacher, priest, or rabbi). What do you think happened there?"

Picture problems

The visual analogue of Verbal Absurdities is *Picture Absurdities* I and II at years VII and XIII (see Fig. 14-5). These subtests depict a logically or practically impossible situation the patient must identify. The *McGill Picture Anomalies Test* (Hebb and Morton, 1943) also depicts practically or logically impossible situations. It consists of two equivalent series of 30 pictures, with instructions to "Show me what is funny or out of place." Patients with surgical lesions of the right temporal lobe tended to make more errors on this test than did other patient groups, and also were slower and more hesitant in their responses, whereas patients with parietal lobe lesions performed well (Milner, 1958). However, these findings were not reflected in another study of patients with temporal lobe epilepsy in which no pre- or postsurgical differences were found (Shalman,

FIG. 14-5. Picture Absurdities I, Card B (Terman and Merrill, 1960). (Courtesy of Houghton Mifflin Co.)

1961). The McGill pictures are dated, and this may well make them unreliable for present-day use, whereas the six Binet pictures seem ageless.

Arithmetic reasoning problems
Besides the usual Arithmetic Story problems, the Binet scales contain some interestingly complex reasoning problems involving arithmetic operations and concepts. These problems may expose subtle difficulties in formulating problems or in conceptual tracking that are not readily apparent in patients whose well-ingrained thinking patterns suffice for handling most test reasoning tasks. *Ingenuity* I and II are arithmetic "brain teasers" such as "(A boy) has to bring back exactly 13 pints of water. He has a 9-pint can and a 5-pint can. Show me how he can measure out exactly 13 pints of water using nothing but these 2 cans and not guessing at the amount." This type of question calls for a "process" rather than content answer, eliciting information about how the patient reasons. The *Enclosed Box Problem* at the SA I level is also a mathematical brain teaser. It is a serial reasoning task that begins with "Let's suppose that this box has 2 smaller boxes inside it, and each one of the smaller boxes contains a

little tiny box. How many boxes are there altogether, counting the big one?" The next three items elaborate on the first, compounding the number of boxes at each step. *Induction* at year XIV involves a serial paper folding and cutting problem in which the number of holes cut increases at an algebraic ratio to the number of folds. After observing the folding and cutting procedure, the patient is asked to state the rule that will enable him to predict the number of holes from the number of folds. *Reasoning* I and II are brain teasers too, requiring the patient to organize a set of numerical facts and deduce their relationship in order to solve the problem.

The *Block Counting* task at age level X, sometimes called *Cube Analysis* (Newcombe, 1969) or *Cube Counting* (McFie and Zangwill, 1960) is another Binet test that lends itself well to the study of reasoning processes. The material consists of two-dimensional drawings of three-dimensional block piles (see Fig. 14-6). The subject must count the total number of blocks in each pile by taking into account the ones hidden from view. Several studies comparing right and left hemisphere patients on this task have found mildly to significantly impaired performances by right hemisphere patients relative to those with left hemisphere lesions (Newcombe, 1969; McFie and Zangwill, 1960; Warrington and Rabin, 1970). Although Newcombe's right and left hemisphere patients' scores did not differ significantly, right hemisphere patients were slower.

Miscellaneous reasoning problems
Codes at AA (Form M, 1937 Revision) and SA II is another kind of reasoning task. Each difficulty level of Codes contains one message, "COME TO LONDON," printed alongside two coded forms of the message. The patient must find the rule for each code. This task requires the subject to deduce a verbal pattern and then translate it.

FIG. 14-6. Sample items from the Block Counting task (Terman and Merrill, 1960). (Courtesy of Houghton Mifflin Co.)

Codes can be sensitive to mild verbal dysfunctions that do not appear on tests involving well-practiced verbal behavior but may show up when the task is complex and unfamiliar.

In Binet *Paper Cutting* subtests at IX, XIII, and AA levels, the examiner cuts holes in folded paper so that the subject can see what he is doing but not how the unfolded paper looks. The subject's task is to draw a picture of how he thinks the paper will look when unfolded. This test was included in a battery for studying the visual space perception of patients with lateralized lesions (McFie and Zangwill, 1960; Paterson and Zangwill, 1944). It discriminated left and right hemisphere damaged patients well: four out of four left hemisphere lesion patients could pass it at the IX year level, whereas only one out of ten right hemisphere damaged patients succeeded.

15
ORIENTATION, ATTENTION, AND SELF-REGULATION

ORIENTATION

Orientation, the awareness of self in relation to one's surroundings, requires consistent and reliable integration of attention, perception, and memory. Impairment of particular perceptual or memory functions can lead to specific defects of orientation; more than mild or transient problems of attention or retention are likely to result in global impairment of orientation. Its dependence on the intactness and integration of so many different mental activities makes orientation exceedingly vulnerable to the effects of brain dysfunction (Schulman et al., 1965).

Orientation defects are among the most frequent symptoms of brain disease, and of these, impaired awareness for time and place are the most common, accompanying every brain disorder in which attention or retention are significantly affected (Gooddy, 1969; McGhie, 1969). It is not difficult to understand the fragility of orientation for time and place, since each depends on both continuity of awareness and the translation of immediate experience into memories of sufficient duration to allow the person to keep in touch with his ongoing history. Thus, impaired orientation for time and place typically occurs with widespread cortical involvement (e.g., in senile dementia or acute brain syndromes), lesions in the limbic system (e.g., Korsakoff's syndrome), or damage to the reticular activating system of the brain stem (e.g., disturbances of consciousness).

Mental Status Questions

Assessment of orientation for time, place, and person is covered in the mental status examination (see pp. 448–450). The reliability or consistency of a patient's orientation for time and place can be determined by asking orientation questions several times in different ways in the course of the examination. By requiring the patient to answer the identification questions that are printed on all standard test forms, the examiner can repeat the orientation assessment without being so obvious as to give offense. One easy way to do this is to ask the subject to write in the answers on the test form. This also provides another sample of reading, writing, and the ability to follow directions.

To test for time orientation, the examiner asks for the date (day, month, year, and day of the week) and the time of day. The patient's sense of temporal continuity should also be assessed, since he may be able to remember the number and name of the present day and yet not have a functional sense of time, particularly if he is in a rehabilitation unit or in the care of a conscientious family whose members make every effort to keep him oriented. On the other hand, some patients will have a generally accurate awareness of the passage of time but be unable to remember the specifics of the date. Questions concerning *duration* will assess the patient's appreciation of temporal continuity. The examiner may ask such questions as "How long have you been in this place?"* "How long is it since you last worked?" "How long since you last saw me?" "What was your last meal (i.e., breakfast, lunch, or dinner)?** How long ago did you have it?"

Assessment of orientation for place generally begins with questions about the name or location of the place in which the patient is

---

* It is important not to give away answers before the questions are asked. The examiner who is testing for time orientation before place must be careful not to ask, "How long have you been in the *hospital?*" or "When did you arrive in *Portland?*"
** Some mental status examinations for recent memory include questions about the foods served at a recent meal. Unless the examiner checks with the family or the dietician, he has no way of knowing whether the patient had chicken for dinner or is drawing on old memory of what people usually eat in the evening. The menu problem is most apparent with breakfast, for the usual variety of breakfasts is so limited it is impossible to tell whether the patient is calling on old memory or new when he reports that he had "toast, cereal, eggs, and coffee."

being examined. The examiner needs to find out if the patient knows the kind of place he is in, e.g., hospital, clinic, office; the name, if it has one, e.g., Veteran's Hospital, Marion County Mental Health Clinic; and where it is located, e.g., city, state. Orientation for place also includes an appreciation of direction and distance. To test for this, the examiner might ask where the patient's home is in relation to the hospital, clinic, etc., in what direction the patient must travel to get home, and how long it takes to get there. The examiner can also check the patient's practical knowledge of the geography of the locale or state and his awareness of the distance and direction of the state capital, another big city, or an adjacent state relative to his present location.

Tests for Orientation

Time

Brief Temporal Orientation Test.   This is a scoring technique in which negative numerical values are assigned to errors in any one of the five basic time orientation elements: day, month, year, day of week, and present clock time (Benton et al., 1964). It has a system of differentially weighted scores for each of the five elements. Errors in naming or numbering days and errors in clock time are given one point for each day difference between the correct and the erroneously stated day and for each 30 minutes between clock time and stated time. Errors in naming months are given 5 points for each month of difference between the present and the named month. Errors in numbering years receive 10 points for each year of difference between the present and the named year. The total error score is subtracted from 100 to obtain the test score. Scores of 60 patients with brain disease were compared with 110 control patients (see Table 15-1).

Both control (patients without cerebral disease) and brain damaged patients most commonly erred by missing the number of the day of the month by one or two. For both groups, the second most common error was misestimating clock time by more than 30 minutes. The brain damaged group miscalled the day of the week with much greater frequency than the control patients. Patients with undifferentiated bilateral cerebral disease performed most poorly of all. Applying this

TABLE 15-1
*Temporal Orientation Test Scores for Control and Brain
Damaged Patients*

Subjects	Score			
	100	99	98–95	94 & below
Control (n = 110)	67 (61%)	33 (30%)	10 (9%)	0
Brain damaged (n = 67)	27 (40%)	6 (9%)	19 (28%)	8 (12%)

(Adapted from Benton et al., 1964)

test to frontal lobe patients, Benton (1968) found that it discriminated between bilaterally and unilaterally brain injured patients, for none of the frontal lobe patients with unilateral lesions and 57% of those with bilateral lesions had defective performances.

Time estimation. Benton and his colleagues (1964) also asked their subjects to estimate the passage of a minute. They report that error scores of 21–22 seconds are in the "average range," an error score of 33 seconds is "moderately inaccurate," and scores over 38 seconds are "extremely inaccurate." For neither the control nor the brain injured patient group was there a relationship between poor scores on the Temporal Orientation Test and size of time estimation error, leading the authors to conclude that "temporal orientation and the ability to estimate brief temporal durations reflect essentially independent behavior processes" (p. 119). Another simple time estimation task requires the patient to guess the length of time taken by a just-completed test session (McFie, 1960). Estimations under one-half the actual time are considered failures. Only one of 15 patients whose lesions were localized on the left temporal lobe failed this task although one-third or more of each of the other groups of patients with localized lesions and one-half of those suffering presenile dementia failed.

Talland (1965) used buzzers in testing time estimation of patients with severe memory impairments. The test involves matching durations of and intervals between buzzer signals. These patients made larger errors of both underestimation and overestimation than the control subjects, but the difference between the two groups was not significant. On another series of time estimation tasks, each given on a different day, both control and memory impaired groups underestimated the time lapse while engaged on a task but the memory impaired patients made larger errors, particularly on the longer (3 minutes) rather than the shorter (30 seconds) time interval. Judgments by control subjects of the amount of lapsed time were much less variable than those of the patients.

Discrimination of Recency task.   This technique was developed to test the hypothesis that memories normally carry "time tags" that facilitate their retrieval (Yntema and Trask, 1963). It has proven useful in identifying the hemisphere side of the lesion when both verbal and nonverbal forms of the test have been administered (Milner, 1971). The verbal form consists of 184 cards on which are printed two spondaic words such as "pitchfork" and "smokestack." Each card has a different word pair, but the same word may occur on a number of cards. At intervals in the deck are cards with a question mark between two words. The subject reads the word pairs aloud, and when he comes to the card with the question mark, his task is to indicate which of the two words he saw more recently. Usually both words have come up previously; occasionally only one had already been seen. The nonverbal form of this task presents paired pictures of abstract art.

On the verbal form of this task, normal control subjects recognized an average of 94% of previously seen words when they were paired with new words and correctly guessed relative recency an average of 71% of the time. Both left fronto-temporal and left temporal groups were significantly impaired on one or both of these tasks relative to the control subjects and right brain injured patients. However, the patients with right-sided lesions were defective relative to controls and left brain injured patient groups on the nonverbal version of this task. Patients with frontal lobe involvement had difficulty with the recency aspect of the task; those with temporal lobe involvement had difficulty with recognition.

Space

"Spatial disorientation" refers to different kinds of defects that in some way interfere with the ability to relate to the position, direction, or movement of objects or points in space. In identifying different kinds of spatial disorientation, Benton (1969b) pointed out that they do not arise from a single defect but are associated with damage to different areas of the brain and involve different functions. With the exception of right-left, topographic, and body schema disorientation, however, most disturbances of spatial orientation occur with lesions of the posterior right hemisphere (Weinstein, 1964). As in every other kind of defective performance, an understanding of the disoriented behavior requires careful analysis of its components to determine the extent to which the problem is one of verbal labeling, specific amnesia, visual scanning, visual agnosia, or a true spatial disorientation. Thus comprehensive testing for spatial disorientation requires a variety of different tests.

Estimations of distance.   Both spatial disorientation (Benton, 1969b) and visual scanning defects (Diller et al., 1974) may be involved in impaired judgment of distances. Benton divides problems of distance estimation into those involving local space, i.e., "within 'grasping distance,' " and those involving points in the space "beyond arm's reach." He notes a tendency for patients with disordered spatial orientation to confuse retinal size with actual size, ignoring the effects of distance.

The task of *bisecting a line* elicits distance judgments in local space. The examiner can draw the line for the patient or ask the patient to copy an already drawn horizontal line. (Diller and his group use a 10 mm line.) He then instructs the patient to divide the line by placing an "x" at the center point. The score is the length by which the patient's estimated center deviates from the actual center. When Diller's technique is used, a second score can be obtained for the deviation in length of the patient's line from that of the copied line. Numerical norms are not available for this technique. Noticeable errors are most often made by patients with visual field defects who tend to overestimate the side of the line on the side of the defective field, although the reverse error appears occasionally (Benton, 1969b).

Spatial dyscalculias.   Difficulty in calculating arithmetic problems in which the relative position of the numbers is a critical element of the problem, as in carrying numbers or long division, tends to occur with posterior right hemisphere lesions (see pp. 57–58). This shows up in distinctive errors of misplacement of numbers relative to one another, confusion of columns or rows of numbers, and neglect of one or more numbers, although the patient understands the operations and appreciates the meaning and value of the mathematical symbols.

Tests for spatial dyscalculia are easily improvised. When making up arithmetic problems to bring out a spatial dyscalculia, the examiner should include several relatively simple addition, subtraction, multiplication, and long division problems using two- to four-digit numbers that require carrying for their solution. The problems should be written in fairly large numbers on blank paper so that the patient cannot use lines for visual guidance.

Spatial dyscalculia may show up on only one or two out of ten or 12 problems, since its severity varies. Any single instance of spatial confusion or mishandling of spatial relationships between numbers signals the possible presence of the problem.

Right-left orientation. Since right-left orientation tends to be disrupted by lesions of the left posterior hemisphere, the communication disabilities of a concomitant aphasia may override the more subtle symptoms of directional disorientation. When verbal communication is sufficiently intact, gross testing of direction sense can be accomplished with a few commands, such as "Place your right hand on your left knee," "Touch your left cheek with your left thumb," or "Touch my left hand with your right hand." A. Smith includes a ten-question test, *Right-Left Body Parts Identification: "Show Me"* in his battery of standard test procedures (see Table 15-2). Because the hand the patient should use to indicate the named body part is not specified, patients with lateralized motor disabilities are not put at a disadvantage.

TABLE 15-2
Right-Left Body Parts Identification: Show Me

"Show Me Your:"	"Show Me My:"
(a) Left Hand	(b) Right Ear
(c) Right Hand	(d) Left Eye
(e) Left Ear	(f) Right Hand
(g) Right Eye	(h) Left Ear
(i) Right Ear	(j) Right Eye

(From A. Smith, undated)

The Standardized Road-Map Test of Direction Sense. This easily administered test provides developmental norms for a quick paper and pencil assessment of directional orientation (Money et al., 1965). As the examiner traces a dotted pathway with his pencil, he asks the subject to tell the direction he takes at each turn, right or left. The test is preceded by a demonstration trial on an abbreviated pathway in a corner of the map. Although adult norms are not available, the authors recommend a cut-off point of ten errors (out of the 32 choice points) for evaluating performance regardless of age. They reason that since patients who make fewer than ten errors are probably not guessing, they must possess a reasonably well-developed and intact direction sense. Almost all brain injured patients who are capable of following simple instructions pass this test so that failure is a clear sign of impaired right-left orientation.

Route finding. A not uncommon problem of organic patients is inability to find their way around familiar places or to learn new routes. The disability can be so severe that it may take days before the alert and ambulatory patient can make his way to the bathroom on his ward. This problem often dissipates as the acute stage of the illness passes, but some confusion about locations and slowness in learning new routes may remain. A test for this disability, the *Extrapersonal Orientation Test,* uses visual and tactile route maps laid out on a nine-point square (Weinstein et al., 1956). The patient's task is to translate the drawn lines of the visual map or the string lines of the tactile map into locomotion by walking the designated pattern on a nine-dot square laid out on the floor. Regardless of the sensory mode of presentation or the side of the lesion, frontal lobe patients showed the least impairment, and parietal lobe patients showed the most impairment on this task (Semmes et al., 1963; Teuber, 1964).

Body schema. Disorientation of personal space (*autotopagnosia*) tends not to be associated with problems of localization in space for it is most apt to occur with left frontal lesions (Teuber, 1964) and is also a common concomitant of aphasia (Diller et al., 1974; Weinstein, 1964). The *Personal Orientation Test* calls for the patient (1) to touch the parts of his body named by the examiner, (2) to name parts of his body touched by the examiner, (3) to touch those parts of the examiner's body the examiner names, (4) to touch his body in imitation of the examiner, and (5) to touch his body according to numbered schematic diagrams of the body (see Fig. 15-1) (Weinstein, 1964). A sixth task tests for astereognosis by asking for the names of seen and felt objects.

A comparison of left and right hemisphere damaged patients' performances on this task indicates that the left hemisphere patients have greatest difficulty following verbal directions, whereas patients with right hemisphere lesions are more likely to ignore the left side of their body or objects presented to their left (Raghaven, 1961). Much of the impaired body orientation associated with left posterior lesions appears to be an aspect of a more global aphasic disorder; or it may follow from incomprehension of how single parts relate to a whole structure (De Renzi and Scotti, 1970). Disturbances of body schema occurring with frontal lesions seem to result from disturbances in scanning, perceptual shifting, and postural mechanisms (Teuber, 1964).

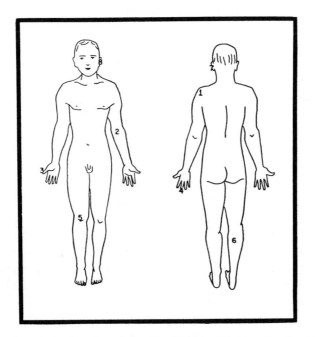

FIG. 15-1. One of the five diagrams of the Personal Orientation Test (Semmes et al., 1963).

Diller and his colleagues (1974) studied body disorientation in relation to scanning problems with the *Body Center Test*. While the examiner taps along the patient's back from shoulder to shoulder, the patient must indicate when he thinks the examiner has reached the center of his back. This procedure is repeated six times, three from each shoulder. Deviations of the guessed center from the actual center are measured in fractions of inches from zero. As on other scanning tests, the performance of patients with severe aphasic disorders was much worse than that of patients with mild aphasia. From the data, it is not possible to determine whether this finding is a function of the severity of the cerebral insult per se or is associated with a sensory disturbance.

MENTAL ACTIVITY VARIABLES

Attention, Concentration, Tracking, and Scanning

Although attention, concentration, and tracking can be differentiated theoretically, in practice they are difficult to separate. Purely attentional defects appear as distractibility or impaired ability for focused behavior of any kind, regardless of the patient's intention. Intact attention is a necessary precondition of both concentration and mental tracking activities. Concentration problems may be due to a simple attentional disturbance, or to inability to maintain a purposeful attentional focus or, as is often the case, to both problems. At the next level of complexity, conceptual tracking can be prevented or interrupted by attention or concentration problems and also by diminished ability to maintain focused attention on one's mental contents while solving problems or following a sequence of ideas.

Most tests of attention and concentration involve some mental or perceptual tracking as well and many of them also involve some form of scanning. The importance of visual scanning in visual perception is well known (Hebb, 1949; Luria, 1966; Weinberg and Diller, 1968; Weinberg et al., 1976). The role of visual scanning in conceptual tracking has only recently become apparent in studies demonstrating the scanning eye movements that accompany the performance of such conceptual tracking tasks as Digits Backward or spelling a long word or name in reverse (Weinberg et al., 1972). Tracking tasks can be complicated by requiring the subject to track two or more stimuli or associated ideas simultaneously, alternatively, or sequentially in what I call *double* or *multiple* tracking behavior. The capacity for double or multiple tracking is one of the first and the one most likely to break down with brain damage. Occasionally, loss of this capacity may be the only documentable mental change following head injury or brain disease. The disturbance appears as difficulty in keeping two or more lines of thought going, as in a cocktail party conversation, in solving two- or three-number addition or multiplication problems mentally, or in remembering one thing while doing another.

Clarifying the nature of an attention problem depends on observations of the patient's general behavior as well as his performance on tests involving concentration and tracking, for only by comparing these various observations can the examiner begin to distinguish the simpler global defects of attention from the more discrete, task-specific problems of concentration and tracking. Further, there is evidence that even impaired attention is not always a global disability but may be specific to the visual or verbal modality and associated with a lesion on the corresponding side of the brain (Diller and Weinberg, 1972).

Verbal tests of attention functions
Two tests make up the classic repertory for the evaluation of attention. One, *Digit Recall*, or *Digit Span*, as it is most usually called (see pp. 208–211), both forward and backward, appears in almost every battery for assessing intelligence, brain damage, or memory, and is an integral part of the mental status examination.

There is little statistical data on the other, *Subtracting Serial Sevens*, for it is not generally used by psychologists. It is part of the mental status examination given by psychiatrists, neurologists, and other medical examiners. The subject is first instructed to "Take seven from 100." When he has done this, he is told, "Now take seven from 93 and continue subtracting sevens until you can't go any further." Patients who are unable to perform Serial Sevens can sometimes handle serial threes ("Take three from 50 . . ."). Patients who cannot perform the simpler serial subtraction task can be asked to count from 20 backwards or say the months of the year backwards, both very simple mental tracking tasks.

A. Smith (1967) gave Serial Sevens to 132 employed adults, most of them with college or professional educations, and found that only 99 performed the task with two errors or less. He thus proved that this test's usefulness in discriminating between normal and brain injured populations does not rest simply on the presence or absence of errors. He also demonstrated that grossly impaired performances are rarely seen in the normal population—only three (2%) of Smith's subjects were unable to complete the task and only six made more than five errors. However, very defective recitations of Serial Sevens are fairly common among brain injured patients (Luria, 1966; Ruesch and Moore, 1943). Serial Sevens can be scored for time taken as well as number of errors by counting pauses that last for five seconds or more. Pauses of more than five seconds between responses also tend to be characteristic of brain injured patients.

Serial Arithmetic. This arithmetic tracking task compounds simple addition and subtraction problems (Talland, 1965). The patient is asked to add or subtract two different kinds of items at a time. For example, the problem could be, "Take six apples and four pears; add three apples and two pears. How many apples and how many pears do you have now?" Increasing the number of items to be added (or subtracted) and using both addition and subtraction adds to the difficulty of the problem. Most of Talland's memory impaired patients could perform this task using paper and pencil; less than half of them could do these problems mentally.

Paced Auditory Serial Addition Test (PASAT). This sensitive test simply requires that the patient add sequentially a series of 60 random digits presented at rates from 1.2 to 2.4 seconds (Gronwall and Wrightson, 1974). For example, if the examiner reads the numbers "2-8-6-1-9," the subject's correct responses, beginning as soon as the examiner says "8," are "10-16-17-26." Scores made by a normal control group are given as percentage correct for each rate of presentation (see Table 15-3). Post-concussion patients consistently performed well below control group averages immediately after injury or return to consciousness. The overwhelming tendency was for their scores to return to normal within 30 to 60 days.

TABLE 15-3
Average PASAT Percent Correct Scores Made by Control Group
at Four Presentation Rates

Presentation rate (seconds)	1.2	1.6	2.0	2.4
Average score (%)	51	66	73	82

(Adapted from Gronwall and Wrightson, 1974)

This technique was developed for taped presentation in order to control the presentation rate but with practice the examiner should be able to deliver the numbers at a reasonably steady one- or two-second rate. The task can also be presented at the subject's response rate, in which case the examiner should record pauses of five seconds and longer. Although the paced delivery format identifies patients whose responses are slowed as well as those who have a tracking disability, the unpaced delivery is more likely to identify those patients whose defective performance is due to a tracking defect.

Nonverbal tests of attention functions
All visual perception tests require visual attention and concentration for successful performance. Visual search and visual scanning tests involve sustained, focused concentration and directed visual shifting. Visual attention functions also enter into the complex scanning and tracking tasks that have proven sensitive to the intellectual impairments resulting from brain injury (see p. 296).

Complex tests of attention functions
   The Symbol Digit Modalities Test (SDMT).   This test preserves the substitution format of Wechsler's Digit Symbol subtest but reverses the presentation of the material so that the symbols are printed and the numbers are written in (see Fig. 15-2) (A. Smith, 1968). This not only enables the patient to respond with the more familiar act of number writing, but also allows a spoken response trial. Both written and oral administrations of the SDMT should be given whenever possible to permit comparisons between the two response modalities. When, in accordance with the instructions, the written administration is given first, the examiner can use the same sheet to record the patient's answers on the oral administration by

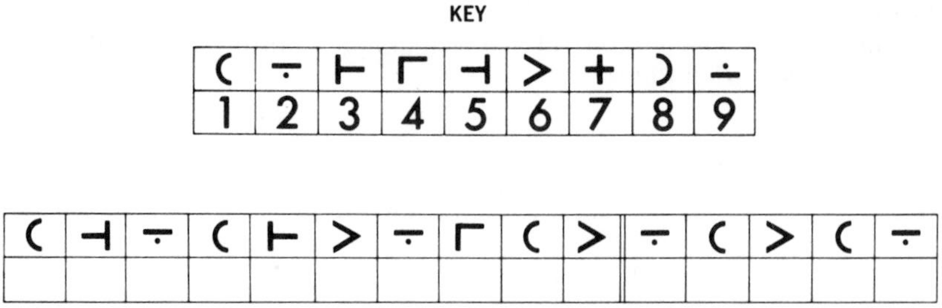

KEY

FIG. 15-2. The Symbol Digit Modalities Test (SDMT). (By Aaron Smith, Ph.D. © 1973 by Western Psychological Services. Reprinted by permission.)

writing them in under the answer spaces. Neither order of presentation nor recency of the first administration appears to affect performance (A. Smith, personal communication). As with the WAIS Digit Symbol subtest, 90 seconds are allowed for each trial; but unlike the WAIS, there are 115 rather than 90 items. The written form of this substitution test also lends itself to group administration for rapid screening of many of the same verbal and visual functions necessary for reading (A. Smith, 1975).

The adult normative population was composed of 420 persons ranging in age from 18 to 74 (see Table 15-4). When applied to 100 patients with "confirmed and chronic" brain lesions, these norms correctly identified 86% of the patient group and 92% of the normal population, using a cut-off point of -1.5 standard deviations below the age norm (A. Smith, personal communication). Smith considers scores below the 1.5 SD cut-off to be "indicative" and those between 1.0 and 1.5 SD's below the age norm to be "suggestive" of cerebral dysfunction. It should be noted that education is positively correlated with the scores of both the written and oral administrations of this test and therefore needs to be taken into account when interpreting the SDMT performance.

A significant performance decrement in one response modality relative to the other naturally points to a dysfunction of that modality. Significant impairment on both administrations reflects visual perceptual, visual scanning (shifting), or oculomotor defects, or general mental or motor slowing (Kaufman, 1968). As with the Digit Symbol subtest, the SDMT is sensitive to the normal effects of aging as well as to brain dysfunction. A complete set of children's norms appears in the test manual (A. Smith, 1973).

TABLE 15-4
Symbol Digit Modalities Test Norms for Ages 18 to 74

Age Group	Mean Educ.	Mean Written Administration	Mean Oral Administration
18–24 (n = 69)	12.7	55.2 (SD 7.5)	62.7 (SD 9.1)
25–34 (n = 72)	13.5	53.6 (SD 6.6)	61.2 (SD 7.8)
35–44 (n = 76)	12.1	51.1 (SD 8.1)	59.7 (SD 9.7)
45–54 (n = 75)	11.7	46.8 (SD 8.4)	54.5 (SD 9.1)
55–64 (n = 67)	11.3	41.5 (SD 8.6)	48.4 (SD 9.1)
65–74 (n = 61)	10.7	37.4 (SD 11.4)	46.2 (SD 12.8)

(Based on Studies by Carmen C. Centofanti)

Trail Making Test (TMT).   This test, originally part of the Army Individual Test Battery (1944), has enjoyed wide use as an easily administered test of visual conceptual and visuomotor tracking. Like most other tests involving attention functions, the *Trail Making Test* is highly vulnerable to the effects of brain injury (Armitage, 1946; Reitan, 1958; Spreen and Benton, 1965). It is given in two parts, A and B (see Fig. 15-3). The patient must first draw lines to connect consecutively numbered circles on one work sheet (Part A) and then connect the same number of consecutively numbered and lettered circles on another work sheet by alternating between the two sequences (Part B).

Some administration and scoring procedures have changed over the years. Originally, the examiner removed the work sheet after three uncorrected errors. Each trial received a score on a ten-point scale depending on the amount of time taken to complete it. Armitage changed this procedure, allowing the patient to finish regardless of the number of errors but accounting for the errors by giving a score of zero to performances in which errors were left uncorrected.

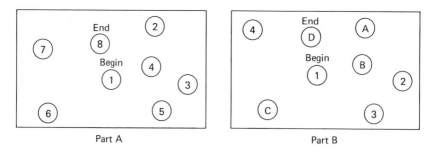

FIG. 15-3. Practice samples of the Trail Making Test.

Reitan (undated) made further changes, requiring the examiner to point out errors as they occur so that the patient could always complete the test without errors and scoring is based on time alone.

This latter method is the one in most common use today. However, the price for a simplified scoring system is paid in diminished reliability, for the measured amount of time includes the examiner's reaction time (in noticing errors), his speed in pointing them out, and the speed with which the patient comprehends and makes the correction. This method penalizes for errors indirectly but does not control for differences in response times and correction styles that can conceivable result in significant biases in the time scores obtained with different examiners.

When interpreting the performance of any test in which response speed contributes significantly to the score, allowances need to be made for the normal slowing of age. The Trail Making Test is no exception, since performance time increases with each succeeding decade (Davies, 1968; Fleming, 1975; Lindsey and Coppinger, 1969) (see Table 15-5). In the single reported study not showing this trend, the average educational level of the control subjects was almost 15 years (Boll and Reitan, 1973). Results of one study suggest that a regular inverse relationship obtains between the amount of time taken to complete either Part A or Part B and intellectual ability as represented by scores on both "verbal" and "nonverbal" tests of intellectual ability (Fleming, 1975). The cutting scores in general use are appropriate for evaluating the performance of younger patients, ages 20 to 39. For this age group, the Trail Making Test performance is within normal limits when Part A is completed in 50 seconds or less, Part B in 79 seconds or less, and the combined

TABLE 15-5
*Distribution of Trail Making Test Scores (in Seconds) for Normal Control
Subjects for the Six Decades Beginning with Age 20*

Age	20 to 39 (n = 180)		40 to 49 (n = 90)		50 to 59 (n = 90)		60 to 69 (n = 90)		70 to 79 (n = 90)	
Part	A	B	A	B	A	B	A	B	A	B
Percentile										
90	21	45	22	49	25	55	29	64	38	79
75	26	55	28	57	29	75	35	89	54	132
50	32	69	34	78	38	98	48	119	80	196
25	42	94	45	100	49	135	67	172	105	292
10	50	129	59	151	67	177	104	282	168	450

(Adapted from Davies, 1968)

time in seconds is 109 or less. However, when applied to normal
control subjects in their seventies, these cutting scores misclassified as brain damaged 92% of the 40 men and 90% of the 40 women
in the group (Davies, 1968). Distributions of scores achieved by
normal older subjects may be used to evaluate the older patients'
performance on this test in lieu of cutting scores.

When the number of seconds taken to complete Part A is relatively much less than that taken to complete Part B, the patient
probably has difficulties in complex—double or multiple—
conceptual tracking. Slow performances at any age on one or both
Parts A and B point to the likelihood of brain damage, but in themselves do not indicate whether the problem is one of motor slowing,
incoordination, visual scanning difficulties, poor motivation, or conceptual confusion.

Reitan and Tarshes (1959) formulated some rules for lateralizing
lesions on the basis of the relationship between the scores on the two
parts of this test. However, using data from this test to lateralize a
lesion is a questionable procedure since 25% of the 44 left hemisphere patients and 28% of the right hemisphere patients making up
the population from which these rules were drawn performed contrary to them. These rules for lateralizing lesions have been supported by some studies (Korman and Blumberg, 1963; Wheeler et al.,
1963). Yet all of a group of seven patients, each unequivocally

diagnosed as having a right hemisphere lesion, were significantly slower on Part B than Part A; Reitan's rules would have called each a left hemisphere patient (Lezak, 1975). It should also be noted that the consistently high diagnostic prediction rates for the Trail Making Test have obtained only when the discrimination has been between brain injured patients and normal control subjects. Its diagnostic effectiveness in differentiating brain injured from psychiatric patients has not been consistent (Brown et al., 1958; Spreen and Benton, 1965; Zimet and Fishman 1970).

Cancellation tasks.   These tests, which require visual selectivity at fast speed on a repetitive motor response task, assess many functions, not least of which is the capacity for sustained concentration. Visual scanning and activation and inhibition of rapid responses are also necessary to the successful performance of cancellation tasks. Thus, lowered scores on these tasks can reflect the general response slowing and inattentiveness of diffuse damage or acute brain conditions or more specific defects of response shifting and motor smoothness or of unilateral spatial neglect.

The basic format for these tests consists of rows of letters or numbers randomly interspersed with a designated target letter or number. The patient is instructed to cross out all target letter or numbers. The performance is scored for errors and for time to completion; or if there is a time limit, scoring is for errors and number of targets crossed out within the allotted time. The possibilities for variations on the basic format are virtually limitless. Several similar tasks can be presented on one page (Weinberg and Diller, 1968). The task can be made more difficult by decreasing the space between target characters or by the number of nontarget characters between the targets (Diller et al., 1974). The task can be made more complex by using gaps in the line as spatial cues (e.g., "cross out every . . . letter that is preceded by a gap" (Talland, 1965)), or by having two target characters instead of one.

Diller and his colleagues (1974) constructed nine different cancellation tasks: two using digits, two using letters, two using easy three-letter words, two using geometric figures (taken from the WISC Coding task), and one using simple pictures. Their basic version of the task consists of six 52-character rows in which the target character is randomly interspersed approximately 18 times in

```
B E I F H E H F E G I C H E I C B D A C H F B E D A C D A F C I H C F E B A F E A C F C H B D C F G H E

C A H E F A C D C F E H B F C A D E H A E I E G D E G H B C A G C I E H C I E F H I C D B C G F D E B A

E B C A F C B E H F A E F E G C H G D E H B A E G D A C H E B A E D G C D A F C B I F E A D C B E A C G


C D G A C H E F B C A F E A B F C H D E F C G A C B E D C F A H E H E F D I C H B I E B C A H C D E F B

A C B C G B I E H A C A F C I C A B E G F B E F A E A B G C G F A C D B E B C H F E A D H C A I E F E G

E D H B C A D G E A D F E B E I G A C G E D A C H G E D C A B A E F B C H D A C G B E H C D F E H A I E
```

FIG. 15-4. Letter Cancellation task: "Cancel C's and E's" (reduced size) (Diller et al., 1974).

each row (see Fig. 15-4). Thirteen control patients had a median error score of 1 on the basic version of the letter and digit cancellation tasks with median performance times of 100 seconds on Letters and 90 seconds on Digits. Stroke patients with right hemisphere lesions were not much slower than the control subjects but had many more errors (median Letters errors = 34, median Digits errors = 24). Patients with left hemisphere lesions made few errors but took up to twice as long (median Letters time = 200 seconds; median Digits time = 160 seconds). Failure on the cancellation tasks appeared to be associated with "spatial neglect" problems of the patients with right hemisphere lesions and with difficulties in the temporal processing of information of left hemisphere patients.

Comparisons between the performances of control subjects and memory impaired patients on a different set of cancellation tasks showed that as a group, the patients worked more slowly and made more errors than the control subjects (Talland, 1965). Their poor performance on this task was attributed to a limited perceptual capacity. However, these patients had all been heavy consumers of alcohol. The growing body of research that implicates an anterior frontal lobe focus in certain of the brain changes associated with alcoholism (Tarter, 1975) raises the possibility that the visual scanning defects of these memory impaired patients may have resulted from motor integration and control problems.

The Sequential Matching Memory Task (SMMT). This task requires "*intense* attention over a considerable period of time" for successful performance (Collier and Levy, undated). It also involves perceptual and response flexibility, since the reference point continually shifts. Although data on this test are limited to one set of experimental studies, it should prove to be an excellent means of measuring the ability to sustain attention.

The *Sequential Matching Memory Task* consists of decks of 3 × 5 inch cards that each have one of two distinctive symbols, such as a plus or a minus. Other than the restriction that four cards with the same symbol not occur in a sequence, the cards are randomly arranged to be exposed to the subject one by one. In a practice trial using 20 cards, the subject must recall the symbol of the card before the previous card (i.e., the card once removed). On test trials, the card to be recalled can be two or more times removed, depending on how difficult the examiner wants the task to be. In the standard administration there are three 35-card trials requiring the subject to remember the card twice removed. In a preliminary study comparing hospitalized epileptic patients and hospitalized postlobotomy patients with a control group of hospitalized psychiatric patients, mostly diagnosed as paranoid schizophrenic, this test differentiated between each patient group and the control group significantly ($p < .01$). The control patients averaged 9+ errors, the epileptic group 13+, and the lobotomized patients 16+ errors per 35-card trial.

SELF-REGULATION

The ability to regulate one's own behavior can be demonstrated both on tests of flexibility and perseverance that require the subject to shift or maintain a course of thought or action according to the demands of the situation. The capacity for flexibility in behavior extends through perceptual, cognitive, and response dimensions. Defects in mental flexibility show up perceptually in defective scanning and inability to change perceptual set easily. Cognitive inflexibility appears in concrete or rigid approaches to understanding and problem solving. Inflexibility of response results in perseverative, stereotyped, nonadaptive behavior and difficulties in regulating and modulating motor acts. In each of these problems there is an inability to shift behavior readily, to conform behavior to rapidly changing demands on the person. This disturbance in the programming of behavior appears in many different contexts and forms and is associated with lesions of the frontal lobes (Luria, 1966; Luria and Homskaya, 1964). Its particular manifestation depends at least in part on the site of the lesion.

Problems in perseverance may also compromise any kind of mental or motor activity. Inability to persevere can result from distractibility, or it may reflect impaired self-control usually associated with frontal lobe damage. In the former case, ongoing behavior is interrupted by some external disturbance; in the latter, dissolution of ongoing activity seems to come from within the patient as he loses interest, slows down, or gives up.

The scanning tests just reviewed are sensitive to a diminished capacity for mental flexibility. The Stroop Test (see pp. 270–271) provides evidence of the ease with which the patient can shift his perceptual set to conform to changing demands. Decreased perceptual shifting also shows up on optical illusions and tests involving visual scanning (see pp. 293–294, 427–434). Analysis of the performance on these and other perceptual tests will enable the examiner to determine whether the disability results from a perceptual defect or from an inability to accommodate to variety and change.

At the cognitive level, mental inflexibility can be more difficult to identify, shading into personality rigidity on the one hand and stupidity on the other. Tests of abstraction that emphasize shifts in concept formation (see pp. 399–405) touch upon mental flexibility.

Another kind of test that assesses inflexibility in thinking is the *Uses of Objects* test, which has also served to identify creativity in bright children (Getzels and Jackson, 1962). The printed instructions ask the subject to write as many uses as he can for five common objects: brick, pencil, paper clip, toothpick, sheet of paper. Two examples are given for each object, such as "Brick—build houses, doorstop," or "Pencil—write, bookmark," with space on the answer sheet for a dozen or more uses to be written in for each object. The tendency to give obvious, conventional responses such as Brick: "to build a wall," or "line a garden path," reflects a search for the "right" or logical solution, which is called *convergent* thinking. In *divergent* thinking, on the other hand, the subject generates many different and often unique and daring ideas without evident concern for satisfying preconceived notions of what is correct or logical. The divergent thinker, for example, might recommend using a brick for a bedwarmer or as a weapon. In recommending this test for use in evaluating mental inflexibility, Zangwill (1966) notes that "frontal lobe patients tend to embroider on the main or conventional use of an object, often failing to think up other, less probable uses. This is somewhat reminiscent of the inability to switch from one principle of classification to another" (p. 397).

Perseverative behavior is one of the hallmarks of response inflexibility. Luria and his group (1966) have developed a number of techniques to elicit perseveration. In one, the patient receives a sheet of paper with several word series typed in rows on it, such as "circle, cross, circle, circle, circle" or "square, cross, circle, cross, cross." The patient is directed to draw the indicated figure above each word as fast as he can. Perseveration problems show up in drawings of a previously commanded figure made to another command, as for instance, continuing to draw a cross to the third, fourth, and fifth command of the first series above. Similar chains of verbal commands will also elicit perseverative tendencies. A variety of figures can be named, including the simple geometric forms, letters, numbers, star, and crescents, etc. Of the common geometric figures, circles are least likely, squares more likely, and triangles most likely to be perseverated (E. Goldberg, 1975).

Difficulties in self-regulation of motor responses can be brought out by tests in which the patient must make converse responses to the examiner's alternating signals (Luria and Homskaya, 1964). For example, if the examiner taps once, the patient must tap twice and vice versa; or if the examiner presses a buzzer to give a long signal, the patient must press for a short signal. Patients with self-regulation problems may irresistibly follow the examiner's response pattern.

Self-regulation problems also appear as difficulty in reversing a motor set. Talland (1965) had both his memory defective patients and his control subjects write S's for 30 seconds, then write reverse S's for 60 seconds and again write standard S's for 60 seconds. On the two 60-second trials, the control subjects wrote an average of 78.2 standard S's and 65.8 reversed S's. The patients produced an average of 78.0 standard S's, but their average of reversed S's was only 35.3.

Similar tests for perseveration, self-regulation, and response control were developed by Tow (1955) to study the effects of frontal lobe surgery. He gave four simple motor tests: (1) The subject writes rows of three small triangles base down alternated with three small triangles base up. (2) The subject writes rows of three H's alternated with rows of three H's on their sides. Pre- and postsurgery error differences on these two tasks were not significant. (3) The subject writes 2 3 4 in one row, the mirror of each digit in the second row, 2 3 4 followed by their mirrors in the third row, and then repeats the three-row sequence. (4) The subject writes a first row of ab cd; a second row of AB CD; and a third row of aAbBcCdD, and again repeats the three-row sequence. On these two tasks, pre- and postsurgery error differences were significant.

Tow coupled these motor set tasks with such tests of perseverance as having the seated patient hold a leg a little above a chair in front of him as long as possible and requiring the patient to write as many three-letter words as he can make up from the letters in the words "constable," "speculate," and "overstate." These three words were chosen because many small words can be formed from each. The words were given one after the other as three separate trials. After surgery, patients tended to let their leg down sooner than before surgery. There was also a decided tendency for their productivity to fall off on the second and third trials of the word task. Tow concluded that "Tests of perseveration measure the tendency of mental processes to lag. Perseveration is involuntary; perseverance implies a voluntary control of the act" (pp. 130–131).

16

BATTERIES AND COMPOSITE TESTS FOR BRAIN DAMAGE

BATTERIES

Two purposes guide the development of neuropsychological test batteries. "Accuracy in prediction is the hallmark of a good diagnostic instrument" (Filskov and Goldstein, 1974), sums up one goal. Tests are chosen—or test data are handled—on the basis of predictive efficiency alone.

A second purpose is the understanding of the nature of organic disabilities. Batteries developed for this purpose provide a standard data collection procedure to include tests that yield a broad behavior sample. Tests in such batteries measure the major intellectual functions across at least auditory and visual, verbal and nonsymbolic modalities, and provide for comparisons between the modalities for each of the major functions (A. Smith, 1975). Test selection may be based as much if not more on usefulness in eliciting different kinds of behavior as on predictive efficiency.

These purposes may appear to be mutually exclusive. In fact, it is possible to construct a test battery that identifies organicity better than chance but still does not cover the major intellectual functions in all significant modalities. However, it is difficult to conceive of a set of tests that could satisfy the requirements of the second purpose but not make good diagnostic discriminations.

There are few formalized batteries for general clinical use although several have been constructed to meet specific clinical or research needs. Among formalized batteries, the best known is the set of tests assembled by Reitan (undated; Reitan and Davison, 1974).

438

Among the batteries constructed for specific purposes are Halstead's battery for testing "biological intelligence" in frontal lobe patients (1947); the Columbia-Greystone battery for studying the intellectual consequences of psychosurgery (Landis, 1952); Benton's six-test frontal lobe battery (1968); and Newcombe's 23-test battery for evaluating the intellectual effects of missile wounds (1969).

Many experienced neuropsychologists assemble their own test batteries for the psychological assessment of brain disorders. A. Smith's (1975) selection of tests for clinical assessment and the set of tests that make up my basic battery (see pp. 443–444 and 89–91) are examples of informal batteries that are subject to change and can be applied flexibly with additions or subtractions to suit the needs of each patient.

In deciding whether to use a ready-made battery, to organize one's own battery, or to reorganize someone else's, the clinician needs to evaluate the battery for suitability, practicability, and usefulness. A battery that is deficient in one of these areas, no matter what its other virtues, will be inadequate for general clinical purposes even though it may satisfy the requirements for some individual cases or research designs.

A *suitable* battery provides an examination that is appropriate to the patient's needs, whether they call for a baseline study, differential diagnosis, rehabilitation planning, or any other type of assessment. Thus, the examination of a patient who seeks help for a memory complaint should contain visual and verbal learning tests and tests of retention and retrieval. Suitability also extends to the specific needs of patients with sensory or motor defects. A suitable battery contains test variations or possibilities for such variations sufficient to provide data on all the major intellectual functions through the handicapped patient's remaining sensory and response modalities.

A *practicable* battery is relatively easy to administer and has inexpensive equipment. It is adaptable to the limitations of the wheel chair or bedridden patient, can be moved by one person, and is transportable by car. Further, a practicable battery does not take so much time as to be prohibitive in cost, exhaust the patient, or greatly limit the number of patients that can be tested by one examiner.

A *useful* battery provides the information the examiner wants. If the examiner decides to rely primarily on one battery of tests for unselected clinical patients, then it must be a multipurpose battery which will aid in diagnosis, give baselines, and supply data for planning and treatment.

There are not now any batteries that satisfy all these criteria, i.e., provide the minimum, maximum, and only set of tests needed in every examination. It is as doubtful whether such a battery can be constructed as whether physicians can devise a single set of examination procedures and laboratory tests that can be efficiently or practicably applied to all patients. Further, although standardized procedures are the heart of reliable assessment, at the present stage of neuropsychological understanding not enough is known to enshrine any set of procedures with a full scale standardization. Present-day batteries, both the informal collections and those for which there are elaborate statistical evaluation procedures, can be no more than early and tentative efforts to deal with the subtle and complex problems of neuropsychological assessment.

Representative Batteries

The Halstead-Reitan Battery
This set of tests has grown by accretion and revision and continues to be revised. It began as a battery of seven tests selected for their power to discriminate between patients with frontal lobe lesions and those with other lesions or normal subjects (Halstead, 1947; Reitan and Davison, 1974).

The Halstead part of the battery consists of the following tests:

1. The *Category Test* is a test of abstracting ability. Stimulus figures, which vary in size, shape, number, intensity, color, and location, and are grouped by abstract principles, are projected on a screen. The subject's task is to figure out the principle relating stimulus subsets and signal his answer by pressing the appropriate key on a simple keyboard. This test is an excellent discriminator between brain damaged and neurologically intact groups (DeWolfe et al., 1971; Shaw, 1966; Spreen and Benton, 1965). The equipment is both expensive and too bulky to be portable.

2. The *Critical Flicker Fusion Test* (CFF) material is a light-flashing stroboscope on which rates of flashing can be adjusted by the subject whose task it is to increase the flash rate until it appears

fused, or steady, to him. It has been dropped from some versions of this battery as being insufficiently discriminating (E. W. Russell et al., 1970).

3. The *Tactual Performance Test* is reviewed on pp. 380–383.

4. The *Rhythm Test* originally appeared in the *Seashore Measures of Musical Talent* (see p. 303).

5. *Speech Sounds Perception Test* is an auditory acuity test, which assesses the subject's ability to discriminate between similar sounding consonants.

6. The *Finger Oscillation Test*, or *Finger Tapping Test*, is also reviewed above (p. 340).

7. The *Time Sense Test* measures the subject's visual-motor reaction time and ability to estimate a just-elapsed time span. The subject is asked to reproduce from sight and then from memory the amount of time required by a sweep hand to rotate around a clock face by pushing a button that starts and stops the sweep hand. The memory component of this test does not discriminate between normal subjects and brain damaged patients and therefore is not in general use although the visual component is part of this battery (Reitan and Davison, 1974).

Other tests in this battery are the *Trail Making Test* (see pp. 429–432); Reitan's modification of the *Aphasia Screening Test by Halstead and Wepman* (see pp. 260–261); a sensory examination that tests for finger agnosia, skin writing recognition, and sensory extinction in the tactile, auditory, and visual modalities; the *Wechsler-Bellevue Intelligence Scale I* or the *WAIS* (see Chapter 8); and the *Minnesota Multiphasic Personality Inventory* (see pp. 464–470). Administration time for the complete Halstead-Reitan Battery runs from six to eight hours.

A distinctive feature of Reitan's handling of the examination data of the Halstead-Reitan Battery has been his reliance on test scores for predicting the nature and the site of the lesion as well as its presence (Wheeler et al., 1963; Wheeler and Reitan, 1963). Reitan preserved Halstead's use of cutting scores and the *Impairment Index* for making gross diagnostic discriminations. The Impairment Index is the number of subtest scores (out of ten) that exceed the cutting scores established by Halstead in his study of frontal lobe patients. Halstead set the cutting score for the Impairment Index at 5 with scores of 4 and lower characterizing the control subjects. Predictions about the site of the lesion and its nature (diffuse or focal, static or changing) are based on statistically identified relationships between test scores. This actuarial approach has encouraged development of computerized interpretations of Halstead-Reitan test protocols (Adams et al., 1975; E. W. Russell et al., 1970).

Halstead developed his norms on a sample of 30 normal control subjects ranging in age from 14 to 50, the average age being 28.3. Subjects over the age of 40 obtain an average Impairment Index score of 5, within the "impaired" range. Older subjects fare most poorly on "tasks requiring the integration of tactile-proprioceptive and perceptual-motor coordination" and on the Category Test (Lewinsohn, 1971; Reitan, 1973).

Evaluations of the Halstead-Reitan battery that have focused on its effectiveness in correctly identifying organic patients, distinguishing them from neurologically intact control subjects, report high rates of correct predictions (S. Goldstein et al., 1973; Lewinsohn, 1973; Reitan, 1955b). However, as with all other psychological tests, prediction rates are less likely to be high when the discriminations to be made are between organic and psychiatric patients. Several studies have questioned whether the Halstead-Reitan battery discriminates between these two kinds of patients better than just one or a few tests. In one, the Bender-Gestalt alone had a higher prediction rate than any of the Halstead tests (Lacks et al., 1970). In another study, only two of 36 discriminations between organic and psychiatric patients made by Halstead test scores proved to be significant, whereas six of 44 WAIS score discriminations were significant (DeWolfe et al., 1971). In a third study, the rate of correct predictions made on the basis of WAIS scores alone was a little better than those made with the full Halstead-Reitan battery (Watson et al., 1968).

Matthews and his coworkers (1966), comparing the efficiency of the individual subtests and the Impairment Index of the Halstead-Reitan battery in separating "neurologic" from "pseudo-neurologic" patients concluded: "In spite of the relatively high levels of statistical significance attained by many of the comparison variables, the use of any single one of them to classify individuals remains a doubtful procedure. Useful cutoff points for the comparison variables could not be established; if raised to a level sufficient to produce a meaningful percentage of correct classifications of brain-damaged subjects, false positives abounded. Even the composite measure, the Impairment Index, was relatively inefficient as a 'yes' or 'no' discriminator. An Impairment Index of 4 or greater correctly classified 91% of the brain damaged patients but misclassified 66% of the 'pseudo-neurologic' subjects. Raising the Impairment Index cutoff point to 6 lowered the frequency of misclassification of 'pseudo-neurologic' subjects to 6% but correct classification of brain-damaged individuals fell to 72%" (p. 250).

Efforts to use the Halstead-Reitan battery for localizing lesions have had equivocal results. This battery does elicit differential performance patterns between patients with left and right hemisphere lesions (Kløve, 1975; Reitan, 1955a). However, these right-left hemisphere differences do not occur with sufficient consistency to warrant basing clinical decisions on the Halstead-Reitan test scores alone (Parsons et al., 1969; Wheeler and Reitan, 1963).

Although the Halstead-Reitan battery has practical limitations in that it is unwieldy, takes a relatively long time to administer, and is not suitable for the thorough examination of patients with sensory or motor handicaps, it does afford one of the more reliable psychological means of identifying patients with brain damage. However, its greatest contribution may not be to diagnostic efficiency, but rather to the practice of neuropsychological assessment, for Reitan undoubtedly has been singularly instrumental in making psychologists aware of the need to test many different kinds of behavior when addressing neuropsychological questions.

Neuropsychological Battery (A. Smith)
The tests that constitute Smith's basic neuropsychological examination (1975) were chosen to provide a well-balanced review of intellectual functions. He includes six standard tests with the WAIS (or WISC for younger subjects): the Visual Organization Test (see p. 286); Raven's Matrices (see pp. 248–251); Administrations A and C of the Benton Visual Retention Test (see pp. 369–374, 325); the Purdue Pegboard Test (see pp. 340–343); the Symbol Digit Modalities Test (see pp. 427–429); and the Peabody Picture Vocabulary Test (see pp. 245–247). In addition, he uses a number of unpublished tests of reading, writing, color naming, identifying body parts, tactile inattention, and memory to round out the battery. The composition of this battery is subject to revision as new tests are developed or

currently used ones prove inadequate for their purpose. The complete battery takes close to three hours to give. There are no norms for the battery as a whole but each test in it has demonstrated sensitivity to a well-defined modality or function impairment or is presently undergoing evaluation.

Luria's Neuropsychological Investigation
Luria's neuropsychological examination techniques have been brought together in a single set of materials comprising a text, manual of instructions, and test cards (Christenson, 1975). Included are the testing instructions and test material for examining the whole range of functions—both neurosensory and intellectual—that he has studied.

COMPOSITE TESTS

Composite tests for brain damage can also be classified according to their purpose. Some are simply screening tests, such as the Hunt-Minnesota Test and the Shipley Institute of Living Scale. These are "two-dimensional" tests in that each measures one class of intellectual activity that tends to be vulnerable to brain damage and another class of intellectual activity that usually remains relatively intact in the presence of brain injury or disease. They purport to do no more than aid in the identification of patients with cerebral disorders by assessing the relative levels of vulnerable and invulnerable activities. In contrast, the Neurological Index of Mental Impairment and the Elizur Test of Psycho-Organicity have additive scoring systems on which cutting scores have been developed. Each of these latter two tests examine a number of different functions thus providing the examiner with a broader range of data for evaluating the patient's disability.

Hunt-Minnesota Test for Organic Brain Damage
This test is based on the observation that brain damage often affects vocabulary and other mental functions differentially (H. F. Hunt, 1943). It contains 16 subtests which, with the exception of the Stanford-Binet Vocabulary subtest, are quite short. All subtests but Vocabulary assess immediate memory, retention, concentration and tracking, or orientation—the functions that tend to be most vulnerable to the effects of chronic diffuse or acute brain disorders. Many of

its items are found in the traditional mental status examination, and all but the Logical Memory subtest of the Wechsler Memory Scale are duplicated in this test.

Evaluations of the Hunt-Minnesota Test have not been encouraging. It has consistently failed to discriminate reliably between normal subjects and patients with organic brain disease, displaying an alarming tendency to call even psychology staff members organic (Aita, Armitage et al., 1947; Yates, 1954).

The Shipley Institute of Living Scale

This test barely qualifies as an organic battery, since it consists of only two subtests (Shipley, 1940, 1946). It was originally developed to screen mentally deteriorated psychiatric patients from other patient groups, but its use has been extended to screening for organicity as well. It is an easily administered paper and pencil test which, like the Hunt-Minnesota Test, is based on the observation that performance on vocabulary tests is often least affected by brain injury. Instead of a comparison between the vocabulary score and memory and attention test results, vocabulary performance is compared with performance on a verbal abstraction test under the assumption that, with mental deterioration, the ability to form abstractions will erode sooner than the basic verbal skills reflected in vocabulary test scores. The test is not standardized for age, sex, or performance on intellectual ability tests, and in fact, the frequency of "organic" scores increases with age (Yates, 1954).

Although this test is still in clinical use (Lubin, 1971), most research studies report that it fails to discriminate between organic patients and normal control subjects as well as between different categories of neuropsychiatric patients (Aita, Armitage et al., 1947; Parker, 1957; Savage, 1970). In one study the Shipley Scale was described as "the most useful single instrument" for separating neurotic from brain concussion patients, but schizophrenic and depressive patients had been eliminated from the patient pool (Abbott et al., 1943). Another study in which the Shipley Scale did identify patients with intellectual impairment indicates that it may be useful for coarse screening of thought disorders without distinguishing between organic and functional problems (Prado and Taub, 1966).

The Neurological Index of Mental Impairment (NIMI)

The NIMI was developed primarily to help medical practitioners evaluate their patients' cerebral functioning by means of a standardized inventory of behavior that can be quickly administered at bedside or in the clinic; it is suitable for reasearch as well (Drake et al., undated; 1973). Although Drake and his colleages identify this test as an instrument for the evaluation of mental status, the NIMI covers both more and less than the traditional mental status examination. Its chief focus is on intellectual functions for which there are 12 different brief subtests. The NIMI also provides for one-word descriptions of the patient's appearance, examination behavior, and emotional status. The unimportance of social and emotional aspects of the patient's behavior relative to intellectual functioning is reflected in the allotment of only 15 of the total possible 170 score points to nonintellectual behavior.

The NIMI is divided into four subsections. The first of these, "Responsiveness," contains multiple-choice descriptions of the patient's appearance, cooperation, self-expression, affect, mood, insight, and level of awareness. The next section is entitled "Auditory Motor." The verbal subsection contains three subtests of (1) immediate verbal recall (of an address and a sentence), (2) interpretation of proverbs, and (3) verbal abstraction (similarities and differences). The numerical part of the "Auditory Motor" section also contains three subtests, of (1) digits forward and backward, (2) addition and subtraction, and (3) the Serial Sevens subtraction subtest. Section three, "Visual Motor," contains three subtests: (1) drawing a clock face, (2) filling in and noting the center of a printed cube, and (3) copying a complex design and then drawing it from memory. Section four concerns "Orientation and Attention." It contains the usual time, place, and person orientation questions, a set of double simultaneous stimulation trials to test for tactile and visual extinction, and question involving right-left orientation, finger recognition, and immediate memory.

A dual scoring system provides point scores for every item and for ten "Impairment Index" scores credited for specific qualitative defects—such as perseveration or certain gross errors on the drawing tests—and for markedly low scores on five test items. By means of the dual scoring system, the examiner should be able to differentiate between persons who are merely dull and those who are brain damaged, for dull persons may get low scores but they are much less likely to exhibit the gross performance defects that merit a score on the Impairment Index. Conversely, bright patients with specific neurological disabilities may achieve high total point scores, but the Impairment Index will call attention to specific behavior dysfunctions associated with brain damage.

Although far from providing a thorough review of intellectual behavior, this test does cover enough of the major functions for most screening purposes. The dual scoring system should minimize both false positive and false negative screening errors. In addition, the multidimensional character of the NIMI affords a behavioral description of the patient to aid in answering critical diagnostic questions concerning the nature and extent of the patient's disabilities. Lack of systematic evaluations of this test precludes much reliance on the scores, but the test certainly appears worthy of clinical trials and systematic study.

The Elizur Test of Psycho-Organicity

This test represents an ambitious effort to "differentiate organics from non-organics" quickly, conveniently, and objectively by a purportedly multidimensional instrument uncontaminated by "intelligence factors" and with broad applicability (Elizur, 1969). It contains two forms (child and adult) for each of three tasks: (1) *Drawing Sub-Test,* four geometric figures drawn from memory following a five-second exposure; (2) *Digits Sub-Test,* oral presentation of a series of 20 numbers of five digits or fewer for immediate recall; and (3) *Blocks Sub-Test,* four Kohs 2 × 2 block designs to copy. Each subtest is scored on a point system but no rationale or data are offered to explain either the kinds of errors selected for scoring or the differences in point values given to the errors.

"Validation Studies" for the adult form are based on two samples of 35 persons each, an "organic group" composed of patients with a variety of neurological diagnoses and a control group matched for age, sex, and "IQ" derived from an unstated source. Statistical comparisons separate these groups at the .01 level but the overlap is considerable. Elizur found cutting scores "suggested by the data" for each subtest and identified better than 80% of both "organics" and "non-organics," using the same two groups of 35 from which he derived the scores. Since the subtests, point system, and cutting scores have not been evaluated by cross-validational studies, the usefulness of the scoring system and the cutting scores for diagnostic purposes remains highly questionable.

17
TESTS OF PERSONAL AND SOCIAL ADJUSTMENT

The assessment of personal and social adjustment contributes to the neuropsychological examination in several important ways. In order to evaluate the patient's performance on the intellectual tests, the examiner needs a basis for estimating the extent to which emotional state, motivation, and characterological predisposition affect the patient's efficiency. In some cases, documentation of emotional and social behavior patterns that are symptomatic of particular brain disorders may play as much or more of a role in the formulation of a diagnosis as do test score patterns of intellectual impairment. Furthermore, subtle aspects of intellectual dysfunction sometimes show up in the patient's responses to relatively unstructured tests of personal and social adjustment when they are masked by the more familiar and well-structured formats of the intellectual tests.

THE MENTAL STATUS EXAMINATION

The mental status examination, a structured interview, usually takes place during the examiner's initial session with the patient. It is the only formal procedure for assessing intellectual functions in psychiatric or neurological examinations. Psychologists often dispense with it since most of the data obtained in the mental status examination is acquired in the course of a thorough neuropsychological evaluation. However, by beginning the examination with the brief review of intellectual and social behavior afforded by the mental status examination, the psychologist may be alerted to problem

448

areas that will need intensive study. He will also quickly learn if the patient's general level of functioning is too low for standard adult assessment techniques, and he is more likely to discover personal idiosyncracies or emotional problems that may interfere with the examination or require special attention or procedural changes.

Some of the mental status information is gained by direct questioning; much of it comes from careful observation of the patient during the course of the interview. Almost every clinical textbook or manual in psychiatry and neurology contains a guide to the mental status examination. Volle (1975) gives examples of a variety of questions, touching upon many different areas of intellectual and social/ emotional functioning, that can be used in a diagnostic interview. Different authors organize the components of the mental status examination in different ways and different examiners ask some of the questions differently, but it always covers the following aspects of the patient's behavior:

1. *Appearance.* The examiner notes the patient's dress, grooming, carriage, facial expressions and eye contact, mannerisms, and any unusual movements.

2. *Orientation.* This concerns the patient's appreciation of time, place, person, and of his present situation (see pp. 416–417). Some examiners also inquire about the patient's awareness of the examiner's role.

3. *Speech.* Observations are made of both delivery and content of speech. The examiner looks for deviations from normal rate, tone quality, articulation, phrasing, and smoothness and ease of delivery as well as for misuse or confusion of words, grammatical and syntactical errors, perseverations, dysnomia, and other defects in word production and organization.

4. *Thinking.* In patients with aphasic disorders or verbal dyspraxias, and in some with severe functional disturbances such as profound depression with motor slowing, it can be difficult to distinguish speech and thought disorders. In most patients, speech can be evaluated separately from such characteristics of thinking as mental confusion, quality and appropriateness of associations, logic, clarity, coherence, rate of thought production, and such specific thinking problems as blocking, confabulation, circumstantiality, or rationalization.

5. *Attention, concentration, and memory.* In this review of immediate, recent, and remote memory, the examiner inquires about the patient's early and recent history, asking for names, dates, places, and events. He gives digit span (see pp. 208–211) and asks for recall of three or four words immediately and again after an intervening task or five more minutes of interview (see p. 345). Serial Sevens (see pp. 425–426) and digits reversed are the standard mental status concentration tasks.

6. *Intellectual functioning.* Estimation of the level of general intellectual functioning is based on quality of vocabulary, reasoning, judgment, and organization of thought as well as answers to questions about topics of general information, fairly simple arithmetic problems, and abstract reasoning tasks. Usually the patient is asked to explain one or two proverbs (see pp. 394–395) and to give "similarities" and "differences" (see pp. 395–397).

7. *Emotional state.* Both *mood* (the patient's prevailing emotional tone) and *affect* (the range and appropriateness of his emotional responses) need to be distinguished and reported. Mood constitutes the ground, affect the figure of the patient's emotional behavior.

8. *Special preoccupations and experiences.* The examiner looks for reports or expressions of bodily concerns, distortions of self-concept, obsessional tendencies, phobias, paranoidal ideation, remorse or suicidal thoughts, delusions, hallucinations, and strange experiences such as dissociations, fugue states, feelings of impersonalization or unreality.

9. *Insight.* This refers to the patient's self-understanding, his appreciation of his condition, and his expectations and plans.

The mental status examination of a reasonably cooperative, verbally intact patient takes 20 to 30 minutes. The examiner's experience and training provide the standards for evaluating much of the patient's responses and behavior, for outside of questions drawn from such standardized tests as the Wechsler or Stanford-Binet scales, there are no quantitative norms.

Many of the mental status items can be integrated into an introductory interview to provide data on most of the behavior covered by a mental status examination in the course of taking the patient's history and discussing his present situation and future plans. For example, the patient's knowledge about his present income, where it comes from, how much he gets from what sources, and his most recent living arrangements reflects the integrity of his recent memory. He will also be performing calculations and indirectly demonstrating the quality of his concentration ability if asked to tell the amount of his total income when it comes from several sources, his annual rent or house payments based on the monthly cost, or the amount of monthly income left after he has paid for housing. Some patients who are concerned about being "crazy" or "dumb" are very touchy about responding to the formal arithmetic questions or memory tests of the mental status examination. These same patients often remain cooperative if they do not perceive the questions as challenging their mental competence.

The Mini-Mental State

This little test is an abbreviated mental status examination (Folstein et al., 1975). It was designed to test cognitive functions simply and quickly and to produce a score that will reflect the severity of intellectual impairment. Administration takes from five to ten minutes. Both administration and scoring are easily learned and are standardized (see Fig. 17-1).

Sixty-three elderly (mean age = 73.9) normal control subjects comprised the standardization population. With a maximum obtainable score of 30, the elderly control subjects and younger patients with functional psychiatric disorders achieved scores in the 24.6 to 27.6 range. Scores of several groups of senile patients ranged from 9.6 to 12.2. There was no overlap between the aged control subjects and the senile patients. This test has proven useful in registering changes in the intellectual functioning of psychiatric patients as they respond to treatment.

PERSONALITY TESTS

The search for "organic" test responses by means of which the examiner can readily identify the brain injured patient has been extended to personality tests as well. Efforts to diagnose brain disease from personality test responses have proceeded in two different directions. Some investigators have sought to identify "organic personalities" from qualitative characteristics or patterns of test responses; others have looked for traces of brain disease in tell-tale "organic signs." Both avenues of investigation have been fruitful. Some tests, such as the MMPI or Draw-a-Person, lend themselves more readily to one kind of data handling than the other; others, such as the Rorschach technique, yield both kinds of data and thus, in some instances, can serve as particularly rich sources of information about the interaction between cognitive deficits, personality characteristics, and personal adjustment.

One major classification of personality tests categorizes them either as objective tests, structured to maximize the likelihood that every subject will interpret the stimuli (test questions) in much the same way, or as projective, "unstructured," tests, which are valuable to the extent that the test stimuli may be variously interpreted. How-

Patient _____

Examiner _____

Date _____

MINI MENTAL STATE

Score   Orientation

( )   What is the (year) (season) (month) (date) (day)? (5 points)

( )   Where are we? (state) (county) (town) (hospital) (floor)
(5 points)

Registration

( )   Name 3 objects: 1 second to say each. Then ask the patient
to repeat all three after you have said
them. 1 point for each correct. Then repeat them until he learns them. Count
trials and record _____.
(3 points)

Attention and Calculation

( )   Serial 7's. 1 point for each correct. Stop at 5 answers.
Or spell "world" backwards. (Number correct equals letters
before first mistake - i.e., d l o r w = 2 correct).
(5 points)

Recall

( )   Ask for the objects above. 1 point for each correct. (3 points)

Language Tests

( )   name - pencil, watch (2 points)

( )   repeat - no ifs, ands or buts (1 point)

( )   follow a 3 stage command: "Take the paper in your right hand,
fold it in half, and put it on the
floor." (3 points)

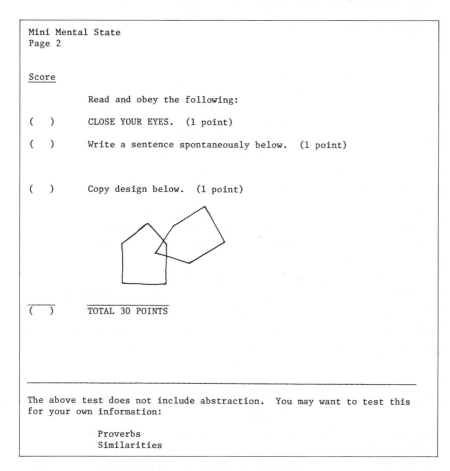

Mini Mental State
Page 2

Score

    Read and obey the following:

(   )   CLOSE YOUR EYES. (1 point)

(   )   Write a sentence spontaneously below. (1 point)

(   )   Copy design below. (1 point)

(   )   TOTAL 30 POINTS

The above test does not include abstraction. You may want to test this
for your own information:

        Proverbs
        Similarities

FIG. 17-1. Mini-Mental State (Folstein et al., 1975).

ever, even the stimulus material of seemingly structured tests, such
as personality questionnaires, can be subject to different interpretations (Carson, 1969b). The distinction here between projective and
objective personality tests follows the common practice of calling
"projective" those tests with relatively less structured stimulus
material that allow the patient open-ended responses, and calling
questionnaire type tests "objective" without regard to the issue of
the extent to which questionnaire test responses also register projection (Cronbach, 1970).

Projective Personality Tests

Clinical psychology's credibility as a science rests on the assumption that a person's behavior is the product of the totality of his experiences, his attitudes, his capacities, and his own uniquely organized perceptual, cognitive, and response characteristics. From this cornerstone derive many of the principles that guide the clinical psychologist's thinking and activities. One of these is the *projective hypothesis,* which holds that when confronted with an ambiguous or unstructured stimulus situation, people tend to *project* their own needs, experiences, and unique way of looking at the world onto it; i.e., they perceive the external stimuli through a reflection of their attitudes, understandings, and perceptual and response tendencies, and interpret the compounded percept as external reality (C. H. Graham, 1965).

Projective testing utilizes this principle to elicit the patient's characteristic response tendencies. A projective test may be comprised of cloud or inkblot pictures, or pictures of persons in vague or ill-defined scenes, or it may consist of a set of instructions to draw a person or to complete sentence stems. The common denominator for all projective tests is that they are techniques that tend "to induce the individual to reveal his way of organizing experience by giving him a field ... with relatively little structure and cultural patterning so that the personality can project upon that plastic field his way of seeing life, his meanings, significances, patterns, and especially his feelings. Thus we elicit a projection of the individual's private world because he has to organize the field, interpret the material, and react affectively to it" (Frank, 1939, p. 391).

The differences in the projective responses between persons, between diagnostic groups, between ages and sexes and cultures, appear in both the *content* of their responses and in the *formal—* structural and organizational—qualities of the content: in the *how* as well as the *what* of a response. Analysis of these complementary aspects of projective productions can often give the examiner a look at the inner workings of the subject's mind that would be difficult to obtain as quickly or in as clear-cut a fashion by any other method.

Projective techniques may be compared to the EEG or any other diagnostic technique which may contribute to the evaluation of a highly complex system in which there are multiple interacting variables, for no single instrument can provide definitive answers to all questions about such a system (J. Fisher and Gonda, 1955). By themselves, EEG findings are of only limited usefulness; but in the context of a complete neurological study, they can be invaluable. The same holds true for the data of a projective study; projective test data alone provide a very incomplete picture of the subject. When taken out of context of interview, history, and medical information, projective test data become insubstantial and unreliable. When used appropriately, projective material complements other kinds of examination data.

Certain projective techniques have contributed significantly to the evaluation and understanding of brain injury. The effects of brain injury may influence the manner in which a person perceives the world, and the ease and flexibility with which he sorts, selects, organizes, or critically evaluates his own mental contents in his efforts to respond to an ambiguous situation. Close and time-consuming observation of the patient as he goes about his daily affairs is the best method of finding out when and how his intellectual impairments affect his behavior. Short of such exacting procedures, projective testing may be the most effective means of answering these questions.

A number of projective response tendencies characterize the behavior of brain damaged persons. Regardless of the technique employed, these response tendencies show up in the *protocols* (the record of test responses) of some brain injured patients and occur much less frequently in the responses of neurologically intact subjects.

1. *Constriction.* Responses become reduced in size. If they are verbal, the patient employs few words, a limited vocabulary, a decreased range of content. If the responses are graphic, drawings are small, unelaborated, and important details may be left out. There will be little if any evidence of creativity, spontaneity, or playfulness in the responses.

2. *Stimulus-boundedness.* Responses tend to stick closely to the bare facts of the stimulus (i.e., to a story telling task with a picture stimulus, "This is a man, this is a woman and a young woman, and there is a horse. It's a farm"; or to an inkblot, "This is an ink splotch; that's all I see. Just an ink splotch"). There may be a "sticky" quality to the patient's handling of the test material in that once he attends to one part of the stimulus, or gives one association, he seems helpless to do much more than reiterate or elaborate on his initial response.

3. *Structure-seeking.* The patient has difficulty in spontaneously making order or sense out of his experiences. He will search for guidance anywhere he can and depend on it uncritically. Structure-seeking is reflected in tendencies to adhere to the edge of the page or to previously drawn figures when drawing (see Fig. 13-4 for a classic example of this tendency), or to seek an inordinate amount of help from the examiner.

4. *Response rigidity.* Difficulty in shifting, in being flexible, in adapting to changing instructions, stimuli, and situations shows up in projective tests as response perseverations (i.e., mostly "bat" or "butterfly" responses to the inkblot cards; an unusual number of identical phrases given to sentence completion stems such as "Most bosses *good*," "Thinking of my mother *good*," "A wife *good*," "When I was a child *good*"). Response rigidity may also show up in failure to produce any response at all in a changing situation, or in poorer quality of response under changing conditions than when repetitively dealing with a similar kind of task or working in the same setting.

5. *Fragmentation.* Fragmented responses are related to the "organic" tendency to *concreteness* and difficulty in organization. Many brain injured patients are unable to take in the whole of a complex situation and organize it to make unified sense out of it, but can only respond in a piecemeal, pedantically matter-of-fact manner. This can be seen in responses that comprehend only part of a total stimulus situation normally grasped in a single gestalt (i.e., a human figure drawing constructed by accretion of the parts; an inkblot response, "leg," to what is commonly perceived not as an isolated leg but as the leg of a whole human).

6. *Simplification.* Simplified responses are poorly differentiated or detailed whole percepts and responses (such as "bat" without details, or "leaf" or "tree stump" to inkblot stimuli; or crudely outlined human figure drawings with minimal elaborations; or six- or eight-word descriptions instead of a creative response on a story telling task).

7. *Conceptual confusion* and *spatial disorientation.* Both organic and functionally disturbed patients may give responses reflecting logical or spatial confusion. Differential diagnosis depends on such other response characteristics as symbolic content, expansiveness, variability of quality, and emotional tone.

8. *Confabulation.* Illogical or inappropriate compounding of otherwise discrete percepts or ideas is a characteristic common to both organic and functional thought disorders. Organic patients are more likely to produce confabulatory responses in which the naturally unrelated percepts or ideas become irrationally linked because of spatial or temporal contiguity, giving them a stimulus-bound or "sticky" quality. Confabulations in which the linkage is based on a conceptual association are more typical of functionally disordered thinking.

9. *Hesitancy and doubt.* Regardless of performance quality or the amount and appropriateness of reassurance, many brain damaged pa-

tients exhibit continuing uncertainty and dissatisfaction about their perceptions and productions.

It is rare to find the protocol of a brain damaged patient in which all of these characteristics occur, although many brain injured persons display at least a few of them. When one type occurs two or three times in a single test, or crops up on several different tests, or when two or three different "organic" characteristics appear in a single test protocol, brain damage should be suspected.

The Rorschach Technique

The Rorschach test is probably the best known of the projective techniques. It was developed in the early 1920's by Hermann Rorschach, a Swiss psychiatrist, who was interested in how his patients' mental disorders affected their perceptual efficiency. He selected the present set of ten inkblots out of approximately 1,000 he made by dropping ink on paper, folding it, and opening it again to get a generally symmetrical design. His criterion for selection was how well the design elicited imaginal responses (Rorschach, 1942).

The subject is shown the blots one card at a time and invited to "tell what the blot looks like, reminds you of, what it might be; tell about everything you see in the blot." The examiner keeps a record of what the patient says. Most examiners note response time for the first response to each card, and many record the total testing time, but there is no time limit. If the patient gives no response or only one response to the first or second blot, the examiner can encourage him to produce more once or twice. I tell patients who offer only one response to the first card that, "Sometimes people can make out more than one thing in a blot." If they still produce only one response to the second blot, I repeat the same statement and then let the matter drop. Other than occasional encouragement as needed, the examiner says nothing during this first, *free association*, phase of the test administration.

After going through all the cards, the examiner conducts the *inquiry* phase in which he questions the patient about what part of the blot was used for each response and what qualities in the blot contributed to each percept. During the inquiry, the examiner also attempts to clarify confusing or vague responses and elicit associations to the responses.

The last part of the Rorschach examination, *testing the limits,* is not always conducted. In this phase, the subject is asked about response categories or card qualities he failed to handle spontaneously, to see if he is capable of making that kind of response at all.

There are a number of scoring systems in general use, all of them variants of Rorschach's original system, and all of them equally effective in the hands of a skilled examiner (Beck, 1961; Beizmann, 1970; Klopfer et al., 1954; Rapaport et al., 1968). The scoring systems are used for categorizing and quantifying the responses in terms of mode of approach and subject matter. Every scoring system includes scoring for the following major response variables:

1. Number of responses.
2. The portion of the inkblot involved in the response: whole, obvious part, or obscure part.
3. Color and shading.
4. Movement (e.g., "*dancing* bears," "*bowing* waiters").
5. Percentage of percepts that are "good," i.e., commonly perceived.
6. Figure-ground reversals.

Responses are also scored for

7. Content, such as human, animal, anatomy, or landscape.
8. Very great frequency or rarity of occurrence.

The scoring pattern and the verbatim content of the responses are then interpreted in terms of actuarial frequencies and the over-all configuration of category scores and content. There are a number of rules of thumb and statistical expectancies, evolved over fifty years of Rorschach experience, which suggest relationships between category scores or score proportions and behavioral or emotional characteristics. These rules and expectancies are only suggestive: any attempt to relate *this* Rorschach response or category score or proportion between scores to *that* specific behavior or mental or emotional characteristic, out of context of the panoply of responses and the total examination situation, is a misuse of this technique. No single Rorschach response or set of responses, taken alone, has any more or less meaning or diagnostic value than any single sentence or gesture taken by itself.

Variables that contribute to the *formal* aspect of the Rorschach performance include the number and appropriateness (form quality) of the responses, use of shape, color, shading, and movement (the *determinants*) in the formulation of a response; and the location, relative size, and frequency of use of identifiable parts of the blots. In analyzing the *content* of the responses, the examiner notes their appropriateness and usualness as well as any repetition or variation of topics, the presence and nature of elaborations on a response, emotional tone, and evidence of thought disorder or special preoccupations. Gratuitous (i.e., unnecessary for clear communication) or extraneous elaborations of a percept may reflect the patient's special preoccupations and concerns. Unusual or idiosyncratic elaborations, particularly of the most common and easily formed percepts (i.e., the whole blot animal—bat or crab—of card I, the "dancing" figures of card III, the "flying" creature of card V, the pink animals at the sides of card VIII, and the tentacled blue creatures of card X) sometimes convey the patient's self-image. Thus, it is not uncommon for a brain injured patient to perceive the "bat" or "butterfly" of card V or the blue "crab" of card X as dead or injured, or to volunteer descriptions of these creatures as "crazy" or "dumb"; e.g., a "crazy bat," a "dumb bunny."

The appeal of a sign system for simple and reliable identification of patients with brain disease has attracted the attention of many Rorschach clinicians and researchers (Burgemeister, 1962; Goldfried et al., 1971). Most Rorschach sign systems are constructed of quantifiable aberrant responses or response tendencies, which have appeared with sufficient frequency in protocols of brain injured patients and sufficient rarity in the protocols of other kinds of patients to warrant the conclusion that they are associated with brain damage to a significant degree. For this reason, organic sign systems share many of the same signs (Hughes, 1948; Piotrowski, 1937; Ross and Ross, 1942).

The most widely used sign system consists of ten signs (Piotrowski, 1937):

1. R. Less than 15 *responses* in all.
2. T. Average *time* per response is greater than one minute.
3. M. There is but one *movement* response if any.
4. Cn. The subject *names colors* (e.g., "a pinkish splotch") instead of forming an association (e.g., "pinkish clouds").
5. F%. Percentage of *good form* responses is below 70 (see pp. 288–289) for a discussion of Rorschach form quality).

6. *P%*. Percentage of *popular* responses is below 25 (see p. 289).

7. *Rpt*. *Repetition* refers to perseveration of an idea in response to several inkblots.

8. *Imp*. *Impotency* is scored when the patient recognizes his response is unsatisfactory but neither withdraws nor improves it.

9. *Plx*. *Perplexity* refers to the hesitancy and doubt displayed by many organic patients about their perceptions.

10. *AP*. The examiner must determine when a pet expression is repeated so often and indiscriminately as to qualify as an *automatic phrase*.

In introducing these signs, Piotrowski notes that "no single sign alone points to abnormality in the psychiatric sense, to say nothing of organic involvement of the brain. It is the accumulation of abnormal signs in a record that points to abnormality" (p. 529). He also recommends that the examiner use caution by not scoring doubtful signs. He considers five to be the minimum number of his signs needed to support an inference of cortical brain disease.

Piotrowski's signs have consistently demonstrated their usefulness in distinguishing brain damaged patients from control subjects; but like so many other "organic" signs, they do not differentiate chronic schizophrenics from organic patients (Goldfried et al., 1971; Suinn, 1969). Thus, psychotic populations will produce a good many false positive protocols. On the other hand, Piotrowski's signs also produce false negatives, for absence of the requisite five signs is no guarantee that the patient is free of brain damage (Sklar, 1963). Yet, with all these problems, the fact that the Piotrowski signs identify the diagnostic category of no fewer than 51% and as many as 97% of the patients (organic and mixed psychiatric) and control subjects in 11 reported studies testifies to its usefulness, particularly with populations in which the frequency of chronic schizophrenia tends to be low. Of the ten Piotrowski signs, all but three—M, P%, and Cn—effectively separate brain injured from nonpsychiatric groups (Goldfried et al., 1971). Four of these—Plx, Imp, Rpt, and AP—have been reported as particularly sensitive to mild and moderate organic conditions (Baker, 1956a).

Dörken and Kral (1952) took another approach to the challenge of identifying organic patients by means of Rorschach indicators. Their seven signs are evidence of the *absence* of organicity; i.e., absence of the intellectual deficits that commonly accompany brain injury. Although these signs differ from Piotrowski's and others using the positive sign approach, three of them have their opposite counter-parts on the positive sign scales. The only study other than the original one reporting on this system indicates that it produces such large numbers of false positives (26.3%) and false negatives (57.9%) that it is not clinically useful (J. Fisher et al., 1955).

Other investigators have developed lists of response and be-havioral aberrations that can be treated as "organic" signs without offering cutting scores or frequency norms. Baker (1956a) reported 23 different signs and response characteristics of organicity, includ-ing four of Piotrowski's signs. Four of her indicators are also among the nine listed by Aita, Reitan, and Ruth (1947) in addition to Piotrowski's ten. Neither Baker nor Aita and his colleagues provided scoring standards for the additional signs. Instead, their signs de-scribe behavior that frequently accompanies brain injury, none of them being diagnostic in itself. The signs common to both lists are (1) *inflexibility*, difficulty in producing alternative interpretations of the same blot, identified as an organic tendency by Lynn et al. (1945) too; (2) *concrete response*, difficulty in organizing whole re-sponses, lack of characterizing or attributing elaboration; (3) *cata-strophic reaction,* emotional reaction to testing so disruptive as to render the patient unable to respond; and (4) *covers part of card,* an uncommon but reliable sign (see p. 289).

Identification of brain injured patients on the basis of clinical interpretations of the Rorschach protocol rests in part on recogni-tion of aberrant responses and in part on the reconstruction of rele-vant dimensions of personality from the content and pattern of re-sponses as well as the patient's nonverbal behavior and extraneous verbalizations (Baker, 1956b; Brussel et al., 1942). M. M. Hall and G. C. Hall (1968) took this approach to evaluate the Rorschach re-sponse characteristics of right and left hemisphere damaged pa-tients by statistical analysis (discriminant functions). They used such data as perplexity, fabulizing (making story elaborations), the total number of responses, and the sum of movement responses to de-scribe the personality characteristics that differentiate patients with right from those with left hemisphere lesions. Harrower-Erickson (1940) studied the personality of brain tumor patients by means of the Rorschach, evaluating their performance by the Piotrowski sign method and also interpreting the behavior and personality implica-tions of such aberrant features as the low number of responses, relative absence of color or movement responses, and lack of shading responses.

The Rorschach is particularly useful in the differential diagnosis of psychiatric patients suspected of having an organic brain disorder. These patients usually carry a diagnosis of schizophrenia because of withdrawn, disruptive, or erratic behavior and complaints of intrusive ideas, mental confusion, or difficulty in thinking. Many have histories of head injury; in others, the behavioral changes just seemed to happen, sometimes following a period of stress, sometimes without apparent reason. The discrimination between an organic and a functional diagnosis is based on the much greater frequency with which schizophrenic patients produce bizarre, symbolic, personalized, or "crazy" associations to the inkblots. The absence of frankly psychotic associations does not rule out the possibility of a functional disorder; many chronic schizophrenics, particularly if they have been institutionalized or have settled into a fairly simple living routine for a long time, tend to produce few, barren, and vague Rorschach responses without frankly psychotic ideation. By the same token, the presence of psychotic thinking does not preclude the possibility of brain damage. However, absence of psychotic thinking tendencies on the Rorschach increases the likelihood that the patient's behavioral disturbances arise at least in part from brain injury.

It is difficult to cast much of the data on which clinical inferences are based, or the inferences themselves, into a form suitable for statistical analysis (Potkay, 1971). However, for clinical purposes, the integration of inferences drawn from both the sign and the clinical interpretation approaches is apt to yield the most information, with each approach serving as a check on the appropriateness of conclusions drawn from the other. By this means, symptomatic cognitive and behavioral defects can be viewed in interaction with personality predispositions so that the broader social and personal implications of the patient's brain injury may be illuminated.

Story telling techniques
Story telling is a particularly rich test medium, since it elicits the flow of verbal behavior, brings out the quality of the patient's abilities to organize and maintain ideas, and may reveal characteristic attitudes and behavioral propensities. Stories told to pictures or

themes can also be analyzed for both their formal and content characteristics (W. E. Henry, 1947; Stein, 1955). Of the several story telling projective tests for adults, the *Thematic Apperception Test (TAT)* (Murray, 1938) is the most widely used (Lubin et al., 1971). Although the familiar test pictures of the TAT have the advantage of known expectations for the kinds and characteristics of stories each elicits (Murstein, 1963), the examiner without TAT or other story test material can easily improvise with illustrations from magazine stories or with photographs.

Stories composed by brain injured patients possess the same response qualities that characterize organic Rorschach protocols. Thus, the brain injured patient is likely to use fewer words and ideas in telling his stories (R).* Response times are apt to be longer with many punctuating pauses (T). Brain injured patients are more likely to describe the picture than make up a story; or if they make up a story, its content is apt to be trite with few characters and little action (M). The organic patient may be satisfied with simple descriptions of discrete elements of the picture and unable to go beyond this level of response when encouraged to do so (Cn). A more than ordinary number of misinterpretations of either elements of the picture or the theme may occur due to tendencies toward confusion, simplification, or vagueness (F%). The organic patient may give relatively few of the most common themes (P%). Perseveration of theme (Rpt) and automatic repetition of certain phrases or words (AP) rarely appear in stories of subjects without brain damage. Inability to change an unsatisfactory response (Imp) and expressions of self-doubt (Plx) may be present. Inflexibility, concrete responses, catastrophic reactions, and difficulties in dealing with the picture as a whole are also likely to be of organic etiology (Fogel, 1967).

Drawing tasks
It is much more difficult to handle the drawings of organic patients as projective material than their verbal products. When perceptual, motor, or practic defects interfere with the ability to execute a drawing, the resultant distortions make doubtful any interpretations based on the projective hypothesis. Even when distortions are slight,

---

* The symbols in parentheses refer to the corresponding Piotrowski organic sign for Rorschach responses (see pp. 459–460).

the examiner cannot tell whether paucity of details, for instance, reflects a barren inner life, or is due to low energy or feelings of uncertainty and self-consciousness, or whether reduced drawing size is a product of life-long habits of constriction or of efforts to compensate for tendencies to spatial disorientation or motor unsteadiness or some interaction between them.

As a rule, formal characteristics of the drawings of brain injured persons, such as size, proportion, angulation, perspective, and line quality, should not be subject to projective interpretations, nor should underdetailing, simplification, or incompleteness. Gratuitous elaborations, on the other hand, may usually be treated as projective material, in which case inferences may be drawn following the principles and practices of projective interpretation (J. N. Buck, 1948; Machover, 1948).

Objective Personality Tests

Objective personality tests are self-report instruments: the patient describes himself by checking those items he wishes to claim to be true about himself. On these tests, the effects of impairment may be manifested through the patient's responses to items concerning intellectual disabilities or personality changes related to his impairment. The two tests that are used most frequently in medical settings, the Minnesota Multiphasic Personality Inventory and the Cornell Medical Index, are appropriate for evaluating personality components of a neuropsychological complaint or disability.

The Minnesota Multiphasic Personality Inventory (MMPI)

This 566-item true-false questionnaire was developed in a medical setting—the University of Minnesota Medical School Hospital and Clinics (Hathaway and McKinley, 1951; Welsh and Dahlstrom, 1956; Dahlstrom et al., 1975). Computerized scoring forms, scoring services, and interpretation systems are available. The MMPI has been translated into other languages, tape-recorded forms have been devised for semiliterates and the visually handicapped, and there is a form for patients who cannot write but may have enough motor coordination to sort item cards. It is an untimed test, suitable for older adolescents and adults. Neither age nor education is taken into consideration in the scoring, but there are separate male and female norms. Verbal comprehension must be at a *low average* or better level for useful results. Very impaired patients who have difficulty following or remembering instructions, who cannot make response shifts readily, or whose verbal comprehension is seriously compromised cannot take this test.

The MMPI was constructed on principles of actuarial prediction. Rigorous statistical discrimination techniques were used to select the items and construct the scales. The criterion for item selection and scale construction was the efficiency with which items discriminated between normal control subjects and persons with diagnosed psychiatric disorders.

The inventory is ordinarily scored for 14 scales: four *validity scales,* which provide information about the subject's competency to take the test, the likelihood that he is malingering or denying real problems, and such test-taking attitudes as defensiveness or help-seeking; and ten *clinical scales* by means of which the patient's responses are compared with those of both the normal control subjects and the different diagnostic groups of psychiatric patients. Interpretation is on the basis of the overall scale *patterns*, not on any one response or the score for any one scale. Dozens of scales other than the 14 in most common use have been developed, but many have not been adequately standardized and most are primarily of research interest.

Spurred by the discriminating power of actuarial predictions (Meehl, 1954; Sines, 1966), numerous investigators have been developing and refining "cookbook" programs for computerized scoring and interpretation of the MMPI (Fowler, 1969). The predictive prowess of these programs is unquestionable when applied to large populations. Their application to the individual case, however, is problematical since the programs in general use interpret the patient's highest but not lowest scores and do not account for age or physical condition (Towbin, 1961), and since every program produces a statistically ascertainable number of false positive and false negative predictions. Use of computerized or "cookbook" interpretations of the MMPI requires sophisticated clinical judgment for the "highly mechanized and 'objective' appearance of an MMPI profile often tempts people to abandon their usual approach in evaluating clinical data and to adopt a kind of rigidly psychometric—sign—actuarial method of interpretation. . . . However, most clinicians who regularly use the MMPI in clinical practice see this as being at best, a relatively barren procedure. At its worst, from the point of view of the individual case, it is productive of sometimes serious diagnostic errors" (Carson, 1969a).

The problem of purely actuarial handling of MMPI responses is demonstrated in the computer interpretation of the MMPI profile of the victim of a car accident, a 23-year-old male high school graduate.

He suffered left sided weakness with some left sided tremor and spasticity, dysarthria, and a tendency to convulsions which was adequately controlled by medication. Intellectual impairment was minimal, showing up mostly in mild concentration and attention problems, weakened retention of newly learned material, and some visuopractic distortions.

The program developed by Dr. Harold Gilberstadt for the Veterans' Administration (1970) produced the following interpretation of his MMPI profile (see Fig. 17-2):

"The patient's current state appears to be characterized by hypomania. Test taking attitude seems to reveal naïveté. Professes rigid adherence to social mores. Sees self as conforming, self-controlled. Normal defensiveness and/or ego strength.

"Single and pair-wise scale analysis suggests the possibility of the following traits and characteristics: histrionic, emotionally labile, may develop atypical symptoms which may yield to superficial treatment, may have episodic attacks of acute distress, may develop symptoms impossible to reconcile with organic etiology. Behavior controls may be tenuous. Veneer of gaiety and friendliness but may be irascible, restless and impulsive, hostile, hyperactive, grandiose, talkative.

"The following should be looked for among trait and diagnostic alternatives: hostile, emotionally labile personality."

This print-out gives a very good description of the young man except that his significant coordination and motor disabilities and his mild intellectual impairment are not included, nor is his history of chronic conflict with his father which tends to generalize into conflict with other persons in positions of authority.

This example illustrates both the strengths and weaknesses of the computerized MMPI. The patient tends to deny disability and social difficulties and therefore did not respond as a disabled person. The computerized interpretation accords well with the patient's perception of himself as whole and on top of things. It correctly identifies him as angry and having some behavioral control problems. However, it does not register the very significant discrepancy between the patient's self-concept and reality, except to indicate the possibility of grandiosity and, by implication ("histrionic," "veneer of gaiety"), the patient's

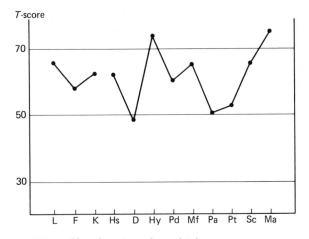

FIG. 17-2. MMPI profile of patient described on pp. 466–467.

tendency to deny unpleasantness at the expense of reality. Further-more, not only does it not identify the central problem of organicity, but it suggests that the possibility of organic etiology of his complaints should be viewed rather skeptically.

Following the actuarial principles underlying this test, there have been a number of efforts to develop MMPI scales that would effec-tively predict the likelihood of brain damage. Hovey's five-item scale (1964) has met with mixed success. This scale consists of four items marked *false* (10, 51, 192, and 274) and one (159) marked *true*. Four is the cutting score for organicity. Hovey recommends that this scale be used only when the K-scale score is 8 or above to minimize the likelihood of false positive errors. In one study, the Hovey scale identified only 28% of a small (n = 25) mixed "brain damaged" group, but 64% of a similar sized group of patients diag-nosed as having multiple sclerosis (Jortner, 1965). Jortner questioned the discriminating power of item 274, "My eyesight is as good as it has been for years," for persons over age 40. Another study (Watson, 1971) found Hovey's scale to be ineffectual in differentiating schizo-phrenic from organic patients and speculated on the importance of regional differences in the application of MMPI scales to local hos-pital populations. A misdiagnosis rate greater than chance (71.5% false negatives, 28% false positives) was reported for 28 patients with mixed organic etiology and 25 normal control subjects (Weingold et al., 1965). Zimmerman (1965), however, found that Hovey's scale identified 62% of severely damaged patients seven years after injury, but only 29% and 25%, respectively, of moderately and mildly injured patients. He concluded that "Hovey's five MMPI items identify the permanent or residual impairment due to severe brain damage."

Two other scales that purport to differentiate brain damaged from other patients illustrate the problem of using clinical scales for individual diagnosis. A 17-item *Pseudo-Neurologic Scale* (Shaw and Matthews, 1965), designed to identify patients whose neurological complaints are not supported by positive neurological findings, contains five items marked *true* (38, 47, 108, 238, 253) and 12 *false* (3, 8, 68, 171, 173, 175, 188, 190, 230, 237, 238, and 243) with a cutting score of 7 in the scored direction. In the original study, this scale differentiated 81% of the patients with symptoms suggestive of brain damage who had negative neurological work-ups while misclassifying 25% of those with unequivocal neurological disease. But cross-validation results, although statistically significant ($p < .01$), were less successful, since there were 33% false negatives (pseudoneurologic patients classified as brain damaged) and 22% false positives. The *Sc-O* scale, composed of 80 items with a 30-item short form, uses a weighting system (Watson, 1971). These scales were studied for their effectiveness in differentiating hospitalized schizophrenic from brain damaged patients. Again, significant results were obtained when these scales were applied to groups, but their prediction rates—which ranged from 72 to 75% for the male patients—make their application to the individual case a questionable procedure.

Efforts to use the MMPI for differential diagnosis of organic defects have produced a variety of scales. Several epilepsy scales have been developed, but none has held up well under cross-validation studies (Dahlstrom and Welsh, 1960; Rosenman and Lucik, 1970). S. H. Friedman constructed a 32-item *Parietal-frontal* (*Pf*) scale (1950) and H. L. Williams a *Caudality* (*Ca*) scale (1952). Both provide some discrimination between brain injured patients with anterior lesions and those with posterior lesions (Dahlstrom and Welsh, 1960; Meier, 1969) although Reitan (1976) reports that more recent research on this problem has not supported the earlier findings.

A sign approach to the identification of epileptic patients on the basis of the standard 14 MMPI scales has not met with more success than has scale development (Hovey et al., 1959; Jordan, 1963; Weingold et al., 1965). Fourteen signs involving two- and three-scale relationships were selected on the basis of how well they differentiated epileptic patients from a group of patients with complaints of "spells" and "blackouts" whose EEG tracings were within normal limits. The signs significantly differentiated epileptic from several functional psychiatric groups but produced no cutting score that would satisfactorily minimize either false positives or false negatives. Response inconsistency, as measured by likeness of responses to the 16 pairs of identical items in the MMPI booklet, tends to characterize the MMPI performance of brain injured patients (Krug, 1967), but further study of this phenomenon is needed before it can be considered a sign of organicity.

The sheer variety of brain injuries and of problems attendant upon organicity probably helps explain the unsatisfactory results of MMPI scale and sign approaches. Moreover, the MMPI was not constructed for neuropsychological assessment and may be inherently inappropriate for this purpose. It would certainly appear to be an inefficient instrument for identifying or localizing cerebral lesions, particularly when so many other more effective methods have been specifically developed to perform these diagnostic tasks.

Nevertheless, there are very general *pattern* tendencies that characterize the responses of many patients with neurological disorders. To some extent, the pattern of MMPI profiles of brain damaged patients is an artifact of the test items and scale composition. Among the 51 items of the 357 scored items on the short form of the MMPI (omitting scale *Si* and all items normally not scored) referrable to symptoms of physical disease, 26 relate to central nervous system diseases and 8 describe problems associated with being ill (Lezak and Glaudin, 1969). Most of the "neurological symptom" items appear on the *Sc* scale, and many have double and triple scale loadings, particularly on scales *Hs, D,* and *Hy*. As a result, nonpsychiatric patients with central nervous system disease tend to have an elevated "neurotic triad" (*Hs, D, Hy*) and higher than average *Sc* scores (see Fig. 17-3).

The tendency for *Sc* to be the highest or one of the highest scales has been noted for epileptic patients (Kløve and Doehring, 1962; Meier, 1969), and high scores on the neurotic triad have character-

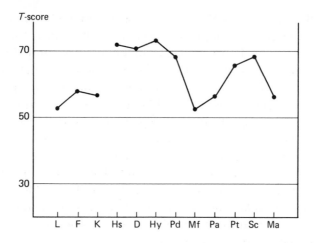

FIG. 17-3. Mean MMPI profile for 25 patients with diagnosed brain disease (Lezak and Glaudin, 1969).

ized the MMPI profiles of patients with multiple sclerosis (Dahlstrom and Welsh, 1960). However, acknowledgment of specific symptoms accounts for only some of the elevation of specific scales; both premorbid personality tendencies and the patient's reactions to his disabilities contribute to his MMPI profile. The combination of symptom description, the anxiety and distress occasioned by central nervous system defects, and the need for heroic psychological adaptive measures probably account for the frequency with which brain damaged patients produce neurotic profiles (A. L. Anderson and Hanvik, 1950; Doehring and Reitan, 1960; Kløve and Doehring, 1962; Lezak and Glaudin, 1969).

The Cornell Medical Index (CMI)
The *Cornell Medical Index Health Questionnaire* is a set of true-false self-descriptive statements (Brodman, 1953; Brodman et al., 1949). The CMI items are specific questions about a wide variety of physical ailments and psychiatric and psychosomatic problems. They cover the same topics, using much the same wording, as does a physician conducting a thorough initial interview. The two forms of the test are identical except for six questions in the genitourinary section that differ for men and women.

The CMI provides an overall score based on the sum of "yes" responses. A cutting score separates normal persons, who may or may not have physical problems, from emotionally disturbed persons, who also may or may not have physical problems. The questions are presented in categories that enable the examiner to determine at a glance which organ systems are the focus of the patient's complaints (see Table 17-1). Twenty-five or more "yes" responses indicate the likelihood of a serious medical or psychiatric problem. If the "yes" responses are mostly confined to one or two of the medical symptom subsections (A through H), the problem is probably primarily medical and the examiner can gain a general idea of its nature from the distribution of "yes" responses. Many "yes" responses scattered throughout sections A through H suggest an emotional or personality disturbance with physical complaints; many "yes" responses in sections I to R suggest psychiatric symptoms. The CMI is thus useful for routine medical—including neurological—screen-

TABLE 17-1
Sections on the Cornell Medical Index

Section	Questions Referring to	Number of Questions
A	Eyes and ears	9
B	Respiratory system	18
C	Cardiovascular system	13
D	Digestive tract	23
E	Musculoskeletal system	8
F	Skin	7
G	Nervous system	18
H	Genitourinary system	11
I	Fatigability	7
J	Frequency of illness	9
K	Miscellaneous diseases	15
L	Habits	6
	Mood and Feeling Patterns:	
M	Inadequacy	12
N	Depression	6
O	Anxiety	9
P	Sensitivity	6
Q	Anger	9
R	Tension	9
	Total	195

ing as well as for identifying emotionally disturbed, neurotic, and malingering patients.

DEVELOPMENTAL SCALES

If a severely impaired patient is unable to respond consistently to examination questions or tasks, it is possible to obtain a standardized evaluation of his behavioral status by using one of the infant and child developmental scales. These scales are inventories of behavior expected at specified ages based on large-scale normative observations. The examiner obtains much of the information about the child (patient) from interviews with a parent (nurse, family member). Some information is obtained through observation, and some from tests for specific responses or skills.

The Gesell Developmental Schedules (Gesell, 1940; Gesell et al., 1949) are probably the most famous of the developmental scales. They cover the age range from four weeks to six years. No score or overall value is computed. Rather, the child's (patient's developmental level can be compared with normative data for the many age levels reported in each of four major areas of behavior: motor, language, adaptive, and personal-social.

An easily administered scale that tests behavior in the three areas of motor, communication, and self-sufficiency skills from birth through the seventh year is the Boyd Developmental Progress Scale (1974) (see Fig. 17-4). This scale focuses on the adaptive aspects of behavior in each of the three test areas so that its data can be immediately useful in rehabilitation planning and training. Some of the items are inappropriate for adult patients (e.g., "Rides Tricycle" at 2 to 3 years) but most are very relevant (e.g., "Cuts with Scissors," or "Feeds—Uses Fork to Spear" at the 2- to 3-year level). The arrangement of test items on the record sheet facilitates both the conduct of the examination and interpretation of the data for it allows comparisons of performance by age and by behavioral area. The communication age scale correlates .95 with the mental age score of the Stanford-Binet (1972 norms) (Boyd, personal communication).

The Vineland Social Maturity Scale ranges from birth to age 25 and over, and includes items assessing the social-adaptive behavior of normal adults, children, and infants (Doll, 1953, 1965). The eight categories in which the Vineland Scale measures social competence are (1) General Self-Help, (2) Self-Help in Eating, (3) Self-Help in Dressing, (4) Self-Direction, (5) Occupation, (6) Communication, (7) Locomotion, and (8) Socialization. The test yields a Social Age score from which a Social Quotient can be derived. The focus of the test is on personal responsibility and independence; the evaluation of motor and communication skills is incidental. Item answers are obtained by interviewing informants or the subject himself rather than from direct observation.

Other developmental scales emphasize different functions, focus on different age groups, or base their standardization on larger or smaller, more or less random populations. Most of them will satisfy the neuropsychological examiner's need for some kind of norms against which he can compare the behavior of a severely impaired patient (Shakespeare, 1970).

TESTS FOR FUNCTIONAL COMPLAINTS

The direct financial benefits of illnesses and injuries related to job, service, or accident, and the indirect emotional and social rewards of invalidism make malingering and functional disabilities an attractive solution to all kinds of social, economic, and personal problems for some people. Functional disorders frequently take the form of neurological symptoms and complaints since many neurological conditions are easily confused with the psychogenic complaints accompanying common emotional disturbances, such as headaches, "blackouts," and memory or sensory problems. The differential diagnosis is further complicated by the fact that early neurological disease often does not show up on physical examination or in laboratory studies.

Another problem complicating diagnosis is that the distinction between unconscious symptom production and the conscious decision to feign illness for personal gain is often blurred, for both conscious and unconscious motivations may contribute to the pseudo-symptoms of physical disease. Moreover, even the issue of whether a complaint is psychogenic is not simple for often the patient presents a mixture of functional and organic symptoms or of organic disabilities with a functional reaction to his handicaps that increases their severity or interferes with treatment or rehabilitation of the organic problem. Therefore, motivation will not be dealt with here;

BOYD DEVELOPMENTAL PROGRESS SCALE

Robert D. Boyd, Ph.D.

NAME _____

UNIT NO. _____

DATE   Year _____ Month _____ Date _____

BIRTH _____ _____ _____

AGE   _____ _____ _____

MOTOR SKILLS

B	6 mos.	1	18 mos.	2	3	4	5	6	7	8
Follows object	Takes two cubes	Builds tower of 2 blocks	Builds tower of 4 blocks		Builds bridge of 3 blocks	10 pellets in bottle 30 sec.	Catches ball, bounced 2/3	10 pellets in bottle 20 sec.	Rides bicycle	Arranges material neatly
Rolls over	Sits without support	Walks alone	Walks upstairs		Cuts with scissors	Alternates downstairs	Cuts—follows simple outline	1Prints first name	1Prints full name	Cuts round outline well
Grasps object	Walks holding on	Walks backwards	Jumps		Balances on 1 foot 1 sec.	Balances on 1 foot 5 sec.	Balances on 1 foot 10 sec.	Builds steps of 6 blocks	1Prints 1-20 few reversals	1Prints 1-20 no revs. 1/2 inch
Bears weight	Stands alone	Stoops and recovers	Throws overhand		Rides tricycle	Hops on 1 foot	2Draws Man 4 parts	2Draws Man 6 parts	2Draws Man 9 parts	Writes full name (cursive)
Transfers objects	Pincer grasp	Scribbles	1Imitates line		Copies circle	Copies cross	Copies square	Copies triangle	Copies vertical diamond	Constructs objects/cooks

1On back of drawing sheet

2On back of this sheet

COMMUNICATION SKILLS

	B	6 mos.	1	18 mos.	2	3	4	5	6	7	8
	Responds to bell	Says—mama, dada	Plays ball	Show-mouth, eyes, hair, nose 1/4	Show-mouth, eyes, hair nose 4/4	[2]What do we— 6/7	Made of-car window, dress 2/3	Made of-car door, shoe 2/3	Made of-fork door, shoe 3/3	[2]Names animals 1 min. 9	Names days of week
	Babbles	Imitates Sounds	Uses 3 to 5 words	Block-on table to me; on floor 2/3	Block-on, under, front back 2/4	Block-on, under, front, back 3/4		[2]Completes analogies 2/3	[2]Definitions 6/9	Alike—boat/airplane; hat/shoe 1/2	Tells own address
	Follows person visually	Responds to no-no, bye-bye	Indicates specific wants	Combines words	Uses plurals	Do—tired, cold, hungry 2/3	Do—cross street		[3]Reads .5 grade level	[3]Reads 1.5 grade level	[3]Reads 2.5 grade level
	Smiles	Hesitates with strangers	Mimics chores	Brings objects on request	Gives full name	Show—"longer" 3/3 or 5/6	Show—"smoother" 3/3 or 5/6	Show—R-ear, L-eye, R-leg, L-arm 4/4	When—breakfast, bed, afternoon 3/3		Show-upper R, lower L; middle 3/3
	Turns to whisper	1 Word—not mama, dada	Solitary play	Parallel play	Cooperative play	Separates—without fuss	Tells age	Plays competitive games		Answers phone—takes message	Plays organized group games

[2]On back of this sheet
[3]Use WRAT

SELF SUFFICIENCY SKILLS

	B	6 mos.	1	18 mos.	2	3	4	5	6	7	8
	Head upright and steady	Drinks from cup with help	Feeds—scoops with spoon (or fork)	Discriminates edible substances	Feeds—uses fork to spear	Feeds—cuts with fork	Brushes own teeth	Names—penny, dime, nickel 2/3	Spreads own bread	Cuts own meat (knife)	
	Recovers toy from chest	Uncovers face	Chews food	Unwraps candy or gum	Blocks—give "just one"	Counts—2 blocks/pellets 2/2	Counts—4 and 3 blocks 2/2	Counts—10 and 8 blocks 2/2	Solves—$2+1$, $3+2$, $5-1$ 2/3	Solves—$8+6$, $9-5$, $7+4$ 2/3	
	Reaches for objects	Works for toy	Drinks without help	Solves pellet bottle	Washes, dries own hands	Ident.—blue, yellow, red, green 3/4	Washes own face	Blows own nose	Bathes self, complete	Buys with money	
	Occupies self, unattended	Pulls self upright	Opens closed doors	Goes about house	Avoids danger—street	Cares for self at toilet	Goes about within block	Goes about, crosses streets	Goes to bed unassisted	Tells time, quarter hour	
	Feeds self cracker	Gets to sitting position	Removes clothing	Puts on some clothing	Gets own drink	Dresses without help	Buttons—correct, complete	Errands outside home	Ties own shoes	Grooms self	

FIG. 17-4. The Boyd Developmental Progress Scale.

only the question of determining whether the patient's complaints are likely to be psychogenic.

In clinical practice, the determination of whether there is a functional component to the patient's symptoms usually rests (1) on evidence of inconsistency in the history or examination; (2) on the likelihood that the set of symptoms and complaints the patient brings makes medical sense, i.e., fits a reasonable disease pattern; (3) on an understanding of the patient's present situation, personal-social history, and emotional predispositions, i.e., his personality "dynamics"; and (4) on his emotional reactions to his complaints, particularly if he presents the classic *la belle indifference* (the beautiful unconcern) characteristic of patients whose symptoms, due to conversion hysteria, are at least in part unconsciously motivated and usually bring significant secondary gains. In addition, there are a few tests of dissimulation that can be given to patients complaining of cognitive or memory defects when their motivations or complaints are suspect. The first four tests have been devised by André Rey and, with the exception of the 15-item "memory" test, are reported in *L'examen psychologique dans les cas d'encéphalopathie traumatique* (1941).

Memorization of 15 items
This technique can be used to test the validity of a memory complaint (1964). The principle underlying it is that the patient who consciously or unconsciously wishes to appear impaired will fail at a task that all but the most severely brain damaged or retarded patients perform easily.

The task is presented as a test requiring the memorization of 15 *different* items. In the instructions, the number "15" is stressed to make the test appear to be difficult. In reality, the patient need remember only three or four ideas to recall most of the items. The examiner marks on a piece of paper the following, in five rows of three character to a line:

A	B	C
1	2	3
a	b	c
○	□	△
I	II	III

The patient sees this display for 10 seconds whereupon the examiner withdraws it and asks the patient to copy what he remembers. A 10- or 15-second quiet delay period can be interpolated. Anyone who is not significantly deteriorated can recall at least three of the five character sets.

Dot Counting: ungrouped dots

This test can be used with patients complaining of general intellectual impairment or specific visual-perceptual defects. It is based on the technique of randomizing stimulus intensity or difficulty levels to determine whether the patient's failures are regularly associated with the altered intensity (as in audiometric examination) or level of difficulty of a task.

The test material consists of six serially numbered 3×5 inch cards on which are printed (1) 7, (2) 11, (3) 15, (4) 19, (5) 23, and (6) 27 dots, respectively. The cards are shown to the patient, one at a time, in the order: 2, 4, 3, 5, 6, 1. The patient is told to count and tell the number of the dots as quickly as he can, and his response times are noted. His response times can then be compared with those made by normal adult subjects (percentiles 25 to 100, Table 17-2) and brain injured patients (percentile 0, Table 17-2). The cooperative patient's time will increase gradually with the increased number of dots. More than one pronounced deviation from this pattern raises the likelihood that the patient is not acting in good faith.

Dot Counting: grouped and ungrouped dots

This test adds six more numbered cards to the Dot Counting task. These cards contain (1) 8, (2) 12, (3) 16, (4) 20, (5) 24, and (6) 28 dots respectively, arranged as follows: (1) two 4-dot squares; (2) two 5-dot squares and two separate dots; (3) four 4-dot diamonds; (4) four 5-dot squares; (5) four 6-dot rectangles; and (6) four 5-dot squares and two 4-dot squares. Again the cards are presented in the order, 2, 4, 3, 5, 6, 1. For this set of cards, however, because the dots are grouped, the time taken to count the dots is much less than for the ungrouped dots (see Table 17-3).

The patient's performance is evaluated in terms of the difference between the total time for the two performances. When there is little difference or the time taken to count the grouped dots exceeds that for the ungrouped dots, the subject's cooperation becomes suspect.

TABLE 17-2
Percentile Norms for Time (in Seconds) Taken to Count Ungrouped Dots

Card	Dots	Percentile				
		100	75	50	25	0
1	7	1	2	4	5	11
2	11	2	3	4	5	17
3	15	3	4	6	7	17
4	19	4	6	7	9	19
5	23	5	8	10	12	30
6	27	6	9	11	16	30

(Adapted from Rey, 1941)

Word Recognition

This is a memory test based on the principle that recognition is easier than recall. It involves a 15-word stimulus list and a 30-word list that contains the 15 words of the stimulus list mixed in with 15 other words. First the word recognition test is given by reading the stimulus words at a one per second rate in the following order:

> half, camel, mistake, toy, morning, hair, wax, grain, cookie, fly, place, cherry, door, knee, state

After 5 seconds, the examiner hands the patient a sheet of paper on which appear the 30 words with the instructions to underline with a pencil all the words he remembers being used.

hello	today	door	thread	light
gift	grain	concert	wall	knee
camel	power	grass	hair	fly
morning	toy	bottle	cheese	mistake
half	style	cookie	horse	cherry
airplane	wax	place	smile	state

Some time later (at least 10 minutes), the examiner gives Rey's Auditory-Verbal Learning Test (see pp. 352–356).

The number of words recalled on the first trial of this test is then compared with the number of words recognized on the word recognition task. A performance in which the number of words recalled equals or exceeds the number of words recognized raises the possibility that the patient is feigning a memory defect or is not cooperating fully or consistently.

TABLE 17-3
Percentile Norms for Time (in Seconds) Taken to Count Grouped Dots

		Percentile				
Card	Dots	100	75	50	25	0
1	8	0.5	1	1	2	3
2	12	1	2	2	2	3
3	16	1	2	2	4	5
4	20	1	1	2	4	5
5	24	2	2	2	5	6
6	28	2	2	3	5	7

(Adapted from Rey, 1941)

The Symptom Validity Test

This simple procedure may be used to evaluate the validity of symptoms and complaints involving perception and short-term memory (Pankratz et al., 1975). It is presented as a test of whatever disability the patient claims to have. It requires the patient to make 100 forced-choice decisions of a simple, two-alternative problem involving his symptom or complaint. By chance alone, approximately 50 percent of the patient's choices will be correct. This is the expected result when the patient's complaints are valid, e.g., when he is deaf or has an impaired short-term memory or no position sense in his toes. Since so many trials are conducted, small deviations from the expected value become significant (Siegel, 1956). When the patient's percent correct score runs much below 40, the examiner can suspect a functional etiology; if he is in doubt, a second set of 100 trials should clarify the question, for the likelihood that the percent correct score would be significantly lower than chance on two sets of 100 trials is so slight as to be highly improbable. Percent correct scores that run significantly above the chance expectation obviously indicate that the patient is able to perform the task.

The adaptability of this task to perceptual and memory complaints is probably limited only by the examiner's imagination. The task is always presented to the patient as a straightforward test of the claimed disability. Loss of feeling on the hand, for example, can be tested by having the patient tell whether he was touched on the palm or the back, or on his thumb or his middle finger. A patient with a visual complaint, such as eyesight too blurry for reading, can be shown two cards, each containing a different simple word or phrase. For testing "blurred" vision, we use cards with the statements "This card is number one" and "Number two is this card" printed in small type. The patient's task is to identify the card he is shown as "one" or "two." Short-term memory can be tested by presenting the patient with one of two similar visual or auditory stimuli, such as colored lights or four- or five-digit numbers, and then having him perform an intervening task, such as counting backwards for ten seconds, before reporting which stimulus he remembered. Even if the patient insists he cannot perform the task at all, he can be required to make the 100 choices.

The Symptom Validity Test confronts malingering patients quite directly for it is difficult to maintain a properly randomized response pattern that will result in a score within the range of chance for 100 trials. Since the examiner reports to the patient whether his choice was correct after each trial, patients may get the impression that they are doing better than they thought they could when half the time they hear that they are correct. The impression of doing well can have an unsettling effect on malingerers. Patients who attempt to avoid the confrontation by giving most or all of one kind of answer are obviously uncooperative. Those who naively give a wrong answer more often than chance betray their competency.

Skillful use of this technique can encourage some functionally disabled patients to experience "recovery" without loss of dignity. The task may be presented as being difficult. For example, the examiner can introduce it by saying, "A lot of people have trouble getting many correct answers." Or the examiner can emphasize that the task is difficult for persons with the patient's disability. The examiner can applaud a naive patient who has demonstrated the functional nature of his complaint by making only 20 or 30% correct responses and reassure him that his performance demonstrated that he can recover the "lost" or weakened function. On subsequent trials, the examiner can encourage him to increase his percent correct score gradually. Higher percent correct scores then become evidence of "improvement," increasing the patient's expectation of "recovery." When this procedure is followed for a series of trials, conducted in a supportive setting, the suggestible patient may be able to relinquish his symptoms within a few days with little threat to his self-esteem.

REFERENCES

Abbott, W. D., Due, F. O., & Nosik, W. A. Subdural hematoma and effusion as a result of blast injuries. *Journal of the American Medical Association*, 1943, *121*, 739–741.

Adams, K., Rennick, P., & Rosenbaum, G. Automated clinical interpretation of the neuropsychological battery: an ability-based approach. Paper presented at the meeting of the International Neuropsychological Society, Tampa, Fla., Feb. 1975.

Adams, R. D., Collins, G. H., & Victor, M. Trouble de la mémoire et de l'apprentissage chez l'homme. Leurs relations avec des lésions des lobes temporaux et du diencéphale. In *Physiologie de l'hippocampe* (Colloques Internationaux du Centre National de la Recherche Scientifique, No. 107). Paris: C. N. R. S., 1961.

Aita, J. A., Armitage, S. G., Reitan, R. M., & Rabinowitz, A. The use of certain psychological tests in the evaluation of brain injury. *Journal of General Psychology*, 1947, *37*, 25–44.

Aita, J. A., Reitan, R. M., & Ruth, J. M. Rorschach test as a diagnostic aid in brain injury. *American Journal of Psychiatry*, 1947, *103*, 770–779.

Ajuriaguerra, J. de, Richard, J., Rodriguez, R., & Tissot, R. Quelques aspects de la désintegration des praxies idéomotrices dans les demences du grand âge, *Cortex*, 1966, *2*, 438–462.

Allen, R. M. The test performance of the brain injured. *Journal of Clinical Psychology*, 1947, *3*, 225–230.

Allison, J., Blatt, S. J., & Zimet, C. N. *The interpretation of psychological tests*. New York: Harper & Row, 1968.

Allison, R. S. Chronic amnesic syndrome in the elderly. *Proceedings of the Royal Society of Medicine*, 1961, *54*, 961–965.

Ammons, R. B. & Ammons, C. H. The Quick Test (QT): Provisional Manual. *Psychological Reports*, Monograph Supplement 1-VII, 1962.

Ammons, R. B. & Ammons, H. S. *The Full-Range Picture Vocabulary Test*. Missoula, Mont.: Psychological Test Specialists, 1948.

Anastasi, A. *Differential psychology* (3rd ed.). New York: Wiley, 1965.

Anastasi, A. *Psychological testing* (3rd ed.). New York: Macmillan, 1968.

Anderson, A. L. The effect of laterality localization of brain damage on Wechsler-Bellevue indices of deterioration. *Journal of Clinical Psychology*, 1950, *6*, 191–194.

Anderson, A. L. & Hanvik, L. J. The psychometric localization of brain lesions: the

481

differential effects of frontal and parietal lesions on MMPI profiles. *Journal of Clinical Psychology,* 1950, *6*, 177–180.

Anderson, C. Chronic head cases. *Lancet,* 1942, *243*, 1–4.

Annett, M. The binomial distribution of right, mixed, and left handedness. *Quarterly Journal of Experimental Psychology,* 1967, *19*, 327–333.

Anttinen, E. E. On the apoplectic conditions occurring among brain injured veterans. *Acta Psychiatrica et Neurologica Scandinavica,* 1960, *35*, Suppl. 143.

Archibald, Y. M., Wepman, J. M. & Jones, L. V. Performance on nonverbal cognitive tests following unilateral cortical injury to the right and left hemispheres. *Journal of Nervous and Mental Disease,* 1967, *145*, 25–36.

Armitage, S. G. An analysis of certain psychological tests used for the evaluation of brain injury. *Psychological Monographs,* 1946, *60* (Whole No. 277).

Army General Classification Test. Chicago: Science Research Associates, 1948.

Army Individual Test. Manual of directions and scoring. Washington, D. C.: War Department, Adjutant General's Office, 1944.

Arnold, M. B. Mind, memory, and the brain. Presidential address presented at the meeting of Division 24, American Psychological Association, New Orleans, Sept. 1974.

Arrigoni, G. & De Renzi, E. Constructional apraxia and hemispheric locus of lesion. *Cortex,* 1964, *1*, 170–197.

Arthur, G. *A Point Scale of Performance Tests.* Rev. Form II. New York: Psychological Corporation, 1947.

Atkinson, R. C. & Shiffrin, R. M. Human memory: a proposed system and its control processes. In *The psychology of learning and motivation* (Vol. 2). New York: Academic Press, 1968.

Atwell, C. R. & Wells, F. L. Wide range multiple-choice vocabulary tests. *Journal of Applied Psychology,* 1937, *21*, 550–555.

Atwell, C. R. & Wells, F. L. *Wide Range Vocabulary Test.* New York: Psychological Corporation, undated.

Aylaian, A. & Meltzer, M. L. The Bender Gestalt Test and intelligence. *Journal of Consulting Psychology,* 1962, *26*, 483.

Baer, P. E. Cognitive changes in aging: competence and incompetence. In C. M. Gaitz (Ed.), *Aging and the brain.* New York: Plenum Press, 1972.

Baker, G. Diagnosis of organic brain damage in the adult. In B. Klopfer (Ed.), *Developments in the Rorschach technique.* New York: World Book, 1956a.

Baker, G. Diagnostic case studies of organic brain damage. In B. Klopfer (Ed.), *Developments in the Rorschach technique.* New York: World Book, 1956b.

Bannister, R. *Brain's clinical neurology* (4th ed.). London: Oxford University Press, 1973.

Barbizet, J. Defect of memorizing of hippocampal-mammillary origin: a review. *Journal of Neurology, Neurosurgery, and Psychiatry,* 1963, *26*, 127–135.

Barbizet, J. *Human memory and its pathology.* San Francisco: W. H. Freeman, 1970.

Barbizet, J. & Cany, E. Clinical and psychometrical study of a patient with memory disturbances. *International Journal of Neurology,* 1968, *7*, 44–54.

Battersby, W. S., Bender, M. B., Pollack, M., & Kahn, R. L. Unilateral "spatial agnosia" ("inattention") in patients with cortical lesions. *Brain,* 1956, *79*, 68–93.

Beard, R. M. The structure of perception: a factorial study. *British Journal of Educational Psychology,* 1965, *35*, 210–221.

Beck, S. J., Beck, A. G., Levitt, E. E., & Molish, H. B. *Rorschach's test: basic processes* (3rd ed.). New York: Grune & Stratton, 1961.

Beizmann, C. [*Handbook for scorings of Rorschach responses*] (S. J. Beck, trans.). New York: Grune & Stratton, 1970.

Ben-Yishay, Y. Diller, L., Mandleberg, I., Gordon, W., & Gerstman, L. J. Similarities and differences in Block Design performances between older normal and brain injured persons: a task analysis. *Journal of Abnormal Psychology*, 1971, *78*, 17–25.

Bender, L. A visual motor gestalt test and its clinical use. *American Orthopsychiatric Association Research Monographs*, 1938, No. 3.

Bender, L. Instructions for the use of the Visual Motor Gestalt test. New York: American Orthopsychiatric Association, 1946.

Bennett, G. K., Bennett, M. G., Wallace, W. L. & Wesman, A. G. *College Qualification Tests*. New York: Psychological Corporation, 1961.

Bennett, G. K., Seashore, H. G., & Wesman, A. G. *Differential Aptitude Tests Manual* (5th ed.). New York: Psychological Corporation, 1972.

Benson, D. F. Fluency in aphasia. *Cortex*, 1967, *3*, 373–394.

Benson, D. F. & Barton, M. I. Disturbances in constructional ability. *Cortex*, 1970, *6*, 19–46.

Benton, A. L. A multiple choice type of visual retention test. *Archives of Neurology and Psychiatry*, 1950, *64*, 699–707.

Benton, A. L. *The Revised Visual Retention Test*. New York: Psychological Corporation, 1963.

Benton, A. L. *Manuel du Test de Rétention Visuelle: applications cliniques et experimentales* (2éme ed.). Paris: Centre de Psychologie Appliquée, 1965).

Benton, A. L. Constructional apraxia and the minor hemisphere. *Confinia Neurologica*, 1967a, *29*, 1–16.

Benton, A. L. Problems in test construction in the field of aphasia. *Cortex*, 1967b, *3*, 32–58.

Benton, A. L. Differential behavioral effects in frontal lobe disease. *Neuropsychologia*, 1968, *6*, 53–60.

Benton, A. L. Constructional apraxia: some unanswered questions. In A. L. Benton, *Contributions to clinical neuropsychology*. New York: Aldine, 1969a.

Benton, A. L. Disorders of spatial orientation. In P. J. Vinken & G. W. Bruyn (Eds.), *Handbook of clinical neurology* (Vol. 3, *Disorders of higher nervous activity*). New York: Wiley, 1969b.

Benton, A. L. The measurement of aphasic disorders. In A. Cáceres Velasquez, *Aspectos patólogicos del lengage*. Lima: Centro Neuropsicologico, 1973a.

Benton, A. L. Test of three-dimensional constructional praxis. Manual. Neurosensory Center Publication No. 286. University of Iowa, 1973b.

Benton, A. L. *The Revised Visual Retention Test* (4th ed.). New York: Psychological Corporation, 1974.

Benton, A. L., Elithorn, A., Fogel, M L., & Kerr, M. A perceptual maze test sensitive to brain damage. *Journal of Neurology, Neurosurgery, and Psychiatry*, 1963, *26*, 540–543.

Benton, A. L. & Fogel, M. L. Three-dimensional constructional praxis: a clinical test. *Archives of Neurology*, 1962, *7*, 347.

Benton, A. L. & Van Allen, M. W. Impairment in facial recognition in patients with cerebral disease. *Cortex*, 1968, *4*, 344–358.

Benton, A. L. & Van Allen, M. W. Aspects of neuropsychological assessment in patients with cerebral disease. In C. M. Gaitz (Ed.), *Aging and the brain*. New York: Plenum Press, 1972.

Benton, A. L. & Van Allen, M. W. Test of Facial Recognition. Manual. Neurosensory Center Publication No. 287. University of Iowa, 1973.

Benton, A. L., Van Allen, M. W., & Fogel, M. L. Temporal orientation in cerebral disease. *Journal of Nervous and Mental Disease,* 1964, *139,* 110–119.

Berg, E. A. A simple objective technique for measuring flexibility in thinking. *Journal of General Psychology,* 1948, *39,* 15–22.

Bersoff, D. N. The revised deterioration formula for the WAIS. *Journal of Clinical Psychology,* 1970, *26,* 71–73.

Bilash, I. & Zubek, J. P. The effects of age on factorially "pure" mental abilities. *Journal of Gerontology,* 1960, *15,* 175–182.

Billingslea, F. Y. The Bender-Gestalt. A review and a perspective. *Psychological Bulletin,* 1963, *60,* 233–251.

Binet, A. Le dévelopment de intelligence chez les enfants. *L'Année psychologique,* 1908, *14,* 1–94.

Birren, J. E. Research on the psychologic aspects of aging. *Geriatrics,* 1963, *18,* 393–403.

Blake, R. R. & McCarty, B. S. A comparative evaluation of the Bellevue-Wechsler Mental Deterioration Index distributions of Allen's brain injured patients and of normal subjects. *Journal of Clinical Psychology,* 1948, *4,* 415–418.

Blakemore, C. & Falconer, M. A. Long term effects of anterior temporal lobectomy on certain cognitive functions. *Journal of Neurology, Neurosurgery, and Psychiatry,* 1967, *30,* 364–367.

Blakemore, C., Iversen, S. D., & Zangwill, O. L. Brain functions. *Annual Review of Psychology,* 1972, *23,* 413–456.

Blinkov, S. M. & Glezer, I. I. *The human brain in figures and tables.* New York: Plenum Press & Basic Books, 1968.

Blumer, D. & Benson, D. F. Personality changes in frontal and temporal lobe lesions. In D. F. Benson & D. Blumer (Eds.), *Psychiatric aspects of neurologic disorders.* New York: Grune & Stratton, 1975.

Bogen, J. E. The other side of the brain I: Dysgraphia and dyscopia following cerebral commissurotomy. *Bulletin of the Los Angeles Neurological Societies,* 1969a, *34,* 73–105.

Bogen, J. E. The other side of the brain II: An appositional mind. *Bulletin of the Los Angeles Neurological Societies,* 1969b, *34,* 135–162.

Bogen, J. E. & Gordon, H. W. Musical tests for functional lateralization with intra-carotid amobarbitol. *Nature,* 1971, *230,* 524.

Bolgar, H. The case study method. In. B. B. Wolman (Ed.), *Handbook of clinical psychology.* New York: McGraw-Hill, 1965.

Bolin, B. J. A comparison of Raven's Progressive Matrices (1938) with the A.C.E. Psychological Examination and the Otis Gamma Mental Ability Test. *Journal of Consulting Psychology,* 1955, *19,* 400.

Boll, T. J. & Reitan, R. M. Effect of age on performance of the Trail Making Test. *Perceptual and Motor Skills,* 1973, *36,* 691–694.

Boller, F., & Vignolo, L. A. Latent sensory aphasia in hemisphere-damaged patients: an experimental study with the Token Test. *Brain,* 1966, *89,* 815–831.

Bolton, N., Britton, P. G., & Savage, R. D. Some normative data on the W.A.I.S. and its indices in an aged population. *Journal of Clinical Psychology,* 1966, *22,* 184–188.

Bolton, N., Savage, R. D., & Roth, M. The Modified Word Learning Test and the aged psychiatric patient. *British Journal of Psychiatry,* 1967, *113,* 1139–1140.

Bonin, G. von. Anatomical asymmetries of the cerebral hemispheres. In V. B. Mountcastle (Ed.), *Interhemispheric relations and cerebral dominance*. Baltimore: Johns Hopkins University Press, 1962a.

Bonin, G. Von. Brain and mind. In S. Koch (Ed.), *Psychology: a study of a science* (Vol. 4, *Biologically oriented fields*). New York: McGraw-Hill, 1962b.

Bonner, F. Cobb, S., Sweet, W. H., & White, J. C. Frontal lobe surgery. *Psychiatric Treatment. Proceedings of the Association for Research in Nervous and Mental Disease*, 1953, *31*, 392–421.

Borkowski, J. G., Benton, A. L., & Spreen, O. Word fluency and brain damage. *Neuropsychologia*, 1967, *5*, 135–140.

Bortner, M. & Birch, H. G. Perceptual and perceptual-motor dissociation in brain-damaged patients. *Journal of Nervous and Mental Disease*, 1962, *134*, 103–108.

Boyd, R. D. *The Boyd Developmental Progress Scale*. San Bernadino, Calif.: Inland Counties Regional Center, 1974.

Brain, R. Disorders of memory. In R. Brain & M. Wilkinson (Eds.), *Recent advances in neurology and neuropsychiatry*. Boston: Little, Brown, 1969.

Branch, C., Milner, B., & Rasmussen, T. Intracarotid sodium amytal for the lateralization of cerebral speech dominance. *Journal of Neurosurgery*, 1964, *21*, 399–405.

Brierly, J. B. The neuropathology of amnesic states. In C. W. M. Whitty & O. L. Zangwill (Eds.), *Amnesia*, London: Butterworth, 1966.

Briggs, P. F. The validity of WAIS performance subtests completed with one hand. *Journal of Clinical Psychology*. 1960, *16*, 318–319.

Briggs, P. F. The validity of the Porteus Maze Test completed with the non-dominant hand. *Journal of Clinical Psychology*, 1963, *19*, 169–171.

Brilliant, P. J. & Gynther, M. D. Relationships between performance on three tests for organicity and selected patient variables. *Journal of Consulting Psychology*. 1963, *27*, 474–479.

Broadbent, D. E. Recent analyses of short-term memory. In K. H. Pribram & D. E. Broadbent (Eds.), *Biology of Memory*. New York: Academic Press, 1970.

Brodal, A. *Neurological anatomy* (2nd ed.). New York: Oxford University Press, 1969.

Brodman, K. Cornell Medical Index—Health Questionnaire. In A. Weider (Ed.), *Contributions toward medical psychology* (Vol. 2). New York: Ronald Press, 1953.

Brodman, K., Erdmann, A. J. Jr., Lorge, I., & Wolff, H. G. The Cornell Medical Index: an adjunct to medical interview. *Journal of the American Medical Association*, 1949, *140*, 530–534.

Brookshire, R. H. *An introduction to aphasia*. Minneapolis, Minn.: BRK Publishers, 1973.

Brown, E. C., Casey, A., Fisch, R. I., & Neuringer, C. Trail Making Test as a screening device for the detection of brain damage. *Journal of Consulting Psychology*, 1958, *22*, 469–474.

Brown, J. W. Language, cognition, and the thalamus. *Confinia Neurologica*, 1974, *36*, 33–60.

Brussel, I. A., Grassi, J. P., & Melniker, A. A. The Rorschach method and post-concussion syndrome. *Psychiatric Quarterly*, 1942, *16*, 706–743.

Buck, J. N. The H-T-P test. *Journal of Clinical Psychology*, 1948, *4*, 151–159.

Buck, M. W. *Dysphasia*. Englewood Cliffs, N. J.: Prentice-Hall, 1968.

Burgemeister, B. B. *Psychological techniques in neurological diagnosis*. New York: Harper & Row, 1962.

Buros, O. K. *The seventh mental measurements yearbook*. Highland Park, N. J.: The Gryphon Press, 1972.

Buschke, H. & Fuld, P. A. Evaluating storage, retention, and retrieval in disordered memory and learning. *Neurology*, 1974, *11*, 1019–1025.

Butler, H. M., Rice, L. N., & Wagstaff, A. K. *Quantitative naturalistic research.* Englewood Cliffs, N. J.: Prentice-Hall, 1963.

Butters, N. An analysis of the Korsakoff patient's memory disorder. Paper presented at the American Psychological Association Convention, Washington, D. C., 1971.

Butters, N. & Barton, M. Effect of parietal lobe damage on the performance of reversible operations in space. *Neuropsychologia*, 1970, *8*, 205–214.

Butters, N. & Cermak, L. S. The role of cognitive factors in the memory disorders of alcoholic patients with the Korsakoff syndrome. *Annals of the New York Academy of Science*, 1974, *233*, 61–75.

Butters, N., Samuels, I., Goodglass, H. & Brody, B. Short-term visual and auditory memory disorders after parietal and frontal lobe damage. *Cortex*, 1970, *6*, 440–459.

Canter, A. H. Direct and indirect measurement of psychological deficit in multiple sclerosis: Parts I and II. *Journal of General Psychology*, 1951, *44*, 3–25, 27–50.

Carson, R. C. Interpretive manual to the MMPI. In J. N. Butcher (Ed.), *MMPI: Research developments and clinical applications.* New York: McGraw-Hill, 1969a.

Carson, R. C. Issues in the teaching of clinical MMPI interpretation. In J. N. Butcher (Ed.), *MMPI: Research developments and clinical applications.* New York: McGraw-Hill, 1969b.

Carter, J. W., Jr. & Bowles, J. W. A manual on qualitative aspects of psychological examining. *Clinical Psychology Monographs* (No. 2). *Journal of Clinical Psychology*, 1948, *4*, 110–150.

Cassel, R. H. The order of the tests in the battery. *Journal of Clinical Psychology*, 1962, *18*, 464–465.

Chapman, L. F., Thetford, W. N., Berlin, L. Guthrie, T. C., & Wolff, H. G. Highest integrative functions in man during stress. In H. C. Solomon, S. Cobb, & W. Penfield (Eds.), *The brain and human behavior. Research Publication of the Association for Nervous and Mental Disease*, 1958, *36*, 491–534.

Chapman, L. F. & Wolff, H. G. The cerebral hemispheres and the highest integrative functions of man. *A. M. A. Archives of Neurology*, 1959, *1*, 357–424.

Chassan, J. B. Statistical inference and the single case in clinical design. *Psychiatry*, 1960, *23*, 173–184.

Christenson, A.-L. *Luria's neuropsychological investigation: text, manual, and test cards.* New York: Spectrum (Halsted Press, John Wiley & Sons, distributor), 1975.

Chusid, J. G. *Correlative neuroanatomy and functional neurology* (15th ed.). Los Altos, Calif.: Lange, 1973.

Clark, J. W. The aging dimension: a factorial analysis of individual differences with age on psychological and physiological measurements. *Journal of Gerontology*, 1960, *15*, 183–187.

Cohen, J., Wechsler Memory Scale performance of psychoneurotic, organic, and schizophrenic groups. *Journal of Consulting Psychology*, 1950, *14*, 371–375.

Cohen, J. Factor-analytically based rationale for Wechsler Adult Intelligence Scale. *Journal of Consulting Psychology*, 1957a, *21*, 451–457.

Cohen, J. The factorial structure of the WAIS between early adulthood and old age. *Journal of Consulting Psychology*, 1957b, *21*, 283–290.

Cohen, L. Perception of reversible figures after brain injury. *A.M.A. Archives of Neurology and Psychiatry*, 1959, *81*, 765–775.

Cohn, R. Role of "body image concept" in pattern of ipsilateral clinical extinction. *A. M. A. Archives of Neurology and Psychiatry*, 1953, *70*, 503–509.

Collier, H. L. & Levy, N. A preliminary study employing the Sequential Matching Memory task in an attempt to differentially diagnose brain damage. Unpublished manuscript, undated.

Colonna, A. & Faglioni, P. The performance of hemisphere-damaged patients on spatial intelligence tests. *Cortex*, 1966, *2*, 293–307.

Cooperative School and College Ability Tests (SCAT). Princeton, N. J.: Educational Testing Service, 1966.

Corkin, S. Acquisition of motor skill after bilateral-medial temporal lobe excision. *Neuropsychologia*, 1968, *6*, 255–266.

Costa, L. D. The relation of visuospatial dysfunction to digit span performance in patients with cerebral lesions. *Cortex*, 1975, *11*, 31–36.

Costa, L. D. & Vaughan, H. G., Jr. Performance of patients with lateralized cerebral lesions. I. Verbal and perceptual tests. *Journal of Nervous and Mental Disease*, 1962, *134*, 162–168.

Costa, L. D., Vaughan, H. G., Levita, E., & Farber, N. Purdue Pegboard as a predictor of the presence and laterality of cerebral lesions. *Journal of Consulting Psychology*, 1963, *27*, 133–137.

Critchley, M. *The parietal lobes*. Baltimore: Williams & Wilkins, 1953.

Critchley, M. Disorders of highest nervous activity: introductory remarks. In P. J. Vinken & G. W. Bruyn (Eds.), *Handbook of clinical neurology* (Vol. 3, *Disorders of higher nervous activity*). New York: Wiley, 1969.

Cronbach, L. J. *Essentials of psychological testing* (3rd ed.). New York: Harper & Row, 1970.

Cronholm, B. & Molander, L. Memory disturbances after electroconvulsive therapy. *Acta Psychiatrica et Neurologica Scandinavica*, 1957, *32*, 280–306.

Cronholm, B. & Ottoson, J.-O. Reliability and validity of a memory test battery. *Acta Psychiatrica Scandinavica*, 1963, *39*, 218–234.

Crosby, E. C., Humphrey, T., & Lauer, E. H. *Correlative anatomy of the nervous system*. New York: Macmillan, 1962.

Crow, C. M. & Lewinsohn, P. M. Performance of left hemiplegic stroke patients on the Benton Visual Retention Test. Doctoral dissertation, University of Oregon, 1969.

Cutter, F. Intelligence: a heuristic frame of reference. *American Psychologist*, 1957, *12*, 650–651.

Dahlstrom, W. G. & Welsh, G. S. *An MMPI handbook*. Minneapolis: University of Minnesota Press, 1960.

Dahlstrom, W. G., Welsh, G. S., & Dahlstrom, L. E. *An MMPI handbook* (Vol. 1. *Clinical Interpretation*) (Rev. Ed.). Minneapolis: University of Minnesota Press, 1975.

Darley, F. L. Apraxia of speech: 107 years of terminological confusion. Paper presented at the annual convention of the American Speech and Hearing Association, Chicago, 1967.

Darley, F. L. The efficacy of language rehabilitation. *Journal of Speech and Hearing Disorders*, 1972, *37*, 3–21.

Davidson, R. E. & Adams, J. R. Verbal and imagery processes in children's paired-associate learning. *Journal of Experimental Child Psychology*, 1970, *9*, 429–435.

Davies, A. The influence of age on Trial Making test performance. *Journal of Clinical Psychology*, 1968, *24*, 96–98.

DeArmond, S. J., Fusco, M. M., & Dewey, M. M. *Structure of the human brain*. New York: Oxford University Press, 1974.

Dee, H. L. Visuoconstructive and visuoperceptive deficit in patients with unilateral cerebral lesions. *Neuropsychologia*, 1970, *8*, 305–314.

Dee, H. L. & Fontenot, D. J. Use of the non-preferred hand in graphomotor performance: a methodological study. *Confinia Neurologica,* 1969, *31,* 273–280.

Dee, H. L. & Fontenot, D. J. Cerebral dominance and lateral differences in perception and memory. *Neuropsychologia,* 1973, *11,* 167–173.

Delp, H. A. Psychological evaluation: some problems and suggestions. *The Training School Bulletin,* 1959, *56*(3), 79–84.

Dennerll, R. D. Cognitive deficits and lateral brain dysfunction in temporal lobe epilepsy. *Epilepsia,* 1964, *5,* 177–191.

Denny-Brown, D., Meyer, J. S., & Horenstein, S. The significance of perceptual rivalry resulting from parietal lesion. *Brain,* 1952, *75,* 433–471.

De Renzi, E. Nonverbal memory and hemispheric side of lesion. *Neuropsychologia,* 1968, *6,* 181–189.

De Renzi, E. & Faglioni, P. The comparative efficiency of intelligence and vigilance tests in detecting hemispheric cerebral damage. *Cortex,* 1965, *1,* 410–433.

De Renzi, E. & Faglioni, P. The relationships between visuospatial impairment and constructional apraxia. *Cortex,* 1967, *3,* 327–341.

De Renzi, E., Faglioni, P., Savoiardo, M., & Vignolo, L. A. The influence of aphasia and of the hemisphere side of the cerebral lesion on abstract thinking. *Cortex,* 1966, *2,* 399–420.

De Renzi, E., Pieczuro, A., & Vignolo, L. A. Ideational apraxia: a quantitative study. *Neuropsychologia,* 1968, *6,* 41–52.

De Renzi, E. & Scotti, G. Autotopagnosia: fiction or reality? *A.M.A. Archives of Neurology,* 1970, *23,* 221–227.

De Renzi, E. & Spinnler, H. Impaired performance on color tasks in patients with hemisphere damage. *Cortex,* 1967, *3,* 194–217.

De Renzi, E. & Vignolo, L. A. The Token Test: a sensitive test to detect disturbances in aphasics. *Brain,* 1962, *85,* 665–678.

Deutsch, J. A. *The structural basis of behavior.* Chicago: University of Chicago Press, 1960.

DeWolfe, A. S., Barrell, R. P., Becker, B. C., & Spaner, F. E. Intellectual deficit in chronic schizophrenia and brain damage. *Journal of Consulting and Clinical Psychology,* 1971, *36,* 197–204.

Diller, L. Hemiplegia. In J. F. Garrett & E. S. Levine (Eds.), *Psychological practices with the physically disabled.* New York: Columbia University Press, 1962.

Diller, L. Brain damage, spatial orientation, and rehabilitation. In S. J. Freedman (Ed.), *The neuropsychology of spatially oriented behavior.* Homewood, Ill.: Dorsey, 1968.

Diller, L., Ben-Yishay, Y., Gerstman, L. J., Goodkin, R., Gordon, W., & Weinberg, J. *Studies in cognition and rehabilitation in hemiplegia* (Rehabilitation Monograph No. 50). New York: New York University Medical Center Institute of Rehabilitation Medicine, 1974.

Diller, L. & Weinberg, J. Evidence for accident-prone behavior in hemiplegic patients. *Archives of Physical Medicine and Rehabilitation,* 1970, *51,* 358–363.

Diller, L. & Weinberg, J. Differential aspects of attention in brain-damaged persons. *Perceptual and Motor Skills,* 1972, *35,* 71–81.

Doehring, D. G. & Reitan, R. M. MMPI performance of aphasic and nonaphasic brain-damaged patients. *Journal of Clinical Psychology,* 1960, *16,* 307–309.

Dörken, H., Jr. & Kral, V. A. The psychological differentiation of organic brain lesions and their localization by means of the Rorschach test. *American Journal of Psychiatry,* 1952, *108,* 764–770.

Doll, E. A. *Measurement of social competence.* Minneapolis: Educational Publishers, 1953.

Doll, E. A. *Vineland Social Maturity Scale: Manual of directions* (Rev. ed.). Minneapolis: American Guidance Service, 1965.

Doppelt, J. E. How accurate is a test score? In D. A. Payne & R. F. McMorris (Eds.), *Educational and psychological measurement.* Waltham, Mass.: Blaisdell, 1967.

Drachman, D. A. & Arbit, J. Memory and the hippocampal complex. II. Is memory a multiple process? *Archives of Neurology,* 1966, *15,* 52–61.

Drake, W. E., Jr. Blumenkrantz, J., Dahlgren, H., & Borum, E. *A neuropsychological approach to the assessment of intellectual impairment. Manual for the Neurological Index of Mental Impairment.* Unpublished manuscript. (Available from W. E. Drake, Jr., 908 Sir Francis Drake Blvd., Kentfield, Calif. 94904.)

Drake, W. E., Jr., Blumenkrantz, J., & Vitale, J. H. *Analysis of interpretation of the Neurological Index of Mental Impairment.* Unpublished manuscript, 1973. (Available from W. E. Drake, Jr., see above citation.)

Drewe, E. A. The effect of type and area of brain lesion on Wisconsin Card Sorting Test performance. *Cortex,* 1974, *10,* 159–170.

Duke, R. B. Intellectual evaluation of brain-damaged patients with a WAIS short form. *Psychological Reports,* 1967, *20,* 858.

Dunn, L. M. *Expanded manual for the Peabody Picture Vocabulary Test.* Circle Pines, Minn.: American Guidance Service, 1965.

Dunn, L. M. & Markwardt, F. C., Jr. *Manual. Peabody Individual Achievement Test.* Circle Pines, Minn.: American Guidance Service, 1970.

Dvorine, I. *Dvorine Pseudo-Isochromatic Plates* (2nd ed.,). Baltimore: Waverly Press, 1953.

Eigenbrod, F. E. *Psychological examination for organicity.* Tuskegee, Ala.: Psychology Service, Veterans Administration Hospital, undated.

Eisenson, J. *Examining for aphasia. A manual for the examination of aphasia and related disturbances.* New York: Psychological Corporation, 1954.

Eisenson, J. Language and intellectual modifications associated with right cerebral damage. *Language and Speech,* 1962, *5,* 49–53.

Eisenson, J. *Adult aphasia.* New York: Appleton-Century-Crofts, 1973.

Elithorn, A., Jones, D., Kerr., M. & Lee, D. The effects of the variation of two physical parameters on empirical difficulty in a perceptual maze test. *British Journal of Psychology,* 1964, *55,* 31–37.

Elizur, A. *The psycho-organic syndrome: its assessment and treatment including manual for the Elizur Test of Psycho-Organicity.* Los Angeles: Western Psychological Services, 1969.

English, W. H. Alzheimer's disease: its incidence and recognition. *Psychiatric Quarterly,* 1942, *16,* 91–106.

Eysenck, M. D. An exploratory study of mental organization in senility. *Journal of Neurology and Psychiatry,* 1945a, *8,* 15–21.

Eysenck, M. D. A study of certain qualitative aspects of problem solving behavior in senile dementia patients. *Journal of Mental Science,* 1945b, *91,* 337–345.

Farnsworth, D. Farnsworth-Munsell 100-hue and dichotomous test for color vision. *Journal of the Optical Society of America,* 1943, *33,* 568–578.

Field, J. G. Two types of tables for use with Wechsler's Intelligence Scales. *Journal of Clinical Psychology,* 1960, *16,* 3–7.

Filskov, S. B. & Goldstein, S. G. Diagnostic validity of the Halstead-Reitan Neuropsychological Battery. *Journal of Consulting and Clinical Psychology,* 1974, *42,* 382–388.

Fisher, G. C. Selective and differentially accelerated intellectual dysfunctions in specific brain damage. *Journal of Clinical Psychology*, 1958, *14*, 395–398.

Fisher, J. & Gonda, T. A. Neurologic techniques and Rorschach test in detecting brain pathology. *A.M.A. Archives of Neurology and Psychiatry*, 1955, *79*, 117–124.

Fisher, J., Gonda, T. & Little, K. B. The Rorschach and central nervous system pathology. *American Journal of Psychiatry*, 1955, *111*, 486–492.

Fitzhugh, K. B., Fitzhugh, L. C. & Reitan, R. M. Psychological deficits in relation to acuteness of brain dysfunction. *Journal of Consulting Psychology*, 1961, *25*, 61–66.

Fleming, M. The Trail Making Test with industrially injured workers. Unpublished paper, Sept., 1975.

Fogel, M. L. The Gerstmann syndrome and the parietal symptom complex. *The Psychological Record*, 1962, *12*, 85–99.

Fogel, M. L. The Proverbs Test in the appraisal of cerebral disease. *Journal of General Psychology*, 1965, *72*, 269–275.

Fogel, M. L. Picture description and interpretation in brain-damaged patients. *Cortex*, 1967, *3*, 433–448.

Folstein, M. F., Folstein, S. E., & McHugh, P. R. "Mini-Mental State." *Journal of Psychiatric Research*, 1975, *12*, 189–198.

Fowler, R. D., Jr. Automated interpretation of personality test data. In J. N. Butcher (Ed.), *MMPI: research developments and clinical applications*. New York: McGraw-Hill, 1969.

Frank, L. K. Projective methods for the study of personality. *Journal of Psychology*, 1939, *8*, 389–413.

French, J. L. *Manual. Pictorial Test of Intelligence*. New York: Houghton Mifflin, 1964.

Friedman, A. S. Minimal effects of severe depression on cognitive functioning. *Journal of Abnormal and Social Psychology*, 1964, *69*, 237–243.

Friedman, S. H. Psychometric effects of frontal and parietal lobe brain damage. (Doctoral Dissertation). University of Minnesota, 1950.

Fuld, P. A. Storage, retention, and retrieval in Korsakoff's syndrome. Paper presented at the meeting of the International Neuropsychological Society, Tampa, Fla., Feb. 1975.

Fuller, G. B. *The Minnesota Percepto-Diagnostic Test* (Rev. ed.). Brandon, Vt.: Clinical Psychology Publishing Co., 1969.

Fuller, G. B. & Laird, J. T. The Minnesota Percepto-Diagnostic Test. *Journal of Clinical Psychology. Monograph Supplement*, 1963, No. 16.

Gainotti, G. Emotional behavior and hemispheric side of the brain. *Cortex*, 1972, *8*, 41–55.

Gainotti, G. & Tiacci, C. Patterns of drawing disability in right and left hemisphere patients. *Neuropsychologia*, 1970, 379–384.

Galin, D. Implications for psychiatry of left and right cerebral specialization. *Archives of General Psychiatry*, 1974, *31*, 572–583.

Gardner, E. *Fundamentals of Neurology* (5th ed.). Philadelphia: W. B. Saunders, 1968.

Gardner, R. W. Jackson, D. N., & Messick, S. J. Personality organization in cognitive controls and intellectual abilities. *Psychological Issues*, 1960, *2*, Monograph 8.

Garrett, H. E. A developmental theory of intelligence. *American Psychologist*, 1946. *1*, 372–378.

Garron, D. C. & Cheifetz, D. I. Comment on "Bender Gestalt discernment of organic pathology." *Psychological Bulletin*, 1965, *63*, 197–200.

Gates, A. I. & MacGinitie, W. H. *Gates-MacGinitie Reading Tests*. New York: Teachers College Press, Teachers College, Columbia University, 1965, 1969.

Gazzaniga, M. S. *The bisected brain*. New York: Appleton-Century-Crofts, 1970.

General Aptitude Test Battery. Washington, D. C.: U. S. Department of Labor, 1965.

Gerstmann, J. Syndrome of finger agnosia, disorientation for right and left, agraphia, and acalculia. *Archives of Neurology and Psychiatry*, 1940, *44*, 398–408.

Gerstmann, J. Problems of imperception of disease and of impaired body territories with organic lesions. *Archives of Neurology and Psychiatry*, 1942, *48*, 890–913.

Gerstmann, J. Some notes on the Gerstmann syndrome. *Neurology*, 1957, *7*, 866–869.

Geschwind, N. Disconnexion syndromes in animals and man. *Brain*, 1965, *88*, 237–294.

Geschwind, N. Problems in the anatomical understanding of the aphasias. In A. L. Benton (Ed.), *Contributions to clinical neuropsychology*. Chicago: Aldine, 1969.

Geschwind, N. The organization of language and the brain. *Science*, 1970, *170*, 940–944.

Geschwind, N. Language and the brain. *Scientific American*, 1972, *226*, 76–83.

Geschwind, N. & Levitsky, W. Human brain: left-right asymmetries in temporal speech region. *Science*, 1968, *161*, 186–187.

Gesell, A. *The first five years of life*. New York: Harper & Row, 1940.

Gesell, A. & Associates. *Gesell Developmental Schedules*. New York: Psychological Corporation, 1949.

Getzels, J. W. & Jackson, P. W. *Creativity and intelligence*. New York: Wiley, 1962.

Ghent, L., Weinstein, S., Semmes, J., & Teuber, H.-L. Effect of unilateral brain injury in man on learning of tactual discrimination. *Journal of Comparative and Physiological Psychology*, 1955, *48*, 478–481.

Gilberstadt, H. *Comprehensive MMPI code book for males*. Minneapolis: MMPI Research Laboratory, Veterans Administration Hospital, 1970.

Glaser, G. H. Convulsive disorders (epilepsy). In H. H. Merritt, *A textbook of neurology* (5th ed.). Philadelphia: Lea & Febiger, 1973.

Glaudin, V., Lezak, M. D., & Pankratz, L. *The self-administered battery (SAB)*. Unpublished test, 1972.

Gloning, I., Gloning, K., & Hoff, H. *Neuropsychological symptoms and syndromes in lesions of the occipital lobe and adjacent areas*. Paris: Gauthier-Villars, 1968.

Gloning, K. & Hoff, H. Cerebral localisation of disorders of higher nervous activity. In P. J. Vinken & G. W. Bruyn (Eds.), *Handbook of clinical neurology* (Vol. 3, *Disorders of higher nervous activity*). New York: Wiley, 1969.

Gloning, K. & Quatember, R. Statistical evidence of neuropsychological syndromes in left-handed and ambidextrous patients. *Cortex*, 1966, *2*, 484–488.

Glowinski, H. Cognitive deficits in temporal lobe epilepsy. *Journal of Nervous and Mental Disease*, 1973, *157*, 129–137.

Goldberg, E. Motor perseverations and languages of coding visual information. Paper presented at the meeting of the International Neuropsychological Society, Tampa Fla., 1975.

Goldberg, L. R. The effectiveness of clinicians' judgments: the diagnosis of organic brain disease from the Bender-Gestalt test. *Journal of Consulting Psychology*, 1959, *23*, 25–33.

Goldfried, M. R., Stricker, G., & Weiner, I. B. *Rorschach handbook of clinical and research applications*. Englewood Cliffs, N. J.: Prentice-Hall, 1971.

Goldstein, G. & Chotlos, J. W. Dependency and brain damage in alcoholics. *Perceptual and Motor Skills*, 1965, *21*, 135–150.

Goldstein, G. & Shelly, C. H. Similarities and differences between psychological deficit in aging and brain damage. *Journal of Gerontology*. 1975, *30*, 448–455.

Goldstein, K. H. *The organism*. New York: American Book Co., 1939.

Goldstein, K. H. *Aftereffects of brain injuries in war*. New York: Grune & Stratton, 1942.

Goldstein, K. H. & Scheerer, M. Abstract and concrete behavior; an experimental study with special tests. *Psychological Monographs*, 1941, *53*, No. 2 (Whole No. 239).

Goldstein, K. H. & Scheerer, M. Tests of abstract and concrete behavior. In A. Weider (Ed.), *Contributions to medical psychology* (Vol. 2). New York: Ronald Press, 1953.

Goldstein, S. G., Deysack, R. E., & Kleinknecht, R. A. Effect of experience and amount of information on identification of cerebral impairment. *Journal of Consulting and Clinical Psychology*, 1973, *41*, 30–34.

Gonen, J. Y. The use of Wechsler's Deterioration Quotient in cases of diffuse and symmetrical cerebral atrophy. *Journal of Clinical Psychology*, 1970, *26*, 174–177.

Gonen, J. Y. & Brown, L. Role of vocabulary in deterioration and restitution of mental functioning. *Proceedings of the 76th Annual Convention of the American Psychological Association*, 1968, *3*, 469–470. (Summary)

Gooddy, W. Disorders of the time sense. In P. J. Vinken & G. W. Bruyn (Eds.), *Handbook of clinical neurology* (Vol. 3, *Disorders of higher nervous activity*). New York: Wiley, 1969.

Goodglass, H. Psychological effects of diffuse versus focal lesions. Paper presented at the Annual Convention of the American Psychological Association, Montreal, Aug., 1973.

Goodglass, H. & Quadfasel, F. A. Language laterality in left-handed aphasics. *Brain*, 1954, *77*, 521–548.

Gorham, D. R. A Proverbs Test for clinical and experimental use. *Psychological Reports, Monograph Supplement*, No. 1, 1956, *2*, 1–12.

Graham, C. H. Visual form perception. In C. H. Graham (Ed.), *Vision and visual perception*. New York: Wiley, 1965.

Graham, F. K. & Kendall, B. S. Memory-for-Designs Test: Revised general manual. *Perceptual and Motor Skills, Monograph Supplement*, No. 2-VII, 1960, *11*, 147–188.

Grant, D. A. & Berg, E. A. A behavioral analysis of degree of reinforcement and ease of shifting to new responses in a Weigl-type card-sorting problem. *Journal of Experimental Psychology*, 1948, *38*, 404–411.

Grassi, J. R. *The Grassi Block Substitution Test for measuring organic brain pathology*. Springfield, Ill.: C. C. Thomas, 1953.

Green, J. D. The hippocampus. *Physiology Review*, 1964, *44*, 562–608.

Grewel, F. Acalculia. *Brain*, 1952, *75*, 397–407.

Grinker, R. R. & Sahs, A. L. *Neurology* (6th ed.). Springfield, Ill.: C. C. Thomas, 1966.

Gronwall, D. & Wrightson, P. Recovery after minor head injury. *Lancet*, 14 Dec. 1974, *2* (7894), 1452.

Grundvig, J. L., Needham, W. E., & Ajax, E. T. Comparisons of different scoring and administration procedures for the Memory-for-Designs Test. *Journal of Clinical Psychology*, 1970, *26*, 353–357.

Guertin, W. H., Ladd, C. E., Frank, G. H., Rabin, A. I., & Hiester, D. S. Research with the Wechsler Intelligence Scales for Adults: 1960–1965. *Psychological Bulletin*, 1966, *66*, 385–409.

Gutman, B. The application of of the Wechsler-Bellevue Scale in the diagnosis of organic brain disorders. *Journal of Clinical Psychology*, 1950, *6*, 195–198.

Hain, J. D. Scoring system for the Bender Gestalt test: Preliminary manual. Unpublished manuscript, 1963.

Hain, J. D. The Bender Gestalt Test: A scoring method for identifying brain damage. *Journal of Consulting Psychology*, 1964, *28*, 34–40.

Hall, J.C. Correlation of modified form of Raven's Progressive Matrices (1938) with the Wechsler Adult Intelligence Scale. *Journal of Consulting Psychology,* 1957a, *21,* 23–26.

Hall, J. C. Reliability (internal consistency) of the Wechsler Memory Scale and correlation with the Wechsler-Bellevue Intelligence Scale. *Journal of Consulting Psychology,* 1957b, *21,* 131–135.

Hall, M. M. & Hall, G. C. Antithetical ideational modes of left versus right unilateral hemisphere lesions as demonstrated on the Rorschach. *Proceedings of the 76th Annual Convention of the American Psychological Association,* 1968, *3,* 657–658.

Halstead, W. C. *Brain and intelligence.* Chicago: University of Chicago Press, 1947.

Halstead, W. C. & Wepman, J. M. The Halstead-Wepman Aphasia Screening Test. *Journal of Speech and Hearing Disorders,* 1959, *14,* 9–15.

Hamlin, R. M. Intellectual function 14 years after frontal lobe surgery. *Cortex,* 1970, *6,* 299–307.

Hanfmann, E. Concept Formation Test. In A. Weider (Ed.), *Contributions toward medical psychology.* New York: Ronald Press, 1953.

Hardy, C. H., Rand, G., & Rittler, J. M. C. *H-R-R Pseudoisochromatic Plates.* Buffalo, N. Y.: American Optical Co., 1955.

Harris, D. B. *Children's drawings as measures of intellectual maturity.* New York: Harcourt, Brace, & World, 1963.

Harris, G. W., Michael, R. R., & Scott, P. Neurological site of action of stilboestrol in eliciting sexual behavior. In K. H. Pribram (Ed.), *Brain and behavior* (Vol. 1., *Mood, states and mind*). Baltimore: Penguin Books, 1969.

Harrison, D. M. & Chagnon, J. G. The effect of age, sex, and language on the Minnesota Percepto-Diagnostic Test. *Journal of Clinical Psychology,* 1966, *22,* 302–303.

Harrower-Erickson, M. R. Personality changes accompanying cerebral lesions. *Archives of Neurology and Psychiatry,* 1940, *43,* 859–890.

Harrower, M. R. Differential diagnosis. In B. B. Wolman (Ed.), *Handbook of clinical psychology.* New York: McGraw-Hill, 1965.

Hathaway, S. R. & McKinley, J. C. *The Minnesota Multiphasic Personality Inventory Manual* (Rev.). New York: Psychological Corporation, 1951.

Hebb, D. O. The effect of early and late brain injury upon test scores, and the nature of normal adult intelligence. *Proceedings of the American Philsophical Society,* 1942, *85,* 275–292.

Hebb, D. O. *Organization of behavior.* New York: Wiley, 1949.

Hebb, D. O. & Morton, N. W. The McGill Adult Comprehension Examination: "Verbal Situation" and "Picture Anomaly" series. *Journal of Educational Psychology,* 1943, *34,* 16–25.

Hécaen, H. Clinical symptomatology in right and left hemisphere lesions. In V. B. Mountcastle (Ed.), *Interhemispheric relations and cerebral dominance in man.* Baltimore: Johns Hopkins University Press, 1962.

Hécaen, H. Mental symptoms associated with tumors of the frontal lobe. In J. M. Warren & K. Akert (Eds.), *The frontal granular cortex and behavior.* New York: McGraw-Hill, 1964.

Hécaen, H. Cerebral localization of mental functions and their disorders. In P. J. Vinken & G. W. Bruyn (Eds.), *Handbook of clinical neurology* (Vol. 3, *Disorders of higher nervous activity*). New York: Wiley, 1969.

Hécaen, H. & Ajuriaguerra, J. de. *Left-handedness.* New York: Grune & Stratton, 1964.

Hécaen, H., Ajuriaguerra, J. de, & Massonnet, J. Les troubles visuo-constructifs par lesion pariéto-occipitale droite. *L'Encéphale,* 1951, *40,* 122–179.

Hécaen, H. & Assal, G. A comparison of constructive deficits following right and left hemisphere lesions. *Neuropsychologia*, 1970, *8*, 289–303.

Heilbrun, A. B., Jr. Specificity of immediate memory function associated with cerebral cortex damage. *Journal of Mental Science*, 1960, *106*, 241–245.

Heimburger, R. F. & Reitan, R. M. Easily administered written test for lateralizing brain lesions. *Journal of Neurosurgery*, 1961, *18*, 301–312.

Henry, G. M., Weingartner, H., and Murphy, D. L. Influence of affective states and psychoactive drugs on verbal learning and memory. *American Journal of Psychiatry*, 1973, *130*, 966–971.

Henry, W. E. The Thematic Apperception Technique in the study of cultural-personal relations. *Genetic Psychology Monographs*, 1947, *35*, 3–135.

Hetherington, R. A neologism learning test. *British Journal of Psychiatry*, 1967, *113*, 1133–1137.

Hewson, L. The Wechsler-Bellevue Scale and the Substitution Test as aids in neuropsychiatric diagnosis. *Journal of Nervous and Mental Disease*, 1949, *109* (Part 1), 158–183; (Part 2), 246–266.

Hillbom, E. After-effects of brain injuries. *Acta Psychiatrica et Neurologica Scandinavica*, 1960, *35*, Suppl. 142.

Hirschenfang, S. A comparison of Bender Gestalt reproductions of right and left hemiplegic patients. *Journal of Clinical Psychology*, 1960a, *16*, 439.

Hirschenfang, S. A comparison of WAIS scores of hemiplegic patients with and without aphasia. *Journal of Clinical Psychology*, 1960b, *16*, 351.

Hirschenfang, S., Silber, M., & Benton, J. G. Psychosocial factors influencing the rehabilitation of the hemiplegic patient. *Diseases of the Nervous System*, 1968, *29*, 373–379.

Hoffman, W. C. Memory grows. *Kybernetik*, 1971, *9*, 151–157.

Hooper, H. E. *The Hooper Visual Organization Test. Manual.* Los Angeles: Western Psychological Services, 1958.

Hopkins, B. & Post, F. The significance of abstract and concrete behavior in elderly psychiatric patients and control subjects. *Journal of Mental Science*, 1955, *101*, 841–850.

Hopkins, B. & Roth, M. Psychological test performance in patients over 60. II. Paraphrenia, arteriosclerotic psychoses, and acute confusion. *Journal of Mental Science*, 1953, *99*, 451–463.

Hovey, H. B. Brain lesions and five MMPI items. *Journal of Consulting Psychology*, 1964, *28*, 78–79.

Hovey, H. B. & Kooi, K. A. Transient disturbance of thought processes and epilepsy. *A.M.A. Archives of Neurology and Psychiatry*, 1955, *74*, 287–291.

Hovey, H. G., Kooi, K. A., & Thomas, M. H. MMPI profiles of epileptics. *Journal of Consulting Psychology*, 1959, *23*, 155–159.

Hsia, Y. & Graham, C. H. Color blindness. In C. H. Graham (Ed.), *Vision and visual perception*. New York: Wiley, 1965.

Hughes, R. M. Rorschach signs for the diagnosis of organic pathology. *Rorschach Research Exchange and Journal of Projective Techniques*, 1948, *12*, 165–167.

Hulicka, I. M. Age differences in Wechsler Memory Scale scores. *Journal of Genetic Psychology*, 1966, *109*, 135–145.

Humphrey, M. E. & Zangwill, O. L. Dysphasia in left-handed patients with unilateral brain lesions. *Journal of Neurology, Neurosurgery, and Psychiatry*, 1952, *15*, 184–193.

Humphreys, L. G. The organization of human abilities. *American Psychologist*, 1962, *17*, 475–483.

Hunt, H. F. A practical clinical test for organic brain damage. *Journal of Applied Psychology*, 1943, *27*, 375–386.

Hunt, J. McV. & Cofer, C. N. Psychological deficit. In J. McV. Hunt (Ed.), *Personality and the behavior disorders* (Vol. 2). New York: Ronald Press, 1944.

Hunt, W. L. The relative rates of decline of Wechsler-Bellevue "hold" and "don't hold" tests. *Journal of Consulting Psychology*, 1949, *13*, 440–443.

Hutt, M. *The Hutt adaptation of the Bender-Gestalt test* (2nd ed.). New York: Grune & Stratton, 1969.

Hutt, M. L. & Gibby, R. G. *An atlas for the Hutt adaptation of the Bender-Gestalt test.* New York: Grune & Stratton, 1970.

Hydén, H. The question of a molecular basis for the memory trace. In K. H. Pribram & D. E. Broadbent (Eds.), *Biology of memory.* New York: Academic Press, 1970.

Ingham, J. G. Memory and intelligence. *British Journal of Psychiatry*, 1952, *43*, 20–32.

Inglis, J. An experimental study of learning and "memory function" in elderly psychiatric patients. *Journal of Mental Science*, 1957, *103*, 796–803.

Inglis, J. A paired-associate learning test for use with elderly psychiatric patients. *Journal of Mental Science*, 1959, *105*, 440–443.

Isaacs, B. & Kennie, A. T. The Set Test as an aid to the detection of dementia in old people. *British Journal of Psychiatry*, 1973, *123*, 467–470.

Ishihara, S. *Tests for color-blindness* (11th ed.). Tokyo: Kanehara Shuppan, 1964.

Jarvie, H. Problem solving deficits following wounds of the brain. *Journal of Mental Science*, 1960, *106*, 1377–1382.

Jarvik, L. F. Thoughts on the psychobiology of aging. *American Psychologist*, 1975, *30*, 576–583.

Jarvik, L. F., Eisdorfer, C., & Blum, J. E. (Eds.). *Intellectual functioning in adults.* New York: Springer, 1973.

Jastak, J. F. A rigorous criterion of feeblemindedness. *Journal of Abnormal and Social Psychology*, 1949, *44*, 367–378.

Jastak, J. F. & Jastak, S. R. *The Wide Range Achievement Test manual.* Wilmington, Delaware: Guidance Associates, 1965.

Jonsson, C.-O., Cronholm, B., & Izikowitz, S. Intellectual changes in alcoholics. *Quarterly Journal of Studies on Alcoholism*, 1962, *23*, 221–242.

Jordan, E. J., Jr. MMPI profiles of epileptics. *Journal of Consulting Psychology*, 1963, *27*, 267–269.

Jortner, S. A test of Hovey's MMPI Scale for CNS disorders. *Journal of Clinical Psychology*, 1965, *21*, 285.

Kaplan, J. & Waltz, J. R. *The trial of Jack Ruby.* New York: Macmillan, 1965.

Kaufman, A. The substitution test: a survey of studies on organic mental impairment and the role of learning and motor factors in test performance. *Cortex*, 1968, *4*, 47–63.

Kay, D. W. K. Epidemiological aspects of organic brain disease in the aged. In C. M. Gaitz (Ed.), *Aging and the brain.* New York: Plenum Press, 1972.

Kee, D. W., Guy, K. C., & Rohwer, W. D. *Paired-associate learning efficiency as a function of response mode, age, and elaboration.* (Report of NIMH Project HD03869). Berkeley, Calif: University of California, Institute of Human Learning, 1971.

Kiernan, R. & Matthews, C. Impairment index versus T-score averaging in neuro-psychological assessment. Paper presented at the meeting of the International Neuropsychological Society, Tampa, Fla., 1975.

Kimura, D. Some effects of temporal lobe damage on auditory perception. *Canadian Journal of Psychology*, 1961, *15*, 156–165.

Kimura, D. Right temporal lobe damage. *Archives of Neurology, Chicago,* 1963, *8,* 264–271.

Kimura, D. Dual function asymmetry of the brain in visual perception. *Neuropsychologia,* 1966, *4,* 275–285.

Kimura, D. Functional asymmetry of the brain in dichotic listening. *Cortex,* 1967, *3,* 163–178.

Kinsbourne, M. The minor cerebral hemisphere as a source of aphasic speech. *Archives of Neurology,* 1971, *25,* 302–306.

Kinsbourne, M. & Warrington, E. K. A study of finger agnosia. *Brain,* 1962, *85,* 47–66.

Kish, G. B. Alcoholics' GATB and Shipley profiles and their interrelationships. *Journal of Clinical Psychology,* 1970, *26,* 482–484.

Klebanoff, S. G., Singer, J. L., & Wilensky, H. Psychological consequences of brain lesions and ablations. *Psychological Bulletin,* 1954, *51,* 1–41.

Klopfer, B., Ainsworth, M., Klopfer, W. G., & Holt, R. R. *Developments in the Rorschach technique* (Vol. 1. *Technique and theory).* Yonkers, N. Y.: World Book, 1954.

Klopfer, B. & Davidson, H. H. *Rorschach technique: an introductory manual.* New York: Harcourt, Brace, & World, 1962.

Kløve, H. Relationship of differential electroencephalographic patterns to distributions of Wechsler-Bellevue scores. *Neurology,* 1959, *9,* 871–876.

Kløve, H. Validation studies in adult clinical neuropsychology. In R. M. Reitan & L. A. Davison (Eds.), *Clinical neuropsychology.* Washington, D. C.: Winston, 1974.

Kløve, H. & Doehring, D. G. MMPI in epileptic groups with differential etiology. *Journal of Clinical Psychology,* 1962, *18,* 149–153.

Kløve, H. & Fitzhugh, K. B. The relationship of differential electroencephalographic patterns to the distribution of Wechsler-Bellevue scores in a chronic epileptic population. *Journal of Clinical Psychology,* 1962, *18,* 334–337.

Kløve, H. & Matthews, C. G. Neuropsychological studies of patients with epilepsy. In R. M. Reitan & L. A. Davison (Eds.), *Clinical neuropsychology.* Washington, D. C.: Winston, 1974.

Knapp, M. E. Problems in rehabilitation of the hemiplegic patient. *Journal of the American Medical Association,* 1959, *169* (no. 3), 224–229.

Knehr, C. A. Revised approach to detection of cerebral damage: Progressive Matrices revisited. *Psychological Reports,* 1965, *17,* 71–77.

Kooi, K. A. & Hovey, H. B. Alterations in mental function and paroxysmal cerebral activity. *A.M.A. Archives of Neurology and Psychiatry,* 1957, *78,* 264–271.

Koppitz, E. M. *The Bender Gestalt test for young children.* New York: Grune & Stratton, 1964.

Korman, M. & Blumberg, S. Comparative efficiency of some tests of cerebral damage. *Journal of Consulting Psychology,* 1963, *27,* 303–309.

Kostlan, A. & Van Couvering, N. Clinical indications of organic brain dysfunction. *Proceedings of the 80th Annual Convention of the American Psychological Association,* 1972, *7,* 423–424. (Summary)

Kreindler, A., Fradis, A., & Sevastopol, N. La repartition de dominance hemispherique. *Neuropsychologia,* 1966, *4,* 143–149.

Krug, R. S. MMPI response inconsistency of brain damaged individuals. *Journal of Clinical Psychology,* 1967, *23,* 366.

Lacks, P. B., Harrow, M., Colbert, J., & Levine, J. Further evidence concerning the diagnostic accuracy of the Halstead organic test battery. *Journal of Clinical Psychology,* 1970, *26,* 480–481.

Lambert, N. M., Wilcox, M. R., & Gleason, W. P. *The educationally retarded child.* New York: Grune & Stratton, 1974.

Landis, C. Remarks on psychological findings attendant on psychosurgery. In *The biology of mental health and disease.* New York: Hoeber, 1952.

Lansdell, H. Mooney's Closure Faces Test, instructions. Unpublished manuscript, undated.

Lansdell, H. C. Effect of extent of temporal lobe ablations on two lateralized deficits. *Physiology and Behavior,* 1968a, *3*, 271–273.

Lansdell, H. C. Evidence for a symmetrical hemisphere contribution to an intellectual function. *Proceedings of the 76th Annual Convention of the American Psychological Association,* 1968b, *3*, 337–338.

Lansdell, H. C. Relation of extent of temporal removals to closure and visuomotor factors. *Perceptual and Motor Skills,* 1970, *31*, 491–498.

Lansdell, H. C. A general intellectual factor affected by temporal lobe dysfunction. *Journal of Clinical Psychology,* 1971, *27*, 182–184.

Lansdell, H. C. Effect of neurosurgery on the ability to identify popular word associations. *Journal of Abnormal Psychology,* 1973, *81*, 255–258.

Lansdell, H. C. & Mirsky, A. F. Attention in focal and centrencephalic epilepsy. *Experimental Neurology,* 1964, *9*, 463–469.

Lansdell, H. C. & Smith, F. J. Effect of focus of cerebral injury on WAIS factors and the course of their recovery. Paper presented at the American Psychological Association Convention, Honolulu, 1972.

Lashley, K. S. Factors limiting recovery after central nervous lesions. *Journal of Nervous and Mental Disease.* 1938, *88*, 733–755.

Leiter, R. G. *Examiner's manual for the Leiter International Performance Scale.* Chicago: Stoelting, 1969a.

Leiter, R. G. *General instructions for the Leiter International Performance Scale.* Chicago: Stoelting, 1969b.

Levitt, E. E. & Truumaa, A. *The Rorschach technique with adolescents and children.* New York: Grune & Stratton, 1972.

Levy-Agresti, J. & Sperry, R. W. Differential perceptual capacities in major and minor hemispheres. *Proceedings of the National Academy of Science,* 1968, *61*, 1151. (Summary)

Lewinsohn. P. M. *Psychological assessment of patients with brain injury.* Unpublished manuscript, 1973.

Lewinsohn, P. M., Danaher, B., Barrera, M., Glasgow, R., & Reicher, G. Assessment and remediation of memory disorder. Paper presented at the 83rd Annual Convention of the American Psychological Association, Chicago, Sept. 1975.

Lewinsohn, P. M., Zieler, R. E. Libet, J., Eyeberg, S., & Nielson, G. Short-term memory. *Journal of Comparative and Physiological Psychology,* 1972, *81*, 248–255.

Lewis, A. Amnesic syndromes. *Proceedings of the Royal Society of Medicine,* 1961, *54*, 955–961.

Lezak, M. D. *The Personal History Inventory.* Paper presented at the 76th Annual Convention of the American Psychological Association, San Francisco, Sept. 1968.

Lezak, M. D. When right is wrong. Vicissitudes of patients with right hemisphere lesions. Paper presented at the biennial spring meeting of the Oregon and Washington Psychological Associations, Salishan, Ore., April 1975.

Lezak, M. D. & Glaudin, V. Differential effects of physical illness on MMPI profiles. *Newsletter for Research in Psychology,* 1969, *11*, 27–28.

Likert, R. & Quasha, W. H. *The Revised Minnesota Paper Form Board Test. Manual.* New York: Psychological Corporation, 1970.

Lilliston, L. Dimensions of schizophrenia as a function of performance on tests of cerebral damage. Paper presented at the meeting of the Eastern Psychological Association, Philadelphia, April 1969.

Lilliston, L. Schizophrenic symptomatology as a function of probability of cerebral damage. *Journal of Abnormal Psychology*, 1973, *82*, 377–381.

Lindsey, B. A. & Coppinger, N. W. Age-related deficits in simple capabilities and their consequences for Trail Making performance. *Journal of Clinical Psychology*, 1969, *25*, 156–159.

Lishman, W. A. Brain damage in relation to psychiatric disability after head injury. *British Journal of Psychiatry*, 1968, *114*, 373–410.

Lorge, I. The influence of the test upon the nature of mental decline as a function of age. *Journal of Educational Psychology*, 1936, *27*, 100–110.

Lubin, B., Wallis, R. R., & Paine, C. Patterns of psychological test usage in the United States: 1935–1969. *Professional Psychology*, 1971, *2*, 70–74.

Luria, A. R. Neuropsychological analysis of focal brain lesions. In B. B. Wolman (Ed.), *Handbook of clinical psychology*. New York: McGraw-Hill, 1965a.

Luria, A. R. Neuropsychology in the local diagnosis of brain damage. *Cortex*, 1965b, *1*, 2–18.

Luria, A. R. *Higher cortical functions in man*. New York: Basic Books, 1966.

Luria, A. R. [*The working brain.*] (B. Haigh, trans.). New York: Basic Books, 1974.

Luria, A. R. & Homskaya, E. D. Disturbances in the regulative role of speech with frontal lobe lesions. In J. M. Warren & K. Akert (Eds.), *The frontal granular cortex and behavior*. New York: McGraw-Hill, 1964.

Lyman, H. B. *Test scores and what they mean*. Englewood Cliffs, N. J.: Prentice-Hall, 1963.

Lynn, J. G., Levine, K. N., & Hewson, L. R. Psychologic tests for the clinical evaluation of late 'diffuse organic,' 'neurotic,' and 'normal' reactions after closed head injury. *Trauma of the central nervous system. Research Publication of the Association of Nervous and Mental Disease*. Baltimore: Williams & Wilkins, 1945.

Machover, K. *Personality projection in the drawing of the human figure*. Springfield, Ill.: C. C. Thomas, 1948.

Magoun, H. G. Neural plasticity and the memory process. In M. Rinkel (Ed.), *Biological treatment of mental illness*. New York: L. C. Page, 1966.

Maher, B. A. Intelligence and brain damage. In N. R. Ellis (Ed.), *Handbook of mental deficiency*. New York: McGraw-Hill, 1963.

Malamud, N. Neuropathology of organic brain syndromes associated with aging. In C. M. Gaitz (Ed.), *Aging and the brain*. New York: Plenum Press, 1972.

Malamud, N. Organic brain disease mistaken for psychiatric disorder: A clinico-pathologic study. In D. F. Benson & D. Blumer (Eds.), *Psychiatric aspects of neurologic disease*. New York: Grune & Stratton, 1975.

Matarazzo, J. D. *Wechsler's measurement and appraisal of adult intelligence* (5th ed.). Baltimore: Williams & Wilkins, 1972.

Matthews, C. G., Guertin, W. H., & Reitan, R. M. Wechsler-Bellevue subtest mean rank orders in diverse diagnostic groups. *Psychological Reports*, 1962, *11*, 3–9.

Matthews, C. G., Shaw, D. G., & Kløve, H. Psychological test performances in neurologic and "pseudo-neurologic" subjects. *Cortex*, 1966, *2*, 244–253.

Maxwell, A. E. Obtaining factor scores on the WAIS. *Journal of Mental Science*, 1960, *106*, 1060–1062.

McAlpine, D., Lumsden, C. D., & Acheson, E. D. *Multiple sclerosis* (2nd ed.). Edinburgh, London: Churchill Livingstone, 1972.

McFarland, R. A. Anoxia: its effects on the physiology and biochemistry of the brain and on behavior. In *The biology of mental health and disease.* New York: Hoeber, 1952.

McFie, J. Psychological testing in clinical neurology. *Journal of Nervous and Mental Disease,* 1960, *131,* 383–393.

McFie, J. Recent advances in phrenology. *Lancet,* Aug. 1961, *2,* 360–363.

McFie, J. The diagnostic significance of disorders of higher nervous activity. Syndromes related to frontal, temporal, parietal, and occipital lesions. In P. J. Vinken & G. W. Bruyn (Eds.), *Handbook of clinical neurology* (Vol. 3, *Disorders of higher nervous activity).* New York: Wiley, 1969.

McFie, J. & Piercy, M. F. The relation of laterality of lesion to performance on Weigl's sorting test. *Journal of Mental Science,* 1952, *98,* 299–305.

McFie, J., Piercy, M. F., & Zangwill, O. C. Visual-spatial agnosia associated with lesions of the right cerebral hemisphere. *Brain,* 1950, *73,* 167–190.

McFie, J. & Zangwill, O. L. Visual-constructive disabilities associated with lesions of the left cerebral hemispheres. *Brain,* 1960, *83,* 243–260.

McGaugh, J. L. Time-dependent processes in memory storage. *Science,* 1966, *153,* 1351–1358.

McGhie, A. Psychological aspects of attention and its disorders. In P. J. Vinken & G. W. Bruyn (Eds.), *Handbook of clinical neurology* (Vol. 3, *Disorders of higher nervous activity).* New York: Wiley, 1969.

McGlone, J. Functional brain asymmetry studied in patients with lateralized lesions. Paper presented at the International Neuropsychological Society meeting, Toronto, 1976.

McNemar, Q. Lost: Our intelligence? Why? *American Psychologist,* 1965, *20,* 871–882.

McReynolds, P. & Weide, M. Psychological measures as used to predict psychiatric improvement and to assess behavioral changes following prefrontal lobotomy. *Journal of Mental Science,* 1960, *106,* 256–280.

Meehl, P. E. *Clinical versus statistical prediction.* Minneapolis: University of Minnesota Press, 1954.

Meehl, P. E. & Rosen, A. Antecedent probability and the efficiency of psychometric signs, patterns, or cutting scores. In D. N. Jackson & S. Messick (Eds.), *Problems in human assessment.* New York: McGraw-Hill, 1967.

Meier, M. J. The regional localization hypothesis and personality changes associated with focal cerebral lesions and ablations. In J. N. Butcher (Ed.), *MMPI: research developments and clinical applications.* New York: McGraw-Hill, 1969.

Meier, M. J. Neuropsychological predictors of motor recovery after cerebral infarction. Paper read at the 82nd Annual Convention of the American Psychological Association. New Orleans, Sept. 1974.

Merritt, H. H. *A textbook of neurology* (5th ed.) Philadelphia: Lea & Febiger, 1973.

Merskey, H. & Woodforde, J. M. Psychiatric sequelae of minor head injury, *Brain,* 1972, *95,* 521–528.

Meyer, V. Psychological effects of brain damage. In H. J. Eysenck (Ed.), *Handbook of abnormal psychology.* New York: Basic Books, 1961.

Meyer, V. & Falconer, M. A. Defects of learning ability with massive lesions of the temporal lobe. *Journal of Mental Science,* 1960, *106,* 472–477.

Meyer, V. & Jones, H. G. Patterns of cognitive test performance as functions of the lateral localization of cerebral abnormalities in the temporal lobe. *Journal of Mental Science,* 1957, *103,* 758–772.

Meyer, V. & Yates, A. J. Intellectual changes following temporal lobectomy for psychomotor epilepsy. *Journal of Neurology, Neurosurgery, and Psychiatry,* 1955, *18,* 44–52.

Miller, E. Handedness and the pattern of human ability. *British Journal of Psychology,* 1971, *62,* 111–112.

Miller, E. *Clinical neuropsychology.* Harmondsworth, England: Penguin Books, 1972.

Miller, E. Short- and long-term memory in patients with presenile dementia (Alzheimer's disease). *Psychological Medicine,* 1973, *3,* 221–224.

Milner, B. Intellectual function of the temporal lobes. *Psychological Bulletin,* 1954, *51,* 42–62.

Milner, B. Psychological defects with temporal lobe excision. In H. C. Solomon, S. Cobb, & W. Penfield (Eds.), *The brain and human behavior.* Baltimore: Williams & Wilkins, 1958.

Milner, B. Laterality effects in audition. In V. B. Mountcastle (Ed.), *Interhemispheric relations and cerebral dominance.* Baltimore: Johns Hopkins University Press, 1962.

Milner, B. Effects of different brain lesions on card sorting. *Archives of Neurology,* 1963, *9,* 90–100.

Milner, B. Some effects of frontal lobectomy in man. In J. M. Warren & K. Akert (Eds.), *The frontal granular cortex and behavior.* New York: McGraw-Hill, 1964.

Milner, B. Brain mechanisms suggested by studies of temporal lobes. In C. H. Millikan & F. L. Darley (Eds.), *Brain mechanisms underlying speech and language.* New York: Grune & Stratton, 1967a.

Milner, B. Discussion of the subject: Experimental analysis of cerebral dominance in man. In C. H. Millikan & F. L. Darley (Eds.), *Brain mechanisms underlying speech and language.* New York: Grune & Stratton, 1967b.

Milner, B. Visual recognition and recall after right temporal lobe excision in man. *Neuropsychologia,* 1968, *6,* 191–209.

Milner, B. Residual intellectual and memory deficits after head injury. In A. E. Walker, W. F. Caveness, & M. Critchley (Eds.), *The late effects of head injury.* Springfield, Ill.: C. C. Thomas, 1969.

Milner, B. Memory and the medial temporal regions of the brain. In K. H. Pribram & D. E. Broadbent (Eds.), *Biology of memory.* New York: Academic Press, 1970.

Milner, B. Interhemispheric differences in the localization of psychological processes in man. *British Medical Bulletin,* 1971, *27*(3), 272–277.

Milner, B. & Teuber, H.-L. Alteration of perception and memory in man: reflections on methods. In L. Weiskrantz (Ed.), *Analysis of behavior change.* New York: Harper & Row, 1968.

Mirsky, A. F., Primac, D. W., Marson, C. A., Rosvold, H. E., & Stevens, J. R. A comparison of the psychological test performance of patients with focal and nonfocal epilepsy. *Experimental Neurology,* 1960, *2,* 75–89.

Moldawsky, S. & Moldawsky, P. C. Digit Span as an anxiety indicator. *Journal of Consulting Psychology,* 1952, *16,* 115–118.

Money, J., Alexander, D., & Walker, H. T., Jr. *Manual for A Standardized Road-Map Test of Direction Sense.* Baltimore: Johns Hopkins University Press, 1965.

Montague, E. K., Williams, H. L., Lubin, A., & Gieseking, C. F. Army tests for assessment of intellectual deficit. *U. S. Armed Forces Medical Journal,* 1957, *8,* 883–892.

Mooney, C. M. Age in the development of closure ability in children. *Canadian Journal of Psychology,* 1957, *2,* 219–226.

Moore, B. E. & Ruesch, J. Prolonged disturbances of consciousness following head injury. *New England Journal of Medicine,* 1944, *230,* 445–452.

Morgan, C. T. *Physiological psychology.* New York: McGraw-Hill, 1943.

Morrow, R. S. & Mark, J. C. The correlation of intelligence and neurological findings on 22 patients autopsied for brain damage. *Journal of Consulting Psychology*, 1955, *19*, 283–289.

Moscovitch, M. Language and the cerebral hemispheres: reaction-time studies and their implications for models of cerebral dominance. *Communication and affect*. New York: Academic Press, 1973.

Mulder, D. W. & Daly, D. Psychiatric symptoms associated with lesions of the temporal lobe. *Journal of the American Medical Association*, 1952, *150*, 173–176.

Murray, H. A. *Explorations in personality*. New York: Oxford University Press, 1938.

Murstein, B. I. *Theory and research in projective techniques, emphasizing the TAT*. New York: Wiley, 1963.

Murstein, B. I. & Leipold, W. D. The role of learning and motor abilities in the Wechsler-Bellevue Digit Symbol test. *Educational and Psychological Measurement*, 1961, *21*, 103–112.

Myers, R. E. Cerebral connectionism and brain function. In C. H. Millikan & F. L. Darley (Eds.), *Brain mechanisms underlying speech and language*. New York: Grune & Stratton, 1967.

Nauta, W. J. H. Some brain structures and functions related to memory. *Neurosciences Research Progress Bulletin*, 1964, *2* (5), 1–20.

Nauta, W. J. H., in R. B. Livingston (Chairman), Brain mechanisms in conditioning and learning. *Neurosciences Research Progress Bulletin*, 1966, *4*, 235–347.

Nebes, R. D. Hemispheric specialization in commissurotomized man. *Psychological Bulletin*, 1974, *81* (1), 1–14.

Nehemkis, A. M. & Lewinsohn, P. M. Effects of left and right hemisphere lesions on the naming process. *Perceptual and Motor Skills*, 1972, *35*, 787–798.

Newcombe, F. *Missile wounds of the brain*. London: Oxford University Press, 1969.

Newcombe, F., Marshall, J. C., Carrivick, P. J., & Hiorns, R. W. Recovery curves in acquired dyslexia. *Journal of the Neurological Sciences*, 1975, *24*, 127–133.

Nielsen, J. M. The cortical motor pattern apraxias. In *The frontal lobes. Research Publication of the Association of Nervous and Mental Disease* (Vol. 24). Baltimore: Williams & Wilkins, 1948.

Nielsen, J. M. Agnosias, apraxias, speech, and aphasia. In A. B. Baker (Ed.), *Clinical neurology* (2nd ed.). New York: Hoeber-Harper, 1962.

Noback, C. R. *The human nervous system*. New York: McGraw-Hill, 1967.

Noble, C. E. Measurements of association value (a), rated associations (a¹), and scaled meaningfulness (m¹) for 2100 CVC combinations of the English alphabet. *Psychological Reports*, 1961, *8*, 487–521.

Norman, R. D. A revised deterioration formula for the Wechsler Adult Intelligence Scale. *Journal of Clinical Psychology*, 1966, *22*, 287–294.

North, R. D. & Zubin, J. Complex mental functions. In N. D. C. Lewis, C. Landis, & H. E. King (Eds.), *Studies in topectomy*. New York: Grune & Stratton, 1956.

Nyssen, R. Contribution expérimentale à l'étude de "l'amnésie de fixation" dans la maladie de Korsakow d'origine alcoolique. *Acta Neurologica et Psychiatrica Belgica*, 1957, *57*, 639–665.

Ojemann, R. G. Correlations between specific human brain lesions and memory changes. *Neurosciences Research Progress Bulletin*, 1966, *4* (Supplement), 1–70.

Oppenheimer, D. R. Microscopic lesions in the brain following head injury. *Journal of Neurology, Neurosurgery, and Psychiatry*, 1968, *31*, 299–306.

Orme, J. E., Lee, D. & Smith, M. P. Psychological assessment of brain damage and intellectual impairment in elderly psychiatric patients. *British Journal of Social and Clinical Psychology*, 1964, *3*, 161–167.

Osgood, C. E. & Miron, M. S. *Approaches to the study of aphasia.* Urbana, Ill.: University of Illinois Press, 1963.

Osterrieth, P. A. Le test de copie d'une figure complexe. *Archives de Psychologie,* 1944, *30,* 206–356.

Ostreicher, H. Memory for unrelated sentences. Unpublished manuscript, 1973.

Ota, Y. Psychiatric studies on civilian head injuries. In A. E. Walker, W. F. Caveness, & M. Critchley (Eds.), *The late effects of head injury.* Springfield, Ill.: C. C. Thomas, 1969.

Oxbury, J. M., Campbell, D. C., & Oxbury, S. M. Unilateral spatial neglect and impairments of spatial analysis and visual perception. *Brain,* 1974, *97,* 551–564.

Oxbury, J. M. & Oxbury, S. M. Effects of temporal lobectomy on the report of dichotically presented digits. *Cortex,* 1969, *5,* 3–14.

Pankratz, L., Fausti, S. A., & Peed, S. A forced-choice technique to evaluate deafness in the hysterical or malingering patient. *Journal of Consulting and Clinical Psychology,* 1975, *43,* 421–422.

Parker, J. W. The validity of some current tests for organicity. *Journal of Consulting Psychology,* 1957, *21,* 425–428.

Parsons, O. A. Brain damage in alcoholics: altered states of unconsciousness. In M. M. Gross (Ed.), *Alcohol intoxication and withdrawal.* New York: Plenum Press, 1975.

Parsons, O. A. & Stewart, K. D. Effects of supportive versus disinterested interviews on perceptual motor performance in brain-damaged and neurotic patients. *Journal of Consulting Psychology,* 1966, *30,* 260–266.

Parsons, O. A., Tarter, R. E., & Jones, B. Cognitive deficits in chronic alcoholics. Paper presented at the International Congress of Social Psychiatry, Jerusalem, June 1972.

Parsons, O. A., Vega, A., Jr., & Burn, J. Different psychological effects of lateralized brain damage. *Journal of Consulting and Clinical Psychology,* 1969, *33,* 551–557.

Pascal, G. R. & Suttell, B. J. *The Bender-Gestalt test: quantification and validity for adults.* New York: Grune & Stratton, 1951.

Paterson, A. & Zangwill, O. L. Disorders of visual space perception associated with lesions of the right cerebral hemisphere. *Brain,* 1944, *67,* 331–358.

Payne, D. A. & Lehmann, I. J. A brief WAIS analysis. *Journal of Clinical Psychology,* 1966, *22,* 296–297.

Payne, R. W. Cognitive abnormalities. In H. J. Eysenck (Ed.), *Handbook of abnormal psychology.* New York: Basic Books, 1961.

Payne, R. W. & Hewlett, J. H. G. Thought disorder in psychotic patients. In H. J. Eysenck (Ed.), *Experiments in personality* (Vol. 2, *Psychodiagnostics and psychodynamics*). New York: Humanities Press, 1960.

Payne, R. W. & Jones, H. G. Statistics for the investigation of individual cases. *Journal of Clinical Psychology,* 1957, *13,* 115–121.

Peck, D. F. The conversion of Progressive Matrices and Mill Hill vocabulary raw scores into deviation IQ's. *Journal of Clinical Psychology,* 1970, *26,* 67–70.

Penfield, W. Engrams in the human brain. *Proceedings of the Royal Society of Medicine,* 1968, *61,* 831–840.

Penfield, W. & Perot, P. The brain's record of auditory and visual experience. *Brain,* 1963, *86,* 595–696.

Penfield, W. & Rasmussen, T. *The cerebral cortex of man.* New York: Macmillan, 1950.

Penfield, W. & Roberts, L. *Speech and brain-mechanisms.* Princeton, N. J.: Princeton University Press, 1959.

Peoples, C. & Moll, R. P. Bender-Gestalt performance as a function of drawing ability, school performance, and intelligence. *Journal of Clinical Psychology*, 1962, *18*, 106–107.

Peterson, L. R. Short-term memory. *Scientific American*, 1966, *215*, 90–95.

Peterson, L. R. & Peterson, M. J. Short-term retention of individual verbal items. *Journal of Experimental Psychology*, 1959, *58*, 193–198.

Piercy, M. The effects of cerebral lesions on intellectual functions: a review of current research trends. *British Journal of Psychiatry*, 1964, *110*, 310–352.

Piercy, M., Hécaen, H., & Ajuriaguerra, J. de. Constructional apraxia associated with unilateral cerebral lesions—left and right sided cases compared. *Brain*, 1960, *83*, 225–242.

Piercy, M. & Smyth, V. Right hemisphere dominance for certain non-verbal intellectual skills. *Brain*, 1962, *85*, 775–790.

Pincus, J. H. & Tucker, G. *Behavioral neurology*. New York: Oxford University Press, 1974.

Piotrowski, Z. The Rorschach inkblot method in organic disturbances of the central nervous system. *Journal of Nervous and Mental Disease*, 1937, *86*, 525–537.

Poeck, K. Modern trends in neuropsychology. In A. L. Benton (Ed.), *Contributions to clinical neuropsychology*. Chicago: Aldine, 1969.

Polyakov, G. I. Modern data on the structural organization of the cerebral cortex. In A. R. Luria, *Higher cortical functions in man*. New York: Basic Books, 1966.

Porch, B. E. *Porch Index of Communicative Ability*. Palo Alto, Calif.: Consulting Psychologists Press, 1967.

Porch, B. E. Multidimensional scoring in aphasia tests. *Journal of Speech and Hearing Research*, 1971, *14*, 776–792.

Porteus, S. D. *The maze test and clinical psychology*. Palo Alto, Calif.: Pacific Books, 1959.

Post, F. Dementia, depression, and pseudodementia. In D. F. Benson & D. Blumer (Eds.), *Psychiatric aspects of neurologic disease*. New York: Grune & Stratton, 1975.

Potkay, C. R. *The Rorschach clinician*. New York: Grune & Stratton, 1971.

Prado, W. M. & Taub, D. V. Accurate prediction of individual intellectual functioning by the Shipley-Hartford. *Journal of Clinical Psychology*, 1966, *22*, 294–296.

Pribram, K. H. The amnestic syndromes: disturbances in coding? In G. A. Talland & N. C. Waugh (Eds.), *The pathology of memory*. New York: Academic Press, 1969.

Purdue Research Foundation. *Examiner's manual for the Purdue Pegboard*. Chicago: Science Research Associates, 1948.

Pyke, S. & Agnew, N. McK. Digit Span performance as a function of noxious stimulation. *Journal of Consulting Psychology*, 1963, *27*, 281.

Quattlebaum, L. F. A brief note on the relationship between two psychomotor tests. *Journal of Clinical Psychology*, 1968, *24*, 198–199.

Rabin, I. A. Diagnostic use of intelligence tests. In B. B. Wolman (Ed.), *Handbook of clinical psychology*. New York: McGraw-Hill, 1965.

Raghaven, S. A comparison of the performance of right and left hemiplegics on verbal and nonverbal body image tasks. Master's Thesis. Northampton, Mass.: Smith College, 1961.

Ramier, A.-M. & Hécaen, H. Rôle respectif des atteintes frontales et de la latéralisation lésionnelle dans les déficits de la "fluence verbale." *Revue Neurologique, Paris*, 1970, *123*, 17–22.

Rapaport, D., Gill, M. M., & Schafer, R. *Diagnostic psychological testing* (Rev. ed.; R. R. Holt, Ed.). New York: International Universities Press, 1968.

Raven, J. C. *Mill Hill Vocabulary Scale* (2nd ed.). London: H. K. Lewis, 1958.

Raven, J. C. Guide to the Standard Progressive Matrices. London: H. K. Lewis, 1960.

Reed, H. B. C., Jr. & Reitan, R. M. A comparison of the effects of the normal aging process with the effects of organic brain damage on adaptive abilities. Journal of Gerontology, 1963, 18, 177–179.

Reed, H. B. C., Jr. & Reitan, R. M. Intelligence test performances of brain-damaged subjects with lateralized motor deficits. Journal of Consulting Psychology, 1963, 27, 102–106.

Reitan, R. M. Instructions and procedures for administering the Neuropsychological Test Battery used at the Neuropsychology Laboratory, Indiana University Medical Center. Unpublished manuscript, undated.

Reitan, R. M. Certain differential effects of left and right cerebral lesions in human adults. Journal of Comparative and Physiological Psychology, 1955a, 48, 474–477.

Reitan, R. M. Investigation of the validity of Halstead's measures of biological intelligence. A.M.A. Archives of Neurology and Psychiatry, 1955b, 73, 28–35.

Reitan, R. M. Validity of the Trail Making Test as an indicator of organic brain damage. Perceptual and Motor Skills, 1958, 8, 271–276.

Reitan, R. M. Psychological deficit. Annual Review of Psychology, 1962, 13, 415–444.

Reitan, R. M. Psychological deficits resulting from cerebral lesions in man. In J. M. Warren & K. Akert (Eds.), The frontal granular cortex and behavior. New York: McGraw-Hill, 1964.

Reitan, R. M. Problems and prospects in studying the psychological correlates of brain lesions. Cortex, 1966, 2, 127–154.

Reitan, R. M. Psychological changes associated with aging and with cerebral damage. Mayo Clinic Proceedings, 1967, 42, 653–673.

Reitan, R. M. Psychological assessment of deficits associated with brain lesions in subjects with normal and subnormal intelligence. In J. L. Khanna (Ed.), Brain damage and mental retardation. Springfield, Ill.: C. C. Thomas, 1968.

Reitan, R. M. Behavioral manifestations of impaired brain functions in aging. Paper presented at the 81st Annual Convention of the American Psychological Association, Montreal, Sept., 1973.

Reitan, R. M. Neurological and physiological bases of psychopathology. Annual Review of Psychology, 1976, 27, 189–216.

Reitan, R. M. & Davison, L. A. Clinical neuropsychology: current status and applications. New York: Winston/Wiley, 1974.

Reitan, R. M. & Kløve, H. Hypotheses supported by clinical evidence that are under current investigation. Unpublished manuscript, 1959.

Reitan, R. M. & Tarshes, E. L. Differential effects of lateralized brain lesions on the Trail Making Test. Journal of Nervous and Mental Disease, 1959, 129, 257–262.

Rey, A. L'examen psychologique dans les cas d'encéphalopathie traumatique. Archives de Psychologie, 1941, 28, No. 112, 286–340.

Rey, A. Sollicitation de la mémoire de fixation par des mots et des objets présentés simultanément. Archives de Psychologie, 1959, 37, 126–139.

Rey, A. L'examen clinique en psychologie. Paris: Presses Universitaires de France, 1964.

Reznikoff, M. & Tomblen, D. The use of human figure drawings in the diagnosis of organic pathology. Journal of Consulting Psychology, 1956, 20, 467–470.

Riklan, M. & Cooper, I. S. Psychometric studies of verbal functions following thalamic lesions in humans. Brain and Language, 1975, 2, 45–64.

Riklan, M., & Levita, E. Subcortical correlates of human behavior. Baltimore: Williams & Wilkins, 1969.

Rohwer, W. D., Jr. Images and pictures in children's learning. *Psychological Bulletin*, 1970, *73*, 393–403.

Rorschach, H. [*Psychodiagnostics: a diagnostic test based on perception*] (P. Lemkau & B. Kronenburg, trans.). Berne: Huber, 1942 (U.S. distributor, Grune & Stratton).

Rosenman, M. F. & Lucik, T. W. A failure to replicate an epilepsy scale of the MMPI. *Journal of Clinical Psychology*, 1970, *26*, 372.

Rosenzweig, M. R., Bennet, E. L., & Diamond, M. C. Brain changes in response to experience. *Scientific American*, 1972, *226*, 22–29.

Rosenzweig, M. R. & Leiman, A. L. Brain functions. *Annual Review of Psychology*, 1968, *19*, 55–98.

Ross, W. D. & Ross, S. Some Rorschach ratings of clinical value. *Rorschach Research Exchange*, 1942, *8*, 1–9.

Rossi, G. F. & Rosadini, G. Experimental analysis of cerebral dominance in man. In C. H. Millikan & F. L. Darley (Eds.), *Brain mechanisms underlying speech and language*. New York: Grune & Stratton, 1967.

Roth, M. & Hopkins, B. Psychological test performance in patients over 60. I. Senile psychoses and the affective disorders of old age. *Journal of Mental Science*, 1953, *99*, 439–450.

Ruesch, J. & Moore. B. E. The measurement of intellectual functions in the acute stage of head injury. *Archives of Neurology and Psychiatry*, 1943, *50*, 165–170.

Russell, E. W. Effect of acute lateralized brain damage on a factor analysis of the Wechsler-Bellevue intelligence test. *Proceedings of the 80th Annual Convention of the American Psychological Association*, 1972a, *7*, 421–422.

Russell, E. W. WAIS factor analysis with brain-damaged subjects using criterion measures. *Journal of Consulting and Clinical Psychology*, 1972b, *39*, 133–139.

Russell, E. W., Neuringer, C. & Goldstein, G. *Assessment of brain damage. A neuropsychological key approach.* New York: Wiley-Interscience, 1970.

Russell, W. R. The after-effects of head injury. *Edinburgh Medical Journal*, 1934, *41*, 129–141.

Russell, W. R. *Traumatic aphasia*. London: Oxford University Press, 1961.

Russell, W. R. Some anatomical aspects of aphasia. *Lancet*, 1963, *1*, 1173–1177.

Russell, W. R. & Smith, A. Post-traumatic amnesia in closed head injury. *Archives of Neurology*, 1961, *5*, 4–17.

Salvatore, A., Strait, M., & Brookshire, R. Effects of patient characteristics on delivery of the Token Test commands by experienced and inexperienced examiners. Paper presented at the Fifth Conference on Clinical Aphasiology. Sante Fe, New Mexico, April 30, 1975.

Samuels, I., Butters, N., & Fedio, P. Short term memory disorders following temporal lobe removals in humans. *Cortex*, 1972, *8*, 283–298.

Sands, E., Sarno, M. T., & Shankweiler, D. Long-term assessment of language function in aphasia due to stroke. *Archives of Physical Medicine and Rehabilitation*, 1969, *50*, 202–206.

Sarno, M. T. *The Functional Communication Profile: manual of directions*. New York: Institute of Rehabilitation Medicine, New York University Medical Center, 1969.

Sattler, J. M. Analysis of the 1960 Stanford-Binet Intelligence Scale, Form L-M. *Journal of Clinical Psychology*, 1965, *21*, 173–179.

Sattler, J. M. *Assessment of children's intelligence*. Philadelphia: W. B. Saunders Co., 1974.

Satz, P. A block rotation task: the application of multivariate and decision theory analysis for the prediction of organic brain disorder. *Psychological Monographs.* 1966a, *80* (21, Whole No. 629).

Satz, P. Specific and nonspecific effects of brain lesions in man. *Journal of Abnormal Psychology*, 1966b, *71*, 65–70.

Satz, P., Achenbach, K., & Fennell, E. Correlations between assessed manual laterality and predicted speech laterality in a normal population. *Neuropsychologia*, 1967, *5*, 295–310.

Satz, P., Fennell, E., & Reilly, C. Predictive validity of six neurodiagnostic tests. *Journal of Consulting and Clinical Psychology*, 1970, *34*, 375–381.

Saunders, D. R. A factor analysis of the Information and Arithmetic items of the WAIS. *Psychological Reports*, 1960a, *6*, 367–383.

Saunders, D. R. A factor analysis of the Picture Completion items of the WAIS. *Journal of Clinical Psychology*, 1960b, *16*, 146–149.

Savage, R. D. Intellectual assessment. In P. Mittler (Ed.), *The psychological assessment of mental and physical handicaps.* London: Methuen, 1970.

Scherer, I. W., Klett, C. J., & Winne, J. F. Psychological changes over a five year period following bilateral frontal lobotomy. *Journal of Consulting Psychology*, 1957, *21*, 291–295.

Scherer, I. W., Winne, J. F., & Baker, R. W. Psychological changes over a three year period following bilateral prefrontal lobotomy. *Journal of Consulting Psychology*, 1955, *19*, 291–298.

Scherer, I. W., Winne, J. F., Clancy, D. D., & Baker, R. W. Psychological changes during the first year following prefrontal lobotomy. *Psychological Monographs*, 1953, *67* (7, Whole No. 357).

Schmidt, R. P. & Wilder, B. J. *Epilepsy.* Philadelphia: F. A. Davis, 1968.

Schuell, H. Diagnosis and prognosis in aphasia. *A.M.A. Archives of Neurology and Psychiatry*, 1955, *74*, 308–315.

Schuell, H. *Differential diagnosis of aphasia with the Minnesota Test.* Minneapolis: University of Minnesota Press, 1965.

Schulman, J. C., Kaspar, J. C., & Throne, F. M. *Brain damage and behavior.* Springfield, Ill.: C. C. Thomas, 1965.

Seashore, C. E., Lewis, D., & Saetveit, D. L. *Seashore measures of musical talents* (Rev. ed.). New York: Psychological Corporation, 1960.

Semmes, J. Hemispheric specialization: a possible clue to mechanism. *Neuropsychologia*, 1968, *6*, 11–26.

Semmes, J., Weinstein, S., Ghent, L., & Teuber, H.-L. Correlates of impaired orientation in personal and extrapersonal space. *Brain*, 1963, *86*, 747–772.

Shakespeare, R. Severely subnormal children. In P. Mittler (Ed.), *The psychological assessment of mental and physical handicaps.* London: Methuen, 1970.

Shalman, D. C. The diagnostic use of the McGill Picture Anomalies Test in temporal lobe epilepsy. *Journal of Neurology, Neurosurgery, and Psychiatry*, 1961, *24*, 220–222.

Shankweiler, D. Effects of temporal lobe damage on perception of dichotically presented melodies. *Journal of Comparative and Physiological Psychology*, 1966, *62*, 115.

Shapiro, M. B. Experimental studies of a perceptual anomaly. III. The testing of an explanatory theory. *Journal of Mental Science*, 1953, *99*, 394–409.

Shaw, D. J. The reliability and validity of the Halstead Category Test. *Journal of Clinical Psychology*, 1966, *22*, 176–180.

Shaw, D. J. & Matthews, C. B. Differential MMPI performance of brain-damaged versus pseudo-neurologic groups. *Journal of Clinical Psychology*, 1965, *21*, 405–408.

Sheer, D. E. Psychometric studies. In N. D. C. Lewis, C. Landis, & H. E. King (Eds.), *Studies in topectomy*. New York: Grune & Stratton, 1956.

Sherrington, C. *Man on his nature* (2nd ed.). Garden City, N. Y.: Doubleday Anchor Books, 1955.

Shiffrin, R. M. & Atkinson, R. C. Storage and retrieval processes in long-term memory. *Psychological Review*, 1969, *76*, 179–193.

Shipley, W. C. *Institute of Living Scale*. Los Angeles, Calif.: Western Psychological Services, 1946.

Shipley, W. C. A self-administering scale for measuring intellectual impairment and deterioration. *Journal of Psychology*, 1940, *9*, 371–377.

Shipley, W. C. & Burlingame, C. C. A convenient self-administered scale for measuring intellectual impairment in psychotics. *American Journal of Psychiatry*, 1941, *97*, 1313–1325.

Shure, G. H. & Halstead, W. C. Cerebral localization of intellectual processes. *Psychological Monographs*, 1958, *72* (12, Whole No. 465.).

Siegel, S. *Nonparametric statistics*. New York: McGraw-Hill, 1956.

Sim, M., Turner, E., & Smith, W. T. Cerebral biopsy in the investigation of presenile dementia. *British Journal of Psychiatry*, 1966, *112*, 119–125.

Simpson, C. D. & Vega, A. Unilateral brain damage and patterns of age-corrected WAIS subtest scores. *Journal of Clinical Psychology*, 1971, *27*, 204–208.

Sines, J. O. Actuarial methods and personality assessment. In B. A. Maher (Ed.), *Progress in experimental personality research*. New York: Academic Press, 1966.

Sklar, M. Relation of psychological and language test scores and autopsy findings in aphasia. *Journal of Speech and Hearing Research*, 1963, *6*, 84–90.

Small, L. *Neuropsychodiagnostics in psychotherapy*. New York: Brunner/Mazel, 1973.

Smith, A. Changes in Porteus Maze scores of brain-operated schizophrenics after an eight year interval. *Journal of Mental Science*, 1960, *106*, 967–978.

Smith, A. Duration of impaired consciousness as an index of severity in closed head injuries. *Diseases of the Nervous System*, 1961, *22*, 1–6.

Smith, A. Ambiguities in concepts and studies of "brain damage" and "organicity." *Journal of Nervous and Mental Disease*, 1962a, *135*, 311–326.

Smith, A. Psychodiagnosis of patients with brain tumors. *Journal of Nervous and Mental Disease*, 1962b, *135*, 513–533.

Smith, A. Changing effects of frontal lesions. *Journal of Neurology, Neurosurgery, and Psychiatry*, 1964, *27*, 511–515.

Smith, A. Certain hypothesized hemispheric differences in languages and visual functions in human adults. *Cortex*, 1966a, *2*, 109–126.

Smith, A. Intellectual functions in patients with lateralized frontal tumors. *Journal of Neurology, Neurosurgery, and Psychiatry*, 1966b, *29*, 52–59.

Smith, A. The serial sevens subtraction test. *Archives of Neurology*, 1967, *17*, 78–80.

Smith, A. The Symbol Digit Modalities Test: a neuropsychologic test for economic screening of learning and other cerebral disorders. *Learning Disorders*, 1968, *3*, 83–91.

Smith, A. Dominant and nondominant hemispherectomy. In W. S. Smith (Ed.), *Drugs, development and cerebral function*. Springfield, Ill.: C. C. Thomas, 1972.

Smith, A. *Symbol Digit Modalities Test*. Los Angeles: Western Psychological Services, 1973.

Smith, A. Neuropsychological testing in neurological disorders. In W. J. Friedlander (Ed.), *Advances in neurology* (Vol. 7.). New York: Raven Press, 1975.

Smith, A. & Kinder, E. Changes in psychological test performances of brain-operated subjects after eight years. *Science*, 1959, *129*, 149–150.

Smith, E. Influence of site of impact on cognitive impairment persisting long after severe closed head injury. *Journal of Neurology, Neurosurgery, and Psychiatry*, 1974, *37*, 726.

Smith, W. L. Psychometric instruments for detection of brain damage. In W. L. Smith & M. J. Philippus (Eds.), *Neuropsychological testing in organic brain dysfunction*. Springfield, Ill.: C. C. Thomas, 1969.

Snelbecker, G. E., Sherman, L. J. & Schwaab, E. L. Validation study of the Organic Integrity Test. *Perceptual and Motor Skills*, 1968, *27*, 427–430.

Sommerhoff, G. *Logic of the living brain*. New York: Wiley, 1974.

Spearman, C. *The abilities of man*. London: Macmillan, 1927.

Spearman, C. & Wynne Jones, L. L. *Human abilities*. London: Macmillan, 1950.

Spellacy, F. J. & Spreen, O. A short form of the Token Test. *Cortex*, 1969, *5*, 390–397.

Spence, J. T. Patterns of performance on WAIS Similarities in schizophrenic, brain-damaged, and normal subjects. *Psychological Reports*, 1963, *13*, 431–436.

Sperry, R. W. Problems outstanding in the evolution of brain function. James Arthur Lecture on the evolution of the human brain. New York: American Museum of Natural History, 1964.

Sperry, R. W. Cerebral dominance in perception. In F. A. Young & D. B. Lindsley (Eds.), *Early experience and visual information processing in perceptual and reading disorders*. Washington, D. C.: National Academy of Sciences, 1970.

Spiker, C. C. & McCandless, B. R. The concept of intelligence and the philosophy of science. *Psychological Review*, 1954, *61*, 255–266.

Spreen, O. & Benton, A. L. Comparative studies of some psychological tests for cerebral damage. *Journal of Nervous and Mental Disease*, 1965, *140*, 323–333.

Spreen, O. & Benton, A. L. *Neurosensory Center Comprehensive Examination for Aphasia*. Victoria, B. C.: Neuropsychology Laboratory, Department of Psychology, University of Victoria, 1969.

Stein, M. I. *The Thematic Apperception Test*. (Rev. ed.). Reading, Mass.: Addison-Wesley, 1955.

Sternberg, D. E. & Jarvik, M. E. Memory functions in depression. *Archives of General Psychiatry*, 1976, *33*, 219–224.

Sterne, D. M. The Knox Cubes as a test of memory and intelligence with male adults. *Journal of Clinical Psychology*, 1966, *22*, 191–193.

Stone, C. P., Girdner, J., and Albrecht, R. An alternate form of the The Wechsler Memory Scale. *Journal of Psychology*, 1946, *22*, 199–206.

Street, R. F. *A Gestalt completion test. Contributions to education*, No. 481. New York: Bureau of Publications, Teachers College, Columbia University, 1931.

Strich, S. J. The pathology of brain damage due to blunt head injuries. In A. E. Walker, W. F. Caveness, & M. Critchley (Eds.), *The late effects of head injury*. Springfield, Ill.: C. C. Thomas, 1969.

Stroop, J. R. Studies of interference in serial verbal reactions. *Journal of Experimental Psychology*, 1935, *18*, 643–662.

Suinn, R. M. *The predictive validity of projective measures*. Springfield, Ill.: C. C. Thomas, 1969.

Sullivan, E. T., Clark, W. W., & Tiegs, E. W. *California Short-Form Test of Mental Maturity* (1963 revision). New York: McGraw-Hill, 1963.

Symonds, C. P. Mental disorder following head injury. *Proceedings of the Royal Society of Medicine*, 1937, *30*, 1081–1092.

Symonds, C. P. & Russell, W. R. Accidental head injuries; prognosis in service patients. *Lancet*, Jan. 2, 1943, *1*, 7–10.

Talland, G. A. Psychology's concern with brain damage. *Journal of Nervous and Mental Disease*, 1963, *136*, 344–351.

Talland, G. A. *Deranged memory.* New York: Academic Press, 1965.

Talland, G. A. Some observations on the psychological mechanisms impaired in the amnesic syndrome. *International Journal of Neurology*, 1968, *7*, 21–30.

Tarter, R. E. Intellectual and adaptive functioning in epilepsy. *Diseases of the Nervous System*, 1972, *33*, 759–770.

Tarter, R. E. An analysis of cognitive deficits in chronic alcoholics. *Journal of Nervous and Mental Disease*, 1973, *157*, 138–147.

Tarter, R. E. Psychological deficit in chronic alcoholics: a review. *International Journal of Addiction*, 1975, *10*, 327–368.

Tarter, R. E. & Jones, B. N. Motor impairment in chronic alcoholics. *Diseases of the Nervous System*, 1971, *32*, 632–636.

Taylor, A. R. The cerebral circulatory disturbance associated with the late effects of head injury. In A. E. Walker, W. F. Caveness, & M. Critchley (Eds.), *The late effects of head injury.* Springfield, Ill.: C. C. Thomas, 1969.

Taylor, A. R. & Bell, T. K. Slowing of cerebral circulation after concussional head injury. *Lancet*, 1966, *2*, 178–180.

Taylor, E. M. *Psychological appraisal of children with cerebral defects.* Cambridge, Mass.: Harvard University Press, 1959.

Taylor, M. L. A measurement of functional communication in aphasia. *Archives of Physical Medicine and Rehabilitation*, 1965, *46*, 101–107.

Tellegen, A. The performance of chronic seizure patients on the General Aptitude Test Battery. *Journal of Clinical Psychology*, 1965, *21*, 180–184.

Terman, L. M. *The measurement of intelligence.* Boston: Houghton Mifflin, 1916.

Terman, L. M. & Merrill, M. A. *Measuring intelligence,* Boston: Houghton Mifflin, 1937.

Terman, L. M. & Merrill, M. A. *Stanford-Binet Intelligence Scale. Manual for the third revision Form L-M.* Boston: Houghton Mifflin, 1960.

Terman, L. M. & Merrill, M. A. *The Stanford-Binet Intelligence Scale* (1972 norms edition). Boston: Houghton Mifflin, 1973.

Teuber, H.-L. Some alterations in behavior after cerebral lesions in man. In A. D. Bass (Ed.), *Evolution of nervous control.* Washington, D. C.: American Association for the Advancement of Science, 1959.

Teuber, H.-L. The riddle of frontal lobe function in man. In J. M. Warren & K. Akert (Eds.), *The frontal granular cortex and behavior.* New York: McGraw-Hill, 1964.

Teuber, H.-L. Neglected aspects of the posttraumatic syndrome. In A. E. Walker, W. F. Caveness, & M. Critchley (Eds.), *The late effects of head injury.* Springfield, Ill.: C. C. Thomas, 1969.

Teuber, H.-L., Battersby, W. S., & Bender, M. B. Performance of complex visual tasks after cerebral lesions. *Journal of Nervous and Mental Disease*, 1951, *114*, 413–429.

Teuber, H.-L. Battersby, W. S., & Bender M. B. *Visual field defects after penetrating missile wounds of the brain.* Cambridge, Mass.: Published for the Commonwealth Fund by Harvard University Press, 1960.

Teuber, H.-L. & Weinstein, S. Performance on a formboard task after penetrating brain injury. *Journal of Psychology*, 1954, *38*, 177–190.

Teuber, H.-L. & Weinstein, S. Ability to discover hidden figures after cerebral lesions. *A.M.A. Archives of Neurology and Psychiatry*, 1956, *76*, 369–379.

Thomas, C. A. An application of the Grassi Block Substitution Test in the determination of organicity. *Journal of Clinical Psychology*, 1963, *19*, 84–87.

Thompson, R. F., Patterson, M. M., & Teylor, T. J. The neurophysiology of learning. *Annual Review of Psychology*, 1972, *23*, 73–104.

Thorndike, E. L. & Lorge, I. *The teacher's book of 30,000 words*. New York: Columbia University Press, 1944.

Thorp, T. R. & Mahrer, A. R. Predicting potential intelligence. *Journal of Clinical Psychology*, 1959, *15*, 286–288.

Thurstone, L. L. *Primary mental abilities*. Chicago: University of Chicago Press, 1938.

Thurstone, L. L. *A factorial study of perception*. Chicago: University of Chicago Press, 1944.

Thurstone, L. L. Psychological implications of factor analysis. *American Psychologist*, 1948, *3*, 402–408.

Thurstone, L. L. & Thurstone, T. G. *American Council on Education Psychological Examination (ACE)*. Princeton, N. J.: Educational Testing Service, 1953, 1954.

Thurstone, L. L. & Thurstone, T. G. *Primary Mental Abilities* (Rev.). Chicago: Science Research Associates, 1962.

Tien, H. C. Organic Integrity Test (OIT). *Archives of General Psychiatry*, 1960, *3*, 43–52.

Tiffin, J. *Purdue Pegboard examiner's manual*. Chicago: Science Research Associates, 1968.

Tolor, A. A comparison of the Bender-Gestalt test and the Digit-Span test as measures of recall. *Journal of Consulting Psychology*, 1956, *20*, 305–309.

Tolor, A. Further studies on the Bender-Gestalt test and the Digit-Span as measures of recall. *Journal of Clinical Psychology*, 1958, *14*, 14–18.

Tow, P. M. *Personality changes following frontal leucotomy*. London: Oxford University Press, 1955.

Towbin, A. P. When are cookbooks useful? In J. R. Brown (Ed.), *Clinical psychology in transition*. Cleveland: Howard Allen, 1961.

Traxler, A. J. Negative transfer effects in paired associate learning in young and elderly adults. *Proceedings of the 80th Annual Convention of the American Psychological Association*, 1972, *7*, 655–666. (Summary)

Tzavaras, A., Hécaen, H., & Le Bras, H. Le problème de la spécificité du déficit de la reconnaissance du visage humain lors des lesions hémispheriques unilaterales. *Neuropsychologia*, 1970, *8*, 403–416.

Urmer, A. H., Morris, A. B., & Wendland, L. U. The effect of brain-damage on Raven's Progressive Matrices. *Journal of Clinical Psychology*, 1960, *16*, 182–185.

Uyeno, E. Differentiating psychotics from organics on the Minnesota Percepto-Diagnostic Test. *Journal of Consulting Psychology*, 1963, *27*, 462.

Valenstein, E. S. *Brain control*. New York: Wiley, 1973.

Vanderplas, J. M. & Garvin, E. A. The association value of random shapes. *Journal of Experimental Psychology*, 1959, *57*, 147–154.

Vaughan, H. G., Jr. & Costa, L. D. Performance of patients with lateralized cerebral lesions. II Sensory and motor tests. *Journal of Nervous and Mental Disease*, 1962, *134*, 237–243.

Vega, A., Jr. & Parsons, O. A. Relationships between sensory-motor deficits and

WAIS verbal and performance scores in unilateral brain damage. *Cortex,* 1969, 5, 229–241.

Vellutino, F. R. & Hogan, T. P. Relationship between the Ammons and WAIS test performances of unselected psychiatric patients. *Journal of Clinical Psychology,* 1966, 22, 69–71.

Vernon, P. E. *The structure of human abilities.* New York: Wiley, 1950.

Victor, M., Adams, R. D., & Collins, G. H. *The Wernicke-Korsakoff syndrome.* Philadelphia: F. A. Davis, 1971.

Victor, M., Talland, G. A., & Adams, R. D. Psychological studies of Korsakoff's psychosis. I. General intellectual functions. *Journal of Nervous and Mental Disease,* 1959, 128, 528–537.

Vignolo, L. A. Auditory agnosia: a review and report of recent evidence. In A. L. Benton (Ed.), *Contributions to clinical neuropsychology.* Chicago: Aldine, 1969.

Vinken, P. J. & Bruyn, G. W. (Eds.). *Disorders of speech, perception, and symbolic behavior* (Vol. 4). In *Handbook of clinical neurology.* New York: Wiley, 1969.

Vivian, T. N., Goldstein, G., & Shelly, C. Reaction time and motor speed in chronic alcoholics. *Perceptual and Motor Skills,* 1973, 36, 136–138.

Volle, F. O. *Mental evaluation of the disability claimant.* Springfield, Ill.: C. C. Thomas, 1975.

Wada, J. & Rasmussen, T. Intracarotid injection of sodium amytal for the lateralization of cerebral speech dominance. *Journal of Neurosurgery,* 1960, 17, 266–282.

Wahl, C. W., Golden, J. S., Liston, E. H., Rimer, D. G., Rose, A. S., Sogher, D., & Solomon, D. H. Toxic and functional psychoses. *Annals of Internal Medicine,* 1967, 66, 989–1007.

Walker, A. E. & Jablon, S. A follow-up of head-injured men of World War II. *Journal of Neurosurgery,* 1959, 16, 600–610.

Walker, R. E., Hunt, W. A., & Schwartz, M. L. The difficulty of WAIS Comprehension scoring. *Journal of Clinical Psychology,* 1965, 21, 427–429.

Walton, D. & Black, D. A. The validity of a psychological test of brain-damage. *British Journal of Medical Psychology,* 1957, 30, 270–279.

Walton, D. & Mather, M. D. A further study of the predictive validity of a psychological test of brain damage. *British Journal of Medical Psychology,* 1961, 34, 73–75.

Walton, D., White, J. G., Black, D. A., & Young, A. J. The Modified Word-Learning Test: a cross-validation study. *British Journal of Medical Psychology,* 1959, 32, 213–220.

Wang, H. S. Cerebral correlates of intellectual function in senescence. In L. F. Jarvik, C. Eisdorfer, & J. E. Blum (Eds.), *Intellectual functioning in adults.* New York: Springer, 1973.

Warrington, E. K. & James, M. Disorders of visual perception in patients with localized cerebral lesions. *Neuropsychologia,* 1967a, 5, 253–266.

Warrington, E. K. & James, M. An experimental investigation of facial recognition in patients with unilateral cerebral lesions. *Cortex,* 1967b, 3, 317–326.

Warrington, E. K., James, M., & Kinsbourne, M. Drawing disability in relation to laterality of cerebral lesion. *Brain,* 1966, 89, 53–82.

Warrington, E. K. & Rabin, P. Perceptual matching in patients with cerebral lesions. *Neuropsychologia,* 1970, 8, 475–487.

Warrington, E. K. & Weiskrantz, L. New method of testing long-term retention with special reference to amnesic patients. *Nature,* 1968, 217, 972–974.

Watson, C. G. The separation of neuropsychiatric hospital organics from schizophrenics with three visual motor screening tests. *Journal of Clinical Psychology,* 1968, *24,* 412–414.

Watson, C. G. An MMPI scale to separate brain-damaged from schizophrenic men. *Journal of Consulting and Clinical Psychology,* 1971, *36,* 121–125.

Watson, C. G., Thomas, R. W., Anderson, D., & Felling, J. Differentiation of organics from schizophrenics at two chronicity levels by use of the Reitan-Halstead organic test battery. *Journal of Consulting and Clinical Psychology,* 1968, *32,* 679–684.

Watts, C. C. & Haerer, A. F. The Organic Integrity Test evaluated. *Journal of Clinical Psychology,* 1970, *26,* 77.

Wechsler, D. *The measurement of adult intelligence* (3rd ed.). Baltimore: Williams & Wilkins, 1944.

Wechsler, D. A standardized memory scale for clinical use. *Journal of Psychology,* 1945, *19,* 87–95.

Wechsler, D. *Wechsler Intelligence Scale for Children. Manual.* New York: Psychological Corporation, 1949.

Wechsler, D. *Wechsler Adult Intelligence Scale. Manual.* New York: Psychological Corporation, 1955.

Wechsler, D. *The measurement and appraisal of adult intelligence* (4th ed.). Baltimore: Williams & Wilkins, 1958.

Wechsler, D. Psychological diagnosis. In I. S. Wechsler, *Clinical neurology.* Philadelphia: W. B. Saunders, 1963.

Wechsler, D. *Wechsler Preschool and Primary Scale of Intelligence.* New York: Psychological Corporation, 1967.

Wechsler, D. *WISC-R manual. Wechsler Intelligence Scale for Children—Revised.* New York: Psychological Corporation, 1974.

Weigl, E. On the psychology of so-called processes of abstraction. *Journal of Abnormal and Social Psychology,* 1941, *36,* 3–33.

Weinberg, J. & Diller, L. On reading newspapers by hemiplegics—denial of visual disability. *Proceedings of the 76th Annual Convention of the American Psychological Association,* 1968, *3,* 655–656.

Weinberg, J., Diller, L., Gerstman, L., & Schulman, P. Digit span in right and left hemiplegics. *Journal of Clinical Psychology,* 1972, *28,* 361.

Weinberg, J., Diller, L., Lakin, P., & Hodges, G. Perceptual problems in right brain damage: The case for treatment. Paper presented at the International Neuropsychological Society meeting, Toronto, 1976.

Weingold, H. P., Dawson, J. G., & Kael, H. C. Further examination of Hovey's "index" for identification of brain lesions: validation study. *Psychological Reports,* 1965, *16,* 1098.

Weinstein, S. Deficits concomitant with aphasia or lesions of either cerebral hemisphere. *Cortex,* 1964, *1,* 151–169.

Weinstein, S., Semmes, J., Ghent, L., & Teuber, H.-L. Spatial orientation in man after cerebral injury: II Analysis according to concomitant defects. *Journal of Psychology,* 1956, *42,* 249–263.

Weinstein, S., & Teuber, H.-L. Effects of penetrating brain injury on intelligence test scores. *Science,* 1957, *125,* 1036–1037.

Weiskrantz, L. Experimental studies of amnesia. In C. W. M. Whitty & O. L. Zangwill (Eds.), *Amnesia.* London & Washington, D. C.: Butterworth, 1966.

Weiskrantz, L. Treatments, inferences, and brain function. In L. Weiskrantz (Ed.), *Analysis of behavioral change.* New York: Harper & Row, 1968.

Welsh, G. S. & Dahlstrom, W. G. (Eds.). *Basic readings on the MMPI in psychology and medicine.* Minneapolis: University of Minnesota Press, 1956.

Wepman, J. M. *Recovery from aphasia.* New York: Ronald Press Co., 1951.

Wepman, J. M. *Auditory Discrimination Test, Form I, II.* Chicago, Ill.: Language Research Associates, 1958.

Wepman, J. M. & Jones, L. V. *Studies in aphasia: an approach to testing.* Chicago: University of Chicago Education-Industry Service, 1961.

Wepman, J. M. & Jones, L. V. Aphasia: diagnostic description and therapy. In W. S. Fields & W. A. Spencer (Eds.), *Stroke rehabilitation.* St. Louis, Mo.: W. H. Green, 1967.

Wepman, J. M., Jones, L. V., Bock, R. D., & Van Pelt, D. Studies in aphasia: background and theoretical formulations. *Journal of Speech and Hearing Disorders,* 1960, *25,* 323–332.

Wheeler, L., Burke, C. H., & Reitan, R. M. An application of discriminant functions to the problem of predicting brain damage using behavioral variables. *Perceptual and Motor Skills,* 1963, *16,* 417–440 (Monograph Supplement).

Wheeler, L. & Reitan, R. M. Discriminant functions applied to the problem of predicting cerebral damage from behavioral testing: a cross-validation study. *Perceptual and Motor Skills,* 1963, *16,* 681–701.

Whitty, C. W. M. & Lishman, W. A. Amnesia in cerebral disease. In C. W. M. Whitty & O. L. Zangwill (Eds.), *Amnesia.* London & Washington, D. C.: Butterworth, 1966.

Williams, H. L. The development of a caudality scale for the MMPI. *Journal of Clinical Psychology,* 1952, *8,* 293–297.

Williams, H. L. Psychologic testing. In A. B. Baker (Ed.), *Clinical neurology* (2nd ed.) (Vol. 1). New York: Hoeber-Harper, 1962.

Williams, H. L., Lubin, A., & Gieseking, C. F. Direct measurement of cognitive deficit in brain-injured patients. *Journal of Consulting Psychology,* 1959, *23,* 300–305.

Williams, J. D., Ray, C. G., & Overall, J. F. Mental aging and organicity in an alcoholic population. *Journal of Consulting and Clinical Psychology,* 1973, *41,* 392–396.

Williams, M. *Mental testing in clinical practice.* Oxford: Pergamon, 1965.

Williams, M. *Brain damage and the mind.* Baltimore: Penguin Books, 1970a.

Williams, M. Geriatric patients. In P. Mittler (Ed.), *The psychological assessment of mental and physical handicaps.* London: Methuen, 1970b.

Williams, M. & Pennybacker, J. Memory disturbances in third ventricle tumors. *Journal of Neurology, Neurosurgery, and Psychiatry,* 1954, *17,* 115–123.

Woltman, H. W. Late neurologic complications of injury to the nervous system. *Wisconsin Medical Journal,* 1942, *41,* 385–391.

Wood, L. & Shulman, E. The Ellis Visual Designs Test, *Journal of Educational Psychology,* 1940, *31,* 591–602.

Woody, R. H. Inter-judge reliability in clinical electroencephalography. *Journal of Clinical Psychology,* 1968, *24,* 251–256.

Woolf, B. B. The application of the Hewson Ratios to the WAIS as an aid in the differential diagnosis of cerebral pathology. *Journal of Nervous and Mental Disease,* 1960, *130,* 98–109.

Worden, F. G. Attention and auditory electrophysiology. In E. Stellar & J. M. Sprague (Eds.), *Progress in physiological psychology* (Vol. 1). New York: Academic Press, 1966.

Wrightsman, L. S. The effects of anxiety, achievement motivation, and task importance on intelligence test performance. *Journal of Educational Psychology,* 1962, *53,* 150–156.

Yacorzynski, G. K. Organic mental disorders. In B. B. Wolman (Ed.), *Handbook of clinical psychology.* New York: McGraw-Hill, 1965.

Yates, A. J. The validity of some psychological tests of brain damage. *Psychological Bulletin,* 1954, *51*, 359–379.

Yates, A. J. Psychological deficit. *Annual Review of Psychology,* 1966, *17*, 111–144.

Yntema, D. B. & Trask, F. P. Recall as a search process. *Journal of Verbal Learning and Verbal Behavior,* 1963, *2*, 65–74.

Zangwill, O. L. *Cerebral dominance and its relation to psychological function.* London: Oliver & Boyd, 1960.

Zangwill, O. L. Psychological deficits associated with frontal lobe lesions. *International Journal of Neurology,* 1966, *5*, 395–402.

Zimet, C. N. & Fishman, D. B. Psychological deficit in schizophrenia and brain damage. *Annual Review of Psychology,* 1970, *21*, 113–154.

Zimmerman, I. L. Residual effects of brain damage and five MMPI items. *Journal of Consulting Psychology,* 1965, *29*, 394.

Zimmerman, I. L. & Woo-Sam, J. M. *Clinical interpretation of the Wechsler Adult Intelligence Scale.* New York: Grune & Stratton, 1973.

Zytowski, D. G. & Hudson, J. The validity of split-half abbreviations of the WAIS. *Journal of Clinical Psychology,* 1965, *21*, 292–294.

NAME INDEX

TEST INDEX

525

SUBJECT INDEX

Page numbers for definitions are in italics

533

Aneurysm. *See* Cerebrovascular accident
Angiography, *12*
Anosognosia, *58*, 155–56. *See also* Denial of disability
Anoxia, *153*, 158
Anterior commissure, 61
Anterior cortex. *See* Frontal lobe(s)
Anterograde amnesia, *61*, 159
Anxiety, 28, 47, 160–61
  and intellectual functioning, 78, 111, 151
  relief from, 29, 65, 69
  with temporal lobe epilepsy, 62–63
  and test performance, 107, 111, 151, 210
Apathy, 28, 37, 158
  in chronic brain conditions, 178
  with frontal lobe lesions, 66, 169
  in Korsakoff's psychosis, 176
Aphasia, *26*, 56, 57, 71. *See also* Communication disorders; Verbal dysfunction
  and auditory comprehension, 304, 305–6
  and body orientation, 421, 422–24
  examining for, 255–56, 301–4, 305–6
  expressive, *26*. *See also* Verbal apraxia
  fluent, *59*
  and handedness, 162–63
  motor, *64*
  sensory, *59*
  and serialization defects, 54–55
  and test performance, 264, 271, 276, 298, 323, 402
  and verbal dysfunction, 81, 277
  Wernicke's, *59*
Apperceptive visual agnosia, *52*
Appositional capacity, *46–47*
Apraxia, *25–26*
  agraphia, *26–27*, 56
  avocalia, *64*
  constructional, *26*, 331. *See also* Constructional apraxia
  for dressing, *58*
  dysnomia, *59*
  expressive amusia, *64*
  ideational, *56*, *64*, 264
  ideomotor, *25–26*, *56*
  motor aphasia, *64*
  motor pattern, *64*
  verbal, *26*, 59, *64*, 67–68
Apraxias and posterior cortex lesions, 54–58
Arithmetic, *24*. *See also* Mathematical reasoning
Arithmetic dysfunctions. *See* Acalculia;

Alexia, for numbers; Anarithmetria
Arithmetic performance, interpretation of, 105–6, 145, 206–7
Arteriosclerotic brain disease, 153, 166
Association areas, cortical, 38–39, 41–42, 49–50, 62
Association fibers, *37*
Associative visual agnosia, *52*
Astereognosis, *56*, 307
Asymmetry, cerebral, *42–48*, 54, 59, 162–63, 179
Attentional activities, *27*, 36, 60–61, 415. *See also* Concentration; Tracking
  in aging, 428–29, 430–31, 442
  in Korsakoff's psychosis, 176
Attentional defects, *27*, 423–25
  in acute brain conditions, 159, 177
  in aging, 170
  in chronic brain conditions, 160, 178
  in diffuse injury, 150, 153
  in epilepsy, 174
  in psychotic disorders, 168
  and test performance, 105, 109, 110, 113, 210–11, 426–27, 431, 432
Audiological assessment, 304–5
Auditory agnosia, 26, 59
Auditory defects, 40, 42, 112, 304–5. *See also* Auditory functions, defects of; Hearing, defects of
Auditory functions, 40–42, 59–60, 301–6
  defects of, 19, 26, 59–60, 302–3, 304–6
Auditory system, 36, 40
  cortical organization, 34, 39, 40–42, 56, 303
  primary auditory cortex, 40–41, 51
Automatisms, 104–5, *347*
Autonomic nervous system, 34, *37*
Autotopagnosia, *422–23*
Avocalia, *64*
Axons, *33*

Barbiturates, inactivation of brain with, 47, 49, 162
Basal ganglia, *37*, 156–57
Baseline examination, 88, 158. *See also* Longitudinal studies
Batteries, test, 101–2, 181–82, 184, 438–40. *See also* Batteries in Test Index
Behavior, functional systems of, 12–13
Behavior-brain relationship. *See* Brain-behavior relationship
Behavior disturbances
  and brain damage, 28–30, 48–49, 69–70, 151, 168–70
  of chronic patients, 160–61, 178
  and hemisphere side of lesion, 47–48

double (multiple), 27, *210*, *425*
double, defects and test performance, 431
Concrete thinking, *24*, 197–98, 392–94
  in chronic brain conditions, 178
  in diffuse brain conditions, 150, 153
  with prefrontal lesions, 65–66, 434
  on projective tests, 456, 461, 463
  as sign of brain damage, 135, 136
  and test-taking problems, 108
Confabulation, 156, 176, 456
Confidentiality, 103
Confusion, 5, 27, 37, 155
  in acute brain conditions, 177
  with frontal lobe tumors, 169
  in senility, 171
  in test responses, 456, 463
Consciousness, 27–28, 36
  disorders of, 28, 35, 62, 154, 415
Consolidation, *22*, 60–62
Constriction, 375, *455*, 464
Construction, spatial, 41, 54, 331
Constructional apraxia, *26*, 331
  differences with side of lesion, 54, 220, 326–27, 328, 330, 337–38
  examples, 45, 337
  frequency with side of lesion, 54, 320, 325, 334–35, 338
  with parietal lobe lesions, 54–55, 57, 220, 320
  and perceptual accuracy, 281
  with prefrontal lesions, 67, 325, 335
  with right hemisphere lesions, 26, 224
  rotational errors in, 136, 167, 333
Contrecoup injury, *163*
Control functions, 12, 28, 30
  disorders of, 30, 64–66, 149, 151, 434–37
  evaluation of, 71, 169, 434–37
  and mental deterioration, 160
Convergent thinking, *435*
Conversion hysteria, 166–67, 476
Coordination, visual-motor, 214
Copying (drawing), 310
  hemispheric differences in, 43, 54, 320, 326–27
Corpus callosum, 35, *38*
Corpus striatum, *37*, 38
Cortex, cerebral. See Cerebral cortex
Cortical stimulation, 60, 63, 162
Creativity and brain damage, 66, 435–36, 455
Cutting scores, *137–39*, 441

Data base of examination, 117, 121
Deficit measurement

comparison standards for, 71–75, 189–91
  direct methods, *74*, *76*, *82*
  indirect methods, *74*, *76–77*, 79–84
  in neuropsychology, 69–71, 141
Deficit measurement paradigm, 71, 82–84
Deficit, patterns of. See Impairment patterns
Delusions, 156
Dementia. See *also* Mental deterioration
  and depression, 171–72
  with frontal lobe tumors, 154–55, 169
  presenile, *86*, 94–96, 158, 323
  senile, *170–72*, 323, 415, 451
Dendrites, *33*
Denial of disability, 48, 58, 155–56, 161
Dependency, 164, 166
Depression, 28, 47–48, 161. See *also* Mourning reactions
  problems of differential diagnosis, 167, 169, 171–72, 346
  and senile dementia, 171–72
  with temporal lobe epilepsy, 62–63
  and test performance, 114–15, 151
Depth perception, 46
Derived scores, *125*
Descriptive evaluations, 4–5, 8, 88–89. See *also* Examination questions
Deterioration. See Mental deterioration
Deterioration ratios, *80*, 193–95
Deviation IQ, 124–26, *129–30*. See *also* IQ score
Diabetes mellitus, 153
Diagnosis, 67–68. See *also* Test interpretation
  impairment patterns in, 83–84, 148–50, 167, 168, 193–97
  and neuropsychological assessment, 4, 69, 88, 134, 438
  pattern analysis in, 134, 141–50, 196–99
  screening techniques in, 134–41, 193–96
Diagnosis, differential. See Differential diagnosis
Diagnostic efficiency
  of screening techniques, 135–41, 165, 454–55
  of test batteries, 165, 438, 442–43
Diagnostic evaluations, 4, 7–8, 86–88, 152. See *also* Examination questions
Diagonality and right hemisphere lesions, 54, 327
Diaschisis, *155*
Dichotic listening, *306*